More Work Than Glory

Buffalo Soldiers in the United States Army, 1866–1916

John P. Langellier

Helion & Company

'If history were taught in the form of stories, it would never be forgotten.'
Rudyard Kipling, *The Collected Works*

Dedicated To Three Wise Men:
Jon Covington, William Gwaltney and Kevin Mulroy

Helion & Company Limited
Unit 8 Amherst Business Centre
Budbrooke Road
Warwick
CV34 5WE
England
Tel. 01926 499 619
Email: info@helion.co.uk
Website: www.helion.co.uk
Twitter: @helionbooks
Visit our blog at blog.helion.co.uk

Published by Helion & Company 2023
Designed and typeset by Mach 3 Solutions (www.mach3solutions.co.uk)
Cover designed by Paul Hewitt, Battlefield Design (www.battlefield-design.co.uk)

Text © John P. Langellier 2023
Images © as individually credited
Maps © John P. Langellier 2023

Every reasonable effort has been made to trace copyright holders and to obtain their permission for the use of copyright material. The author and publisher apologize for any errors or omissions in this work and would be grateful if notified of any corrections that should be incorporated in future reprints or editions of this book.

ISBN 978-1-804513-34-7

British Library Cataloguing-in-Publication Data.
A catalogue record for this book is available from the British Library.

All rights reserved. No part of this publication may be reproduced, stored in a retrieval system, or transmitted, in any form, or by any means, electronic, mechanical, photocopying, recording or otherwise, without the express written consent of Helion & Company Limited.

For details of other military history titles published by Helion & Company Limited contact the above address or visit our website: http://www.helion.co.uk.

We always welcome receipt of book proposals from prospective authors.

Contents

Acknowledgements		iv
Abbreviations		v
Preface		vii
Introduction		ix
1	The Men Who Joined the Ranks	13
2	Commissioned Officers	83
3	Multiple Missions	136
4	Army Garrisons	193
5	Segregation, Discrimination and Race Relations	227
6	Myths, Memorials and Meanings	268
Bibliography		284
Index		309

Acknowledgements

Many individuals contributed to this project. Among them were: Hannah Ablebeck; Bob Boze Bell; Jack Blades; Robert Bluthardt; Ryan Booth; Stephen Brown; RaNae Calder; Tamia Clardy; Cynthia Clark; Rick Collins; Jon Covington; Jonathan Deiss; Ephriam D. Dickson III; Coi Drummond-Gehrig; Shelly Dudley; Barbara Dunn; Bettye Gardner; Omar Earton-Martinez; Ward Eldredge; George Elmore; Sheila Fabrizio; Mark Fritch; Al Gonzales; Samantha T. Goza; Katie Gray; Stephen Gregory; William 'Bill' Gwaltney; Salome Hernandez, Lindsey Hillgartner; Katie Horstman , Larry Johnson; Sandra M. Johnston; Mark Kasal; Robert Kochian; Blaine Lamb; Evelyn Lemons; Turkiya Lowe; Thomas Marshall; Deborah Mitchell; James Ogden; Leo Oliva; Kay Phillips, Michael 'Bo' Phillips; Thomas Phillips; Melodie Pointer; Cory Robinson; Mary Robinson; Paul F. Rogers; Karen Roles; Eric Rossborough; Brian Shellum; Mackenzie Snare; Eileen Starr; Tammy Stoeber; Sheila Stubler; Homer Theil, Jonathan Waltmire; Mike Weinstein; Clark Whitehorn; and Charles Young. I most appreciate the efforts of series editor Dr Christopher Brice and copy editor Carla Rosenthal at Helion & Company for bringing this project to press To these and many others, I owe a debt of gratitude. In particular this project was made possible by the sponsorship of the National Park Service and the Association for the Study of African American Life and History. Despite such extensive support and assistance, all errors, omissions and statements made in the following document are the sole responsibility of the author and do not reflect the opinions or official positions of any other individual or institutions.

Abbreviations

AGO	Adjutant General's Office
A&NJ	Army and Navy Journal
A&NR	Army and Navy Register
ARSW	Annual Report of the Secretary of War
Ch.	Chapter
Cong.	Congress
GCM	General Courts-Martial
GO	General Orders
M	Microfilm
MC	Manuscript Collection
MS	Manuscript
NARA	National Archives and Records Administration
RG	Record Group
Sess.	Session

Many who served made good the words from Frederick Douglass's July 6, 1863 speech: 'Once let the black man get upon his person the brass letters US, let him get an eagle on his button and a musket on his shoulder and bullets in his pocket and there is no power on earth or under the earth which can deny that he has earned the right of citizenship in the United States.' Among these stalwart freedom fighters was the formerly enslaved Private William Wright of Company H, 114th US Colored Troops (USCT) Infantry Regiment. (Courtesy Library of Congress)

Preface

Following the Civil War, Congress authorized the formation of two cavalry regiments and four infantry regiments (which were soon reduced to two) composed of African American soldiers. These regiments, the Ninth and Tenth Cavalry and the Twenty-Fouth and Twenty-Fifth Infantry [regiments], were stationed throughout the West, where they saw action in countless battles and skirmishes during the Indian Wars. The American Indians nicknamed the members of these regiments 'Buffalo Soldiers.'

The Buffalo Soldiers performed outstanding service to the United States not only during the Indian Wars, but the Spanish American War, the Philippine Insurrection and the raids against Pancho Villa. In addition, Buffalo Soldiers built forts, escorted wagon trains, mail stages and railroad crews, drew maps, located sources of water and were largely responsible for opening millions of square miles of western land to settlement. Twenty Congressional Medals of Honor were awarded to Buffalo Soldiers.[1]

While African Americans boast a long and notable presence in the nation's military past, the involvement of Blacks in the armed forces of the United States, in the eighteenth through the mid-twentieth centuries, previously received limited recognition. This situation particularly applied to Black troops serving in the post-Civil War American West, who have come to be known as 'Buffalo Soldiers.' As James N. Leiker observed: 'For much of the past century, both popular culture and professional historians overlooked the buffalo soldiers.'[2]

That is not to say these Black members of the United States Army, who served during the mid-1860s through first decade and a half of the 1900s, had been ignored completely. In fact, among other late Victorian era individuals, Frederic Remington, 'made a large, important and even influential segment of the reading public aware of their presence.'[3] Remington's contemporary, powerful imagemaker of the American West, William F. 'Buffalo Bill' Cody, also included Black veterans in his Congress of Rough Riders, who traveled throughout the United States and

---

1 Buffalo Soldiers Commemoration Act of 2005. March 9, 2005. Calendar No. 36. 109th Cong. 1st sess. Senate Report 109–24 (Washington, DC: US Government Publishing Office. 2005).
2 James N. Leiker 'Black Soldiers at Fort Hays, Kansas, 1867–1869: A Study in Civilian and Military Violence,' *Great Plains Quarterly* 17 (Winter 1997): 3.
3 According to Thomas Phillips, co-author of one of the most authoritative histories of the African American military experience of the late Nineteenth century, as quoted in John P. Langellier, *Scouting with the Buffalo Soldiers: Lieutenant Powhattan Clarke, Frederic Remington, and the Tenth US Cavalry in the Southwest* (Denton: University of North Texas Press, 2020), 6 and 303n16.

portions of Europe where vast audiences experienced former frontier troopers turned troupers in the arena.[4]

Arguably, however, it was William H. Leckie's *The Buffalo Soldiers: A Narrative of the Negro Cavalry in the West* (Norman: University of Oklahoma Press, 1967) that captured the imagination of generations. As Bruce Glasrud concluded: 'What Leckie accomplished was to inspire a host of other studies of the role of black soldiers in the American West.'[5] Some of Leckie's success followed his lead with emphasis on military campaigning. This aspect, while rousing and important, represented only a portion of a broader story.[6] Indeed, Michael Tate's thesis that: 'The army spent relatively little time in armed conflict with Native Americans. In truth, the overwhelming majority of its attention was devoted to performing tasks which played an even larger, holistic role in the development of the West' aptly applied to both whites and Blacks who constituted a segment of Tate's 'multipurpose army.'[7]

Although not entirely ignoring the engagements against the earlier inhabitants of the Trans-Mississippi frontier and later deployments to Cuba and the Philippines, the thrust of *More Work Than Glory* chiefly explores the non-combat missions of Blacks in the United States. Moreover, not just the missions, but the men themselves, occupies much of the chronicle in order to humanize the rank and file, provide some concept of individuality and reveal both continuity and change found among the soldiers during the Gilded Age and shortly thereafter. Finally, over time, misinformation that occasionally evolved in persistent legends or even myths, deserved consideration. Concurrent efforts to honor the bravery of the Buffalo Soldiers, or conversely to dismiss them as willing agents of 'settler colonialism' a perspective that explores westward expansion in a critical light, further fueled the following treatment.[8] Thus, the saga of the Black regulars between 1866 through 1916 is a rich, complex saga worthy of re-examination.

4   John Langellier, 'Blacks in Army Blue: Early Depictions by Frederic Remington and William F. Cody,' *Points West* (Fall/Winter 2018), 10–13.
5   For the full text read: Bruce A. Glasrud, 'Western Black Soldiers Since *The Buffalo Soldiers*: A Review of the Literature,' *Social Science Journal* 36 (1999): 251–70.
6   For instance, the first brief published narratives of the Ninth and Tenth Cavalry regiments and Twenty-Fourth and Twenty-Fifth Infantry regiments that formed part of the anthology by Theo. F. Rodenbough and William L. Haskin, eds., *The Army of the United States: Historical Sketches of the Staff and Line with Portraits of the Generals-in-Chief* (New York: Maynard, Merrill, & Co., 1896), 280–87; 288–300; 695–96; 697–99, focused on clashes with Native Americans as did many other writers in future accounts. Among these later writings was Steven D. Smith and James A. Zeidler, eds., *A Historic Context for the African American Military Experience* (Champaign, IL: US Army Construction Engineering Research Laboratories, 1998), 82–111; 133–6; 138–40; and 143–6, which encapsulated the combat and campaign role of the Black soldier on the frontier, in Cuba, the Philippines, and Mexico.
7   Michael L. Tate, *The Frontier Army in the Settlement of the West* (Norman: University of Oklahoma Press, 1999), x.
8   The *Oxford English Dictionary* defines settler colonialism is 'the policy or practice of acquiring full or partial political control over another country, occupying it with settlers, and exploiting it economically.' The concept applies both within the United States and many other areas of the globe. Specific examples related to the Black military experience appeared in such texts as Anthony W. Wood, *Black Montana: Settler Colonialism and Erosion of the Racial Frontier, 1877–1930* (Lincoln University of Nebraska Press, 2021), 9; Roxanne Dunbar-Ortiz, *An Indigenous Peoples' History of the United States* (Boston: Beacon, 2014), 146–8.; and Patrick Wolfe, 'Settler Colonialism and the Elimination of the Native,' *Journal of Genocide Research* 8 no. 4 (December 2006): 387–409.

Introduction

Blacks, both freemen and enslaved, served in every war fought by forces of the present day United States. In fact, even before the emergence of an independent nation, periodic recourse to arming Blacks arose. This meant that by the Revolutionary War, thousands of Blacks took up the cause against Great Britain. Admittedly others joined the Crown.

An estimated 5,000 Black patriots, in the main from the northern colonies, fought for independence, albeit with few reaping rewards for their service.[1] Despite this fact, during the second war with Great Britain, in 1812, Blacks once again rallied to the republic. Laws were passed, especially in New York, authorizing the formation of regiments of Black enlisted personnel under white officers, a formula that would be repeated elsewhere and over time with few exceptions.

During the War of 1812, records indicated 2,000 Blacks served on land and sea with the United States. Some 500 of this number stood fast behind the cotton bale bulwarks at New Orleans under Andrew Jackson including some Black officers.[2] Three decades later, African Americans took part in the War with Mexico (1846–1848) although in a limited capacity.[3] Approximately 1,000 Black sailors served in the US Navy while a small number of infantrymen, guides, and musicians dotted the ranks of the US Army and units of state volunteers.[4]

---

1   Peter M. Voelz, *Slave and Soldier: The Military Impact of Blacks in the Colonial Americas* (New York: Garland, 1993); and Woody Holton, *Black Americans in the Revolutionary Era: A Brief History with Documents* (Boston: Bedford/St. Martin, 2009) number among numerous publications recounting the presence and participation of Blacks in the Revolutionary War both in the colonists' camp and with the British. Also review Philip S. Foner, *Blacks in the American Revolution* (Westport, CT: Greenwood Press, 1975).

2   Jesse J. Johnson, *A Pictorial History of Black Soldiers (1619–1969) in Peace and War* (Hampton, VA: Hampton Institute, 1969), 29–40; Bernard C. Nalty, *Strength for the Fight: A History of Black Americans in the Military* (New York: Free Press, New York 1986), 23; Laura E. Wilkes, 'Missing Pages in American History, Revealing the Services of Negroes in the early Wars of the United States of America, 1641–1815,' in *The Negro Soldier: A Select Compilation* (Boston: Robert F. Walcutt, 1861), 65–66; and Joseph T. Wilson, *The Black Phalanx: A History of the Negro Soldiers of the United States in the Wars of 1775–1812, 1861–1865* (Boston: Robert F. Walcutt, 1865), 84

3   L.D. Reddick 'The Negro Policy of the United States Army, 1775–1945,' *Journal of Negro History* 34 no 1: 15.

4   Johnson, *A Pictorial History of Black Soldiers*, 43–50 provides some examples of men in the US Army and volunteers whose enlistment papers described skin color as 'black,' 'black complexion,' and 'colored' who presumably were of African American decent. Moreover, Robert E. May, 'Invisible Men: Blacks and the US Army in the Mexican War,' *Historian* 49 no. 4 (August 1987): 463–477, offers a succinct analysis of the conflict related to Blacks who were engaged in the Mexican American War.

In 1866, the US Congress authorized four infantry regiments, the Thirty-Eighth, Thirty-Ninth, Fortieth, and Forty-First, which consisted of Black enlisted personnel. (Courtesy John Langellier)

After hostilities commenced between North and South, a familiar scenario reemerged. Much as had been the case at the outbreak of the Revolutionary War, Abraham Lincoln's administration banned Blacks. Once more, pragmatic and political considerations led to a change of course. Both under Black officers at Port Hudson and serving with white officers on a hundred other battlefields, more than 180,000 African Americans earned emancipation rather than just accepted it at the stroke of the presidential pen.

Their actions disproved the contention that Blacks would not stand up in combat. As but one illustration of this fact, Major-General James G. Blunt's description of the First Colored Regiment at the Battle of Honey Springs, Arkansas indicated the will and ability to face fire. Blunt challenged, 'let me here say that I never saw such fighting as was done by that Negro regiment. They fought like veterans, with a coolness and valor that is unsurpassed ... The question that Negroes will fight is settled; besides, they make better soldiers in every respect than any troops I have ever had under my command.'[5] To a great degree, such proven performance within

---

5   George Washington Williams, *A History of the Negro Troops in the War of the Rebellion, 1861–1865* (New York: Harper & Brothers, 1888), 322.

both the Union Navy and Army bolstered by many regiments of US Colored Troops, paved the way for Blacks to take a permanent place in the US Army.[6]

Indeed, by 1866, as part of many US constitutional amendments and congressional legislation enacted during the Civil War and post war Reconstruction, the federal government established six regiments of African Americans within the Regular Army. Thus, for the first time Blacks entered the ranks of the US Army during peacetime, but only as privates and non-commissioned officers.[7] At first, the Army Reorganization Act of 1866, provided for two mounted units, the Ninth and Tenth Cavalry regiments and four regiments of infantrymen, the Thirty-Eighth through Forty-First Infantry. As the *Army and Navy Journal*, a semi-official periodical opined: 'The services of the colored troops were thought to deserve reward, and it was with all these objects in view that the reorganization was made in 1866.'[8] Yet another reorganization and further reduction of an already minuscule national military establishment took place in 1869. The former Thirty-Eighth through Forty-First Infantry regiments were consolidated to become the Twenty-Fourth and Twenty-Fifth Infantry regiments. The Ninth and Tenth Cavalry regiments remained intact.[9]

These units' formation represented one of the Reconstruction's lasting effects. In fact, the presence of Black regulars outlasted most of the initial short-lived efforts by Congress to address the loathsome wrongs of slavery. The very existence and accomplishment of these troops would come to represent a milestone on the circuitous road to equality and civil rights in the United States. Conversely, the fact that the regiments were segregated demonstrated one of the prevailing major hurdles in the battle for racial justice.

Consequently, the post-Civil War Black soldier played an essential part in the nation's history. They helped maintain law and order in the West. They often campaigned in a harsh environment against determined enemies who fought to preserve their traditional ways of life. Later, they faced well entrenched foes in the Spanish American War in Cuba and afterwards, they engaged Filipinos who sought independence. In 1916, they deployed against elusive Mexican raiders and revolutionaries. In short, they formed a viable, valuable cadre of westward expansion

---

6   An article titled 'White Troops and Colored Troops,' *Army and Navy Journal*, January 19, 1867, 348 (hereafter referred to as *A&NJ*), summarized statistics about Black and white soldiers in the Union Army, and drew favorable conclusions about incorporating African Americans into the military during peacetime. For more on the subject consult, William A. Dobak, *Freedom by the Sword: The US Colored Troops, 1862–1867* (Washington, DC: Center of Military History United States Army, 2011).

7   Gary Donaldson, *The History of African-Americans in the Military: Double V* (Malabar, FL: Krieger Pub Co., 1991), 50. This enactment was in keeping with the Thirteenth, Fourteenth, and Fifteenth Amendments of the United States Constitution as well as various so-called 'Reconstruction acts.' The first two such acts promulgated in 1867 'divided the South into five military districts, each to be commanded by a general.' These officers were charged with the protection of 'the civil and property rights of all persons; to suppress insurrection, disorder, and violence; and to punish or cause to be punished, all criminal actions.' William L. Richter, *The Army in Texas During Reconstruction 1865–1870* (College Station: Texas A&M, 1987), 92. For context see: Eric Foner, *Forever Free: The Story of Emancipation and Reconstruction: America's Unfinished Revolution* (New York: Alfred A. Knopf, 2005).

8   *A&NJ*, October 27, 1877, 184.

9   Bernard C. Nalty and Morris J. MacGregor, *Blacks in the Military: Essential Documents* (Wilmington, DE: Scholarly Resources, 1981), 47; Arlen L. Fowler, *The Black Infantry in the American West, 1869–1891* (Westport, CT: Greenwood, 1971), 12; and William A. Dobak and Thomas D. Phillips, *The Black Regulars, 1866–1898* (Norman: University of Oklahoma Press, 2001), 3 and 17.

on the frontier as part of the constabulary fielded west of the Mississippi River for over three decades after the Civil War. Thereafter, their role and that of the United States Army evolved into a new function. The country emerged as an international power with a martial force that from the late 1890s onward, would be dispatched beyond the Continental United States to far off engagements around the globe in Asia, Africa, Europe, and Latin America.

During the Gilded Age, some Black soldiers received recognition for their performance above and beyond the call of duty. Their valor under fire gained this elite body the Medal of Honor – their nation's highest military decoration for combat heroism. Others secured different types of acknowledgement for their deeds. Further, during their formative years, the Black regulars undertook the same varied, often tedious – sometimes dangerous – duties assigned to their white comrades. This included an array of efforts. Among these, Black soldiers often served in the capacity as law enforcement. For many decades, they guarded the international boundary between Mexico and its northern neighbor, long before the establishment of the United States Border Patrol. Similarly, Black infantrymen and cavalrymen occasionally patrolled and protected national parks which helped make it possible for visitors to enjoy these incredible treasures more than a decade in advance of the National Park Service's creation.

Those men who took up army life from 1866 through 1916 did so for many reasons. Whatever the wide-ranging intentions for volunteering, their individual stories are varied and enlightening. Viewed together, the picture that emerged portrayed struggle, sacrifice, fortitude, failure, and success, in the face of numerous intimidating impediments. Forming these regiments entailed selecting individuals with the capability to perform in the ranks, finding capable officers, and retaining a competent enlisted core to work alongside those in command. These goals presented significant challenges that would be met and overcome on many occasions.[10]

In the end, as one observer pronounced, these Black regulars became 'a credit to the service' and faithful to their calling. Their 'very high *esprit de corps*' and the pride they took in 'their profession,' he observed, was so important to them that many enlisted 'practically for life.' Overall, their, 'discipline, fidelity, neatness, sobriety,' and perhaps above all, their bravery, were all 'very estimable qualities.'[11] Considering the writer was a white officer, who never commanded Black troops during his long, distinguished raise from West Point cadet to general, such candor offered an unvarnished assessment of the Black soldier as he emerged in the half century after the Civil War.

---

10 Dobak and Phillips, *The Black Regulars*, 5–11, 16–24, 44–49, 68–69, 72, 86–87, 156, 267, 285 n1, 296n4, and 296–7n8, ably discusses recruiting and the process in a sufficient manner as to require little further detail in the present study. For comparison and context for recruiting in general during the immediate post-Civil War until after the Wounded Knee affray read: Douglas C. McChristian, *Regular Army O! Soldiering on the Western Frontier 1865–1891* (Norman: University of Oklahoma Press, 2017), 13–78.
11 James Parker, *The Old Army: Memories, 1872–1918* (Philadelphia: Dorrance and Company 1929), 92–93.

1

The Men Who Joined the Ranks

The year 1866 represented several milestones in the nation's military history. One of these landmarks was due to an increase of the United States' land forces by nearly five-fold from its antebellum antecedents. Just prior to the clash between North and South, during early 1861, the US Army consisted of less than 13,000 officers and men. Four years later, 1,034,064 federal volunteers had to be mustered out of the Union Army between May 1, 1865, through 1867.[1] At its height, actual immediate post-Civil strength reached about 57,000 personnel of all grades and ranks as of September 30, 1867. That figure slightly exceeded congressional limits.

Thereafter, through the Spanish American War, a downward trend remained the norm. Indeed, as early as 1869, Congress consolidated the 45 infantry regiments, into 25 units with an authorized strength of no more than 45,000. By 1876, once more the threshold declined. This time the authorization totaled 27,442, which continued as the status quo for over two decades.[2] In fact, actual levels typically tended to fall below that number.

Given the vast expanses of a sprawling country and an array of assignments, meant that through the late 1800s, Uncle Sam's thin blue line often stretched to breaking point. Troops would be called upon to serve in the South as occupation forces during Reconstruction.[3] They would be dispatched in considerable numbers to Texas in response to Emperor Napoleon III's establishment of a puppet government in Mexico that triggered opposition under Benito Juarez and others. Even after the Mexicans dispatched the European interlopers, turmoil continued for many decades. In fact, the border between Mexico and the United States long remained a

---

1   Under the act of March 3, 1855, the aggregate ceiling for the US Army was 12,698 of which 11,658 were enlisted personnel. This was the basis for the Union Army at the outbreak of the American Civil War. The act of July 28, 1866, allowed for no more than 54,641 officers and men with 51,605 of that number being enlisted. By the March 5, 1869, act the aggregate had fallen to 37,313. Francis B. Heitman, *Historical Register and Dictionary of the United States Army, 1789–1903* (Washington, DC: US Government Printing Office, 1903) 2, 596–7; 604, 608.
2   Richard W. Stewart, gen. ed., *American Military History: The United States Army and the Forging of a Nation, 1775–1917*, I (Washington, DC: Center of Military History, United States Army, 2009), 308.
3   For a general overview consult, James E. Sefton, *The United States Army and Reconstruction, 1865–1877* (Baton Rouge: Louisiana state University Press, 1967). For a study focused on a region particularly germane to Black soldiers obtain Richter, *The Army in Texas During Reconstruction*, 32, 67, 83, and 180–81.

James H. Kornegay, enlisted around July 1881. His second enlistment was in May 1886 at Fort Reno for a term of five years when he was assigned to Company A, Twenty-Fourth US Infantry. Described as 31 years old, born New Berne, North Carolina, he listed soldier his occupation. He had black hair, black eyes and a black complexion and stood 5' 6½" tall. Kornegay was discharged on May 16, 1891, by expiration of term of service at Fort Bayard, New Mexico as a sergeant. (Courtesy John Langellier)

reason for the presence of the US Army from Texas to California. Occasionally, domestic disturbances demanded military responses.[4] Coastal defense along the Eastern seaboard, the Gulf of Mexico and the West Coast required considerable outlay of funds to build fortifications and furnish them with artillery and artillerymen.[5] Perhaps paramount among their myriad missions resulting from demanding service in the trans-Mississippi West that took many, distinct forms.[6]

Forming the Black Regiments

To assist in fulfilling the array of tasks it faced, for the first time, the Regular Army admitted African Americans into its ranks. Except for posting to coast defense in the 1860s and for years thereafter, Black regulars received the same varied taskings as their white counterparts. In most respects, these Black troops differed little from their white contemporaries. As an early study concluded, except for desertion and some other distinctions, including lower incidences of drunkenness and segregation, the regiments with Black enlisted men generally resembled those comprised of white troops.[7]

Filling the ranks of the regiments with Blacks presented many obstacles. As an early member of the National Association for the Advancement of Colored People (NAACP), Oswald Garrison Villard, summarized, 'a motley mixture of veterans of volunteer organizations, newly released slaves and some freedmen of several years' standing but without military experience' responded to the recruiters. Villard indicated: 'They were eager to learn and soon showed the same traits which distinguish the black regiments to-day [early twentieth century] – loyalty to their officers and to their colors, sobriety and courage and a notable pride in the efficiency of their corps.'[8]

The seminal study, *Black Regulars*, reinforced Villard's observations. The authors stated: 'About half of the black men who joined the Regular Army in the late 1860s had served during

---

4 Robert W. Coakley, *The Role of Federal Military Forces in Domestic Disorders, 1789–1878* (Washington, DC: US Army Center of Military History, 1988); and Jerry M. Cooper, *The Army and Civil Disorder: Federal Military Intervention in Labor Disputes, 1877–1900* (Westport, CT: Greenwood Press, 1980), provide background on this subject.
5 Emanuel Raymond Lewis, *Seacoast Fortifications of the United States: An Introductory History* (Washington, DC: Smithsonian Institution Press, 1970), remains a useful primer.
6 As previously noted, Tate, *The Frontier Army in the Settlement of the West*, emphasized the non-combat aspects of the military beyond the Mississippi. Numerous other authors concentrated on battles and campaigns such as early efforts by Fairfax Downey, *Indian Fighting Army* (New York: Charles Scribner's Sons, 1941); and Paul I. Wellman, *The Indian Wars of the West* (Garden City: NY: Doubleday & Company, Inc., 1956). These early narratives, aimed at a popular audience, gave way to more analytical, scholarly works such as Robert M. Utley, *Frontier Regulars: The United States Army and the Indians, 1866–1891* (New York: Macmillan, 1973), and a host of other titles that followed.
7 Erwin N. Thompson, 'The Negro Regiments of the US Regular Army, 1866–1900, MA thesis, University of California, Berkeley, 1966, 96. Comparisons of studies of Blacks within the overall narrative provided by McChristian's *Regular Army O!* lend further credence to Thompson's conclusion. Relative to alcoholism among Black troops, Miles V. Lynx, *The Black Troopers; or, The Daring Heroism of the Negro Soldiers in the Spanish-American War* (Jackson, TN: M.V. Lynx Publishing House, 1899), 18–19, offered some, salient statistics that underscored a more positive record among African Americans regarding the use of liquor and associated health consequences
8 Oswald G. Villard, 'The Negro in the Regular Army,' *Atlantic Monthly* 91 (June 1903), 722.

the Civil War.'[9] Statistics of the enlistees who entered the Black regiments in 1866 substantiated this assertion in that out of approximately 2,100 men who signed on in that year, 562 listed their former occupation as soldier or discharged soldier, while many likewise indicated that their civilian occupation had been a farmer or laborer. (See Table 1) Other patterns emerged as well. These men tended to stand, 'about five foot, six inches tall, [and] claimed to be in his early twenties.' Few could sign their names. Over time, more literate enrollees tended to be found by recruiters in Northern cities. Finally, almost all the early inductees were southern born and as indicted previously were held in enslavement.[10]

Table 1: Occupations Listed by Black US Army Enlistees, 1866[11]

Occupation	Count	Occupation	Count
Baker	2	Distiller	1
Barber	26	Drummer	2
Barkeeper	1	Engineer	1
Blacksmith	18	Farmer	487
Boatman/Steam Boatman	55	Farrier	1
Bookkeeper	1	Fireman	2
Bricklayer/Brick Mason	6	Fuller	1
Brick Maker	1	Furman	2
Brick Moulder	1	Gardner	1
Bugler	3	Groom	1
Butcher	3	Hackman	1
Butler	1	Herder	5
Cattle Driver	1	Hostler	16
Carpenter	16	Iron Worker	1
Cart Man	1	Joiner	1
Cigar Maker	2	Kettle Sitter	1
Clerk	3	Laborer	589
Coachman	5	Machinist	2
Coalman	1	Mason	3
Cook	28	Mattress Maker	1
Cooper	1	Mechanic	1
Confectioner	1	Merchant	1
Dentist	1	Miller	5
		Musician	9

9   Dobak and Phillips, *Black Regulars*, 24.
10 Dobak and Phillips, *Black Regulars*, 10 and 23. *Annual Report of the Secretary of War, 1866*, I, (Washington, DC: Government Printing Office, 1866), 2. Hereafter this source will be cited as *ARSW* with pertinent identification data.
11 For an extensive compilation of the Register of Enlistments for 1866 providing names and other data on early enlistees to the black regiments consult: Anthony Powell, *For the Love of Liberty: The African American Soldier in the Post Civil War Army, 1866–1897* (San Jose, CA: Portraits in Black, 2020). Also review, Virgil D. White, *Index to Pension Applications for Indian War Service between 1817 and 1898* (Waynesboro, TN: The National Historical Publishing Company, 1997).

Painter	7	Soldier/Discharged Soldier	562
Paperhanger	1	Spinner	2
Plasterer	1	Steward	5
Porter	1	Stockman	1
Poston Railer	1	Sugarman	1
Oiler	2	Tanner	2
Ostler	2	Teamster	21
Riverman	11	Tinner	1
Sailor/Mariner	44	Tobacco Stemmer	1
Servant	31	Wagoner	6
Shoemaker	9	Waiter	64
Slater	3		

While the majority of the first candidates signed on at southern locales near their homes, freedmen and the formerly enslaved, also responded from the northern states. (Table 2) A few others came from the West, after their volunteer duty beyond the Mississippi ended. Among these, some members of the Fifty-Seventh US Colored Troops (USCT) in New Mexico agreed to travel eastward where they would link up with the Tenth Cavalry at Fort Leavenworth, Kansas, the regimental rendezvous site, or continued to Jefferson Barracks, Missouri to enter the Thirty-Eighth Infantry.[12]

---

12 SO, No. 35, Head Quarters District of New Mexico, October 6, 1866, called on officers in New Mexico to '…canvass the 57th US Colored Troops now in the District and enlist from the for the 10th US Colored Cavalry and 38th US Colored Infantry, as prescribed by par. 3rd of General orders No. 6, current series from the Head Quarters, Military District of the Mississippi.' This order likewise designated Fort Union as the recruiting station. RG 98, Records of US Army Commands, District of New Mexico Orders, vol. 41, 144–6, NARA. As a follow on, SO No. 39, Head Quarters District of New Mexico, October 21, 1866, noted: 'All recruits which have been enlisted from the 57th US Colored Troops, for the 10th US Colored Cavalry and 38th US Colored Infantry, will be sent with the troops still remaining of the 57th US Colored Troops. to Fort Riley, where orders will be received from higher authority, as to their further movements.' RG 98, Records of US Army Commands, District of New Mexico Orders, vol. 41, 150–2, NARA. As indicated by Letter 478, Head Quarters District of New Mexico, October 27, 1866 to Adjutant General Head Quarters Department of the Missouri, 'the mere skeleton' remaining personnel of the 57th US Colored Troops desired to return to their homes in Arkansas. The commanding officer directed them to proceed as a group to Fort Riley, Kansas. RG 98, Records of US Army Commands, District of New Mexico Letters, vol. 16, 631, NARA.

Table 2: Birth Places Black US Army Enlistees, 1866[13]

Africa	1	Massachusetts	38
Alabama	62	Mexico	1
Arkansas	10	Mississippi	110
Canada	4	Missouri	128
Connecticut	4	New Jersey	6
Cuba	1	New York	20
Washington, DC	53	North Carolina	59
Delaware	5	Ohio	13
Florida	10	Pennsylvania	30
Georgia	46	Rhode Island	1
Kentucky	536	Santo Domingo	1
Illinois	7	South Carolina	92
Indian Territory	2	Tennessee	89
Indiana	5	Texas	5
Jamaica	5	Vermont	2
Louisiana	357	Virginia	198
Maine	1	West Virginia	2
Maryland	93	Wisconsin	1

Despite considerable effort, filing quotas presented one of many challenges. For instance, at first, the Fortieth Infantry cast a wide net from Baltimore and Washington, DC to Smithville, North Carolina and Charleston, South Carolina and preliminary reports claimed satisfactory results.[14] Disappointingly, as of October 1, 1866, only 76 names appeared on the Fortieth's regimental roster in contrast to the Ninth Cavalry's 266 total, which resulted chiefly from work in Louisiana. A nineteenth century historical sketch of the Ninth maintained that these figures belied the nature of these inductees who supposedly were an 'ignorant, entirely helpless' lot 'filled with superstition' a depiction disputed over a century later by a scholarly monograph.[15]

---

13 RG 94, Records of the Office of the Adjutant General, Register of Enlistments in the United States Army, 1866, Vols. 62–64 (M233), NARA.

14 *ARSW, 1866*, I, 59. Indeed, this same source contained information about rotation of sites for recruiting depots depending on which communities or locales might prove the most likely to furnish recruits. See for instance: *ARSW, 1870*, I, 65.; *1879*, 33–34; *1887*, 83; *1888*, 74; as well as Dobak and Phillips, *Black Regulars*, 49.

15 Grote Hutcheson, 'The Ninth Regiment of Cavalry' in Rodenbough and Haskin, *The Army of the United States: Historical Sketches*, 280–2. Charles L. Kenner, *Buffalo Soldiers and Officers of the Ninth Cavalry, 1867–1898: Black and White Together* (Norman: University of Oklahoma Press, 1999), 11, countered Hutcheson indicating: 'almost 40 precent of its [Ninth Cavalry] recruits had prior military service. The majority tended to be laborers and farmers, but 'more than 10 percent were artisans or domestic servants. Louisiana recruits predominated during 1866, but afterwards more were from Kentucky, Virginia, and the rest of the upper South.'

The Forty-First Infantry also vied for prospects in the same area as the Ninth Cavalry, particularly dispatching recruiting parties to Baton Rouge and Greenville, although later Kentucky furnished men as well. The Tenth Cavalry fanned out among urban areas such as Boston, Louisville, Memphis and Philadelphia, yet the initial return was an unpromising 27 future troopers.[16] By the end of 1866, just 64 unassigned names were on the Tenth's rolls.[17] Perhaps the regimental commander's insistence on 'quality' inductees, a mandate shared by his counterpart in the Forty-First Infantry, at first inhibited progress.[18]

What was meant by 'quality' centered around the level of education and skills required to maintain a unit. Antebellum laws in the South that forbade education of the enslaved, ran contrary to this goal. From the outset, the prevalence of inadequate formal schooling required ongoing efforts to eliminate this deficiency given that few willing enlistees met the desired standards.[19] To address the need for suitable individuals who would become corporals and sergeants, the Tenth Cavalry's commander dispatched an officer to Philadelphia. He was to seek, 'colored men sufficiently educated to fill the positions of non-commissioned officers, clerks and mechanics' with an additional directive to locate 'superior men … who will do credit to the regiment.'[20] As late as the Spanish American War and deployment to the Philippines, however, inducting illiterate men in time of conflict presented no bar to enlistment.[21]

Adding to concerns, many of those who once suffered under the 'peculiar institution', paid a price from being overworked, malnourished and long treated as inferior. This led one senior officer in the Thirty-Ninth Infantry to depict his subordinates as, 'the very ignorant class of negroes … of the lowest type of the race.'[22] Besides damaging self-image and sometimes initiative, enslavement took its toll physically. Efforts to preclude the entry of infirmed or the disabled meant that several of the first who joined, at a time when medical officers were limited, only underwent perfunctory procedures. Lackluster approaches included observing an applicant

---

16 *ARSW 1866*, I, 13; and William H. Leckie and Shirley A. Leckie, *The Buffalo Soldiers: A Narrative of the Black Cavalry in the West.* (Norman: University of Oklahoma Press, 2003), !3–14.
17 John Bigelow, Jr., 'The Tenth Regiment of Cavalry' in Rodenbough and Haskin, *The Army of the United States*, 289
18 Leckie and Leckie, *Buffalo Soldiers*, 13; and Dobak and Phillips, *Black Regulars*, 9.
19 Dobak and Phillips, *Black Regulars*, 50.
20 Bigelow, 'The Tenth Regiment of Cavalry,' 290.
21 Morris J. MacGregor and Bernard C. Nalty, eds., *Blacks in the Military: Basic Documents* III, (Wilmington, DE: Scholarly Resources, 1977), 160–1.
22 As quoted by Edward M. Coffman, *The Old Army: A Portrait of the American Army in Peacetime, 1784–1898* (New York: Oxford University Press, 1986), 331. The *Annual Reports of the Secretary of War* contain considerable medical statistics and details about the health of Black troops and comparisons to white soldiers. For examples during much of the Indian wars consult volume 1 for each of the following years with their relevant pages: 1869: 79, 422–23; 1870, 272–73; 1871: 238–39; 1872: 8, 300; 1874, 233–33; 1882, 473–74; 1883, 608–9; 1884, 114, 127, 720–23; 1886: 6, 289, 586–7, 589, 592, 599–600, 608–9; 1887:238–9, 624, 646–49; 1888: 642–3, 651–2, 666, 676, 693; 1889: 733–4; 777–9, 792, 795–6; 797, 799–800, 850; 1890: 881, 894, 902–4, 944; 1891: 578–80, 588, 590, 6431; and 1893: 417–18, 437–8, 456, 458–9. Further, by the early twentieth century, *Crisis* 5 (December 1912): 67, indicated: 'According to the annual report of Surgeon-General George H. Herney, the non-efficiency rate of the colored soldier was 25.88, while that of the white soldier was 33.60. The colored soldiers also were in the hospital less.'

walking and hopping to determine their soundness that differed little from a cursory inspection at the slave block.[23]

One other impediment arose, this time from an internal US Army mandate to avoid draining the workforce destined to return to southern fields.[24] The caveat sometimes overrode military manpower requirements. Essential contract laborers or sharecroppers who replaced the system of slavery that made plantations and other enterprises possible, took precedent over martial matters.

Immediate Post-Civil War Troops

Regardless of such barriers, officers had to convince thousands of men to become part of the six new regiments. Although often men who once had worked the fields responded, freeman, Alexander 'Sandy' Cheatham also signed on for similar reasons. He distained the back breaking, constant cycle of farm life that had been his lot. Born in Alexandria, Virginia on March 1, 1848, the strapping 6'2" sixteen-year-old must have appeared old enough to join Company C, Twenty-Eighth USCT. He had tired of 'milking any more cows' plus he wanted to do his part to free fellow Blacks long struggling under the yoke of enslavement. Late in 1865, Cheatham mustered out with thousands of other Union veterans. Avoiding a return to the farm, he worked as a deckhand on a Baltimore-based harbor boat. The lure of the military pulled Cheatham away. On September 3, 1867, the Civil War veteran returned to the army, this time in Company L, Tenth Cavalry. Over the next 28 years, he remained on duty until his retirement as a sergeant on March 18, 1895. Given many deterrents to marrying, Cheatham remained a bachelor, until just two weeks after leaving the army. At that time, he married 23 year-old Annie Ball, another native of Alexandria, at Israel Methodist Church in Washington, DC. Over the years, Cheatham supported his spouse and their children with his retirement and a salary as a mailman.

When he died on April 8, 1914, Annie Cheatham did not receive her husband's pension. Nearly destitute, the widow of this 'honest and respectable man' who had gained a reputation herself as an 'honest hardworking woman' faced difficult times not only for herself, but also for their three children. In desperation, she wrote to the commissioner of pensions. She had, 'no money and in winter time right at my door with nothing to pay the rent.' This poverty forced her to look for a home to place her children, but to no avail. She pointed out: 'I did not know there was such a place in Washington City that would treat a poor lone woman like that.' Eventually, after considerable red tape, she secured a $16 a month pension, which she added to by work as a domestic until her death on July 8, 1936.[25]

Like Alexander Cheatham, Charles Creek turned to the army as a means to cease his grind as a field hand. Creek frankly stated: 'I got tired of looking at mules in the face from sunrise to sunset, thought there must be a better living in this world.'[26] So, too, had William Givens

---

23 Dobak and Phillips, *Black Regulars*, 7–8; 47–48; and 288, n11.
24 *ARSW, 1866*, I, 2.
25 Alexander 'Sandy' Cheatham Biographical File, Fort Verde State Park, Camp Verde, AZ.
26 Don Rickey, Jr., 'Negro Regulars in the American Army: An Indian Wars Combat Record.,' 4. Photocopied typescript, Falls Church, VA, May 1965, 4, Fort Union National Monument, New Mexico.

of Cynthiana, Kentucky, born on March 10, 1853, been a 'farmer in boyhood.' He abandoned these labors to spend four years as a construction worker. Finally, Givens enlisted on August 20, 1869, reporting to Company B, Tenth Cavalry. He served his full enlistment until his honorable discharge as a sergeant on August 20, 1874. Givens returned to service on August 1, 1876, again with Company B, Tenth Cavalry from which he would be discharged as first sergeant, on August 3, 1881. Next, he reported to Company K, Tenth Cavalry on November 8, 1881, remaining with the outfit as first sergeant until his expiration of service on November 12, 1892. More than a year passed before another reenlistment on November 14, 1893, took him to Troop F, Ninth Cavalry where he received an appointment as a lance corporal. By May 1894, he transferred back to his old regiment with Troop H, Tenth Cavalry. In due course, he would be appointed a sergeant with Troop D.

In January of 1898, Givens regained his position as top sergeant. On August 6, 1898, the 5'8 ½" 169lb Givens remained in Cuba after participating in the fighting there. Evidently, despite occasional breaks in service, he professed, 'I like the army and think I cannot do better in civil life.'

Indeed, Givens demonstrated his unswerving commitment to the profession of arms, first with the regiment in Texas where he served on the border during the grueling Victorio Campaign. Over decades, he ambitiously sought advancement through competitive examinations for various non-commissioned staff positions. While these efforts failed to bear fruit, he demonstrated his mettle during the Spanish American War in Cuba. As a first sergeant, he received a recommendation for a Certificate of Merit based on assuming command of the company in combat at Santiago. John Bigelow, Givens' captain, reported the stalwart soldier exercised, 'a steadying and encouraging influence upon his men.'[27]

As Bigelow's proposed commendation worked its way up the chain of command, Givens accepted a second lieutenant's commission in the Tenth US Volunteer Infantry.[28] He was one of the few Black officers with this unit manned by African American enlisted personnel. At one point, Givens received orders to take command of Company A. Demonstrating awareness of prevalent racial attitudes of the era, he asked that the detail be rescinded. He demurred because the company had a first lieutenant who should lead the unit in the 'absence of his captain.' Moreover, he contended it would be humiliating 'to the [white] officer of Company A,' and did not think assumption of command would be in the best interest of the service.[29]

Givens' responses did not stem from a lack of leadership abilities. Instead, he displayed a realistic recognition of the prejudicial mores of his times. Tellingly, his May 1898 efficiency report gave him high marks for his zeal and ability. For these traits and his capacity for command, he received an 'Excellent' rating. Despite the approbation of Givens' superiors, when the volunteers mustered out, he was forced to resume his rank as an enlisted man (a private) in the Tenth

---

27 *ARSW, 1898*, I, 711.
28 Edward L. Baker, *Roster of Non-Commissioned Officers of the Tenth Cavalry with Some Regimental Reminiscences, Appendices, Etc. connected with the Early History of the Regiment* (St Paul, MN: Wm. Kennedy Printing Co., 1897), 27; and givens_william_10us_vol_inf_cmsr-spanam (1), RG 94, NARA.
29 William H. Givens to Adjutant Tenth Volunteer Infantry, January 4, 1899, RG 94, Givens, William, Composite Service Record, NARA.

Cavalry. By the same token, a board reviewing the recommendation for Givens to receive the Certificate of Merit denied the request as it also did for a Medal of Honor.

Givens retired in June 1901 with 30 years' service. He died at Bellingham, Washington in 1907.[30] At least Givens had the satisfaction of knowing about Bigelow's efforts to recognize this commendable non-commissioned officer for his extraordinary actions.[31]

It should be noted, during decades as a soldier, Givens suffered from his share of illnesses such as acute diarrhea and acute rheumatism, both infirmities possibly arising from the rigors of frontier duty, inadequate diet and poor sanitation. More certainly, malarial fever and acute dermatitis on both feet stemmed from conditions faced in Cuba, causing service-connected ailments. So, too, was 'chronic orchitis traumatic' incurred by striking his 'testicle against the saddle while drilling.'[32]

As with William Givens, Charles H. Chinn pursued the military as a career. This quest resulted in considerable success.[33] Chinn volunteered as a private in the Twenty-Third USCT, which fought in Virginia and probably was the first full regiment of Blacks in the Army of the Potomac to see action against the vaunted Army of Northern Virginia.[34] Chinn later enlisted in the Twenty-Eighth USCT.[35] After the war, he began his five-year commitment, first as a private with the Company L, Ninth Cavalry. (Note the term company was the official designation for

---

30 *East Oregonian* (Pendleton, OR) February 12, 1907, Daily Evening Edition.
31 Schubert, *On the Trail of the Buffalo Soldiers*, I, 164–5. Note William A, Richardson, ed., *Supplement to the Revised Statutes of The United States I Second Edition Revised and Continued. 1874–1891* (Washington, DC: US Government Printing Office, 1891), 889, indicated that holders of the Certificate of Merit would receive $2 a month extra pay during his tie in service from the date of for which he was cited. Also, consult Adjutant General's Office Circular No. 2, February 11, 1892, which stipulated 'certificates of merit should, under law, be awarded for distinguished service, whether in action or otherwise, of a valuable character to the United States as, for example, extraordinary exertion in the preservation of human life, or in the preservation of public property, or rescuing public property from destruction by fire or otherwise, or any hazardous service by which the Government is saved loss in men or material. This was the only other recognition for enlisted men save the Medal of Honor during this period and had been personally commended by General Miles for bravery in the Indian wars.' Span amwar.com/Tenth cav.htm.
32 Givens, William, Composite Service Record, RG 94, NARA. While at Fort Assiniboine, Montana with Troop H, Tenth Cavalry, was one of several army wide candidates examined for advancement to ordnance sergeant, but he would not receive such an appointment. *A&NJ*, November 16, 1895, 179.
33 starexponent.com/news/local/freedom-foundation-plans-to-spruce-up-historic-shiloh-church-cemetery/article_0e936026-b618-53bb-93ee-8d2a66526139. According to Irene Schubert and Frank N. Schubert, *On the Trail of the Buffalo Soldiers: New and Revised Biographies of African-Americans in the US Army, 1866–1917* (Lanham, MD: The Scarecrow Press, 2004), 56, Chinn was a native of Kentucky.
34 A report from Ninth Army Corps, Fourth Division made by Brigadier General Edward Ferrero on May 15, 1864 referred to a superior force from the Army of Northern Virginia that the 2nd Ohio Cavalry repulsed. In response, the general 'marched the Twenty-third US Colored Troops to support the cavalry' which they did 'in line of battle … and drove the enemy in perfect rout.' spotsylvania.va.us/783/23rd-US-Colored-Troops.
35 For more on this regiment recruited extensively from Indiana and which saw at the controversial Battle of the Crater on July 30, 1864, consult: William Robert Forstchen, 'The Twenty-Eighth United States Colored Troops: Indiana's African Americans go to war, 1863–1865,' Ph.D. diss., Purdue University, 1994.

the basic tactical unit of era consisting of a maximum of 100 men of both cavalry and infantry regiments until 1883.)

By the mid-1870s, Chinn possessed two skills that assisted him as he advanced up the enlisted ranks. First, he became a saddler sergeant, an essential skilled worker charged with repairing and maintaining horse equipage along with various other types of leather used by cavalry units. Moreover, he was literate as demonstrated in 1874. He chaired a committee of fellow enlisted men from the Ninth Cavalry as well as the Twenty-Fourth Infantry at Ringgold Barracks, Texas. Soon after the death of Massachusetts Senator Charles Sumner, these soldiers met with Chinn presiding. They unanimously adopted a resolution expressing their condolences and admiration for this staunch abolitionist. Chinn authored the document.[36]

As for the deceased, in 1856, South Carolina Congressman Preston Brooks savagely caned Sumner because of an impassioned 'Crime against Kansas' speech the Massachusetts lawmaker made in the United States Senate. Years later, Sumner returned to Congress. He took up his empty desk where among his accomplishments, in 1865, he championed the Thirteenth Amendment to the US Constitution. Not content to stop there, Sumner sought additional legislation to gain a greater political voice and standing for Blacks, including his drafting of the country's first civil rights bills.[37]

The soldiers at Ringgold Barracks knew of these efforts. They praised Sumner as, 'the advocator of our equal rights with all men.' Their resolution acknowledged the passing, 'of such a noble friend … to our race' and 'his history which is part of the history of the country for the past 30 years' that had ended resulting in the loss of 'a true friend' to 'the colored people of the United States.' The committee intended to send copies of their resolution to four key newspapers hoping they would be published. Chinn's imprimatur appeared at the end of the submission as chairman.[38]

By 1877, Chinn no longer held the position of saddler sergeant. Instead, he advanced to first sergeant of Company C, Ninth Cavalry – the top non-commissioned officer within a company.[39] Nearly a decade later, the *Army and Navy Journal* listed him as the Twenty-Fourth Infantry's sergeant major, the highest enlisted position within a regiment, the next higher level of organization consisting of 10 to 12 companies, depending on the era. He, as did many other enlisted men who occasionally transferred within the regiments comprised of Blacks, performed concurrent duty as post sergeant major of Fort Sill, Indian Territory (Oklahoma).[40]

Although Chinn reverted to first sergeant in Company E, Twenty-Fourth Infantry, he sought a position as a senior non-commissioned staff officer. While at Fort Sill, he underwent an examination to determine his qualifications for the position of a post quartermaster sergeant – a desirable administrative assignment charged with oversight of a wide array of tasks. Quartermaster sergeants issued uniforms, barracks furnishings, cookware, as well as being responsible for

---

36 Frank N. Schubert, ed. and comp., *Voices of the Buffalo Soldiers: Record, Reports and Recollections of Military Life and Service in the West* (Albuquerque: University of New Mexico Press, 2003), 63–64.
37 senate.gov/senators/FeaturedBios/Featured_Bio Sumner.htm.
38 *A&NJ*, April 25, 1874, 580.
39 Schubert and Schubert, *On the Trail of the Buffalo Soldiers*, 57.
40 *A&NJ*, December 18, 1886, 410.

draught animals and wheeled vehicles to name but a few of their many details. The position required organizational skills, accounting aptitude and literacy.[41]

While the outcome of this test is unknown, Chinn eventually secured a billet in another desirable capacity as a post ordnance sergeant – one other complex non-commissioned specialty like that of the quartermaster. In this case, the occupation concentrated on accoutrements, armament and ammunition. In all these instances, these promotions to the upper non-commissioned officer echelons typically represented the pinnacle for enlisted men's advancement.[42] During this era, making the leap from the ranks to an appointment as a commissioned officer in the US Army, presented a monumental challenge for white enlisted men and an impossible feat for Black soldiers in the nineteenth century. For all intents, the route to higher pay and status as a staff non-commissioned officer was the only one opened to Chinn. Even then, he faced incredible odds.

In some respects, that success nearly proved Chinn's undoing. While stationed at Fort Pulaski outside Savannah, Georgia, by then more or less a mothballed installation, Ordnance Sergeant Chinn attacked an unsuspected enemy with nearly fatal consequences. In a battle against a hoard of invading mosquitoes, he resorted to extreme measures that resulted in a second bombardment of the brick fortress with a potentially disastrous outcome. As a newspaper account indicated, one morning the sergeant left his quarters for chores. He headed to the storeroom that held his materials and tools. Soon afterwards, an explosion concerned one of the other staff members at the fort. The cause was Chinn's novel approach to eradicate, 'the swarms of mosquitoes in the store room.' His solution to rid the facility of the pests involved, 'a handful of powder from one of the open casks in the corner of the room, dampened it and laid it in the middle of the floor. This he ignited, so that the smoke would drive out the pesky insects.'

The strategy literally, backfired. That initial small discharge jumped to a larger source – 400lbs of black powder, which exploded. A chain reaction ignited ammunition detonating at intervals. For an entire day, two sections of the fort burned, consuming considerable government property and threatening worse destruction. Another adjacent storage magazine containing two tons of volatile explosives threatened even a worse eruption.

Beside this possibility, one more concern arose. It appeared the injuries Chinn sustained during the conflagration would result in his death after being, 'knocked down three times in his effort to reach the door.' With his clothes torched as was much of his body including his hair, eyebrows and, 'from his head down below his waist he was horribly scorched and burned,' he

41 This examination was held in accordance with Special Order 109, October 14, 1887, Department of the Missouri. *A&NJ*, October 29, 1887, 263. Later that year, *A&NJ*, December 17, 1887, 403, indicated Chinn had been granted what seemed an unusually lengthy furlough for an enlisted man 'of four months' as first sergeant of Co. E, Twenty-Fourth Infantry per '(SO 142, Dec. 12, Div. M.).'
42 According to the *Weekly Arizona Miner* (Prescott) June 19, 1885, 'John Fitzgerald, a strapping colored soldier' was aboard a train headed to Fort Bowie, Arizona 'to take a position as post ordnance sergeant – to which he has been promoted, he being the first colored soldier ever promoted to that position.' Although, Fitzgerald was an eighteen-year army veteran when he secured this promotion that brought him to a garrison manned by white troops. He was not the only Black ordnance sergeant assigned to a garrison with white enlisted personnel. Among others, Moses Williams was detailed in a similar capacity at Fort Whipple, Arizona. For more about this former cavalryman and Medal of Honor recipient consult: Donald Richard Whitbeck, *A Man Named Moses: The Military Life of a Heroic Buffalo Soldier* (Los Angeles: WT Records and Publishing, 1996).

finally reached an area where a medicine chest and oil could be accessed. The post doctor soon attended the unfortunate victim.

A newspaper reporter speculated Chinn would, 'have to be court martialed for this loss of government property, due to his carelessness.' Given that the fort's medical officer thought it impossible for Chinn to survive, it appeared the sergeant would not face disciplinary actions. In fact, this incident did not end the career of the long service soldier who had, 'been considered an able and faithful officer in his position.'[43]

He survived. Three years later, decades of dedication allowed him to retire. Acting on final orders, he entrained to Fort McPherson, Georgia to complete the necessary out-processing for his honorable discharge. From there, he was to travel at government expense, to Brandy Station, Virginia, which he had selected as his retirement residence. The journey added one last laurel to his proud decades in uniform. While in transit, Chinn experienced Jim Crow laws in Georgia. In response, he refused to accept the harassment of being seated in a car restricted to Blacks. Although most Blacks acquiesced to this widespread prejudicial practice, Chinn balked at the slight. He took legal action against both the railroad and the state of Georgia, but Chinn's appeal to the court failed to bring about the justice he sought in an era when the fictitious 'separate but equal' rule prevailed throughout the nation.[44] Nonetheless, Chinn did reach Virginia. He remained there in peaceful retirement until 1927, when he died and was laid to rest in Culpeper County's Shiloh Baptist Church Cemetery in Elkwood.[45]

On one hand, Chinn represented scores of formerly enslaved individuals who looked to the US Army to emerge from their past and make a new life as a soldier. Unlike a goodly number of these men, however, Chinn secured a coveted, rare position as a staff non-commissioned officer, an opportunity available to a limited number of whites and even fewer Blacks, the majority of who had been freeborn Northerners.[46]

Of note, Chinn was not the first Black to gain advancement as a staff non-commissioned officer. This occurred in 1879, when two men James, W. Sullivant and David B. Jeffers, obtained this distinction as post commissary sergeants. The latter of the pair, Jeffers, somewhat paralleled Chinn's path, albeit one which predated the race conscious ordnance sergeant. A number of years after his Civil War, after Jeffers' Civil War experience with the Thirty-Second USCT, influenced the Indiana native to return to the military at Cincinnati, Ohio. At first, he did a stint with the Twenty-Fourth Infantry where he received his warrant as a sergeant. Transferring to the Ninth Cavalry, he secured an appointment as the regimental quartermaster sergeant that provided a steppingstone to one of the nearly 150 billets for commissary sergeants. On June 5, 1879, he assumed this position and remained active for 30 years until his retirement from Fort Custer, Montana in May of 1897. Barely a year later, the retiree returned to the army as a first lieutenant in the Forty-eighth Volunteer Infantry, one of several temporary units established with Black soldiers and a few Black officers necessitated by the Spanish American War.[47]

---

43 *Morning News* (Savannah, GA) July 21, 1894.
44 *A&NJ*, April 17, 1897, 603.
45 starexponent.com/news/local/freedom-foundation-plans-to-spruce-up-historic-shiloh-church-cemetery/article_0e936026-b618-53bb-93ee-8d2a66526139.html.
46 Dobak and Phillips, *Black Regulars*, 81–83.
47 Schubert and Schubert, *On the Trail of the Buffalo Soldiers*, 152. In contrast, Sullivant served only briefly as a commissary sergeant because of a conviction for embezzlement in 1879 by general court-

Joseph Parker was another of those fortunate few individuals who possessed special skills, trades and above all, the ability to read and write that were uncommon among the early enlistees.[48] During the Civil War, Parker wore the lozenge and three chevrons of a first sergeant with the First USCT. Two years after the war ended, he entered the Tenth Cavalry, on May 8, 1867, as a private. Parker then became a saddler sergeant. By 1873, he earned the top non-commissioned officer's slot with the regiment as its sergeant major, a position he retained until his death in 1882.[49]

Correspondingly, Mexican born Stephen Starr drew on his time with the Sixty-Fifth US Colored Infantry's Company I, where he was wounded in action. This background provided a solid foundation for a later 30 year career with the Regular Army. A former cowboy and sheepherder, Starr entered as a foot soldier with the Forty-First US Infantry. In 1869, as part of the reorganization and reduction of army manpower, he would become a fixture of the Twenty-Fourth Infantry. During the Spanish American War, like Jeffers, he accepted a wartime commission with the Black Ninth Infantry, US Volunteers, but not before receiving a second combat wound, this time with the Twenty-Fourth Infantry at San Juan Hill.

Robert Anderson's tenure with the US Colored Troops also placed him among the Civil War survivors who continued to wear Uncle Sam's blue. In his autobiography, *From Slavery to Affluence* Anderson recorded: 'My company was ordered to Kansas and became part of the army that corralled the Indians on the reservation in what was known as Indian Territory,' where he and his comrades in arms crossed the country afoot, but not without incident. About a month after Anderson and his unit marched from Missouri towards Texas, a raiding party appeared. Anderson's account read much like a passage from a pulp novel: 'We expected a battle and the [supply] wagons were all drawn in a circle and the horse and mules staked inside the circle and the regiment drawn up in battle formation.' Thinking better of striking, the Native Americans did not attack. Understandably cautious, that night, the infantrymen remained in their makeshift bastion. As Anderson confessed, 'none of us slept much.'[50]

One more soldier surnamed Anderson, whose given name was Richard, also decided to remain with army life after the Civil War. Richard Anderson soldiered with the Sixty-Fifth USCT (formerly the Second Regiment of Missouri Colored Infantry from his native state).[51] In

---

martial that led to an eight-year prison sentence. He never served the term. On June 25, 1879, after his arraignment, Sullivant escaped from guard house at Fort McIntosh, Texas. *ARSW, 1879*, I, 209.
48   Dobak and Phillips, *Black Regulars*, 50–53.
49   *Ibid.*, 82; and Schubert and Schubert, *On the Trail of the Buffalo Soldiers*, 151–2.
50   Robert B. Anderson, *From Slavery to Affluence: Memoirs of Robert Anderson, Ex-Slave* (Hemingford, NE: n.p., 1927), 45.
51   Second Regiment Colored Infantry was organized at Benton Barracks December 18, 1863 to January 16, 1864. The regiment remained there on duty until March 1864. The designation changed to Sixty-Fifth Regiment United States Colored Troops on March 11, 1864. Attached to Dept. of Missouri to June, 1864. Provisional Brigade, District of Morganza, Louisiana, Department of the Gulf, to September, 1864. 2nd Brigade, 1st Division, United States Colored Troops, District of Morganza, Department of the Gulf, to February, 1865. 1st Brigade, 1st Division, United States Colored Troops, District of Morganza, Louisiana Department of the Gulf, to May, 1865. Northern District of Louisiana and Department of the Gulf to January, 1867. Garrison duty at Morganza, Louisiana until May 1865. Ordered to Port Hudson, Louisiana. Garrison duty there and at Baton Rouge and in Northern District of Louisiana until January, 1867. Mustered out January 8, 1867. nps.gov/civilwar/search-battle-units-detail.htm?battle UnitCode= UUS0065RI00C.

1866, he signed on in Baton Rouge, Louisiana with the Ninth Cavalry where he reported as a private to Company B. He must have demonstrated ability. After his first five-year enlistment, he had risen to sergeant, once more chiefly because he was literate. With his term expired, the sergeant left the army to make his way to St. Louis, Missouri.

Anderson spent less than a year as a civilian before reenlisting in the Ninth for a second tour of duty. This time he earned his first sergeant's chevrons. The register of enlistments for 1877 and 1882 continued to trace Anderson's whereabouts and status. During the former year, he stated he was 37 years of age and was serving at Fort Bayard, New Mexico with the Ninth Cavalry. His eyes, hair and completion were described as black and his height recorded at 5'7½". When discharged on August 2, 1882, Anderson had been his company's first sergeant. At the expiration of these five years as a non-commissioned, his character was rated as, 'highly exemplary.' He then made his way to Fort Hays, Kansas where he reenlisted for another five years, which ended on August 2, 1887, with Troop B, Ninth Cavalry at Fort Selden, New Mexico. In both instances, like many careermen, he listed his occupation as 'soldier.'[52]

Between these two terms, Anderson took part in the Victorio Campaign. During this dangerous deployment, he displayed credible valor. It was in August 1881 at Gavilan Canyon, New Mexico where he faced the elderly, yet highly capable Nana and his fellow Apache.[53] By February 5, 1885 Anderson became the Ninth's regimental quartermaster sergeant. From there he succeeded in passing his examination for post quartermaster sergeant, which brought about his transfer from Fort Riley Kansas to Fort Selden, New Mexico, at that time garrisoned solely by white troops. While rare, this situation occasionally occurred for other Black staff non-commissioned.[54] After three years, word came for Anderson to move on to Fort Apache, Arizona. There he returned to the familiar environment of Black soldiers – men of the Tenth Cavalry.

Not long thereafter, Anderson made his way back to New Mexico as a member of the non-commissioned staff of Fort Marcy in Santa Fe.[55] By this time, he transitioned to post commissary sergeant, a rank he held upon retirement, which took place on August 20, 1892, at his own request.[56] His multiple talents bespoke of an exceptional soldier. Anderson also stood out in that he numbered among an extremely rare group of Black enlisted men who left accounts of their combat experiences when he briefly recorded his campaigning against Victorio.[57]

Anderson was remarkable in another way. Unlike most staff non-commissioned officers through the 1880s, who tended to be freeborn northern men, Andersons' southern roots differed from the norm. A likelihood existed that he had been enslaved prior to the war. Nevertheless, Anderson could be considered, 'typical of the twenty-five non-commissioned officers from the

---

52 RG 94, Register of Enlistments, Alphabetical Listing 'A', 46 Line No. 59, 1877; 26 Line No. 124, 1882, NARA.
53 Monroe Lee Billington, *New Mexico's Buffalo Soldiers, 1866–1900* (Niwot: University Press of Colorado, 1991), 106–7; Kenner, *Buffalo Soldiers and Officers of the Ninth*, 230.
54 'Post Q.M. Sergt. Richard Anderson will be relieved from duty at Fort Riley, and will proceed to Fort Selden for duty (SO Sept 4, H.Q.A.)' *A&NJ*, September 19, 1885, 121.
55 *A&NJ*, September 22, 1888, 65, reported this transfer promulgated by Special Orders, HQA, September 13, 1888.
56 *A&NJ*, August 6, 1892, 862 per Special Orders, HQA, August 1, 1892.
57 T.G. Steward, *The Colored Regulars in the United States Army* (Philadelphia: A.M.E Book Concern, 1904), 317–20.

black regiments who … were able to join the staff departments.' This situation allowed them to receive, 'better pay and long-term assignment to one post,' plus under certain circumstances, 'a private dwelling, however shabby, instead of the crowded and sometimes dangerous communal life of the barracks.'[58] The advantages accrued increased the likelihood that these men could abandon bachelorhood to begin a family – a relatively rare option in that military policy discouraged marriage in many ways.

James D. Walker exemplified another frequent path followed by USCT veterans who continued military life after the Civil War. His post-1865 service did not result in a decades-long stint on active duty. Walker numbered among many others whose time in the ranks ended after one or two tours. This native of Jessamine County, Kentucky, first enlisted on July 6, 1864. As with many formerly enslaved individuals, he could not state his date of birth. He first went to Camp Nelson, Kentucky as a private in the 116th USCT. After his discharge in late 1866, Walker made the transition from what amounted to temporary duty as a Union volunteer, to the fulltime status of a member of the US Army. He spent the next five years with the Ninth Cavalry. At the expiration of his service in 1871, he received an honorable discharge at Fort McKavett, Texas. Subsequently, Walker married Catherine Brown (nee Johnson). They raised a family and as early as 1875, he began preaching. Walker served as an African Methodist minister both in El Paso and in San Angelo, Texas. Walker's remuneration from his congregations would have been insubstantial at best. In 1900, the cavalrymen turned clergyman would be admitted to the National Soldiers Home at Leavenworth, Kansas due to rheumatism and debilitating ailments that sometimes caused him to end his homily in the middle of a sermon.[59]

Thomas Braddock offered another example of the hardships endured by Black soldiers and subsequent physical ailments. Born in 1855 in Howard County, Maryland, he listed his occupation as a laborer on October 4, 1881, at the recruiters in Baltimore. He was also probably one of many survivors of enslavement. On December 31, 1881, the 5'7 ½" Braddock arrived at Fort Davis, Texas as a new member of Company I, Tenth Cavalry. Barely a year into service, rheumatism plagued Braddock. This was not an uncommon complaint among horse soldiers in particular.

Over the coming years, he received rudimentary treatment for his left shoulder and knees. Nonetheless, once Braddock transferred to Arizona with the entire regiment in 1885, he went into the field. He did so again in 1886, which may have further aggravated his medical condition and possibly contributed to his discharge at the end of his sole enlistment. After his departure, on October 30, 1886, he went to Prescott, Arizona. By 1890, Braddock headed to Phoenix. For a time, he served as a janitor for Phoenix's Mayor James D. Monihan, who thoughtfully put Braddock on light duty because of his infirmities. His ailments worsened and the old trooper developed a heart murmur. Braddock turned to patent medicine to ease his pain. These heavily alcohol-based remedies may have shortened his life. Braddock, who was literate, unlike many of those who had been formerly enslaved, died at age 55 on March 4, 1910.[60]

While Braddock's ailments could be attributed to stramineous military duty, that seemingly was not the case for William Cathay. On November 15, 1866, Cathay (or Cathey), who was

---

58 Dobak and Phillips, *Black Regulars*, 82–83.
59 James Walker, Biographical File, Fort Concho National Landmark and Museum Library, San Angelo, TX.
60 Thomas Braddock, Biographical File, Fort Verde State Park, Camp Verde, Arizona.

one of a number of individuals without prior military experience, entered service at St. Louis. Described as being 22 years of age, standing 5'9" with black eyes, hair and complexion, the newly admitted recruit reported to nearby Jefferson Barracks. Missouri. By February 13, 1867, Private Cathay mustered into Company A, Thirty-Eighth Infantry.[61]

That same month, the first of several periods of hospitalization appeared in Cathay's records. The recruit had contracted smallpox. Another admission to hospital followed in April; this time at Fort Riley, after departing Jefferson Barracks for an overland trek from Missouri through Kansas and on to New Mexico.

At the end of the journey, Cathay arrived at Fort Cummings, New Mexico. On 27 January 1868, the private soon spent three days at that post's medical facility due to a complaint diagnosed as rheumatism. By March 20, another three days of hospitalization brought about a diagnosis for the same malady. After a transfer to Fort Bayard, New Mexico, Cathay went to the post hospital for a month with neuralgia. On October 14, 1868, Fort Bayard's surgeon issued a certificate of disability pronouncing the patient both mentally and physically feeble and noting the private had spent numerous periods on sick call that frequently resulted in being pronounced unfit for duty. As one biographical sketch indicated, Cathay entered four hospitals at five different times and for varied time periods.[62]

Cathay departed the military with an undistinguished record, possibly reflecting the actions of a malingerer or alternately, as was not uncommon within the ranks, as one with considerable preexisting medical issues. Either way, the discharged infantryman returned to civilian pursuits, assumed the name of Cathy Williams and adopted the garb of a woman. The erstwhile former foot soldier undertook various jobs including, during 1869–70, as an officer's cook at Fort Union, New Mexico. In due course, Williams possibly moved to Pueblo, Colorado and for two years, worked in a local laundry. After Pueblo, Las Animas was the next stopover as a laundress.[63]

By 1876, Cathay resided in Trinidad, Colorado. There, the local laundress consented to an interview that found its way into a St. Louis Paper. The resultant article became the basis for much of the misunderstood and misrepresented saga.[64] Williams' self-portrayal to the reporter

---

61 RG 94, Records of the Adjutant General's Office, Regular Army Muster Rolls, Company A, 38th Infantry, December 1866-October 1868, NARA.
62 RG 94, Adjutant General's Office, Carded Medical Records, Regular Army, 1821–1884, NARA, contains six cards relating to William Cathey. Further, DeAnne Blanton, 'Cathay Williams: Black Woman Soldier 1866–1868,' *Minerva* 10 nos. 3, 4 (Fall-Winter 1992): 1–12 delves into the medical records in the National Archives in detail questioning if 'racism or sexism' caused denial of the claim for disability 'during the pension application and review process?' The author somewhat dilutes this line of inquiry acknowledging 'that nowhere in her pension application file are any written statements that can be perceived, even marginally, as racist or sexist, and there are no derogatory remarks written about the applicant herself.' Further, Blanton adds one telltale other detail when indicating that among the causes for 'denying a pension was that the service was not legal. The Pension Bureau could have denied the disability application immediately, because the former soldier in question was a woman. Enlistment of women in the military was illegal. Just as likely, denial stemmed not from gender bias, but was based on a determination that the ailments delineated either preexisted military service or appeared after time in the military without tangible relation to being service connected.
63 Mary Williams, 'Cathay Williams Female Buffalo Soldier,' Fort Davis National Historic Site, www.buffalosoldier.net.
64 *St. Louis Daily Times*, January 2, 1876. The article indicated that during the interview with 'Kate' the reporter described his subject as a 'powerfully built black as night, masculine looking, and has a

Some secondary sources presumed William Cathay died in the early 1890s and further labelled the individual as the 'only female buffalo soldier' known by the name Cathy Williams. The 1910 United States Census indicated that these authors erred on such details. (Courtesy National Archives and Records Administration)

was that of a good soldier, who never went to the guardhouse as a prisoner, carried the musket and performed the duties assigned. There was no mention of frequent absences from duty while in hospital. Tiring of the military, supposedly in an effort to end service earlier than the required time allotted, Williams used complaints of frequent pains in the side and rheumatism to obtain a medical release. The fair-weather private also declared that the surgeon discovered a not so well-kept secret. Williams asserted: 'the men all wanted to get rid of me after they found out I was a woman.' Women were barred from military service and would be for decades to come. Thus, this factor would have been grounds for immediate dismissal.

Nonetheless, producing a copy of the US Army discharge papers seemingly convinced the reporter of the veracity of these claims. Among other details, the supposed native of Missouri related the family and their alleged slave master lived near Jefferson City. After the man 'died there and when the war broke out and the United States soldiers came to Jefferson City they took me and other colored folks with them to Little Rock,' Williams related. Williams added names of some high-ranking Union officer-employers to underpin the claim.

Based on this uncollaborated article, more than a century later, several writers and the general accepted the article. Some dubbed Williams as 'the only documented black woman to serve in the regular Army during the nineteenth century.[65] Likewise, a few biographers referenced Williams' unsuccessful efforts to obtain a military pension.[66] The late 1890s' medical affidavit accompanying the application for disability, clearly marked through references as 'he' and 'him' and substituted 'she' and 'her' as amendments. Further, the physician noted the applicant stood 5'7" tall, weighted 160lbs, had a large, stout physique and was 49 years old. There was no deafness, or indication of rheumatism or neuralgia, but all the toes on both feet had been amputated, which required the use of crutches. The doctor provided no explanation or details concerning the cause of amputation. More to the point, he concluded that no reason existed to grant a disability pension. How he reached this verdict is unknown, as is whether he or two other physicians involved in the review even conducted a complete physical examination given emphasis solely on the feet.[67] The military denied the application for medical benefits for lack of evidence that

---

very independent air both in conversation and action.' Furthermore, the writer reported if Williams 'dressed in male attire … would readily pass as a man.'

65 blackpast.org/african-american-histor593–4, y/williams-cathay–1850. Also see, Philip Thomas Tucker, *Cathy Williams: From Slave to Female Buffalo Soldier* (Mechanicsburg, PA: Stackpole Books, 2002); and *America's Female Buffalo Soldier: A New Look at the Life of Cathy Williams in History and Memory* (n.p.: n.d., 2017), as well as a more insightful article by Gabriel Arkles, 'No One Is Disposable: Going Beyond the Trans Military Inclusion Debate,' *Seattle Journal for Social Justice* 13 no. 2 (2014): 459–514. Numerous online websites repeat the story and various versions of the declaration such as 'Cathay Williams Defied Her Time to Become the Only Known Female Buffalo Soldier' and 'Cathay Williams Was the Army's Only Female Buffalo Soldier and First Black Female Enlistee.' newsroom.woundedwarriorproject.org/The-Only-Known-Female-Buffalo-Soldier-Cathay-Williams; military.com/history/ cathay-williams-was- armys-only-female-buffalo-soldier-and-first-black-female-enlistee.html, as but two of many erroneous contentions.

66 Schubert and Schubert, *On the Trail of the Buffalo Soldiers*, 322–23; Schubert, *Voices of the Buffalo Soldiers*, 33–35; Dobak and Phillips, *Black Regulars*, 288 n 12.

67 RG 15, Records of the Veterans Administration, pension application, Cathay Williams, Surgeon's Certificate in the case of Cathay Williams alias William Cathay, September 9, 1891, and Original Invalid Claim, Cathay Williams alias William Cathay, February 19, 1892, Pension File SO 1032593. Cathay William. NARA. Although the three doctors described Williams as 'a large stout woman' and used

the health issues were service connected. Additionally, there was no mention that the original discharge came about because of Williams being discovered to be woman.

Indeed, Cathy Williams was William Cathay who was a biological male. Somehow this fact escaped those who failed to question the 1876 article. More than two decades later, however, another reporter published an exposé under the headline 'WILLIAM CATHAY'S WHIM. For Twenty Years He Masqueraded as a Woman.' The gist was that Williams had long been, 'employed by many of the most prominent families as a laundress' in Pueblo. Employers described Cathay as: 'Thoroughly deferential in every way she was a typical servant of the South during the antebellum days.'[68]

The 1880 census listed Kate Williams as a 'Black Female Age 37 washer woman. Married, Born New Mexico; Parents Born New Mexico.'[69] Four years earlier, Williams told the St. Louis reporter of being from Missouri and that her husband had attempted to run off with her money, wagon, mules and a watch, that led to his arrest. Thus, the 1880 census did not square with these portions of the 1876 account.

Further, the 1897 article reported the court pronounced the subject insane. During the first hearing, the judge sent Williams to an asylum wearing the garb of a woman in which the respondent had appeared before the bench. Upon the new patient's arrival at the institution, the staff 'told the attending physician that there was no place for her as she was a man.' Nonetheless, Williams remained clothed in a dress as authorities at the facility expressed a concern for the 'possible effect on the disease for which the patient was suffering.'

Not long thereafter, 'the same individual appeared at Trinidad as William Cathay and was adjudged insane and returned here to-day and committed to the asylum as a man.' Regardless, Cathay kept insisting that 'he served through the war as a body servant to Generals Grant and Sherman.' The article added that Cathay, 'donned woman's clothes in a moment of whim and continued to wear them' after the Civil War had concluded. Nevertheless, until his death on September 27, 1911, official records in the institution carried the name William Cather, who was listed as a male.[70] In the final analysis, Cathay brought about no change within the United States military of the era, a stronghold of homophobia.

gender specific terms such as 'her' there is no indication that the patient disrobed. If not, the three acted on Williams' statement of being a woman and possibly drew that conclusion as well from her attire.
68 *Rocky Mountain News* (Denver) April 22, 1897.
69 10th Census 1880 Trinidad, Las Animas County, Colorado. Enumeration District No.66, Page 14.
70 Note that some sources postulated 'Cathy Williams' died around 1893 in Trinidad, Colorado. The official death certificate indicated he was a single, colored male passing away at age 69. His place of birth was listed as Ohio. The listed cause of death at the asylum in Pueblo was 'chronic nephritis.' Committal papers from court in Trinidad papers bear the date April 26, 1897 and refer to William Cather (the name in which the individual was recorded at the institution) as 'he' and 'him.' Likewise, the accompanying order to commit stated also Cather was a native of Ohio, and was 55 when he entered the facility for 'chronic mania.' Documents provided Colorado Mental Health Institute at Pueblo, May 6, 2022. The 1900 and 1910 census added the date of birth as March of 1842, repeated the place of birth as Ohio, and indicated in the former instance the occupation as laborer as well as reported the inability to read and write. 12th Census 1900 2nd Precinct, Colorado State Insane Asylum, Pueblo County, Colorado, Enumeration District158, Sheet No. 4; 13th Census 1910 2nd Precinct, Colorado State Insane Asylum, Pueblo County, Colorado, Enumeration District 158, Sheet No. 3b.

While unusual in several respects, William Cathay's story revealed several factors of a broader nature. For one thing, admitting physically unfit applicants periodically led to early discharge or subsequent efforts to obtain medical pensions, a course initiated by Cathay. Next, like many soldiers, whether Black or white, Cathay returned to civilian life before or after their initial three or five-year commitment.[71] Nonetheless, the tendency to reenlist ran higher in the regiments with Black personnel. Several hundred of them continued, 'for more than two enlistments' as they possibly 'found greater rewards in the army than they would in civilian life.'[72] According to one overarching review of the US, Army in the West from 1866 through the early 1890s: 'the higher reenlistment rate could be explained by the fact that black soldiers were well-respected and highly regarded within the black community. The opposite was true of the white population's attitude towards white soldiers. Most white civilians looked upon the soldier with contempt regardless of race.'[73]

However, other reasons prompted Blacks to enlist or reenlist, as Cathay's 1876 interview also revealed. The erstwhile infantryman said: 'I wanted to make my own living and not be dependent on relatives or friends.'[74] Despite being unique in many ways, William Cathay's desire for economic betterment and advancement both for monetary gain and elevation of social standing would be shared by many Black recruits.[75] Making a living, however, was only one incentive.

Motives and Motivation

Consequently, numerous Blacks, many of whom previously had been enslaved, as well as displaced by the Civil War, looked at the military variously not only as a source of income, but it also offered food, shelter, clothing and more. Some of them perceived the US Army as an honorable profession with a potential to achieve what would be viewed in the future as a springboard for upward mobility. Decades after the first Black regiments formed, Secretary of War Redfield Proctor addressed this topic, writing: 'To the colored man the service offers a career; to the white man too often only a refuge.'[76] Also, for some, the military opened a means to seek adventure, or even escape from an old way of life, such as prosecution by the law, racial threats in the defeated South and elsewhere, marital issues and unemployment.

Other impetuses spurred enlistment depending on individual circumstances, such as the primary reason why Joshua Johnson became a private in the Tenth Cavalry. He developed

---

71 Dobak and Phillips, *Black Regulars*, 47–48; 267.
72 *Ibid.*, 58.
73 Utley, *Frontier Regulars*, 22 and 26. As another example of a long-time early member of the Black regiments, Benjamin F. Davis appeared on the rolls as an original member of Company, Tenth Cavalry as of October 15, 1867. Born in Chester County, Pennsylvania, Davis served in the Civil War before entering in the US Army. He retired on April 23, 1895 with 31 years active duty to his credit, 19 of which was as either the Ninth Cavalry's regimental sergeant major, or as a post quartermaster sergeant, another of the sought-after staff NCO positions. Another telling detail was that he remained in contact with an old comrade, Robert Benjamin. Of equal interest, he joined the NAACP. Schubert and Schubert, *On the Trail of the Buffalo Soldiers*, 73.
74 *St. Louis Daily Times*, January 2, 1876.
75 Rickey, 'Negro Regulars in the American Army,' 4.
76 *ARSW, 1889*, I, 9.

hemorrhoids during his service in the Union Army and upon mustering out of the USCT, he did not have the money for a physician. Johnson was able to avoid detection of his preexisting condition, which later required a military doctor to treat him after he reported for duty.[77]

Another Civil War veteran, George Washington Williams, recounted that a patriotic spirit induced him to flee from Bedford Springs, Pennsylvania to take up soldiering. The 14 year-old son of free Blacks never knew the sting of an overseer's lash, yet he was intent on striking a blow against the Confederacy. To do so, he was among many throughout the decades, who falsified their ages.[78] This subterfuge may have accounted for his use of an assumed name when he entered Company C, Forty-First USCT. The ploy succeeded. This under-aged impostor soon discovered that his decision had serious consequences. During September of 1864, he participated in the assault against Fort Harrison, Virginia and sustained a wound. Although a

casualty, he quickly headed back to the front to engage in some of the final fierce fighting of the war.

After surviving shot and shell during the war, Williams spent a 'few months at home with books.' The brief respite wore thin. He longed, 'for the outdoor, lively exhilarating exercise of military life.' Leaving home, Williams reached Pittsburgh and on August 9, 1867, he signed on for five years with the Tenth Cavalry. After he had reported to Carlisle Barracks, in the eastern part of the state, as an experienced non-commissioned officer he drilled recruits before being dispatched to Kansas for duty with regimental headquarters.[79] At 18 years of age, the callow youth was promoted to the highest enlisted rank as the regimental sergeant major! In his new position, Williams conceded his days: 'would flow merrily away at headquarters, with but little to do, far away from the Indian's deadly arrow.'[80]

After the regiment's organization concluded, Williams departed for Fort Arbuckle, Indian Territory (Oklahoma). For the most part, the three companies sent there spent much of the time in rebuilding the post. This tedious duty meant Williams and his fellow troopers lived in relative safety, but inexplicably, on May 19, 1868, a bullet entered his left lung.[81]

It is unknown how Williams sustained his wound. After a period of hospitalization, he obtained a certificate of disability for the injury received, 'not in the line of duty rendering him unfit to perform the duties of a soldier.' Consequently, on September 4, 1868, he returned to civilian status once more. The 19 year-old Williams went on to became a distinguished Baptist minister, authored the first book treating the history of Blacks in the United States, was elected as an Ohio state legislator and worked as a respected newspaper columnist.[82]

---

77   Dobak and Phillips, *Black Regulars*, 47.
78   Many 'minors found their way into the black regiments.' Indeed, at various times the threshold was either 18 or 21 years of age for the minimum allowed without consent of a parent or guardian. The one exception was for musicians. Dobak and Phillips, *Black Regulars*, 23; and McChristian, *Regular Army O!*, 33.
79   Dobak and Phillips, *Black Regulars*, 85.
80   'Military Life on the Plains,' *Cincinnati Commercial*, January 6, 1877, written under Williams' *nom de plume*, Áristides.
81   RG 94, Records of the Adjutant General's Office, Special Orders, Fort Arbuckle, Indian Territory, May 19, 1868, NARA.
82   John Hope Franklin, *George Washington Williams: A Biography* (Chicago: University of Chicago Press, 1985), 1–11. In contrast, Kentuckian Corporal Edward Scott did receive disability payments for his wounds, which was so severe that it required amputation of his right leg, which he stoically

Somewhat akin to Williams, as a child during the Civil War, Madison Bruin had observed both northern and southern troops in his home state of Kentucky. Unlike Williams, Bruin could not pass as older than his actual age. Thus, he had to wait for his chance. He recollected: 'What did I think when I seed al them sojers? I wants to be one too. I didn't care what side, I 'jis wants a gun and a hoss and be a sojer.'[83] As access to horses and firearms had been the domain of the master class, Bruin desired to take on the trappings of those who once ruled his life. He probably was not alone in this aspiration.

Jerry Jenkins agreed with Bruin. After his first enlistment, he briefly left for the civilian world. He quickly decided to head back to his old outfit, the Twenty-Fourth Infantry. Writing to Lieutenant John L. Bullis, he informed his commanding officer: 'I much Wrother Souldier then to do Any thing else.'[84]

While referring to a slightly later period, Sampson Man's impetus differed from Jenkins and Bruin. He went to the recruiter out of 'devilment.' After Mann's mother found that her son was 'doin' wrong' by selling 'moonshine' to the neighbors, she demonstrated her displeasure and 'whomped' him twice. As Mann was told at the recruiting station, 'how good it was in the Army,' he thought the military might be better than facing maternal wrath.[85] Somewhat similar to Mann, 26 year-old George Bentley recalled joining, '… the army simply to get away from his mother and a brother, neither of whom he liked.'[86]

Then there was Mansfield Robinson. 'On a lark,' he approached a recruiter in Evansville, Indiana. A friend, who wanted to enlist, talked Robinson into accompanying him. The officer on duty convinced the disinterested lad into taking the entrance examination. Although his companion did not pass the test, Robinson succeeded. He 'decided on the spot to enlist and stayed in the army until retirement.'[87] Sometimes family members also spurred their relatives to accompany them into the military.[88]

One universal asset assured to all who entered the ranks, was decent clothing which had been denied to most of the millions of the formerly enslaved. In this regard, the comments of the US Army's quartermaster general, Samuel B. Holabird, opined that to Black soldiers, 'the uniform in his eyes sets him apart as a conspicuous man among his kind.'[89] This incentive may well have been valid in a number of instances. Underscoring this thesis, one African American recruit recalled: 'It was the uniform' that enticed him to join because of 'the feeling that it gave me.'[90]

A 1980 study added to this notion. Supposedly: 'Black military organizations projected images that met their members' deepest needs. Prestige, dress and bearing, of course varied

---

bore and continued to lead his life, which included marriage and raising a family with her as well as contributed to the household income until his death in 1919 at 62-years of age. Allan Radbourne, *Corporal Edward Scott, Frontier Cavalryman* (London: English Westerners' Society, 2014), 24–29.
83 Federal Writers' Project: Slave Narrative Project, 16, Texas, Pt. 1, 171.
84 Dobak and Phillips, *Black Regulars*, 52.
85 Don Rickey, 'Interview with Sampson Mann' reprinted in Schubert, *Voices of the Buffalo Soldiers*, 153–58.
86 Thompson, 'The Negro Soldiers on the Frontier,' 226.
87 Coffman, *The Old Army*, 335–36.
88 Dobak and Phillips, *Black Regulars*, 49–50.
89 Samuel B. Holabird, *Some Considerations Respecting Desertion in the Army*, Ordnance Notes No. 232 (Washington, DC: US Government Printing Office, 1882), 16.
90 Anthony Powell, Lecture, Smithsonian, September 29, 2016, si.edu/object/ytpBofRUraUMY.

with rank and insignia, but all men in uniform were differentiated from the anonymous souls that walked the streets in ordinary garments, in search of themselves and companionship.'[91] Presenting a positive image to the world seemed of great importance for a significant number of Blacks during and after the Civil War. Dress was one factor of the equation.[92] Arguably, 'to the oppressed black man, the military uniform meant a chance to change who he was.' It represented 'a chance for a new identity, one of pride and hopefulness, a chance to change his social position.'[93]

There also was another critical psychological element influencing several Black soldiers – that of expressing masculinity. This stimulus arose from generations of treatment as subhuman or inferiors that had oppressed all enslaved individuals. Both during the Civil War and thereafter, some African Americans looked to their military service as a powerful means to override the negative views held by many whites who considered Blacks as inferior beings. By donning martial trappings, they, 'forged a new identity as freedom fighters, demanding the rights of full citizenship and manhood.'[94]

As noted elsewhere, another outgrowth of oppression revolved around the denial of education to the enslaved; educational opportunities for some knowledge-thirsty men, who viewed formal learning as a worthwhile objective. This group could particularly look to the military after the Freedmen's Bureau ceased to exist. For instance, George Conrad, Jr. stated that when he entered the Ninth United States Cavalry, he was illiterate, but like his father whom 'the white folks learned … how to read and write' he would acquire the same skills after he entered service.[95]

As such, the reasons to seek out the military varied greatly from one would-be soldier to the next. Everything from practical to psychological components played a part. With the passage of time, new reasons would be added. Furthermore, the sources for manpower evolved. At first, until the Great Migration, the majority of African Americans resided in the Deep South, a region that once provided a primary pool for Black soldiers. As early as 1870, however, 'a disproportionately larger number of those in the army were from border states or the North.' In that year, a census of Fort McKavett, Texas, which at that time ranked among, 'the largest black garrisons' where a half dozen companies variously represented the Ninth Cavalry, Twenty-Fourth Infantry and Twenty-Fifth Infantry, revealed important statistics. Of the post's military population: 'Only 22 (6.5 percent) listed Alabama, Georgia, South Carolina, Mississippi, or Florida as their birthplaces, while 21 came from Pennsylvania and New York. The 117

---

91   Douglas Henry Daniels, *Pioneer Urbanites: A Social and Cultural History of Blacks in San Francisco* (Philadelphia: Temple University Press, 1980), 133.
92   Monica L, Miller, *Slaves to Fashion: Black Dandyism and the Styling of Black Diasporic Identity* (Durham: Duke University Press, 2009), exhaustively explored the topic of dress within the Black community.
93   Kevin Bair, 'Power of the Hero Image: The Uniform, The Black Soldier and the Ku Klux Klan,' historywithkev.com/2019/09/10/power-of-the-hero-image-the-uniform-the-black-soldier-and-the-ku-klux-klan.
94   For more see: Sherri Arnold Mehta, 'The Civil War, Black Masculinity, Black Nationalism, and a Black Male Epistolary Tradition,' Ph.D. diss, Michigan State University, 2019; and the essential study on the topic, Le'Trice D. Donaldson, *Duty Beyond the Battlefield African American Soldiers Fight for Racial Uplift, Citizenship, and Manhood, 1870–1920* (Carbondale: Southern Illinois University Press, 2020).
95   George P. Rawick, ed., *The American Slave: A Composite Autobiography* (Westport, CT: Greenwood, 1972) 7, pt. 1, 41

Kentuckians (34.8 percent) far outnumbered natives of even the next highest state, Virginia, with its 47 (13.9 percent) soldiers.'[96] (See Table 3)

Table 3: Nativity of Blacks Accepted as Recruits 1880[97]

State	Infantry	Cavalry
Alabama	11	1
Delaware	2	4
DC	7	1
Georgia	7	2
Illinois	2	2
Kentucky	15	29
Louisiana		3
Maine	2	
Maryland	42	72
Massachusetts	1	
Mississippi	5	1
Missouri		5
New Jersey		1
New York	1	2
North Carolina	1	2
Ohio	4	10
Pennsylvania	25	13
Rhode Island		1
South Carolina	4	5
Tennessee	59	3
Virginia	54	52
West Virginia	2	1
Canada		3
West Indies	1	

A Second Phalanx

Demographic swings equated to but one component of evolution within the Black military community. Concurrent corollaries appeared – a trend towards better educated applicants along with decreasing numbers of previously enslaved individuals. However, for many years both categories could be found in varying numbers and did not disappear until well into the

---

96 Coffman, *Old Army*, 331–2. Of interest, the same source mentioned that 142 (42.2 percent) of the men received the classification 'mulatto' versus the standard 'colored' in reference to race indicative of the era's nuanced perspective on the subject.
97 *ARSW, 1880*, I, 43.

future.⁹⁸ Nonetheless, Mineral Point, Wisconsin native Charles Burrill Turner characterized the new developments in terms of birthplace, freeborn status and education. Soon after he joined the army on November 15, 1875, at Indianapolis, Indiana, Turner possessed sufficient literacy to become the company clerk. Before he could do so, he required parental permission because he was only 16, which fell below the minimum age that varied between either 18 or 21 years of age depending on the requitements that changed from time to time. Otherwise, US Army regulations required the consent of a parent or guardian. The one exception was for musicians.⁹⁹

Turner's first assignment in July of 1876, brought him to Company E, Tenth Cavalry as a private along the Pecos River, Texas. By November 20, 1879, he advanced to corporal, then rose to sergeant, the rank he held late in 1887, when he underwent an examination at Fort Grant to become the regimental quartermaster sergeant. During the following year, he passed a board, 'for the position of post quartermaster, but for some unknown cause, the board did not recommend him for an appointment.'¹⁰⁰

While unsuccessful in his bid to be selected as a non-commissioned staff officer, Turner did become Troop E's first sergeant while at Fort Apache, Arizona. By August of 1892, he subsequently tested for the position of commissary sergeant. Once more, this second effort to attain a higher rank did not come to pass. Turner remained in the Tenth. After the Spanish American War brought all four regiments of Black soldiers into the fray, Turner stayed behind in the United States on recruiting duty in Kentucky. He would assist in signing up 325 new men.¹⁰¹

Turner's diverse abilities would be recognized with a temporary promotion to second lieutenant in Forty-Eighth Volunteer Infantry. When that unit disbanded, he found his way back to the Tenth Cavalry, but as was typical, at the lower pay grade. In Turner's case he reverted to corporal, although he would advance to the second squadron's sergeant major as of December 27, 1902. Less than 11 months later, he retired and received transportation to Louisville, Kentucky.¹⁰² While in service, like many others, Turner participated in the National Regular Army and Navy Union, United Order of Odd Fellows and the Masons, as a member of the historically Black Prince Hall order. His membership in various veterans and fraternal organizations mirrored many other Black soldiers.

Likewise, William Hallett Greene represented transformational trends. This first African American graduate of City College of New York received liberal applause on June 26, 1886,

---

98 Caleb Benson was one of many who signed his enlistment with an 'X'. Nonetheless, after his induction in 1875, he remained in the military for a lengthy, exemplary career. Thomas R. Buecker, 'One Soldier's Service: Caleb Benson in the Ninth and Tenth Cavalry, 1875–1908,' *Nebraska History* 74 no. 2 (Summer 1993): 54 to 62.
99 McChristian, *Regular Army O!*, 33.
100 *A&NJ*, October 29, 1887, 262; January 7, 1888; and Herschel V. Cashin, Charles Alexander, William T. Anderson, Arthur M. Brown, and Horace W. Bivins, *Under Fire with the Tenth US Cavalry: A Brief, Comprehensive Review of the Negro's Participation in the Wars of the United States* (New York and London: F.T. Neely, 1899), 314–15.
101 *A&NJ*, November 8, 1890, 170; June 6, 1892, 692 and August 6, 1892, 863; Cashin, *Under Fire with the Tenth US Cavalry*, 315–16.
102 *A&NJ*, October 7, 1899, 147; Delilah L. Beasley, *The Negro Trail Blazers of California: a Compilation of Records From the California Archives In the Bancroft Library At the University of California, In Berkeley, And From the Diaries, Old Papers And Conversations of Old Pioneers In the State of California: It Is a True Record of Facts, As They Pertain to the History of the Pioneer And Present Day Negroes of California* (Los Angeles: Mirror Printing, 1919), 284; and Schubert, *On the Trail of the Buffalo Soldiers* I, 433.

during the ceremony where he his took his Bachelor of Science diploma in hand. Nicknamed 'Greeny' by his fellow students, he had been elected his class's secretary and by all accounts was popular. Armed with his new degree and having indicated in the campus newspaper that his favorite person was 'Uncle Sam' it seemed logical for Greene to consider the US Army as a means to a earn a living.

As a teenager, he sought and obtained written permission from his father to enlist. Rather than set his sights on the infantry or cavalry, he gravitated to the Signal Corps – a small, specialized branch of only a few hundred enlisted men and a handful of officers. Technical in nature and limited in numbers, applicants had to pass an examination before they could be considered for an appointment in an organization that assumed not only responsibility for various forms of military communication, but also performed weather recording and reporting before the National Meteorological Service existed. At that time, the rolls of the Signal Corps contained no Black personnel.

Consequently, Greene embarked on a precedent breaking course. Before long, he reached a roadblock in the form of the head of the Signal Corps, Brigadier General William B. Hazen. The general concluded that legislation limited Blacks solely to inclusion in the four segregated line regiments. Based on his reading of Congressional intent, Hazen dismissed the application. The matter did not end there.

New York City College's president, Alexander S. Webb, a graduate of the United States Military Academy and a Medal of Honor recipient for his actions at Gettysburg, intervened. Webb wrote to Secretary of War Robert Lincoln, son of the 'Great Emancipator.' In response, Lincoln overruled Hazen, who disagreed and required a written order instructing him to admit Greene, provided that the candidate met the requirements. Hazen complied with Lincoln's official directive, plus made it clear that he based his past actions purely on his understanding of policy and not from, 'prejudice on account of color.'

After his official paperwork had been processed on September 29, 1884, Greene's way was clear to attend the signal school at Fort Myer, Virginia. Notably, his military forms indicated he was, 'a colored man enlisted for the Signal Corps, US Army by order of the Secretary of War.' Afterwards, Greene completed the rather demanding curriculum, standing number two in his class of eight. Having performed well in the classroom, he awaited assignment on station duty. The opportunity arose when the Signal Service observer at Pensacola asked for an assistant. Greene received orders to report there.

Responding to his first posting, Greene arranged for lodgings and attended to other matters so that he would be ready for work upon arrival. After his arrival in Pensacola, Florida, he reported to the signal service sergeant who, 'refused to receive him because of his color.' This non-commissioned officer who barred Greene received a summons to Washington to explain his actions. This left Greene in charge of the office. Soon, First Class Private W. H. Greene relieved the recalcitrant sergeant who had protested against working with a Black assistant. That non-commissioned would be sent elsewhere.

Subsequently, Greene obeyed his next orders, dated November 14, 1885, to travel from Pensacola north to Rochester, New York. This detail placed him closer to family and acquaintances. At first, the relocation seemed welcome, but not for long. On August 22, 1886, Private Greene again came to the attention of General Hazen based on charges from Signal Corps inspector Lieutenant F. M. M. Beall. Supposedly, the lieutenant arrived at Greene's post only to find the soldier absent. Beall called Greene back from the telegraph office where he was dispatching a cable with his 3:00 p.m. weather observations. The inspector questioned the private, then charged him with falsifying a report as the official information form stated the data had been gathered at precisely three o'clock. Beall insisted he had arrived at exactly 2:59 p.m., which meant Greene had lied. Beall recommended the private, 'be severely censured in General Orders,' and warned that any repetition of this behaviour would lead to courts-martial proceedings.

Greene rebutted, stating he routinely filled out the time and affixed his signature to the weather form in advance to concentrate on 'the observation itself.' Greene concluded his reclaimer with a plea for 'leniency in action' in order to have 'a chance to prove' himself 'by the strictest obedience to orders and faithful performance of duty in the future.' Given his unblemished record to that date, Greene's superiors took no action. His efficiency report revealed previously had been rated generally as good, as was his intelligence, industry, studiousness, amenability to discipline and temperance. Additionally, Greene did not gamble for money, nor was he in debt. Finally, he kept his hair short and neatly trimmed and overall presented a soldierly appearance. With these attributes, Greene's immediate superior felt he should remain at his station despite Beall's allegations of unreliability and inadequacy as a weather observer.

Had the situation concluded there, Greene should have completed his first enlistment. Thereafter, he could consider his future, if any, in the army. That possibility never arose due to several factors, which began to hound him after New Year 1887. At that time, his troubles emerged anew. First, Greene slid into debt. He had bought an overcoat and a suit which he had altered. Unable to settle his accounts, Greene sent a letter to the merchant indicating he had been ill but would make good his balance by mid-February. When he failed to do so, James Henderson, to whom Greene owed the funds, brought the matter to attention of the non-commissioned officer to whom the private reported. Henderson informed Sergeant Edward McGann that six months had passed without restitution. Again, Greene assured that he would pay, but a visit from his mother had resulted in some unexpected expenses.

More likely, in spite of an efficiency report that indicted he was temperate and did not gamble, Greene managed to run up gaming tabs totaling $160, a substantial sum on his private's pay. He pawned his watch. This brought only a fraction of what he owed. In desperation he turned to his Sergeant McGann to arrange for the NCO to make instalments from Greene's pay with the pledge that he swore to end his gambling as well as added 'any deceit or lie' on his part would 'be enough to break this contract and make my conduct publicly known.'

Greene's word meant little. He borrowed money from prominent local men with the falsehood that his military pay had not arrived. In reality, Greene's arrest, 'at 2 o'clock one morning in a low colored gambling resort' demonstrated his continued downward spiral. Conviction by a Rochester magistrate followed as did action by the US Army, but not as expected. While Signal Corps officials carefully weighed their course of action, on May 20, 1887, Greene requested a discharge. The military quickly obliged. They released him by general orders dated June 10, 1887. With a stroke of the pen, an early although unintended effort at integration in the US Army came to an unfortunate conclusion.[103] Not until after the Second World War did presidential action by Harry S Truman begin to sweep away the separate status of Blacks in the US armed forces, ushering in desegregation of the nation's military.

---

103 The narrative related to William Greene was taken from his service record in RG94, NARA; GO 120, AGO, May 25, 1887; *Army and Navy Register*, June 21, 1884, 142; and MacGregor and Nalty, *Blacks in the Military*, III, 29–31.

Even though Greene's service ended abruptly, one biographer suggested the US Army's first Black signal corpsman and pioneer meteorologist: 'opened the way for the acceptance of a handful of Black enlisted men into other technical branches, such as the Hospital Corps, the Ordnance Department and the Quartermaster and Commissary Departments.'[104] Lamentably, Greene's departure in many respects mirrored the fates of two pioneer commissioned officers – Henry O. Flipper and Henry V. Plummer. (See Chapter 2)

Happily, Walter H. Loving of Virginia, during his military career, fared better than Greene. He attended high school in Washington, D.C. and had been a member of the High School Cadets, along with several other youths including Benjamin O. Davis.[105] Prior to his June 22, 1893 enlisting in the US Army, at St. Paul, Minnesota, Loving had made his living as a musician. The 5'9" 21-year-old would start his active duty at Fort Bayard, New Mexico. He became a member of the Twenty-Fourth Infantry regimental band for a time, until he transferred to Company D.[106]

Loving's devotion to music remained strong. He would return to the band, as well as providing private singing lessons for free, directing concerts and generally playing a prominent part in the musical scene when stationed at Fort Douglas in Salt Lake City, Utah.[107] He also advocated a quest for talented Blacks who could replace white bandmasters in the four regiments, going so far as to contact Booker T. Washington's assistant, E. J. Scott, to promote this effort. His theory was that only topnotch candidates for these coveted positions could break the color barrier.[108] Early in the twentieth century, Scott successfully completed this crusade, which in due course resulted in Black band leaders serving in all the regiments staffed by African Americans.[109]

To some degree, Loving benefitted from the movement he promoted. He eventually became a major in the Philippine Constabulary heading its band for 20 years. With retirement nearing, he gave a farewell concert enjoyed by a record-breaking crowd. Showing their appreciation, after the concert reached its finale, appropriately Loving received, 'a handsome watch on behalf of the Manila community and with a beautiful loving cup from the members of the band.' His successor took the baton from the veteran bandmaster with appropriate praise for all his predecessor's accomplishments. Loving, he lauded, trained his musicians so well as to achieve lasting fame 'wherever great music is heard. But more than this, you have wrought this success with a modesty which has been becoming.'[110]

---

104 blackoncampus.com/2008/09/09/the-troubling-case-of-william-hallett-greene.
105 *Evening Star* (Washington, DC) May 28, 1905.
106 Schubert, *On the Trail of the Buffalo Soldier*, I, 271.
107 *Salt Lake Tribune*, January 23, 1898, and February 6, 1898.
108 Marvin E. Fletcher, *The Black Soldier and Officer the United States Army 1891–1917* (Columbia: University of Missouri Press, 1974), 72.
109 Fletcher, *The Black Soldier and Officer*, 70–71.
110 *Crisis* 12 (June 1916): 67; and 29 (January 1925): 25. For additional biographical information and analysis review, Roger D. Cunningham, "The Loving Touch': Walter H. Loving Five Decades of Military Music,' *Army History: The Professional Bulletin of Army History* 64 (Summer 2007): 4–25. (Online Link: jstor.org/stable/26295292? seq=1# metadata_info_ tab_contents). Cunningham points out that: 'Until the early twentieth century … white chief musicians led the Regular Army's regimental bands. Evidence suggests that the belated decision to appoint black chief musicians was influenced by the extraordinary music of Walter H. Loving, who rose from poverty in the rural South to spend more than seven years as an Army musician.'

Horace W. Bivins provided a fourth example of the second wave of Black regulars. Born on May 8, 1866, in the post-Civil War era, he would leave his home in Accomack County, Virginia at the age of 19 to enter Hampton Institute. There, Bivins received his first taste of military training in the cadet program included in the college's curriculum. He remained at college for two years as a preliminary for fulfilling his parents' wishes to attend a theological seminary.[111] However, he eschewed an ecclesiastical calling to pursue another vocation.

Much like George Washington Williams, Bivins had, 'a great desire for adventure.' Bivins longed, 'to see the wild West.'[112] Then, too, he may have been motivated by a reaction to rabid racism. Bivins' father had helped build a church and a school in their hometown of Pungoteague, Virginia, which ended with the torching of the structure and a threat of lynching for its founder.

Whatever his reasons, Bivins enlisted in 1888. 'After receiving a few lessons in mounted and dismounted drill' at Jefferson Barracks, Missouri and as so many recruits before and after him would do, he headed to west. On June 19, 1888, Bivins' name appeared on the roster of Troop E, Tenth Cavalry at Fort Grant, Arizona. From there, he went to San Carlos Reservation where his education assured an appointment as a clerk. It was at San Carlos that he also participated in target practice. He scored second highest out of the 60 men although this was the first time that he, 'ever had shot a rifle.' Afterwards, he led his troop in marksmanship year after year, representing the unit in, '1892, '93 and '94, winning eight medals and badges at the department competition,' following in 1894 when he, 'won three gold medals' representing 'the Department of the Dakotas at the army competition at Fort Sheridan and carried off the first gold medal.'[113]

Previously, at Fort Apache, on June 15, 1890, he became a corporal. His promotion, performance as a crack shot and high level of education must have impressed his commander. This officer granted not easily obtainable permission for the corporal to wed. On October 15, 1890, the ceremony took place with the post chaplain uniting Horace Bivins and Maria Neuman in the bounds of matrimony. She was nearly five years Bivins' senior and would be the first of his three wives. What happened to this original spouse remains unresolved. After the regiment rotated to Montana, it seems she did not accompany Bivins.

Bivins's marital situation aside, he ultimately developed into one of the army's top marksmen of his era.[114] According to an interview given decades after the fact, in 1896, William 'Buffalo Bill' Cody attempted to lure Bivins away from the military as a member of the colorful wild west extravaganza. Supposedly, Bivins would compete against the show's star – Annie Oakley. Bivins rejected the offer. He preferred, 'the army routine to circus life.'[115]

Declining show business seemed a wise decision. Proficiency with both revolvers and long arms contributed to steady promotions in his troop and on the regimental non-commissioned

---

111 *Baltimore Evening Sun*, December 8, 1960.
112 Cashin, *Under Fire with the Tenth US Cavalry*, 58–59. Note that Bivins served as one of the authors in this anthology.
113 *Ibid.*, 58 and 60; *A&NJ*, October 6, 1894, 87.
114 Baker, *Roster of Non-Commissioned Officers*, 51; *A&NJ*, July 4, 1891, 765, and October 20, 1894, 119; *St. Paul Daily Globe*, September 30, 1894, 6; *Cleveland Gazette*, November 3, 1894; and *Indianapolis Freeman*, July 10, 1897, which indicated he was the only man to earn three gold medals for marksmanship in one year. As an interesting aside, Bivins' record might be evaluated against Nicholas Johnson's, *Negroes and the Gun: The Black Tradition of Arms* (Amherst, NY: Prometheus Books, 2014).
115 *Billings Gazette*, March 3, 1935.

staff, leading to a 1901 appointment as a post ordnance sergeant.[116] This desirable duty brought quarters and higher pay. Bivins again could entertain marriage. He did so in 1904 to Deadwood, South Dakota native Claudia M. Browning, 'daughter of Walker Browning one of the oldest and most highly respected colored citizens of Billings.' The couple then started their wedded life at Fort Missoula, Montana. They remained together until her death in 1944.[117]

Bivins' postings would take the couple to many diverse places such as New York and Vermont.[118] That is not to say the pair constantly stayed under the same roof as one of his deployments was to Cuba, where he earned recognition for valor. He went also to the Philippines, as well as other duty stations that resulted in temporary separations for the couple and their children.[119] During one of these overseas assignments, Bivins left a brief account of his actions. He recorded the clash with the Spanish at San Juan Hill.[120]

In 1913, a wish to care for his ageing mother (who now resided with the family) and his own failing health, prompted Bivins to seek retirement.[121] Remaining enamored with the West where Bivins spent much of his 25 years of active duty, he settled in Montana. There he farmed successfully; took up taxidermy; offered his collection of seashells and various preserved specimens of fauna gathered in the Philippines to the Parmly Billings Memorial Library, said to be valued at $1,500 and of interest to the Smithsonian; and evidently emerged as a well-regarded pillar among the local Black and white communities alike – if favorable newspaper coverage that indicated the family's place in the community was accurate.[122]

Even in retirement, Bivins maintained his connection to the military. During the First World War, he returned to duty and pinned on the bars of a captain, He spent a brief time at Fort Dix, New Jersey where he was looked upon as a role model.[123] After that, Bivins returned to Montana, but due to illness in the early 1920s, he spent six months at Walter Reed Hospital in Washington, DC, 'where he underwent a serious operation.'[124] Decades later, although Bivins was in his 70s, he once more offered his sword as the Second World War loomed on the horizon![125] When not recalled, he opened his home for religious services where all would be welcomed.[126]

After his beloved Claudia's death, he eventually married a third time, in this instance to Julia E. West, possibly the daughter of a Hampton classmate. The nuptials took place on September 10, 1950. The union must have been a brief one. In 1951, Captain Bivins moved to Baltimore

---

116 Schubert, *On the Trail of the Buffalo Soldiers*, I, 39.
117 *Missoulian*, March 4, 1904; *Billings Gazette*, March 18, 1904; and *Helena Independent Record*, August 8, 1944.
118 For example, as indicated in the *Army and Navy Register*, December 31, 1910, 19. 'Ord. Sergt. Horace W. Bivins, Fort Ontario, will be sent to Fort Ethan Allen for duty. W.D., Dec. 27.' Hereinafter cited as *A&NR*.
119 *St. Paul Appeal*, September 23, 1899.
120 See Horace W. Bivins, 'The Battle of San Juan Hill by a Gunner of the 10th Cavalry,' *Southern Workman* 27 (November 1898), 219–20.
121 *Evening Star* (DC) July 16, 1913.
122 *Billings Gazette*, June 12, 1908; May 21, 1909; September 22, 1918; April 9, 1933; April 7, 1935; March 3, 1935; November 4, 1940; April 10, 1946; *Butte Miner*, March 3, 1920; *Wolf Point Herald* (MT) August 14, 1924; *Circle Banner* (MT) August 15, 1924; *Review* (Kevin, MT) August 14, 1924; October 8, 1925; and October 15, 1925, 2.
123 *Southern Workman*, 48 (March, 1919), 160; and *Crisis* (May, 1930), 168.
124 *Seattle Northwest Enterprise*, November 12, 1931.
125 *Montana Oil and Mining Journal* (Great Falls, MT) December 7, 1940.
126 *Omaha Guide*, June 10, 1944.

to live with a niece.[127] Some nine years later, the veteran of 32 years as a proud, capable soldier ended. He was 94 when laid to rest in December of 1960 at the Baltimore National Cemetery.[128]

Comradery and Community

As one other aspect of Bivins' life, he added another example found within the Black military cadre. His brother-in-law through marriage was Sergeant William McCabe – indicative of the cohesive ties that periodically emerged among Black enlisted men.[129] In this same light, Bivins, along with McCabe, served as two of the pallbearers for James Baltimore, 'one of the pioneer negro residents of Billings.' McCabe, like Bivins, was 'an Indian war veteran.' Baltimore had been in poor health. He died while at the Warm Springs, Arkansas government medical facility.[130]

Several examples of former soldiers such as Bivins, McCabe and Baltimore settling near each other after departing the military, existed. San Angelo and Fort Concho, Texas offered a prime pattern for old soldiers becoming neighbors in civilian communities adjacent to military installations. Four former frontier soldiers gravitated there. William Ellis, whose presumed birthdate was 1838, had entered Company E, Twenty-Fifth Infantry as a private. On August 30, 1870, he appeared before a recruiter at Cheshire, Ohio. Ellis ended up at Fort Concho. Less than two years later, while on a patrol near Kickpoo Springs, the 5'2" enlisted man, who did not meet the minimum height requirement by one inch, became extremely ill.[131] Concerned for Ellis' health, his comrades brought the ailing doughboy back to the post hospital. While in the ward, he appeared to expire, being pronounced dead at 9 a.m. After hospital attendants moved the 'corpse' to the morgue, some of Ellis' friends gathered there to mourn the dearly departed. With a pot of coffee and two jugs of whiskey to help them through the impromptu wake, they began singing spirituals.

Around 11 a.m. while crooning 'Are You Coming Home Tonight. Are You Coming Home to Jesus. Are You Coming Out of the Darkness into the Light' one choir member decided to peer into the adjacent room to view the body. Ellis' hands and feet had been bound, which meant when the curious comrade saw movements, he exclaimed: 'That man ain't dead; he's movin.

He's getting up.'

In fact, when a hospital steward responded, he confirmed the surprising event. Ellis was alive. After a week in hospital, Ellis returned to duty. From Fort Concho he transferred to Fort Davis, Texas where he ended his one tour of duty in 1875. Bearing the nickname 'Dead' Ellis, he moved back to San Angelo as one of the first African American residents of the civilian community neighboring Fort Concho. He became a local fixture. Following a brief unsuccessful marriage, Ellis remained in town as an eccentric who became a 'public charge' until his death

---

127 *Baltimore Evening Sun*, December 30, 1955.
128 *Baltimore Evening Sun*, December 8, 1960.
129 *Seattle Northwest Enterprise*, April 11, 1935. Presumably, this was the Sergeant William McCabe who served in Troop E, Ninth Cavalry. Schubert, *On the Trail of the Buffalo Soldiers*, I, 276.
130 *Seattle Enterprise*, October 28, 1927.
131 In fact, Ellis was nearing the cut off of 35 years of age for a first enlistment. McChristian, *Regular Army O!*, 33 and 633 n54.

Elijah Cox was born a freeman in Michigan as his parents boldly escaped enslavement and made their way first Canada, then Mackinaw. During a skirmish fought with Native Americans between Forts Quitman and Davis in Texas, Cox sustained a wound that ended his short time as infantryman. He, like Mazique, after his discharge took up residence in San Angelo. He especially became known for his musical talents. The Library of Congress field services even recorded one of Cox' performances. (Courtesy Library of Congress)

on December 11, 1928, as one of the oldest residents in the town.[132] Attendees at his funeral did not witness a second resurrection.

Elijah Cox knew Ellis. Cox's parents had escaped enslavement by making their way to Canada. They halted short of the border as their son was born in Mackinaw, Michigan. Apparently, his family had resettled there. During the Civil War, an officer in the Sixth Illinois Cavalry hired Cox as a servant. After Robert E. Lee surrendered, Cox journeyed home to try his hand at carpentry. The trade did not appeal to him. He signed as a sailor working on the Great Lakes. This pursuit had little attraction as well. On July 1, 1870, Cox decided to enlist in the US Army at Detroit.

Also, just 5'2" tall, Cox, like Ellis, fell just below the minimum height. He listed his occupation as musician, which served him later in life. In Company D, Twenty-Fifth Infantry, however, it is not clear whether his musical skills were used, but assuredly he did see action. During a skirmish fought with Native Americans at a site between Forts Quitman and Davis in Texas, he sustained a wound that ended his short time as an infantryman. On June 30, 1871, Cox also made his way to San Angelo, Texas where he remained until his death on 20 January 1941, at age 98. For decades, he eked out a living as a bartender, buffalo hunter, carpenter, cook, entertainer

132 *San Angelo Evening Standard*, December 12. 1928.

In 1875, Sancho Mazique joined the Tenth Cavalry. It is probable that he had been enslaved in his native South Carolina where he learned carpentry. The military availed itself of his skills at Fort Concho, Texas. After his honorable discharge, Mazique remained in the nearby town of San Angelo, where he died at age 101. (Courtesy Fort Concho National Landmark)

and musician, having mastered the guitar and fiddle. He even made a recording of three tunes.[133] Perhaps it was 'Old Cox's' musical gifts that left the most lasting memory for this one-time soldier turned jack of all trades. Proudly, he recalled his musical performances at Fort Concho where he could 'play 300 waltzes, all different without stopping.'[134]

Another event that remained vivid in Cox's mind was the fact that he had been one of witnesses to 'Dead' Ellis' return from beyond. Appropriately, both men became minor local celebrities and would be buried in San Angelo's Fairmount Cemetery with two other Black enlisted men who dwelled in the Texas town after they left the military.

One of these was Jacob Wilks (AKA Wilkes). The third member of this distinct foursome had been from Kentucky and spent 45 months fighting for the Union as a member of the 116th USCT. Now a seasoned soldier, when his unit disbanded, Wilks, soon after the formation in 1866 of the Ninth Cavalry, became one of the regiment's early members. He remained with the regiment for the next decade with stints at Fort McKavett, Texas and Fort Selden, New Mexico. After Sergeant Wilks' honorable discharge, he stayed in New Mexico. In due course, Wilks relocated to San Angelo, Texas where he died in 1922 as the town's 'oldest black citizen'

---

133 Elijah Cox, Biographical File, Fort Concho National Landmark and Museum Library (San Angelo, TX); Bill Wynn, 'Old Cox,' *Junior Historian* 6 No. 5 (May 1946):1–4; *San Angelo Standard Times*, January 21, 1941. For these recording access poddtoppen.se/podcast/ 1375326879/jack-dappa-blues-podcast/the-african-american-folklorist-ep-2-elijah-cox.

134 *San Angelo Standard Times*, May 3, 1924.

a distinction he would surrender to the final African American Indian Wars veteran in the town.[135]

Edward (Sancho) Mazique (also spelled Maziche and Mozique) likewise made San Angelo home after leaving the military. Born on June 10, 1849, in Columbia, South Carolina to a French Creole father and enslaved mother, his early story underscored the cavalier attitude of some slave holders. The widow, who had held Mazique, his mother and six siblings in enslavement, made a wedding present of what she viewed as little more than disposable goods. She gifted the family to a nephew, who brought all eight of his new holdings to his home in Spartanburg, South Carolina. In bondage during the Civil War, Mazique had been, 'taught to fear the blue-coated Union soldiers' whom he avoided at first.[136]

Eventually, following the war's end, he adopted a different attitude. After peace returned, Mazique and his family went to Columbia, South Carolina. He sought employment there at a boarding house frequented by students at the local medical school where he plied his skills as a carpenter. Nearly a decade passed before he and three other Black youths in Columbia decided to enlist, which he did on February 23, 1875.

After reporting to the recruit rendezvous at Jefferson Barracks, Missouri, he came down on a levy destined for Fort Concho. Mazique arrived there on July 9, 1875. His perfunctory military training would have been inadequate if sent on campaign. That shortcoming never mattered. Mazique's invaluable carpentry skills kept him safe and relatively comfortable in garrison rather than taking to the field with Company E. This assignment likewise earned him an additional $10 extra duty pay per month.[137] Furthermore, Mazique made additional money by selling buffalo hides, steaks and tongues from kills he downed with his cavalry carbine, indicating he must have been a competent marksman.[138]

Not all his outside efforts brought additional revenue. On at least one occasion, he presented the regimental commander's family with wild turkey hunted with one of the officers.[139] Possibly Mazique enjoyed a special place with regimental commander Benjamin Grierson and his family for such kindnesses. His other duty as a member of the Tenth Cavalry's band may have gained preference also as these military musicians numbered among the colonel's favorites – him being a former music schoolteacher in civilian life.[140] Mazique had also been present at the death of the Grierson's teenage daughter Edith. After she passed, Mazique helped make her coffin. Decades later, after his own death in 1951, he would join Edith Grierson along with Cox, Ellis and Wilkes in San Angelo's Fairmount Cemetery.

---

135 Schubert, *Voices of the Buffalo Soldiers*, 40–46; and *Frontier Times* 4 (April 1927), 9–11. Also see: Jacob Wilkes, Biographical File, Fort Concho National Landmark and Museum Library, San Angelo, TX.
136 *San Angelo Standard Times*, April 2, 1951.
137 McChristian, *Regular Army O!*, 108 and 657 n34; and Rickey, *Forty Miles a Day*, 95 and 110 discuss extra duty. For some specific examples, review MC46 Fort Assiniboine Vol. 103, Post Orders, 1902–1904.
138 *San Angelo Standard Times*, June 10, 1949.
139 Sancho Mazique Biographical File, Fort Concho Library, San Angelo, Texas with a portion of a typescript dated November 1879 from Alice Grierson.
140 Thomas C. Railsback and John P. Langellier, *The Drums Would Roll: A Pictorial History of US Army Bands on the American Frontier 1866–1900* (London: Arms and Armour Press, 1987), 16; and Leckie, *Buffalo Soldiers*, 40.

There were other examples of soldiers who remained behind to take up residence in nearby civilian communities close to their former garrisons. Fort Davis offered similar cases such as George Bentley, who after leaving Company K, Ninth Cavalry, in 1871, married a local Latina. Four years later, he would be elected town constable. Bentley stayed a fixture of the town throughout his life. Then, like James Walker, upon departing Company I, Ninth Cavalry, Robert Fair adopted a new vocation as a Methodist lay preacher in the town of Fort Davis.[141]

In like manner, it is known that at least a trio of past Tenth Cavalry soldiers adopted Tucson, Arizona after their regiment relocated to the territory from Texas.[142] Richard Holt, born in Richmond, Virginia around 1861, enlisted at Chicago, Illinois. The 23 year-old laborer, who most likely had been enslaved, was assigned to Troop E, Tenth Cavalry. After a posting to Texas for approximately a year, in 1885, he moved with the unit to Arizona. While Fort Grant would be his official home, he spent nine months on detached service at Bonita Canyon. The mission of Troop E was to cut, 'the Indians off at their stronghold' and keep them in 'abeyance.' As part of his duties, Holt carried mail from the railroad to the interior. With expiration of his service in 1889, Holt worked on a southern Arizona cattle ranch through 1897 for $30 a month, plus room and board, more than twice his army pay. Later, he found employment in mining camps, hotels and with private families. He never owned property, remained a bachelor although he had a common law wife. The couple had two children and his net worth was approximately $50. His $40 a month government disability pension from the military kept him from destitution.[143]

William Varnon (also known as Henry Varnom) came from Georgetown, Kentucky. He was approximately 17 when he enlisted in 1876. He may have had experience as a barber; if so, Varnon exchanged a razor for a saber in the Tenth Cavalry. By 1882, he reenlisted with Company G at Fort Concho. During the final phases of the Geronimo campaign in Arizona (as a member of Troop E) he spent a brief time at Camp Bonita in the Chiricahua Mountains.[144] In 1892, following his discharge at Fort Grant, Arizona, he obtained a position as a porter in

---

141 Katrina Christiana Loening Eichner, 'Queering Frontier Identities: Archaeological Investigations at a Nineteenth-Century US Army Laundresses' Quarters in Fort Davis,' Ph.D. diss., University of California, Berkeley, 2017, 51.
142 James Walter Yancy, 'The Negro of Tucson, Past and Present,' MA thesis, University of Arizona, 1933, 34, which mentioned: 'Many of the Negroes who lived in Tucson came here in the United States Army and after being discharged made this their home.' Regrettably he only provided three examples to support his statement. The first of these evidently was William 'Curly' Neal, who supposedly took up residence in Tucson in 1878 having come here with the army. As there were no black troops stationed in the area until the mid-1880s the date of association with the military unless he was engaged as a servant of performed some other function. Some of Neal's other assertions also seem spurious such as being a fellow scout with William F. 'Buffalo Bill' Cody, although his statement that he obtained a government contract to carry mail from Tucson to Oracle received partial verification in the *Arizona Weekly Citizen* (Tucson) June 26, 1886, 3. See both Yancy, 'The Negro of Tucson,' 25–27, and MS 579, Neal, William, 1849–1936 Collection, Arizona Historical Society Library, Tucson, the related finding aid which is found at arizonahistoricalsociety.org/wp-content/upLoads/library_Neal-William.pdf. In 1895, Curly and his wife Annie Magdalen Box Neal opened the Mountain View Hotel in Oracle. For details read: Barbara Marriott, *Annie's Guests: Tales From a Frontier Hotel* (Tucson: Catymatt Productions, 2000). Further, Cody actually was a guest at the hotel. Thus, Curly's claim about an association with Buffalo Bill may have had a basis in fact.
143 Yancy, 'The Negro of Tucson,' 35–36. Holt filed for his disability on April 18, 1924, which he subsequently received. nps.gov/chir/learn/historyculture/soldier-roster.htm.
144 nps.gov/chir/learn/historyculture/soldier-roster.htm.

a Phoenix hotel. Later, Varnon – who by now was married to a white woman 'of the Mormon faith' – sought employment in Tucson. The couple's days there allowed them to set aside sufficient money from his $8 a week plus board working for Henrietta Herring Franklin, the spouse of Selim M. Franklin, at their stately brick Main Street residence. The Varnons managed to raise three children and acquire a half lot for $100 where they built their own home.[145]

Thomas Grant, the third known former Tenth cavalryman who elected to stay in the vicinity of Old Pueblo, was born in Germantown, Kentucky, in 1848. His first source of income upon discharge from the cavalry came when he was hired by John L. Martin, an attorney located at Court Street. Although he remained in Martin's employ thereafter, Grant tried his hand at homesteading on 22 acres adjacent to Fort Huachuca, until a severe case of mental illness caused him to be institutionalized. When Grant returned, his cattle, horses and wagons had been taken by unknown parties. The determined Grant managed to purchase an adobe house at a Main Street lot just outside the Tucson city limits for a total of $125. For an undiscovered reason, he lost title to this property. During his final years, Grant combined his government pension with $18 a month from Martin, along with a free room. Like many an old soldier of the era, he barely made a subsistence living.[146]

Elsewhere, Salt Lake City appealed to a few other former soldiers. One of these was another possibly enslaved youth, who took freedom into his own hands – Soloman ('Black Sol') Black. Born on August 10, 1854, in Rome, Georgia, the self-proclaimed, 'youngest soldier' in the Civil War' still wore 'knee pants when he went in as a drummer boy.'[147] Records indicate that Black enlisted in Company E, Forty-Fourth USCT on June 5, 1865, nearly two months after the war had ended.[148]

Within three years, Black entered the Twenty-Fourth Infantry. He did so on December 10, 1870, even though he was only 16, possibly as a musician. Most of his subsequent postings were with the Twenty-Fourth, although he spent six years with the Tenth Cavalry. While on active duty, which ended in 1897, he had married twice.[149] Evidently no children resulted from either union. After several years in Salt Lake City, he ultimately headed back to Texas where he died at age 78.[150]

Kentuckian Lee Shipman's master was promised a bounty for the service of his former chattel and namesake. The Twenty-Fourth USCT, organized at Camp Nelson, Kentucky from January 1 to April 27, 1865, was Shipman's first step in a long martial career. The regiment never saw combat. It spent its entire existence on garrison and guard duty until being mustered out on December 20, 1867.[151] After Private Shipman's name had been added to the rolls, during February 1865, only a few months passed before his promotion to sergeant. Whatever attributes earned

---

145 *Ibid.*, 34.
146 *Ibid.*, 36.
147 *Salt Lake Tribune*, May 9, 1897.
148 Michael James Tins Clark, 'A History of the Twenty-fourth United States Infantry Regiment in Utah, 1896–1900,' Ph.D. diss. University of Utah, 1979, 74; and M589, roll 7 plaque number: c–57 nps.gov/civilwar/search-soldiers-detail.htm?soldierId=C8B6E682-DC7A-DF11-BF36-B8AC6F5D926A.
149 The announcement of Musician Sol Black, Company G, Twenty-Fourth Infantry retired appeared in *A&NJ*, May 1, 1897, 645.
150 Clark, 'A History of the Twenty-fourth United States Infantry Regiment,' 76.
151 nps.gov/civilwar/search-battle-units-detail.htm?battleUnitCode=UUS0124RI00C.

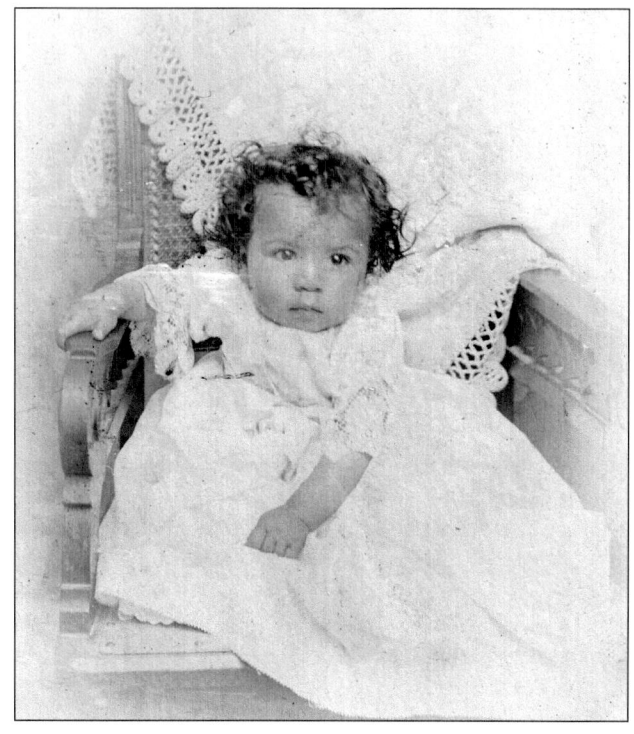

After Sergeant Pollard Cole retired, he and his spouse Estephana soon moved to El Paso. In late 1894, their son was born there. Emblematic of the closeknit communities that sometimes developed among Black soldiers of the era, they sent an old comrade, Tenth Cavalry Sergeant Charles Faulkner, a photograph of the infant. (Courtesy John Langellier)

him this advancement did not offset his reduction to private due to 'conduct prejudicial to good order and military discipline.'[152] That setback failed to inhibit Shipman from volunteering for duty with the Twenty-Fourth Infantry, where he accumulated eight enlistments with the unit until his retirement in Salt Lake, on March 31, 1897.[153] He had little time to enjoy civilian life because within three months the 'veteran of 30 years and three months service' entered the 'post hospital where he departed from this life. The deceased was greatly liked and honored by all his comrades and it was with deep regret that they heard 'taps' blown over his grave,' according to his Company A comrades.[154]

A third Salt Lake transplant, Parker Buford of Pulaski, Tennessee was about 20 years old when he joined the Twenty-Fourth Infantry, after its establishment in 1869. The fact that he was married at the time and had a newborn son, James, differed from the norm because single men usually were enrolled, at least for the first enlistment. Nonetheless, he succeeded in being accepted. Both spouse and child accompanied him to Texas and later to Arizona. Indeed, James Buford followed in his father's footsteps. He enlisted in the Twenty-Fourth while at San Carlos, Arizona on March 31, 1891. Meanwhile, the senior Buford continued soldiering until his retirement on September 20, 1900. Two years earlier, Parker and Eliza received devastating news. Their son James had died in 1898.

The Bufords weathered this storm. After Parker's discharge, having completed his 30 years requirement for retirement, they bought a home on 1333 East 7th South in Salt Lake. They remained there until his death in February 1911.[155] Two of Parker's comrades from the Twenty-

---

152 M589 ROLL 78 FILE NUMBER: D–129, nps.gov/civilwar/search-soldiers-detail.htm?soldierId=8E6104D0-DC7A-DF11-BF36-B8AC6F5D926A.
153 Clark, 'A History of the Twenty-fourth United States Infantry Regiment,' 76–77.
154 *Salt Lake Herald*, June 7, 1897.
155 Clark, 'A History of the Twenty-fourth United States Infantry Regiment,' 77–78.

Kentuckian Brent Woods existed among an elite 22 African American soldiers, who between 1877 and 1898, displayed extraordinary valor that earned each of them the Medal of Honor. Woods posed for a photograph in the early 1890s. It was a dozen years when he received his long overdue acknowledgement of an heroic performance in New Mexico. (Courtesy Library of Congress.)

Fourth Infantry, who likewise made Salt Lake their post-military residence, witnessed Eliza's application for a widow's pension, attesting that they had known her and the deceased for 25 years and 18 years respectively as evidence of the tightknit community formed among some Black regulars.

The two men were Corporals Thornton Jackson and Squire Williams of Companies C and D, respectively. Jackson's daughter recollected her father was a 'very stern, very noisy person' who liked Fort Douglas. One of his closest friends was yet one more former non-commissioned officer – Sergeant Alfred Rucker. After retirement, starting in 1900, Jackson drove a light wheeled conveyance to transport officers' families around the post and to town. Incidentally, the corporal's daughter, Viola Jackson, wedded the son of a Ninth Cavalry trooper of the Fort Duchesne, Utah garrison, representative of marriages that periodically took place between family members of soldiers.[156]

The other witness for Eliza Buford's pension petition, Corporal Squire Williams, held a Certificate of Merit (NB: the only form of recognition for valor available to soldiers except for the Medal of Honor during this period) for 'gallant and meritorious' action in Arizona during an onslaught by highwaymen in 1890 to rob the US Army pay under Major Joseph Wham.[157]

156 Ibid., 79–80.
157 Spanamwar.com/Tenth cav.htm. Also, consult Adjutant General's Office Circular No. 2, February 11, 1892, which stipulated 'certificates of merit should, under law, be awarded for distinguished service, whether in action or otherwise, of a valuable character to the United States as, for example, extraordinary exertion in the preservation of human life, or in the preservation of public property, or rescuing public property from destruction by fire or otherwise, or any hazardous service by which the

He had been with the regiment in other postings including Fort Douglas where he lived nearby after his retirement in June 1901.[158]

Another instance of veterans electing to stay behind in the vicinity of their last Garrison, took place at Fort Ethan Allen, Vermont. Several Black soldiers adopted civilian life at Colchester (now Winooski), Vermont to earn their livings, achieve respect as community members and rear families including some of their descendants who still lived in the area into the twenty-first century. Among them were four former members of the Tenth Cavalry, who formed part of the congregation of what became the Winooski United Methodist Church – Sergeant Willis Hatcher (wounded in action in Santiago, Cuba); Sergeant and one-time farrier Silas Johnson; Private John Ralph Lyons (awarded a Certificate of Merit for saving a comrade from drowning in Mallets Bay); and Corporal Beverly Thornton, who was related to Sergeant Major E.P. Frierson of the Tenth Cavalry by marriage.[159]

While Tucson, Salt Lake and Winooski came to be new homes for former soldiers somewhat by happenstance, one community was unique as a post-military haven – Allensworth, California. Named for its most notable founder, the regimental chaplain of the Twenty-Fourth Infantry, Allen Allensworth, the settlement located south of Hanford in Tulare County, emerged after 1908 with the establishment of The California Colony and Home-Promotion Association.[160] As the title implied, the organization built a community complete with a school, church, mercantile and other appurtenances of a small town to cater for its agriculturally based citizens. Additionally, Reverend Allensworth specifically sought out soldiers and their families for the commune, whom the residents referred to as 'The Sergeants.'[161]

The chaplain's quest for former military men stemmed from many considerations. Henry Singleton, whose father owned the store, shared one of the motives to underpin the population with seasoned soldiers: 'In 1910, when we came to Allensworth, there was a good deal of prejudice against Negroes. When we came … there was a lot of fear on those days. The particular group of pioneers didn't know how people in these little white towns were going to react toward them. Allensworth, being an Army man, was interested in in having soldiers settle in Allensworth.'[162]

It was not uncommon in the antebellum north for Blacks to congregate in urban areas not only due to pressure from whites to segregate, but also as there was a degree of safety in numbers when fugitive slave laws even led to the kidnapping of a freeman. In this regard, Elizabeth Payne McGhee, whose father William Payne was an early Allensworth townsman stated:

> Since so many ex-soldiers were there, they formed protective groups. They even went so far as to drill and they had signals so if anything happened in the town and we had to get

---

Government is saved loss in men or material. Note, Richardson, *Supplement to the Revised Statutes of The United States* I, 889, indicated that holders of the Certificate of Merit would receive $2 a month extra pay during his tie in service from the date of for which he was cited.

158 *A&NJ*, June 15, 1901, 1019, and Schubert, *On the Trail of the Buffalo Soldier* I, 474.
159 winooskiunitedmethodistchurch.org/the-buffalo-soldiers.html; blackpast.org/african-american-history/buffalo-soldiers-vermont–1909–1913.
160 Beasley, *The Negro Trail Blazers of California*, 154. Elsewhere the author mentions several other Black veterans, chiefly from the Spanish American War and Philippine service, who took up life in California. Beasley, *The Negro Trail Blazers*, 278–300.
161 Alice C. Royal, *Allensworth The Freedom Colony* (Berkely: Heyday, 2008), 16.
162 Royal, *Allensworth The Freedom Colony*, 16.

together for protection, they had signals they'd give and people a mile and a half away would get together. They trained and got real good, but they never once said anything about the little town – but they were ready.

McGhee added two other salient details. Several veterans came from Fort Huachuca, 'with money, to build and buy farm equipment.'[163]

In fact, most of the experienced non-commissioned officers had been with the chaplain's Twenty-Fourth Infantry. The roster included Sergeants Joseph Brown, Thomas Hamlin, George Hixon, Robert Howard, William Jenkins, Joseph Lee and John Taylor.[164] Then there was Sergeant George Carver, formerly of Company E, Twenty-Fourth Infantry, who ranked number 52 among expert riflemen in the army during 1904. He exchanged a rifle for a glove as the first baseman on the town's ball team.[165] Another man, named Nash, must have had a more than passing knowledge of firearms as he managed the gun club for wealthy whites a number of miles to the south of the colony.[166]

William Fox of Company B, Twenty-Fourth Infantry had been reduced from sergeant to private while in Company D and fined $30 for threatening his first sergeant and assaulting a corporal.[167] As an unassigned recruit at Fort Bayard, he came down on a levy under Order 246, December 19, 1893, along with three other privates bound for Fort Huachuca. By 1904, he was at Fort Niobrara, Nebraska.[168] Evidently, Fox had mended his ways sufficiently to be accepted by Chaplain Allensworth for the colony.

James Phillips, who enlisted in Chicago on August 14, 1893, first joined Fox with Company B, Twenty-Fourth Infantry at Fort Huachuca. Phillips later went to Company H. He saw action in Cuba during 1898, then received his discharge with an 'excellent' character. Later that year, on September 26, Phillips reenlisted at Fort Douglas. It was there he served as a special duty laborer in the subsistence department beginning on October 2, 1898. Upon his discharge, on January 29 1899, at Salt Lake City garrison as a single man of 'good' character, he reenlisted the next day to return to the same special detail. In 1905, as a private with Company M, Twenty-Fourth Infantry, he ranked number 51 among rifle experts with a score of 76 out of 100 possible.[169]

At Allensworth, Phillips and his family lived in a prefabricated house that locals assisted in erecting. This structure stood just behind Chaplain Allensworth's home.[170] Phillips died in San Francisco. At that time, the chaplain's daughter, Josephine Allensworth along with, 'Sarah Hindsman, Cora Overr, Sarah Porter (mother of Mrs. Birdie Phillips) and Laura Smith – helped Phillip's widow [Birdie] petition the Army' for her survivor's pension of $12 a month.

---

163 *Ibid.*
164 Royal, *Allensworth The Freedom Colony*, 137–38. John Taylor may have been the first sergeant of Troop E, Tenth Cavalry, 'who was shot in the leg as he was going up San Juan Hill.' *Colored American Magazine* 17 (August 1909), 125.
165 Schubert, *On the Trail of the Buffalo Soldier* I, 84; and Royal, *Allensworth The Freedom Colony*, 16.
166 Royal, *Allensworth The Freedom Colony*, 16.
167 *A&NJ*, February 4, 1893, 395.
168 Schubert, *On the Trail of the Buffalo Soldier* I, 151.
169 *Ibid.*, 329.
170 Royal, *Allensworth The Freedom Colony*, 16.

Once again, this assistance offered yet one more example of cohesion often found within the military community even after leaving service.[171]

Phillips also was a comrade in arms at Fort Huachuca with John R. Green, a sergeant in Company A, Twenty-Fourth Infantry. While at Fort Apache, Private Green met Chaplain Allensworth. After Green transferred to Fort Bayard, New Mexico, the clergyman had him appointed as the post schoolteacher.[172] Later, Green taught at Fort Huachuca, but would be relieved from this extra duty per Order 66, Fort Huachuca, May 7, 1893.[173]

Another telling point about Green, while at Fort Huachuca, he and his wife each donated $1 as a contribution to the defence fund for three Black women charged with murder in Lunenburg County, Virginia. Fellow Company A Sergeant Frank Banks and his wife matched the Greens in this effort. Green, who signed the letter with the accompanying donation that remarked: 'While we earnestly believe the women to be innocent, the murder was committed by some one and this alone is enough to inspire every Afro-American to do all in their power to clear the innocent and let the guilty be punished.'[174]

Yet one more sergeant, James 'Bunky' Grimes from the Twenty-Fourth Infantry, who had been wounded in Cuba, retired to Allensworth. He acquired an impressive 11 and a half acres.[175] Similarly, Twenty-Fourth Sergeant G.W. Hicks, held three city lots and a 10-acre ranch in alfalfa.[176] Anderson Bird, formerly a member of Company D, Twenty-Fifth Infantry, moved his family to Allensworth. He purchased five acres of land on which he succeeded in raising sugar beets.[177] Generally speaking, a number of the Allensworth pioneers fared fairly well after leaving the military. They were a fortunate few. In reality, however, as seen by previous examples, veterans of the half century after the Civil War regularly faced financial hardship.

One more instance of associations carried on after retirement involved Thomas Goodloe. For nearly a half century, he maintained contact with Archy Wall, another Maury County, Tennessee native whom he knew since childhood. Goodloe and Wall had both spent time with the Twenty-Fourth Infantry. Even after moving on to other regiments, they periodically saw each other or otherwise communicated periodically.[178]

Banner Bearers of Empire

Many of the residents of Allensworth came into the army as part of a third wave of Black soldiers, who appeared coincidently to what Historian Frederick Jackson Turner viewed as the

---

171 *Ibid.*, 17. Of note, Cora Overr's husband Oscar was a Spanish American War veteran who held a commission as a lieutenant in the 23rd Kansas Volunteer Infantry
172 Monroe Lee Billington, *New Mexico's Buffalo Soldiers, 1866–1900* (Niwot: University Press of Colorado, 1991), 162.
173 Schubert, *On the Trail of the Buffalo Soldier* I, 174.
174 *Richmond Planet*, January 11, 1896.
175 Beasley, *The Negro Trail Blazers*, 156; William G. Müller, *Twenty-Fourth Infantry Past and Present a Brief History of the Regiment Compiled from Official Records, Under the Direction of the Regimental Commander* (n.p., 1923), 18.
176 Beasley, *The Negro Trail Blazers*, 156.
177 *Ibid.*, 160.
178 Schubert, *On the Trail of the Buffalo Soldier* I, 167.

closing of the frontier in 1890. Even as constabulary duty in the West drew to its end, the United States soon morphed from continental colonialism to an international imperialism triggered by the Spanish American War and forays into the Pacific especially the Philippines and Hawaii as well as Alaska. When the nation emerged as a global power, so did its armed forces on land and sea transform accordingly. From 1898, when the US Army, Navy and Marines set out for Cuba and during more than a dozen years thereafter, the country's military expanded to project power to far flung destinations.

Among this iteration of Black regulars were a few who pursued distinctive courses. For example, some followed Bandmaster Lovings' lead and achieved notice along with promotion based on musical aptitude. While each regiment boasted a band, the leaders of these martial music makers, like the first officers and the early chaplains, all were white. Conversely, the accomplished bandsmen they led such as, 'Alexander Sewall a musician bearing excellent endorsements from members of the Marine Band,' were Black.[179] By the early twentieth century, that paradigm shifted. All but the Twenty-Fourth Infantry at Madison Barracks, New York had Black bandmasters.[180] Sewell applied for the position to assail this last holdout.

He stood in good company. Previously, Wade H. Hammond earned laurels as chief musician of the Ninth Cavalry Band. Hammond, born in Alabama, in 1895, graduated from the Agricultural and Mechanical College. He earned a livelihood both as musician and tailor but would become bandmaster at his alma mater and then at Western University, from which place he joined the Ninth Cavalry in 1909. His regiment sent him to the Royal Military School of Music in London at their expense, which permitted him to travel to other countries. After two months, Hammond returned to resume his position as bandmaster with the Ninth.[181]

Before Hammond crisscrossed the Atlantic, a Cheyenne, Wyoming newspaper championed him as: 'the most accomplished negro musician in the service.'[182] A few years later, while the regiment resided in Arizona, the mayor of Douglas presented Hammond, 'with a gold medal set with diamonds.' This medal was purchased by popular subscription to express 'the gratitude of the citizens for the services of the band during the last two years.' It bore, as part of the inscription: 'Keep step to the music of the Union.'[183] Nearly a decade later, Hammond, still served at

---

179 *A&NJ*, January 30, 1909, 5.
180 *Washington Bee*, January 30, 1909.
181 *Cheyenne State Leader*, August 24, 1912; and *Crisis* 12 (November 1916): 13. Black bandsmen also could be found outside the military once they left the ranks including at 'The commencement exercises of the Institute of Musical Art in the City of New York, of which Mr. Frank Damrosch is director, were held in Aeolian Hall on June 1. Mr. Alfred J. Thomas, the only colored member of the graduating class, was formerly a leader in the United States Tenth Cavalry Band.' *Crisis* 8 (August 1914): 163. Similarly, reporting on President Theodore Roosevelt's visit to Tuskegee, the *Evening Star* (Washington, DC) for October 24, 1905, indicated that the formal welcome was started by 'the Institute Band, led by Elbert B. Williams, bandmaster, member of the 9th Cavalry, U.S.A., which saw service with the President's Rough Riders at Santiago, who is detailed by the War Department to Tuskegee, followed by the nearly 1,000 students of the school in two divisions.'
182 *Cheyenne Daily Leader*, March 23, 1910. The next year Hammond demonstrated his commitment to civil rights by serving on Fort D.A. Russell, Wyoming soldiers' trolley boycott committee. *Cheyenne Daily Leader*, January 15, 1911.
183 *Crisis* 9 (March 1915): 218.

Fort Huachuca where he became one of the first Black warrant officers. He continued to be a popular figure there and throughout the southwest.[184]

Hammond's contemporary, John R. Anderson, was born November 25, 1880, in Thaxton, Virginia. He elected on his own recognizance to leave Company L, Twenty-Fourth Infantry in 1899 for the cavalry. Two years later, Anderson reenlisted with Troop L, Ninth Cavalry, stating that his occupation was a carpenter. He remained with the regiment until his discharge in 1904 at the Presidio of San Francisco, California. By October 24, 1906, Anderson decided to return to the military at Fort McDowell, California as private serving variously with Troops E and F, Tenth Cavalry. He accompanied the regiment to Fort Ethan Allen, Vermont where he was discharged on October 23, 1909, as a sergeant rated with an excellent character. When he reenlisted that year for a final tour of duty, he now reported his occupation, as did hundreds of others, as a soldier. From Vermont he went on to the Army War College Detachment at Fort Meyer, Virginia. Among other assignments he worked as a janitor in the post administration building.

On January 27, 1911, he obtained his final discharge 'by purchase.' Thereafter he resided quietly in Washington, DC with his spouse, the former Rosa E. Buckner. There was one exception in that in his late 30s, Anderson sailed to France as a member of the 350th Field Artillery, making the trip home after the First World War as the regimental colour sergeant on February 16, 1919, from Brest, France. Anderson died on June 8, 1962 and would be buried in Arlington National Cemetery.[185] For the most par,t Anderson exemplified the third generation of Black regulars.

Over the course of four decades in the ranks (from 1887 to 1937), Samuel Waller complied a record that essentially paralleled Anderson's. The illiterate country lad from Memphis, Tennessee was not yet 14 years of age when he managed to pass as an older applicant. After entering the military, Waller became eligible to attend a post school. According to his grandson, Waller looked to the army as the means to achieve: 'the only part of the American dream that the nation would let him share in.' He, like many, supposedly, 'did not join because of patriotism.' Instead, the military provided, 'a way up and a way out' and proffered freedom, as well as 'economic stability,' plus an 'opportunity to do things that would be impossible otherwise' for a Black man during that era.[186] Samuel Waller epitomized several of the intrepid African

---

184 Schubert, *On the Trail of the Buffalo Soldier*, I, 185.
185 A John R. Anderson enlisted in 1898 as a private in Company H, Twenty-Fourth Infantry at Camp Wikoff, New York with four years continuous service. Shortly thereafter he took a furlough because of illness. He would recover sufficiently to be placed on special duty as a teamster and carried on in this capacity until being discharged on January 29, 1899 as a single man with an excellent character. He again enlisted the next day at Fort Douglas, Utah remaining with the Twenty-Fourth Infantry. Schubert, *On the Trail of the Buffalo Soldiers*, I, 12. It is highly probable that this is the same John R. Anderson who on January 24, 1901, once more signed on for duty, this time in Troop L, Ninth Cavalry while in Washington, DC. RG393, Returns From Regular Army Cavalry Regiments, 1833–1916 microfilm publication M744, Roll 9. Records of US Regular Army Mobile Units, 1821–1942, NARA. The remainder of Anderson's military record based on various items in the National Archives was furnished by a family member, William Gwaltney via an email to the author on January 13, 2022.
186 Anthony Powell, Lecture, Smithsonian Institution National Postal Museum, September 29, 2016, si.edu/object/ytpBofRUraUMY. Powell stated Waller, at one time or the other, served in all four of the 'buffalo soldier' regiments (Twenty-fourth and Twenty-fifth US Infantry; Ninth and Tenth US Cavalry) with posting in the American West, Cuba, four tours in Philippines, Mexico in 1916, WWI, and the Siberian Expedition of 1919–1920, spending 40 years as an enlisted man.

Vance H. Marchbanks, photographed here with his spouse, the former 'Callie' Hatton, married at Fort Apache, Arizona. They spent much of his four decades in the US Army together. Marchbanks began his military career as a private in the Ninth Cavalry. During 1897, he temporarily transferred to the hospital corps, but returned to the cavalry where he became a non-commissioned officer. During the First World War, the globe-trotting professional soldier received a commission as a captain. His memoirs offer one of the most detailed accounts of an enlisted Black regular known from the pre-World War II era. (Courtesy Fort Huachuca Museum)

American enlisted men who proudly viewed service in the military as a profession. He reenlisted multiple times. In fact, extraordinarily, he at one time or another, served in all four Black regiments moving back and forth over the years.

Vance Hunter Marchbank, Sr. was another model of devotion to duty. Marchbank recollected being, 'brought up on a farm in the back-woods of Putnam County, Tennessee.' He had seen soldiers only once, 'but the Soldier bug had bitten me at sometime, because when I was a small boy, I would long to be a soldier and to go out West and fight the Indians.'[187]

Marchbank accumulated four decades in the military. In the process, he left behind one of the most detailed known accounts of a Black regular.[188] Along the way, he experienced many places unfamiliar to most people in the United States at the time such as the Suez Canal, Singapore, Aden, Arabia, Port Said, Egypt, Malta and Gibraltar, on a protracted voyage with his regiment, the Tenth Cavalry, that brought him to New York City.[189] It was such adventures that may have inspired his son to follow in his father as a career military man, as would a few other offspring of professional soldiers. From March 1934 to October 1939, the senior Marchbanks' duty with the seedbed of many Black soldiers, Washington High School Cadet Corps in Washington, DC, made it possible for his son to enter medical school while the family lived in the city and had military pay to maintain them. The younger Marchbank went on to hold a commission as a doctor in the United States Air Force.

Not everyone born into a Black military family followed in their father's martial calling. Charles Mingus, Jr., choose a different destiny. Born on April 22, 1922, in Nogales, Arizona, Mingus' father was a sergeant posted there at the time. Rather than enlist, the talented son became a renowned jazz musician and composer instead of a soldier.

His father was born in, 'Swain County, North Carolina, on February 4, 1877, the great-great-grandson of the family's founding patriarch, Jacob Mingus' who, with his spouse Sarah, allegedly were 'the first whites to settle in North Carolina's Oconaluftee valley around 1790.' Of mixed parentage (a Black father and white mother), family lore had it that their offspring, the senior Charles Mingus, 'didn't like the situation up there at the plantation,' where he was born. According to his daughter Grace: 'he put his age up and joined the service. Somebody sent word to him in the service and he went back one time on leave and they had a big celebration. But he was leery of staying there; he was afraid for his life, because of the racial thing. So, he left and went back into the service.'

Another daughter, Vivian, recalled her stepmother saying that Mingus: 'ran away when he was about fourteen and joined the army.' Supposedly, he first enlisted at Richmond.[190] This was on November 5, 1892, with the Tenth Cavalry as a private. By March 14, 1897, he had advanced to corporal in Troop G of the regiment, while posted to Fort Assiniboine, Montana.[191] It seems there was an 18 month break in service, 'long enough to head back to the Mingus family homestead to see where he fit, if at all.' Mingus's family accounts make his ambivalence unclear.

---

187 Vance Hunter Marchbank, Sr., 'Forty Years in the Army,' unpublished MS c, 1940, transcription, Fort Huachuca Museum, 2006, 6.
188 These dates and time in service were by his own calculations. Marchbank, 'Forty Years in Army,' 109.
189 Marchbank, 'Forty Years in Army,' 82.
190 For more detail read, Gene Santoro, *Myself When I am Real: The Life and Music of Charles Mingus* (Oxford University Press, 1994), 16.
191 Schubert, *On the Trail of the Buffalo Soldiers*, I, 297.

What is known is that on June 12, 1902, he reenlisted. This time he joined the Twenty-Fourth Infantry. He went with this regiment from Montana to New York and in time, to the Southwest, as well as the Philippines and Fort Wright, Washington, 'until his twenty-year-plus time was up and his second wife wanted to move to Los Angeles to be with her family.'[192] This was Harriet, who died when Charles Mingus, Jr. was not yet two years old. By that time, Staff Sergeant Charles Mingus, Sr., 'retired from the army, after logging in twenty-seven years, eleven months and twenty-one days – including his two years, one month and twenty-seven days in the Philippines.' As foreign service counted for double time, Sergeant Mingus spent some 23 years on active duty thereby entitling him to his full army pension as a sergeant in the quartermaster department.[193]

Ernest Stokes (c.1870–1936) of Chattanooga, Tennessee came from the same generation as Charles Mingus, Sr. He likewise, made the US Army his home for several decades. His granddaughter recounted that Stokes: 'wanted to escape from the South, where he experienced oppressive racial prejudice.' In 1898, Stokes availed himself, 'of an opportunity for an overseas assignment, hoping for a life free from discrimination in another country. He responded to a call for volunteers for the Spanish-American War in the Philippines.'[194]

Stokes and other Tennesseans trained at the Presidio of San Francisco before shipping across the Pacific. He was assigned to the Ninth Cavalry. With the regiment, he braved the long overseas voyage. As Stokes later related to a family member, he did so to pursue: "a new destiny, a better life than here [the United States].' His dreams would not be realized, at least while in the US Army. Nonetheless, he remained in the military, although not as a bachelor as had been the case when he first entered the army. In 1902, he married Maria Bunag from Peñaranda, Nueva Ecija. They would have three daughters, all born at Fort Stotsenberg, later known as Clark Air Force Base. Sometime in the late 1920s or early 1930s, Stokes headed back to the United States. At this crossing, a widower since 1917, he brought his second spouse to the United States. Ernest and Roberta Stokes settled in the West Oakland, California.

There, like other veterans and family members before them, they linked up with old comrades. They passed many an evening, 'partying and playing cards together' with their wives, whom the old soldiers had 'taught to play poker.' Stokes' descendants remained in the Bay Area generations after his death.

---

192 Santoro, *Myself When I am Real*, 17. In part, this information coincides with Charles Mingus (Sr.) being carried on the roster of Company A, Twenty-Fourth Infantry in Cuba from June through December 1898. www. spanamwar.com/24thinf.htm.
193 *Ibid.*, At Camp Stephen D. Little in Nogales, Arizona (Charles Mingus, Jr.'s birthplace) his father received praise from the commanding colonel relative to the construction of the post theater. He noted: 'After the work had progressed to a certain stage tbs money ran so short and we had to pay Mr. Lovell [who had been in charge of the project] so much that I had to let him go. And then we got a black man – a negro – Sergeant Mingus of the quartermaster department, and he took charge of the work, superintended it and prosecuted it to a conclusion. I want you all to take your hats off to Sergeant Mingus, and to know that there is such a man here who can do that kind of work. (Applause.) To Sergeant Mingus I wish to publicly extend the thanks of the regiment.' *Daily Morning Oasis* (Nogales, AZ) December 26, 1920.
194 Evangeline Canonizado Buell, *Twenty-five Chickens and a Pig for a Bride: Growing Up in a Filipino Immigrant Family* (San Francisco: T'Boli Publishing and Distributor, 2006), 16–20 provided the sources for all quotations related to Sergeant Stokes.

Private James Harrison, like many other Black soldiers, spent only one tour of duty in the army. Nonetheless, he managed to see more of the world than many of his contemporaries. Soon after his January 28, 1907, enlistment, he sailed far from his native Carbondale, Illinois for the Philippines. (Courtesy John Langellier)

An unknown number of Stokes' comrades sailed to the islands during the late 1800s and early 1900s to serve in the so-called Philippine Insurrection and thereafter, as a long-standing occupation force. Over several decades, the number of Blacks who did so numbered in the thousands.[195] Most of the men who deployed overseas in the late nineteenth and early twentieth centuries, however, returned to the Continental United States. Among them was John H. Graine. At 14 years of age, Graine took up the printer's trade, which he followed for about 20 years. During some of that time, he worked on his local newspaper, *The True Northerner*, in various positions. He also functioned as a foreman and assistant editor of a prominent African American paper, *The Chicago Conservatory*. In the late 1890s, Graine briefly set aside these pursuits to enlist as a 'faithful soldier in the Ninth Cavalry in the Spanish American War and served until he was honorably discharged.' Soon afterwards, he returned to his former occupations, married and started a family.[196]

Melvin McCaw offered another perspective. From 1896 to 1917, combining an assortment of military and civilian sources offered a window into this Columbia, Tennessee native's military service. McCaw's army career began approximately three decades after his birth in 1867. He took part in fighting in Cuba at San Juan Hill and the siege of Santiago de Cuba, as well as the US occupation of the Philippines in 1900. In 1907, he reported to the United States Military Academy as a non-commissioned officer with the first detachment of African American troops assigned there, in part because of the high level of desertion among the white enlisted cadre at West Point. McCaw qualified as marksman and a sharpshooter, received appraisals by his superiors as an intelligent and loyal soldier of good character and unlike the majority of those who

---

195 Buell, *Twenty-five Chickens*, 17, maintains '6,000 African-Americans were sent to the Philippines in 1898' but that figure likely far exceeds the actual number.
196 *True Northerner* (Paw Paw, MI) February 18, 1916.

came before him, enjoyed domestic life with his spouse and their two children. Also, he entered the rolls of an impressive legion of those who retired after 30 years of uninterrupted service.[197]

Augustus Snoten likewise widely vagabonded during his three decades on duty that took him from Puerto Rico to Alaska and many places in between. Edward Bordinghammer, another 30 year man, went from New York to Alaska to Texas.[198] James Harrison did some globe-trotting as well. He enlisted on January 28, 1907, and 'With good conduct and self behavior' he recorded his time would expire, 'Jan 29th year of 1910.' Born in 1881 at Carbondale Illinois, Harrison sought enlistment at Lynchburg, Virginia, thereby demonstrating a certain penchant for travel even before his days with the military. From the recruiting station, he went to Columbus, Ohio for cursory training, until February 19, 1907. His introduction to service was followed by a brief rendezvous with the Twenty-Fifth Infantry at Fort Reno, Oklahoma. Barely settled into barracks and the daily martial routine, on August 4, Harrison and the regiment started for San Francisco, then steamed on to Honolulu and the Port of Nagasaki. Laying over there from September 5 for two days, the ship sailed for Manila making its landing on September 13. The unit received its awaited orders the following day.

Harrison and the regiment again were at sea until September 16, when they made a brief stopover at Zamboanga, Mindanao. At last, the men departed for their destination of Parang. On September 17, they disembarked at the port for a two-year posting. He was with Company B, Twenty-Fifth Infantry. Just over 24 months passed before Harrison and his comrades completed their tour of duty in the Philippines. As he did at the beginning in his journal-scrapbook, Harrison recorded his departure in telegraphic spurts, writing in the third person and paying sparse attention to spelling and punctuation. Nonetheless, he captured the homeward journey thusly:

> The 25 Infy Rgt in witch he is serving was relieve on Sept 1 09 and sail for Zamboanga arrived Sept 7th taken in four company and Band Twenty-fifth Infy head quarters and command sail on evening of 7th for Manila arrived in Manila until leaving of 15 sail for quarantine station 3 hours run and arrive at 3 oclock sailing for Nagasaki Japan on next day Sept 11th at noon 5 days at sea weather bad arrive Nagasaki on Sept 16th stop over Two days and departure for Seattle Wash on the 18th inst weather condition for two weeks bad on the 8 day from Japan past island near Nome Alaska 2 thousand miles from Seattle 2 hundred miles from Nome 3 thousand mi from Japan.
>
> Arrive Seattle on Oct 5 –09 departed from transport Sheridan and taken station Fort Lawton Wash same inst Total time between Parang Island of Mindinao and Settle Wash Twenty five days and 8 hours In witch four days 18 hours was consumed for stop over. Condition of weather bad for twenty two days and 9 hours.[199]

Except for African American porters and other workers on the railroads, few Blacks, or whites for that matter, boasted such an extensive movement across the United States and beyond its shores than the widely traveled Black soldiers including Harrison and thousands of others. In

---

197 archives.nypl.org/scm/20643#access_use.
198 Brian Shellum, *Buffalo Soldiers in Alaska: Company L, Twenty-Fourth Infantry in Skagway, 1899–1902* (Lincoln: University of Nebraska Press, 2021), 17–18; 27, 242–24, and 272 n28.
199 James Harrison Scrapbook and Album, Author's Collection.

fact, generally the wealthy class enjoyed such a luxury. As such, in some respects, Black regulars stood in the vanguard of the later 'Great Migration.'

Some of them never returned from these ventures to foreign climes. One of these was David Fagen, perhaps the most controversial of the soldiers who landed in the Philippines. As a biographical sketch related: 'David Fagen was by far the best known of the ... Black soldiers who deserted the US Army in the Philippines at the turn of the twentieth century and defected to the enemy.'[200] Fagen's saga began on June 4, 1898, when he agreed to enlist for a term of three years. His transition from laborer to soldier brought him to the Twenty-Fourth Infantry as a private. In order to enlist, Fagen 'had to provide two character references, people who knew the family and lived nearby. He chose the carpenter Samuel Bryant and the laborer William Hicks, both residents of the Scrub [the early Black community in Tampa, Florida]. William Hicks remains obscure, but Samuel Bryant was a significant member of the black community.'[201] Consequently, Fagen's family must have enjoyed a degree status in their neighborhood, at least in the case of being able to list Bryant as a reference.

Beyond that, Fagen seemed to craft some of his personal history to suit the recruiter's requirements such as stating he was 22 years old when more than likely he was 19. Furthermore, he had declined to reveal that he had been married and still may have been, a fact that could have barred him from being accepted. Fagen also swore that he did not drink, 'intoxicating liquors.' The next year, he reported, 'moderate use of spirits.' Adding to the less than accurate picture, he found a willing accomplice in Lieutenant Charles Tayman, the white recruiting officer, who stated: 'Fagen spoke, read and wrote the English language "satisfactorily." ' Ironically, the applicant 'verified this by signing the official enlistment document with an "X," ' which suggested Fagen likely could not write.[202]

Although illiterate, which demonstrated that issue had not been irradicated entirely, Fagen was not without abilities and sensibilities. These factors evidently emerged after he reached the Philippines. There, a possible anti-authoritarian bent and a sense of racial injustice, led him to the realization (one shared with many other Black American soldiers in the islands) that, 'this conflict pitted them against a nonwhite population for which some of them felt a genuine

---

200 Michael C. Robinson and Frank N. Schubert, 'Seeking David Fagen: The Search for a Black Rebel's Florida Roots,' *Tampa Bay History* 22 no. 1 (2008): 19. For additional analysis by these two scholars read: Michael C. Robinson and Frank N. Schubert, 'David Fagen: An Afro-American Rebel in the Philippines, 1899–191,' *Pacific Historical Review* 44 no. 1 (February, 1975): 68–83, the two articles taken together providing the most balanced evaluation of this polemic figure. Previously, D. B. McKay, *Pioneer Florida* (Tampa: Southern Publishing, 1959), 1: 238, derided Fagen, while more recent efforts tend to be more sympathetic such as Philip W. Hoffman, *David Fagen: Turncoat Hero* (Staunton: American History Press, 2017); Michael Morey, *Fagen: An African American Renegade in the Philippine-American War* (Madison: University of Wisconsin Press, 2019). Also see Scott Brown, 'White Backlash and the Aftermath of Fagen's Rebellion: The Fates of Three African-American Soldiers in the Philippines, 1901–1902,' *Contributions to Black Studies* (1995/1996) 13/14 Article 5: 165–73.and E. San Juan, Jr., 'An African American Soldier in the Philippine Revolution: An Homage to David Fagen.' academia.edu/242727/a.homage_to_david_ fagen_ african_american_ soldier_in_ the philippine_revolution.
201 Robinson and Schubert, 'Seeking David Fagen:' 20, 24, and 27.
202 *Ibid.*, 27.

sympathy.'²⁰³ Regardless of whether race consciousness stirred Fagen, on November 17, 1899, he decided to desert. He then cast his lot with the Filipinos.²⁰⁴ Little time passed before Fagen emerged as an infamous *cause célèbre*. For several years, newspaper ink flowed combining fact with fiction, such as one article that claimed Fagen: 'is one of- the most daring and bloodthirsty of the Filipino generals. He is charged with torturing American prisoners.'²⁰⁵

Crime and Punishment

While Fagen attained notoriety, he was not the sole soldier to desert in the Philippines. Figures differ among some scholars, but certainly whites regularly continued to flee since the 1860s in higher numbers than Blacks. Be that as it may, Black soldiers were human. Black or white, as the commanding general of the US Army mused in 1889, occasionally, 'men creep into the ranks … who are known to have committed heinous crimes and continued to do so.'²⁰⁶ Such individuals, another officer concluded, were 'restless, uneasy characters and are not inclined to stay anywhere for any length of time.' Indeed, many studies contained considerable evidence about crimes committed by Black soldiers, but these infractions were no greater than existed among white troops.²⁰⁷

In this light, as W. Sherman Savage indicated not, 'all black soldiers were exemplary.'²⁰⁸ When they strayed, like all soldiers, they, 'could be subject to military and civil law, or both.' Civil courts had jurisdiction over capital crimes. On occasion, general courts-martial convened, 'to try officers or enlisted men charged with capital offenses.' Garrison courts were far more common and presided over, 'less than capital offenses' with limited sentencing power 'of not more than thirty days' general confinement or fourteen days solitary.'²⁰⁹ Regardless of the level of court-martial, they addressed offenses between soldiers, matters of government property, or infractions of a variety of specifically military rules or regulations such as desertion.

Beginning with garrison courts-martial, which ran gamut of offenses, one soldier stationed at Fort Davis postulated that these tribunals exacerbated desertion. He said that being, 'fined $5 to $10 for missing roll call, failing to stand at attention, or appearing with his blouse unbuttoned could cause a man straightaway to be marched to the guardhouse.' These tribunals were

---

203 *Ibid.*, 32. Richard E. Welch, Jr., 'American Atrocities in the Philippines: The Indictment and the Response,' *Pacific Historical Review* 43 no. 2 (May, 1974): 233–253, offers a review at one of the reasons why Black soldiers and some of their white comrades recoiled at fighting against Filipinos, who sought to free their land from yet another imperial power, as the United States appeared to replace Spain as an overlord.
204 Schubert, *On the Trail of the Buffalo Soldiers*, I, 139.
205 *Cook County Herald* (Grand Marais, MN) November 10, 1900.
206 *ARSW 1889*, I, 101.
207 Stephen Bonsal, 'The Negro Soldiers in War and Peace,' *North American Review* 185 (June 7, 1907): 321–27; Billington, *New Mexico's Buffalo Soldiers*, 163–73; Dobak and Phillips, *Black Regulars*, 160–223; Frank N. Schubert, *Buffalo Soldiers, Braves, and the Brass* (Shippensburg, PA: White Mane Publishing Company Inc., 1993), 83–92; and Shellum, *Buffalo Soldiers in Alaska*, 160–64, are among some of the best documented published works on the subject of crime and punishment related to Black soldiers during the last quarter of the nineteenth century.
208 W. Sherman Savage, *Blacks in the West* (Westport, CT: Greenwood Press, 1976), 50.
209 McChristian, *Regular Army O!*, 381–2.

the enlisted man's bane. Worsening the matter, he thought: 'was being locked up for what might be a considerable period while awaiting his case to be heard.'[210] One historian added to this opinion. He postulated that some deserters may have done so as, 'a way of protesting the conditions under which they lived and the officers under whom they worked.'[211]

One specific example of a garrison court-martial involved a hearing to determine if Farrier Benjamin Buckner of Troop C, Tenth Cavalry was guilty of, 'marrying a notorious strumpet to the scandal and disgrace of the service.'[212] He was acquitted.

Sergeant Alfred Pride, Troop K, Ninth Cavalry, proved less fortunate. For allowing a prisoner to escape while he served as sergeant of the guard, Pride received the sentence of a reduction in rank to a private and a $20 fine. The court noted punitive actions would have been more stringent had he not exhibited a record of 'long service and good character.'[213]

Garrison court-martial proceedings often were serious, but on occasion could be frivolous or sometimes humorous. Typically, general courts-martial proved more consequential. A litany of charges, such as desertion, gambling, illicit sex, violence, liquor and occasionally narcotics, resulted in the convening of general courts-martial boards.[214] Despite the fact that Black soldiers tended to be less inclined to the use of alcohol, that statistic did not equate to a total lack of issues that arose from drinking.[215]

Nor did their more reliable record when it came to serving out their complete term of enlistment, apply to everyone. Random reviews of these military documents demonstrated several trends. As one baseline, between 1882 and 1884, records related to the Ninth Cavalry for general courts-martial (GCM) indicated that 20 were for negligence; 18 for absence without leave; 17 for theft; 10 for assault; nine for desertion, six for intoxication; and one for sexual deviance.[216] By 1886, GCM throughout the US Army included desertion by 10 Black soldiers, one of whom surrendered and nine others who were apprehended. All were tried, convicted and received similar sentences. (Table 4)

210 *A&NJ*, June 26, 1886, 989.
211 Billington, *New Mexico's Buffalo Soldiers*, 37
212 Schubert, *On the Trail of the Buffalo Soldiers*, 67, and *AN&J*, July 28, 1894, 842.
213 *A&NJ*, November 8, 1890, 170.
214 McChristian, *Regular Army Oh!*, 366–67.
215 According to *A&NJ*, May 11, 1901, 886–7, a US Army doctor made 'a comparison of liquor drinking among white and black troops' and concluded 'that there is approximately only one-tenth as much sickness from the use of alcohol among the negro as the white troops … Coming to the delicate subject of venereal diseases … While the colored troops show a higher moral rate in the matter of liquor, they are decidedly the weaker brother in this connection, being doubly touched by this disease.' Further a Tenth Cavalry officer recorded that: 'A man was made to walk [on patrol leading his horse] for having unfitted himself for duty by getting drunk.' This 'punishment was illegal, but sanctioned by the custom of the service.' John Bigelow, Jr. *On the Trail of Geronimo* (Tucson: Westernlore Press, 1986), 6.
216 Kenner, *Buffalo Soldiers and Officers*, 24. This same source summarized the number of desertions in the regiment between 1885 through 1887 was 99. Kenner, *Buffalo Soldiers and Officers*, 26.

Table 4: Sample Courts-Martial

GCM Orders No. 2, HQA January 3, 1883 Recruit Charles McCoy Colored Detachment, General Mounted Service 47th Article of War desertion November 5, 1882 and surrendered November 28, 1882 sentenced to dishonorable discharge, forfeiture of all pay due and four years hard labor.
GCM Orders No. 3, HQA January 12, 1886 Private Henry Wilson Troop E, Ninth Cavalry 47th Article of War desertion on June 30, 1885 and apprehended November 16, 1885 sentenced to dishonorable discharge, forfeiture of all pay due and confined three years hard labor.
GCM Orders No. 3, HQA January 12, Recruit Leonis Trent Colored Detachment, General Mounted Service 47th Article of War desertion from Jefferson Barracks about September 9, 1885 and apprehended in Memphis on or about November 4, 1885 sentenced to dishonorable discharge, forfeiture of all pay due, and three years hard labor.
GCM Orders No. 7, HQA January 16, 1883 Private Jeremiah Spencer Troop H, Ninth Cavalry 47th Article of War desertion June 18, 1881 and apprehended October 31, 1882 sentenced to dishonorable discharge, forfeiture of all pay due and four years hard labor.
GCM Orders No. 9, HQA February 6, 1886. Private George Browne Troop E, Ninth Cavalry 47th Article of War desertion on August 4, 1884 and apprehended December 30, 1885 sentenced to dishonorable discharge, forfeiture of all pay due and confined three years hard labor.
GCM Orders No. 39, HQA August 27, 1883 Recruit Albert Huff Troop G, Ninth Cavalry 47th Article of War desertion from June 25, 1883 sentenced to dishonorable discharge, forfeiture of all pay due and three years hard labor.
GCM Orders No. 39, HQA August 27, 1883 Private Charles Schuller Company C, Twenty-Fifth Infantry deserted May 29, 1883 and surrendered July 29, 1883 sentenced to dishonorable discharge, forfeiture of all pay due and two years hard labor.
GCM Orders No. 52, HQA November 14, 1883 Samuel Thompson Troop I, Ninth Cavalry 47th Article of War desertion from June 25, 1883 sentenced to dishonorable discharge, forfeiture of all pay due and two years hard labor.
GCM Orders No. 71, HQA August 19, 1886 Private Andrew Washington Company I, Twenty-Fifth Infantry 47th Article of War desertion on May 18, 1886 and apprehended July 4, 1886 sentenced to dishonorable discharge, forfeiture of all pay due and confined five years hard labor.
GCM Orders No. 91, HQA October 29, 1886 Recruit Joseph Lee Troop H. Ninth Cavalry 47th Article of War desertion on May 11, 1883 and apprehended August 12, 1884 1885 sentenced to dishonorable discharge, forfeiture of all pay due and confined four years hard labor.
GCM Orders No. 94, HQA November 10, 1886 Recruit Charles Miller Colored Detachment, General Mounted Service 47th Article of War desertion on September 14, 1886 and apprehended September, 18, 1886 by police officer at Carondelet, Missouri plus disposed of a pair of mounted trousers and suspenders he borrowed from a fellow recruit plus a pair of his own issued shoes; sentenced to dishonorable discharge, forfeiture of all pay due and confined four years hard labor.

In the early 1900s, during the US Army's deployment to the Philippines, white and Black enlisted men alike acted on various motives to leave the ranks. Some of those captured faced execution. Edward A. Dubose and Lewis Russell, both from Company E, Ninth Cavalry, accused of defection to the enemy, faced the death sentence.[217] The hangman's knot awaited others besides deserters. Indeed, murder was an odious offense punishable under civilian and military law alike.

---

217 *Billings Gazette*. February 11, 1902; *Arizona Republican* (Phoenix, AZ) February 11, 1902; *Rosebud County News* (Forsyth, MT) February 13, 1902; and *Butler Weekly Times* (Butler, MO) February 20, 1902.

Homicides regularly received press coverage. One of the first of these appeared in early 1869. A terse paragraph in the *New York Herald* under the headline: 'White Man Murdered by Negro Soldiers – The Murderers Hung by a Vigilance Committee' told a far too common tale in the American South, but less so in the West at least as far as members of the US Army were concerned. Three Black privates from Thirty-Eighth were some of the earliest to succumb to a mob in this instance that formed in Hays City, Kansas. The trio died at the hands of the crowd without benefit of trial.[218]

A similar distasteful fate befell Robert Robertson of the Twenty-Fifth Infantry. When Robertson's company transferred from Fort Sisseton, South Dakota to Fort Shaw, Montana, the soldier paid for the transportation of, 'a sporting woman, Quennie Montgomery' to join him. Once Montgomery arrived, she was barred from, 'post owing to her character. So she went to Sun River to live.'[219] Before long, a white infantrymen entered the picture. He boasted: 'he had lots of money' to persuade her to leave Robertson. A jealous Robertson sought out his rival, but mistook, 'another man, Charles McGuire, walking along the road' as Montgomery's new lover. He fired at McGuire and killed the stranger. At first Robertson went to the guard house. In due course, military authorities delivered the shooter to local civil authorities in Sun River for trial. During the 'night a masked body of men overpowered Deputy Sheriff John Hurley and took the prisoner out in the alley back of the stone store and hung him to a beam.'

More often, however, manslaughter and murder resulted in due process by the civil courts. Further, perpetrators often attacked fellow soldiers with fatal results. In truth, nearly as many Black soldiers were murdered then killed in combat on the frontier. Representative, random cases, tried in civilian courts, bear witness to this statement. One of these occurred during the mid-1880s. Tenth Cavalry Private John R. Scott killed a comrade at Camp Verde, Arizona. Scott changed his original not guilty plea to guilty in the hope that he would avoid execution and instead serve life imprisonment in a 'Detroit house of correction.'[220]

Far to the north, at Fort McKinney, Wyoming, a pair of Ninth Cavalry privates, One Hall and Amos Parmer, 'exchanged a few words while on the road between Buffalo' and the post. During their return to the garrison, Parmer called his companion, 'a regular sucker.' Hall was unarmed at the time. Upon reaching the fort, he obtained a revolver and sought out Parmer. Hall found Parmer. He fired two shots. Parmer died a few hours later.[221] Hall escaped the gallows. Instead, he was convicted of manslaughter and sentenced to four years in the penitentiary.[222]

During the fall of 1888, Ninth Cavalry Private Tom Collins from Fort Duchesne, Utah shot and killed a sergeant from his regiment. After awaiting trial in the state penitentiary, Collins claimed he acted in self-defense.[223] Without witnesses, Collins' assertion was impossible to refute in order to determine his guilt beyond a reasonable doubt.

---

218 *New York Herald*, January 12, 1869.
219 *Cheyenne Daily Leader*, June 12, 1888; and *Missoula Gazette*, June 23, 1888. The *Omaha Daily Bee*, June 12, 1888, cavalierly dubbed this incident a 'Dose of Montana Justice.'
220 *Mohave County Miner* (Mineral Park, AZ) December 6, 1885.
221 *Cheyenne Daily Leader*, November 9, 1887.
222 *Ibid.*, December 25, 1887.
223 *Salt Lake Herald*, March 27, 1888. For a few other examples of Black soldiers committing murder or manslaughter see: *Weekly Missoulian*, March 19, 1890; *New North-west* (Deer Lodge, MT) June 19, 1896; *Ravalli Republican* (Stevensville, MT) April 21, 1897, and August 24, 1898; *Butte Inter Mountain*, May 24, 1899; *Philipsburg Mail* (Philipsburg, MT) June 23, 1899; *San Francisco Call*, June

That was not true for Private David Lemmons of Company A, Twenty-Fourth Infantry.[224] At Fort Reno in today's Oklahoma, Lemmons avowed that he killed Sergeant Peter Webster of his company in self-defense. This time witnesses were present. The gist of the affray appeared to be rooted in a rivalry between the two men over a local prostitute. After Webster learned that Lemmons, in clear violation of orders, 'took his gun and walked from the barracks down towards the laundry' the NCO responded. The sergeant dispatched a corporal's guard. When the detail arrived, Lemmons refused to be disarmed. He then threatened the guard. Leaving a pair of privates behind, the corporal hastened back to Webster. He made his report. In reply, Webster stated that he: 'would go down and arrest the man. He started across the area and as he approached Lemmons the latter ordered him to come no nearer at the peril of his life.' Undeterred, the NCO ordered the private to drop his weapon. Lemmons leveled his rifle at his superior. He boldly demanded that the sergeant, 'unload his gun. Webster replied that his piece was empty.' As Webster came near, Lemmons pulled the trigger. The round struck Webster on the left side killing him almost instantly.

Lemmons fled, concealing himself in a tent where there was a child inside. Consequently, as soldiers surrounded the makeshift structure, they called upon Lemmons to surrender. Their demand went unheeded. A temporary stand-off ensued. The soldiers feared they might kill or injure the child. A mob quickly gathered and fearing they might turn on him, Lemmons finally surrendered to an officer from his company.[225]

In September, a grand jury convened. Lemmons' attorney maintained that Webster had threatened to shoot his client on sight. He added: 'the two men held an enmity toward each other' for some time. Then, the jurors heard testimony from several eyewitnesses. The first of those called to the stand was a private from Company K. He reported the events from the time of his arrival with the corporal's guard until the point when Lemmons demanded that the sergeant unload his Springfield rifle. At that point Lemmons retorted: 'Go away and leave me or I will shoot you; by G – d I'll shoot you anyway.' He then fired on Webster who fell and

---

26, 1899, June 27, 1899, and May 17, 1903; *A&NJ*, July 1, 1899, 1047; *Houston Daily Post*, February 23, 1900, Mailable Edition; *El Paso Daily Herald*, February 26, and March 2, 1900; *Kalispell Bee*, August 22, 1902; *Prairie Chronicle* (Cottonwood, ID) November 7, 1902, and November 4, 1904; *River Press* (Fort Benton, MT) November 12, 1902, and November 19, 1902; *New North-west* (Deer Lodge, MT) November 19, 1902, December 31, 1902, March 16, 1904, April 5, 1905, May 3, 1905, August 2, 1905, August 16, 1905, December 13, 1905, February 28, 1906, and July 31, 1907; *Rosebud County News* (Forsyth, MT) December 4, 1902; *Western News* (Stevensville, MT) December 30, 1903; *Butte Inter Mountain*, December 18, 1903; *New Era* (Monterey, CA) May 11, 1904; *Santa Fe Daily New Mexican*, October 20, 1904; *Daily Evening Bulletin* (Maysville, KY) October 22, 1904; *Kootenai Herald* (Kootenai, ID) November 4, 1904; *Pullman Herald* (Pullman, WA) November 5, 1904; *East Oregonian* (Pendleton, OR) December 16, 1904, Daily Evening Edition; *Taney County Republican* (Forsyth, MO) December 29, 1904, and March 2, 1906; *Rock Island Daily Argus*, August 23, 1905; *Havre Herald*, December 15, 1905; *River Press* (Fort Benton, MT) February 7, 1906; *Tombstone Epitaph*, December 24, 1916, Weekly Edition; and *Spokane Press*, November 26, 1910, and December 16, 1910.

224 Note, the earliest newspaper accounts variously reported the perpetrator's name as David Simons, Davis Simons, David Simonson, and David Simmons and his victim as Porter Webster, all of which were incorrect. See *Emporia Weekly News*, May 17, 1888; *West Tennessee Star* (Bolivar, TN) May 25, 1888; *St. Landry Democrat* (Opelousas, LA) May 26, 1888; *Belmont Chronicle* (St. Clairsville, OH) May 24, 1888; *Daily Evening Bulletin* (Maysville, KY) May 17, 1888; *Russellville Democrat* (Russellville, AR) May 24, 1888; and *Evening Capital Journal* (Salem, OR) May 17, 1888.

225 *Wichita Daily Eagle*, May 26, 1888; and *St. Paul Daily Globe*, June 3, 1888.

immediately expired. The next man to appear under oath, the corporal of the guard first sent to apprehend the defendant, recounted much the same story but added that after Lemmons killed Webster, the corporal of the guard pursued the assailant. He fired twice but missed both times.

Another pair of witnesses offered similar accounts. One of them added that he met Lemmons, who was crying while in search of, 'a woman named Sally Brown' with whom the private 'had quarreled earlier in the day.' The woman, who was in a tent, hid under a table piled with clothing. Her makeshift hideout succeeded. Lemmons did not discover her and continued his search. It was after his failure to locate Sally Brown that he encountered Webster, said the final witness.[226] These accounts led the jury to conclude Lemmons was guilty beyond the shadow of a doubt. In accordance with their verdict, the judge called for the death sentence.

A native of Leavenworth, Kansas where he was born on January 1, 1869, Lemmons had been described as, 'a light mulatto, of good appearance and does not look like a 'bad man." He enlisted on November 25, 1884, joining his regiment in Indian Territory soon thereafter. It seemed he would not live to see his 21st birthday in that his execution was set for November 6, 1889. On that day, a telegram from President Benjamin Harrison announced a stay, 'until Wednesday, January eighth, next'[227] On that date, the president again intervened. He commuted the sentence to imprisonment for life. The ghastly testing by a marshal of, 'the rope with a sandbag to see that it was equal to the job' proved unnecessary.[228]

Then there was the matter of Phillip Lashley. He had fled Fort Huachuca, Arizona in the wake of murdering a private from his company. Authorities first believed Lashley had struck out for Sonora, Mexico. That conjecture proved incorrect. Regardless, a reward of $125 was offered for the arrest and delivery of this deserter from Company C, Twenty-Fourth Infantry.[229]

A Danish national from the Caribbean, Lashley had previously been a sailor. Sergeant Lashley and a Private John Sanders, vied for the affections of the same woman, Mrs. Maggie Jennings, the spouse of yet a third Black soldier stationed at the fort.[230] The post commander, Captain Charles Dodge, employed her at his quarters. It was there that Lashley confronted Sanders. On the night of April 13, 1896, Lashley, who supposedly previously had threatened Sanders, pulled his pistol, declaring: '"I promised to kill you and I'll do it." Three balls entered his body, Sanders dying immediately.' Lashley walked out of the garrison and remained absent for four days. At that point, he returned. Fearing being mobbed, he gave himself up to the commanding officer for protection.[231]

Although Lashley maintained his innocence. His lawyer introduced witnesses to collaborate his guiltlessness. Nonetheless, his trial ended with a verdict of 'willful murder.' The death penalty was imposed. An appeal to the territorial supreme court sustained the lower court's finding. Another attempt to overturn the punishment by seeking the Danish consul general's intervention brought no relief.[232] On July 15, 1897, with incredible bravado, Lashley

---

226 *Ibid.*, September 4, 1889. The paper referred to the prisoner as David Lemons.
227 *Ibid.*, November 6, 1889.
228 *Columbus Journal* (Columbus, NE) January 15, 1890.
229 *Arizona Republican* (Phoenix, AZ) April 24, 1896.
230 *Tombstone Epitaph*, January 31, 1897, Sunday Edition.
231 *Arizona Republican* (Phoenix, AZ) April 30, 1896.
232 *Oasis* (Nogales, AZ) April 10, 1896, June 20, 1896, and June 26, 1896; *Arizona Sentinel* (Yuma, AZ) October 3, 1896; *Graham Guardian* (Safford, AZ) June 11, 1897; *Florence Tribune*, June 12, 1897; *Arizona Weekly Citizen* (Tucson, AZ) June 20, 1896; *Tombstone Epitaph*, January 17, 1897, Sunday

mounted the scaffold. He fairly bounded up the steps almost at a run, made a rambling last speech peppered with profanity, cursed those who had condemned him and defiantly danced a near jig before the trap sprung.[233] At least one of those whom Lashley threatened to return from the grave to haunt, temporarily succumbed to the murderer's curse. The accursed told a newspaper the executed man, 'had been a nightly visitor to his bedside ever since the fourth night after' the hanging.[234]

Another Black enlisted man accused of murder in Arizona, Private William Jefferson of Troop E, Tenth Cavalry, became somewhat of a celebrity in the aftermath of being apprehended. He supposedly clubbed Private William Fleming to death. At first, wild stories circulated that the crime was a conspiracy involving a trio of hired assassins, or so charged William Varnum, also of Troop E. Varnum was one of the suspects arrested soon after the bludgeoning took place at San Carlos, Arizona. Subsequently, he testified for the prosecution. Varnum's wild, erratic stories called his veracity into question. To begin with, he wove a fanciful tale that the assailants had taken payment from a secret society within the troop, 'similar to the Mollie Maguires or Ku Klux.'[235] He named the co-conspirators as troop barber David Edwards along with Privates Primas Douglass and Jefferson Wilson, who purportedly dealt the death blow. Initially, Varnum confessed he served as the decoy to lure Fleming to his doom.

In late 1889, 'the examination of the negro soldiers from San Carlos, charged with the murder of the man Fleming several weeks ago,' set in motion a long series of hearings and legal maneuvers. O.T. Rouse defended Wilson, who requested to be tried separate from the others.[236] By late May of the following year, after six hours of deliberation, a 15 person grand jury found Wilson guilty. He was to be hanged.

During the trial, Varnum took the stand. There he changed his original deposition. He 'denied all knowledge, practically, of Fleming's murder,' but the prosecutor succeeded in eliciting what appeared to be damning evidence from him. His statements, along with some bloodstained clothing produced as exhibits, convinced the jurors that Wilson murdered Fleming.[237]

The case might have been closed had it not been for Wilson's counselors, who argued that under a new statute passed by the 15th Arizona Territorial legislature, there had to be no less

---

Edition, January 31, 1897, Sunday Edition, February 28, 1897, Sunday Edition, April 18, 1897, Sunday Edition, July 10, 1897, Sunday Edition, and June 27, 1897; *Phoenix Weekly Herald*, July 1, 1897, July 15, 1897, and July 29, 1897; and RG21 Records of District Courts of the United States Agency or Division: US Territorial Court for the First Judicial District of Arizona, Series: Criminal Case Files, 1882–1912, Folder Title: C–1114 Philip Lashley Box Number: 70, National Archives at Riverside, CA, NARA.

233 *Flagstaff Sun-Democrat*, July 1, 1897; *Tombstone Prospector*, July 7, 1897, and July 10, 1897; *Arizona Silver Belt* (Globe, AZ) July 15, 1897; *Graham Guardian* (Safford, AZ) July 16, 1897; *Phoenix Weekly Herald*, July 15, 1897; *Border Vidette* (Nogales, AZ) July 17, 1897: and *St. Johns Herald* (St. Johns, AZ) July 17, 1897. See also the *Helena Independent*, December 4, 1894, for the case of Thad Robinson, the Black soldier charged with the murder of James Williams, a fellow soldier, at Fort Custer. *Leavenworth Echo* (Leavenworth, WA)

234 *Oasis* (Nogales, AZ) November 13, 1897; *Florence Tribune*, November 13, 1897; *Mesa Free Press*, November 19, 1897; and *Phoenix Weekly Herald*, November 18, 1897.

235 *Arizona Silver Belt* (Globe, AZ) September 7, 1889. The *Arizona Weekly Enterprise* (Florence, AZ) September 14, 1889; *Tombstone Daily Epitaph*, September 10, 1889; and *Arizona Weekly Citizen* (Tucson, AZ) September 14, 1889, also carried variations of the account.

236 *Arizona Weekly Citizen* (Tucson, AZ) October 5, 1889.

237 *Arizona Republican* (Phoenix, AZ) May 30, 1890; and *Arizona Silver Belt* (Globe, AZ) June 7, 1890.

than 17 or more than 23 members of a grand jury.[238] The attorneys managed to appeal their case before the United States Supreme Court.[239] The justices denied the petitioner and the arguments made by his attorneys, which relied heavily on habeas corpus precedents.[240] The matter went back to Arizona, thereby precipitating a further legal tussle. It appeared that another trial would be convened in 1892. The year came and went without a new date being for a hearing to be set.[241]

By 1893, additional legal technicalities arose that transferred the proposed venue first to Florence, Arizona. However, as the presiding judge there had been one of Wilson's lawyers, he was disqualified. Once more, the trial was set for yet another locality, which was to be at Tucson.[242] Meanwhile, Wilson languished in the Maricopa County Jail in Phoenix. The condemned man became a model prisoner. He was described as the 'father' of jail where he was 'allowed more privileges than had ever before been accorded a man under sentence of death. He never abused his privileges, but on several occasions prevented outbreaks of prisoners.' Among other actions, he allegedly thwarted the escape of the notorious horse thief John Clay. Wilson gave the alarm, which prevented the jail break. He incurred Clay's wrath, but the rustler's attempt at vengeance ended when Wilson defended himself and almost fatally cut Clay with a razor 'which he had concealed in his cell in some unaccountable manner.'[243]

One report asserted that unlike the other suspects, Wilson had no motive to commit murder. Another newspaper article mentioned the victim had: 'held himself aloof from his colored brethren and incurred the enmity of Wilson and his co-conspirators who were jealous of Fleming because his attention to an Apache woman,' on the reservation had been favorably received. Whatever the truth, all the others associated with the killing had been released. Conversely, Wilson remained incarcerated for years. If the less than dependable William Varnum could be believed, after they were set free, all of them died tragic deaths.[244]

Perhaps there was some validity to this, however, as no one who appeared at the 1889 hearing could be located including US Army surgeon E.C. Mann, who had testified in earlier proceedings to provide details about his medical findings.[245] With the long lapse

---

238 *Arizona Silver Belt* (Globe, AZ) January 3, 1891.
239 *St. Johns Herald* (St. Johns, AZ) January 8, 1891, and May 21, 1891; Related coverage appeared in *Arizona Republican* (Phoenix, AZ) January 28, 1891, May 2, 1891, May 3, 1891, and May 10, 1891; *Tombstone Epitaph*, February 1, 1891; *Mohave County Miner* (Mineral Park, AZ) May 9, 1891; and *Arizona Silver Belt* (Globe, AZ) May 9, 1891.
240 *Arizona Republican* (Phoenix, AZ) May 25, 1891. For the high court's decision obtain *Cases Argued and Decided in the Supreme Court of the United States, October Terms, 1890, 1891, in 134, 140, 141, 142, US Book 35, Lawyer's* Edition (Rochester, NY: The Lawyer's Co-operative Publication Company, 1901), 575–585.
241 *Ibid.*, (Phoenix, AZ) July 13, 1892.
242 *Iibid*, (Phoenix, AZ) May 18, 1893; *Arizona Silver Belt* (Globe, AZ) May 27, 1893; *Oasis* (Nogales, AZ) June 8, 1893; and *Arizona Weekly Citizen* (Tucson, AZ) June 17, 1893.
243 *Ibid.*, (Phoenix, AZ) July 13, 1892, May 18, 1893, June17, 1893, and January 24, 1896.
244 *Ibid* (Phoenix, AZ) May 18, 1893. Both the *Arizona Republican* (Phoenix, AZ) May 30, 1890, and *Arizona Silver Belt* (Globe, AZ) June 7, 1890, cited another party named Logan. Troop E's first sergeant was James Logan, who was at Camp Bonita, and whose name appeared on the so-called 'Garfield Monument.' Martin D. Tagg, *The Camp at Bonita Cañon: A Buffalo Soldier Camp in Chiricahua National Monument Arizona* (Tucson: Western Archeological and Conservation Center, 1987), 231. Further, the *Arizona Republican*, July 13, 1892, alluded to 'a subordinate officer of the company whose name does not appear in the record of Wilson's trial' as well as indicated Wilson, Varnum, Douglass, and 'the colored sergeant were at once arrested.' Presumably, this was Logan.
245 *Ibid.*, (Phoenix, AZ) July 13, 1892.

between trials, one Arizona daily concluded Wilson's culpability remained unproven. The reporter speculated: 'Hence his release upon his individual bond for the alleged reason of the impossibility for the prosecution, at this late day, to obtain witnesses to establish his guilt.' Apparently with the end of Wilson's term of enlistment and due to other circumstances, he would be released on his own recognizance.[246] Also, acquittal seemed likely, so much so that when he returned to Phoenix awaiting further legal actions, the penniless ex-soldier, 'was staked by A. Barry, who was under sheriff during the time of his confinement in this country.' Additionally, the former county sheriff offered Wilson employment![247] By late October, the murder charge was a dismissed.[248] Fleming's killer, or killers, never paid for the deed.

At large at last, Wilson went into business. He operated a small store in Phoenix near the train depot. This establishment became the target of two thieves who robbed 'the ex-San Carlos soldier who came into prominence as defendant in a murder trial' of $22.50, some of which may have been in their procession when police captured them.[249] According to another newspaper account, Wilson had a partner in this enterprise – José Apadaca. Wilson's choice of a business associate was questionable at best. One night in August 1894, Apadaca was cut down by a shotgun blast from a night watchman at another store in town. At the end of the story, the reporter noted the dead burglar had figured frequently in police and justice's courts for minor offenses. The article ran: 'He and Jeff Wilson, the colored murderer, kept a store near the depot since Wilson's release from jail until a year ago.'[250] Even though the courts had not convicted Wilson, at least in some minds he was viewed as Fleming's killer.

Another unsolved murder involved non-commissioned officer, Emanuel Stance. He traced his roots in the US Army to October 2, 1866, when with 50 other men in Lake Providence, Louisiana, Stance added his name to the roster of the Ninth Cavalry. The recruit enjoyed an advantage over most of this levy in that he could read and write. Armed with this advantage, by March 1867, Stance rose to sergeant, He remained a non-commissioned officer for the remainder of his career.

Subsequently, Stance became the first African American soldier to be awarded the Medal of Honor in the post-Civil War era. While brave in battle, the formerly enslaved Stance, who was born in Carroll Parish, Louisiana, during 1844, was not an ideal soldier in peace. In December 1872, he engaged in a brawl with his sergeant, Henry Green, who had reported him drunk while on duty. Stance bit off part of Green's lower lip. Stance temporarily lost his stripes and spent six months in the guardhouse.

Despite Stance's lack of respect for military decorum, after he regained his rank, he himself became a strict disciplinarian expecting complete obedience from subordinates. Not surprisingly, his leadership style entailed bullying men. By the late 1880s, that approach resulted in dire consequences. Towards the end of 1887, while at Fort Robinson, Stance engaged in disputes and

---

246 *Arizona Silver Belt* (Globe, AZ) June 24, 1893.
247 *Arizona Republican* (Phoenix, AZ) June 17, 1893. According to the *Arizona Weekly Citizen* (Tucson, AZ) June 24, 1893: 'Jeff Wilson, the prisoner released yesterday after being in custody four years, left last night for Phoenix, where he made many friends, to look for employment.'
248 *Arizona Weekly Citizen* (Tucson, AZ) October 7, 1893.
249 *Arizona Republican* (Phoenix, AZ) January 30, 1894.
250 *Ibid.*, (Phoenix, AZ) August 19, 1894.

scuffles within Troop F. On December 25 of that year, a passer-by found Stance's body on the road between the post and the town of Crawford. Nearby, a service revolver, which perhaps was the murder weapon, was found.[251] Neither the pistol nor the perpetrator or perpetrators were identified. The ensuring investigation lasted for nearly a year, but before justice could be served, like the Fleming incident, by the time a hearing arrived, 'some witnesses had died, while others had been discharged and could not be located.'[252]

A less grim incident emerged from an attempt on Civil War USCT veteran and one of the earliest enlistees in the Tenth Cavalry, Sergeant Shelvin Shropshire. In 1898, while encamped readying for deployment to Cuba, Private John Henson of Troop H allegedly assaulted the sergeant with pistol. Previously, on the train trip from Montana, where the troop had been posted before callup, Henson had hurled insulting epithets at the sergeant. Brought before court-martial, the officers found the offending soldier guilty.[253]

Although Shropshire evidently did not resort to Stance's heavy-handed ways, he nonetheless was not without enemies. Whether out of resentment for Henson's treatment at Chickamauga, or for some other cause, in 1900, another court convened. Called into order at Fort Sam Houston, Texas, the tribunal focused on 25 members of the Tenth United States Cavalry. Their purpose for convening 'grew out of the attempted killing of Sergeant Shropshire … on the night of August 3rd' at another Texas post – Fort Clark. While the old sergeant played 'his violin in his quarters' two shots came through the window but missed the target. Although the matter was to, 'be probed to the bottom' the assailant or assailants went undiscovered.[254]

Violence by Black soldiers against their comrades indicated that as with all groups and cultures, these men did not form a monolithic society. Envy, romantic rivalry, hatred due to maltreatment, real or imagined, actions under the influence of alcohol and a variety of motives erupted among Black regulars just as they did within the ranks of white soldiers. Dissension that sometimes ended in homicide, as one scholar indicated, provided: 'some insights into the factors which divided blacks against each other and in some cases thwarted efforts to establish unity.' Even so, as many, if not more endeavors to achieve cohesion, could be cited, 'ranging from establishment of their own fraternal organizations to threats of violence against' an entire local civilian community.[255]

Soldier Mayhem Committed on Civilians

Killings and violent assaults with deadly weapons were not restricted to confrontations between or among soldiers. Civilians, including women and in at least one case, a child, numbered among the unfortunate fatalities. Soon after leaving the service, Frank Nelson, who had spent 10 years in Company C, Twenty-Fourth Infantry, became infatuated with a woman. In a fit of jealousy, he killed the woman and her child. Before his hanging, Nelson harangued: 'I was aggravated and whiskey helped the aggravation.' He claimed that during his decade in uniform

---

251 www.nps.gov/people/emanuel-stance.htm.
252 Schubert, *Buffalo Soldiers, Braves, and the Brass*, 84–86.
253 *Abendblatt* (Chicago) May 5, 1898; *Omaha Daily Bee*, May 5, 1898; and *Sun* (New York) May 5, 1898.
254 *El Paso Daily Herald*, August 28, 1900, and *Freie Presse für Texas* (San Antonio) August 27, 1900.
255 Schubert, *Buffalo Soldiers, Braves, and the Brass*, 83.

he posted a good record, 'except only where a woman was concerned.' The murdered woman was not his wife. She was the spouse of a soldier in Company A of the regiment. Despite her marital status, Nelson stated: 'she was a public woman.' He blamed his woes on such women, whom he wanted barred from military posts. If the US Army prohibited their presence, he argued, 'there would be less trouble.' He preached: 'all trouble amongst the men were tracable [sic] to that source.' Not accepting personal responsibility, he claimed, 'if it were not for these women, the men would not be so apt to get drunk and act foolishly so frequently.'[256]

Another member of the Twenty-Fourth Infantry, Levi Johnson, was charged with murder of a Black woman at Fort Sill, Oklahoma.[257] Yet a third infantryman from the Twenty-Fourth, a Sergeant Burrows at Fort Thomas, Arizona, 'shot Belle Blakely, a prostitute' known to be 'a hard character.'[258] Prior to this shooting, Blakely had been incarcerated for 18 months. Coincidentally, Frank Nelson was held in a cell near Blakely where the two accused murderers had opportunities to speak. Unlike Nelson, Blakely was not convicted, nor were two possible accomplices, a woman named Kate McClelland and a Private Allen from Fort Thomas.[259]

Units from the Tenth Cavalry also served at that post. A trooper from the Fort Thomas 'attempted murder of a woman.' He discharged four rounds from his revolver firing 'through a window while she was lying in bed.'[260] None of his rounds struck the intended target. Turning the tables, Fannie Oliver, a Black 'countesan [sic] at the "hog ranch" just off the Fort Grant,' Arizona killed a soldier named Johnston.[261] She escaped and briefly avoided capture until being apprehended near the fort.[262]

Scores of other episodes in which fighting, that frequently entailed the use of weapons from razors and knives to revolvers, led to injuries that were not lethal.[263] Nor were assaults

---

256 *Arizona Republican* (Phoenix, AZ) July 3, 1891; *Arizona Weekly Citizen* (Tucson, AZ) August 9, 1890; and *Mohave County Miner* (Mineral Park, AZ) November 8, 1890. According to the *Fergus County Argus* (Lewiston, MT) March 9, 1893, First Sergeant Jonas Cox of Company H, Twenty-Fifth Infantry suspected his spouse of an extramarital affair. Evidently, he encountered the supposed lover. Cox was shot through the face at a ranch about, 'a mile and a half from Fort Missoula' then 'walked into the post grounds, covered with blood. The ball, which was from a government rife, entered the corner of the mouth and passed through the opposite cheek.' His rival may have been the shooter.
257 *Mohave County Miner* (Mineral Park, AZ) June 7, 1888.
258 *Arizona Weekly Citizen* (Tucson, AZ) May 28, 1892; and *Arizona Silver Belt* (Globe, AZ) May 28, 1892.
259 *Arizona Weekly Enterprise* (Florence, AZ) June 28, 1890; *Arizona Silver Belt* (Globe, AZ) May 31, 1890; *St. Johns Herald* (St. Johns, AZ) June 12, 1890; *Arizona Republican* (Phoenix, AZ) June 20, 1891; and *Arizona Weekly Citizen* (Tucson, AZ) October 31, 1891.
260 *Clifton Clarion* (Clifton, AZ) May 8, 1889.
261 *Arizona Silver Belt* (Globe, AZ) March 23, 1889. In another shooting at a hog ranch (slang for houses of prostitution where liquor and gambling also regularly could be found) Fort Huachuca's version was the site of a killing by its proprietor, John Riley. Private Jim Easly of Company C, Twenty-Fourth Infantry fired a number of rounds at Riley. He replied with a salvo from his Winchester that killed his attacker. Riley's actions were deemed justifiable homicide. *Tombstone Epitaph*, April 12, 1893; *Arizona Weekly Citizen* (Tucson, AZ) April 15, 1893; and *St. Johns Herald* (St. Johns, AZ) April 20, 1893.
262 *Arizona Silver Belt* (Globe, AZ) March 30, 1889.
263 While not comprehensive the following sources offer illustrations of an array of murders, aggressive behaviour, and conflicts: GCM Orders No. 40, HQA June 9, 1869, Orders No. 51, HQA August 12, 1869, and Orders No. 106, HQA December 28, 1886; *Omaha Daily Bee*, August 16, 1886, and January 6, 1888; GCM Orders No. 101, HQA December 8, 1886; *Santa Fe Daily New Mexican*, July 19, 1889; *Sun* (New York, NY) February 2, 1890; *Pittsburg Dispatch*, February 2, 1890; *Weekly*

restricted to weapons and fist-fighting. Sexual assault raised the irrational, erroneous, racist specter of Black males as brutes fixated on raping white women. Newspapers of the mid-nineteenth through mid-twentieth centuries regularly ran sensationalized stories about Black attackers and all too common retaliatory incidents of lynching. One of these appeared in 1867, when a trio of deserters from the Thirty-Eighth Infantry at Fort Hays were charged with entering the house of P. J. Peterson. They found Mrs. Peterson there and supposedly, 'dragged her into the cellar and outraged her person in a horrible manner.' When located, the three men understandably staged 'a desperate resistance.' After being taken into custody, 'they confessed their guilt and while being taken to jail were rescued by a mob and killed and their bodies thrown into the river.'[264]

During the next decade, one study underscored the widespread anxieties found among many officers of the Ninth Cavalry who 'feared their men might assault white women.' Consequently, they thought the worst when Corporal Daniel Talliaferro of the Ninth Cavalry, at Fort Davis, Texas climbed into the window of Lieutenant Fred Kendell's quarters. While the lieutenant was absent on detached duty, his spouse awoke to find the intruder attempting to enter the bedroom. She snatched a revolver from the bedstand and fired with mortal effect. The bullet shattered Talliaferro's skull. Officers at the post, 'had no doubt that it was an intended rape.' The commanding officer, Colonel George Andrews, supported this conclusion. He wrote that during the 17 months he had served with Black troops, purported similar actions existed at other Texas posts including Forts Clark, Davis, Duncan and Stockton and possibly at Forts Concho and McKavett.[265]

That same year, again at Fort Davis, Twenty-Fifth Infantry bandsman Martin Pedee faced court-martial for attempted rape of a fellow soldier's white wife – Annie Williams. Sentenced to be dishonorably discharged and imprisoned for seven years at hard labor, the evidence was flimsy. A review of the case overturned Pedee's dismissal. Despite that, there was no conclusive 'evidence either to prove there had been "an attempt at rape" or to establish the identity of the intruder' and the alleged perpetrator served 12 months at hard labor.[266]

Two soldiers arrested in Valentine, Nebraska received even harsher punishment. They rapidly fell into the hands of the law with only 36 hours elapsing from the time they reportedly ravished a local woman. After a swift hearing, the convicted pair received a sentence of 20 years each in the penitentiary.[267] In neighboring Montana, a quick-thinking ranch woman residing near Havre, talked her assailant into sparing her. After being thrown down by a Black man, who presumably came from Fort Assiniboine, she pleaded with the intruder 'and offered him what money there was in the house.'[268] He took the cash and fled. Notifying the family on the next

---

Missoulian, March 19, 1890; *Red Lodge Picket* (Red Lodge, MT) February 27, 1897; *Arizona Silver Belt* (Globe, AZ) November 15, 1898; *River Press* (Fort Benton, MT) September 3, 1902; *New North-west* (Deer Lodge, MT) December 3, 1902, and November 18, 1903; and *San Francisco Call,* June 6, 1903. MC46, Fort Assiniboine Records, Vol. 9, 159.

264 *Evening Star* (Washington, DC) June 3, 1867.
265 Kenner, *Buffalo Soldiers and Officers,* 58–9, and 323n15; *San Antonio Daily Herald,* December 5, 1872, that indicated Talliaferro was a District of Columbia native who had completed his third of five year's enlistment at the time of his killing; Also see, Thompson, 'Negro Soldiers,' 231–32.
266 Kenner, *Buffalo Soldiers and Officers,* 58.
267 *Omaha Daily Bee,* January 1, 1888.
268 *Great Falls Weekly Tribune,* December 28, 1894.

Not long after he reported to his first posting with the Twenty-Fifth Infantry in Washington, Private Nathaniel Bledser increased racial tensions because of his criminal activities. (Courtesy Library of Congress)

ranch of the event, they contacted officers at the fort. She traveled to the garrison in hopes of identifying the guilty party. Regrettably, she could not offer conclusive evidence to single out the preparator.

There was no doubt about the identity of an interloper from the Twenty-Fifth Infantry, who entered a Seattle, Washington home. He was Private Nathaniel Bledser. While on pass to the city from Fort Lawton, he became inebriated. Bledser first 'drank some whisky at the post, then went to a grocery and drank a gallon of beer and after that was in a mood for any wickedness.'[269] Eventually, he broke into a house, then returned to the fort where he confessed. Bledser's imprisonment for 'assault on a white woman' resulted in 'an indeterminate sentence of from four to ten years in the state penitentiary.'[270]

Another battalion of the Twenty-Fifth Infantry served at Fort George Wright in Spokane, Washington. A newcomer to the post, raw recruit Private George McElroy, arrived from Chicago. A few weeks later, the police arrested him on the charge of 'assaulting Sampa Swain, a 14-year-old girl.' He was said to have intimidated, 'the girl by brandishing a pistol and a knife.' Had McElroy joined Company H, to which he had been assigned and shipped out to battle forest fires, he might have avoided the sordid affair. At the time, he was in hospital, however and remained behind at the fort.[271]

McElroy attacked the teenager while she enjoyed a party with, 'friends on the river towards the south end of the reservation.' Her cries for help brought another Twenty-Fifth Infantryman, Green E. N. Wokcoff, to her assistance. As Wokcoff, approached, McElroy ran. In the aftermath, Swain went to post headquarters where she described her attacker. A detail from the fort went in search of the culprit. Reportedly, 'from the commanding officer to the humblest recruit' they all desired 'that the guilty party be punished, if a crime has been committed.'[272] Miss Swain failed to make a positive identification. The matter then transferred to civil authorities to obtain further evidence. Despite direct testimony provided by Private Wokcoff, no conviction resulted. One interested party outside the military and law enforcement chain believed he had evidence

---

269 *Salt Lake Tribune*, June 9, 1910.
270 *Newport Miner* (Newport, WA) October 27, 1910.
271 *Arizona Republican* (Phoenix, AZ) August 24, 1910; and *Spokane Press*, August 23, 1910.
272 *Tonopah Daily Bonanza*, August 24, 1910.

of a conspiracy that some soldiers afforded McElroy an 'alibi and the crime was laid on a man by the name of Allen Thompson, a recruit that was in no way guilty.'[273]

Meanwhile, McElroy avoided consequences until he decided to desert. He may have done so because of a further scrutiny into the rape. Regardless, while fleeing, he lured two teenage boys away from their homes promising 'to give them some army clothes.' McElroy told the boys that he was a deserter. Then fearing they would report his whereabouts, he compelled them to accompany him. After being released, the youngsters informed authorities of their abduction. That led to McElroy's capture and trial. His desertion and kidnapping resulted in a sentence, 'of nine years at hard labor in the Walla Walla penitentiary.'[274]

What motivated McElroy to seize the boys? Given widely held Victorian era taboos against homosexuality, did he intend to molest them? Either he did not do so, or the details were not reported. Indicative of the subject's sensitivity, when military authorities learned that a non-commissioned officer molested two young recruits who reported to Fort Missoula, they euphemistically dealt with the issue. The officers mentioned Oscar Wilde and referenced Scripture to skirt the nature of the offense.[275] For the protection of the two victims' reputations, the reviewers decided to discharge the abuser quietly for the good of the service.

More public acknowledgements of professed unwanted sexual advances came to light in three courts-martials held by the Ninth Cavalry between 1881 and 1882. The last of these ended the career of Company D's top NCO. Three privates stepped forward. They swore First Sergeant Richard Dickerson made sexual advances towards them and much more. He replied in a 12 page written refutation. Dickerson denied engaging in such 'an unnatural and beastly crime.' His plea did not sway the court. Discharged without honor, he nevertheless received no other punishment although he could have been imprisoned.[276]

If the US Army broadly displayed homophobic tendencies, official military policy was even more critical of mutiny. During the Civil War, intermittent outbreaks by Black soldiers took place. While less frequent during the period between 1866 and 1916, several munities of varying degrees erupted. Arguably none of them rose to the intensity of the 1917 outburst, which terrorized Houston, Texas.[277] One of the earliest post-Civil War uprisings was said to have resulted when a sergeant in the Ninth Cavalry at San Antonio, Texas was slated to be reduced to the ranks. He took fatal pre-emptive action and with the backing of 14 comrades, murdered a lieutenant 'and was then killed himself.'[278]

---

273 *Leavenworth Echo* (WA) August 5, 1911.
274 *Ibid.*, (WA) August 11, 1911, and August 18, 1911.
275 MC46, Fort Assiniboine Records. Another possible example that may have been coded language for homosexual actions referred to the Private George Suter, Troop I, Tenth Cavalry. He received a dishonorable discharge for 'moral degradation.' *A&NJ*, February 20, 1874, 444.
276 MC46, Fort Assiniboine Records; and Kenner, *Buffalo Soldiers and Officers*, 268–76. For a brief discussion of homosexuality in the post-Civil War US Army see: McChristian, *Regular Army O!*, 367–9 and 680nn 18, 19, 20, which among other topics treats in some detail the rather well known story of Mrs. Nash, who variously was a laundress and provided other services at a few frontier military posts. Also review, Kenner, *Buffalo Soldiers and Officers of the Ninth Cavalry*, 288–7; 272–7; and 364n5.
277 To date, Scott F. Thompson, "'The Negro had been run over long enough by white men, and it was time they defend themselves': African-American Mutinies and the Long Emancipation, 1861–1974," Ph.D. diss., West Virginia University, 2021, stands as the most comprehensive overview of this subject.
278 *New York Herald*, May 22, 1867; and reprinted in the *New York Dispatch*, May 26, 1867.

What this garbled, inaccurate newspaper report referred to was a clash between a Ninth Cavalry lieutenant, Edward Heyl and a band of his men. Heyl's high-handed treatment of soldiers in Company E provoked some soldiers to take up arms against him. In the melee, both officers and enlisted men received wounds. One also died – Sergeant Harrison Bradford, who had assembled several troopers and started out for the tent of the regiment's lieutenant colonel where they sought to address their grievances. On the column's way to speak to the senior officer in camp, Heyl intercepted them. He opened fire. One of his rounds struck Bradford in the temple, killing him but not before Braford lashed out with his saber and slashed Heyl. The officer survived. He not only avoided the consequences of maltreating his troops, but also, continued his career and became a colonel in the inspector general's department.[279]

The men with Bradford dispersed and 10 deserted to avoid the consequences of their actions. It took over a week to capture and return the deserters to face judgement. Amazingly, their counsels mounted an effective defence. They convinced the military tribunal of Heyl's cruel treatment and brutal enforcement of discipline, as well as succeeded in raising some legal technicalities. In the end, two non-coms charged as ringleaders, were deemed responsible for the 'mutiny.' They received death sentences. Eventually, they were restored to duty as would their comrades after spending prison time at Fort Massachusetts on Ship Island in the Gulf of Mexico.[280]

Two years later, Civil War veteran Second Lieutenant Bernard Herkness chanced upon Privates Jesse Reeves of Company D and Hugh Anthony of Company I, both of Thirty-Eighth Infantry. The soldiers were in the process of desertion. On April 23, 1869, the men fired their breech-loading Springfield rifles. They mortally wounded the lieutenant. Reeves was sentenced to dishonorable discharge, forfeiture of all pay due and was to be hanged. Likewise, Anthony was dishonorably discharged, forfeited all pay due and was to serve five years' imprisonment. The sentences were commuted to 10 years and three years' imprisonment, respectively.[281]

Not every breaking of the law ended in death or injury. Larceny of various sorts and differing degrees placed many a Black soldier in confinement. Tenth Cavalry officer John Bigelow demonstrated a certain level of disdain for his men when he emphatically and unfairly charged that the 'cardinal vice of the negro, stealing' was at the heart of many losses of equipment in his troop.[282] There was no denying that some men made off with government property, which they illegally sold or used as barter. Such larceny existed in all units of the era, both where Blacks and whites alike served.

'Recruit James Williams Colored Detachment, General Mounted Service,' numbered among these petty criminals. He appeared before a GCM for dual violations related to the 32nd and 17th Articles of War. The first infraction stemmed from Williams being absent without leave from Jefferson Barracks. While away from the post, he sold a cavalry greatcoat for which he had a pay deduction of $6.18 for two months as reimbursement. Added to his punishment, he was placed on hard labor for the same two months and held in the post guard house.[283]

---

279 Heitman, *Historical Register* I, 527.
280 Byron Price, 'Mutiny at San Pedro Springs,' *By Valor and Arms* 1 no. 3 (Spring 1975): 31–34, ranks among the best summations of this event.
281 GCM Orders No. 70, HQA December 16, 1869. Of interest, the majority of general courts-martial for that year were for officers.
282 Bigelow, *On the Trail of Geronimo*, 88.
283 GCM Orders No. 7, HQA January 16, 1883.

Recruit Leonis Trent, who also was punished for desertion that year, was placed on hard labor under guard for six months and drew half play until he made restitution for an army blanket, two shirts, blouse, overcoat and shoes he had sold valued at $25.26.[284] Happily Recruit William Vrooman was exonerated of an accusation that he attempted to steal an overcoat from another soldier.[285]

Not only government issue items disappeared as illegal cash supplements. Private Klide Adam from Fort Missoula, Montana, the headquarters of the Twenty-Fifth Infantry, fled after robbing the quartermaster's safe. He had been on guard all day and requested that the quartermaster give him the key to where the safe was kept. Adam said he would clean the room. Finishing the task, Adam returned the key. The next morning, he did not answer roll call. Upon investigation, he had managed to work the safe's combination and extracted $500 in cash and $300 in checks.[286]

In the southwest, John Smith from Fort Grant, Arizona was accused of robbing the US mail.[287] Whether he came to justice for the robbery is unknown. Private Louis Russum, Troop D, Tenth Cavalry stole a diamond ring valued at $200 from Lieutenant Charles Grierson, the son of his regimental commander. Dishonorably discharged, Russum forfeited all pay due him and faced one year in prison.[288] One enterprising, unscrupulous Black soldier posted to San Carlos, Arizona even might have played a part in illicit sales of liquor to the Apache on the reservation.[289] The accusation may have been hearsay.

A crime spree in Honolulu, Hawaii that included, 'a series of burglaries, holdups and other lesser offenses, apparently committed by members of the Twenty-Fifth Infantry' brought stern action by the commanding general in the area. Although attributed to recruits, the general threatened, 'to increase the provost guard and, if necessary, confine the entire regiment to barracks'[290]

Then there was a far more sophisticated, nineteenth century version of white-collar crime. George Lewis, who enlisted during 1880 in Washington, DC, later was described as 'a fine athletic specimen of manhood, six feet one inch in height, broad shouldered, slender waisted, with an erect, military carriage, lithe as a cat.' Born in Virginia, he was in his early 20s when he went to the recruiter. Having a much better education than most Blacks of the era and writing 'a fine business hand … he was found to be so clever with the pen that he was detailed as work in the office of the auditor general of the war department and learned things about the office.' That experience proved useful, but not in his capacity as an enlisted man. Following his detail in the War Department, Lewis left for the Twenty-Fourth Infantry. He quickly received a promotion to corporal. Lewis then successively became a sergeant and thereafter the regimental sergeant

---

284 GCM Orders No. 3, HQA January 12, 1886.
285 GCM Orders No. 33, HQA May 8, 1886.87
286 *New North-west* (Deer Lodge, MT) May 24, 1905.
287 *Arizona Weekly Citizen* (Tucson, AZ) April 27, 1889.
288 GCM Orders No. 46, HQA June 15, 1886.
289 *Tombstone Daily Prospector*, November 29, 1890.
290 *Ogden Standard*, April 17, 1914, City Edition. The general also vowed 'to put an end to the series of petty crimes' that perhaps not so coincidentally followed 'the third escape of Private Herman Lewis, who is facing cumulative sentences amounting to 80 years on charges of highway robbery. It is believed that Lewis has been able to effect [*sic*] his escape through the connivance of follow soldiers.' *Pierre Weekly Free Press*, April 23, 1914.

During 1899 and 1900, Company B, Twenty-Fourth Infantry garrisoned Vancouver Barracks, Washington. This portrait of an unidentified private offers one of the few tangible reminders of their service at this venerable post. (Courtesy Library of Congress)

major. As did many soldiers in the Black regulars, he sought a transfer in this case to the Ninth Cavalry. Given that ranks were not permanent during this era, he reverted to private. Not long after Lewis joined Troop I, Ninth Cavalry, he sported corporal's chevrons. He held that rank when he deserted. In 1889, upon capture, Lewis went to the Fort Robinson's guardhouse under dual charges of desertion and forgery. Among Lewis' convoluted schemes that brought him to fall from grace, was a bogus claim against a fabricated paymaster account from which he drew a $150 advance.

His conviction for forgery and theft resulted in five years in the penitentiary at Lansing, Kansas.[291] Even from his cell, he continued to spin a deceptive web, which gained him the dubious honor of being styled, 'the smartest all-round forger in this country' whose cleverness also was portrayed as 'unparalleled in the history of crime.' Lewis' machinations proved possible because the conman worked his way into the confidence of prison authorities. This permitted securing everything necessary to establish what appeared to be a legitimate bank account with a $20,000 balance – a staggering sum in the days compared to the $13 monthly pay for a private.

Working with an accomplice who recently had completed his five-year prison sentence, Lewis concocted the last part of his plan. He forged, 'a formidable document from the secretary of war addressed to the warden' announcing reinstatement to active duty and a pardon. The ruse almost gained Lewis' freedom, except for one flaw. Although the warden believed the veracity of the correspondence, he wanted to keep the original despite the requirement that it was to be given, 'to the discharged prisoner as a means of identification' when he reported to obtain his back pay. A reply from the War Department made it clear that Lewis had carried out another hoax.

---

291 *Omaha Daily Bee*, March 16, 1889, and June 20, 1891; *A&NJ*, March 30, 1889, 620; and Schubert, *On the Trail of the Buffalo Soldiers*, 265.

He remained in custody, but his misdeeds were recounted in the *New York Herald* followed by reprints of the story in other newspapers.[292]

By no means was this chronicle of lawless activities definitive. Furthermore, for every account of illegal conduct, many more instances of admirable behaviour could be cited. Returning to W. Sherman Savage, the eminent historian suggested Blacks in the post-Civil War were, 'much like soldiers in general' in that they 'displayed the virtues and vices and common to humanity.'[293] Even so, this area remains a valuable field for future study.

A Complex Portrait

Most of those who took up military life during the half century after the Civil War were neither heroes nor villains, although there was a fair share of both. Sometimes these characteristics even existed in the same individual. Moreover, while denied full participation in the American dream, as a group, these Black soldiers made inroads that contributed to positive changes in the fight for equality wrested by incredible effort and persistence. Furthermore, they would not be frozen in time. Indeed, as one of the earliest observers of the Black regulars in the post-Civil War summarized: 'As the years passed the character of the colored soldiers naturally changed. In place of the war veterans and of the men whose chains of servitude had just been struck off, came young men from the North and East with more education and more self-reliance.'

Additionally, as General John Pope concluded: 'Everything that men could do they did and it is little to say that their services in the field were marked by hardships and difficulties. Their duties were performed with zeal and intelligence and they are worthy of consideration.'[294] Even Elizabeth Bacon Custer, who shared the negative opinion with her soldier spouse George Armstrong Custer about the inferiority of Blacks, concurred with General Pope in at least this one instance. She conceded: 'they were determined that no soldiering should be carried on in which their valor was not proved.'[295]

Chaplain G.G. Mullins, a white clergyman who frequently denigrated his Black soldier flock from the Twenty-Fifth Infantry, also acquiesced: 'The ambition to be all that soldiers should be is not confined to a few of these sons of an unfortunate race. They are possessed of the notion that the colored people of the whole country are more or less affected by their conduct in the army.'[296] Another officer with the Twenty-Fifth was more effusive. Colonel Burt proclaimed his men were 'the best soldiers in the world.'[297] The *Army and Navy Journal* weighed in with an encomium from the early 1900s insisting: 'They are of a class who are ashamed of neither their color or their hair and among the infantry many are large and tall. Generally, they are well

---

292 *Sully County Watchman* (Clifton, SD) June 20, 1891; *Wood County Reporter* (Grand Rapids, WI) June 18, 1891; *Mineral Point Tribune* (Mineral Point, WI) June 20, 1891; and *A&NJ*, March 18, 1893, 429.
293 Savage, *Blacks in the West*, 50. For comparative purposes also consult John A. Haymond, *The American Soldier, 1866–1916: The Enlisted Man and the Transformation of the United States Army* (Jefferson, NC: McFarland & Company, Inc., Publishers, 2018).
294 *ARSW, 1880*, I, 83.
295 Elizabeth Bacon Custer, *Tenting on the Plains or General Custer in Kansas and Texas* (New York: Charles L. Webster & Company, 1887), 678–79.
296 'The Morals of the Colored Troops,' *A&NJ*, January 27, 1877, 395.
297 Terrell, 'A Sketch of Mingo Saunders,' 131.

After his 1906 dismissal from service, Sergeant Mingo Sanders numbered among many old soldiers who struggled to survive once they left the US Army. (Courtesy Library of Congress)

proportioned and possessed of the full complement of muscular strength. As to conduct, they are not surpassed in the Army.'[298]

Over the decades, several men who made the military a career, proudly listed 'soldier' on their enlistment papers under the column marked 'profession.' More spent far less time in uniform, but nonetheless sometimes contributed during their service.[299] They made good soldiers, 'in drill, fidelity and smartness' said one source.[300] By the 1890s, Zenas Bliss, who once disparaged Black troops as the 'lowest type of the race,' after two decades commanding them, reversed his past pronouncement. He noted: 'The improvement' within the Black regiments that had 'been wonderful and they now rank among the best soldiers on the frontier.'[301]

One historian seconded Colonel Bliss when he added: 'Despite the many similarities between the men who served in the Tenth between 1892 and 1918 and those of the previous era, the soldiers who joined the Tenth Cavalry after 1892 were significantly different in several respects.' For one, because of opportunities afforded to them in the service, post-Civil War soldiers enjoyed better educations, being able to read and write on at least a rudimentary

---

298 *A&NJ*, November 14, 1903, 280.
299 Schubert, *On the Trail of the Buffalo Soldiers*, I, 509, charts the number of Black enlisted men between 1867 and 1916, which ranged as low as 256 in 1870 to a high of 1849 in 1915, both totals being for the Twenty-Fourth Infantry. Lows and highs for the Twenty-Fifth Infantry were 319 (1875) and 1808 (1915) while the range for the Ninth Cavalry was 611 (1894) to 1219 (1900) as compared to the Tenth Cavalry, which were 488 (1892) to 1239 (1899), a figure that coincides with the deployment after departing Cuba for duty in the Philippines.
300 Villard, 'The Negro in the Regular Army,' 722–23.
301 As quoted by Coffman, *Old Army*, 332.

level.[302] This analysis might be applied across the board to all four of the regiments of Black regulars as the late Victorian era through the eve of the First World War.

Further, Chaplain Theophilus Steward wrote of his soldier congregation: 'among those who had faced Spanish bullets at El Kaney [sic] a feeling that there were limitations to a soldiers' submission to insults and outrages, although all were willing to endure much for the good of the regiment.'[303] Viewing with additional decades of perspective, one historian determined that by the early twentieth century, 'soldiers better understood the connection between military performance and civil rights … For many, this translated into a refusal to tolerate abuse whether from civilians, enemy soldiers, or even their own officers.'[304]

Continuing the discourse, the author reached another salient deduction about the progress of 'African American men' who entered the US Army 'in 1905 for many of the same reasons they did in 1870 – status, need for employment, lack of civilian opportunities.' While certain factors remained the same, during the early 1900s, 'the significance of that service had changed. Valor in combat and participation in national endeavors now inspired the hope of elevating their race to a greater level of equality with whites. Henceforth, the goals of protecting their nation from foreign aggression and lifting themselves to the position of 'leading minority' became intertwined.'[305]

Sweeping conclusions aside, during the dynamic half century between the late 1860s through 1916, Black soldiers formed a substantial portion of the US Army. Of the upwards of 20,000 who served, they came from different backgrounds.[306] They encountered assorted, occasionally unique experiences. By weaving together scattered newspaper articles, official records, personal effects, photos and rare family stories, these frequently anonymous figures emerge as individuals rather than an amorphous mass.

Finally, Black soldiers became more independent with the passage of time. Their achievements appeared more impressive given the nature of segregation and differing degrees of discrimination faced in the insular, hierarchical, racially charged society in which they operated. In the process, they persevered, as well as attained, a laudable reputation. Along the way, not a few achieved a sense of race consciousness that evolved in the Black community at large and which presaged later movements towards equal rights.

Above all, Howard University Professor Rayford Logan offered a poignant summation when he wrote: 'Negroes had little at the turn of the century to help us sustain our faith in ourselves except the pride that we took in the Ninth and Tenth Cavalry, the Twenty-Fourth and Twenty Fifth Infantry. They were our Ralph Bunche, Marian Anderson, Joe Louis and Jackie Robinson.'[307]

---

302 David K. Work, 'The Fighting Tenth Cavalry: Black Soldiers in the United States Army 1892–1918,' MA thesis, Oklahoma State University, 1998, 32–33.
303 T.G. Steward, *Thirty Years of Gospel Ministry From 1864 to 1914* (Philadelphia: A.M.E. Book Concern, 1921), 360.
304 James N. Leiker, *Racial Borders: Black Soldiers Along the Rio Grande* (College Station: Texas A&M University Press, 2002), 110.
305 Leiker, *Racial Borders*, 117.
306 Schubert, *On the Trail of the Buffalo Soldiers*, 509.
307 Rayford Logan, *Betrayal of the Negro, from Rutherford B. Hayes to Woodrow Wilson* (New York, Collier Books, 1965), 335.

2

Commissioned Officers

During the Civil War, with but rare exceptions, white officers commanded USCT troops. On occasion, a few Blacks served as doctors and functioned as chaplains. This fact supported the widely held notion that Blacks, while potential fighters, were not capable of leadership. Many instances in combat belied this contention. Nonetheless, the practice remained after the establishment of the six segregated Regular Army regiments in 1866. Indeed, from that year through 1916, only a fortunate few Blacks would be commissioned among nearly 1000 officers who received assignments to these units.[1]

White Commanders

In the beginning, many of the white men who accepted appointments to Black regiments had served with the USCT during the war. For instance, Captains William Danilson and John Thompson, were both veterans of the First South Carolina Infantry, one of the original regiments consisting of Black rank and file. They secured commissions in the Fortieth US Infantry and Thirty-Eighth US Infantry regiments respectively.[2] Similarly, former Union enlisted musi-

---

[1] This figure. while not complete, represents an estimated 95 percent or more of officers assigned to the Thirty-Eight, Thirty-Ninth, Fortieth and Forty-First Infantry regiments (later consolidated as the Twenty-Fourth and Twenty-Fifth Infantry regiments) and the Ninth and Tenth Cavalry regiments. Names and related background information were derived from the following sources: George W. Cullum, *Biographical Register of the Officers and Graduates of the US Military Academy at West Point, NY, from its establishment, in 1802, to 1890; with the Early History of the United States Military Academy* (Boston, Houghton, Mifflin and Company, 1891) II; (1891) III: (1901) IV; (1910) V; (1920) VI a; (1920) VI b; and (1930) VII; Francis B. Heitman, *Historical Register and Dictionary of the United States Army, from its Organization, September 29, 1789, to March 2, 1903* (Washington, DC: Government Printing Officer, 1903) I; William H. Powell, *List of Officers of the Army of the United States from 1779 to 1900 Embracing a Register of All Appointments by the President of the United States in the Volunteer Service During the Civil War and of Volunteer Officers in the Service of the United States June 1, 1900.* (New York: L R. Hamersly & CO., 1900); William H. Powell, *Powell's Records of Living Officers of the United States Army* (Philadelphia, L.R. Hamersly, 1890); and *US Army Register* (Washington, DC: United States Army) for the years 1866–1916.

[2] Thomas Wentworth Higginson, *Army Life in a Black Regiment* (Williamstown, MA: Cornerhouse Publishers, 1984), 270. First published in 1870, this minor classic, sheds considerable light on some

cian Charles D. Beyers obtained a lieutenancy in the Eighty-First USCT. With the 1866 Reorganization Act, he would become a captain in the Forty-First Infantry. Later, on November 11, 1869, after the next congressional reorganization, he joined the Twenty-Fourth Infantry, followed by a transfer on January 1, 1871, to command of Company C, Ninth Cavalry. He remained there until his dismissal from service on November 21, 1884.[3]

The fact that such individuals continued to command Black troops could be traced to the same motives that prompted them to continue military duty after 1865. Not a few sought an opportunity to advance from the ranks to receive higher pay and increased status as an officer, which for varying reasons was not always an option available in regiments consisting of white soldiers. While perhaps much fewer in number, there were others who embraced the cause of hard-won Black freedom that emerged from the four years of fighting. In essence, they were the descendants of antebellum abolitionists.

After his 1866 appointment as the Ninth US Cavalry regiment's commanding colonel, Edward Hatch remained with of his unit the rest of his life. (Courtesy Library of Congress)

In fact, numerous candidates willingly commanded Black soldiers.[4] This meant there were sufficient men who fulfilled the required quotas for the lowest vacancy in the hierarchy of second lieutenant to the top tier of colonel.[5] In a greatly reduced military force, openings were limited. Those who desired to remain in uniform during the first quarter century after 1865, had limited options for appointments.[6]

---

    aspects that continued to be germane after the Civil War relative to Black regulars.
3   Christina Joslin, *Fort Bayard: A Post on the Apache Frontier* 3rd ed (n.p: 2009), 41.
4   Thompson, 'The Negro Regiments of the US Regular Army, 1866–1900,' 150, provided a sampling of 200 officers assigned between 1866 and 1876 to the cavalry (100) and infantry (100) in the US Army. Half served in white regiments and an equal number in Black regiments, Of these, 169 had been in the Union Army, 17 received medals of and 36 officers, 18 in cavalry and 18 in infantry transferred from duty with Back troops to assignments with white troops. In turn, nine cavalrymen and four infantrymen left white regiments for commands with Blacks.
5   Fairfax Downey, *The Buffalo Soldiers in the Indian Wars* (New York: McGraw-Hill Book Company, 1969), 24.
6   As one example, 'Of the original officers of the [Twenty-Fifth Infantry] regiment there are now but six on the rolls, viz.: Captains John W. French, Charles Bentzoni (bvt. lieutenant-colonel) and Gaines Lawson (bvt. lieutenant-colonel), and Second Lieutenants (now captains) David B. Wilson, Owen J.

Regardless of what motivated them, certain statistics can be gleaned to produce a composite picture. For instance, less than 10 percent of the officers whose records were surveyed, traced their births to other nations beyond the United States. Scotsman Francis Moore, who had commanded Black soldiers both during and after the Civil War, was one of these foreign-born exceptions. On September 10, 1861, he began as a private of Company M, First Colorado Cavalry. Moore became a sergeant on December 31, 1862. Less than a year passed when he gained a captaincy in the Sixty-Fifth USCT. By the time Moore mustered out of the Union Volunteers, he was one of the regiment's majors.

During the summer of 1866, he reported as a second lieutenant in the Ninth Cavalry characteristic of the downsizing of the nation's armed forces, which meant most of those who wished to continue their military status did so at lesser grades. That next May, Moore became the regimental commissary officer. He remained in that assignment through July 15, 1870. Along the way, Moore advanced to first lieutenant. On August 24, 1872, he quickly gained his captain's bars. By his retirement on April 5, 1905, he had risen to brigadier general, his climb from private to general being one of the most impressive of those officers who served with Black regulars.[7]

The majority of officers in the post-Civil War, however, were born in the United States. As a sample of over 900 officers, they traced their roots to nearly every state and territory in the 'Lower Forty-eight.' (Table 5) Not surprisingly, the largest numbers came from the most populous states of the era with New York and Pennsylvania heading the list. Of these, during the first decade of Black regular regiment existed, a substantial number of their officers were Civil War veterans. Given that rank and advancement depended largely on seniority and for the years immediately following Appomattox, on Republican political patronage, this group gained the lion's share of the captaincies and above. Further, almost 45 percent were from West Point (384). Most of them were new graduates who assumed vacancies as second lieutenants when these positions came available due to retirement, resignation, promotion, transfer, or dismissal of the first wave of officers. The remainder of the candidates, although fewer in number, entered the military directly from civilian life:[8]

Bethel Moore Custer (no relation to the better-known members of the Seventh Cavalry) could be singled out as rather typical. He came up through the ranks as a private, advanced to sergeant in a Pennsylvania volunteer regiment, then was commissioned as a second lieutenant in the Thirty-Second USCT on March 4, 1864. By November of that year, Custer ranked as a first lieutenant with the regiment, a grade he retained when entering the Eleventh USCT on October 22, 1865. After mustering out of the Union Army, on July 28, 1866, he secured a second lieutenancy with the Thirty-Eighth Infantry. On November 11, 1869, Custer made his

---

Sweet and Henry P. Ritzius. It may also be interesting to note that Colonel Andrews, who has been colonel of the regiment for over 20 years, is the only colonel who ever commanded it; that during its 22 years of existence, the whole regiment has been together but fourteen days, and that but one captain (Van Valzah) has attained his majority by regular promotion.' George Andrews. 'The Twenty-Fifth Regiment of Infantry,' *Journal of the Military Service Institution of the United States* (January 1892): 226. See Appendix 1 for the full text.

7 Heitman, *Historical Register* I, 712; *Army Register, 1908*, 437.
8 According to Rodenbaugh and Haskins, *The Army of the United States*, 282: 'The original vacancies in the grades of first and second lieutenant were to be filled by selection from among the officers and soldiers of volunteer cavalry; two-thirds of the original vacancies in the higher grades by selection from among the officers of volunteer cavalry; and one-third from among officers of the regular army.'

Table 5: Birthplaces of White Officers Serving in Black Regiments, 1866–1916

Alabama	9	North Carolina	16
Arizona	2	North Dakota	4
Arkansas	5	Ohio	75
California	16	Oklahoma (Indian Territory)	3
Connecticut	15	Oregon	4
Dakota Territory	2	Pennsylvania	95
Delaware	2	Rhode Island	12
District of Columbia	18	South Carolina	10
Florida	4	South Dakota	4
Georgia	15	Tennessee	20
Idaho	1	Texas	17
Illinois	44	Utah	1
Indiana	28	Vermont	16
Iowa	17	Virginia	37
Kansas	6	West Virginia	2
Kentucky	25	Wisconsin	14
Louisiana	10	Wyoming	5
Maine	25	Asia	2
Maryland	19	Austria	2
Massachusetts	44	Germany	11
Michigan	24	Prussia	9
Minnesota	11	Ireland	20
Mississippi	5	Canada	12
Missouri	25	England	7
Montana	4	Scotland	7
Nebraska	4	Madera	1
Nevada	3	Poland	1
New Hampshire	8	Sweden	1
New Jersey	21	South America	1
New York	135	France	1

transition to the Twenty-Fourth Infantry where he would become a first lieutenant on March 1, 1871. He would be appointed regimental quartermaster on May 15, 1877 to April 30, 1880 and made captain by June 18, 1880, a grade he held at his death on December 22, 1887.[9]

Francis Dodge was yet another former enlisted man who gained a commission while commanding Black troops during the Civil War. From first lieutenant in the Second United States Colored Cavalry on December 20, 1863, he advanced to company commander as a

---

9   Heitman, *Historical Register* I, 348. Also consult James Carsten, *Another Custer: Bethel Moore Custer and the Buffalo Soldiers, 1867–1887* (n.p.: n.p., 2013).

captain on July 6, 1865. Just a little over a year later, he accepted an appointment as a first lieutenant with the Ninth Cavalry. By July 31, 1867, Dodge again sported the twin bars of a captain. In that grade he experienced extensive field service that included exhibiting exceptional valor, which led to his receipt of the Medal of Honor. Dodge would leave the Ninth upon promotion to major in the Paymaster Department on January 13, 1880.[10]

As noted, such veterans dominated in the decades immediately after the war. In fact, more than half of the Regular Army officer corps of the late 1860s through early 1890s consisted of Union men, several of whom graduated from West Point and many of whom served during the clash between North and South, with little or no previous military experience. Among the appointments made to the six regiments during 1866, 106 had been with the USCT.[11]

As noted, with the passage of time, newly commissioned West Pointers assumed a more prominent presence. Of these, 18 cadets stood dead last academically as the 'goat' of their classes among 442 graduates who received commissions in the last quarter of the nineteenth century from the Academy and who reported to command Black soldiers. Also, 23 more, did not graduate, but later became officers. Once they entered active duty, low academic standing did not always coincide with poor performance in active service. Indeed, some of them achieved accolades including five who received the Medal of Honor while leading Black troops.[12]

Furthermore, placement of those with lower grades and higher demerits was not the exclusive domain of cadets sent to the Black regiments. This proved true for cavalry and infantry regiments manned by white troops as well. Assignments simply coincided with vacancies requiring replacements. In turn, those with highest grades and least demerits usually sought billets with the engineers and artillery. Significant exceptions existed based on a variety of factors.[13]

Just as an evolutionary process existed for enlisted personnel, so too was it with the officer corps. Eventually a mix of West Point graduates and 'old hands' from the Civil War resulted

---

10   Powell, *List*, 177.
11   Dobak and Phillips, *The Black Regulars*, 31.
12   They were: George Ritter Burnett for his actions at Cuchillo Negro, New Mexico, August 16, 1881; Louis Henry Carpenter 'for distinguished conduct during the Indian campaign in Kansas and Colorado, September and October, 1868 and in the forced march September 23–25, 1868 to the relief of Forsyth's scouts while serving as Captain, Tenth Cavalry commanding Troop H;' Powhatan Henry Clarke of the Tenth Cavalry, who on May 12, 1891, was recognized 'for having rushed to the rescue of a soldier who was severely wounded and lay disabled exposed to the enemy's fire and carried him to a place of safety at Pinito Mountains Mexico May 3, 1886;' Lieutenant Matthias Walter Day for bravery 'in action against hostile Apache Indians at Las Animas Cañon, New Mexico September 18, 1879 in singly advancing into the enemy's line and carrying a wounded soldier of his command on his back down a rocky trail under a hot fire, after he had been ordered to retreat; while serving as Second Lieutenant Ninth Cavalry;' and Robert Temple Emmet 'For distinguished gallantry in action against hostile Indians, Las Animas Cañon, New Mexico, Sept. 18, 1879, while 2d Lieutenant, Ninth U. S. Cavalry.' Another 15 officers held the Medal of Honor from actions during the Civil War. For a full listing of all Medal of Honor recipients during the Civil War and Indian Wars visit army.mil/medalofhonor/ citations1.html; army.mil/medalofhonor/citations2.html; army,mil/medalofhonor/citations3.html.
13   Dobak and Phillips, *Black Regulars*, 37–38, provides background on rationale for accepting a position in a cavalry regiment whether with Black or white troops. Moreover, the authors ably summarize the salient points related to officers serving with buffalo soldiers through the Spanish American War, thereby negating the need for a lengthy discussion in this chapter except for Black commissioned officers. Dobak and *Phillips, Black Regulars*, 24–43.

John J. 'Black Jack' Pershing was one of nearly 1000 commissioned officers who spent part of their military careers with African American troops, in his case with the Tenth Cavalry. (Courtesy Library of Congress)

with the junior officers largely being drawn from the Academy. David William Fulton of Ohio offered an example of the changing face of the officer corps during the last decades of the nineteenth century. Ranking 77 in a class of 77 this 'goat' of the cadets commissioned in 1886 was to be a second lieutenant in the Twenty-Fourth Infantry.[14] He first reported to Fort Supply, Oklahoma where he took command of Company B of the Indian scouts through 1888. The following March, orders detailed him to Fort Bowie, Arizona to serve on a courts-martial board, after which he reported to Fort Bayard, New Mexico for his next long-term assignment.

Unfortunately, he developed pneumonia and Fulton died on March 28, 1889. Thereby ending his short, nearly forgotten place with the regiment, except for his West Point album, commission and class ring displayed by the Fort Bayard Historic Preservation Society.[15] Except for his early death, Fulton typified the growing number of US Military Academy graduates who, over the half century after the Civil War, replaced veterans of that conflict, as did those in later times who served during the campaigns in Cuba and the Philippines.

Another member of the Class of 1886, who lived far longer and achieved fame after his service with Black troops, was Missourian John J. Pershing, who ranked 30 out of 77 and first served in the Sixth US Cavalry. On October 20, 1892, with his promotion to first lieutenant and under a new policy of advancement based on seniority within the individual's branch of service rather than regiment, he was transferred from the Sixth Cavalry to the Tenth Cavalry. At that juncture, Pershing applied for an exception. He requested to remain with his old regiment rather than report to the new assignment. He even began to question whether he should

---

14 James S. Robbins, *Last in Their Class: Custer, Pickett and the Goats of West Point* (New York: Encounter Books, 2006)
15 Heitman, *Historical Register* I, 440; Cullum, *Biographical Register*, VII, 249.

resign his commission to pursue civilian opportunities because of the painfully slow prospects for promotion in the peacetime army. Pershing calculated that it would take another 15 years to reach captain.[16]

Later, Pershing even attempted to exchange his cavalryman's spurs for placement as a staff officer, where improved prospects for promotion, or at least a more comfortable life free from field duty, existed. He petitioned for a move to Commissary Department, Judge Advocate General Department, or the Quartermaster Department, going so far as to apply for leave to pursue this last-named goal at higher headquarters in San Francisco.[17] In all cases, his efforts failed.

Did he dislike serving with Blacks, or did he think he had better prospects for advancement elsewhere? Regardless of his reasons, had Pershing secured a position in another branch, his career probably would have taken a dramatically different direction rather than reaching the heights he did when selected as the commander of the American Expeditionary Force (AEF) during the First World War with the exalted title of 'general of the armies.'

Others besides Pershing found their appointment to Black regiments, stepping-stones for successful careers. Such was the case for Ranald Slidell Mackenzie, who graduated first in his West Point class of twenty-eight in 1862. After stellar performances against the Confederates, McKenzie received recognition with his appointment as colonel of the Forty-First Infantry headquartered at Baton Rouge, Louisiana. During March of 1869, he transferred to the newly constituted Twenty-Fourth Infantry as its colonel and briefly held this position until reassignment to Fourth Cavalry on December 15, 1869.[18]

With McKenzie's departure, Abner Doubleday (sometimes erroneously referred as the 'father of baseball') assumed the Twenty-Fourth's regimental reins. His second in command, Lieutenant Colonel William Shafter, was an active, hard-fighting officer who afterwards served in both the Twenty-Fourth and then Twenty-Fifth Infantry. Subsequently, he transferred to the First US Infantry as the regimental commander of this white regiment. Later, during the Spanish American War, he led the US Army in Cuba.[19]

Correspondingly, after an impressive career during the Civil War, Wesley Merritt (West Point Class of 1860) would be appointed lieutenant colonel of the Ninth Cavalry. Assuming his post on July 28, 1866, Merritt first spent time on inspection duty from his station at the headquarters of the Department of the Gulf. In February 1867, he assumed the command of his regiment at New Orleans. From there, like McKenzie, he proceeded to Texas, serving at San Antonio followed by a move to Fort Davis. He took a leave of absence in 1870 until October 1871, but returned to Texas where he resumed command of his regiment that led to postings to Forts Stockton and Clark, then Fort Concho, until May 1874. On July 1, 1876, with his promotion to colonel of the Fifth Cavalry, he ended his tenure with the Ninth.

---

16 Frank E. Vandiver, *Jack: The Life and Times of John J. Pershing* I (College Station: Texas A&M Press, 1977), 124–5.
17 Vandiver, *Black Jack*, 133, 155; and MC46 Vol. 20, Post Letters Received, Montana Historical Society, Helena.
18 Cullum, *Biographical Register* II, 840.
19 Powell, *Living Officers*, 395–7; and 536; Cullum, *Biographical Register* II, 132; and Downey, *The Buffalo Soldiers*, 23. Further, Shafter had been the lieutenant colonel of the Forty-First Infantry and with two years was reassigned to Twenty-Fourth Infantry on April 14, 1869. For more on his life read: Paul H. Carlson, *'Pecos Bill' A Military Biography of William R. Shafter* (College Station, TX: Texas A&M University Press, 1989).

Others like McKenzie, who would be carried on the regimental rolls for only a brief period, or never actually served with one of the units comprised of Black regulars, would obtain fame. This included George S. Patton Jr., who appeared on regimental reports of the Tenth Cavalry for a scant few months from June to December 1916, but never actually served with the regiment.[20] In contrast, some of his fellow officers, who would wear stars during the Second World War, such as George C. Marshall and Carl Spazt, spent some of their early days in the military with Black troops, albeit again for relatively brief periods.[21] Other notables who served part of their apprenticeships as officers with Black enlisted men, included Frank Ross McCoy whose extraordinary performance in and out of uniform, included duties as acting military aide to President Theodore Roosevelt, head of the United States relief expedition activated after the 1932 Kanto, Japan earthquake and other military as well as diplomatic duties.[22]

A considerable number of officers, while not as well known as Pershing, Patton, or Marshall, long stayed the course in command of Blacks, as lieutenants and captains. They endured sluggish promotion rather than leave the military. In this regard and other aspects, the nearly 1,000 officers who served with the Black regulars compared to their contemporaries from other regiments, differed little from those detailed to white units. That is not to say significant differences did not exist. Most significantly, as historians William Dobak and Thomas Phillips underscored: 'Of all the colonels in the army' the two assigned in 1866 to command the Ninth and Tenth Cavalry Edward Hatch and Benjamin Grierson, 'had the longest continuous service' of any regimental commanders during the Indian Wars.[23] While the commanding officer regularly changed in the other eight cavalry regiments, the Ninth and Tenth proved the exceptions, once more indicative of dedication by some officers to their men.[24] However, ready acceptance of an assignment with Africans Americans was not universal.

---

20   The Punitive Expedition's commander, John J. Pershing, purposely left Patton's own regiment, the Eighth Cavalry, out of his strike force into Mexico because he lacked confidence in the aged commanding colonel. Patton managed to be attached to the 13th Cavalry in Federico, Mexico and upon promotion from second lieutenant to first lieutenant to rank from May 21, 1916, he would be assigned to Tenth Cavalry. He never joined the unit as this was a 'paper' assignment. Cullum, *Biographical Register*, 1434 and RG393, Returns Regular Army Cavalry Regiments 1833–1916 Tenth Cavalry 1910–1916, June–December, 1916, Microcopy No. 744, Roll 102, NARA. For Patton's actual participation and status Pershing's incursion into Mexico review Vernon L. Williams, *Lieutenant Patton: George S Patton, Jr. and the American Army in the Mexican Punitive Expedition, 1915–1916* (Abilene: TX: Old Segundo Companion Book, 2003).
21   When George Catlett Marshall, Jr. received his promotion to first lieutenant on March 7, 1907, he transferred from the Thirtieth Infantry to the Twenty-Fourth Infantry, remaining on the regimental rolls until June 1, 1911. *US Army Register, 1916*, 366. In turn, Carl Spatz, who graduated 57 in his West Point class of 107, would be assigned on June 12, 1914, as a second lieutenant in the Twenty-Fifth Infantry. He served at Schofield Barracks, Hawaii with the regiment from October 4, 1914, to October 13, 1915, when orders to report to San Diego, California as a student officer at Signal Corps Aviation School changed the trajectory of his military career. Cullum, *Biographical Register*, VI b, 1696–7.
22   McCoy graduated 34 out of 67 graduates of his West Point Class of 1897 joining the Tenth Cavalry the next year. Cullum, *Biographical Register*, V, 583. His papers in the Library of Congress bespeak of amazing service for which see loc.gov/item/mm78031989.
23   Dobak and Phillips, *Black Regulars*, 34.
24   Once again, Thompson, 'The Negro Regiments,' 148–73, offered useful statistics that within his sample of 200 officers little difference existed between promotions for individuals serving with white units versus those assigned to regiments with Black enlisted personnel.

Commissioned Officers 91

Pallbearers for Colonel Edward Hatch's 1889 funeral at Fort Robinson, Nebraska consisted of distinguished non-commissioned officers who paid their final honors to their respected regimental commander. They were: (Back Row Left to Right) First Sergeant George Wilson; First Sergeant David Badie; Medal of Honor recipient First Sergeant Thomas Shaw; Sergeant Nathan Fletcher. (Front Row Left to Right) Chief Trumpeter Stephen Taylor; Sergeant Edmund McKinzie; Sergeant Robert Burley; Sergeant Zekiel Sykes. Courtesy United States Military Academy)

In 1866, former music teacher turned Union volunteer general, Benjamin Grierson, gained the colonelcy of the Tenth US Cavalry. (Courtesy Library of Congress)

Attitudes and Opinions

George Armstrong Custer stood out among several officers who declined a commission that would have resulted in commanding African Americans. He refused a lieutenant colonelcy in one of the two cavalry regiments formed in 1866 with Black troopers. Instead, he opted for the Seventh Cavalry at the same grade.[25] Ironically, eschewing a position in a Black regiment was one of his few commonalities with his Georgia-born combative subordinate, Captain Frederick W. Benteen. Benteen rejected a majority in the Ninth Cavalry to accept a lesser grade as a captain with the Seventh Cavalry. Ironically, when his promotion to major occurred, long after Little Bighorn, it was to the Ninth![26]

Custer was not alone in declining duty with African Americans. Evidence of like actions for lesser-known Civil War veterans also exists.[27] Perhaps these men shared Lieutenant Colonel Eugene Asa Carr's views, who would forgo a 'chance for a rapid promotion' despite being urged by friends to accept a billet with Blacks. Like Custer, he set his sights on a regiment with white enlisted men, the Fifth Cavalry. Not surprisingly, Carr contended Black men were unfit to be soldiers.[28]

While is impossible to determine how many shared Carr's bias, five advertisements, which appeared in the personal column of the influential *Army and Navy Journal* for 1871, demonstrated an array of attitudes towards Black troops.[29] The first four that ran in April betrayed little prejudice simply stating: 'TRANSFER – A CAPTAIN OF CAVALRY, colored regiment, well up on the list, wishes to transfer into infantry.' The second posting, however, indicated a definite biased attitude from a first lieutenant 'OF INFANTRY (white) serving in a pleasant post in the South,' who sought a 'transfer with any first lieutenant serving upon the Plains or Pacific coast. Would transfer into a colored regiment above the fourth file [ranking within the regiment].' Yet

---

25 T. J. Stiles, *Custer's Trials: A Life on the Frontier of a New America* (New York: Alfred A. Knopf, 2015), 220, 229–33, 235, 246. 252, 368–9, 417, and 435, presents many examples of Custer's ambivalent perspective about Blacks, which in certain aspects coincided with the views of many other military men of his generation.

26 Dobak and Phillips, *The Black Regulars*, 27–28, and 30.

27 Examples of Civil War veterans who demurred included: Virginian Edward Albert Belge, declined a captaincy in the Forty-First US Infantry on July 28, 1866. Likewise, Henry G. Thomas, born in Maine, who had previous experience with US Colored Troops, did not accept a position as major in the Forty-First Infantry. Pennsylvanian Joel Graham Trimble, who began his military career during the antebellum era with the First US Dragoons and by February 19, 1863, had gained a commission as a second lieutenant would on July 28, 1866, decline a proposed captaincy in the Ninth US Cavalry. Trimble's refusal to accept meant he waited until December 26, 1868, for a commission at that grade in a regiment comprised of white enlisted men. In July 1866, New Yorker Gulian Verplanck Weir turned down a captaincy in the Thirty-Ninth Infantry, which contributed to his remaining a first lieutenant until November 10, 1874. On August 31, 1867, Maryland native Hiram F. Winchester rejected an offer as a second lieutenant in the Tenth Cavalry. The next month he agreed to the same grade, but with Sixth US Cavalry manned by white troops. Powell, *List*, 188; 626–27; 636–37; 661–62; and 682.

28 James T. King, *War Eagle: A Life of General Eugene A. Carr* (University of Nebraska Press, 1963), 77 and 275 n19.

29 By Donald Nevius Bigelow, *William Conant Church & The Army and Navy Journal.* (New York: Columbia University Press, 1952), remains the quintessential study on this semi-official military publication and its editor.

another infantryman, in this case a captain, indicated he belonged, 'to one of the oldest and best white regiments serving at a most agreeable post in the East' but qualified that he was 'desirous of negotiating a transfer' with a cavalry captain serving in a unit with white troops. Similarly, 'A CAPTAIN IN ONE OF THE BEST OLD WHITE Infantry regiments, located at a pleasant and healthy post on the frontier' wished a transfer to the cavalry and would accept an exchange in a regiment with either 'white or colored troops.'[30]

A few months later, yet another variation on the theme read: 'A FIRST LIEUTENANT OF INFANTRY (white), stationed at a very desirable post in the Department of the South, desires to transfer with an officer of the same grade on equal terms it in a white regiment, but if in a colored regiment, a reasonable bonus would be expected.'[31] One newspaper article went so far as to allege that graduating West Point cadets, 'are fighting bitterly against such details' with Black troops 'and many of them would prefer to remain as additionals (West Point graduates awaiting an appointment) for years rather than accept appointments to these regiments.'[32]

It seems that over time, however, if one mid-1880s' newspaper article was to be believed, prejudice against assignments to command Blacks gradually dissipated with even Southerners, 'to whom such service would naturally be distasteful' willing to accept a commission in one of the four regiments. The reason given was that Blacks, if properly led and fairly treated, made 'model soldiers.'[33] Andrew Burt, one-time colonel commanding the Twenty-Fifth Infantry, reached that conclusion. He even made his views known in a nationally published laudatory article.[34]

While some avoided duty with Blacks or pursued a transfer to a white unit, occasionally an officer might seek such an assignment. This is what George Rodney did. He revealed that in 1916, the Tenth Cavalry, 'had two captains who hated Arizona and who greatly desired an Eastern station.' In turn, 'personal reasons' induced Rodney to swap posts from Fort Leavenworth, Kansas with a discontented Tenth Cavalry captain serving at Naco, Arizona, 'about twenty-five miles east on the railroad: from Fort Huachuca.' After Rodney made his way to Arizona, he reported to the squadron commander and indicated his wish to join his troop. The major 'cut me short' recalled Rodney. He indicated: 'You can attend to that later. The troop runs itself. Rather the First Sergeant runs it like a clock. He's been more than thirty years in the regiment.'[35]

This conversation spoke on two points. Even after decades since the establishment of the Black regulars, many an enlisted man remained career oriented. Moreover, savvy officers knew they could trust these topnotch veterans to do their jobs and do them well, the major among them. Another long service officer strongly agreed with this point of view.

Reinforcing the trust, authority and the responsibility bestowed on senior sergeants by some officers, Colonel Charles A. Romeyn wrote in the *US Cavalry Journal* about William Barnes. He cited Barnes as one of his two ideals of a first sergeant – 'one colored, one white.' He underscored: 'Both men were sober (absolutely teetotalers); loyal, on the job at all times' as well as being crack shots, physically fit, fine horseman, capable of dealing with alcoholics and 'either

---

30 *A&NJ*, April 29, 1871, 588.
31 *Ibid.*, June 3, 1871, 868.
32 *Yorkville Enquirer* (SC) July 3, 1889.
33 *Indianapolis Journal*, November 1, 1886.
34 Andrew S. Burt, 'The Negro Soldier.' *Crisis* 1 (February 1911): 23–25.
35 George Brydges Rodney, *As a Cavalryman Remembers* (Caldwell, ID: Caxton Printers, Ltd., 1944), 247 and 249.

reformed or drove out the drunkards.' Supposedly, these model top soldiers possessed a litany of other incredible traits.[36]

Decades earlier, an admiring Frederic Remington also singled out another member of this special breed of 'top soldiers.' He praised Alabaman Shelvin Shropshire, formerly of Company F, Fifteenth USCT and later, 'a constituent member of C company, organized at Fort Leavenworth, Kansas May 19, 1867 and … a conspicuous member of the regimental since.'[37] Remington associated Shropshire with 'Some of the old sergeants' who had 'been taught their battle tactics in a school where the fellows who were not quick at learning are dead.'[38] Appropriately, Shropshire ended his 33 years in the Tenth Cavalry with a fete staged by comrades consisting of a sumptuous dinner dance. His retirement that dated October 11, 1902, saw this fixture of Troop H close a, 'magnificent record of … arduous, zealous and faithful service …' He had served in, 'three wars and three countries … with greatest credit to himself, to the cavalry service and the army.' His commanding officer further lauded Shropshire for being: 'Faithful to every trust and obligation imposed upon him, of irreproachable, character, brave capable, proud of and true to his country. He is a man who has always carried American arms to victory and the highest type of that backbone of the army: the non- commissioned officer.'[39]

Blacks at West Point

Even with such complimentary reflection on the leadership capabilities of Black NCOs, actual command regularly remained the prerogative of whites. Strong stereotypes about the ability of Blacks to take charge of troops prevailed. That situation changed, although slowly, with the unprecedented admission of Blacks to the United States Military Academy. Just as the radical wing of the Republican party enacted legislation to include African Americans in the Regular Army, they likewise secured appointments that in the past had barred promising candidates of color from attending the United States Military Academy. In 1870, Mississippian Michael Howard and South Carolinian James Webster Smith changed the face of West Point forever. For various reasons, sometimes including the poor treatment experienced at the Academy at the hands of follow cadets, this pair of pioneers and another 18 Black cadets, who followed, never completed their studies.[40] It was more than just the daunting curriculum and regimented life of cadets that kept these aspirants from graduating. Black cadets faced four years ostracism whereby they would only be spoken to in the strictest of military requirements and treated as outcasts or as nonexistent because of racial profiling.[41]

---

36 Charles A. Romeyn, 'The First Sergeant,' *Cavalry Journal* No. 140 (July 1925): 296–98.
37 Schubert, *On the Trail of the Buffalo Soldiers*, I, 379; and Edward L. Baker, *Roster Non-Commissioned Officers of the Tenth US Cavalry with Some Regimental Reminiscences, Appendices, Etc., Connected with the Early History of the Regiment* (St. Paul, MN: Kennedy Printing Co.1897), 17.
38 Frederic Remington, 'Vagabonding with the Tenth Horse,' *Cosmopolitan* (February 1897), 349.
39 *Colored American* (Washington, DC) November 1, 1902.
40 John F. Marszalek, *Court Martial: A Black Man in America* (New York: Charles Scribner's Sons, 1972), 18.
41 Jeremy Wayne James, 'Alone in the Profession of Arms: America's First Three African American West Point Graduates,' MA thesis, Texas A&M University, 2007, 5.

Second Lieutenant Henry O. Flipper, Class of 1877, became the first African American graduate of the United States Military Academy. While on duty at Fort Davis, Texas, this distinction did not preclude him from standing court-martial. Found guilty of conduct unbecoming an officer, the court sentenced Flipper to dismissed from the US Army. 111-SC–2668824. (Courtesy US National Archives)

One of West Point's most highly respected professors, Peter S. Michie, not only condoned this treatment, but also published an apologia for its necessity. He argued: 'the fact that, in any altercation, where a colored cadet was a party, punishment of the white cadet was more certain, more severe and speedy' strict separation was essential. The practice of shunning a Black stemmed not from hatred, claimed Michie. It arose to avoid possible consequences of interactions that might lead to trouble. Another West Point instructor, George L. Andrews, concurred with Michie. He further reinforced his fellow faulty member's defence with his own perspectives. Both men voiced their views openly in articles that appeared in nationally prominent periodicals of the era.[42] Despite such protestations and incredible barriers, the day of the Black officer was about to emerge.

Henry O. Flipper
Henry Ossian Flipper succeeded as the first African American graduate of the United States Military Academy. This was no easy feat. Gaining admission to the storied school was one thing. Once there, Flipper endured daunting obstacles. During his time at West Point, he bore personnel insults from white cadets. As with those who came before him and failed to graduate for sundry reasons, the Cadet Corps shunned him. Few ever uttered a word to him except when military propriety dictated.[43]

---

42 Petters S. Michie, 'Caste at West Point,' *North American Review* (June 1880), 604–13; George L. Andrews, 'West Point and the Colored Cadets,' *International Review* (November 1880), 477–89.
43 Theodore Delano Harris, 'Henry Ossian Flipper: The First Black Graduate of West Point,' Ph.D. diss., University of Minnesota, 1971, 78–79. While Harris's early work on Flipper remains the

Keeping a record of his trying four years at West Point, shortly after graduation, Flipper shared his experiences in the form of a rare autobiography titled: *The Colored Cadet at West Point*. In the narrative, he set forth his view on equality in the United States. With the end of Reconstruction on the horizon, Flipper felt that the government would not be able to achieve the goals of Radical Republicans by legislation alone. To Flipper, the process would be a long, evolutionary one before Blacks could participate fully in American society, a point of view not too distant from that later adopted by Booker T. Washington.

The conclusion of Reconstruction signaled a reversal in the gains that had been made by and for Blacks up to that juncture. This deterioration of status for Blacks continued well into the twentieth century and beyond. Flipper's fate partially characterized the problems of the period. In 1877, after reporting to the Tenth Cavalry, the newly commissioned second lieutenant took up traditional daily life at a Western fort. He mainly performed routine garrison assignments, but he did not pass all of his time in Texas in garrison.

For instance, Flipper and two of his men rode 98 miles in 22 hours to deliver dispatches to Colonel Grierson. Having made this taxing journey, Flipper rolled into his blankets for a few hours of sleep before departing the next morning to retrace his route from Eagle Springs to old Fort Quitman, Texas. After Flipper rejoined his company, news arrived via a mounted messenger. Grierson, his son and eight men, who earlier had set out from Fort Davis, Texas, encountered an enemy force with superior numbers.

Grierson's detail had camped at a waterhole known as *Tinaja de las Palmas*. There, the colonel ordered his small band to pile up rocks to form three hasty barricades. Entrenched, the command watched and waited for Victorio and his Apache followers to arrive. During the early morning of July 30, Lieutenant Leighton Finley joined the colonel, adding another 11 carbines to the defence. By 9:00 a.m. the understrength defenders clashed with an advance party on their return from Mexico.

Spotting the trap, the Apache's leading element attempted to flee. Grierson dispatched Finley and his 10 troopers to sever the enemy's escape route. In the meantime, Company C, with Flipper as second in command, hastened towards the fray. Flipper recalled: 'We came in a swinging gallop for fifteen or twenty miles. When we arrived we found 'G' Troop had already come and the fight was on.' The ensuing clash produced casualties on both sides, some men possibly being struck by friendly fire as two relief columns converged to aid Grierson. In the aftermath, Flipper noted: 'We buried the soldiers where they fell. I was detailed to read the Episcopal service over them, after which a volley was fired and the buglers sounded taps. This was the first and only time I was under fire.'[44]

---

standard reference, another academic source offers further details – Donald B. McClung, 'Henry O. Flipper: First Negro Officer in the United States Army,' MA thesis, East Texas State University, 1970. Other biographies include titles such as Lowell D. and Sara H. Black, *An Officer and A Gentleman: The Military Career of Lieutenant Henry O. Flipper* (Dayton. OH: The Lora Company, Ltd., 1985); Don Cusic, *The Trials of Henry O. Flipper, First Black Graduate of West Point* (Jefferson, NC: McFarland & Co., 2009), and Jane Eppinga, *Henry Ossian Flipper: West Points' First Black Graduate* (Fort Worth, TX: Wild Horse Press, 2015) all aimed at a popular audience, but added little to previous efforts by Harris and McClung.

44 Henry O. Flipper, *Black Frontiersman: The Memoirs of Henry O. Flipper, First Black Graduate of West Point*, compiled and edited with introduction and notes by Theodore D. Harris (Fort Worth: Texas Christian University Press, 1997), 34.

After nearly four years of gaining experience in garrison and on campaign, Flipper's place within the military came to an abrupt halt. When William R. Shafter arrived at Fort Davis, Texas where Flipper then was posted, the new commander informed the lieutenant that he would be replaced as acting assistant quartermaster at the post. Later, Shafter told the junior officer he also was to be removed as commissary of subsistence, a decision made in light of charges leveled for alleged embezzlement and conduct unbecoming an officer and a gentleman.

At that point, Shafter placed Flipper in the guardhouse, somewhat atypical, but not an unheard of action when it came to officers, who customarily were restricted to their quarters while awaiting legal procedures. Upon learning of this form of incarceration, the departmental commander, Brigadier General Christopher C. Augur, instructed Shafter to release Flipper and to, 'treat him like a white man.'[45] This meant the lieutenant was to be placed under house arrest. Although Shafter complied, Flipper's fortunes did not improve because after being released from the guardhouse he was confined to quarters, 'which were barricaded, nailed up and made as secure as the guardhouse was … and was guarded night and day by an armed sentinel.'[46]

Likewise, Shafter curbed Flipper's postal and visitation privileges along with denying him credit to purchase goods at the commissary. As all of Flipper's property and funds had been seized, these measures compounded his difficulties. Fortunately, several members of the local community believed the lieutenant to be innocent and they advanced funds. Also, Flipper attempted to raise money to hire a civilian attorney. He failed to obtain the minimum of $1,000 to engage a lawyer, a retainer that nearly equaled his annual pay. Captain Merritt Barber of the Sixteenth United States Infantry then stepped forward. He offered a *pro bono* defence. Barber's opposition, Twenty-Fourth United States Infantry Captain John W. Clous, conducted the prosecution as judge advocate.[47]

Several weeks passed. The court, which was held in the chapel at Fort Davis, eventually exonerated Flipper on the charge of embezzlement. They did find him guilty of conduct unbecoming an officer. With this verdict, Flipper lost his commission with a dismissal from service and a dishonorable discharge. Flipper had no recourse but to leave the Tenth Cavalry. He attempted for much of his remaining life to overturn the conviction.[48]

Sixteen years passed before Flipper's appeal reached the United States Congress. In his request reinstatement, he plead for permission to 'apply the training and ability acquired by

---

45 Parker, *The Old Army Memories*, 93.
46 Black, *An Officer and A Gentleman*, 120.
47 Born in Germany, Clous served the US Army as private in Company K and the band of Ninth Infantry from February 2, 1857, to November 5, 1860. Just before the Civil War erupted, he transferred to the Sixth Infantry as a non-commissioned, but by November 29, 1862, he was a second lieutenant and them a first lieutenant in the regiment from where he became a captain Thirty-Eighth Infantry on January 22, 1867. November 11, 1869, found him in the Twenty-Fourth Infantry where he remained until April 1, 1886, when his promotion to major began an advance as a military attorney ultimately becoming the Army's judge advocate general on May 22, 1901. He retired as a brigadier general two days later. Heitman, *Historical Register* I, 311.
48 Flipper carried on many civilian pursuits as well as exhibited an interest in mining operations. He never married, although one intriguing article stated: 'Lucy Barbee the well known janitress of the Sheldon block is dangerously ill at the Sister's hospital from blood poisoning. It is understood that she is engaged to be married to Ex Lieutenant H. O. Flipper of the 10th US cavalry, a West Point graduate. *El Paso Daily Herald*, April 26, 1898.

The second Black graduate of West Point, John Hanks Alexander, managed better than Henry O. Flipper to navigate the prejudice he faced. Upon his commissioning in June 1887, he traveled west to join the Ninth Cavalry as a second lieutenant. Alexander would be praised for: 'his ability and energy' both attributes that would have served him well in his duty as the military instructor at Wilberforce University. Regrettably, not long after Alexander reported to the school, he suffered what appeared to be a heart attack and died. (Negroes for a New Century 1900)

me at the Military Academy to the service of the government.'[49] Later, in 1898, the cashiered lieutenant proffered his sword to the nation after it declared war on Spain. This petition and one that surfaced in 1921, allowing Flipper to be placed on the army retirement list as a colonel, failed. Not until late 1976, did he receive his final day in court when a United States Army board reviewed his case. In a vote of four to one, they concluded the first Black graduate of West Point should receive a retroactive honorable discharge.

John Hanks Alexander
Not long before Flipper's dismissal, he in part inspired the next Black West Point aspirant, John Hanks Alexander. Cognizant of Flipper's admission as a cadet and subsequent graduation from the United States Military Academy, Alexander decided to follow the lead of his much-publicized predecessor.[50] Alexander was born on January 6, 1864, in Arkansas to formerly enslaved parents. His father and mother sought better lives for the family. In fact, as Alexander related, his father James Alexander 'by hard work, had accumulated a little money and about 1850 he bought himself and my mother and three children out of slavery' first freeing himself and eventually purchasing the freedom of the all the other members of the household in their native Virginia before relocating to Arkansas.[51] Subsequently, four more children expanded the family with John being the eldest among the new additions.

---

49   Cusic, *The Trials of Henry O. Flipper*, 137.
50   *Cleveland Gazette*, July 2, 1887.
51   *Omaha Daily Bee*, June 27, 1883.

To maintain the family, both parents contributed income needed to support a household of nine people. His mother Frances, affectionately known as 'Fannie' by her intimates, found employment as a domestic. His father established a dry goods business. Towards the end of the 1865–1867 recession, 'which caused so much distress and havoc,' the store closed.

Besides endeavoring to provide for the household, James Alexander, a stalwart Republican, participated in politics. This included serving as a justice of the peace in Arkansas and by his son's account, James was the first Black to do so. He also became a representative to the state legislature for Phillips County by appointment from the governor. In 1871, the ambitious patriarch died leaving his widow and several young children, including seven-year-old John, to fend for themselves.[52]

John's mother continued to rear the youngsters. In the process, she achieved respect in their community, as well as inspired John, who attributed 'whatever success he has gained' to her.[53] Evidently, although uneducated, Fannie encouraged John to avail himself of schooling, which he did. After his graduation from Helena High School in his Arkansas hometown, he delivered an address that expressed a moral tone and demonstrated a keen ability both in oral and written communication. He then accepted a brief teaching position in Mississippi.[54] Six months as a schoolmaster, during the fall of 1880, ended with his admission to Oberlin College. Alexander had completed two years there when he learned of the competitive examinations for the United States Military Academy.[55]

On May 14, 1883, Alexander and three others tested. Only two hopefuls passed this preliminary trial with Alexander achieving the highest scores. Supposedly, because of a 'physical condition described by an acquaintance as "pigeon breasted" ' he became the alternate to the white candidate, 'William Waites, the son of Ohio's chief justice.' The second hurdle came at West Point when both Alexander and Waites, 'passed the physical examination, but Waites failed the academic portion in which Alexander excelled.' Consequently, Alexander's local congressman designated him as his appointee.[56]

This successful bid for West Point received mention in the *New York World*. A *World's* reporter noted that when Alexander appeared in the dining room of a West Point hotel, during his visit to the Academy for the examinations, no one associated with him. However, after a lengthy conversation with Alexander, the reporter concluded that he was 'a clever and very intelligent young man fully equal in appearance and manners to any of the candidates I have met and superior to many.'[57]

Four years passed. One official at West Point claimed Alexander was 'making a better record than any other colored cadet ever admitted' proving himself to be a 'splendid scholar, getting along finely.'[58] His academic performance and a relatively small number of demerits meant

---

52 *Cleveland Gazette*, March 29, 1884.
53 *Ibid.*, January 18, 1887.
54 'Principles of Life,' December 19, 1879, Alexander Collection, Papers of the Alexander Family of Helena, AK, HM 28885–28913, Huntington Library, San Marino, CA.
55 *Cleveland Gazette*, June 18, 1883.
56 Willard B. Gatewood, Jr., 'John Hanks Alexander of Arkansas: Second Black Graduate of West Point,' *Arkansas Historical Quarterly* 41 no. 2 (Summer 1982): 117. This same source reveals considerable background about both Alexander and his family for which see pages 103–28.
57 *New York Daily Tribune*, June 23, 1883; *New York Times*, June 13, 1883.
58 *New York Globe*, January 26, 1884.

Alexander graduated 32nd in a class of 64, a respectable placing which theoretically should have afforded him a choice of cavalry regiments where a vacancy existed. Nonetheless, Second Lieutenant Alexander went to the Ninth Cavalry.

Probably this biased point meant little to one of the members of the audience. On June 11, 1887, 'a tall, stately black women' and 'former slave, Frances Alexander' was on hand to witness one of the proudest moments in her life – the graduation of her son John from West Point. She must have been elated after her long trek from Arkansas, especially when John Hanks Alexander received his diploma from General Philip Sheridan that engendered, 'thunderous hand-clapping' as a reward for a 'strikingly handsome young man whose trim fitting gray uniform accentuated his muscular litheness and whose "majestic carriage" ' had weathered the isolation he faced for four years.[59]

While at West Point: 'His color precluded social intercourse with white cadets and prevented his participation in certain extra-curricular activities.' To combat this, 'Alexander attempted to cope with his loneliness by writing and receiving letters.'[60] Finally, those days had ended. Following the graduation, Alexander took a brief leave to visit family and friends in time to witness 'commencement week at Oberlin,' which he had attended for nearly two years.[61] With the short reunion concluded, Alexander began frontier military life.

First, he was to be sent to Fort Niobrara, Nebraska with the Ninth Cavalry's Troop A.[62] Then, from September 30, 1887 to March 14, 1888, he served at Fort Robinson, Nebraska as the post's junior subaltern.[63] It was there he penned one of his few known surviving letters. The contents revealed only minor details of the changes he experienced from his cadet days, but evidenced that he provided financial support to his mother and the remaining children at home.[64] Furthermore, he had incurred debts of his own, a not uncommon plight of young officers who had to procure their personal mounts, an array of costly uniforms, weapons and accoutrements as a second lieutenant to replace their West Point kit, along with other requirements once commissioned.

His time at Fort Robinson ended in March of 1888. He again packed his meager belongings to shuttle off for Fort Washakie, Wyoming.[65] Alexander remained only a few weeks at Fort Washakie. In June, he accompanied his Troop C and their mounts to another assignment at recently established Fort Duchesne, Utah.[66]

59 *Chicago Tribune*, June 12, 1887; *Memphis Daily Appeal*, June 12, 1887; *New York Times*, June 12, 1887; *Cleveland Gazette*, June 18, 1887; *New York Freeman*, June 18, 1887.
60 Gatewood, 'John Hanks Alexander of Arkansas:' 119.
61 *Springfield Daily Republic*, July 7, 1887.
62 *A&NJ*, August 6, 1887, 23.
63 *Ibid.*, March 24, 1888, 694.
64 After Alexander's death in 1894 his mother applied for his pension and explained how his insurance received prior to this application were expended from house repairs and paying for her son's funeral as well as his debts including loans from two of his brothers. She also indicated he had contributed upwards of $400 as financial assist to her and the two youngest children including funds for his siblings' education. RG 94, Records of the Adjutant General's Office, Alexander_John_pension-WC517000-part0001(3) NARA
65 *A&NJ*, March 24, 1888, 694.
66 Of this incident the *Salt Lake Herald*, August 14, 1889, announced: 'LIEUTENANT J. H. ALEXANDER, Ninth Cavalry, U.S.A. is in the city en route to Fort Duchesne from Fort Robinson, Neb., where he went in charge of wagon train.'

Before their departure from Wyoming, some of Alexander's men visited the nearby civilian community of Lander where they 'fought bravely at the gaming tables.' In turn, the day before Alexander departed, he took tea with one of the town's residents, a Miss Roberts, as befitted his status as an officer and a gentleman. Concluding their distinctly different farewells in town, Alexander and his horse soldiers set out overland to Utah.

This was the lieutenant's first field duty. He relished the experience. Alexander charted this excursion in a pocket diary where he jotted down highlights in pencil. On June 11, 1888, Alexander and the other members of the Ninth rode westward from Wyoming to Utah. By June 26, the caravan passed, 'thro' fine scenery.' The trip was nearly completed as the column intended to march to the fort on the next day. This left him: 'Feeling bully but am glad that we are as near our journey's end.'

Their anticipated June 27 arrival proved correct. Once there, Alexander found his latest billet, 'a terrible dusty hot post, very uninviting at the first glance.' At least the officers were 'very genial men.' Conversely, Alexander discovered a common concern. Insufficient quarters existed, 'so I am camped out as usual. Not comfortable these hot days in a tent.'

Although Alexander's accommodations left something to be desired, once he arrived in Utah, he settled into garrison life. During his days at Fort Duchesne, Alexander, undertook a variety of assignments. One of these chores entailed the establishment and supervision of the 'government saw mill (Slab Town)' where his troops cut 'lumber for the sidewalks to be erected around the post.'[67] Other chores included building and maintaining a telegraph line to Price, Utah, directing fatigue details, leading a patrol to evict squatters on government land and commanding troops on practice marches. Likewise, fighting fires that broke out with some frequency at the fort, may have required his attention.[68] As an aside, supposedly men of the Ninth constructed Nine Mile Canyon Road that linked Fort Duchesne to the railroad at Price, Utah, but no evidence exists that Alexander took part in what was a fairly common assignment for frontier troops.

When not carrying out official projects, a list at the end of his pocket diary revealed a tantalizing array of individuals whom he wrote in his spare time. Alexander directed his correspondence to his mother and sister plus friends and acquaintances, sadly probably all lost, as is his official personnel file in the National Archives. To some extent the lack of these materials explains the reason why no full-length comprehensive biography exists.[69]

What can be deduced is that in between routine at Fort Duchesne, he periodically traveled from Utah on detached duty or for personal reasons.[70] For instance, during the summer of 1889, Alexander received orders to return from Fort Sidney, Nebraska to his post in Utah.[71] Later

---

67 *Salt Lake Herald*, December 7, 1890.
68 Ronald G. Coleman, 'The Buffalo Soldiers: Guardians of the Unitah Frontier 1886–1901,' *Utah Historical Quarterly* 47 no. 4 (Fall 1979): 433; Michael J. Clark, *US Army Pioneers; Black Soldiers in Nineteenth-century Utah* (Salt Lake City: Fort Douglas Military Museum, 1988), 6.
69 James, 'Alone in the Profession of Arms,' 7. As James indicated, John H. Alexander, RG 94, Records of the Adjutant General's Office, File Number 3279, ACP 1887, NARA, has been missing since 1981.
70 See for instance *Appeal: A National Afro-American Newspaper* (Saint Paul, MN) February 8, 1890, which the heading 'ST. LOUIS' reported 'Lieutenant J. H. Alexander passed through the city Monday.'
71 *Omaha Daily Bee*, August 10, 1889.

that year, he conducted prisoners to Fort Omaha, Nebraska from November 5 to 12, 1889. Thereafter he took leave until February 5, 1890.[72]

Likewise, as almost all officers did, he sat on courts-martial boards in both Utah and Nebraska.[73] Another detail took him much farther afield when he set out for a national guard summer camp of the African American Charlotte Light Infantry in Raleigh, North Carolina as an inspector and instructor from November 2 through 7, 1891.[74] One more leave followed until January 12, 1892, at which time he journeyed to Fort Robinson for a second assignment there with the Ninth Cavalry.[75] Among other minor events, he transferred from Troop M to I.[76] He also fulfilled collateral responsibilities as the post exchange officer, which an inspector deemed, 'well supplied and properly conducted' and the operation 'under Lieut. Alexander ... who has been recently appointed, it is thought will make a success of it as he has taken hold of matters with a zeal and watchfulness.'[77]

Adding to his workload, Alexander assumed the position of acting adjutant of Fort Robinson while the officer holding that posting was absent.[78] Then, too, he received another temporary appointment as judge advocate, a responsibility he previously held at Fort Duchesne where among other defendants whom he prosecuted, was Medal of Honor recipient Sergeant John Denny.[79] Additionally, at Fort Leavenworth, Kansas, Alexander passed his examination for promotion to first lieutenant.[80] When a vacancy occurred based on his place in seniority, he would be eligible to add a silver bar to his shoulder straps at this higher grade.

As previously mentioned, Alexander wrote letters as well. For one of thes,e he availed himself of a Fort Robinson officers' club letterhead to transcribe a holiday message to his mother.[81] All the while, Alexander continued as, 'Acting Commissary of Subsistence and as Officer in charge of the Post Exchange' through January 25, 1894, when his detail ended effective January 31.[82] In the routine relief of Lieutenant Alexander, his commanding officer conveyed, 'his appreciation of the business-like methods which have governed his administration of affairs, while in charge of these Departments.'

The reason for terminating this assignment arose from Alexander's latest of several transfers. Probably this one came as more welcomed news. The army dispatched the 'talented colored officer, to the Professorship of Military Science and Tactics at Wilberforce University,

---

72 RG 94, Records of the Adjutant General's Office, Alexander_John_pension-WC517000-part0001(3) NARA; *Omaha Daily Bee*, October 4, 1889.
73 *Omaha Daily Bee*, August 6, 1891; May 23, 1893.
74 *Cleveland Gazette*, October 31, 1891.
75 RG 94, Records of the Adjutant General's Office, Alexander_John_pension-WC517000-part0001(3) NARA. Alexander went on another leave for 30 days during the summer of 1893, which brought him to Omaha as part of his time away for the regiment. *Omaha Daily Bee*, August 15, 1893.
76 *Omaha Daily Bee*, February 5, 1892.
77 RG 94, Entry 25, Box 480, 18833prd 1893, NARA.
78 *Cleveland Gazette*, February 18, 1893.
79 *Omaha Daily Bee*, January 17, 1894.
80 *Cleveland Gazette*, November 11, 1893.
81 RG 94, Records of the Adjutant General's Office, John H. Alexander to Mother [Fannie E. Alexander] Fort Robinson, Nebraska, December 26, 1892. Alexander_John_pension-WC517000-part0001(3) NARA.
82 Orders No. 7 Regimental Series, Fort Robinson, Nebraska, January 25, 1894.

Wilberforce, Ohio,' which constituted a 'first of its kind to be made in this country.'[83] On the surface, the groundbreaking posting of a Black officer to this pioneering institution of higher education for African Americans could be construed as recognition for his past 'efficiency and credit.'[84] On the other hand, this move may have been a maneuver by the War Department to offset rumblings within the Ninth Cavalry about the regiment being the only one to have Black officers in its midst.[85]

W. E. Annin, post trader at Fort Robinson, provided a window into the unenviable situation Alexander faced as a Black line officer. The white merchant, who held a license to sell to the garrison from his store, recollected that the lieutenant's commission:

> ... gave him a life-long position as an officer and his shoulder straps and uniforms delegated him authority equal to that of any other officer of his rank. But outside of that the poorest white laborer was more to be envied in some respects than the brainy, soldier-looking mullato ... There was no open ostracism, no expression of antagonism, no insults or studied cuts. But the line was everywhere drawn at official intercourse.

He self-isolated, making no social, 'calls upon families of brother officers. He was not expected at receptions and balls. If he came and stayed for a moment, as a matter of form, he always quietly withdrew. He messed by himself, although most of the remaining unmarried officers used the officers' mess and enjoyed the comradeship which it brought, he lived more or less alone.'

Alexander told Annin: 'I have not fault to find.' The lieutenant further confessed: 'No man can force himself on to society anywhere.' For this reason, he kept himself, 'in the background and not intruding myself where possible I may not be wanted. I have often declined invitations of a social of semi-social nature' with at least the one exception of sharing a Christmas dinner with a white infantry officer and family, 'so as not to give offense to anyone.' Perhaps Henry O. Flipper's fate and that of William H. Greene influenced his acquiesce to the well-defined racial barriers of the times, which caused him to, 'keep within my own lines.' In so doing, he did not consider himself 'a martyr' nor did he feel he was 'ostracized by the garrison.'[86]

Alexander may not have revealed all his convictions and attitudes to the post trader. Regardless, the professorship at Wilberforce afforded a new world of possibilities. Perhaps he could even find a perspective bride, something he had considered at least in passing. Barely a month after arriving at Wilberforce, on March 26, he traveled to Springfield, Ohio to attend, 'a meeting of the Knights Templars.' He was awaiting his turn to be shaved at Coates barbershop where he, 'complained of a pain in his head. As he rose to take his place in the chair he fell to

---

83 *New York Tribune*, January 18, 1894. The story appeared in several other sources including one of first in the *Omaha Daily Bee*, January 9, 1894 followed by such publications as *A&NJ*, January 17, 1894, 376; *Waterbury Evening Democrat*, January 27, 1894; *Daily Kennebec Journal* (Augusta, ME) January 31, 1894; *San Francisco Morning Call*, February 1, 1894; *The Roanoke Times*, February 10, 1894; *Lincoln County Leader* (Toledo, OR) February 15, 1894; *Fisherman & Farmer* (Edenton, NC) February 23, 1894.
84 *A&NJ*, March 31, 1894, 542.
85 For negative reactions to Lieutenants John Alexander and Charles Young both being on the rolls of the Ninth Cavalry review *A&NJ*, November 16, 1889, 229 and January 18, 1890, 402.
86 *Crawford Tribune*, April 6, 1894.

the floor and was dead before any one could reach him.' At the local undertaker's 'where a post mortem examination' followed, the cause of death given was, 'the rupture of one of the large arteries near the heart.' When the War Department 'gave no instructions as to an escort' for the deceased, Company A, of the Ninth Battalion of Infantry, Ohio National Guard, 'a colored company, was called upon. The remains were taken by his friends to Wilberforce March 27.'[87]

In recognition of Alexander's passing, Topeka, Kansas' *American Citizen* elegized:

> Negroes of the United States can ill afford to lose a man … His sudden death is a shock to us and we sincerely mourn his untimely end. A young man of unusual brilliancy, with a long and useful career before him, to be cut down just at the beginning of life, as it were, is a sad blow to the whole race.

The *Indianapolis Courier* reaffirmed: 'the race loses probably its greatest military light.' Back in Arkansas the *Freeman* pronounced:

> His death was a severe shock to Helena, his home. Not only to home and relatives, but throughout the Northern States. Lieutenant Alexander was just about to do great work with the promotion President Cleveland had given him, Professor of Military Science at Wilberforce University, the only one in the United States for colored boys.[88]

One headline even proclaimed: 'NOTED COLORED OFFICER DEAD'[89] In spite of positive and glowing words at Alexander's passing and earlier predictions of his potential, actually he had been inconspicuous, leaving little to remember him by except perhaps his placement at Wilberforce. He would be the first, but not the last, Black officer to be sent there as a sort of limbo during a period when the military had yet to come to grips with the advancement of Black officers.

Charles Young

Not long before Wilberforce's up and coming professor of military sciences' death, one line appeared in Montana paper summarizing: 'There are two colored officers in the regular army, Lieutenants J. H. Alexander and Charles Young of the Ninth Cavalry, which is composed of colored troops.'[90] With Alexander's demise, only one Black officer in the combat arms remained

---

87 *A&NJ*, March 31, 1894, 542. His official pension file reported he died 'from apoplexy contracted in service.' RG 94, Records of the Adjutant General's Office, Alexander_John _pension-WC517000-part0001(3) NARA.
88 These newspapers were quoted in 'John H. Alexander, No. 3205 Class of 1887,' *The Association of Graduates of the United States Military Academy Annual Reunion June 12th 1894* (Saginaw, MI: Seeman & Peters, Inc. Printers, 1894), 73. As an indication of a certain degree of fame Alexander had achieved many similar accounts appear such as *Waterbury Evening Democrat*, March 27, 1894; *Omaha Daily Bee*, March 27, 1894; *Salt Lake Herald*, March 29, 1894' *Democratic Northwest and Henry County News* (Napoleon, OH) March 29, 1894; *Red Cloud Chief* (NE) March 30, 1894; *North Platte Tribune*, April 4, 1894; *Western Kansas World* (WaKeeney) April 7, 1894; *Omaha Daily Bee*, April 4, 1894; *New-York Tribune*, April 8, 1894, 22.
89 *Jersey City News*, March 29, 1894.
90 *Yellowstone Journal* (Miles City, MT) December 30, 1893.

Symbolic of the isolation Charles Young and all African American cadets experienced at the United States Military Academy, he is relegated to a separate position from the main formation during summer camp of 1887. (Courtesy US Military Academy)

– the aforementioned Charles Young, who briefly had been Alexander's roommate at West Point.

Indeed, in some respects, Young's path mirrored that of Alexander. What most set the two apart was that the third and last Black graduate of West Point in the nineteenth century, enjoyed a much longer career and arguably, a highly productive one both in and out of the military. Young, who was the son of a veteran from the USCT, was born on March 12, 1864, in May's Lick, Kentucky. He moved with his parents to the North where he performed well as a diligent student. After completing high school, Young briefly served as a teacher in his adopted hometown of Ripley, Ohio. During this period, he considered applying for admission to a Jesuit college. When the opportunity arose for the West Point competitive examination, he abandoned that goal. Young passed the test. In 1884, word came for him to join his class in New York.

One of his classmates, Charles Dudley Rhodes, remembered Young in his cadet days as 'a rather awkward, overgrown lad, large-boned and robust in physique and of a nervous impulsive temperament.' Life at the Academy was lonely as after John Alexander graduated and the discharge of other Black cadets for insufficient grades, Young remained as the sole African American at West Point. With no comrades, he seemed, 'impelled to talk with anyone who would take an interest in his conversation' forcing him to engage in an uncharacteristic activity. He conversed with German-born boot blacks at the Academy in their native language just to communicate with another human beyond official exchanges. In this instance, Young's 'good working knowledge of Latin, Greek, French, Spanish and German' paid practical dividends.

During these first years of isolation, Young had few occasions to break through the racial wall erected around him by the 'silencing' of his fellow cadets. Nevertheless, Young persisted. Gradually, his perseverance started to win over at least some of his classmates. They 'began to acknowledge and respect his finer traits of character; while a spirit of fair play induced many cadets ... to treat Young with the kindness and consideration long his due.'[91]

After he received his commission in 1889, Young followed Alexander's route to Fort Robinson. Purportedly he continued to, 'face the same loneliness and isolation he would experience at West Point.' At another station, Fort Duchesne, an annual efficiency report stated Young was 'liked and respected very much' and remained 'alone socially.'[92] At least Young and Alexander briefly served together there. This rare opportunity provided some moments for the two men to share a comradeship that they had been denied them in the white dominated officer corps of the times. In contrast to the Black rank and file who 'worked, went to school, drank, gambled and frequented the Strip together' African American West Point cadets and officers, 'were in the tradition of the army discouraged from fraternizing with the enlisted men and at the same time not fully accepted by their white fellow officers.'[93]

Even then, during this fleeting overlap, they seldom performed duties together for any length of time.[94] One happy coincidence, however, gave them an unheard of, even though temporary chance, to serve in the same troop as superior and subordinate. Their posting at Fort Duchesne corresponded with a new phase in US Army history. The long-fought Indian wars had all but concluded and eventually led to a closure of many posts.

At this point, the preponderance of cavalrymen remained west of the Mississippi, but in reduced numbers. The perspective that many of the old outposts had outlived their usefulness to some extent carried over into a parallel action – the reduction of the number of enlisted men per company, as well as the elimination of Troops L and M from each mounted regiment and a similar downsizing of infantry regiments.[95] This meant a shuffling among the officers who now outnumbered eligible commands. As part of the restructuring, Captain Frank B. Taylor of Young's Troop B reported to Fort Robinson on detached duty. Once again, this change meant Alexander took command of the troop from November 1890 to February 1891 with Young as his direct subordinate.[96]

Interestingly, prior to that time, when Alexander learned of Young's pending addition to the Ninth Cavalry, he balked. Alexander felt paring them in the same regiment would offer 'no

---

91 [Charles D.] Rhodes, 'Charles Young No. 3330 Class of 1888,' *Annual Report of the Association of the Graduates United States Military Academy June 12, 1922* (Saginaw: Association of the Graduates United States Military Academy, 1922), 152. Brian G. Shellum, *Black Cadet in a White Bastion: Charles Young at West Point* (Lincoln: University of Nebraska Press, 2006) is a must-read to appreciate Young's early life.
92 As quoted by Nancy G. Heinl, 'Colonel Charles Young Pointman,' *Army* (March 1977), 31.
93 Clark, *US Army Pioneers*, 5.
94 *Ibid.*, 6.
95 Mary Lee Stubbs and Stanley Russell Connor, *Armor-Cavalry Part I: Regular Army and Army Reserve* (Washington, DC: Office of the Chief of Military History United States Army, 1969), 23.
96 Brian G. Shellum, *Black Officer in a Buffalo Soldier Regiment: The Military Career of Charles Young* (Lincoln: University of Nebraska Press, 2010), 38–39. Of the numerous biographies and biographical sketches related to Charles Young, Shellum's work ranks in the top tier.

Major Charles Young and Captain John R. Barber converse in Mexico during the 1916 Punitive Expedition. Young's military advancement upward to colonel threatened white superiority advocates. (Courtesy National Archives and Records Administration)

benefits to ... efforts to advance the race.' Similarly, Young did not view Alexander and he both being assigned to the Ninth Cavalry as beneficial for Blacks.[97] Alexander's untimely death ended this discourse. Young then remained the only Black line officer in the army. Thereafter, his upward assent was a matter of considerable interest to many African Americans. Indeed, when he came into consideration for his major's gold oak leaves, the NAACP's *Crisis Magazine* carried his picture on the cover along with a thumbnail sketch of his military accomplishments to date. The article also announced: 'Captain Young is now being examined at Fort Riley for his majority and is detailed to go as the United States military attaché in Liberia.'[98] After attaining that grade, when the next rung of the military ladder approached, one newspaper somewhat inaccurately noted: 'THE PROMOTION OF MAJOR YOUNG Noted Tenth Cavalryman Made Lieutenant Colonel ... Commander of Squadron of His Regiment In General Pershing's Expedition in Mexico – Reaches Highest Rank Ever Attained by Any Colored Man In United States Army.'[99]

Ultimately, Young replaced the deceased Alexander at Wilberforce University as a professor of military science and tactics; temporarily commanded a battalion of the Ohio national guard; assumed the acting superintendency of Sequoia National Park; as well as became a military

---

97 Shellum, *Black Officer*, 4 and 39. Upon learning of Alexander's opposition to both Black officers being assigned to the Ninth, an editorial rebuttal in the *A&NJ*, January 18, 1890, 170, indicated that an officer had the right to ask for a transfer to another regiment. Thus, the implication was Alexander could do so if he felt strongly about the matter.
98 *Crisis*, 4 (February 1912): 146–7.
99 *Denver Star*, September 9, 1916, 4. For an earlier report of this promotion see *Evening Star* (Washington, DC) August 16, 1916.

attaché first in Haiti and later in Liberia. While impressive, some of these posting reflected the concern of military authorities that he would command white officers, a prospect fraught with implications that would challenge racial norms of the era. Sending him away from regimental duties temporarily forestalled this situation that eventually arose during the 1916 Punitive Expedition into Mexico.

This campaign triggered by Francisco 'Pancho' Villa's lethal 1915 attack on Columbus, New Mexico, resulted in Young's first and only taste of command in combat. When Brigadier John J. Pershing crossed into the Republic of Mexico, his strike forces included the Twenty-Fourth Infantry and Tenth Cavalry. On April 1, 1916, the lead elements of the latter unit under Colonel William C. Brown, 'headed south to Agua Caliente ranch, about 20 miles away. In the vanguard rode Major Charles F. Young, commanding F and G troops.'

This meant, that while the rank and file were Blacks, all the officers under Young were whites. At about noon, Young's advance guard struck 150 *Villistas* near Agua Caliente. Once both troops arrived on the scene, Young maneuvered around the enemy's left flank, then attacked which routed the *Villistas*. Two Mexican dead remained on field, as did, 'a machine gun and a pack saddle – valuable botty. The Buffalo Soldiers continued to pursue the scattered enemy for a full two hours and the Mexicans found a strong position in a ravine that Young considered too strong to attack without reinforcement.'

Rather than withdraw, during the next morning the entire regiment, resumed the attack. After the squadrons formed as, 'a line of skirmishers, Colonel Brown ordered all to open fire. The enemy did not budge. Finally, Brown ordered Young to flank the Mexicans again, in a maneuver similar to the one he had executed the day before.' Young responded by remounting his two troops from their previous skirmish line afoot. He then 'formed his troopers abreast, in a "line of foragers," and started down a steep hill. On Young's signal, the troopers broke into a pistol charge' aimed at the *Villistas*' 'right flank, supported by machine gun fire over their heads.' The rapid-fire weapons and the determined charge on horseback, scattered the defenders. In the process, 'Young's troopers never had to fire a shot from their pistol chambers, but the Buffalo Soldiers had introduced a new technique: overhead machine-gun fire.'[100]

While Young made history as a man of action, he also possessed intellectual acumen. A prolific author, his impressive bibliography included *Military Morale of Nations and Races* (Kansas City, MO: Franklin Hudson Pub. Co., 1912) a treatise that among other things championed the accomplishments of Blacks as soldiers. As for his non-military accomplishments, Young played organ, piano and violin plus wrote music. All this prompted Young's prestigious contemporary and close friend, W. E. B. DuBois, to eulogize: 'The life of Charles Young was a triumph of tragedy.' While these achievements were worthy of note, perhaps Young's highest honor was as a leader and role model. As one of his classmates wrote: 'He loved his men and they loved him.'[101]

---

100 The above recapitulation was taken from: John S.D. Eisenhower, *Intervention! The United States and the Mexican Revolution 1913–1917* (New York: W.W. Norton & Company, 1995), 265–6.
101 Rhodes, 'Charles Young,' 154.

Up from the Ranks

While Charles Young would be denied a general's star, one of his subordinates would be the first Black to attain that goal. During his posting at Fort Duchesne, Young encountered an ambitious Ninth Cavalry squadron sergeant major named Benjamin O. Davis. Young helped prepare the able enlisted man for the examination to obtain a direct commission from the ranks – an uncommon incidence for whites and at that time, an unheard of accomplishment for Blacks. The two men, mentor and student, made history. Young ended his military days as the first African American colonel in the US Army. Davis, after passing his examanination, decades later, became the first Black brigadier general.

Davis' story is well known from his high school days in Washington, DC as an officer of the cadet corps, to his commission as a second lieutenant in the US Army 'being the first Afro-American who has ever risen from the ranks to a commissioned grade.'[102] In fact, Davis was the first to succeed in gaining a direct commission from the ranks although nearly three decades earlier, an attempt to promote a pair of other African American enlisted men failed.[103]

Benjamin O. Davis, Sr., represented a rare example of a Black enlisted man who received an officer's commission from the ranks. With the assistance of Charles Young, Squadron Sergeant Major Davis of the Ninth Cavalry, studied for the required examination. He passed with high marks and eventually became the first African American US Army brigadier general. (Courtesy United States Army Heritage and Education Center)

---

102 *Appeal: A National Afro-American Newspaper* (Saint Paul, MN) May 4, 1901. For further details consult: Marvin E. Fletcher, *American's First Black General: Benjamin O. Davis, Sr., 1880–1970* (Lawrence: University Press of Kansas, 1989).
103 Sergeant Charles E. Layman, of the Twenty-Fourth Infantry, and Sergeant Thomas H. McGuire, of the Twenty-Fifth Infantry received nominations' as second lieutenants, which according to one biased report was initiated 'to placate a certain public sentiment.' These men, if promoted, would 'have just as much rank and swagger as the best man of this date from West Point. What are we coming to, pray?' queried the editor of the racist tinged *Omaha Daily Bee*, February 13, 1888.

After passing 'with honors, averaging 91 percent' Davis assuredly took advantage of past educational opportunities. As one African American-owned paper predicted, his success would 'greatly encourage the negro soldiers who have not heretofore believed it possible for one of their race to get into the regular establishment as a commissioned officer.'[104] The *Colored American* optimistically indicated: 'Yes, the soldier white or black, who appears before an Examining Board physically and mentally unqualified will be turned down. We have in the service who will be able to do just what Mr. Davis has done if they get down to study. The door is open, who will be next?'[105]

In point of fact, Davis was one of two African American enlisted men who overcame the formidable obstructions that long barred them from becoming officers. He would be joined by 'Sergeant Green, of the Twenty-Fourth Infantry,' who 'took the examination in the Philippines and having passed with a high percentage' earned a place as 'a second lieutenant in the regular army.'[106] In 1901, John Ernest Green, born in Tennessee on April 27, 1878, numbered among 300 enlisted men who sought a commission along with Davis.[107] The two stood among the handful who earned their place from enlisted ranks.[108]

Green first came into the army via Walden University in Nashville after being recruited during the Spanish American War by Chaplain Allen Allensworth. Given Green's level of education, the regimental chaplain wisely made him his clerk, although the soldier officially appeared on the roster of Company H, Twenty-Fourth Infantry from April 27, 1899 to July 7, 1901.[109] It was while serving with the regiment in the Philippines that Green reached an unusual goal, when he received his commission as a second lieutenant in the Twenty-Fifth US Infantry on February 2, 1901. For the next 27 years, he trod a familiar road remaining with the Twenty-Fifth for most of his military service. He underwent periodic assignments to Wilberforce and Liberia and on occasion, other temporary details such as serving as a judge for a drill competition of high school military cadets at the educational institution once attended by B. O. Davis.[110] His promotion to first lieutenant came on July 15, 1907.

104 *Appeal: A National Afro-American Newspaper* (Saint Paul, MN) March 26, 1901, under the headline 'A COLORED MAN'S ACHIEVEMENT.'
105 *Colored American* (Washington, DC) July 13, 1901.
106 *Appeal: A National Afro-American Newspaper* (Saint Paul, MN) April 27, 1901. Also see: *San Francisco Call*, March 22, 1901; *Evening Times-Republican* (Marshalltown, IA) March 25, 1901; *Iowa State Bystander* (Des Moines, IA) April 19, 1901; *Colored American* (Washington, DC) May 18, 1901; *Cook County Herald* (Grand Marais, MN) July 6, 1901; *Freeland Tribune* (PA) July 22, 1901; *Colored American* (Washington, DC) May 18, 1901.
107 Marvin E. Fletcher, *The Black Soldier and Office in the United States Army, 1891–1917* (Columbia: University of Missouri Press, 1974), 165.
108 The *Denver Star*, September 9, 1916, noted: 'Captain Davis and Captain Green both received their commissions through competitive examination. Captain Davis was a first lieutenant in the Eighth United States Volunteer Infantry from July 1898, until March 1899, and the following June enlisted in the Ninth Cavalry. He underwent the examination for second lieutenant and was appointed in May 1901, being assigned to the Tenth Cavalry. Captain Benjamin O. Davis is serving as professor of military science and tactics at Wilberforce university, Wilberforce. O. Captain Green also served in the ranks in the army, enlisting in the Twenty-Fourth Infantry in April 1899. He was commissioned a second lieutenant in the Twenty-Fifth Infantry in 1901. Captain Green is serving as military attaché to Liberia, where he succeeded Major Young, who is now a lieutenant colonel.'
109 Charles Alexander, *The Battles and Victories of Allen Allensworth* (Boston: Sherman, French, and Co., 1914), 364, 392.
110 *Cleveland Gazette*, May 17, 1913; November 18, 1916; *Crisis*, 12 (June 1916): 62–63; *Washington Herald*, May 4, 1913.

Less than a decade later, during the 1916 Punitive Expedition, he was on the Mexican Border.¹¹¹ The borderlands became familiar to Green. In fact, as a lieutenant colonel, he commanded Camp Henry J. Jones, Arizona, a rare opportunity for a Black officer of the era. He retired from there in 1929.¹¹²

Politics Paves the Way

Perhaps the most unusual path taken by an African American to receive a commission in the Regular Army during the 1800s, was that of an enslaved youth born near the Vidalia, Louisiana. On September 10, 1847, his Irish immigrant father, Patrick Lynch, who managed the Tacony Plantation and his mother, Catherine White of mixed-ethnicity and enslaved at the time, became the parents of their third son – John Roy Lynch. Before long, young John Lynch 'became the personal valet of … Mississippian Alfred W. Davis' until 1862 when the slaveholder left for the Confederate Army. After emancipation, Lynch worked as a cook for the Forty-Ninth Illinois Volunteers 'and performed other odd jobs.' With the war's end, he made his living in a variety of ways besides becoming a Republican Party faithful that eventually, resulted in his election from Mississippi to the House of Representatives to the 43rd Congress. At 26 years of age, he was the youngest member to take his seat for the years 1873 through 1875.

While the demise of Reconstruction changed his fortunes and that of the Republicans in the South, Lynch remained active in the party. In 1880, some five years after he had left Congress, Lynch once more made a bid for a place in Washington. His Democratic rival rode on the coat-tails of the 'Solid South' winning, 'with 63 percent of the vote,' after he obtained, '9,172 votes to Lynch's 5,393. Lynch contested the election.' He argued 'that in five counties, more than 5,000 of his votes had been counted' for the Democratic candidate. Lynch further asserted, 'several thousand Republican ballots had been thrown out after a secret hearing because of technicalities such as a clerical failure to send a list of names with the returns and the presence of unusual marks on the ballots.'¹¹³

Lynch prevailed, partially due to his opponent's open remarks that he was 'in favor of using every means short of violence to preserve [for] intelligent white people of Mississippi supreme control of political affairs.' Reviewing the matter, House members voted 125 to 83 to seat Lynch and defeat white supremacy and election fraud.¹¹⁴ This would be Lynch's final time to hold elected office. Defeated for reelection, Lynch returned to his personal business ventures.

After the United States went to war with Spain, Lynch's political connections with the Republican Party brought an unexpected offer from President William McKinley – a wartime temporary slot as paymaster in the US Volunteers. He served as a major until May 13, 1901, when he left the service.¹¹⁵ Soon afterwards, Lynch secured a captaincy in the US Army as a

---

111 *US Army Register, 1916*, 422.
112 Schubert, *On the Trail of the Buffalo Soldiers* I, 173–4.
113 history.house.gov/People/Detail/17259. John Roy Lynch, *Reminiscences of an Active Life: The Autobiography of John Roy Lynch* (Chicago: University of Chicago Press, 1970) provides further details.
114 *Congressional Record*, House, 47th Cong., 1st sess. April 27, 1882: 3376–94.
115 Lynch, *Reminiscences of an Active Life*, 404–6. After the treaty of peace with Spain ended hostilities, McKinley offered Lynch a commission as captain in the US Army Pay Department.

paymaster.[116] During the course of his military duties, he spent three years in Cuba, then would be stationed in Nebraska, California, Hawaii and the Philippines.[117] A heart condition brought about early retirement as a major in 1911, a grade he obtained on September 13, 1906.[118] Despite this disability, Lynch was 92 when he died in Chicago, on November 2, 1939.

Regimental Chaplains

Political influence also existed in more than one instance related to those men appointed to spread the gospel and offer educational and other sundry services at frontier forts. These were the army chaplains who preached, provided spiritual guidance, oversaw the post bakery and other varied duties, one of the most significant being superintending the garrison's school. The last duty proved most critical. Immediately after the Civil War, numerous Black and white soldiers who came into Uncle Sam's army, could not read or write. The 1866 congressional legislation that created the Black regiments offered one advantage not provided to the white rank and file. These six units would be assigned regimental chaplains rather than the standard practice of the period, which entailed posting of a chaplain to select garrisons.[119] Whether it was the severe strictures in the South against enslaved people acquiring literacy during the antebellum era, or cases such as that of Henry McIntyre, who during the Civil War was a sergeant in the First South Carolina infantry and 'deliberately refrained from learning to read, because that knowledge exposed slaves to so much more watching and suspicion' most Black soldiers lacked schooling.[120] This situation remained the norm for many years after 1866.

While the army made special efforts towards education, unfortunately it seemed that it gave little to no thought 'to the black soldiers' religious tradition or to the appointment

In 1884, Reverend Henry V. Plummer was the first African American to receive an appointment as a chaplain in the US Army. His tenure lasted less than a decade when a court-martial resulted in a questionable dismissal from the Ninth Cavalry. (Courtesy Moorland-Springam Research Center, Howard University)

116 Heitman, *Historical Register*, I, 649; *Denver Colorado Statesman*, April 14, 1906.
117 Lynch, *Reminiscences of an Active Life*, 437–94.
118 history.house.gov/People/Detail/17259; *US Army Register, 1910*, 71.
119 Alan K. Lamm, *Five Black Preachers in Army Blue, 1884–1901: The Buffalo Soldier Chaplains* (Lewiston, NY: Mellen Press, 1998), 57–86 summarizes the history of chaplains serving in Union Army regiments with Black troops as their soldier congregations.
120 Higginson, *Army Life in a Black Regiment*, 252–3.

of a black chaplain who understood that tradition.'[121] As such, at first, none of the original six appointees were Blacks. (Table 6) The clerics selected for the earliest appointments, while earnest in many cases, tended to make a limited impact on the soldiers to whom they ministered. More than a dozen years passed before efforts to correct this situation emerged. Motives ranged from enhancing the effectiveness of the regimental chaplains to securing Black votes for the Republican party who relied considerably on this portion of the electorate to secure offices.

Table 6: White Regimental Chaplains

Name	Born	Appointed From	Regiment	Date of Appointment
John N. Schultz	New Jersey	Indiana	38th Infantry	July 28, 1866
	Transferred to Twenty-Fourth Infantry November 11, 1869; Resigned July 23, 1875			
D. Eglinton Barr	Scotland	New York	39th Infantry	July 28, 1866
	Transferred to Twenty-Fifth Infantry April 20, 1872; Resigned September 2, 1872			
George W. Pepper	Ireland	Ohio	40th Infantry	January 7, 1867
	Unassigned April 15, 1869; Assigned Tenth Cavalry December 21, 1870; Honorably discharged at own request December 31, 1870			
Elijah Guion	New York	Louisiana	41st Infantry	July 28, 1866
	Unassigned November 11, 1869; Assigned Tenth Cavalry December 31, 1870; Died January 17, 1879			
John C. Jacobi	Poland	Connecticut	9th Cavalry	March 9, 1867
	Retired July 29, 1868; Died February 9, 1874;			
Washington M. Grimes	Ohio	Ohio	10th Cavalry	February 7, 1867
	Resigned March 19, 1869			

---

121 Earl F. Stover, *Up from Handymen: The United States Army Chaplaincy, 1865–1920* (Washington, DC: The Office of Chief of Chaplains, 1977), 88. For relevant background on African Americans and early Christianity review Lamm, *Five Black Preachers*, 9–56.

Black Chaplains

In 1884, both these factors played a part in the appointment of Henry V. Plummer, the first Black chaplain to receive a commission in the US Army. In this instance, he would join the Ninth Cavalry. Born on June 30, 1844, Plummer's lot was that of formerly enslaved field worker in Prince George County, Maryland. The Civil War offered a means to break his chains of bondage. During that conflict, Plummer joined the US Navy. He served for 16 months until his honorable discharge during the summer of 1865. While in the navy, he learned to read and write. Thereafter, Plummer continued his education as best he could, while working as a night watchman in a Washington DC post office. Plummer managed to save the funds from this job and his outside income as a political worker that enabled him to attend Wayland Seminary. In addition: 'Before, during and after his course of study at the seminary, he served as a Baptist pastor or missionary in Maryland and Washington, DC'[122]

Based upon these varied experiences, Plummer secured letters of recommendation from numerous clergymen and significantly, one from Frederick Douglass to support his bid for a chaplaincy. When white Chaplain Charles C. Pierce resigned from the Ninth, Plummer acted and secured the appointment. With the shepherd's crooks of a chaplain upon his shoulder straps, he reported to his first military billet at Fort Riley, Kansas.

Upon Plummer's arrival, the July 12, 1884 edition of the local Junction City *Union* noted the clergyman 'well merits the office given to him.' The new member of Fort Riley's garrison soon found ample work to occupy his days. Typical of other military chaplains of the time, beyond his religious ministrations, he served as superintendent of post schools as well as managed the fort's bakery. His first year in Kansas passed with considerable success in all areas of responsibility, so much so that he drew favorable attention from another newspaper correspondent. The reporter attended one of the chaplain's services where he hear, 'one of the best sermons and prayers' he could remember from any preacher.[123]

In 1885, Plummer transferred to Wyoming with the Ninth Cavalry. There, the chaplain remained dedicated to the educational needs of his soldier-students. He made a number of important recommendations aimed at improvements, not the least of which was a request for adequate funds to purchase supplies and equipment, as well as establish a 'Bureau of Education and Literature' to oversee army wide standards for books and furnishings to outfit the enlisted men's schools and post libraries.

Ever ready to take on more challenges, Plummer joined the 'Chaplain's Movement' the brainchild of Post Chaplain Orville J. Nave of Fort Omaha, Nebraska. By 1891, Nave called for his 34 counterparts to meet at Leavenworth, Kansas. A half dozen of his colleagues responded, Plummer among them. At their sessions: 'They made three resolutions that dealt with the sale or use of alcoholic beverages.'[124]

At Fort Robinson, Nebraska, he also oversaw the publication of the short-lived post newspaper, which in one issue carried the recipe for a hefty, liquor-based libation served at the officers' mess, dubbed 'Fort Robinson Punch.' While a crusader against liquor, the paper printed the contents

---

122 Earl F. Stover, *Chaplain Henry V. Plummer, His Ministry and His Court Martial* (Lincoln, NE: Nebraska Historical Society, 1975), 1.
123 As reported in *A&NJ*, November 29, 1884, 342.
124 Stover, *Chaplain Henry V. Plummer*, 5–6.

Born into enslavement, during the Civil War, Kentuckian Allen Allensworth escaped and eventually served with the United States Navy. He then went on to obtain an impressive education. Allensworth's credentials led to a chaplaincy with the Twenty-Fourth Infantry. He retired as a lieutenant colonel, the first African American to achieve this grade in the US armed forces. (Courtesy John P. Langellier)

that included champagne to finish the concoction. Ironically, alcohol contributed to Plummer's undoing in the military. Allegedly, on June 2, 1894, he took part in a promotion celebration at the quarters of Sergeant Major Jeremiah Jones, where he was accused of drinking, supplying liquor to enlisted men, using vulgar language and engaging in other disgraceful conduct. These complaints came from Saddler Sergeant Robert Benjamin, an individual whom the chaplain previously had disciplined for failure to perform duties connected with Fort Riley's bakery. Perhaps a long simmering grudge caused Benjamin to turn on Plummer. In addition, the post commander at Fort Robinson distrusted Plummer.

Both that officer and the regimental commander evidently viewed the clergyman as a disruptive force. Suspecting Plummer of distributing a circular to the troops at that installation, which spoke out against discrimination in nearby Crawford, Nebraska, and believing the chaplain penned anonymous editorials about 'racial injustices' experienced by the Black troops, Plummer's superiors pressed charges against their subordinate. They considered Plummer a 'disturbing element' within the command. More damning, they accused him of conduct unbecoming an officer.[125] After an 11-day hearing, the court pronounced him guilty. Just as had been true for Flipper and Greene, Plummer's dismissal brought an abrupt end to his promising military career.

The next African American man of the cloth to assume a regimental chaplaincy, Allen Allensworth, hailed from Kentucky. Like Plummer, he had been enslaved before the Civil War,

---

125 Stover, *Up from Handymen*, 89–90.

escaped from his bondage and fled north. For a time, he served with the Illinois Volunteers and assisted with hospital work. Eventually, he also joined the United States Navy. Before war's end, he was a petty officer.

As a young lad before the war, Allensworth's thirst for knowledge caused him to learn the illegal arts of reading and writing while 'playing school' with a slave owner's child. He continued to seek self-improvement in post-Civil War civilian life.[126] After a brief time with the Freedman's Bureau, Allensworth entered school to complete a degree in divinity. With his studies completed, the minister turned his full attention to preaching. By 1885, when a vacancy for chaplain of the Twenty-Fourth Infantry opened, Allensworth set about to secure his commission.

Allensworth realized that he must gain political support for his cause. Mustering his allies, he wrote to President Grover Cleveland, a Democrat who briefly held the presidency during a long period dominated by the Republicans. In his carefully worded letter to the commander in chief, Allensworth stated, 'a number of my Democratic friends, who desire to strengthen your administration among the colored people, particularly in the south and to show the good feelings which exist and is growing between the two races, have encouraged me to ask for an appointment.' Allensworth suggested he could, 'secure good discipline and gentlemanly conduct among the soldiers.' Further, he felt that such an appointment would demonstrate the administration's support of deserving, able men from the Black community. Given that Southern Democrats of this period tended to be no friend to African Americans, this final statement might have struck a resounding chord. Here was a potential means to secure the Black vote.

Allensworth assured Cleveland that he relished the 'opportunity to show, in behalf of the race, that a Negro can be an officer and a gentleman.' Allensworth's carefully reasoned concluding remarks reflected the bias he realized existed. He ended: 'I know where the official ends and where the Social life begins and therefore gaurded [sic] against social intrusion … and am prepared to gaurd [sic] against allowing myself in any position to give offense.'

Mindful of the extant powerful color line, once Reverend Allensworth actually secured his appointment as chaplain, he continually balanced his own vision of the future for African Americans with the harsh political and social realities of his times. This he did from the outset. Thereafter, his record remained impeccable, yet often required caution.

After his 1886 appointment, news appeared in such announcements as one printed in a paper from his native state, The story indicated:

> Rev. Allen Allensworth the well-known colored minister and politician of Bowling Green was accepted as chaplain of the Twenty-Fourth Infantry … This is the first colored appointment given to Kentucky and there is only one other colored man who is a commissioned officer in the army Henry. V. Plumber [sic], of Maryland and is stationed at Fort McKinney, Wyoming Territory.[127]

Allensworth, the article went on to say, was:

---

126 The basis of the narrative and sources for all quotations found in this biographical sketch were drawn from John P. Langellier and Alan M. Osur, *Chaplain Allen Allensworth and the Twenty-Fourth Infantry 1886–1906* (Tucson: Tucson Corral of the Westerners, 1980).
127 *Semi-weekly South Kentuckian* (Hopkinsville) June 1, 1886.

… a good speaker very ready-witted and a hard worker. In speaking of his appointment yesterday he said: 'I feel very much honored at being selected for this place and feel the appointment was secured through the intercession of my white friends. I have worked hard to try and elevate the colored race, always teaching one doctrine – that when a colored man displays refinement and intelligence the whites will surely recognize it.'

In an unusual aside, the paper mentioned: 'Mrs. A.V. Starbird, Mr. Allensworth's old mistress, joined in the petition for his appointment … and he was a servant in her family for several years.' Adding to the strange mix, the article divulged Reverend Allensworth had 'also been engaged in preparing a book entitled "The Bright Side of Slavery," which he contemplates publishing in a few months.' The manuscript, however, never reached print. It seems to have been lost, perhaps on purpose if he rethought the implications of such a piece.

What is known, despite the constraints Allensworth faced, his two decades in uniform found him a constant bearer of the double-edged sword of a man of God and mentor for his martial congregation. In the latter instance, while at Fort Bayard, New Mexico, he prepared one of the first army manuals on education for enlisted personnel. He proved innovative and diligent in this and all his endeavors and as a disciple of Booker T. Washington in his devotion to industrial training.

In this pursuit, he received personal leave to attend 'the National Educational Association, of which he is a director,' said one newspaper account. The article, which unabashedly proselytized military service at length indicated 'young men who sought to distinguish themselves on a preparatory field for a successful career can find it in the Army that in the army as in civil life there is room at the top for all who reach it.' After extolling the virtues of spending five or 10 years in uniform, the reporter advised, 'our young men of a patriotic turn of mind to write to the Chaplain at Fort Bayard N. M. for further information on the subject.'[128]

Later, the chaplain took leave from the regiment on an unusual detail to be present 'at the world's Columbian exposition.' He remained at this prestigious, highly visible international fair in Chicago for nearly nine months before his return to the Twenty-Fourth.[129] At least one newspaper derided his posting. It questioned: 'Among the thirty army officers detailed for duty at the world's fair is Captain Allen Allensworth, colored, of the 24th infantry. Army officers and the general public are wondering what possible duty an army chaplain would be called upon to perform at Chicago during the big show?'[130]

Regardless of this snipe, the chaplain once again departed from the regiment, this time during the Spanish American War, when the clergyman turned army recruiter. After the Twenty-Fourth triumphantly came back to the post it had occupied before overseas deployment – Fort Douglas in Salt Lake City, Utah – once more, their spiritual leader soon left for yet a second temporary recruiting stint.[131]

128 *Appeal: A National Afro-American Newspaper* (Saint Paul, MN) July 26, 1890. After this Chaplain Allensworth spent time in his native Kentucky, which was the first time in three years, before returning to Fort Bayard.' *Hopkinsville Kentuckian*, August 22, 1890.
129 *Evening Star* (Washington, DC) February 17, 1893; October 31, 1893.
130 *Chariton Courier* (Keytesville, MO) March 3, 1893.
131 *Salt Lake Herald*, April 26, 1899.

While keen on bringing in new and impressive blood to the regiment, the chaplain never lost sight of his religious obligations nor his determination to share pride in a rich Black heritage with his congregation. For instance, he played a significant part during 'a very impressive and appropriate programme … rendered at the post chapel … in honor of Mr. Frederick Douglass.' The regimental band 'furnished music' followed by Allensworth's delivering 'a very fine address.'[132]

Additionally, the avid educator looked to varied means of conveying his messages whether sacred or secular. As an example, during his lecture on 'Old Testament Characters,' he illustrated his text by means of a stereopticon presented to the regiment by a 'Philadelphia philanthropist.'[133]

He, however, required no extra means to make his message clear in that he was a confident orator. Nowhere was this more evident than at a gathering of the National African American Press Association that met in St. Paul, Minnesota where he appeared among a lengthy list of speakers. Each of these worthies received no more than three minutes to deliver, 'rapid-fire speeches' on 'The Outlook for the Race.' Why the chaplain, who was not a journalist, attended this convocation remains a mystery, although he published *The Kiss*, a title and its contents evidently having been lost like his slavery manuscript.[134]

More typically, the chaplain tended to his military assignments. Once, he even would be singled out for an unprecedented honor near the end of his tenure at Fort Douglas. When the 'entire garrison turned … to witness the presentation of the flag handed the regiment by the White Rose society of New York City.' The flag was to be handed to the chaplain and one of the regiment's senior captains. In turn, they passed the flag to the regimental color sergeant followed by a grand review. Fulfilling his prestigious charge: 'Chaplain Allensworth, with an orderly bearing the colors, advanced from the flagstaff, halted about faced and received the flag from the orderly. At the command "backward march," the orderly stepped back five feet, the chaplain lowered the flag and the casing was removed by the orderly the chaplain again about faced, unfurled the flag and presented it' to the assembled honor guard.[135]

The martial pomp came in advance of the regiment's next transfer to the Philippines where all four of the regiments with a Black rank and file soon sailed. In early May, as the first stopover on the way to the islands, the chaplain encamped with the Twenty-Fourth for their temporary marshalling at the Presidio of San Francisco. After his arrival there, his spouse briefly joined him.[136]

While the regiment remained in the Bay Area, in recognition of the respect the Allensworth had gained within the Black community at large, the chaplain periodically accepted invitations to preach at local churches. Sometimes he made 'appeals to his race' in sermons such as one where, 'he called attention to the fact that the negro had fought in all of the great wars of the nation and has won for himself and to the nation of which he is a part, an imperishable record.' He emphasized, 'the splendid work done by the colored troops at San Juan and other notable fights in the late war with Spain. He added, 'they were again called to go to Manila' where they

---

132 *Ibid.*, February 16, 1899.
133 *Ibid.*, February 19, 1899.
134 *Appeal: A National Afro-American Newspaper* (Saint Paul, MN) February 10, 1900; February 17, 1900; and February 24, 1899, all included Allensworth in an alphabetic listing of African American authors and the titles of their work.
135 *Salt Lake Herald*, March 18, 1899.
136 *Salt Lake Herald*, May 2, 1899, and May 4, 1899.

were expected to 'bear a share in the conflict and he said they were ready. That whenever a call upon them was made they responded "Here I am. send me."'

Further, the chaplain called on the young men in the pews 'to educate themselves, intellectually, morally and religiously; to become men of good, sound moral character, honest in all things and above all honest to themselves and their race. He impressed this advice on their minds as being a great duty which he hoped every man would fulfill.' Similarly, he urged the women in attendance, 'to maintain pure and virtuous characters, without which the standard of the race could not be maintained with a degree of dignity which it ought to have as a race.'[137] At another congregation, he took as his text as the 'Hidden Principles of Influence.'[138] This was only a few weeks after he had marched in San Francisco's 4th of July parade with the regiment's first battalion and band.[139] Towards the end of the month, Allensworth and the Twenty-Fourth Infantry were in step once again. They proceeded to *City of Para* and boarded the steamer for the Philippines.[140]

As with most of the men going abroad, his family remained behind. That separation soon ended. Not long after landing in the Philippines, the chaplain experienced health problems. His medical condition resulted in his sailing eastward to the Bay Area. There, he rejoined the family at the Presidio of San Francisco. He remained at the post through October 25, 1900. Then the Allensworths steamed across the bay to Fort McDowell on Angel Island. Just before departing, he addressed another civilian flock at the Bethel AME (African Methodist Episcopal) Church between Powell and Jackson.[141]

The chaplain subsequently took up a temporary assignment on Angel Island. His medical leave eventually extended for many months.[142] The reason for his unanticipated absence resulted from infirmities that required him to use a cane in order to remain ambulatory. On January 21, 1901, his physical condition worsened. As reported: 'while walking the cane used to support his left knee slipped and he fell, fracturing the patella of his left knee.' Despite the setback and a good deal of pain, 'during the Chaplain's stay at Angel Island he never lost sight of his commitment to the education within the Twenty-fourth.' This passion manifested itself in the form of his securing of '2,000 pounds of reading matter and a quantity of stationery, which he … forwarded to his regiment in the Philippines.'[143] This effort indicated a much higher level of literacy than had been the norm in times past.

Finally, on March 15, 1901, the chaplain's health improved to the degree that he could rejoin his regiment.[144] Before that, while at Angel Island, his temporary responsibility as a post chaplain presented an exceptional example of crossing the color line. There, by one account, he preached, 'a very interesting and instructive picture sermon' to white members of the garrison, both officers and men. Supposedly his homily was 'thoroughly enjoyed by all.'[145]

---

137 *San Francisco Call*, June 19, 1899.
138 *Ibid.,*, July 2, 1899.
139 *Ibid.*, July 4, 1899.
140 *Hawaiian Star*, July 21, 1899.
141 *San Francisco Call*, September 16, 1900.
142 *Salt Lake Herald*, November 11, 1900; *A&NJ*, November 10, 1900, 251.
143 *A&NJ*, February 2, 1901, 552. Once back in the Philippines he sustained another injury that added to his already frail health. *Evening Star* (Washington, DC) April 16, 1904, Part 2.
144 *Evening Star* (Washington, DC) December 6, 1900; *A&NJ*, December 8, 1900, 347; *Salt Lake Herald*, December 9, 1900.
145 *A&NJ*, November 24, 19, 304.

Beside this one of many distinctions, because of his service in the Civil War, Allensworth occasionally took part in veterans' programs. For instance, while in Salt Lake he was selected by Utah Department of the Grand Army of the Republic (GAR) as alternate delegate to the national encampment, which was an annual convention of this influential veterans' organization.[146] He also remained a party loyal. In 1904, the well-traveled chaplain attended the Republican national convention in Chicago.[147] Political contacts and his Civil War active duty combined with steadfast service, brought a promotion to major. A Salt Lake newspaper article noted this advancement came about 'under the new act of Congress' which resulted in the fact that Allensworth 'jumped' every other army chaplain and 'was made the senior major.' Revealing support for the move, the reporter deemed Allensworth, 'one of the most intelligent men and best speakers in the corps of chaplains … He is at present the only colored man in the regular army holding the rank of major.'[148]

Adding to the discussion, another observer predicted this step would end with Chaplain Allensworth likely retiring with the rank of lieutenant colonel.[149] That forecast provoked a salvo of refutations arguing why this would not be the case, nor supposedly was it the US Army's intent under the new promotion scheme for chaplains to advance to any higher grade. Purportedly, even if Chaplain Allensworth's service in the Union Navy:

> … seemed to entitle him to advancement to a lieutenant colonelcy upon his retirement if the War Department had known of his civil war record before his advancement it is probable, he would not have been advanced to a major's rank. This advancement would have been withheld until his retirement and the right of a chaplain to act in a lieutenant colonelcy would not have been discussed.[150]

Several months of speculation and wrangling ensued. Rumors that President Theodore Roosevelt had 'determined that chaplains should enjoy the rank of major and not be promoted to lieutenant colonel,' stated the *Washington Times*.[151] Even as Roosevelt's administration wrestled with

---

146 *Salt Lake Herald*, February 24, 1899. *Salt Lake Tribune*, May 31, 1904, listed Allensworth as a member of the G.A.R. J.B. McKeen Post No. 1 in Salt Lake since the founding of the organization.
147 *Appeal: A National Afro-American Newspaper* (Saint Paul, MN) June 25, 1904.
148 As the *Deseret Evening News* (Salt Lake, UT) August 29, 1904, Last Edition. Also see *Evening Star* (Washington, DC) June 14, 1904; *Washington Times*, June 14, 1904; *Omaha Daily Bee*, June 23, 1904; *Appeal: A National Afro-American Newspaper* (Saint Paul, MN) June 25, 1904. For background on the change of policy to allow chaplains to advance to the grade of major read *Evening Star* (Washington, DC) April 16, 1904. 'SOLDIER PREACHERS Proposition to Give Some Rank of Major.' RG 94_e25_391443_chaplains_in_service_1901 (2), NARA lists all US chaplains citing their assignments and denominations during 1901 including Allensworth with the Twenty-Fourth Infantry and his Baptist affiliation as opposed to Anderson, Prioleau, and Steward, who were African American Episcopal. The dates of appointments also appear indicating Allensworth was fifth in seniority of all army chaplains. Further, RG 94, Records of the Adjutant General's Office_e25_1176413_ chaplains _denominations_1906 (1), NARA indicated the same affiliations remained with Anderson, Prioleau, and Steward being listed as A.M.E. and Chaplain Gladden who had followed Allensworth as being a Baptist. In that year there were 120 applications for but three vacancies in the chaplains' corps.
149 *Washington Times*, August 1, 1904.
150 *Ibid.*, August 7, 1904; *St. Louis Republic*, August 8, 1904, repeated the story.
151 *Ibid.*, July 30, 1904.

the matter, Allensworth soldiered on as best as he could. Nonetheless, ill health continued to plague him, although not inhibiting him from travel to such places as St. Paul and Fort Snelling, Minnesota as well as Chicago. For the most part, he remained on duty with the Twenty-Fourth, which by that time, headquartered at Fort Harrison, Montana.[152]

Finally, during the summer of 1905, orders called for this 'oldest chaplain on the active list in the army' to leave his post after two decades and proceed to his home to await retirement as an end to his remarkable climb from enslavement to a nationally recognized religious figure and educator. At that juncture, he again took leave. He passed through Salt Lake for a 'vacation in East and was registered at the White House for a visit.'[153] Was it possible that he thought he could meet with Roosevelt to persuade the chief executive to reverse the president's supposed stand against chaplains advancing beyond major?

Regardless of the intent of this trip, he eventually would be placed on the retired list as of April 7, 1906, 'with the advanced rank of lieutenant colonel on account of his civil war record. He has the distinction of holding the highest rank of any colored man in the army.' Just before the chaplain retired, he numbered among the last 65 Union veterans who remained on duty as officers out of the legions who continued to serve after the conflict's conclusion.[154]

As Allensworth awaited his honorable discharge and promotion to be processed, the family began to settle at their new Los Angeles home. Even before retiring in Southern California, preliminary discussion about a colonization 'scheme' in Colorado drew notice.[155] One of these articles tinged with racist overtones ran, 'another black cloud is rising over yonder: A self-governing negro colony, of which there are but thirteen in the entire country, will be established in Colorado within the next year. A tract of 10,000 acres will be purchased to set up the black crest of Ethiopia in the Arkansas valley.' A trio of men headed by, 'Allen Allensworth, chaplain of the Twenty-Fifth [sic] United States infantry' who was to serve as 'president of the colony' Reverend J. E. Ford, pastor of Zion Baptist church was to be vice president and John Adams, editor of the *Western Appeal*, was slated for secretary.[156] This preliminary concept gave way to seeking a site in the Golden State. That effort occasioned the founding of a Black, self-sustaining community in the San Joaquin Valley that bore Allensworth's name and long years later, became a California state park.[157]

In addition to efforts for the establishment of a town, he previously participated in Los Angeles politics and duties as a citizen. Allensworth would be called on as one of 60 jurors for duty in the superior court. Such a summons would have been unheard of during his youth.[158] Further, when in 1906 the devasting earthquake and fire struck San Francisco, he volunteered as member of a committee of Black citizens dedicated to raising funds for victim relief.[159]

---

152 *St. Paul Globe*, June 19, 1904, and November 23, 1904; *Appeal: A National Afro-American Newspaper* (Saint Paul, MN) December 17, 1904.
153 *Salt Lake Tribune*, July 20, 1905.
154 *Omaha Daily Bee*. March 25, 1906.
155 *Colorado Statesman* (Denver) March 31, 1905.
156 *Las Vegas Daily Optic* (NM) April 14, 1905.
157 *Broad Ax* (Salt Lake) June 23, 1906. Also, *Los Angeles Herald*, August 2, 1908, 7, Part 2 ran an article headlined as 'Negro Colony to Be Formed' and indicated the role Allensworth would play.
158 See for example the *Los Angeles Herald*., October 5, 1906, 'NEGRO REPUBLICANS ORGANIZE FOR LOCAL AND STATE ELECTIONS. Executive committee included Allen Allensworth 'the retired chaplain' U.S.A.' Los Angeles Herald, September 4, 1909, 2, Part 2.
159 *Los Angeles Herald*, April 21, 1906.

Moreover, justly proud of his status as a Civil War veteran, he periodically appeared at various integrated GAR events as an honored guest. He occasionally offered invocations, or provided Lincoln's Birthday remarks, in one case alongside another speaker – an ex-confederate officer.[160] From time to time, he returned to the pulpit. His sermons took such titles as the 'Five Manly Virtues,' 'Lincoln and the Colored Soldier' and a discourse on army life in which interestingl,y he opposed the post canteen that supposedly had been instituted as a haven for off duty soldiers designed to keep them away from neighboring civilian dens of iniquity.[161]

This negative view of an official US Army policy was not the only time Lieutenant Colonel Allensworth took a stance that ran contrary to military chapter and verse. Conversely, he endorsed the army's handling of the 1906 Brownsville Affair. He personally sought to convince African Americans 'of the justice and necessity of the action of the [War] Department' seemed contradictory to decades of support for Black soldiers. This stand spoke volumes about his complex loyalty to the US Army on one hand and to the men whom he had served as minister and mentor on the other side of the coin.[162]

Allensworth typically had to tread carefully. Throughout his chaplaincy, he regularly addressed the restrictive racial mores of his era as best as he could under cumbersome circumstances. He took advantage of the measure of opportunity afforded Blacks in the military where a greater semblance of equality existed, although limited in many ways, than could be gained from any other institutions or within the nation as a whole. His death on September 14, 1914, in Monrovia, California, after being struck by a motorcycle, brought down the curtain on a noteworthy exemplar, who truly lived up to his philosophy of influencing others, 'through a tolerant, genial and kindly attitude toward all men.' In so doing, he gained respect from many Black and white contemporaries with whom he came in contact [163]

While Chaplain Allensworth received considerable praise and much deserved contemporary recognition, his fellow military clergyman, who joined the Twenty-Fifth Infantry in 1891, was no less admired. Born on April 17, 1843, the apply christened Theophilus Gould Steward traced his lineage as a free Black to pre-Revolutionary War roots. Steward's extraordinary resume before, during and after his days in the US Army revealed a life of achievement from his days spent as a school teacher; to work in a bank; extensive travel including to Haiti; graduation at the top of his class in divinity school; several notable and successful civilian pastorates; performance as a missionary; and at the end of his military career, he accepted a prestigious professorship and position as an administrator at Wilberforce University. He served there until his death on January 11, 1924.[164] It is little wonder that he has been the subject of two thoughtful biographies whose titles reveal his passionate championship of racial justice.[165]

160 *Ibid.*, December 31, 1905; May 31, 1908, Part 2; February 13, 1910, Part 2
161 *Ibid.*, January 27, 1907, Part 3; February 13, 1906; November 25, 1905.
162 Allen Allensworth to Military Secretary, December 24, 1906, AGO, File 670, ACP RG 94, A. Allensworth, NARA.
163 Colonel A.C. Markley, Letter of Commendation, August 2, 1902, AGO, File 670, ACP RG 94, A. Allensworth, NARA. Another white officer, Brigadier General James A. Buchanan, made it a point to seek out his old comrade when visiting Southern California upon his return from the Philippines. *Los Angeles Herald*, August 1, 1906,
164 RG 94, AGO, File 4634, ACP RG 94, T.G. Steward, NARA; Schubert and Schubert, *On the Trail*, 275; Lamm, *Five Black Preachers in Army Blue*, 193–226.
165 William Seraile, *Voice of Dissent: Theophilus Gould Steward (1843–1924) and Black America* (Brooklyn, NY: Carlson Publishing, Inc., 1991); and Albert G. Miller, *Elevating the Race: Theophilus G. Steward,*

The highly learned, prolific author, Chaplain Theophilus G. Steward, assumed the chaplaincy of the Twenty-Fifth Infantry. During August 1891, he reported to regimental headquarters at Fort Assiniboine, Montana. Among his extensive writings was an optimistic pronouncement that he looked forward to a future where there would: 'be no more colored soldiers in the army of the United States ... but simply Americans – all.' (Courtesy Library of Congress)

Steward also received mention as a 'literary worker, whose productions find ready acceptance with editors of magazines and leading journals. Such men as these verify the statements that the mental development required in military tactics enables the soldier to enter the literary world and successfully compete with the most logical writer of the present day.'[166] The *Cleveland Gazette* of August 8, 1891, further proclaimed that he was, 'one of the most scholarly ministers of the A.M.E. Church.'

Assuredly, this Army chaplain proved a prolific, powerful writer, whose prose often supported his soldier flock. In fact, among his articles was the 'The Colored American Soldier' for *The United Service* in April of 1894, 'Morality of Negro' for the *Social Economist* in 1895 and other short submissions that set the stage for a more ambitious effort. In 1904, Steward's *The Colored Regulars in the United States Army With a Sketch of the History of the Colored American and an Account of His Services in the Wars of the Country from the Period of the Revolutionary War to 1899* represented a milestone in the historiography related to the Black military experience in the United States. This publication reflected the chaplain's continual advocacy for the 'four regiments of colored troops in the service' that had demonstrated 'during peace the high character or good order and military discipline that their friends expected and that in the encounters with the Indians they have shown a skill and bravery equal to white troops.'[167]

Furthermore, Chaplain Steward's martial ministry revealed one more rather interesting detail. Often, family members, particularly the spouses of chaplains, greatly aided them. This assuredly proved true for Steward. In 1866, he wed his first wife, the former Elizabeth Gladden. Regrettably, she had little time to join in his work. She died on November 2, 1893, just a few years after the couple began their days with the army. His second marriage, in 1896, to Dr. Susan McKinney, who had been a physician at Wilberforce, again blessed him with another amazing life partner. The Indianapolis *Freeman* for April 30, 1898 referred to Dr. Steward as, 'a thorough scholar' who also was 'a musician.' Indeed, she was this and more. Among her other accomplishments the doctor was, 'one of the first women in the North America to graduate from medical school.'[168]

Yet another individual connected to Wilberforce received a chaplaincy in the 1890s. Born on May 15, 1856, into enslavement in Charleston, South Carolina, George W. Prioleau, completed his early education in the public schools of his native city, then went on to Cardoza Military Academy, Clafin University and Wilberforce University. A member of the A.M.E. Church, prior to his commissioning, from 1889 to 1895, Reverend Prioleau taught as a professor of Pastoral Theology and Homiletics at Payne Theological Seminary, Wilberforce University. Once appointed an army chaplain, he traveled to Fort Robinson, Nebraska. There, he reported to the Ninth Cavalry's regimental headquarters. When the United States went to war with Spain, as the case with Chaplains Allensworth and Steward, he set off on special recruiting service. This meant he did not embark for Cuba with the unit. He did sail to the Philippines, however, where he spent two tours of duty with the Ninth Cavalry.[169] Prioleau later transferred to the Tenth Cavalry with postings along the United States-Mexico border.

Black Theology, and the Making of an African American Civil Society, 1865–1924 (Knoxville: The University of Tennessee Press, 2003).
166 Cephas C. Bateman, 'A Group of Army Authors,' *The Californian* 4 (October, 1893): 692–93.
167 *Fort Worth Daily Gazette*, May 6, 1894. Mailable Edition, Pt. 2.
168 Schubert, *Voices of the Buffalo Soldiers*, 173.
169 *Colored American Magazine* 15 (April 1909): 223–24. Interestingly the headline of this article read: 'Sky Pilots of Our Colored Troops.'

George W. Prioleau followed Reverend Plummer as the Ninth Cavalry's spiritual leader and educator. He defined his role with the regiment as fostering 'agreeable associations' of homelife amid 'an atmosphere pregnated with evil and sin.' (Courtesy John P. Langellier)

Throughout his chaplaincy Reverend Prioleau perceived his main mission entailed encouragement of his enlisted congregation, whom he viewed as being separated from 'agreeable associations' of their families and homes to be thrust into bachelor barracks amid 'an atmosphere pregnated [*sic*] with evil and sin.'[170] Elsewhere, he privately shared his philosophy of the rather tenuous perch on which he balanced as a Black commissioned officer standing between his white peers and his African American enlisted congregation. He saw the stratified and segregated society of a nineteenth century military post as a compartmentalized world:

1. Commissioned officers and families to themselves.
2. Chaplains and families to themselves, with a few exceptions.
3. Enlisted men and families to themselves, with a few exceptions.
4. White civilian employees and their families to themselves.'

Even through this restrictive lens, Chaplain Prioleau maintained that Black and white enlisted men drew 'no social line of distinction.'[171] His contention seemed more a hopeful promise than a reflection of reality, although he was not blind to the racism that surrounded him and Blacks in general.

One thoughtful biographer's analysis of this inspirational individual concluded Prioleau, 'had been born into slavery but had risen to the ranks of the upper-middle-class black community' to become 'one of only a handful of commissioned army officers' of African ancestry. While realizing, 'patriotic service and military duty would not erase the color line in the minds of many white Americans,' he nonetheless could be viewed as 'intelligent, well educated, articulate and obviously gifted man and leader,' despite frustrations and slights. He saw the army as a vital means for the advancement of Blacks. After transferring regiments, this time to the Twenty-Fifth Infantry

---

170 G.W. Prioleau, 'Is the Chaplain's Work a Necessity?' in T.G. Steward, ed., *Active Service, or, Religious Work Among US soldiers. A series of Papers by Our Post and Regimental Chaplains* (New York: US Army Aid Association, 1897), 27–28.
171 As quoted by Stover, *Up From Handymen*, 91.

In 1898, when the Tenth Cavalry departed Fort Assiniboine, Montana for Chickamauga, Georgia and then sailed on to Cuba, regimental Chaplain William T. Anderson remained behind at the fort. He assumed a variety of additional duties, including as acting post commander – a first for an African American in the US Army. (Courtesy Library of Congress)

at Schofield Barracks, Hawaii, he played a key part in raising $3,200 for the relief of the Black victims of the violent East St. Louis, Illinois race riot.[172] Retiring as a major (promoted August 9, 1917) on May 15, 1920, Prioleau devoted the last seven years of his life in Los Angeles where the ever-indefatigable humanitarian and true believer labored to establish a new A.M.E. church in his neighborhood.[173]

Another 'sky-pilot' who weathered enslavement and subsequently became associated with the pivotal Wilberforce University was born in Seguin, Texas, on August 20, 1859. William T. Anderson attended Wilberforce before moving on to Howard University, Washington, DC and Cleveland Homeopathic Medical Clinic where he was, 'the first of a very large class' to receive his MD. Further, on June 27, 1896, Wilberforce granted him a Doctor of Divinity degree making him, 'perhaps the most educated African American chaplain of his era.'[174]

Anderson's academic credentials permitted him to carry on a medical practice while he simultaneously performed as pastor to several congregations of the A.M.E. Church including St. John's Church in Cleveland. It was there, in August 1897, based on his notable credentials, connections within the Republican Party and because of impressive supporters the likes of Booker T. Washington and the presidents of Howard and Wilberforce Universities, that he secured a commission.

Soon Reverend Dr. Anderson joined the Tenth Cavalry at Fort Assiniboine, Montana. Once on duty, he may have been surprised by the support of the regimental commander and adjutant along 'with the people in general' who stood behind his military vicarage and gave him the

172 *Crisis* 12 (July 1916): 117; (September 1916): 247.
173 Lamm, *Five Black Preachers in Army Blue*, 134–36; *US Army Register, 1924* (Washington, DC: US Government Printing Office, 1924), 748.
174 Lamm, *Five Black Preachers in Army Blue*, 149.

latitude to institute a weekly Thursday evening lyceum for the, 'intellectual, moral and social improvement of the non-commissioned officers.'[175]

In all these endeavors Anderson resembled his fellow Black army chaplains. Yet, he stood apart from his clergymen contemporaries in several ways. First, when the Tenth Cavalry departed in 1898, from Fort Assiniboine for combat in Cuba, he remained behind and shouldered the unprecedented tasks of holding the fort as post exchange officer, quartermaster and commissary while concurrently assuming command of the post. In so doing, he was the first known African American to command a US Army installation.[176] Not until nearly a decade later would Charles Young assume such a responsibility at Fort Huachuca, Arizona.

Beyond that, Anderson would be 'the only African American chaplain sent to a foreign land' during the Spanish American War. All the other Black chaplains remained stateside on recruiting duty. In this regard Anderson became one of the few chaplains who, 'for the first time … accompanied American troops into a land not contiguous to the United States' as official non-combatants defined by Articles I and II in accordance with the 1864 Geneva Convention.[177]

In Cuba Anderson witnessed the horrors of combat and pestilence that killed more troops from disease than those who succumbed to Spanish bullets.[178] Rather than recoiling, Anderson set to 'work on the field' achieving 'much praise from brother officers' for his ministry, use of his medical training, establishment of a post library, along with his deft handling of details as school inspector and chief of the sanitary operations for the Department of Manzanillo, Cuba. This last extraordinary delegation brought special mention in the reports of the departmental inspector general and his commanding officer. It was from such special commendations that after 10 years as captain, during August 1907 Anderson rose to major.

At that grade, his duties went beyond those strictly associated with chaplains. While at Fort William McKinley in the Philippines, he temporarily served as post treasurer. Later, he took charge of the United States morgue in Manila.[179] Mortuary records carried the names of nearly 8,000 soldiers, officers, marines, scouts, civilian employees and members of officers' families since the time the United States occupied the islands. The remains of soldiers and officers all had to be prepared, processed and transported home.[180]

Likewise, Anderson and his wife, Sada, returned to the United States, fortunately alive and well. They accompanied the Tenth Cavalry to Fort Ethan Allen, Vermont from where he retired on January 10, 1910. The couple set up household at Wilberforce followed by travel abroad. He remained active until age 85. The exemplary Christian soldier passed quietly on August 21, 1934. Veterans in his final home of Cleveland, Ohio named an American Legion post in his honor.[181]

While Anderson achieved much merited acknowledgement, another young clergyman joined the Black regulars to fill the void left by Lieutenant Colonel Allensworth's retirement.[182] South

---

175 William Anderson to Adjutant General, Department of Dakota, May 10, 1898, Selected ACP, AGO RG 94, WT Anderson, NARA.
176 Lamm, *Five Black Preachers in Army Blue*, 151.
177 Stover, *Up From Handymen*, 111.
178 Lamm, *Five Black Preachers in Army Blue*, 152.
179 RG395_e2683_box001_anderson_william (2), NARA.
180 *Colored American Magazine* 15 (April 1909): 224.
181 Lamm, *Five Black Preachers in Army Blue*, 157–8.
182 *Montana Plaindealer* (Helena) April 6, 1906. According to the *Colorado Statesman* (Denver) March 24, 1906: 'Now comes the first national appointment of the race from Colorado. The honors fall upon

Carolinian Washington W.E. Gladden was born on June 23, 1866. Nearly four decades later, on May 21, 1906, his appointment to the chaplaincy of the Twenty-Fourth Infantry capped his education at Western College in Macon, Missouri where he dual majored in science and theology. After pastoring several Baptist churches in neighboring Kansas, he traveled to Colorado Springs, Colorado. He gathered a large congregation and built a handsome new house of worship there. He and his spouse, the former Adelaide Louise Walker, joined the Twenty-Fourth Infantry in the Philippines after which, they went with the unit to Madison Barracks, New York.[183] According to one account, he soon began, 'doing good work for his regiment and race.'[184]

Upon his return with the Twenty-Fourth to the Philippines, in 1913 as a captain (where he remained for the next three years), an enlisted man validated this approbatory comment.[185] The anonymous individual observed the clergyman's effort in Manila gave, 'warm testimony' when the soldiers expressed the view that Chaplain Gladden was "solving the religious problem.' To illustrate his statement, he sent, 'a picture of a church service with 457 auditors, including Filipinos. 'Our Sunday school consists of four classes and the attendance is very large. The chaplain is well thought of and is carrying his good work on among the young men as well as the old. He is well known to all and is held in the highest esteem.'[186]

Not only did Chaplain Gladden accompany the Twenty-Fourth to the Philippines, but also, when the United States dispatched the regiment along with others to Mexico in 1916, like Chaplain Anderson during the Spanish American War, he accompanied the fighting forces abroad as a non-combatant. There he performed additional functions as postmaster and property office for the regiment.[187] With the conclusion of this final overseas deployment, orders dispatched him to an army retiring board at the Presidio of San Francisco, California. The chaplain's examination there subsequently led to his discharge due to medical disability in line of duty. On May 22, 1917, he left the army. He died in Los Angeles, California on March 11, 1922.[188]

One of the final members to be added to this exclusive fraternity of Black chaplains from the pre First World War era was Gallipolis, Ohio native Oscar J.W. Scott. Born on July 31, 1867, Scott attended public schools, which had been established there the year after his birth.

---

the honored shoulders of Rev. W. E. Gladden of Colorado Springs who was appointed Wednesday Chaplain of the 25th [sic] Infantry to succeed Chaplain Allen Allensworth retired. Rev Gladden was indorsed by every white and colored Baptist organization in the country and by all classes and kinds of men. Congressman Brooks has stood behind Rev. Gladden and left no stone unturned to see that his appointment was assured.'

183 RG 94_e541_birthrecords-gladden_washington (1), NARA.
184 *Colored American Magazine* 15 (April 1909): 224.
185 RG 94, Records of the Adjutant General's Office_e106_box03-gladden_washington (1). This same document showed he had been in the Philippines previously from September 1906 to February 1908 with the Twenty-Fourth Infantry and after that at Fort George Wright, Washington from October 1907 with the Twenty-Fifth Infantry. As an aside he states under special skills that he had 12 years' experience in stationary steam engineering, an atypical background for a chaplain.
186 *Crisis* 5 (March 1913): 225; and (April 1916): 284.
187 Stover, *Up from Handymen*, 173.
188 *Evening Star* (Washington, DC) April 14, 1917; *Army and Navy Register*, March 25, 1922, 277; Monroe N. Work, ed., *Negro Year Book: An Encyclopedia of the Negro 1921–1922* (Tuskegee: The Negro Year Book Publishing Company, 1922), 194; RG 94, Records of the Adjutant General's Office Chaplain Washington W. E. Gladden to the Adjutant General, U.S.A., Washington, D.C., August 2, 1910, AGODF No. 1549808, NARA.

After that, he received training at the Columbus Business College and the Defiance Normal College. Scott went on to graduate from the classical department of Ohio Wesleyan University. He undertook further education at Drew Theological Seminary as well as the Theological and Oratorical departments of the University of Denver. Scott ultimately obtained his Doctor of Divinity degree.

Before his appointment as a first lieutenant and the chaplaincy of the Twenty-Fifth Infantry, on April 17, 1907 (somewhat ironically by appointment of President Theodore Roosevelt in the aftermath of the Brownville Affair), Reverend Scott had pastored AME churches in Delaware, Ohio, at Madison, New Jersey, in Denver, Colorado's Shorter Chapel, as well as Allen Chapel, Kansas City, Missouri and Metropolitan Church, Washington, DC This last vicarage represented one of the largest Black churches in the nation during this time. It was that pulpit from which he would accept his commission with the Twenty-Fifth Infantry. The chaplain, his spouse and their three children traveled to Fort Macintosh, Texas. They soon packed again and this time, the destination was far away, 'Mindanao, Philippine Islands, the home of the warlike Moros.'[189]

Seven years later, he became a captain. After that, he served 'with his regiment in Texas in the Philippines in the State of Washington' and by 1914, in Hawaii. It was there that he came into his own, gaining a reputation as, 'a successful preacher' who 'worked hard to improve the social and physical condition of his soldiers.' He would be counted among the African American US Army chaplains who, 'almost without exception had so good a record for manliness and morality.'[190]

Like Chaplain Allensworth, Chaplain Scott selected Abraham Lincoln as a subject during February 1914. His address, titled 'Abraham Lincoln the Ideal American" was to be open to members of Schofield Barracks' YMCA and their guests. The announcement of this lecture included the positive perspective that, 'Because of Chaplain Scott's ability as a speaker the lecture promises to be of unusual interest.'[191] Evidently, he lived up to the advance press in that:

> The lecture was well attended and the chaplain, speaking straight from the shoulder, paid many glowing tributes to the martyred president. Interestingly little stories of the South cropped into his remarks. He touched lightly on slavery and in a forceful manner traced the life of Lincoln from a humble log cabin to a seat in the presidential chair.

One member in the audience was quoted as stating: 'I have heard many addresses on Abraham Lincoln, but the one delivered by Chaplain Oscar Scott at the YMCA last evening was by far the best I ever listened to.'[192]

Another time, the chaplain lectured from direct experience after having been asked to deliver an address about the recently deceased scion of Tuskegee in a presentation he called 'Booker T. Washington As I Knew Him.' He spoke authoritatively of his 'personal friend and of whom the

---

189 *Honolulu Star-Bulletin*, May 24, 1916, 2:30 Edition; *Indianapolis Recorder*, May 4, 1907; *A&NJ*, August 25, 1907, 1398; *Colored American Magazine* 15 (April 1909): 224; mydailysentinel.com/news/60432/black-history-month-the-relics-of-separate-but-equal.
190 *Crisis* 6 (December 1914), 67.
191 *Ibid.*, February 9, 1914, 2:30 Edition; February 11, 1914, 2:30.
192 *Ibid.*, February 13, 1914, 2:30 Edition; February 13, 1914, 3:30.

chaplain could reveal many details.'¹⁹³ Appropriately, when as 'a part in the movement of people of the United States to erect a memorial for the late Booker T. Washington, boys of the 25th Infantry, Schofield Barracks … raised $125' and planned further donations, Chaplain Scott took 'charge of the contributions for the memorial' that was to take 'the form of a beautiful building rather than a mere monument of stone.'¹⁹⁴

Although personally inspiring, he went beyond Chaplain Allensworth in his employment of visual aids. Occasionally he incorporated silent films into his service including the three-reel *The Trials of Joseph* proceeded with sacred music provided by Chief Musician Leslie King as just one instance of weaving the regimental band into his impactful church services.¹⁹⁵

During the Yuletide holidays in 1915, the chaplain noted every man, woman and child at Schofield Barracks would have a Christmas present under the three trees set up at the post.¹⁹⁶ At Easter of the following year, as another mark of his success and popularity, he 'conducted Easter services in the regimental amusement hall' where 'fully 1800 men, many of them accompanied by their families attending. Sacred selections were played by the regimental band and a program of Easter music was presented. "Believing the Easter Story" was the theme of Chaplain Scott's address.'¹⁹⁷ Once again, 'the regimental band conducted by chief musician Leslie King' set the tone. Afterwards, Chaplain Scott, 'had the house darkened and the movie machine threw old familiar songs upon the screen' at what the headlines called 'a gathering that will go down in history as one of the greatest ever held in this regiment, not only from the stand point of numbers present but also from its impressiveness, due to the splendid manner in which the program was carried out by the chaplain.'¹⁹⁸

Aware of the moving picture's power, little wonder that Scott appeared in the forefront to ban the Honolulu screening of the prejudicial *Birth of A Nation*. He challenged that the movie did 'an injustice to the negroes showings scenes which, though they may have occurred in fact, are not typical.' Scott contended: 'the picture, stirs race feeling and would have a bad effect on the men of the 25th Infantry.' Additionally, he took part in patriotic gatherings, officiated at weddings, emerged as the principal force behind a successful literary society for the men and took charge, 'of the much neglected graveyard of the post and turned it into a veritable garden spot.'¹⁹⁹

Both the chaplain and his spouse made a marked impression on the regiment and were a popular couple.²⁰⁰ Among other things, Ethel Stafford Prioleau lent her musical talents, along with arranging entertainment for the children and participating in recitals for the adults.²⁰¹ When it was learned of an exchange of positions with the Tenth Cavalry's Chaplain Prioleau, which at that point served in Mexico with the Punitive Expedition, many expressed their

---

193 *Ibid.*, December 18, 1915, 3:30 Edition.
194 *Ibid.*, April 24, 1916, 3:30 Edition.
195 *Ibid.*, January 14, 1916, 3:30 Edition; February 20, 1914, 2:30 Edition; February 23, 1914, 3:30 Edition.
196 *Ibid.*, December 18, 1915, 3:30 Edition.
197 *Ibid.*, April 25, 1916. Both he and Chaplain Gladden were listed among the Black officers on duty in that same year. *Crisis* 5 (April 1916), 284.
198 *Ibid.*, April 29, 1916, 3:30 Edition.
199 *Ibid.*, February 21, 1916, 3:30 Edition; March 6, 1916, 2:30 Edition; February 24, 1916, 3:30 Edition; December 27, 1915, 2:30 Edition; April 27, 1916, 3:30 Edition.
200 *Ibid.*, April 27, 1916, 3:30 Edition.
201 *Ibid.*, March 6, 1916, 2:30 Edition; March 25, 1916, 2:30 Edition.

regrets at the pending departure.[202] The Scotts' constant efforts on behalf of the men of the regiment both for their spiritual benefit and morale, drew throngs of well-wishers.[203] The congregation from the Twenty-Fifth Infantry gathered en masse to greet the guests of honor with a hearty ovation. The chaplain responded with an address that underscored how he and the family regretted their departure from the regiment. Others followed with laudatory speeches and the band provided music.[204] To cap the occasion, Private Max Poindexter expressed his personal aloha concluding that Chaplain Scott's dedication ranked, 'him out second to none with B. T. Washington as a leader.'[205]

While perhaps not so demonstrative, the troopers of the Tenth Cavalry found their new chaplain exhibited the same zeal he had displayed with the Twenty-Fifth Infantry. After joining them in Mexico for a brief tour, he proceeded stateside with the horse soldiers. Afterwards, he spent much of his remaining active duty days at Fort Huachuca, Arizona. At that installation, he established a new office and study in the post library that offered easy access for soldiers to visit him and for him to illustrate programs with his balopticon, a device utilizing reflected light for projecting images of opaque objects as a sort of precursor to PowerPoint presentations. To inaugurate the facility and piece of equipment, his spouse directed a dance number staged by several of the post's young women, followed by refreshments.[206]

Unlike the Black chaplains of an earlier era, however, a degree of affluence and status had been achieved. By the second decade of the twentieth century, Reverend Scott as well as his family and friends, occasionally motored in comfort to Douglas, Arizona and elsewhere in an automobile.[207] Given that as a senior captain and after April 17, 1921 as a major, the chaplain drew respectable pay commensurate with any other officer of his grade; what previously would have been a luxury to almost all military men now could be obtained if desired. In fact, equal army pay represented one of the salient achievements that overrode other examples of discrimination faced by Black officers and soldiers alike.

Regardless of the economic status that the Scotts enjoyed, it did not guarantee personal health. As had been the experience of several other chaplains and officers, the rigors of service Major Scott endured led to his retirement on May 12, 1922 for disability in line of duty.[208] Upon hearing news of Scott's departing the army, *Crisis* magazine expressed a deep interest in a comment made in the *Army and Navy Register* that with:

> The retirement of Chaplain Oscar J.W. Scott (colored), US Army, on account of physical disability incident to the service, leaves the 10th cavalry (colored) without a chaplain. Under the announced policy of the War Department of making no appointments of chaplains until the excess occasioned by the reduction of the Army to 150,000 is absorbed no colored chaplain will be available to take Chaplain Scott's place.'

---

202 *Ibid.*, February 23, 1916, 3:30 Edition; *Honolulu Star-Bulletin*, March 29, 1916, 3:30 Edition; *Crisis* 5 (November 1916), 30.
203 *Ibid.*, April 27, 1916, 3:30 Edition.
204 *Ibid.*,, May 24, 1916, 2:30 Edition.
205 *Ibid.*, June 3, 1916, 3:30 Edition.
206 *Phoenix Tribune*, July 31, 1920.
207 *Ibid.*, July 31, 1920; December 18, 1920.
208 *US Army Register, 1924* (Washington, DC: US Government Printing Office, 1924), 757.

Possibly a white chaplain would report as a replacement, an experiment the paper vowed to watch 'with interest, for very many officers who have served with colored regiments have expressed the belief that the right kind of white chaplain could be eminently successful in serving Negro troops and at the same time could minister to the white officers and their families.'[209]

To the contrary, even before Chaplain Scott retired, support for a replacement from a member of the A.M.E. denomination had reached President William Howard Taft through the secretary of war. The president favorably acted on this suggestion although none of the names as perspective candidates would be nominated.[210]

Meanwhile, during the next year, Scott officiated at Colonel Charles Young's dignified burial in Arlington National Cemetery.[211] Of Young, the retired chaplain recollected: 'I knew him best perhaps in Mexico.' There, his fellow Black officer, 'used to play the organ in religious services while the regiment was encamped in Colonia Dublan, Mexico.'[212]

The eighth Black appointee to the US Army chaplaincy prior to the First World War, Louis Augustus Carter, was a native of Auburn, Alabama. Born on February 20, 1876, Carter was a freeman from birth, as were many of the enlisted men in the ranks when he entered the army. His early attendance in public schools was followed by advanced education at the Tuskegee Institute (Tuskegee University) from 1895 to 1897 and Selma University between 1897 and 1900. He left both academic establishments without graduating, although in 1899 he was ordained as a Baptist minister. The next year, he enrolled at Virginia Union University where, in 1904, he obtained his Bachelor of Divinity degree. In 1907, Guadalupe College in Texas granted him an honorary Doctor of Divinity degree.

During his student days, he ministered at three churches in Virginia. After receiving his bachelor's degree, 'he accepted the pastorage of Old Mount Zion Church, Knoxville' where he remained from 1905 through 1910.[213] In that year, he pursued an appointment as an US Army chaplain. In support, Carter obtained an impressive array of letters 'from two members of the US House of Representatives, the mayor and former mayors of Knoxville, the president of the East Tennessee Banker's Association, several lawyers and numerous ministers.'[214]

Despite such sterling recommendations, Carter almost failed to be commissioned because of newly adopted, more stringent standards for the selection of chaplains. A successful candidate had to submit support either by confidential letters from representatives of the aspirant's denomination that indicated the clergyman was in good standing, or the individual would be the 'subject of special investigation' before they could be selected. The latter method was employed. A US Army recruiting officer interviewed some locals in the Knoxville area, who told him Carter was a man of 'bad moral character and had secured his letters of recommendation 'by some political deal.' Rather than accept hearsay, Chaplain W.E. Gladden journeyed

---

209 *Crisis* 24 (July 1922): 106.
210 RG 94, Records of the Adjutant General's Office_e25_box5879_1555377_anderson-chaplain (2), NARA.
211 *New York Age*, June 9, 1923.
212 enotes.com/homework-help/what-religion-for-colonel-charles-young–69855.
213 *Programme Farewell Service and Exercise for Louis Augustus Carter Colonel, Chaplain Corps, U.S.A Fort Huachuca, Arizona October 29–30, 1939* copy in the United States Army Chaplain Center and School Library, Columbia, South Carolina.
214 Anthony Appiah and Henry Louis Gates, Jr., eds., *Africana: The Encyclopedia of the African and African American Experience* 2d Edition (Oxford: Oxford University Press, 2005), 758.

to Tennessee to determine the 'truth or falsity of the rumors.'[215] Happily, the accusations were unfounded although the motives for such slander were not clear.

Chaplain Gladden reported favorably to a review committee. Later that summer of 1910, he spent 10 weeks at Madison Barracks and Pine Camp, New York where he shared his experience and tutored Carter, who had been accepted for duty with the Tenth Cavalry. The novice chaplain studied an array of non-theological tracts from Army regulations to the manual of courts-martial, while he also visited the men in their barracks, daily accompanied by Chaplain Carter. They even participated in the field maneuvers before Chaplain Carter's abbreviated apprenticeship ended and he left for Fort Ethan Allen, Vermont.[216] In so doing, soon after Chaplain Anderson's retirement, earlier that year, he joined the regiment. A nearby Vermont newspaper noted the newcomer possessed, 'marvelous oratorical ability and great versatility and to be fertile in expedients to accomplish his ends.'[217]

Carter soon had the opportunity to prove the veracity of this press along with other capabilities. Among these was one of many additional tasks he performed for nearly three decades that included an unusual assignment to manage the Tenth Cavalry's Wild West Show at the post's massive riding hall, during Thanksgiving of 1911.[218] After that, Carter served continuously until his retirement on February 29, 1940, at one time or other with all four regiments of Black regulars. In this, he was unique. Carter's transfers brought him to far flung garrisons including periodic, extensive assignments to Arizona at Fort Huachuca, Douglas and Camp Stephen D. Little, Camp Stotsenburg in the Philippines, the Army Chaplains' School at Fort Leavenworth, Kansas, as well as Fort Benning, Georgia. In the process, he earned a Mexican Border Service Medal, First World War Victory Medal, American Defense Service Medal and an unusual decoration for a non-combatant, an Expert Marksmanship Badge displaying the Pistol-Bar.[219]

In the Philippines, during 1915, Chaplain Carter discovered that the military provided no housing for the family of soldiers, 'below the rank of staff sergeant for the men of the 9th Cavalry.' In response, he convinced Camp Stotsenburg's commander, 'to set aside an area within the camp for married men to build houses at their own expense.' Given that this effort required $200 for a hut and a slightly lesser amount if the soldier undertook the work, even that sum was unaffordable for the men. Once more, the chaplain, 'came to their aid persuading the Quartermaster to assume "certain financial responsibilities" – outside Army regulations' with arrangements for installment repayments.[220] By the next year, while still in the Philippines, he received yet another special assignment. In 1916, when the Ninth Cavalry commemorated its fiftieth anniversary, Chaplain Carter oversaw this celebration.[221]

215 RG 94, Records of the Adjutant General's Office, Memorandum for the Assistant Secretary of War,' Subject: Examination of the Rev. L.A. Carter, a candidate for appointment as chaplain, War Department, Office of the Chief of Staff, Washington, D.C., April 9, 1910, AGHODF No. 154908, L.A. Carter, 1–6, NARA.
216 RG 94, Records of the Adjutant General's Office, Chaplain Washington W.E. Gladden to Adjutant General, US.A., Washington, D.C., August 2, 1910, AGHODF No. 154908, L.A. Carter, NARA.
217 *Burlington Weekly Free Press*, March 24, 1910.
218 Fletcher, *The Black Soldier and Officer*, 80.
219 R.V. Lee, Official State of Military Service and Death of Louis A. Carter Service Number O 4358, Louis A. Carter File, Fort Huachuca Museum, Arizona.
220 Stover, *Up From Handymen*, 164.
221 *Crisis* 5 (November 1916), 30.

Besides these two examples of Carter's dedication to 'the spiritual and physical welfare of the men' he also promoted: 'sports, entertainments ... literary societies and debating clubs' in addition to periodic supervision of post schools and the post library. In the last instance, he saw to it that *The Crisis* and titles relevant to African American history and culture were included to advance 'racial pride and an interest in Black studies' that he reinforced 'by presenting impressive programs during regimental anniversaries that recounted the military successes of the Black soldier,' all of which led to his positive influence on a dedicated 'large congregation.'[222]

Louis Augustus Carter died on June 14, 1941, in Tucson, Arizona at the Veteran's hospital. The retired chaplain numbered among a small cadre of Blacks to attain the rank of colonel in the United States Army. He would be laid to rest 'at Fort Huachuca ... where he last served the army from which he retired in February, 1940.'[223] Flags flew at half-staff. The entire Twenty-Fifth Infantry regiment attended the services.

The course charted by these Black chaplains, the West Pointers and those commissioned from civilian life or the ranks, differed from that taken by the average African American enlisted man. They performed under intense scrutiny, being looked upon as role models and upholders of middleclass values yet did so with a particular perspective of hard-edged experience and sometimes painful observation, fired in the crucible of bigotry and inequality. In part, the fates of Second Lieutenant Henry O. Flipper and Chaplain Henry V. Plummer further indicated that all Black commissioned officers stood on precarious ground. Debatably, Flipper greatly contributed to the end of his own career. Nevertheless, Flipper later claimed that his dismissal was unjust constituting 'a punishment, which, in similar circumstances, would never have been inflicted on a *white* officer.'[224]

Decades later, a study of the Flipper matter supported the lieutenant's argument and emphatically concluded, 'racism affected the sentence.' Conversely, the same author countered, 'it is doubtful that racism was a factor in the charges or verdict.'[225] In so doing, he contradicted his own contention. Regardless of varied points of view, one salient fact remains. Conviction for conduct unbecoming an officer during this era, often brought about dismissal. For instance, based on a review of all US Army GCM for the years 1879 through 1881, some 27 officers were found guilty of this relatively common charge. Of these, 10 remained in service despite all being sentenced to termination of their military careers. A variety of factors allowed them to do so, usually based on length of faithful service or occasionally because of political influence. Tenth Cavalry Captain George Armes twice escaped being ousted because of a combination of both of these factors. Indeed, the combative Armes stood arrest 23 times and faced eight trials, as well as a sanity hearing before being involuntarily retired.

As for Chaplain Plummer's dishonorable discharge, there might be reason to aver racism contributed to his removal. Questions could be asked as to what prompted an adverse testimony

---

222 Appiah and Gates, *Africana*, 759.
223 *Phoenix Index*, June 28, 1941; July 5, 1941. His widow, the former Mary Moss, would be able to be near the grave of her deceased husband because she became the senior hostess officiating at the Fort Huachuca 'service club functions, planning, organizing and supervising social activities for the soldiers on the post.'
224 Barry C. Johnson, *Flipper's Dismissal: The Ruin of Lt. Henry O. Flipper, U.S.A. First Coloured Cadet of West Point* (London: Privately Printed, c. 1980), 110.
225 Charles M. Robinson III, *The Court Martial of Lieutenant Henry Flipper* (El Paso: University of Texas at El Paso, 1994) 112–13.

by one of the Ninth Cavalry's senior enlisted men and why the clergyman's superiors took the actions they did, against him. Even then, one careful review of the chaplain's hearing determined the record of the trial and indicated, 'the evidence rulings were proper and without prejudice to the accused and that he received a vigorous and adequate defence.' The author further remarked: 'Yet the pre-trial investigation and record of court martial leave the impression that the evidence was sufficient to sustain the charge and that the jury did not apply the standard of reasonable doubt.'[226] However, for both Flipper and Plummer, speculation is of no avail.

Regardless of the dismissals of West Point's first Black graduate and the US Army's first Black chaplain, these few men and the other Black officers represented the main differences that set the regiments of Black regulars apart from infantry and cavalry units made up of a white officers and soldiers. As such, if the African American population at large looked to the Black enlisted men as the forerunners of Ralph Bunche, Marian Anderson, Joe Louis and Jackie Robinson, then Flipper, Alexander, Young and the other Black cavalry and infantry officers, might be seen as stellar examples of W. E. B Dubois' 'talented tenth.'[227] As for the Black chaplains, they tended to be energetic disciples of George Washington Carver, who emphasized vocational education to 'elevate the race.' To some degree, they likewise might be viewed as precursors in the struggle for civil rights championed generations later by Dr. Martin Luther King, Jr.

---

226 Stover, *Chaplain Henry V. Plummer, His Ministry and His Court-Martial*, 25.
227 According to Dubois: 'The problem of education, then, among Negroes must first of all deal with the Talented Tenth; it is the problem of developing the Best of this race that they may guide the Mass.' Booker T. Washington, et al, *The Negro Problem: A Series of Articles by Representative American Negroes of Today* (New York: J. Pott & Company, 1903), 33.

3

Multiple Missions

From the time of the American Revolution forward, the land forces of what became the United States stood as 'the sword of the republic' charged with defending the nation from all foes both foreign and domestic, or so the theory ran.[1] In reality, with the exception of two wars with the British, the first to gain independence fought from 1775 to 1787 and the second, the War of 1812, what emerged as the United States Army, took on varied roles. In fact, although costal defences required substantial support well into the Second World War, during the late eighteenth and much of the nineteenth centuries, the Regular Army concentrated its resources and expended much of its energy as 'frontiersmen in blue.'[2] Often miniscule in terms of troop strength, the military moved in the vanguard of expansion north towards Canada; southward to New Spain and its successor Mexico, with whom it eventually clashed and wrested significant territorial gains; and surged onward to the Pacific Ocean behind the Corps of Discovery under the storied infantry officers William Clark and Meriwether Lewis.[3]

'Indian Wars'

Continual endeavors to acquire land and exploit resources resulted in numerous encounters with Native Americans on both sides of the Mississippi River. Frequently, the contact proved peaceful. On many other occasions, however, the two cultures clashed before, during and

---

1 Francis Paul Prucha, *The Sword of the Republic: The United States Army on the frontier, 1783–1846* (Bloomington: Indiana University Press, 1969), stands as the essential introduction to the US Army during its first decades of existence.
2 Refer to the quintessential Robert M. Utley, *Frontiersmen in Blue: The United States Army and the Indian, 1848–1865* (New York, Macmillan, 1967), for background on the military's presence in the West after the Mexican American War through the American Civil War. Utley's companion volume, *Frontier Regulars: The United States Army and the Indian, 1866–1891* (Bloomington: Indiana University Press, 1973), adds further context through the so-called Ghost Dance.
3 While many treatments of the Lewis and Clark Expedition exist, Stephen E. Ambrose, *Undaunted Courage: Meriwether Lewis, Thomas Jefferson, and the Opening of the American West* (New York: Simon & Schuster, 1996), provides a highly readable narrative of this prime example of the US Army's assignments as explorers.

An unknown private from Company G, Twenty-Fifth Infantry appears in the winter campaign kit of the early 1890s. At the time of the photo session, he was stationed at Fort Missoula, Montana, where a half dozen of his comrades from the same company bicycled from that garrison to St. Louis, Missouri. (Courtesy John Langellier)

especially after, the Civil War. It was the two dozen years after that national tragedy when the first Black regulars entered the fray. In fact, during what became known as the Indian Wars, according to one compilation of the approximately 1,296 engagements fought between 1867 through 1890 on the frontier, Black troops and their white officers took part in 168 actions. In other words, they participated in 13.8 percent of all clashes, essentially in keeping with the fact that Blacks composed 12 percent of the US Army fighting force during this period.[4]

Ninth Cavalry – 'We Can, We Will'

The Ninth and Tenth Cavalry regiments bore the brunt of this combat. Records compiled by both units revealed their widespread call to arms. Starting with the Ninth Cavalry, scarcely seven months after forming in New Orleans, Colonel Edward Hatch obeyed orders in March 1867 to take his 12 companies to Texas. The regimental total of 885 men mainly consisted of enlisted personnel and only a handful of officers. This fact led to unfortunate consequence in that enroute to San Antonio, a mutiny erupted. One officer and two enlisted men died in the outbreak.

This episode brought about a response to the colonel's appeal for more officers. Soon thereafter, a pair of companies departed San Antonio for Brownsville, while the remaining 10 companies followed within several weeks bound for Fort Stockton, which was headquarters and garrisoned by four companies. Further, Fort Davis absorbed the other six companies.

Thus began eight years in the region with mandates to protect the mail and stage route from San Antonio to El Paso, maintain law in their operational area and deal with Native Americans.[5] These peoples included Mescalero Apache from the west, Kickapoo and Lipan from Mexico, along with Kiowa and Comanche from the north. The last-named group, who acquired the horse from the Spanish, quickly developed into one of the finest light cavalrymen the world had known. They mastered their mounts to emerge as the lords of the Southern Plains. In the process, the Comanche forged an empire that for a brief time, competed with the United States' expansionist ambitions.[6]

Facing such daunting opposition in west Texas, at first, the Ninth Cavalry lacked the experience and capability to combat the Comanche and other rapid raiders who hit and ran before raw recruits responded. During August and September, small war parties struck with impunity. By October, they killed their first Black soldiers, Corporal Emanuel Wright and Private E.T. Jones. They formed part of a mail escort that 'consisted of six men – two white and four soldiers … The two whites escaped unhurt.' In addition to Wright and Jones, the other two troopers were wounded. A newspaper account reported the corporal was 'said to have fought gallantly,' while supposedly, the surviving Black soldiers, 'adopted the policy of praying for the Indians to be driven away.' The warriors did not scalp the dead bodies.[7] Another Ninth Cavalry private,

---

4   Schubert and Schubert, *On the Trail of the Buffalo Soldiers*, 355–59.
5   Rodenbough and Haskins, *The Army of the United States*, 283.
6   For a superb analysis of these impressive equestrians read: Pekka Hämäläinen, *The Comanche Empire* (New Haven, CT: Yale University Press, 2009).
7   Leckie and Leckie, *Buffalo Soldiers*, 87; and *Dallas Herald*, November 16, 1867.

Nathan Johnson, fell at the hands of a Mescalero band who ambushed an eastbound stagecoach heading out of El Paso.[8]

Not until 1867 neared an end, would Black soldiers begin to make inroads against their diverse adversaries. At that time, they confronted overwhelming odds, facing an estimated 900 Kickapoos, Lipans and Mexicans at Fort Lancaster. Outnumbered a dozen to one, they held their ground behind the remains of the abandoned post where they pushed back their enemies. During the firefight, reportedly: 'The soldiers behaved with great spirit and gallantry.' They killed 20 of the attackers and wounded several other, but not without a cost. The raiders 'captured all of the horses and mules belonging to the Post but 6 or 7, on the sick list,' as well as 'also killed or captured three soldiers.'[9] The three casualties downed in the fierce exchange, Privates Andrew Trimble, William Sharpe and Eli Boyer, 'had been taken by surprise, roped and dragged away.' Three months later, near the encounter, a party found their bodies.[10]

After the engagement at Fort Lancaster, the pair of companies at Brownsville deployed further north along the Rio Grande to Forts Duncan and Clark. Moreover, Hatch directed abandoned Fort Quitman, northwest of Fort Davis, to be 'reoccupied by a strong detachment under aggressive Major Albert P. Morrow.'[11]

The troop transfers better positioned the Ninth to strike the roving enemy, an objective the regimental commander contemplated for the forthcoming spring. Furthermore, his command gradually gained knowledge of the brutal environment of west Texas while simultaneously obtained an appreciation for their enemies' tactics. This experience improved operations as indicated during September1868, when 60 soldiers, commanded by Lieutenant Patrick Cusack, one of the few Irish-born officers in Ninth Cavalry, intercepted approximately 200 Lipan Apache. The strike force boldly set upon the Apache camp. Despite the fact they, 'fought desperately, superior fire power routed them.' The Apache scattered leaving 25 dead, most of their supplies, hundreds of stolen mules, horses and cattle along with two Mexican boys who had been captured. Cusack pursued a short distant before returning to the abandoned battle site to collect the spoils.[12]

The lieutenant praised his subordinates and rightly so. The column accomplished no mean feat in that the proximity of the Mexican border offered a nearby ideal sanctuary for the enemy. Learning of the prohibition against United States' troops from crossing south of the Rio Grande-Rio Bravo, predatory parties, including Native Americans, Comancheros and Mexican nationals – bandits and revolutionaries alike – escaped into Mexico with impunity.

It became obvious that more aggressive actions must be employed to halt what the whites of the era styled, 'depredations.' Before Hatch could launch a full-scale expedition to squelch the marauders, he received a special detail with the Freedman's Bureau, leaving it to his second in command, capable Civil War cavalryman, Lieutenant Colonel Wesley Merritt, to execute an end to warfare in the Ninth Cavalry's zone of operations. Merritt's efforts, 'stretched to the

8   Leckie and Leckie, *Buffalo Soldiers*, 87.
9   *Dallas Herald*, January 18, 1868.
10 Leckie and Leckie, *Buffalo Soldiers*, 87–88.
11 *Ibid.*, 88.
12 Charles L. Kenner, *Buffalo Soldiers and Officers of the Ninth Cavalry, 1867–1898* (Norman: University of Oklahoma Press, 1999), 53.

limit the strength and endurance of his command' to little avail. Once more, elusive, 'small war parties' slipped into Mexico out of reach from their weary, frustrated pursuers.[13]

After performing 18 months of detached service with the Freedman's Bureau in Louisiana, Colonel Hatch resumed leadership of the Ninth. On September 9, 1869, he launched an all-out campaign that coincided with a series of campaigns by former commander of the Forty-First Infantry, Colonel Ranald Mackenzie, who now headed the sub-district of the Pecos with authority over his own regiment, the Fourth Cavalry and a half dozen companies of the Ninth. The mixed command meant that on October 28, 1869, a then rare multiracial force consisting of Company G, Ninth Cavalry reinforced by 26 white Fourth Cavalry troopers and a like number of Tonkawa Indian scouts, readied to engage Native Americans.[14]

By this point, a number of former fieldhands had evolved into combat-hardened veterans ready to engage an elusive enemy. Consequently, during the dead of winter January 1870, elements of the Ninth Cavalry rode out from Fort Davis, but this time, towards Apache territory. For the next five months, they trailed Mescalero Apache west into New Mexico. Few Apache came into their sights, but the destruction of numerous wickiups and capture of considerable livestock, caused great suffering among the *Inde* (Apache). During this campaign, Sergeant Emanuel Stance of Company F earned the first of 18 Medals of Honor presented to Black soldiers on the frontier. (TABLE 7) Of the 417 Medals of Honor awarded between 1865 and the 1890s to recipients who served in the West, approximately four percent of the total went to Black cavalrymen, infantrymen and Seminole Indian Scouts, who were of African ancestry.[15] The figure fell far below the total engagements fought, as compared to instances of white officers and enlisted men who received this prestigious recognition for valor in the West. Nonetheless, if one historian's calculations are accurate, of 2,704 engagements fought by the US Army between 1866 and 1891, against Native Americans, only 141 of these clashes, 'or just over 5 percent of the total' involved African American soldiers.[16] As such, the lesser number of Medals of Honor generally was in keeping with statistical data and not simply a matter of prejudice.[17]

---

13   Leckie and Leckie, *Buffalo Soldiers*, 88.
14   Kenner, *Buffalo Soldiers and Officers*, 54.
15   Frank N. Schubert, *Black Valor: Buffalo Soldiers fand the Medal of Honor, 1870–1898* (Wilmington, DE: Scholarly resources Inc., 1997), sheds considerable light on the subject during the Indian Wars and Spanish American War. The so-called 'Seminole Negro-Indian Scouts' were descendants of individuals who fled enslavement in the southeast came to live with the Seminole people in Florida. After the US government forced the Seminole to the western Indian Territory the formerly enslaved group relocated to the area as well as other places in Texas and Mexico. Between 1870 and 1881, many of offered their expertise as scouts to the US Arm. In this capacity, they took part in no less than 26 expeditions. In the process, they earned four Medals of Honor. Likewise, they a became known for their tracking skills, hardiness, marksmanship, and as formidable adversaries of the Lipan and Mescalero Apache. For more on the Seminole scouts consult, *A&NJ*, August 11, 1877, 5; and Kevin Mulroy, *Freedom on the Border: The Seminole Maroons in Florida, the Indian Territory, Coahuila, and Texas* (Lubbock: Texas Tech University Press, 1993), 113–32; 162; 168, relative to the scouts.
16   Thomas D. Phillips, 'The Black Regulars,' in Alan G. Bogue, ed., *The West of the American People* (Itasca: F.E. Peacock 1970), 141.
17   Schubert, *Black Valor*, 165

Table 7: Medal of Honor Recipients 1870–1890

Rank	Name	Date of Issue
Sergeant	Thomas Boyne	January 6, 1883
Sergeant	Benjamin Brown	February 19, 1890
Sergeant	John Denny	November 27, 1894
Private	Pompey Factor*	May 28, 1875
Corporal	Clinton Greaves	June 26, 1879
Sergeant	Henry Johnson	September 22, 1890
Sergeant	George Jordon	May 7, 1890
Corporal	Isaiah Mays	February 19, 1890
Sergeant	William McBryar	May 15, 1890
Sergeant	Thomas Shaw	December 1890
Private	Adam Payne (aka Paine)*	
Trumpeter	Isaac Payne*	May 28, 1875
Sergeant	Emanuel Stance	June 28, 1870
Private	Augustus Walley**	October 1, 1890
Private	John Ward*	
First Sergeant	Moses Williams	November 12, 1896
Corporal	William O. Wilson	September 17, 1891
Sergeant	Brent Woods	July 12, 1894

*= Seminole Negro Scout
**= A recommendation for a second Medal of Honor for actions in Cuba during the Spanish American War was denied.

Regardless, there would be ample opportunity for Black troops to display their courage; forceful relocation of the Mescalero from west Texas brought no end of clashes with the Kiowa, Comanche, Kickapoo and Lipan, who held fast to their ancestral realm. Hatch and others thought they could only achieve victory through conquest of the various groups such as the Kickapoo and Lipan by hitting them in their Mexican refuges. By December 1870, the colonel lobbied both the United States and Mexican governments for permission to ford the Rio Grande. President Ulysses Grant's administration concurred, but President Benito Juarez, in a struggle to retain his office against General Porfirio Díaz, demurred.

For the time being, west Texas essentially remained a no-man's land. During the eight years on duty there, the Ninth Cavalry attained limited success in quelling the violence that beset the region. Amid relentless patrols and skirmishes, the regiment also participated in some exploration and mapping of vast regions that later paid dividends, when the duel between the empires of the United States and the Comanche at last ended a bloody, regrettable period in the nation's past.

Even as the final acts played out in Texas, the Ninth redeployed. Once more, New Mexico served as the theater of operations. Beginning in the early 1870s, the United States Indian Bureau established reservations for the various subdivisions of the Western Apache who long resided in Arizona and New Mexico. To isolate them, the government sometimes sent them to barren and desolate plots away from their traditional lands. The ill-conceived practice often ignited resistance. The most dissatisfied fled to Mexico.

During 1875, in response, the Ninth Cavalry received orders that transferred regimental headquarters to Santa Fe, New Mexico. Over the following 6 years, the regiment's various companies scattered throughout the territory, taking post at Forts Bayard, McRae, Wingate, Stanton, Union, Selden, in New Mexico and Garland, Colorado, among other duty stations. They embarked on patrols from these outposts, but seldom met with Apache parties who had bolted from the oppressive reservations. Operating with but half their authorized strength, the severely undermanned regiment lacked the manpower required for such a large territory.

Nonetheless, they persevered. During September 1877, their persistence brought about their first major encounter. An estimated 300 Apache warriors, led by the impressive Victorio, bolted from the hated San Carlos reservation in Arizona. Once free, they struck along the Upper Gila River. In response, elements of the regiment closed with Victorio and his band in Arizona's rugged Mogollon Mountains. After a month at liberty, the Apache surrendered. Men of Company B escorted them back to San Carlos, but the return to the status quo soon ended. Once the Black soldiers withdrew and headed to their garrison, Victorio and his followers slipped away once more and returned to raiding.

Again, the Ninth Cavalry took to the field. In February 1878, elements of the regiment troops surrounded the fugitives at Ojo Caliente, New Mexico. After negotiations, Victorio and his band surrendered on the condition that they would not be forced to return to San Carlos, a god-forsaken place that Western writer Owen Wister once described as 'hell on earth.'[18] Arrangements for another, more acceptable reservation site, temporarily saw an end in fighting but Victorio would not remain long quiet.

Even as an uneasy peace had been achieved with Victorio, the Utes in Colorado grew frustrated with their lot. In 1868, the Utes agreed to reside on a reservation in the western part of the territory. For a few brief years, until a silver boom during the 1870s disrupted the calm, they lived peaceably. When miners flooded into their lands, boundary disputes arose. By 1876, with Colorado's statehood, whites pressed the federal government to remove the Utes from their silver-laden reservation. As officials in Washington considered the matter, squatters moved preemptively on to Ute territory. Resistance by the Ute people followed.

By March 1878, units from the Ninth Cavalry responded. They took up position on the reservation's southern border. Without employing force, Colonel Hatch brokered an agreement that ceded a strip of reservation land to the whites. Unfortunately, the arrangement only forestalled conflict. By 1879, the situation worsened. Among other factors, efforts by federal Indian agent Nathan Meeker for the Utes to abandon their traditional nomadic ways and convert to farming, caused further turmoil. The Utes threatened to revolt.

An unduly apprehensive Meeker requested military intervention. The US Army responded. It dispatched details from the Third and Fifth Cavalry regiments and from the Fourth Infantry, all manned by whites. On September 29, 1879, when the soldiers crossed the Milk River, the Utes opened fire. The surprised army troops took up a defensive position.

Later that day, Captain Francis Dodge of Company D, Ninth Cavalry, received an urgent plea for reinforcements. His command saddled their mounts and rapidly rode continuously for 23 hours to lift the siege at reach the Milk River. They joined the embattled whites. For three days, the joint forces held out against the determined Utes. Then, on October 5, a relief column

---

18 Owen Wister, 'Specimen Jones,' *Harper's New Monthly* 80 no. 530 (July 1894), 209.

from the Fifth Cavalry dispatched from Fort D.A. Russell, Wyoming ended the costly clash that left dead and wounded, some who suffered greatly, on both sides of the bitter battle. In the process of the desperate struggle, the especial valor of Ninth Cavalry Sergeant Henry Johnson earned him a Medal of Honor.[19]

The engagement at Milk River was not the only challenge faced by Black soldiers in 1879. One of the most frustrating campaigns engaged in by the Ninth Cavalry and its brother regiment, the Tenth Cavalry, involved Victorio's last effort to escape the stifling imprisonment of the reservation. In late August 1879, Victorio once again struck a final blow for freedom with a group of Mescalero Apache. The initial responses came when Lieutenant George Washington Smith, with 14 men from his company, unsuccessfully attempted to intercept the fugitives. Afterwards, through 1880, Victorio's party cut a swath of destruction and death in the borderlands.

During the campaign, several skirmishes ensued. One of the earliest took place on September 4, 1879, when the Apache daringly attacked Company E, Ninth Cavalry at Ojo Caliente. They killed eight guards and made off with 46 horses. The Ninth dispatched almost every able-bodied man sending virtually every soldier to search for Victorio and his warrior allies. They crossed the border into Mexico but did little more than exhaust their mounts and supplies, as well as themselves, before they returned to garrison. This left the Apache presumably safe in Mexico.

The Mexican Army entered the fray particularly after the Apache killed over two dozen civilians during a pair of attacks at Carrizal. Fearing the Mexicans more than the Americans, in January 1880, Victorio and his men retreated north across the border to the San Andres Mountains. Once intelligence revealed the Apache again were on US soil, Colonel Hatch left regimental headquarters in Santa Fe to assume command of renewed action against Victorio. As part of his strategy, Hatch, who suspected Victorio's fellow Mescalero Apache on the Tularosa Reservation secretly supplied their brethren, disarmed them and confiscated their horses. Rather than aid his cause, Hatch's action incensed the locals. Between 30 to 50 of them elected to link up with Victorio.

While more warriors went over to the enemy camp, the military simultaneously added to its numbers. Five companies from the Tenth Cavalry, one from the Sixth Cavalry (white personnel) and two Indian scout companies arrived from Texas and Arizona to reinforce the Ninth Cavalry. Before the strengthened strike force could mobilize, however, Victorio and his band headed from the San Andres Mountains westward towards their former homeland near the Mogollon range in western New Mexico. Once more, Victorio's group illuded the US Army as they chased him to no avail, through the Mogollon and Black Mountains as far west as San Carlos. Towards the end of May, at last they located the band. Once again, the query melted away across the border into Mexico.

The proven tactic finally failed. Due to the attacks against citizens of Carrizal during the previous year, the Mexicans increased their endeavors to subdue the Apache. In October, Mexican troops ensnared Victorio and his men in a mountain canyon. Refusing to surrender, the Apache fought gallantly, yet they could not escape the Mexican onslaught. Victorio and some 60 of his followers went down in a hail of bullets.

---

19   Details of this incident appear in Russel D. Santala, *The Ute Campaign of 1879: A Study in the Use of the Military Instrument* (Fort Leavenworth: US Army Command and General Staff College, 1994).

Even though the charismatic, competent Victorio had fallen, by October 1880, survivors, under the elderly but hardy Nana (Victorio's former lieutenant), continued to ride roughshod in southern New Mexico. For the next year, troopers of the Ninth Cavalry chased these foes in the all too familiar, cat-and-mouse game in and out of New Mexico's mountains and back and forth across the Mexican border. Their grueling pursuit in New Mexico lasted until late 1881, when Nana and his men drifted westward into Arizona.[20]

Before doing so, the Apache and their Black pursuers met in a deadly clash in New Mexico. The widow of an officer who fell in this fight noted her husband, George W. Smith, who had ridden to no avail in 1879 to interdict Victorio, again led a patrol of from the Ninth Cavalry against 'the Apache Indians, in the Membres [sic] mountains, in Gavolon Canyon, about 25 miles' out from Fort Bayard. On August 19, 1881, two bullets struck the officer. In response, 'his faithful men begged him to dismount, but supposedly his reply was "Never while a breath is in me" and continued to command until he fell from his saddle.' Although their white officer was dead, for the next several hours, his troopers 'continued to fight and by their bravery (God bless them) saved the body of their heroic commander. They were colored troops, soldiers of the 9th US Cavalry and a braver set of men never lived.'[21] Uncle Sam agreed. US Army officials bestowed a Medal of Honor on Sergeant Brent Woods, although one historian has argued the NCO and 'every man in his command should have been recommended' for this same decoration to reflect their heroism.[22]

A decade would pass before another member of the Ninth Cavalry's rank and file would be cited for his extreme courage under fire. Sadly, a series of calamitous events led to the final fight between the Ninth Cavalry and Native Americans and the issuance of another Medal of Honor. The spiral began during the winter of 1889–1890. The particularly harsh season inflicted great suffering on the Lakota (Sioux) confined to a half dozen reservations in North and South Dakota that were but a fraction of the once extensive empire reigned over by these bison hunting horseman. Now, in a greatly constricted environment, the impoverished, hungry and disease plagued people grasped at a faint hope for a better future. Word about a faraway Paiute named Wovoka, who prophesized of a new world in which the Native Americans 'would be reunited with dead friends and relatives in a blissful and eternal life, free of pain, sickness, want and death, free, above all, of white people' converted followers within the distraught Lakota nation.[23]

---

20 For an outline of the movements of various companies during the 1879–1881 campaign against Victorio and Nana review, 'History of the Ninth Regiment US Cavalry, 1935,' 32–42, US Army Heritage and Education Center, Carlisle Barracks, PA. For in-depth details, a pair of monographs by Robert N. Watt, *'I Will Not Surrender the Hair of a Horse's Tail': The Victorio Campaign 1879* (Solihull, West Midlands, England: Helion & Company Limited, 2017); and *'Horses Worn to Mere Shadows': The Victorio Campaign 1880* (Warwick, England: Helion & Company Limited, 2017), are highly recommended; with a third volume concluding the narrative – With *My Face to My Bitter Foes': Nana's War 1880–1881* (Warwick, England: Helion & Company Limited, 2019).

21 Mrs. George. W Smith in Association of Survivors, Regular Brigade, Fourteenth Corps, *Army of the Cumberland Proceedings of reunions held at Pittsburgh, Pa., Sept. 11–12, 1894, Crawfish Springs, Ga., Sept. 18–19, 1895, St. Paul, Minn., Sept. 1–2, 1896, Columbus, Ohio, Sept. 22–23, 1897/Association of Survivors, Regular Brigade, Fourteenth Corps, Army of the Cumberland. Historical sketch/by Frederick Phisterer. Roster of membership and death roll of the brigade during the war. Official reports of the Battle of Stone River, Tenn.* (n.p.: n.p., 1898), 125.

22 Kenner, *Buffalo Soldiers and Officers*, 230.

23 Utley, *Frontiersmen in Blue*, 402.

To revive the former glory days, intense prayer accompanied a physically exhausting 'Ghost Dance' to induce a trancelike state that allegedly allowed the faithful to see into this promised return of bygone times. The Ghost Dance swept throughout the Lakota camps. At first, the movement unfolded peacefully, but the new agent at the Pine Ridge reservation, the inexperienced D. F. Royer, overreacted to the frenzied dancing and chanting. He turned to the military for troops to maintain order. In late November 1890, five troops of the Ninth Cavalry, along with eight companies of white foot soldiers from the Second and Eighth Infantry, filtered into the Pine Ridge and Rosebud reservations.

By that time, the Ninth Cavalry had been on duty for five years at various posts throughout the upper Great Plains. Previously the regiment enjoyed a quiet period at its Fort Robinson, Nebraska headquarters and other troops stationed at Fort Duchesne in Utah, Fort McKinney in Wyoming and Fort Niobrara in Nebraska. By 1896, the regiment consolidated its strength at Forts Robinson and Duchesne.

Being some of the closest horse soldiers to the Lakota reservations, the Ninth offered a ready resource in response to Agent Royer's call. The presence of 600 troops, however, understandably alarmed the Lakota. They soon split into two factions: those who accepted the soldiers and others who intended to defy them. The latter element withdrew to a remote area in the northwest corner of the Pine Ridge reservation. By early December, an estimated 600 Lakota families from Pine Ridge and Rosebud had followed them.

To prevent a similar exodus at the other Lakota reservations, the senior military authority in the area had the two most influential leaders – Sitting Bull and Big Foot – arrested. This pre-emptive action worsened matters. After his arrest by Indian police, Sitting Bull's followers attempted to rescue the holy man. The effort ended in the tragic deaths of Sitting Bull, a half dozen of his Lakota supporters and an equal number of Indian police. In response, the leadership at Pine Ridge called on Big Foot, who remained under the military's watchful eyes, to travel there as a peacemaker. Not realizing that Big Foot left the reservation in response to this request, elements of both the Seventh and Ninth Cavalry regiments set out to intercept him. Two troops of the Seventh Cavalry made first contact and accompanied Big Foot and his entourage to Pine Ridge. When the remainder of the Seventh Cavalry met the escort at Wounded Knee Creek, however, the commander ordered the Lakota to surrender their firearms. The demand ignited the already tense situation and precipitated the infamous Wounded Knee massacre.

Other encounters occurred during the clash of cultures. Among these were a pair of skirmishes between the Lakota and the Ninth Cavalry. The first encounter erupted very soon after patrols from the Ninth failed to find Big Foot and just prior to the Wounded Knee debacle. On December 29, 1890, three of the four troops made their way back to the Pine Ridge Agency. Troop D, however, lagged with the pack train. After a two hour wait at the Agency for Troop D, the other three troops discovered their comrades with the pack animals were engaged in a fire fight. Remounting, they galloped to the relief. After a quick, sharp exchange, they repelled the attackers. In the process, they sustained one casualty.

Concurrently, the Lakota survivors of Wounded Knee and others, sought safety in the northwest corner of the Pine Ridge reservation. In the process, they fired the buildings at the Drexel Mission. In response, troopers from the Seventh Cavalry arrived on the scene. Their commander overlooked a basic military tactic by not securing the surrounding heights in advance of deploying his main body into the valley. The Lakota lost little time in taking advantage of the error. They entrapped whites in the valley and opened a barrage. The reports from these volleys reached the Pine Ridge Agency. Once more, the Ninth Cavalry swung into the saddle. They made a charge that scattered the attackers. Within a little more than 30 hours, the four troops of the Ninth trekked over long, chilling miles, participated in a pair of two skirmishes, suffered only one man and two horses killed, plus added Corporal William O. Wilson's name to the list of regimental Medal of Honor recipients. With this incident, the Ninth Cavalry concluded its fighting against Native Americans.[24]

In turn, several weeks later, the Lakota returned to their reservations.[25] The Ghost Dance ended a century of resistance between the Native Americans in the West and was the last major campaign of the Indian Wars. With that, the Ninth Cavalry, which was the first regiment to take to the in the field in November 1890, became 'the last to leave late the following March.'[26]

Tenth Cavalry – Ready and Forward

After a taxing time forming the Tenth Cavalry at Fort Leavenworth, Kansas, Colonel Benjamin Grierson dispersed the regiment to other posts around Kansas with their main stations at Forts Dodge, Harker, Hays, Larned, Riley and Wallace.[27] As the regiment hopscotched from place to place, like the Ninth Cavalry, it began to confront Native Americans within its operational area. Initially this meant Kansas and Colorado. The first engagement took place on August 2, 1867, when Captain George Armes and Company I, numbering 34 men and two officers, faced what appeared to be 300 Native Americans near Saline River, some 40 miles northeast of Fort Hays, Kansas. After six hours hunkered down in a hollow square, the troops retreated with the loss of Sergeant W. Christy, killed and Captain Armes, wounded. Nearly three weeks later, on August 21, Armes' company consisting of 40 troopers, along with another 90 men from the Eighteenth Kansas Volunteers, exchanged fire with an estimated 500 warriors. Once more the clash took place northeast of Fort Hays, Kansas. Again, one soldier died and was scalped. Thirteen others from Company I sustained wounds, while 15 of the volunteers and two civilian guides also were wounded.[28]

Over a year later, on September 15, 1868, approximately 100 Southern Cheyenne descended on Company I, commanded by Captain George W. Graham. They fought until dark. The company lost 10 horses killed or captured. The Cheyenne paid more dearly, it being reported that seven from their party had been struck. That same day, a nine-member detachment from Company G held off 60 or so Cheyenne, who, before their withdrawal, wounded one private and two civilians with the Tenth Cavalry detail.

---

24 The basis for much of the recapitulation of the Ninth Cavalry during the Ghost dance was drawn from: Alexander W. Perry, 'The Ninth United States Cavalry in the Sioux Campaign of 1890,' *Journal of the United States Cavalry Association* 4 no. 12 (March 1891) :37–40.
25 For a summary and contextual analysis of the Ghost Dance and Wounded Knee refer to: Robert M, Utley, *The Last Sovereigns: Sitting Bull and the Resistance of the Free Lakotas* (Lincoln, NE: Bison Books, 2020).
26 Rodenbough and Haskin, *The Army of the United States*, 287.
27 Leckie and Leckie, *The Buffalo Soldiers*, 8, 13–14, 17, 20, 22; and 30–33.
28 George A. Armes, *Ups and Downs of an Army Officer* (Washington, DC: privately printed, 1900), 243–9.

A day later, about 700 Native Americans with Roman Nose, 'corralled' Lieutenant Colonel George A. Forsyth and dozens of well-armed white scouts on an island in the Republican River. Two of his men slipped through the cordon. They reached Fort Wallace, Kansas with news of the desperate situation. Relief parties mobilized, including Captain Louis H. Carpenter with Company H, as well as Company I. Carpenter's relief force arrived first. They found Forsyth's beleaguered defenders without of rations and 'living on horse-flesh without salt or pepper.' All their officers had fallen or had been wounded and all the horses and mules had been killed. The twice wounded Forsyth, laid in a hastily scooped hole in the sand. The stench of livestock was overpowering. Carpenter ordered tents pitched for the wounded away from the foul air and waited for additional relief that arrived 26 hours later.

By October 14, Carpenter and members of his hard riding Company H, responded to new orders. He was to take his men and those of Company I, under Captain Graham, as an escort for Major Eugene Asa Carr of the Fifth Cavalry. Previously, Carr had expressed a low opinion of Black soldiers. The two companies set out towards Carr's camp on Beaver Creek.[29] En route, on October 18, about 400 Native Americans hit the column of 120 men. Although under fire, they forged ahead until reaching a defensible position. Carpenter halted the troops, drew up the supply wagons as a makeshift bastion and galloped the cavalrymen inside the protective barricade. His men dismounted and secured their horses within the wagon centre. Once afoot, the cavalry quickly formed on the outside of the corral. Then, they volley-fired their Spencer repeating carbines that repelled most of the attackers, even though several valiant warriors stood fast. Such bravery cost the stalwart Cheyenne. Nine died including their mounts and an unknown number of wounded left the field with the others. Three warriors made it to within 50 yards of the wagons. Once the six-hour clash concluded with attackers' withdrawal, the column continued with their three wounded comrades. They turned back to Fort Wallace without further challenge, having travelled 230 miles in about seven days.[30]

From Kansas, Grierson's men eventually took up stations at Forts Sill, Gibson, Arbuckle, Camp Supply and Cheyenne Agency, all in Indian Territory, as well as some elements that remained at Fort Dodge. During April 1873, a shift to Texas began with three companies reporting to Fort Richardson, two to Fort Griffin and another pair to Fort Concho. The other companies remained at Fort Sill and Camp Supply, Indian Territory.

Nonetheless, during the summer of 1873, a brief respite descended on Indian Territory. In contrast, small raiding parties haunted the north Texas border.[31] Their strikes kept the Black horse solders on the move, but rarely did a patrol locate much less close with a well mounted enemy.[32] Even during winter, when Native Americans in Texas commonly went into camp, Comanche and Kiowa raids took place with such frequency that the Tenth Cavalry spent the season stationed at a string of stockaded, temporary fire bases spread out between Fort Sill and

---

29 R. Waller, 10th Cavalry, 1868, 'The fighting Tenth Whipped the Indians at Beaver Creek,' *Winners of the West*, October 1924, 3, offered a first-hand reminiscence of the skirmish.
30 The above accounts represent a composite of Rodenbough and Haskins, *Army of the United States*, 291–2; E.L.N. Glass, comp and ed., *The History of the Tenth Cavalry, 1866–1921* (Fort. Collins, CO: Old Army Press, 1972), 15–16; and *ARSW, 1869*, I, 19–20. Also see: 'Trooper of the Tenth US Cavalry Claims to be the First Man to the Rescue of Beecher Island,' *Winners of the West*, August 1925, 1.
31 H. B. Wharfield, *10th Cavalry & Border Fights* (El Cajon, CA: H. B. Wharfield, 1965), 55–9.
32 Leckie and Leckie, *The Buffalo Soldiers*, 7 and 80–81.

Fort Griffin. These detachments served as a mobile, rapid strike force, to intercept their roving adversaries. Through the spring and summer, hostilities increased. By July, military leaders planned another major campaign similar to the one of 1867–68. Setting out in September, various units including the Tenth, remained active until the following spring.

During this campaign, known as the Red River War, five columns drawn from regiments stationed in the Departments of Texas and Missouri, ranged over a wide-ranging territory. The Tenth Cavalry formed the 'backbone' of one of these columns. After enduring the winter of 1874–1875 with but limited success, the regiment made its way south to Texas.[33]

Over the next 10 years, the Tenth Cavalry continued service in the Lone Star State. As before, hunting small bands of Native Americans entailed many long marches over a great expanse of harsh land, from the northern border of the state and occasionally across the Rio Grande into Mexico.[34] For example, in July 1875, six companies of the Tenth participated in an extensive expedition aimed at sweeping the Native Americans from the region of Texas known as the *Llano Estacado* or Staked Plain. Two years later, elements of the regiment once more entered this forbidding landscape.[35]

During the ensuing years, the regiment would be engaged in scores of small actions against bands of Apache, Lipan and Kickapoo throughout the region culminating in 1880 with rugged field service alongside the Ninth Cavalry during the pursuit of Victorio and his tenacious band. Highlights of the Tenth's participation included a July 30 ambush of Colonel Grierson and a half dozen men (including his young son) forcing them into a stand-off behind a quickly erected barricade between Fort Quitman and Eagle Springs, Texas. Lieutenant Leighton Finley with 15 reinforcements from Troop G, appeared on the scene to bolster the defence. The combined forces engaged the Apache and held them a bay for four hours until relieved by Troops A and C. Seven Apache warriors died while unknown numbers sustained wounds. During the three-hour engagement, one Tenth cavalryman, Private Martin Davis, was the sole fatality among the defenders. Lieutenant Samuel Colladay received a wound, but recovered[36]

As the war party withdrew, the Tenth gave chase to the Rio Grande. A running fight of 15 miles or more under Corporal Asa Weaver of Troop H proved fatal. Private William Tockes, Troop C, was killed. His bucking horse charged directly into the enemy. During the melee, Tockes dropped his horse's reins, aimed his carbine and fired to right and left. Originally listed as missing in action, months later, a patrol discovered his skeleton. Weaver received a promotion to sergeant. Also of note, Captain Thomas Lebo, with Company K, followed a hot trail to the top of the Sierra Diabola. His patrol captured Victorio's supply camp of 25 head of cattle and considerable other provisions on pack animals.[37]

A few days later, Colonel Grierson struck a more decisive blow. While trailing Victorio northwards through the Carriso Mountains, his column veered to the right, made a forced march of 65 miles, swung around the flank of the unawares Apache and delivered a frontal attack that forced them southward. Victorio's fortunes steadily declined until Mexican forces ended his

33 *Ibid.*, 126.
34 Glass, *The History of the Tenth Cavalry*, 20.
35 The latter expedition proved one of incredible hardship, as evidenced by Paul H. Carlson, *The Buffalo Soldier Tragedy of 1877* (College Station: Texas A&M University Press, 2003).
36 *A&NJ*, August 7, 1880, 14.
37 *Ibid.*, August 21, 1880, 48.

bold bid for freedom south of the border.[38] Thereafter, through 1881, the Tenth took part of in trailing Victorio's successor, the venerable Nana, who carried on a determined resistance.

Following these years of extensive field duties, a long-sought peace settled over the Texas-Mexico border region. This brief tranquility allowed the Tenth Cavalry to concentrate its companies at Forts Concho, Stockton and Davis, although the troopers continued to patrol the Rio Grande to the south and the Guadalupe Mountains to the west.[39] As such, from 1882 through 1885, the regiment enjoyed a welcome rest. In fact, the presence of the Tenth and other units greatly declined particularly with the Comanche, Kiowa and Mescalero tightly held to reservations.

By early 1885, the US Army turned to other more turbulent fronts. In the process, the Tenth Cavalry transferred to the Department of Arizona, long a 'dark and bloody ground.' In July of that year, the entire regiment rode overland from Texas across New Mexico and a slice of Mexico for their new home. Once they reached Arizona Territory, the regiment's components dispersed. Regimental headquarters and one troop took station at Whipple Barracks adjacent to Prescott. Another five troops went to Fort Grant, three to Fort Thomas, two to Fort Verde and one to Fort Apache.

Four of the troops from Fort Grant had scarcely settled into their quarters when orders directed them to join the ongoing campaign against Geronimo. A squadron consisting of Troops D, E, H and K, under Major Fredrick Van Vliet, marched from eastern Arizona to Fort Bayard, New Mexico, via the Mogollon Mountains. Their outing produced no results. Meanwhile, most of the regiment took to the field during the entire Geronimo campaign.[40] Several of the officers performed detached duty with Indian scouts at the front. Some, such as Second Lieutenant Powhatan Clarke, combined Indian scouts and handpicked enlisted men from the Tenth, to conduct patrols along the Mexican border. Intermittently, he linked up with his Troop K under command of Captain Lebo. It was on one such occasion, in 1886, that brought Clarke and Troop K into the northern Mexico's Pineto Mountains where his rescue of Corporal Edward Scott, under a hail of enemy bullets, earned him a Medal of Honor.[41] As the account of regimental activities confessed, however: 'Such instances of distinguished service are the more creditable as the opportunities therefor were extremely rare. To the greater part of the regiment the Geronimo campaign was a dismal succession of inglorious days devoted to the guarding of water-holes, mountain passes, etc.'[42]

Nonetheless, for months, elements of the Tenth stayed the course along with their white comrades. Their steadfast efforts took its toll down. During March 1886, Geronimo could no longer sustain his resolute bid to remain at large. He agreed to end the fighting. However, he quickly changed his mind and slipped away again into the wilds of Mexico.

---

38   The above narrative was taken from Rodenbaugh and Haskin, *The Army of the United States*, 295–6. Also, refer to, Kendall D. Gott, *In Search of an Elusive Enemy: The Victorio Campaign, 1879–1880* (Fort Leavenworth: Combat Studies Institute Press, 2004).
39   Leckie and Leckie, *The Buffalo Soldiers*, 239–46.
40   Glass, *The History of the Tenth Cavalry*, 24.
41   For more information on this engagement obtain, John P. Langellier, *Scouting with the Buffalo Soldiers: Lieutenant Powhattan Clarke, Frederic Remington, and the Tenth Cavalry in in the Southwest* (Denton, TX: University of North Texas Press, 2020), 125–32.
42   Rodenbaugh and Haskin, *The Army of the United States*, 296.

Despite a taxing month-long chase by the Fourth and Tenth Cavalry regiments, Geronimo and less than three dozen loyal holdouts avoided capture.[43] To deny aid from the Chiricahua Apache, Geronimo's kinsmen, the government seized those who remained on the reservation at San Carlos. Orders withdrew Tenth Cavalry troopers from the field campaign in order to arrest and transport 400 Chiricahua. These unfortunate victims of war eventually boarded trains as prisoners bound for Florida. Geronimo and his dwindling numbers ultimately joined them in exile. He would never return to the land of his birth and only a small group still eluded capture. Mangus, the son of the impressive of Mangus Coloradas, remained at large with his followers until September 18, 1886. On that day, Troop H, Tenth Cavalry trapped the fugitives. Rather than fight to the death, they too surrendered.[44]

Generally, peace prevailed thereafter. For the most part, the conclusion of campaigning by the Tenth Cavalry came as semi-official history recorded: 'The Indians were … fairly well settled down to farming on their reservations' essentially rang true.[45] With this ceasefire, in late 1886, the regiment's headquarters relocated to Santa Fe. Afterwards, the Tenth Cavalry experienced relative quiet in north-western New Mexico, although intermittent unrest from the Native Americans, who remained in the region after Geronimo's forced removal, required occasional responses. More critical actions took place in 1887, when details from the regiment returned the field, this time on the manhunt for the 'Apache Kid' (*Haskay-bay-nay-ntayl*) a former scout turned renegade – although in many ways, not without provocation.[46]

Supposedly, during June 1887, the Kid and some of his fellow scouts killed 'the former Indian policeman known as Rip.' Complicating matters, the Kid and his detail had been drinking, a common accompaniment to violence at San Carlos. Furthermore, Rip reputedly had killed the Kid's kinsman marking the incident as a not uncommon example of kinship revenge.[47] After Rip's death, orders to disarm the Kid and his group awaited them at the agency. Some of the men surrendered their weapons. Evidently the Kid, 'had not given up his gun yet and made signs to [his men] to take back their [ammunition] belts and their guns too; the belts and the guns.' Sensing trouble, chief of scouts, German-born civilian Al Sieber, rushed 'into his tent to get his Winchester … Just as he stepped through the opened door he fell to one side when a shot went through the door.'[48] The Kid bolted.

Although the Kid and his associates would be captured, tried and sentenced to life imprisonment, General Nelson Miles called for a reduction to 10 year terms for each man. The officer

---

43 First Lieutenant John Bigelow, Troop K, Tenth Cavalry sent serialized accounts to *Outing Magazine*, that captured many details of the final Geronimo campaign from a first-hand perspective. The articles would be edited and compiled Arthur Woodward into the highly readable, *On the Bloody Trail of Geronimo* (Tucson: Westernlore Press, 1986).
44 Rodenbaugh and Haskin, *The Army of the United States*, 296; Leckie and Leckie, *The Buffalo Soldiers*, 251–2.
45 Glass, *The Tenth Cavalry*, 28.
46 According to *A&NJ*, March 15, 1890, 579, '"The Kid" is about 30 years old, tall, slight and very handsome, and one of the brightest Apaches of these Carlos reservation. He was at one time 1st sergeant of the company of Apache scouts, commanded by Mr. [Francis Joseph] Darr, formerly lieutenant of the 12th U. S. Infantry.'
47 Alan Radbourne, *Mickey Free: Apache Captive, Interpreter, and Indian Scout* (Tucson: Arizona Historical Society, 2005), 193.
48 John P. Langellier, ed., and comp., *All My People Were Killed: The Memoir of Mike Burns (Hoomothya) A Captive Indian* (Prescott, AZ: Sharlot Hall Museum, 2010), 40.

who served as defence during the courts-martial, continued the appeal process. He eventually secured their releases from the military prison on Alcatraz. When the Kid returned to Arizona, he would be escorted back to San Carlos. The army determined that he and the other scouts should not have been judged by courts-martial.

Instead, the case was deemed a matter for the civil courts. The Kid and his co-defendants returned to Arizona to face a new trial held at Globe. At his hearing, the Kid, Say-es, Pash- ten -tah (Bach-e-on-al) and Hale (Miguel) were found guilty of the attempted murder of Al Sieber. Convicted of this crime, all these former scouts were sentenced to seven years at the Yuma Territorial Prison. The four and a similar number of other Apache, named Hos-cal-te (Tonto Tag Number 60), El-cahn, Has-ten-tu-du-jay and Bi-the-ja-be-tish-to-ce-an, along with a Mexican convicted of horse rustling, proceeded to the railhead at Casa Grande. Sherriff Glenn Reynolds and W. A. 'Hunkydory' Holmes guarded the group being transported in a wagon driven by a third civilian, Eugene Middleton. At Kelvin Grade in the Tortilla Mountains, the incline became so steep that all the prisoners dismounted their moving jail. It was there that they overcame their guards, both of whom died in the escape attempt. Making good their attack, the prisoners all scattered, leaving behind a wounded Middleton and the stunned horse thief. Snow covered their tracks allowing all of them to disappear despite efforts to apprehend the fugitives.[49]

Some four months later, one of the same escapees, Hale, had been brought to bay. At the time, the Mexican forces encountered him, under the redoubtable Moscow born Emilio Kosterlitzky, they had no idea about the relationship of their two-day battle with the Apache Kid and his fellow runaways.[50] Not until Kosterlitzky sent the watch and chain retrieved at the site to the United States, along with a revolver bearing some initials and a money pouch with US currency, did it become clear that these were all items removed from Sherriff Reynolds' body.[51]

Three days after Kosterlitzky's engagement in Sonora, north of the international line, another two Apache became casualties and three were captured. A like number of survivors, El-Chees-Choos, Nas-good and In-dees-doo-day, remained at large, trailed by an atypical composite force during the days of a segregated army. The patrol consisted of selected Black veteran soldiers from Troop I, K and L Tenth US Cavalry, a small detail of white enlisted men from Troop L, Fourth US Cavalry and Indian scouts, all White Mountain Apache, except for one Yavapai. As

---

49   Several sources provide details, including Phyllis de la Garza, *The Apache Kid* (Tucson: Westernlore Press, 1995); Jess G. Hayes, *Apache Vengeance* (Albuquerque: University of New Mexico Press, 1954); and Charles W, McKenna, Jr., *Renegade of Renegades: Court-Martial of Apache Kid* (Lubbock: Texas Tech University Press, 2009).

50   la Garza, *The Apache Kid*, 297; and *A&NJ* April 5, 1890, 599. The son of a Russian father and German mother, as a youth Kosterlitzsky lived in both countries. He would attend military school in St. Petersburg, Russia. Afterwards he spent a brief time with the Russian Navy from which he deserted during a cruise which put into Cabello, Venezuela. He made his way north to Mexico where in the 1870s he joined the army of that nation quickly becoming a first sergeant. Soon thereafter he received a commission as an ensign (junior lieutenant) and climbed the career ladder ultimately being promoted to colonel in the Mexican National Guard on December 28, 1906. Among other things he performed parallel services in the *Gendarmeria Fiscal*, the famed *Rurales* otherwise known as the mounted police of Sonora. This interesting mercenary-adventurer died in Los Angeles in September 4, 1926. Thrapp, *Frontier Biography*, 795–96; and Cornelius C. Smith, Jr., *Emilio Kosterlitzsky: Eagle of Sonora and the Southwest Border* (Glendale, CA: Arthur H. Clark Co., 1970).

51   Hayes, *Apache Vengeance*, 162–63.

one of the pair of officers with the group, Lieutenant Powhatan Clarke explained, 'an American troop will have in it only a few splendid riders and a lot of men who are absolutely worthless.' This meant that for serious duty such 'as an Indian chase, we take selected men from several troops.'[52] The red, white and Black strike force, under Lieutenant James Watson with Clarke as second in command, closed with the fugitives three miles north of Roggenstrohs's Ranch near the mouth of Cherry Creek at Salt River.[53]

In crisp prose, Tucson's Spanish language newspaper, *El Fronterizo*, recounted that the '5 renegades who murdered the driver George Herbert last week were hit yesterday, 30 miles north of here, by the troops of Lieutenants Watson and Clarke, a rough fight ensued which resulted in the death of two hostiles and the capture of the remaining three.' The clash took place after a chase of, 'more than three hundred miles through the most rugged country of the territory.' The two dead 'Apaches were buried in the same place where they fell,' while the prisoners proceeded to Globe for trial in Graham County.[54]

On the same day (March 15, 1890), a Tucson English language periodical, the *Arizona Weekly Citizen*, provided its version of the confrontation. The paper added details such as the command led by Watson and Clarke, 'overtook the renegades on Salt river, about 30 miles north of Globe in a rugged and almost impenetrable locality. The troops surprised the renegades at 1 o'clock, p.m., on Friday and after the first exchange of shots the renegades took to the rocks and began a determined fight for their lives.' During this clash, 'The troops and scouts displayed great bravery ... although at a disadvantage' in their positions against a well concealed enemy. Rare praise from locals called this 'the best piece of work ever accomplished in the pursuit of Indians in Arizona and the greatest credit is due to the lieutenants for their splendid work and those under them especially "Rowdy" and other scouts, who resolutely stuck to the trail until the fugitives were sighted.'

In fact, another report from Globe's *Silver Belt*, described the intense action as the patrol closed in on the renegades. Both Watson and Clarke led from the front, intent on reaching the mouth of a small cave, which colorfully was described as 'not as deep as a quart mug.' Clarke, the first to appear in front of the enemy hideout shot one of them, 'twice though the body. "Rowdy" the Indian scout shot the Indian, breaking both arms, thus saving the life of "Tucson's own" Lieut Clarke' who had a bullet hole 'through his hat and also one between his legs.'

Likewise, Sergeant James T. Daniels of Troop I, Fourth US Cavalry and Sergeant William McBryar of Clarke's Troop K joined Rowdy in the elite pantheon of Medal of Honor recipients. Daniels would be commended for: 'Untiring energy and cool gallantry under fire in an engagement with Apache Indians.' McBryar would be singled out 'for coolness, bravery and marksmanship while his troop was in pursuit of hostile Apache Indians.'[55] In McBryar's case,

---

52 (New York) *Herald*, May 12, 1892, 5.
53 Berndt Kühn, *Chronicles of War: Apache and Yavapai Resistance in the Southwestern United States and Northern Mexico, 1821–1937* (Tucson: Arizona Historical Society, 2014), 297. Little is known of George Roggenstroh other than a mention that he was a cattleman who bought livestock in Willcox. (Florence) *Arizona Weekly Enterprise*, July 26, 1890, 1.
54 (Tucson) *El Fronterizo*, March 15, 1890, 1.
55 Eric S. Johnson, comp. and ed, *No Greater Calling: A Chronological Record of Sacrifice and Heroism During the Western Indian Wars, 1865–1898* (Atglen, PA: Schiffer Military History, 201), 358. Schubert, *Black Valor*, 101–15; 150, 155; 158; 161, 166–67, outlined the career of this dedicated professional. Also read *Arizona Silver Belt*, June 21, 1890, 3, which indicated the presentation of the

as Frank N. Schubert underscored in *Black Valor*, the army approved his medal 'with almost no delay, making him the first man in the Tenth Cavalry to be so honored.' Schubert postulated: 'The speed with which this award was made suggests that McBryar did indeed distinguish himself. Frequently, years passed before officers got around to submitting recommendations and sometimes the soldiers themselves had to start the process.'[56]

The long-time colonel of the Tenth Cavalry, Benjamin Grierson, recently advanced to brigadier general in command of the Department of Arizona, recommended the prompt award of brevets and medals for distinguished gallantry.[57] Additionally, he echoed others when he stated:

> This is one of the most brilliant affairs of-its kind that has occurred in recent years and has had a very quieting effect upon and will no doubt prove a lasting lesson to, the Indians of the San Carlos Agency. It was, therefore, extremely gratifying to congratulate the commanding officers of San Carlos and Fort Thomas and especially Lieutenants Watson and Clarke and the troops under their command for the persistent pursuit and complete success.[58]

Even Frederic Remington drew on affray. He turned the incident into an article titled 'Two Gallant Young Cavalry Men' for *Harper's Weekly*.

This episode closed the Tenth Cavalry's combat record in Arizona. It did remain in the territory for several more years and included in 1891, a detail who entered the Hopi reservation within the territory to maintain law and order. The previous year, the United States government began to enforcement of a compulsory attendance at Indian agency schools. The Hopi protested. Unrest reached such a level that two troops arrived to assure compliance with the unpopular policy.[59]

Some five years later, during June and July 1896, after the regiment's transfer to Montana, Tenth Cavalry troopers apprehended some 525 Cree, who crossed into the United States from Canada on a raid for horses and cattle. The men of the Tenth spent over 1,000 miles in the saddle on this assignment, which ended with the return to the north of this destitute group who also suffered from disease.[60]

    Medal of Honor to Rowdy on the parade ground at Fort Grant and the bestowal of brevet ranks of captain and first lieutenant on Watson and Clarke respectively, at the same ceremony.
56   Schubert, *Black Valor*, 106, 194 n 11, and 195 n12.
57   Grierson also must have been pleased of a mention in the Santa Fe *Daily New Mexican*, March 22, 1890, 4, that he was the commander officer for Watson and Clarke and made it appear that their colonel deserved some credit for the success of his two subordinates.
58   *ARSW 1890* I, 167. Also, for a synopsis of the operation and Grierson's comments consult *A&NJ*, April 5, 1890, 599. Also note, both officers wrote of this firefight. This first, which received considerable assistance from Frederic Remington, was Powhatan Clarke, 'A Hot Trail,' A Hot Trail,' XVI *Cosmopolitan Magazine* No. 6 (October 1894), 706–16; and James W. Watson, 'Scouting in Arizona,' X *Journal of the US Cavalry Association* (June 1897): 128–134. Curiously, Remington's own attempt to narrate the tale of what happened to the Kid's group, 'How an Apache War Was Won,' remained unpublished in his lifetime. McCracken, *Frederic Remington's Own West*, 49–61. In the story he mentions only Watson. In turn, Watson and Clarke do not mention McBryar by name although they refer to Rowdy.
59   John Bigelow, Jr., *Reminiscence of the Santiago* Campaign (New York and London: Harper & Brothers, 1899), 296–297; Glass, *History of the Tenth Cavalry*, 26–28.
60   One communication noted an officer and a detail from Troop C, Tenth Cavalry brought back 24 Cree. MC46, Letters Sent, Vol. 20, June 18, 1896, Montana Historical Society Library, Helena, MT.

By the next summer, Troops, A, E and K, 'were called out to arrest' several Cheyenne near the Tongue River Agency, but again this duty did not result in a clash between the two groups.[61] By spring 1898, the Indian Agent at the Blackfeet Agency, asked for 150 troops from Fort Assiniboine, Montana. This request had to be denied due to the transfer of most of the garrison in Montana when the war with Spain led to troop withdrawal from the territory for redeployment to the Department of the Gulf, as part of the force destined for the invasion of Cuba.[62]

Except for the disastrous Wounded Knee episode, these various forays of Montana's Black cavalrymen against American Indians were resolved without bloodshed. In fact, by the time African American soldiers reached Montana, a major mission for most of the Victorian era US Army had all but ended – that of providing a combat force to engage the ever-pressed native peoples of the West.

Walk-a-Heaps – Infantrymen Enter the Fray

Although cavalrymen experienced most of the armed conflict in the West, from time to time Black infantrymen took to the field and met with a Native American opponent. Indeed, one of the earliest newspaper accounts of encounters between Native Americans and Black soldiers entailed an encounter with infantrymen. Corporal David Turner of Company K, Thirty-Eighth Infantry, provided an eyewitness account of this episode that occurred in Kansas, on June 26, 1867. Turner and fellow infantrymen had a 'fite with Indians.' The exchange lasted about one and a half hours. After that, the war party withdrew to bury their dead. Turner claimed the enemy's fatalities numbered four including their leader. He also recounted, 'none of our men were hurt the boys fit well and when the Indians made their wild yell the boys ancered them with led.' One non-commissioned officer failed to perform as steadily. Turner confessed: 'ime sorry to say Corprel Smith flich from the fire he stop in camp until the fite was about over and then he come out after the Indians was two miles off and holred give it to em boys.' Turner and his comrades thought that was 'poor encouragement for a non commissioned offercer.'[63]

Although willing to do their part in combat, generally the infantry faced one major disadvantage, that of being afoot against a highly mobile, mounted opponent. A report from 1869 Kansas underscored this and other drawbacks. By the time a company of the Thirty-Eighth left their barracks in response to Native Americans being sighted in the area, 'so much time was consumed in getting' into the field passed and followed by the fact that 'the rations for the expedition … were eaten up,' the result would be that little was 'accomplished by this column.'[64]

See also, MC46, Letters Sent, Vol. 20, June 15, 1896; June 23, 1896; and June 26, 1896, referring to the 'roundup' of the Cree and their deportation to Canada. Glass, *History of the Tenth Cavalry*, 30, noted Lieutenant Pershing and the men of Troop D were 'out all summer, marching over 600 miles' during this assignment.

61 Glass, *History of the Tenth Cavalry*, 30.
62 MC 46, Letters Received, Vol. 20, April 8, 1898; and April 10, 1898.
63 A reprint from Boston *Transcript* in the Richmond *Daily Dispatch*, August 15, 1867. A year later, a detachment in the Hatchet Mountains, New Mexico, August 2, 1868 … wherein three Indians were killed and many wounded, and a large amount of property destroyed and animals captured.' *ARSW, 1869*, I, 773–4.
64 *ARSW, 1869*, I, 18.

Two years later, after the Twenty-Fourth Infantry had been organized, they also found it difficult to close with a fast-moving foe. For instance, during June and July 1871, companies from the regiment gave chase to raiders bound for the White Sands region of southeastern New Mexico. Although unsuccessful in closing with the group or regaining stolen livestock, they became the first members of the United States Army to make their way into the White Sands region and survive.[65]

In 1875, two companies reached an equally formidable environment – *Llano Estacado*. Commanded by Lieutenant Colonel Shafter, they operated under the twin goals to clear the Llano Estacado of Comanche and prepare a detailed map of a little known region, at least to the military and settlers alike. Besides men from the Twenty-Fourth, Shafter's contingent included other Black troops from the Tenth Cavalry and the Twenty-Fifth Infantry, along with two companies of Indian scouts, who possessed invaluable knowledge of the area.

After Shafter gathered his command at Fort Concho, Texas, he eventually led the contingent north to the Fresh Fork of the Brazos River. The first leg of the journey brought them to a previously established camp. Simultaneously, the cavalry and Indian scouts rode westward in quest of the Comanche, intent on the destruction of their villages. For the most part, the Infantry remained at the supply camp, although detachments of foot soldiers ranged to the southwest on patrols. Completing almost five months in the field, in late November, Shafter headed his column to Fort Duncan, Texas. Even though a crippling physical blow had not been struck, the command won a phycological victory by making it clear the Llano Estacado offered no inaccessible sanctuary to the Comanches. Further, the map prepared from their reconnaissance remained in use for three decades.[66]

Not content to rest on these accomplishments, in 1876, the same pair of companies from the Twenty-Fourth Infantry, once again followed Shafter. During the spring of that year, negotiations broke the long-term interdiction by Mexico of US troops crossing into their sovereign territory, at least while pursuing Native Americans fleeing Texas southward. As part of this new situation, in July 1876, Black infantrymen again displayed their mettle. Companies B, E and K crossed into Mexico. A detachment from the regiment, composed of 20 carefully picked, hardy men from Company B under Lieutenant George Evans and 20 Seminole scouts, all under command of Lieutenant John Bullis, Twenty-Fourth Infantry, were selected. They trekked 110 footsore miles in 25 hours. Their rapid advance resulted in surprising a camp 40 miles from the Pecos River that consisted of 23 lodges of Lipan and Kickapoo near Saragossa, Mexico. The lighting strike left 10 enemy dead and four captured, along with an estimated 200 horses. Lighting a huge bonfire, the strike force threw the captured camp material into the flames, followed by heading their prisoners and captured stock back to the main column.[67] While the expedition managed to destroy some villages to ashes, the actions of the American military enraged many Mexican citizens. As the United States troops returned northwards towards the Rio Grande, an unfriendly Mexican Army

---

65 Leckie, *The Buffalo Soldiers*, 96–97.
66 Arlen Fowler, *The Black Infantry in the West, 1869–1891* (Westport, CT: Greenwood Press, 1971) 32–33; Leckie *The Buffalo Soldiers*, 143–48; William G. Müller, *The Twenty Fourth Infantry: Past and Present, 1869–1922* (Ft. Collins, CO: Old Army Press, 1972), 24–26.
67 *New Orleans Republican*, August 5, 1876. For a contextual overview obtain: Kenneth W Porter, 'The Seminole Negro-Indian Scouts, 1870–1881,' *Southwestern Historical Quarterly* (1952) 55: 358–377.

followed close to their rear.⁶⁸ Despite these circumstances, throughout the rest of 1876 and into 1877, the US Army crossed the Rio Grande repeatedly, although admittedly the infantry's primary function was to guard the railroad crossing over the Rio Grande.⁶⁹

Moreover, the Twenty-Fifth Infantry participated in these actions, when in 1878, Company B joined Colonel Ronald Mackenzie's final foray across the Rio Grande. Rather than conduct another search and destroy operation, Mackenzie's chief objective was a show of force for the Mexican government. For nearly three decades, the United States railed against what it perceived as the Mexican government's inactivity to quell violence and lawlessness along the border. Even after Washington's April 1878 official recognition of strongman Porfirio Díaz's regime, the issue remained contentious. President Díaz refused to change his country's policy until the US Army rescinded its orders that permitted American forces to enter Mexico. A stalemate resulted when the US government countered that cross-border operations would not cease until the Díaz government addressed the situation with its own plan of action.

On June 12, 1878, Mackenzie along with eight troops of cavalry, three companies of infantry (one of which was Company B of the Twenty-Fifth Infantry) and three artillery batteries, demonstrated the Americans' ability to maneuver in Mexico at will. On two different occasions, during Mackenzie's nine-day excursion, the Mexican Army dispatched a blocking force to repel the advance of the *norteamericanos*. Twice, US infantry continued the march. Each time, Mexican troops withdrew. Having shown the flag, Mackenzie directed his column north. By June 21, 1878, they crossed the Rio Grande onto US soil. His forces returned to their various duty stations, including Company B that marched to San Felipe, Texas on June 23.⁷⁰

By the 1880s, for all intents, Black infantrymen ceased fighting in the borderlands. Instead, they provided security as camp guards. During the conclusion of the Victorio Campaign, they protected the supply trains for the Tenth Cavalry. In August 1880, however, Black infantrymen contributed to the relief of Grierson at Rattlesnake Springs, that at last ended Victorio's presence in Texas as a final engagement against Native Americans in the region. With that, the days of striking out against Native Americans by African American foot soldiers closed.⁷¹

Cuba – A Hot Time in the Old Town

Now that the Black regulars concluded campaigns on the frontier, it appeared their combat days ended. Then, in 1898, the time came for all four regiments of Black soldiers to mobilize for their first overseas experience. Once more, they would face fire, but this time against a new opponent, the Spanish, who awaited them in Cuba. On the night of February 15, 1898, while riding at anchor in Havana Harbor, an explosion sank USS *Maine*. The death of 260 Americans, of whom 22 were Black seaman, enraged Americans. Revenge against Spain, the purported culprit responsible for the sinking, provoked the public. They rallied to the battle cry: 'Remember the *Maine*! To Hell with Spain!' Diplomacy failed to placate the United States. Many US citizens and the press clamored for war. During April 1898, the jingoists prevailed. The United States

---

68 Leckie, *The Buffalo Soldiers*, 149–50; Müller, *The Twenty Fourth Infantry*, 26–28.
69 Utley, *Frontier Regulars*, 11–12; Müller, *Twenty Fourth Infantry*, 28.
70 Smith and Zeidler, *A Historic Context*, 107–8.
71 Leckie, *The Buffalo Soldiers*, 226–7.

Congress responded in the affirmative to President William McKinley's request to dispatch an armed force to Cuba. Congress not only concurred, but also, declared Cuba to be a free and independent nation rather than a Spanish colony.[72]

The Black regulars received orders as some of the first units to be called up for duty abroad. Gathering in the South from their various posts in the West, the Twenty-Fourth and Twenty-Fifth Infantry regiments, along with the Ninth and Tenth Cavalry regiments joined other units to form the 5th Army Corps, commanded by none other than William R. Shatter, now an overweight, ageing major general. The Ninth and Tenth Calvary served under former Confederate General Joseph Wheeler in his dismounted cavalry division. The Twenty-Fourth Infantry reported to Major General Jacob F. Kent's infantry division, while the Twenty-Fifth Infantry formed under Brigadier General Henry W. Lawton.

After rather hasty preparations and training, for the first time in history, all four Black regiments assembled for combat duty together. On June 15, 1898, they steamed from Tampa Bay for a seven-day voyage to Cuba. Once their transports reached the coastal town of Daiquiri, tempestuous seas hindered the debarkation of materiel and troops. The first causalities of the campaign resulted from efforts to land, claiming the lives of two privates from the Tenth Cavalry, who drowned. Surmounting the challenge of coming ashore, the invasion force rapidly turned inland with the aim of reaching the capital city of Santiago.

To arrive at this objective, they faced their first obstacle, the Spanish defenses at Las Guasimas southeast of the capital. Wheeler's division drew this opening assignment that fell to the First Volunteer Cavalry (Rough Riders) along with the regulars, the First (white) and Tenth (Black) US Cavalry regiments. Forging ahead, these units drew up at Las Guasimas where they readied for the assault. During the early morning of June 24, they attacked the Spanish above them on a hill surrounded by dense vegetation. After an hour or more of brisk fighting, they finally dislodged the Spaniards, who retreated in good order towards Santiago. Heat, humidity and the physical strain of battle in the hot and humid climate left the dismounted US cavalry unable to give chase.

Next, the Americans pushed northwest towards Santiago. As they neared the city's outskirts, they took up position of a plain just below San Juan Heights. Before the Americans appeared, the Spaniards strengthened their defence works on three strategic hills – San Juan, El Pozo (named Kettle Hill by Americans because of a sugar refinery on top, which resembled a kettle from afar) and El Caney. Victory depended on seizing these key positions located on heights enhanced by breastworks, strong entrenchments, barbed wire and an extensive field of fire for Spanish Mausers and machine guns to sweep the onslaught from below. The defenders at El Caney enjoyed the additional advantages of four blockhouses, a stone church and a small fort.

To overcome these well positioned barriers, the US called for the division of forces into two units. With the smaller contingent that included the Twenty-Fifth Infantry, Lawton would undertake dislodging the enemy at El Caney. Unrealistically, believing Lawton's men could storm the position within a matter of minutes, the plan postulated a quick link up with Wheeler's larger body. Wheeler's force would consist of the Ninth and Tenth Cavalry and Kent's infantrymen among whom were the Twenty-Fourth. After combining the two elements, the Americans then could assault San Juan and El Pozo Hills.

---

72 Smith and Zeigler, *A Historic Context*, 129.

With this plan in place, during the early morning of July 1, some 6,600 US troops appeared below San Juan Heights. When Lawton launched his drive against El Caney, over 500 Spanish readied for the clash that opened at dawn. A pre-strike artillery bombardment resulted in little impact. Nevertheless, Lawton called for the main body to advance while the Twenty-Fifth waited in reserve. Fighting lasted until around noon, when the first defence fell amidst numerous casualties on both sides.

As the exhausted first wave rested, Lawton called on his reserves to prepare for the next strike. They did so with vigor. The Twenty-Fifth swarmed forward. Through cactus that tore uniforms and flesh, they clambered past thick underbrush and overcame other obstacles. All the while, Spanish fire killed and wounded the Black infantrymen, who fell by the scores. Despite losses, they reached a slightly sheltered hollow from which they poured volleys into the defenders. Hoping their fire had weakened the Spanish, the American troops made a general advance up the hill. Several hours passed before they secured El Caney.

The target proved far more formidable than envisioned by Shafter. It required 10 hours not 10 minutes to overcome the determined defenders. In the process, nearly 450 American casualties resulted. Furthermore, thus occupied, Lawton's force could not add additional firepower to the San Juan Heights portion of the two-pronged assault. Regardless, the insistent Shafter dispatched his other force against San Juan and El Pozo Hills. Supposedly the Black soldiers 'went to that incline yelling and shouting,' and by so doing, inspired the white troops while at the same time demoralizing some of the enemy.[73] Even so, the Spanish held fast.

Not until mid-afternoon, did the US troops cut through the barbed wire then stormed the Spanish trenches where hand-to-hand fighting ensued. The overrun Spaniards lost the two hills but cut down many of those who faced them that day. More than 1,000 American dead and wounded paid the price. Indeed, the Twenty-Fourth sustained an amazing 40 percent casualty rate.[74] In the aftermath, from atop the San Juan Hill, a Black soldier exclaimed: 'The dead and wounded soldiers! It was indescribable! One would have to see it to know what it was like and having seen it, I truly hope I may never see it again.'[75]

While the Spanish yet remained entrenched around Santiago and their fleet anchored in Havana's harbor, only a matter of time remained before capitulation. On July 3, a truce ended the land war. Later that day, the United States Navy annihilated the Spanish fleet. Two weeks later, the local Spanish commander surrendered Cuba to the conquerors from the United States, among whom were the Black veterans, who had turned from the frontier West to a new chapter as instruments of a new-born international power.[76]

For the brave acts performed in Cuba, during 1898, the Black regulars earned five more Medals of Honor.[77] Matching this courage under fire at Siboney, Black soldiers unselfishly

---

73 Charles Alexander, *Battles and Victories of Allen Allensworth* (Boston: Sherman, French and Co., 1914), 369.
74 Albert Scipio II, *Last Black Regulars: A History of the 24th Infantry Regiment, 1869–1951* (Silver Spring, MD: Roman Publications, 1983), 25.
75 Willard B. Gatewood, Jr., *'Smoked Yankees' and the Struggle for Empire: Letters from Negro Soldiers 1898–1902* (Urbana: University of Illinois Press, 1971), 70.
76 Unless otherwise noted, Smith and Zeidler, *A Historic Context*, 130–35, provided the source for the above summary of operations in Cuba.
77 Among useful references to campaigning in Cuba and the Philippines are Edward A. Johnson, *History of the Negro Soldier in the Spanish American War (and Other Items of Interest)* (Cincinnati, OH:

volunteered to assist at the field hospital inundated by thousands of yellow fever-stricken victims. They responded to the desperate pleas of Colonel Charles Greenleaf, the surgeon in charge of the overwhelmed medical facility.

After eight different regimental commanders refused assistance, the Twenty-Fourth Infantry's colonel answered. He called for volunteers. A grateful Dr. Greenleaf told a reporter: 'There is more real heroism in marching into a fever-stricken tent and staying there day and night … than there is in making a single charge up any hill.' In response to their colonel's request 'every single man in the regiment' came forward.[78] Of those who stepped up, 65 functioned as nurses and another 70 performed as cooks, burial parties and hospital attendants. They did so at a cost. Only two dozen of the generous men avoided illness themselves whilst 31 paid the ultimate price for their sacrifices by death.[79] Later, some of these same stalwarts saw arduous campaigning in the Philippine Islands. Here they returned to what a few of them would have recognized today as counter insurgency operations or even asymmetrical warfare as it would be styled in a later era.

On to the Philippines

It was in an unfamiliar country, but it was a rather familiar type of warfare, to where all four regiments steamed not long after they returned from Cuba. During this same period, the War Department created two regiments of Black volunteers, the Forty-Eighth and Forty-Ninth Infantry, in the fall of 1899, who would be dubbed the 'Immunes.'[80] Whether Regular Army or Volunteers, these, *soldados negro*, as the Filipinos referred to the Black Americans in Army Blue, searched for will of the whisp *insurrectos* as they once did in Texas and elsewhere in the southwest on the trails of Apache, Comanche and other Native Americans. The jungles of the islands, well known to the Filipinos who rebelled against the most recent foreign overlords, the United States having replaced Spain, prevented the newcomers from staging full-fledged battles.

Guerilla warfare, known to some of the older soldiers and their veteran frontier officers, regularly meant responding to sniper fire and hit-and-run assaults. In response, small scouting parties probed the bush beyond the US Army's scattered camps, which sometimes resembled the crude frontier outposts from the immediate post-Civil War era.[81]

On rare occasions, patrols located and fought sizeable enemy forces. On August 12, 1899, one such incident occurred when a detail from the Twenty-Fourth Infantry sighted an enemy at San Mateo. They gave battle with one man killed and four others wounded before the *insurrectos*

W.H. Ferguson Company, Publishers ,1899); Miles V. Lynk, *The Black Troopers or the Daring Heroism of the Negro Soldiers in the Spanish-American War* (Jackson, TN: The M.V. Lynk Publishing House, 1899); Herschel V. Cashin, *Under Fire With the Tenth Cavalry* (Niwot: University Press of Colorado, 1993); Gatewood, Jr., *'Smoked Yankees;'* and Bigelow, *Reminiscence of the Santiago Campaign*. Also review a presentation made by Frank Schubert regarding Black soldiers at San Juan Hill, to wit: history.army.mil/html/documents/ wwspain/buffalos_sjh/schubert.htmlBuffalo.

78 *Leslie's Weekly*, November 3, 1898, 3.
79 Marvin Fletcher, *The Black Soldier and Officer in the United States Army, 1891–1917* (Columbia: University of Missouri Press, 1974), 43.
80 Gatewood, *'Smoked Yankees,'* 240.
81 Fletcher, *Black Soldier and Officer*, 52–53.

fled.⁸² Two years later, during January 1900, more than 1,000 Filipinos struck elements of the Twenty-Fifth Infantry at Iba, Zimbales. In a desperate defence, the Black infantrymen held out against an overwhelming onslaught, whom they drove off, but not before they reportedly killed more than 100 attackers. Miraculously, they avoided taking any casualties within their ranks.⁸³

Another noteworthy operation entailed a force of 350 infantrymen from the Twenty-Fourth following Captain Joseph B. Bachelor on a more than 300-mile trek through almost every imaginable type of terrain found in central Luzon. They intended to close with followers of the major leader of Filipino resistance, Emilio Aguinaldo. Their difficult dual-purpose was to prevent Aguinaldo's escape into the Cayagan Valley and to deal a damaging blow to his followers in the region. Once they reached Naguilian, the strike force discovered numerous well entrenched enemies on a bluff across from them on the Cayagan River. Several daring men volunteered to brave the swift running river, one of whom drowned in the attempt. Their bold action enabled a flanking movement that drove off the enemy from their fortified position. Afterwards, the stalwart men of the Twenty-Fourth continued their advance without further opposition. When they marched into Tugeraroa (Cayagan's capital), General Daniel Tirona, the local Filipino senior officer, surrendered without resistance along with 1,000 of his command.⁸⁴

Back to Mexico

Actions in the Philippines, although similar in some ways to the Indian Wars, especially in Texas and the American southwest, also differed in many ways.⁸⁵ In terms of the Black regulars, operations in the Philippine Islands generally entailed elements from the Twenty-Fourth and Twenty-Fifth Infantry regiments. Just prior to the United States' entry into the First World War, however, the cavalry experienced a brief resurgence after Francisco 'Pancho' Villa swept into the United States with 500 of his *Dorados* in what amounted to a terrorist attack on an American civilian community. Villa's purpose to incite the United States into war against the unstable Mexican government headed by Venustiano Carranza, also stemmed from his grievances against the United States for providing arms to that government's army. His raid resulted in an unforeseen consequence.

The day following the attack, President Woodrow Wilson dispatched John J. Pershing, a former junior officer who leaped from a captaincy in the Tenth Cavalry to don a brigadier general's star and due to Theodore Roosevelt's past patronage, assembled a retaliatory expedition destined for Mexico. His balancing act from the War Department entailed destruction of

---

82 Scipio, *Last Black Regulars*, 33.
83 John Henry Nankivell, *History of the Twenty-Fifth Regiment, United States Infantry, 1866–1926* (Denver: Smith-Brooks Printing, 1926), 91.
84 Fletcher, *Black Soldier and Officer*, 49–52.
85 For a comparison and contracts review, Andrew J. Birtle, *US Army Counterinsurgency and Contingency Operations Doctrine, 1860–1941* (Washington, DC, Center of Military History United States Army 2009), 55–189. For an overall look at Black soldiers in the Philippines study: Christopher M. Redgraves, 'African American Soldiers in the Philippine War: An Examination of the Contributions of Buffalo Soldiers during the Spanish American War and Its Aftermath, 1898–1902,' Ph.D. diss. University of North Texas, 2017.

Villa's force, while at the same time, he must tread with great care to avoid affronting Carranza's government.[86]

Resembling Makenzie and other officers from the past, on March 15, 1916, Pershing's Punitive Expedition made its way into Mexico, on a cold trail left by Villa through northern Mexico.

On March 29, the advance guard made first contact at Guerrero, Mexico. There, 370 officers and men from the Seventh Cavalry sent an estimated 600 Mexican rebels in retreat.[87] Two days later, the Tenth Cavalry also engaged an enemy with Major Charles Young assuming a key part in the clash at Aguas Calientes and a second contest ensued soon thereafter. These skirmishes with the Villistas were the exceptions rather than the rule. Consequently, during early May, Pershing turned to another approach. The general divided northern Mexico into five military districts, with a regiment given responsibility for the search in each region. He assigned the Tenth Cavalry to the Namiquipa district where it settled into a familiar boring camp routine.[88] Except for outpost duty and scouting, inactivity made one day appear much the same as the next until the Carranza government grew weary of the US Army in Mexico. Warned that the Mexican Army would oppose troop movements in any direction except northwards on its return to the United States, Washington paid no heed to the ultimatum. Altercations between Carranza's men and Pershing's units resulted.[89]

Tensions came to a head on June 16, 1916. Word arrived from headquarters for Captain Charles T. Boyd, commander of C Troop and his lieutenant, Hank Adair, to reconnoiter in the vicinity of Ahumada, Chihuahua, Mexico. Their mission required the patrol to obtain intelligence on the local Mexican troop strength, but under no circumstances were they to engage governmental forces from Mexico. Captain Lewis S. Morey, Troop K. commander received similar orders. In response, the two units set out from their individual camps.

Meeting at Santo Domingo Ranch, the combined force advanced together towards Ahumada where a series of events unfolded with deadly results. After approximately an hour at Carrizal, on June 21, 90 members of the Tenth Cavalry confronted over 400 Carranzistas. When the gunfire subsided, both of Troop C's officers were dead, along with 10 enlisted men. Two dozen Black horse soldiers became prisoners among whom were several wounded who suffered from both enemy bullets along with desperate thirst, hunger and exposure to the elements. Others either escaped or briefly avoided capture. Eventually the Mexicans returned the prisoners at El Paso.[90]

With one minor exception, the inopportune Carrizal scrap was the final resort to arms by the Tenth. The exception was a brief encounter at Bear Valley, 25 miles northwest of Nogales, Arizona, two years later which occurred against destitute Yaqui fugitives who made their way north from revolutionary worn Mexico.[91]

---

86 Clarence C. Clendenen, *Blood on the Border* (New York: Macmillan, 1969), 214.
87 *Ibid.*, 237–40.
88 *Ibid.*, 272–3.
89 Glass, *History of the Tenth Cavalry*, 79.
90 For a brief motion picture clip of the return of the Tenth Cavalry prisoners of war by the Mexican government see: youtube.com/watch?v=ukYczBoK9Wg.
91 Wharfield, *10th Cavalry & Border Fights*, 1–15.

Casualties

The dead at Carrizal were only some of the Black regulars who perished in the line of duty. Between 1886 and 1916, relatively few men (120) were killed in action. Just over half of this number fell during the Indian Wars of 1867–1890.[92] Conversely, far more significant were the numbers of soldiers who succumbed to disease, accident, or violence. Such was the case for the ill-stared 1877 excursion that set out from Fort Concho, Texas under Captain Nicholas Nolan of the Tenth Cavalry. This patrol came to be known as the 'Staked Plains Horror,' and also pejoratively referred to as 'Nolan's Lost Nigger Expedition.' Regardless of the sobriquet, the contingent suffered terribly during this ill-fated venture into the Llano Estacado.[93]

More Than Combatants

Combat missions, the *raison d'être* for the military, rightly received considerable emphasis in many narratives. While of importance, these episodes depicted only a portion of the Black soldiers' accomplishments between 1866 and 1916. Indeed, even as Black regulars demonstrated combat prowess, they simultaneously carried on diverse and sometimes demanding duties that required considerable ability. For example, Black soldiers took part in the rescue of lost groups in the vast West.[94] More commonly, they protected Indian lands from white encroachment such as the Mescalero Reservation in New Mexico beset by marauding outlaw bands. More notably though, Black cavalrymen preempted trespassing by whites onto Native American lands in Indian Territory years before the 'land rush' opened Oklahoma for settlement.

During the 1880s, today's Oklahoma had remained a federal government reservation for more than a dozen Native American peoples. Laws prohibited whites from entry, but between 1879 and 1881, considerable numbers of settlers violated. To stem this tide of settlement, the Ninth Cavalry deployed to Kansas and Oklahoma Territory.[95] One of these interlopers, David

---

92 Schubert, *On the Trail of the Buffalo Soldiers*, 514, lists 61 perished during the Indian Wars (44 men from the Ninth Cavalry and 17 from Tenth Cavalry) another 29 were killed by the Spanish in Cuba during 1898, 23 fell in the Philippines, and seven were killed in Mexico during 1916. 5

93 As mentioned in the *New York Herald*, August 7, 1877 'No news has been received from the party that went out from Concho in search of Captain Nolan and his men, lost on the Staked Plains, but there is reason to hope they may turn up yet all right.' Unfortunately this positive prediction proved unfounded as several newspapers around the country would soon report such as: *New York Sun*, August 9, 1877; *Dallas Weekly Herald*, August 11, 1877, September 15, 1877; *New Bloomfield, Pa. Times*, August 14, 1877; *Weekly Democratic Statesman* (Austin, TX) August 16, 1877; *Dallas Daily Herald*, September 9, 1877; *Weekly Herald* (Cleveland, TN) September 13, 1877; *Juniata Sentinel and Republican* (Mifflintown, PA) September 19, 1877; *Times* (New Bloomfield, PA) July 23, 1878. That same year the US Army Surgeon J.H.T. King published the first lengthy account of many under the title *Experience of Troop A, 10th Cavalry On the 'STAKED PLAINS,' Texas July 1877* (Fort Davis, TX: Chas. Krull, Post Printer, 1877). A more recent, scholarly native, Paul H. Carlson, *The Buffalo Soldier Tragedy of 1877* (College Station: Texas A&M University Press, 2003) remains the definitive study.

94 *Anaconda Standard*, June 23, 1894, published the William Carlin hunting party story about abandonment of George Colgate, the group's cook.

95 As reported in the *St. Landry Democrat* (Opelousas, LA) October 10, 1885: 'The War Department has instructed Fred M. Crandall, of the Twenty-Fourth Infantry, to carry out the instructions of the

L. Payne, who many looked to as the leader of 'Oklahoma Movement' (an unofficial organization designed to promote settlement of Oklahoma) paid no head to legal constrains. In 1882 alone, he headed four clandestine excursions into Indian Territory bent on colonization. Each invasion led to his arrest and removal from the area. Rather than deter the would-be settlers, Payne and his followers (known as 'Boomers') grew emboldened, so much so that by August 1882, they refused to leave.

Troops from the Ninth brooked no resistance. They seized the Boomers' belongings, tied the squatters and secured them into their wagons and forcibly removed them from the area. Once more, Payne ignored these efforts. By January 1883, he cavalierly brought 900 settlers back, which repeated the cycle of temporary arrest and removal to Kansas. Six months later, a stubborn Payne attempted another bid to colonize the Indian Territory with the same results. How long Payne would persist is unknown because he died of natural causes while organizing another attempt.

One of Payne's dedicated disciples, William Couch, assumed the leadership. During the second half of 1883, he also made at least three forays. Not surprisingly, the Ninth Cavalry acted as they had done so on previous occasions. Under Couch, they proved no less adamant to the extent that during January 1885, some 300 of them, while ensconced on Stillwater Creek, rebuffed eviction orders from Colonel Edward Hatch. Thereafter, the colonel assembled seven companies from his regiment, bolstered by a company of infantry and two imposing howitzers. With this might, he threatened to attack the encampment. Unscathed, Couch and his band did not leave. Instead, they indicated their intent to stage a defence if the soldiers used force. Hatch wished to advert a confrontation. Rather than resort to violence, he turned to another option. The military surrounded the camp and awaited the inevitable exhaustion of supplies. Less than a week later, the hungry Boomers packed their belongings. Thwarted, they made for Arkansas City. After almost four years of carrying out a task that gained little approbation, but considerable condemnation, the Ninth brought a peaceful end to their seesaw encounter with the Boomers.

Over a dozen years later and far from Oklahoma, orders detailed a non-commissioned officer and nine enlisted men drawn from Company M, Twenty-Fourth Infantry to travel from New Fort Spokane, Washington under the command of a major. They were to proceed to Coeur d'Alene Indian Reservation to 'confer with US Indian Agent ... with reference to the ejectment of trespassers' from tribal lands and march 'to such points on that reservation ... as may be necessary.'[96]

Two other widely separated conflicts that partially entailed land, but in the main arose from economic gain and a struggle political power, also emplaced Black regulars in an uncomfortable position. Both in New Mexico, during the 1870s and nearly two dozen years later in Wyoming, Black troops assumed the role of peacekeepers. Beginning with New Mexico, a pair of clashes

---

Secretary of the Interior concerning the removal of unauthorized persons on the Cherokee lands in the Indian Territory, west of the Arkansas River. The order particularly referred to the removal of 'boomers' and squatters.' George Conrad, Jr., Federal Writers' Project Collection. Ex-Slave Narratives. 1935–1942.B Box 25, Folder 7, M1981.105 location 0924.03, Oklahoma Historical Society, is a rare first-hand account by soldier from Troop G, Ninth Cavalry about the removal of squatters. Also see Leckie and Leckie, *The Buffalo Soldiers*, 204; and Kenner, *Buffalo Soldiers and Officers*, 198–205.

96 *A&NJ*, July 1, 1899, 1047.

involved the Ninth Cavalry. The first encounter emerged from actions by a group that mainly consisted of British business interests to secure a sprawling land grant dating back to the Mexican regime. In 1870, after purchasing almost two million acres, the buyers began to evict miners and settlers who resided on the property. With the help of what became known as the infamous 'Santa Fe Ring' that held considerable economic and political clout in the territory, the consortium provoked the local citizenry. The stakes escalated with the murder of a prominent outspoken critic of the investor group. In turn, one of the murder suspects, Cruz Vega, would be tortured and killed by rancher Clay Allison. The murder incited a vow of vengeance by a member of Vega's family.

During the chaos, rumors spread that Governor Samuel Axtell plotted to use Colonel Edward Hatch's Ninth Cavalry, recently relocated to the territory, as henchmen to challenge the investors and the Santa Fe Ring. President Rutherford B. Hayes eventually removed Axtell, but not before Captain Francis Moore received a directive from Hatch to accompany the county sheriff to Allison's ranch and arrest the owner. Allison surrendered quietly. His acquiesce probably surprised his foes, who possibly hoped he would resist and be killed. In due course, the commander of Fort Union, New Mexico dispatched the remainder of the Moore's company to Cimarron. They remained there, until April 1876, when recalled. The federal government no longer felt the Ninth Cavalry's presence in the raucous region necessary.

As tranquility returned to the north-western part of the territory, to the east, military force again would be called out, this time to Lincoln County. By February 1878, members of the Ninth once more united with local law enforcement. On this occasion, they assisted a deputy US marshal to serve warrants for some members of one of the two opposing parties known as 'The House.' This consortium attempted to monopolize government beef, grain and vegetable contracts for the Mescalero Reservation and to some extent, sought to supply nearby Fort Stanton. English-born John Tunstall and his business partner Alexander McSween coveted this same lucrative trade as did their staunch rivals of The House. Some ethnic and religious undertones added complications.

On this less than welcome mission, with the deputy marshal, three of the horse soldiers suffered frostbite that required hospitalization. Next, Black cavalrymen assisted a deputy marshal, when he searched the residence of a suspect in town. Afterwards, they remained as support, when an armed posse under Lincoln County Sheriff William Brady challenged the deputy. With the backing of troops, he took some of the posse members into confinement. Later, Fort Stanton's commander personally headed a Ninth Cavalry patrol to apprehend suspects implicated as murderers. Then, he turned them over to the courts.[97]

That same month, as hostilities intensified, the territorial governor contacted Colonel Hatch. He asked the colonel to send troops to Lincoln. In response, 25 men from Company H, Ninth Cavalry entered the community. Afterwards, they joined in additional efforts by lawmen, who aligned on both sides of the powerplay. Eventually, on April 20, ferocity reached such proportions that Lieutenant Colonel N. A. M. Dudley, recently arrived commander of Fort Stanton, agreed to dispatch 20 men to town, 'to aid the sheriff in maintaining public order.' The situation continued to deteriorate. At that point, Dudley decided personally to lead four officers, 11 men from the Ninth Cavalry and two dozen white soldiers from the Fifteenth Infantry. The detachment towed a Gatling gun and 12-pound howitzer. To ensure that they were obvious,

97 *Mesilla Valley Independent*, April 27, 1878.

Dudley ordered the detail to don their dress uniforms including the ungainly cavalry helmet topped with yellow horsetail plumes. Professing neutrality, he avowed his presence simply was 'to protect women and children.'[98]

While he professed to be neutral, Dudley leaned towards The House. A newspaper account related the officer prevented McSween's allies from aid by 'pointing a canon towards them.' Previously, Dudley had leveled the fieldpiece in the direction of a residence owned by Ben Ellis, another McSween associate. Furthermore, the lieutenant colonel refused to accept McSween's surrender offer to place himself in the army's custody. He countered that he had no authority to oblige.[99] Denied this option, McSween forted up in his home with compatriots among whom was William 'Billy the Kid' Bonney. Men who worked on behalf of The House torched McSween's residence where he died in the flames.

In late July, Hatch telegrammed Dudley informing the regiment's second in command, 'his actions had been illegal and that he should cease them at once.' Following this censure, Dudley curtailed activities. The territory's recently appointed replacement governor, Lew Wallace, who among other things was a veteran of the Union Army and author of *Ben Hur*, called for Dudley's removal from Fort Stanton. The request went unheeded although Dudley did appear at a board of inquiry.[100]

Arguably, the Ninth Cavalry achieved better results in Wyoming. During a dispute between large corporate cattle ranchers and small landholders, matters worsened. Over the years, the large financially powerful entrepreneurs encroached on the free-range at will. A severe winter, in the mid-1880s, compounded the issue. Tensions heightened. By April 1892, some of the corporate group employed extreme action. They attacked key opponents in Johnson County. Eventually, in June 1892, troops from the Ninth Cavalry established Camp Bettens near the town of Suggs, the epicenter of trouble.[101] The detachment remained on station, until November 1892, when their duty ended after a relatively uneventful stay in so far as dealing with the two factions was concerned.

On the Border

Conflicts over economics and ethnicity, however, erupted outside of New Mexico and Wyoming. For over half a century, from Texas to California, Black soldiers performed their duties in an ethnically diverse world where many cultures converged and sporadically sparred.[102] Several

---

98 *Ibid.*, August 3, 1878, criticized Dudley for not taking actions that could have stopped 'the disgraceful actions' that ended with McSween's being killed while holding up in his burning home.
99 *Las Vegas Gazette* (NM) August 17, 1878.
100 Other otherwise noted the forgoing narrative was derived from Billington, *New Mexico's Buffalo Soldiers*, 61–86. As for the lengthy hearing that shed considerable light on the matter including Dudley's refusal to accept McSween's surrender, even after the merchant's wife attempted to convince the colonel to do so, review R.M. Barron, ed., *Court of Inquiry: Lieutenant Colonel N.A.M. Dudley Fort Stanton, New Mexico may-June-July 1879* (Edina, MN: Beaver's Pond Press, Inc., 2003), 2 vols.
101 For details obtain, Frank N. Schubert, 'The Suggs Affray: The Black Cavalrymen in the Johnson County War,' *Western Historical Quarterly* 4 no. 1 (January 1973): 57–68.
102 James N. Leiker, *Racial Borders: Black Soldiers along the Rio Grande* (College Station: Texas A&M Press, 2002) 112 and 176–7.

instances of violence occurred along the international line established in the wake of the 1848 Treaty of Guadalupe Hidalgo and the subsequent Gadsden Purchase of the early 1850s. Among these was a so-called outbreak of 'Border Outlawry' where allegedly 'an armed mob of 400 Mexicans, 100 of them from the Mexican side of the river' seized a swatch of El Paso County. According to an exaggerated narrative, the invaders threatened, 'to massacre all Americans. They have arrested and jailed the county officers. Several prominent citizens have fled from the county. A small detachment of the Ninth United States Cavalry started for the scene of trouble to-day, to protect the Custom House and government property. The Mexicans claim El Paso county belongs to Mexico.'[103]

This volatile friction, 'grew out of the question to the rights and title to certain salt mines.' Further summarizing, the reporter added: 'No international complications are likely to grow out of this disturbance.' The trouble, one newspaper stated, evolved from the gathering of 'salt from the lakes in El Paso county without restrictions of any kind … These salt lakes have been a source of trouble dating back almost to the first settlement of El Paso county.'[104] In response, Black soldiers from Forts Bayard, Stanton, Davis and troops posted at Santa Fe, made forced marches to quell the mob or insurgents who threatened a makeshift company of Texas Rangers. These *Paseños* (local Latinos) rebelled against a cartel formed by a group of whites bent on securing the profitable local salt deposits. Motivated both to protect this critical source of their income and also fueled by ethnic and nationalistic factors with a touch of xenophobia, the Latino population took up arms. In the process, many died.[105]

The turbulence existing at San Elizario was just one of many examples of the potentially explosive borderlands that challenged both the governments of Mexico and the United States alike. As such, relations between both neighboring nations were often greatly strained.[106] Thus, a case might be made that their presence from the Pacific to the Gulf of Mexico was among the longest-running missions and most lasting contributions of Black soldiers of the late nineteen and early twentieth centuries while they served as precursors to the US Border Patrol, founded in 1924.

In his autobiography, army officer George Rodney imparted the flavor of a posting on the border. Although he presented the story in a somewhat satiric manner, he clearly made his point: 'The Lieutenant takes his men to the hellhole where he's to stay and he calls his sergeant an' tells him: "You take ten men today, Sergeant and ride the border from Point o' Rocks to Saddlers' Wells. You'll take note of all the activities on the Mexican side of the line, especially any movement of troops and above all you'll see to it that the Neutrality Laws are strictly observed."'[107]

---

103 *Tulare Times* (Visalia, CA) October 20, 1877.
104 *Delaware Gazette and State Journal* (Wilmington) December 18, 1877.
105 Paul Cool, *Salt Warriors: Insurgency on the Rio Grande* (College Station: Texas A&M University Press, 2008) offers a balanced, thorough view of the 'Salt Wars.'
106 While far beyond the scope of this study, at a minimum Matt Matthews, *The US Army on the Mexican Border: A Historical Perspective* (Fort Leavenworth, KS: Combat Studies Institute Press, 2007) and Thomas Torrans, *Forging the Tortilla Curtain: Cultural Drift and Change Along the United States-Mexico Border from the Spanish Era To the Present* (Fort Worth: TCU Press, 2000), should be consulted to appreciate the importance of the borderlands to the present.
107 Rodney, *As A Cavalryman Remembers*, 239–40.

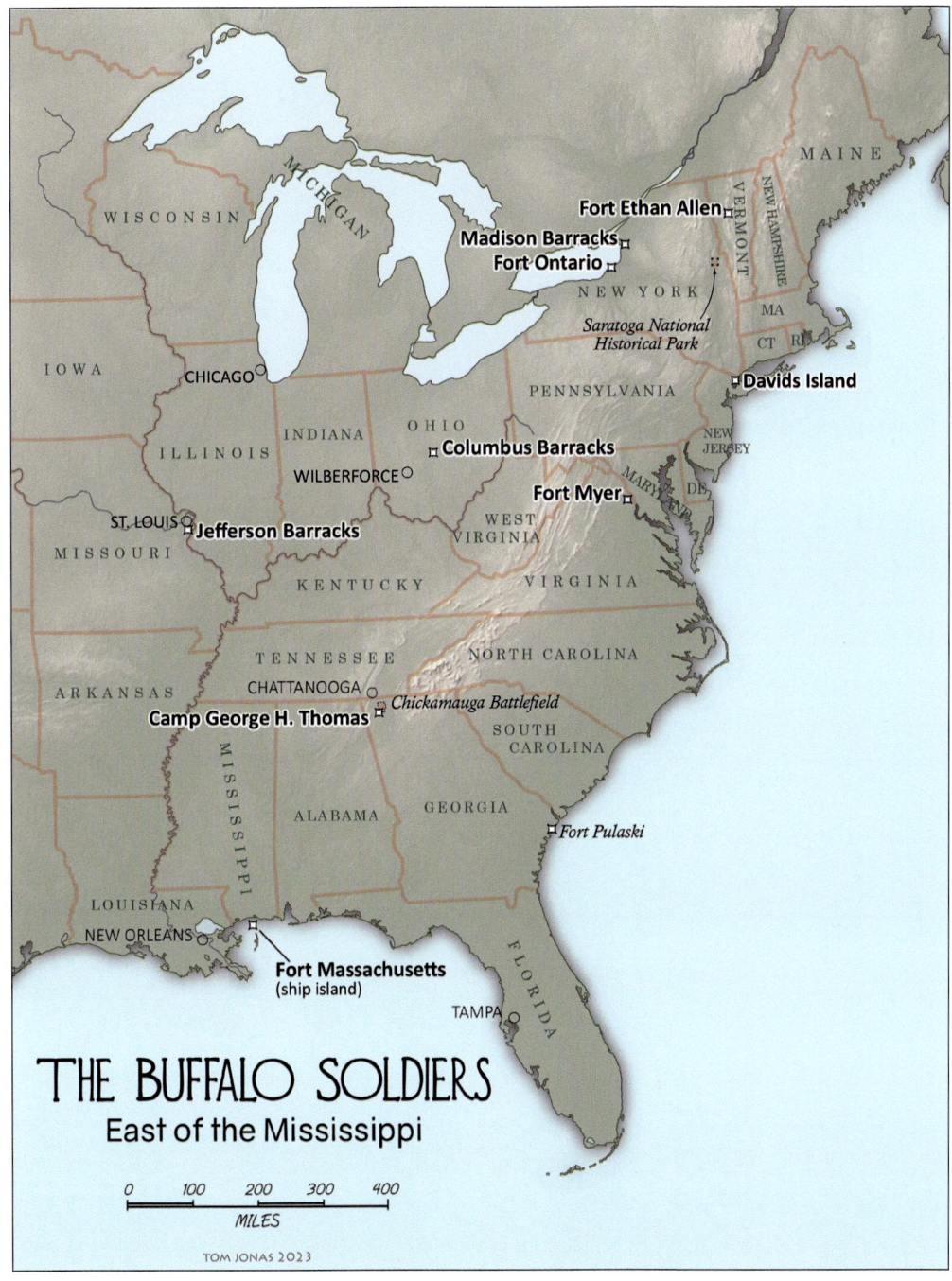

While with few exceptions Black regulars served west of the Mississippi River, beginning with the Spanish American War, that policy shifted slightly with posting of Buffalo Soldiers to more eastern locales. (Courtesy John Langellier, drawn by Tom Jonas)

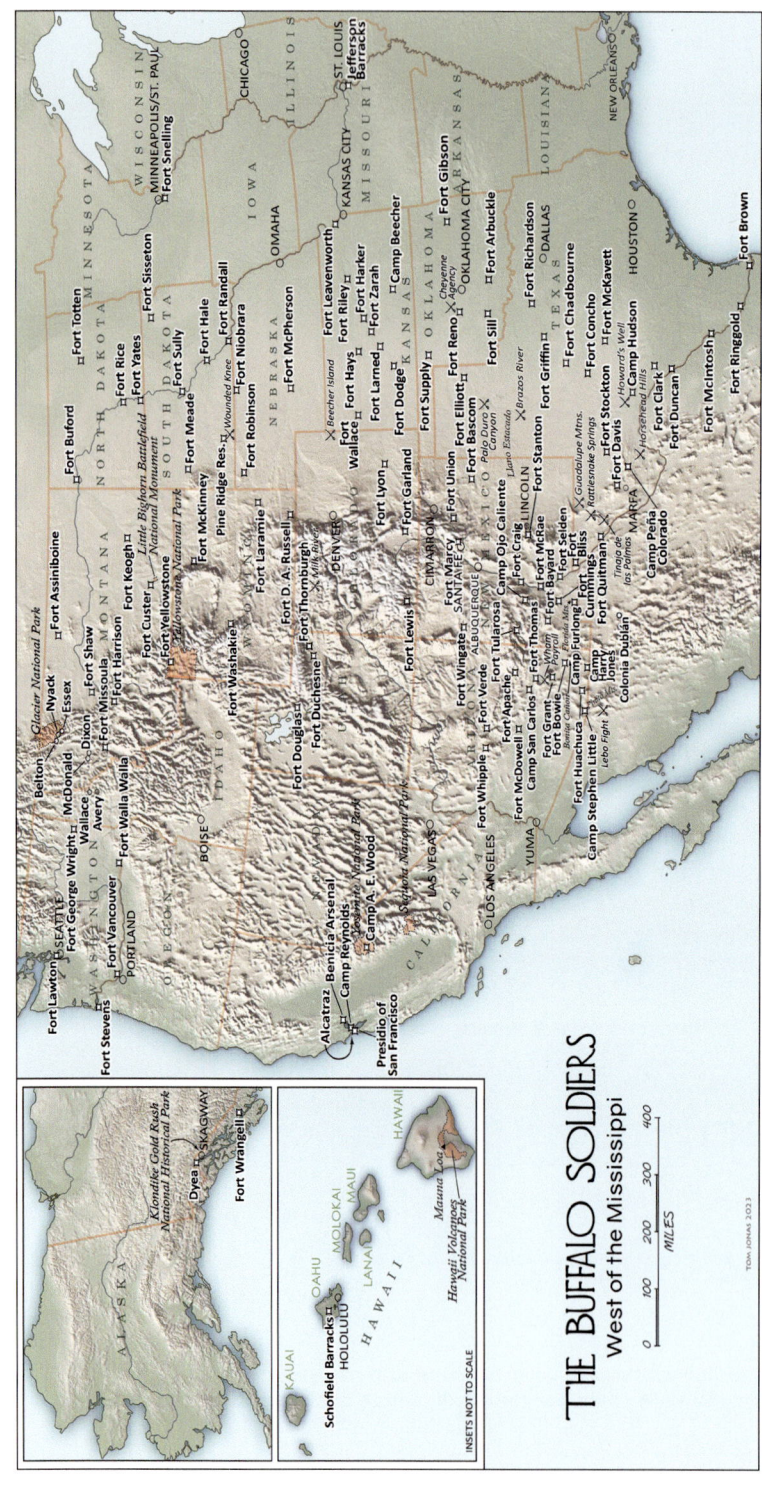

Soon after the Civil War ended, Black regulars reported to the American West. By the early turn of the century, they began to serve beyond the continental United States in Cuba, the Philippines, Alaska, and Hawaii. (Courtesy John Langellier, drawn by Tom Jonas)

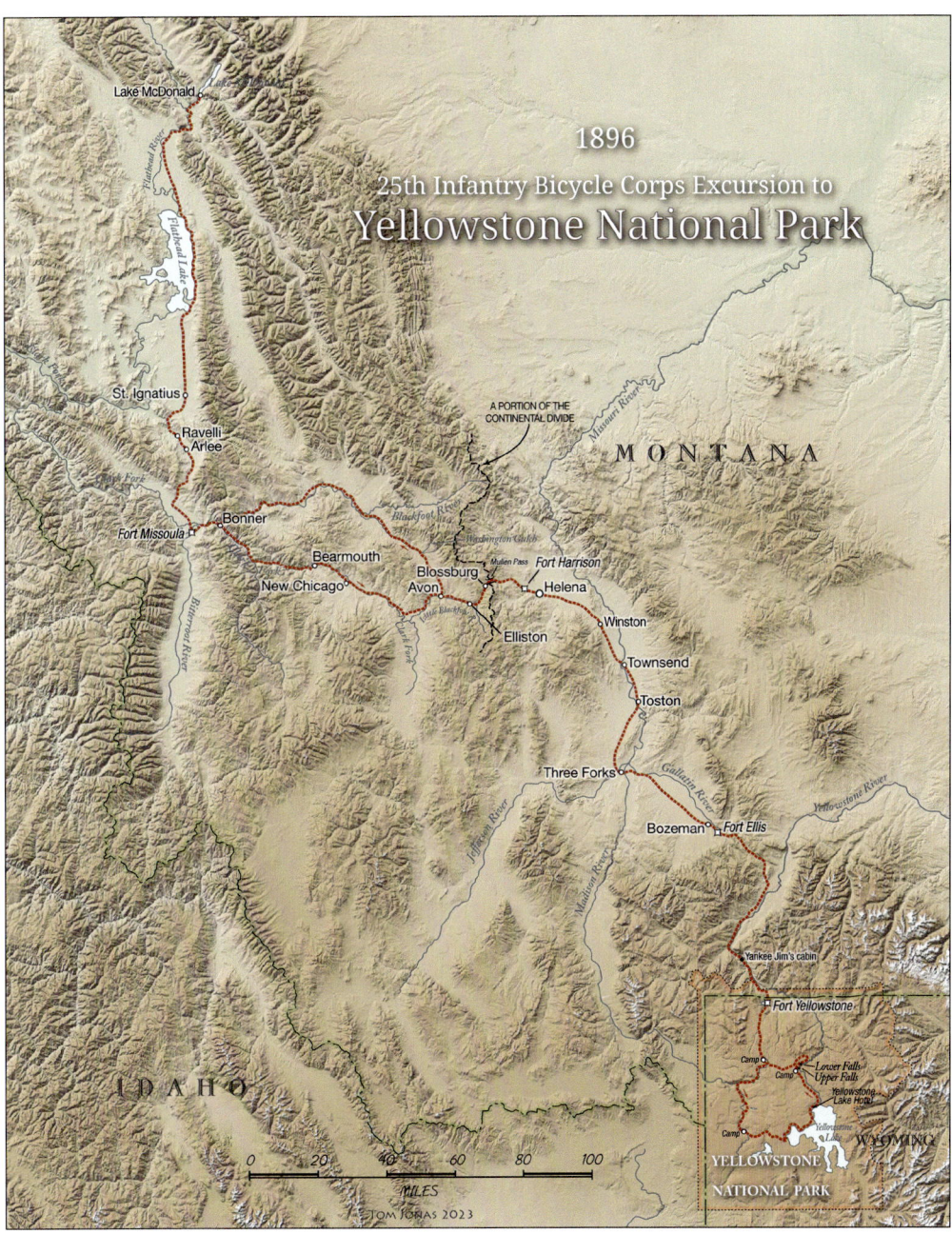

In the late 1890s, a cadre of enlisted men from the Twenty-Fifth Infantry, commanded by Lieutenant James Moss, experimented with bicycles as a means of deploying combat troops. One of their tests took them round trip from Fort Missoula. Montana to majestic Yellowstone National Park. (Courtesy John Langellier, drawn by Tom Jonas)

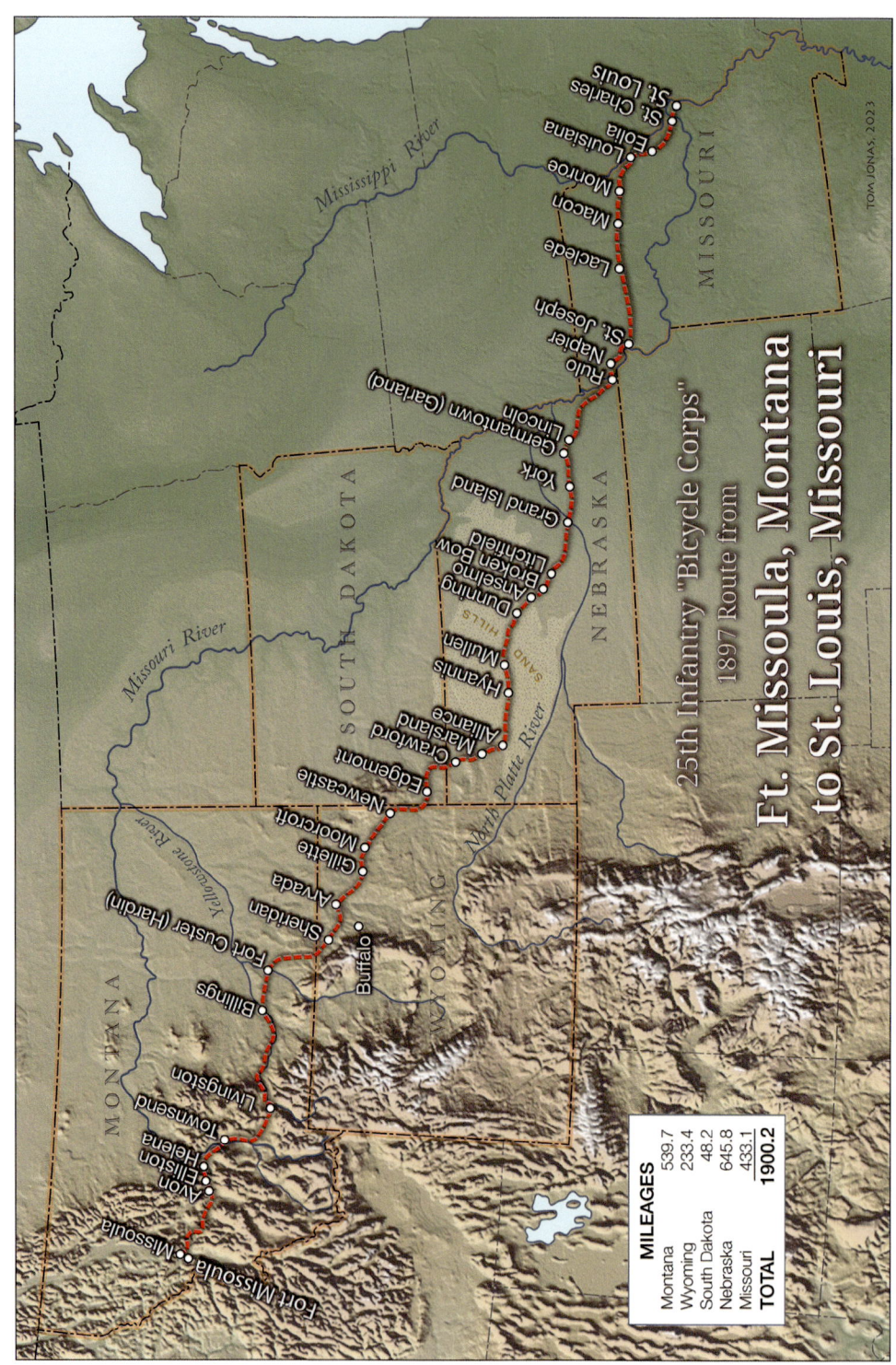

The final experiment of the Fort Missoula-based 'bicycle corps' entailed a grueling 1900 mile trek to St. Louis, Missouri. (Courtesy John Langellier, drawn by Tom Jonas)

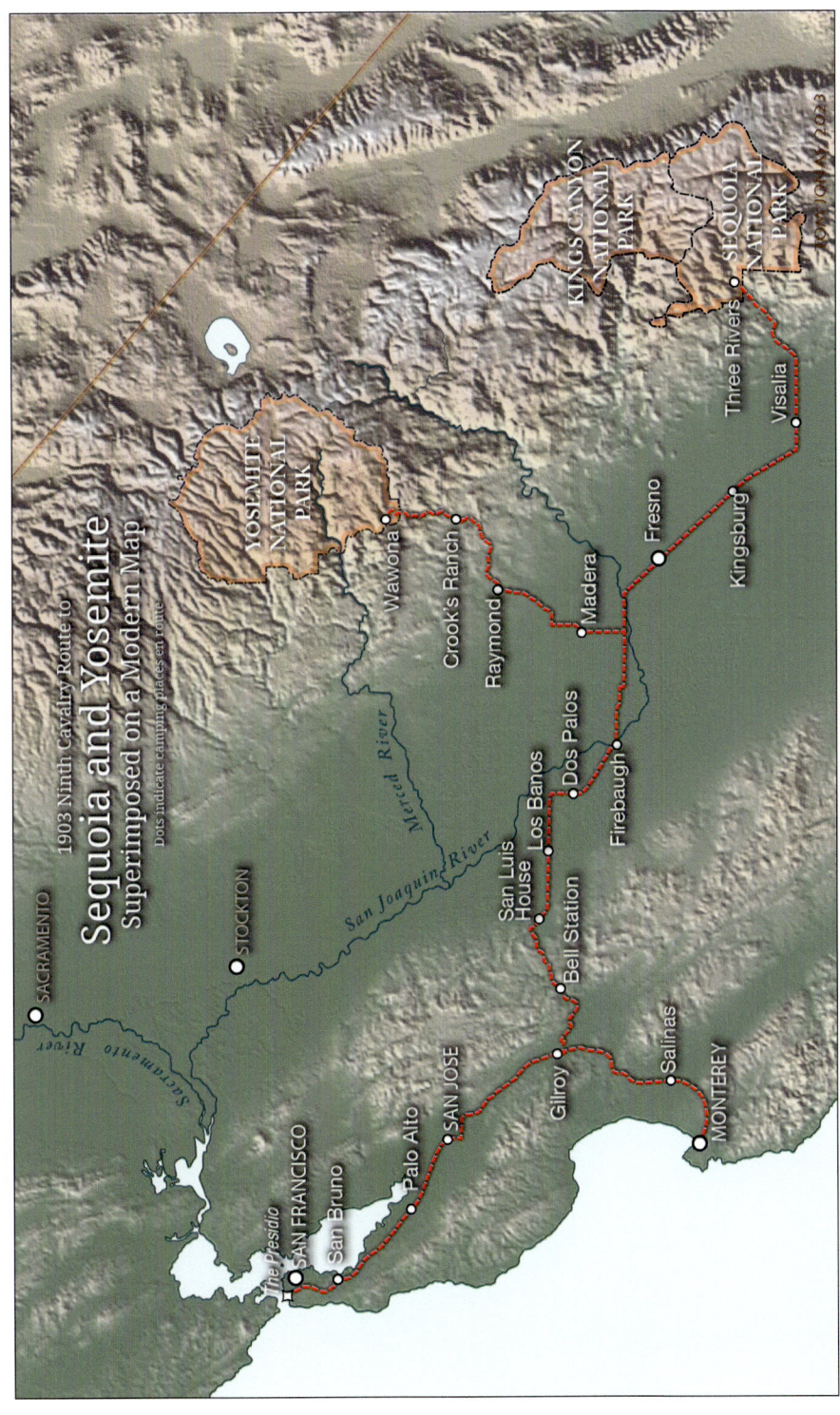

In 1903, troops of the Ninth Cavalry rode from the Presidio of San Francisco to Sequoia National Park where they performed duties that in later times fell to rangers of the National Park Service. During the same period, other contingents of Black cavalrymen took up like assignments in Yosemite National Park. (Courtesy John Langellier, drawn by Tom Jonas)

v

Dozens of US National Park Service sites include Black military history in the nineteenth century. Among them, Fort Larned National Historic Site, Kansas, features a vital living history program depicting the life of the garrison during the 1860s. (Courtesy US National Park Service)

Consequently, the same issues that faced Mackenzie and others in Texas, during the 1870s, remained an agitation to officers serving nearly a half century later. During the early twentieth century, however, it was 'Mexican factions' who engaged 'in bloodless battles within twenty yards of the line [border] and always one faction had its back to the American side, driving families to shelter from the firing.'[108] Stray bullets sometimes struck civilians and military personnel in the United States, but little could be done to counter strife between opposing Mexicans, during many years of revolution. Similar frustrations dogged US Army forces, Black and white, for decades regarding rampant smuggling activities along the seemingly endless miles of the line that included elicit alcohol, drugs, weapons and human trafficking.[109]

While somewhat less complex, in the late 1890s, one company of the Twenty-Fourth Infantry fleetingly acted as in an analogous manner but not as guardians between Mexico and the United States. Instead, they stood watch over the borderlands between Alaska and Canada's Yukon Territory that coincided with efforts at a final establishment of the international boundary between the two countries.[110]

Prison and Policing Efforts

As such, on the border and elsewhere, Black soldiers apprehended criminals or assisted civilian law enforcement beyond New Mexico and Wyoming. As an example, after a deputy federal marshal in Texas, 'attempted to arrest several men in one of the panhandle counties … for alleged violation of the revenue laws' he himself was apprehended 'by the state authorities.' It was not until the law officer obtained military assistance from Fort Elliott that he succeeded in taking the wanted parties into custody. The muscle provided came from Captain Nicholas Nolan and Second Lieutenant Henry O. Flipper of the Tenth Cavalry, who led the troops that made the arrest possible. For their efforts, the two officers: 'were indicted by the grand jury for unlawfully permitting United States soldiers to be used for the above purposes.'[111]

Additionally, Black military personnel both guarded and transported prisoners. This included securing civilians such as Maximo Castillo, 'the Mexican bandit charged with the Cumbre tunnel disaster in which ten Americans and forty-one others lost their lives.' Men from the Ninth Cavalry captured Castillo and brought him to justice along with six of his followers.[112] At another time, a detachment from the Twenty-Fifth Infantry commanded by Lieutenant James Moss escorted the first Spanish prisoners of war from Cuba to the US where they were to be held at Fort McPherson, Georgia, although some racists decried the use of Black soldiers for this purpose.[113] Yet in a third instance, Black troops under Sergeant Charles Conner, Company F, Twenty-Fourth Infantry were charged with taking white deserters to a military prison. Conner,

---

108 Ibid., 241.
109 George T. Díaz, *Border Contraband: A History of Smuggling Across the Rio Grande* (Austin: University of Texas Press, 2015); and Gerald Horne, *Black and Brown: African Americans and the Mexican Revolution, 1910–1920* (New York: New York University Press, 2005), 62–65; 95, summarized smuggling in the borderlands.
110 Shellum, *Buffalo Soldiers in Alaska*, 31.
111 *Emporia Weekly News* (KS) December 19, 1879.
112 *Lindsay Gazette* (CA) February 1, 1914.
113 *Globe-Republican* (Dodge City, KS) May 12, 1898; *Camden Chronicle* (Camden, TN) May 13, 1898.

Ship Island, Mississippi Company C, Second Louisiana Native Guards, was among the first Black military units assigned to this garrison during the Civil War and for a brief period after Reconstruction. Among their duties was service as prison guards. Nathan W. Daniels Diary; Vol. I, mss84934 (Courtesy Library of Congress)

along with his detail of five men, allowed themselves 'to be disarmed by train robbers while en route from Fort Elliott.'[114] Connor faced courts-martial. He and his detachment all would be denounced publicly by their comrades for the 'cowardly, unsoldierly conduct of the party.'[115]

Oversight of inmates was not restricted to traveling with their charges. For a few years after the Civil War, at Ship Island, Mississippi, Black infantrymen guarded both African Americans and whites detained in the fortress' stockade.[116] During a brief period in 1899, Company H, Twenty-Fourth Infantry acted in a similar capacity at the military penitentiary located on Alcatraz.[117]

---

114 *Barton County Democrat* (Great Bend, KS) March 24, 1887.
115 *Evening Star* (Washington, DC) December 13, 1886.
116 Bearss, *Historic Resource Study Ship Island*, 340–2.
117 *Anaconda Standard* (MT) April 8, 1899. The company was to leave for the Presidio effective June 19 'for temporary station, to prepare for embarkation to the Philippine Islands.' In turn, Battery B, Third Artillery, from Angel Island, was to replace them at Alcatraz. *A&NJ*, July 1, 1899, 1047.

In 1903, considerable excitement prevailed in the San Francisco Bay Area, which President Theodore Roosevelt included his cross-country jaunt of that year. The Third Squadron, Ninth Cavalry escorted him to such places as the Presidio as evidenced by the private wheeling near the presidential carriage with a troop from the regiment mounted in the far background. The Ninth Cavalry likewise rode with the commander in chief during a parade through downtown San Francisco that a pioneer motion picture photography filmed for a few fleeing moments. (Courtesy Gordon Chappell Historic Trust)

Guards of Honor and Escort Details

A few years later, in May of 1903, Troops I and M, Ninth Cavalry commanded by Captain Charles Young, provided a guard of honor when President Theodore Roosevelt visited the Bay Area. 'Hearty cheering from citizens' greeted Roosevelt upon his arrival while cavalrymen of the Ninth smartly presented sabers.[118] The next day, two troops of the Ninth Cavalry paraded through the streets of San Francisco. They flanked the commander in chief as his military escort.[119] Remarkably a motion picture cameraman captured them along the route.[120]

Supposedly, as the Black, 'troopers of the 9th Cavalry approached' from the reviewing stand the president acknowledged: 'They were with me at Santiago.'[121] Additionally, during Roosevelt's visit, a detachment from the Third Squadron of the Ninth Cavalry staged, 'a platoon drill, sabre exercises, a sham battle, unsaddling of horses, bareback riding, throwing of horses to the ground by riders, resaddling and skillful Cossack riding.'[122] Interestingly, earlier on Roosevelt's westward train journey to the coast, he received similar honors at Crawford, Nebraska, rendered by a guard from the Tenth Cavalry dispatched from nearby Fort Robinson.

As shown in this photograph from a series taken in October 1912, at today's Saratoga National Park, New York, Troop D, Tenth Cavalry from Fort Ethan Allen, Vermont, staged a sham battle. They were present at dedication of the Saratoga Monument and enlivened this demonstration of civic and patriotic pride. Ironically, they did so in a segregated society where these soldiers did not enjoy the words of the founding fathers that: 'All men are created equal.' (Courtesy National Park Service)

A variety of other reasons required the presence of Black soldiers. They safeguarded settlers and railroad construction crews as they laid and maintained tracks. In turn, troops assisted with

---

118 *San Francisco Call*, May 13, 1903.
119 *Ibid.*,, May 6, 1903, May 8, 1903; May 9, 1903, May 12, 1903, May 14, 1903, May 15, 1903, May 16, 1903.
120 loc.gov/item/00694419.
121 *Evening Star* (Washington, DC) March 6, 1905.
122 *San Francisco Call*, April 3, 1903.

the building of roads plus the erection of telegraph lines. They also accompanied survey parties. Similarly, they performed guard duties and escorted mail carriers, plus traveled on stage lines aboard coaches as well as at remount stations and stops to provide security.[123]

In this vein, accompanying army supply trains or parties changing duty stations were regular events. A pair of accounts from the 1870s and the early 1890s capture polemic versions of this type of assignment from divergent times and places – one fraught with danger and the other routine. The first of these involved a trip from Kansas to Indian Territory via Fort Dodge, Kansas where a diarist's May 31 entry indicated the precarious conditions faced along the way. While encamped near Fort Dodge, the writer related: 'This morning we heard that about 150 Indians had killed 3 men at a ranch 30 miles ahead of us [.] a detachment of Negro soldiers went out early this morning to see about it and … while we were eating our dinner it passed on the way back to the fort [.]' Indeed, the raiders killed three men and wounded one other after appearing at 'the Ranch pretending to be friendly and while they were shaking hands fired on them that man that is wounded [a Black soldier] says he cut one of them [the Indians] rather bad with an axe that was in the house.'[124]

A few days later, 'several men killed the Indians which are going around committing these depredations.' Also, the diarist mentioned, 'another detachment of Soldiers from [Camp] supply have just passed and using their language the Indians have raised hell there within the last two or three days. They have killed several men around camp Supply about three days ago and a band of Indians of about 60 dashed right through the fort firing as they went things are commencing to look rather ruff [sic].'

By June 9, while rolling southward, they, 'looked back on the road and saw 3 wagons coming … very fast[;] a couple of minutes later after we looked back and the plains were just covered with Indians all around the wagons[.] I guess there were more than a hundred.' The officer in charge called for a rescue party. In response, the diarist joined a half dozen Black cavalrymen and one white soldier all of whom: 'volunteered to go and help them out. So, we formed a line so that we would not be in a bunch and advanced toward them' managing to drive off the attackers without a casualty on their part although the Indian was 'nocked [sic] off his horse.' By five o'clock in the afternoon, a Tenth Cavalry company from Camp Supply arrived as reinforcements.

Eventually, the wagon train reached the supposed safety of that outpost. This was not so, as warriors in the vicinity boldly raided the cavalry's herd making off with five horses. In response, a detail from the Tenth Cavalry 'went out … about 5 miles from the Post and have been fighting for an hour and a half there seems to have been a very large number for the[y] took a piece of Artillery out and we can see they are using it by the puffs of smoke.'

Some 21 years later, Mary Elizabeth Allen Richards Almy recounted a more mundane passage. The mother-in-law of Ninth Cavalry officer Lieutenant Montgomery Davis Parker,

---

123 The *Los Angeles Herald*, June 11, 1893, remarked: 'The United States boundary commissioners arrived in Tucson from Yuma several days ago … They came by railroad, while the military escort, in charge of Lieut. W. P. Jackson, Twenty-Fourth Infantry, and Dr. F. A. Winter, medical corps, came overland with the wagons. The escort consists of 23 soldiers of the Second cavalry and Twenty-Fourth Infantry.'
124 'Safe out of Indian Country and very glad of it,' Diary of W.C. Irvine, Carlisle, Cumberland County, Pennsylvania, May 23rd, 1870, Box 3, Folder 1, Coll. 126, John T. Williams Papers, American Heritage Center, University of Wyoming, Laramie. Miraculously this document was discovered in a storage box under the eaves of a barn in 1963.

Mrs Almy, along with her daughter, infant granddaughter and the lieutenant, journeyed from Fort Washakie, Wyoming bound for a new posting at Fort Robinson, Nebraska. During the first phase of the journey, the women rode in an army ambulance, which doubled as a sort of stagecoach with Troop E, Ninth Cavalry as escort.

Setting out on May 18, 1891, they lumbered along for approximately 173 miles. The troopers made the travelers as comfortable as possible. Mrs. Almy remarked how: 'The horde of black men got the seven tents up for the officers, in marvelously quick time. One feels so whole with so much willing, cheery service.'[125] When a six-mule-drawn escort wagon 'piled to the top with canvas cover, with camp outfit, mess wagon – stoves and cooking utensils, etc … wobbled down and turned over' the soldiers descended on the accident. They quickly took off the canvas cover and 'nearly unloaded the wagon, righted it again, reloaded' which allowed the column to continue. While the doting grandmother admired the soldiers' pluck, she did so in racist terms. She likened the rescue party to 'black flies' and recalled 'the big, strong darkies worked so quickly and are worth two white men in such an emergency.' Regardless of her verbiage, she particularly appreciated the two troopers who acted as striker and assistant striker. She admitted, 'we are beautifully cared for.'

Along the route, officers and enlisted men occasionally hunted. One of the soldiers brought down a deer. Mrs. Almy thought: 'How glad the men will be to have some venison. I hope they will remember their captains and their lieutenants … and they did! And they brought us a filet, which we are going to have for dinner tonight.' Later, one of the strikers presented the family with five small fish that he caught in a net from the Platte River. One June 4, having exchanged the rickety ambulance for a more comfortable train car, the trekkers reached Fort Robinson.

Conversely, what should have been uneventful duty terminated in a desperate encounter. In May 1889, US Army paymaster, Major Joseph Wham, proceeded from Fort Grant to Fort Thomas, Arizona. A detachment from the Tenth Cavalry and the Twenty-Fourth Infantry guarded the $28,000 payroll cash. At a carefully selected point where the road could be covered from heights on either side, highwaymen unleashed an ambush. The brisk firefight ended with the robbers carrying off the entire payroll. In the process, the desperados wounded eight of the detail. Two of the unsuccessful defenders earned Medals of Honor. The remainder of the men received Certificates of Merit.[126] In turn, the perpetrators, who all lived in the area, although captured after being pursued by Powhattan Clarke contingent from the Tenth Cavalry and others, were tried, but avoided imprisonment.[127]

---

125 Mary E. Almy, 'A Fitful Journey,' Transcript 1891 Diary from Fort Washakie, WY to Caspar, WY. Coll. 3596, American Heritage Center, University of Wyoming, Laramie. The collection contains a photocopy. The whereabouts of the original manuscript, which covered other periods and which contained photographs, is unknown.
126 As the lengthy title implies, Larry D. Ball, *Ambush at Bloody Run: The Wham Payroll Robbery of 1889: A Story of Politics, Religion, Race, and Banditry in Arizona* (Tucson: Arizona Historical Society, 2000) explores the multi-layered factors related to this dramatic holdup.
127 Langellier, *Scouting with the Buffalo Soldiers*, 208. For transcripts of the trail in the Arizona Historical Society Tucson, of the *United States v. Mark R, Cunningham*, et al, see arizonahistoricalsociety.or/wp-contenet/upLoads/library_Wham-Payroll-Robeery.pdf. Period newspaper accounts included *Evening Star* (Washington, DC) May 14, 1889; *Sacramento Daily Record-Union*, September 28, 1889; *Arizona Silver Belt* (Globe) October 5, 1889; *Los Angeles Daily Herald*, November 16, 1889; and *Arizona Weekly Citizen* (Tucson) September 28, 1899, and May 25, 1891.

Labor Disputes

The payroll robbers' quest for easy riches contrasted with the larger economic stakes and power struggles in place other than Arizona. In the 1890s, several occurrences of labor versus management and business interests, turned Black soldiers out of their snug barracks. In Coeur d' Alene, Idaho, as mining corporations sought higher profits, they cut wages and extended working hours. The miners' union reacted and employers retaliated. They hired strikebreakers and armed guards. Ignoring an injunction from the state's governor and believing the federal government would remain aloof, the workers again responded. Once more, the owners retaliated. Fighting broke out, injuring and killing parties on both sides of the dispute.

Despite the appearance that the federal government would not intervene, state officials convinced President Benjamin Harrison to dispatch white troops from the Fourth Infantry at Fort Sherman, Idaho to Wardner, Idaho. Also, Black soldiers from the Twenty-Fifth Infantry at Fort Missoula, Montana entrained for their destination of Mullin, Idaho. Additional white infantrymen ultimately arrived that brought the number of US Army personnel up to 1,200.[128]

In 1892, although sent to quell labor unrest in the mines, Black infantrymen appeared in the streets of Wallace, Idaho to join locals in commemorating the 4th of July. (Courtesy John Langellier)

128 Clayton D. Laurie and Ronald H. Cole, *The Role of Federal Military Forces in Domestic Disorders 1877–1945* (Washington, DC: Center of Military History US Army, 1997), 153–61.

Newspapers noted troop movements, as well as generally chronicled the ongoing drama.[129] Within weeks, articles began to appear predicting the regulars were to be withdrawn once order returned. These headlines proved true, although two infantry companies stayed behind at Wardner, while another remained in Wallace, Idaho. Likewise, one company took station at the Gem Mine. Army presence seemed superfluous as over the ensuing weeks, they did little more than interact with the townsmen in a friendly manner. They played baseball games against community teams, picnicked with locals and mingled with them in saloons. They did so until early November. When calm prevailed in the Coeur d' Alene region, Uncle Sam sent the soldiers back to their garrisons. Idaho national guardsmen soon followed suit. While the military made errors and in certain cases, violated the 1878 Posse Comitatus Act (Pub.L. 45–263) that bars federal troops from participating in civilian law enforcement except when expressly authorised, by and large, the troops performed reasonably well. As such on November 18, 1892, the governor lifted martial law. For the next two years, 'a fragile peace prevailed.'[130]

However, national events again brought about mobilization sparked by labor issues. After the Panic of 1893, under the banner of Jacob Coxey whose movement took his name, widespread unemployment prompted a march on Washington, DC[131] Simultaneously, workers struck the Pullman Car Company in Chicago. Ripples spread westward that impacted both the railroads and the mines.[132] Perceived threats of possible bloodshed and destruction of property meant men of the Twenty-Fifth Infantry left Fort Missoula along with various other units called up to shield railroad assets.[133]

Captain J. Milton Thompson of the Twenty-Fourth Infantry saw no need for these troops particularly regarding activities in Idaho. He telegraphed: 'Investigations of violent intents of miners claimed by operators is not supported by the facts. Certain parties wish Federal Government to believe the anarchy of 1892 still exists. That is false. Arrival of troops was not the cause of peace. People were capable of handling matters before troops or without them.'[134] A Montana editor added a prejudicial slant when he wrote: 'The fact that colored troops might be used … is very irritating.' The op-ed further professed many citizens thought sending soldiers

---

129 For a running contemporary commentary on the Idaho miners' strike read *Salt Lake Herald*, May 22, 1892 and September 22, 1892; *St. Paul Daily Globe*, July 12, 1892; *Record-Union* (Sacramento, CA, July 13, 1892 and July 21, 1892; *Helena Independent*, July 14, 1892, Morning; *San Francisco Morning Call*, July 14, 1892 and July 15, 1892; *New York Evening World*, July 14, 1892; *Daily Yellowstone Journal* (Miles City) July 16, 1892, July 17, 1892, July 19, 1892, July 20, 1892, July 21, 1892, July 22, 1892, and July 23, 1892.
130 Laurie and Cole, *The Role of Federal Military Forces*, 162.
131 *Helena Independent*, June 6, 1894, noted that at Arlee, Montana 66 Coxeites were taken prisoner and escorted by men from Company G, Twenty-Fifth Infantry to be jailed in Helena in assistant to the federal marshal and his deputies
132 For example, in the Southwest a train of with a detail from the Twenty-Fourth Infantry proceeding from Fort Huachuca, Arizona to Santa Fe, New Mexico 'to aid in suppression of the strike, boarded a train of the Guaymas branch of the Atchison, Topeka & Santa Fe railroad at Huachuca station' only to have the pro-union 'engineer and fireman cut off their engine and came to Benson, leaving the train standing.' *Delaware Gazette and State Journal* (Wilmington) July 19, 1894.
133 *Anaconda Standard*, July 8, 1894. The next day, the July 9 issue of that same newspaper reported that Idaho's two senators met with the president 'to urge federal protection for Wallace, Idaho, where rioting is reported.'
134 Laurie and Cole, *The Role of Federal Military Forces*, 153.

was needless at that time. If the military had to be deployed, civilians much preferred white Troops – or so the paper informed.[135]

In stark contrast to those who opposed the use of the military, Chaplain Theophilus Steward, 'defended the soldier's action when he had 'to bring the bayonet against ... his own countrymen.' The soldier was in these circumstances 'a patriot; true to his oath and loyal to his flag.'"[136] Evidently Steward's superiors concurred. They detached sufficient numbers 'to guard the tunnels and bridges to the west of Helena.' A 'squadron of the Tenth Cavalry ... from Fort Buford to Glendive,' and another three troops from the regiment, left Fort Custer for various positions where they watched over the tunnel at Big Horn or pitched tents at the Billings roundhouse, whose community was considered, 'a center of the malcontents.' As a further precaution, 'the two companies of the Twenty-Fifth Infantry, stationed at Fort Custer, marched to Custer Station to be available for any service after the trains commenced running.' They encamped at Livingston, painted as, 'the worst nest of lawlessness on the entire [Northern Pacific Railroad] line.'[137]

The Black soldiers from Forts Buford, Custer and Missoula, all received the same rules of engagement as their white comrades. Unlike the Johnson County War, however, Blacks were sent mostly because of their proximity to the row, rather than because of an opinion that they would not side with the union. Additionally, they operated under the admonishment that: 'The officers and men must be prudent and cool in the discharge of this delicate duty, but firm and positive in an exigency.'[138]

One commander of white troops focused on the term 'firm' and not the requirement to 'be prudent and cool.' When Captain Benjamin Lockwood and two companies of white infantrymen and a pair of Twenty-Fifth Infantry companies from Fort Custer rolled into Livingston, Montana, 'the whole city turned out and fully 1,000 strikers and sympathizers gathered near the depot, lining the track on either side.' The local press dubbed Lockwood, 'a military despot and a rowdy' who supposedly uttered a curse as he detrained. 'Drawing his sword,' the paper declared, 'he commanded the soldiers to charge the crowd, saying, "Club the God damned sons of bitches." The captain then struck an inoffensive old man with his clenched fist and knocked him down.'[139]

On a more positive note, when the situation heated up and the crowd turned on two of the strikebreakers, who had replaced the Union men, the fearful pair fled. They charged through the encircling Black troops at 'breakneck speed.' The soldiers came 'on the double-quick. They halted in front of the crowd and leveled their pieces.' Their officer, First Lieutenant Joseph O'Neil, whom the reporter pronounced, 'a very gentlemanly fellow, then addressed the crowd and said he had just been informed that a half dozen of the train crew were being murdered by the strikers. The situation was soon explained.' The lieutenant ordered the soldiers to unload

---

135 *Helena Independent,* June 9, 1894.
136 Chaplain Steward traveled to minister at the 'camps set up along the tracks, by tunnels and near bridges' where men from the regiment had been assigned. Shortly after his return from this duty he took exception to the references of 'hired soldiery.' Stover, *Up From Handymen,* 85; Seraile, *Voice of Dissent,* 123. For the full text of the chaplain's views on the subject of the military in labor disputes as well as a companion article see: T.G. Steward, 'Starving Laborers and the 'Hired Soldier,' *The United Service Journal* (October 1895), 363–6 and 'The Reign of the Mob,' *The Independent* (May 11, 1899): 1296–97.
137 *ARSW, 1894,* I, 126.
138 *New York Tribune,* July 10, 1894.
139 *Anaconda Standard,* July 11, 1894.

their rifles and return to the train. After the trains pulled out, O'Neil and 100 of his men remained in Livingston. They established camp near the roundhouse.

While the indignant citizens held a town meeting to redress Lockwood's actions, they displayed no such animosity towards O'Neil and his company. This was telling. Black porters, among others, showed no sympathy for the strike. Consequently, those who supported the Union looked askance at African Americans who remained in the railroad's employ. As such, in Missoula, locals heckled two railroad employees. In response, a Twenty-Fifth Infantry private prodded a man in the crowd with a bayonet. The civilians withdrew. Subsequently the sentry was charged with assault. Some difficulty arose in serving an arrest warrant but did not cause further issues.

Newspaper accounts from Billings also demonstrated mixed views about the army's presence under the command of Captain Robert D. Reade. On one hand, fraternization with residents occurred. Indeed, some of Reade's 'talented choristers' cavalrymen provided an 'open air concert' for townsmen. At another time, they 'gave a highly interesting exhibition of horsemanship and skill.'[140] In like manner, a baseball game between 'a scrub of nine citizens' from Billings and a team selected from the enlisted ranks, took to the diamond with the troops winning.[141] On the surface, the atmosphere between the townsmen and troops seemed cordial.

Yet a negative attitude manifested itself in a denigrating reference by the *Billings Daily Gazette* to Troop K as, 'The Fighting Coons.'[142] Racial bias and a perception that all soldiers were 'hired guns' and strikebreakers, appeared in an editorial that emphasized the requirement for soldiers had passed. Although grateful to the troops for protection during uncertain times, the editor contended that most Americans abhorred 'orders from soldiers of the government, be they white or black.'[143]

Not everyone shared this point of view. For one, a Missoula paper took a middle ground. It set aside the 'question of the advisability of ordering out the troops' to look at another aspect of the strike, the soldiers' conduct. The paper concluded that the men from Fort Missoula performed in an exemplary manner. The article praised 'beyond a doubt the excellence of the negro as soldier. During the entire period that the guard was on duty, no act of the troops was open to criticism and there was not a single instance of unjust exercise of authority.' Railroad owners lauded the troops while allegedly the majority of the strikers admitted 'if the soldiers had to be called out there could have been none better than the companies of the 25th infantry who were encamped here.'

Turning to a linked matter, the writer challenged: 'The prejudice against the colored soldier seems without foundation for if the 25th is an example of the colored regiments, there is no exaggeration in the statement that there are no better troops in service.' In the eyes of this

---

140 *Yellowstone Journal* (Miles City) July 10 and July 16, 1894.
141 *Ibid.*, (Miles City) August 14, 1894.
142 *Billings Daily Gazette*, July 9, 1894.
143 *Ibid.*, July 25, 1894. Despite the commentary, at least Troop K's commander found his stay in town enjoyable enough to bring his spouse back from Fort Custer 'to remain a short time in Billings.' *Billings Daily Gazette*, July 30, 1894. The couple would have been able to remain together there for at least a few weeks because the Tenth Cavalry troopers were not relieved from duty in town until August 18, at which time they were 'to make a practice march returning to Fort Custer by such detours' as Reade selected. The men had until September 1 to make their way back to post based upon the rations they had on hand. *Billings Daily Gazette* August 14, 1894.

newspaperman, the Black troops were 'model soldiers' who displayed an 'excellent spirit.' Both 'orderly and quiet,' the rank and file made the Twenty-Fifth 'a splendid regiment and worthy of unstinted praise.'[144]

Ultimately, the Black military units received compliments for professionalism from their departmental commander, Major General Wesley Merritt. He enthusiastically recognized all troops for rapid movements 'to protect the more important destructible structures and tunnels' along with those onboard trains as guards, 'terminals and important points on the railroad.' The general applauded the 'discipline and management' of men in his command, which gained them, 'the highest praise of all well-disposed people and the well-founded respect of the lawless.'[145]

A half-decade elapsed before a repeat of labor grievances meant troops reappeared in Idaho. As before, wages and working conditions in the mines underpinned unrest. Mine owners further exasperated workers by employing undercover Pinkerton detectives to infiltrate the union. Mine owners also instituted regular dismissal of union card holders. Hostilities brought about the familiar destruction of property, injury, death, arrests and incarceration.[146]

In Idaho, the old tinder boxes of Wardner and Wallace flared up as hot spots. Details from the Twenty-Fourth Infantry dispatched from Washington State, replicated pervious military roles. They assisted law enforcement and functioned as jailers – conflicted duties they did not particularly relish, nor did the miners. One newspaper account reflected the mood. It claimed Captain Joseph Bachelor, Jr., who commanded the company of the Twenty-Fourth Infantry sent to Wardner was 'characterized as a combination of cyclones and wildcats when it comes to fighting.' Unimpressed, 'the miners at Wardner threatened to clean out the first detachment of troops,' but this proved an idle boast.[147]

Unlike Captain Bachelor, First Lieutenant William Murphy did not arrive in Idaho with a dubious reputation. After the polite young officer: 'came out of a house with a veteran miner in custody' his prisoner, whose hair was 'white and his mustache grizzly with many years of toil … turned at the door and kissed his aged wife. "Good-bye. Mother" were his parting words.'

Murphy then walked his charge to bullpen, an outdoor makeshift prison camp. As the lieutenant exited, he told the woman: 'I am very sorry, madam, to be obliged to do this and hope that your husband will soon return, but my orders are to arrest every man.'

Purportedly, when Murphy and his Black infantrymen searched the town, they did so with the 'same courtesy.' At the bullpen, guards chatted with their prisoners. They even, 'explained to them the mechanism of their guns and their accoutrements.' However, each miner knew that when he looked 'down the barrels of a couple of 30-caliber rifles with a colored soldier at the other end of the gun, his first impulse is to stop. His next impulse is to stay stopped.'[148]

---

144 *Anaconda Standard*, August 7, 1894. The August 10, 1894, *Anaconda Standard* followed with an additional positive report indicating the strikers had disperses which meant the troops could return to their posts.
145 *Yellowstone Journal* (Miles City) August 13, 1894.
146 Laurie and Cole, *The Role of Federal Military Forces*, 167–178 encapsulated 'the record of blunders' the US Army made 'against the union in Idaho during 1899 through 1901, which resulted in 'being castigated as the enemy of organized labor.'
147 *Shoshone Journal*, May 12, 1899. For examples of other articles recounting this dispute consult *Coeur d'Alene Press*, April 1, 1899; *Silver Blade* (Rathdrum, ID) May 6, 1899.
148 *Anaconda Standard*, May 7, 1899,

Cordiality went only so far. As one headline read: 'THE SOLDIERS WERE STRICT.' Evidence of this fact existed when in one case, 'a prisoner chanced to put his fingers through a hole inside the prison.' This led to a no-nonsense 'colored soldier on guard on the outside' shoving 'his bayonet at the protruding fingers, inflicting a bloody wound.' One of the residents, detained for many months, purportedly suffered, 'all sorts of indignities.' According to an investigation, 'he was stood up to a post and a bayonet run into his breast by a colored soldier.'[149]

Despite opposing perspectives, the contentious situation ended in 1901. The last troops departed from Idaho. Black soldiers, all of whom were drawn from Twenty-Fourth Infantry, headed for their scattered garrisons in Montana, Utah, Washington and Wyoming before dispersal to other more remote destinations beyond the shores of the Continental United States.[150]

Closing the Frontier and Burying Its Dead

In the last-mentioned state, Wyoming, Black cavalrymen performed an atypical task – the closure of Fort Laramie. As part of the consolidation of former frontier outposts, in the last decade of the nineteenth century, the US Army deemed this venerable garrison surplus. A detail commanded by the Ninth Cavalry's regimental quartermaster, First Lieutenant Charles Taylor, accompanied by a medical officer, Assistant Surgeon Jefferson Kean, two sergeants and 11 privates from Fort Robinson, Nebraska.[151] In March 1890, the detail arrived to salvage anything that could be of use from the abandoned station and hauled everything back with them to Nebraska. This included windows, doors, water piping, sawmill equipment along with roofing and floor materials.[152] The abandonment and dismantling of the fort was 'a stunning blow to the civilians' who long resided in the area.[153] Happily, many of the locals later spearheaded efforts to preserve the historic site, which became a significant addition to the National Park Service's cultural resources in 1938.[154]

Approximately at the same time, troopers from the Ninth Cavalry undertook other pical efforts in neighboring Montana. Company D, Twenty-Fifth Infantry, commanded by Captain Owen Sweet, received orders for their own unusual detail. They were to leave Fort Custer, Montana for the Little Bighorn battlefield. As with Fort Laramie, this sacred site eventually would be administered by the National Park Service. Long before that time, however, Company

---

149 *Butte Intermountain*, March 21, 1900.
150 *ARSW, 1899*, I, Pt 3, 41; L. Scipio, *Last Black Regulars*, 33–35.
151 Post Orders 51, Fort Robinson, Neb. March 17, 1890; Post Orders 63, Fort Robinson, Neb., March 27, 1890; Letter from Department of the Platte to Commanding Officer Fort Robinson, March 11, 1890; Letter from Department of the Platte to Commanding Officer Fort Robinson, March 25, 1890; Douglas McChristian, *Fort Laramie: Military Bastion of the High Plains* (Norman: University of Oklahoma Press, 2009), 394–5; and *Omaha Daily Bee*, April 21, 1890. The *AN&J*, April 19, 1890, 640 also noted: 'Lieut. C.W. Taylor, quartermaster [Ninth Cavalry], is at Fort Laramie superintending its demolition and sale.'
152 *Rawlins Republican*, April 11, 1890. The detail returned to Fort Robinson on April 23, 1890.
153 *Cheyenne Daily Leader*, March 25, 1890.
154 Merrill J. Mattes, *Fort Laramie Park History, 1834–1977* (Denver, CO: Rocky Mountain Regional Office National Park Service, 1980), Pts. II and III.

D was dispatched, 'for the purposes of marking boundaries and placing in position about 300 headstones on the battlefield of the Little Big Horn, where Gen. George A. Custer and the officers and men of his command fell June 25, 1876.'[155]

In the process, they discovered three bodies that had not received burial. One of the skeletons, 'still had on parts of a United States uniform showing that be had been a private soldier.' Speculation led to the conclusion that the unknown trooper, 'had been badly wounded, crawled into the brush and there died. The skulls of the other two men had been broken in above eyes, as if done by a stone mallet.'[156] These soldiers also unearthed an officer's spur, some buttons assumed to be those from a surgeon with the command and other artefacts.[157]

They completed their tasks of fencing the national cemetery along with 'placing head and foot stones of white marble over the graves where Custer's men fell' that bore 'the inscription: Here fell a Soldier of The Seventh United States Cavalry, June 25, 1876.' This assignment entailed setting up 229 markers including ones for 17 officers that were described as 'handsome slabs of marble erected over the spot where they fell.' Later plans included construction of a cottage at the northwest corner of the enclosure for a caretaker. That project went beyond the few weeks spent at the battlefield by Sweet and his soldiers, who remained through late May.[158]

Experiment in Mobility

Soon the labors of this burial detail would be observed by other Black soldiers. That situation existed due to a fascinating footnote of US military history that centred around a fleeting experiment to put American infantrymen on two wheels.[159] Amazingly, one of the army's most junior officers, Second Lieutenant James Moss, not long after his graduation from West Point, successfully contacted the newly appointed US Army's commanding general, Nelson A. Miles. The lieutenant proposed that selected Black infantrymen test the viability of bicycles in the field as means to increase combat mobility.[160]

---

155 *A&NJ*, May 10, 1894, 694.
156 *Santa Fe New Mexican*, May 15, 1890; Great West (St. Paul, MN) May 16, 1890.
157 *Rawlins Republican*, May 16, 1890; *Livingston Enterprise* (Livingston, MT) May 17, 1890; *New Ulm Weekly Review*, May 21, 1890; *Sun* (New York, NY) May 22, 1890.
158 *Livingston Enterprise* (Livingston, MT) May 17, 1890; *Pittsburg Dispatch*, May 20, 1890.
159 Popular narratives abound, but the first-hand account from the 'bicycle corps' commanding officer is highly recommended as follows: James A. Moss, *Military Cycling in the Rocky Mountains* (New York American Sports Pub. Co., 1897) (online Link: brbl-dl.library.yale.edu/ vufind/ Record/4099165). So, too, are a trio of scholarly articles: Marvin E. Fletcher, 'The Black Bicycle Corps,' *Arizona and the West* 16 no. 3 (Autumn 1974): 219–232; Charles M. Dollar, 'Putting the Army on Wheels: The Story of the Twenty-Fifth Infantry Bicycle Corps,' *Prologue* 17 no. 1 (Spring 1985): 7–24; and Alexandra V. Koelle, 'Pedaling on the Periphery: The African American Twenty-Fifth Infantry Bicycle Corps and the Roads of American Expansion,' *Western Historical Quarterly* 41 no. 3 (Autumn 2010): 305–326.
160 Jim Fitzpatrick, *The Bicycle In Wartime: An Illustrated History* (Washington, DC: Brassey's Inc. 1998) among other topics, treats late 1880s through 1890s experiments in France, England, and Germany exploring the use of bicycles, as well as an overland trek from Nelson Miles' headquarters in Chicago to Connecticut by a Signal Corps detachment from that state's national guard. Also consult an online synopsis from the National Archives at rediscovering-black-history.blogs.archives.gov/2022/02/07/iron-riders–25th-infantry-regiment-part-i.

As a recently commissioned second lieutenant, James Moss left West Point for his first duty assignment at Fort Missoula, Montana. There he convinced the commanding general of the US Army to allow him to undertake a series of experiments related to the use of bicycles under campaign conditions. He handpicked a small cadre of enlisted men from the Twenty-Fifth Infantry for his trials. Later, during the Spanish American War, he transferred to the Twenty-Fourth Infantry and saw combat. He became a prolific author and retired as a colonel. (Courtesy Library of Congress)

Where no bridges existed in Yellowstone and elsewhere, the resourceful Twenty-Fifth Infantry bicycle corps had to improvise a means to surmount such obstacles.111SC885170001 (Courtesy National Archives and Records Administration)

On May 12, 1896, Miles endorsed the project. Moss, an enthusiastic cyclist, picked eight men, none of whom previously had cycling experience, to make their first outings from Fort Missoula, Montana to McDonald Lake in the Mission Mountains, sometimes erroneously confused with the body of water bearing the same name in Glacier National Park. By August of 1896, Moss readied a second, more ambitious trip from the fort to Yellowstone National Park and back – 800 miles in all. The 'Bicycle Corps' left Missoula on August 15. Moss kept a detailed log of each day's progress. He noted the types of grades, road conditions and weather encountered along the route. The volunteers peddled their way from Fort Missoula to Fort Harrison, a post that had been built on the northern outskirts of Helena, Montana. Afterwards, they moved on to Fort Yellowstone and Yellowstone National Park where they tested their equipment and stamina before they peddled home.

By early 1897, encouraged by his Yellowstone test, Moss once more sought permission to traverse a more impressive distance – nearly 2,000 from western Montana to St. Louis, Missouri. After Moss received a favorable reply, his expanded command of 23 wheeling riders from the Twenty-Fifth Infantry, an army doctor and a Montana journalist cycled out to tackle rough terrain. Often, they proceeded without trails, or occasionally forded river crossings where no bridges stood. Along their course, they also rode pass the haunting Little Bighorn battle site where years earlier, some of the men from their regiment had marked the graves and boundaries of the grounds. Similarly, Tenth Cavalry troopers encamped on maneuvers at the battlefield just a few years before the bicycle corps.[161] From Montana, the infantrymen peddled on to their destination. They averaged 52 miles a day despite being laden down with equipment and firearms.

En route, the Twenty-Fifth Infantry bicyclists received triumphal greetings at towns where they appeared on their long ride as they would after their arrival in St. Louis, on July 24. Moss intended to continue to Minneapolis. General Miles' absence from his headquarters resulted in his request's denial. Consequently, on August 19, 1897, Moss and his men entrained for Montana. They did so after they complied with instructions to ship their loaned bicycles back to the Spalding Company.

Based on the impressive statics of this sojourn, Moss, on February 7, 1898, sought approval to organize another cycle infantry trial from Fort Missoula to San Francisco. While his regimental commander endorsed the concept, war with Spain loomed. Army officials deemed further bicycle tests unnecessary. Soon, Moss and his men were off to fight in Cuba. With international affairs taking precedent, the bicycle experiment ended.

National Parks

So it was that both Black and white soldiers were no strangers to national parks and forests. As early as 1875, US Army Engineer Corps Captain William Ludlow suggested the use of army personnel to protect Yellowstone, the first national park in the United States. Over a decade later, the secretary of the interior requested that the secretary of war post troops there. Among others, their charge was to stop vandalism and wildlife slaughter, one of several mandates the military fulfilled for more than two decades after Yellowstone's creation.[162]

Likewise, exploration of uncharted or little known areas in future national parks occasionally fell to the military. Among these outings were ones led by Lieutenant George P. Ahern of the Twenty-Fifth Infantry. On September 20, 1888, Ahern received orders to march from Fort Shaw, Montana with four Black enlisted men and proceed 'to the headwaters of the North Fork of Sun River to ascertain if there is a practicable pass through the mountain range at or near this point.'[163] By 1889, Ahern and his party of infantrymen again trudged overland, 'completely

---

161 *Livingston Enterprise* (MT) November 2, 1889, and May 17, 1890; *A&NJ*, May 10, 1890, 694; *Rawlins Republican*, May 16, 190; Pittsburg Dispatch, May 20, 1890; *Reporter and Farmer* (Webster, SD) May 22, 1890; Eugene P. Frierson, 'An Adventure in the Big Horn Mountains or, The Trials and Tribulations of a Recruit,' *Colored American Magazine* 8 (April, May, June, 1905): 196–99; 277–79; 338–40.

162 H. Duane Hampton, *How the US Cavalry Saved Our National Parks* (Bloomington: Indiana University Press, 2017), particularly chapters 3 and 4, summarized the military's role prior in Yellowstone through 1886. For the entire span of US Army involvement in Yellowstone National Park see yellowstone.org/safeguarding-yellowstone-the-us-army–1886–1918.

163 A contemporary reference in the *Great Falls Weekly Tribune*, October 3, 1888, stated: 'Lieut. Ahern ... is now on a scouting expedition to the main range of the Rockies. Much later, the *Choteau Acantha*

mapping the intervening country.'[164] That same year, Ahern's small command was not alone in the field. Comrades from Companies C, E and F of the Twenty-Fifth set out from Fort Shaw making their way to the Blackfoot Crossing of Sun River, on the first leg of the trip. Within three days they camped 'near Bynum then continued until they reached a spot near Marias Pass, where the battalion remained until September 17.' On that date, they marched back to the fort.[165]

In 1890, Ahern tramped in the vanguard of seven Twenty-Fifth infantrymen. This time, G. E. Culver, professor of mineralogy and geology for South Dakota, accompanied the expedition.[166] Their efforts would be lauded as 'completing another of the many tasks assigned to the army as an advance guard in settlement and development of the western frontier.'[167] Ahern's Montana trailblazing would not end with these forays. In 1894, he would be slated, 'to join an Arctic expedition … to explore Ellesmere land and the islands to its west.'[168] Subsequently, he transformed his academic lectures as the professor of forestry at Montana agricultural college into a real-world setting as superintendent of the Bureau of Forestry in the Philippines. According to one newspaper account, because of his experience he spoke, 'eloquently of the forestry interests of the Philippines.'[169]

Ahern and his men contributed to the 1910 establishment of Glacier National Park. Prior to Ahern, however, many individuals partook of the area's wonders, including Brigadier General Wesley Merritt, commander of the Department of Dakota. Merritt and his guests spent, 'several weeks hunting, fishing and climbing the glaciers in that noted region.' The adventurers were well provided for by their able escort, a troop of the Tenth Cavalry from Fort Assiniboine.[170]

In due course, military detachments served in other places destined to be designated national parks, most notably at California's Yosemite, Sequoia and General Grant reserves, as well as eventually, at Hawaii's Volcanoes. Here, like their predecessors on the mainland, they carved out the Mauna Loa Trail. By the 1890s, it was these three sites located in the High Sierras, however, where troops arrived to perform tasks similar to their counterparts in Yellowstone. None other than the pre-eminent conservationist John Muir acknowledged the positive presence of soldiers with admiration:

> After the Yosemite National Park had been guarded four years by a small troop of cavalry, I [John Muir] made an extended excursion through it to see what the effect of this protection

---

(MT) September 10, 1931, provided considerable details about Ahern's several treks in the area including Glacier National Park.
164 *A&NJ*, August 16, 1889, 945. Also see *Great Falls Weekly Tribune*, May 22, 1889, Semi-weekly Edition; and *Helena Independent*, May 21, 1889.
165 Holterman, *The Twenty-Fifth Infantry in Glacier National Park Country*, 2. One recollection indicated that while passing through Glacier the witness came upon a contingent of the Twenty-Fifth Infantry who were, 'lost as a band of bats in daylight.' H. G. Merriam, ed., *Montana Adventure: The Recollections of Frank B. Linderman* (Lincoln: University of Nebraska Press, 1968), 70.
166 *Helena Independent*, August 12, 1890, Morning. For a concise first-hand overview see Garry Eugene Culver, 'Notes on a Little Known Region in North-Western Montana,' *Transactions of the Wisconsin Academy of Sciences, Arts, and Letters* 8 (1892): 187–205.
167 *Choteau Acantha* (MT) September 10, 1931.
168 *Montanian* (Choteau) March 16, 1894.
169 *Montanian and Chronicle* (Choteau) July 12, 1901.
170 *Anaconda Standard* (MT) August 10, 1894.

Placed on detached service from Fort Shafter, Hawaii, work forces from the Twenty-Fifth Infantry encamped on the 'Big Island' to perform backbreaking road building much as their predecessors had done in the post-Civil War American West. (Courtesy US Geodetic Survey)

In 1899, details from Companies H and I, Twenty-Fourth Infantry replaced other units previously sent from the Bay Area to Sequoia and Yosemite National Parks. Their brief posting represented a new mission for them, which required the foot soldiers to draw mounts and horse equipage to make their rounds through the vast expanses of both preserves. An unknown photographer captured four infantrymen from Company H near Wawona in the environs of Yosemite. They were among the first Buffalo Soldiers to serve in a national park. (Courtesy National Park Service)

was. Before the military assumed control the forest floor was swept as bare as the driest desert at the end of every summer and the sky was full of dust and smoke. Now the ground is covered with grass and flowers like a garden.

The sage conservationist attributed to 'a mere handful of soldiers, without friction or noise' worthy accomplishments. He praised: 'A single soldier armed with the authority of the United States and a gun would suffice to protect a hundred thousand acres of the Sierra forests, however difficult and rough the topography' or so he believed.[171]

As was true in Yellowstone, the first detachments in California consisted of white soldiers. That was until the late 1890s.[172] At that time, Black infantrymen, temporarily staging in the San Francisco Bay Area for eventual Pacific postings, reported for a few months to Yosemite, Sequoia and General Grant Parks. These movements warranted notice in an 1899 San Francisco paper that indicated: 'A detachment of colored troops has been ordered to report for guard duty at Yosemite National Park. It is composed of fifty men and will be under command of Lieutenants George H. McMaster,' and none other than James A. Moss, who had been promoted to first lieutenant by that time, along with a transfer to the Twenty-Fourth Infantry. Twenty-five soldiers from the regiment proceeded to Sequoia Park and the others headed to General Grant Park.[173] Very soon, the detachments, who had been issued horses to perform as mounted infantrymen, completed their brief deployment in the parks. They boarded a train for the Bay Area, destined for assignments beyond California. White artillerymen, drawn from garrisons in San Diego and the San Francisco area, relieved them.[174]

Not until 1903 would Black regulars reappear in the Sierras. Replacing white US Army personnel and state volunteer infantry units, who previously had been dispatched there, four troops of the Ninth Cavalry's Third Squadron made positive impressions and contributions. From the Presidio of San Francisco, they proceeded on horseback for, 'summer service in the National Parks of California. Troops I and M ... marching for the Sequoia Park on May 20th and Troops E and L for the Yosemite Park on April 25th.' Their duties featured patrols to protect the parks from sheepherders and others.[175]

---

171 *Harper's Weekly*, June 5, 1897, 566.
172 Harvey Meyerson, *Nature's Army: When Soldiers Fought for Yosemite* (Lawrence: University Press of Kansas, 2001). Note, this study makes no reference to the presence of Black infantrymen in the park but does contain some information about the Ninth Cavalry under Major John Bigelow. Despite the fine work by Hampton and Meyerson, no definitive study about the role of the US Army in the national parks has been published.
173 *San Francisco Call*, April 30, 1899; *A&NJ*, May 13, 1899, 874; *Report of the Acting Superintendent of the Yosemite National Park to the Secretary of the Interior 1899*, 3–4 (online link: npgallery.nps.gov/GetAsset/d7bbac 44256942fe874 ae 7206b5b7396).
174 *San Francisco Call*, June 18, 1899; *A&NJ*, July 1, 1899, 1047. Interestingly, one of the enlisted artillery replacements at Yosemite, A. B. Bailey, sent a few pithy submissions to the *Wilson Times* (NC) July 7, 1899, August 4, 1899, August 25, 1899. For more details also see, Buffalo Soldier Collection, Collection YOSE 6901/YOSE 120175, Box 1 Rosters and Biographical Files; Box 2 Biographical Files Continued, Yosemite National Park Museum Archives, El Portal, CA.
175 George F. Hamilton, 'History of the Ninth Regiment US Cavalry,' unpublished Mss United States Military Academy Library, n.d. RG 22.25A. The Buffalo Soldier Collection, Collection YOSE 6901/YOSE 120175, Box 1 Rosters and Biographical Files; Box 2 Biographical Files Continued, Yosemite National Park Museum Archives, El Portal, CA; RG94, Entry 53, Boxes 1112, 1113, 1125, and 1126

A half dozen horse soldiers from Troop I, Ninth Cavalry enjoyed a respite from their mission to protect Sequoia and King's Canyon National Parks, during the summer of 1903. (Courtesy Monterey County Historical Society)

The Sequoia contingent particularly received considerable positive press.[176] In great part, this acknowledgement could be attributed to their commanding officer – Captain Charles Young. By that time, he had gained national visibility along with attaining considerable local popularity.

Young's presence also resulted in one of the few known enlisted men's memoirs penned during the first four decades in the history of the Black regulars. In this case, Sergeant W. M. Nicholas, one of the non-commissioned officers who was a member of Troop I, who served in the giant redwood. He extoled his captain's virtues. Nicholas also added many salient specifics.

NAR; and Sergeant W. M. Nicholas, Troop I, Ninth US Cavalry, written in Santa Rosa, California, January 1945, Charles Young Collection, National Afro-American Museum and Cultural Center, Wilberforce, OH, also all should be reviewed to add to the operations in California's national park by the Ninth Cavalry.

176 *Washington Times*, May 2, 1903; *Daily Visalia Delta*, June 3, June 20, June 23, July 11, August 20, September 2, September 17, September 22, October 13, October 18, November 4, 1903; *Fargo Forum and Daily Republican*, November 9, 1903; *San Francisco Call*, November 9, December 18, 1903; *Elk Mountain Pilot* (Irwin, CO) November 17, 1903; *New York Tribune*, December 27, 1903.

For example, he recalled:

> On May 15 Troops I and M, Ninth Cavalry, were ordered by the War Department to proceed overland, mounted, from San Francisco to Sequoia National Park, Tulare County, California, as distance of 285 miles, for Park guard duty under the Department of Interior, for the protection and preservation of the Wild Game, during the travel season of Tourists and Hunters of Big Game.

The observant NCO added: 'Captain Young purchased a Fruit and Stock Ranch consisting of 480 acres on which there was 15 acres of Apples and various other Fruits Trees such as Lemons, Oranges, Nuts and Berries sufficient for a 10 room House, Barn for 8 Horses and a Storage House for 40 Tons of Apples.' Sergeant Nicholas continued: 'Captain Young bought 160 acres in Inyo County, California.' Following their commanding officer's lead, Nicholas and another sergeant 'homesteaded 160 acres adjacent to this property – all level land and at the expiration of our term of enlistments, December 1903' and the two former soldiers temporarily operated these ranches.[177]

The fact that the captain invested in local real estate was a not uncommon action for army officers posted to various sites in the West. Furthermore, this action indicated his personal interest in the area and its potential which he described in glowing terms.[178] Young did more than invest in the area's real estate market and inspire some of his men to do likewise. Of more importance, during the summer of 1903, the two troops in Sequoia and General Grant, undertook many successful projects for which Young recognized his command. He stated: 'I would fail in my duty toward the officers and men if I did not commend the hearty cooperation and efficiency of the former and the faithfulness to duty and good conduct of the latter, a fact that was commented upon by both visitors to the park and the residents in the neighborhood of the camps.'[179]

The range of activities included naming of:

> ... three trees (giant sequoia) in Sequoia Park ... One "G.A.R." tree, in honor of the Grand Army of the Republic; another, from its peculiar growth of three large trees from one big trunk, was named "I.O.O.F.," for the Odd Fellows of the country; and the third, after repeated requests from visitors and the wishes of the workmen who finished the Giant Forest road, was named for that great and good American, Booker T. Washington.[180]

In this regard, one paper ran a bold headline: 'OFFICER LABELS THE WRONG TREE Name of Booker Washington Misplaced in Kaweah Park.'[181]

---

177 Sergeant W. M. Nicholas, Troop I, Ninth US Cavalry, written in Santa Rosa, California, January 1945, Charles Young Collection, National Afro-American Museum and Cultural Center, Wilberforce, OH
178 *Daily Visalia Delta*, August 9, 1903; Sophie Britten, *Pioneers in Paradise: A Historical and Biographical Record of Early Days in Three Rivers, California 1850 to 1950s* (Indianapolis: Dear Ear Press, 2013), 168.
179 *New York Times*, November 9, 1903.
180 *Evening Star* (Washington, DC) November 9, 1903.
181 *San Francisco Call*, November 11, 1903.

This faux pas aside, Young's command supplied yeoman service. Among their accomplishments was the determined completion of the first usable road into Giant Forest and a significant first trail to the summit of Mt. Whitney, the tallest peak in the contiguous United States.[182] The team could be proud of what they had completed. Their captain celebrated their toil with a barbeque where the enlisted men and local dignitaries met under the awesome canopy of the sequoias.[183] Their labors deserved such a celebration particularly because of the 'road, bridge and trail building in the vicinity of Mt. Whitney and 'within its shadow' that made 1903 a record year for the park.[184]

Sharing the fruits of hard work, Captain Young (seated in the centre) joined foreman George Welch, who stood directly behind the officer, with some of the many soldiers and civilians who completed numerous projects during the summer of 1903 that outstripped the achievements of the previous three seasons combined. (Courtesy National Park Service)

182 nps.gov/yose/learn/historyculture/buffalo-soldiers.htm. Also consult Eldredge, *In the Summer of 1903*, for a recapitulation of this season and Young's presence in the park. More information exists in *Report of the Acting Superintendent of Sequoia and General Grant National Parks California, Sequoia and General Grant National Parks Office of the Acting Superintendent Kaweah, Cal October 15, 1903*, in *Annual Reports of the Department of the Interior, for the Fiscal Year Ended June 30, 1903*, 3, pt. 1 (Washington, DC: US Government Printing Office, 1903).
183 *Daily Visalia Delta*, August 15, 1903; August 28, 1903; August 29, 1903.
184 For an excellent contemporary appraisal of the work read *Mount Whitney Club Journal* (1903): 106, 121, and 130–31.

During the 1904 season, the First Squadron, Ninth Cavalry headquartered at Ord Barracks in Monterey, California sent soldier guardians to the parks. This included Troop D, Ninth Cavalry, who formed in two ranks for a photograph with the dramatic Fallen Monarch in Mariposa Grove at Wawona, California.
(Courtesy National Park Service)

The following season, the Ninth Cavalry's First Squadron drew duty in the Sierras. Among their accomplishments, during 1904, was the completion of an arboretum in Yosemite National Park near the south fork of the Merced River.[185] In that year, Major John Bigelow, the park's acting superintendent, praised Assistant Surgeon Henry F. Pipes. Although having, 'no particular training as a botanist but interested in his work' Pipes headed the labeling of trees

---

185 nps.gov/yose/learn/historyculture/buffalo-soldiers.htm.

with English and Latin names. This possibly was the first nature trail in the United States, while the arboretum established the foundation for a museum and library at Camp A.E. Wood (Camp Hoyle) near Wawona under the young physician aided by Black cavalrymen from the two troops deployed under Bigelow's command.[186]

During the seasons of 1903 and 1904, the presence of some 500 Black regulars benefitted Sequoia and Yosemite. Far across the Pacific, other Black soldiers made their mark, in this case at road building – a staple task for soldiers dating back many generations. In Hawaii, not long before the United States entered the trenches in France during the First World War, companies rotating from the Twenty-Fifth Infantry based at Schofield Barracks landed at Kīlauea. Between 1915 and 1917, they labored mightily to build trails that opened this dramatic wonderland to future tourists. In certain respects, they were among the first in a long line of awestruck visitors to the future national park.[187]

National Forests

In some instances, troops posted to the parks engaged a non-human enemy – forest fires. Several references in the reports from officers serving as acting superintendents noted this dangerous duty, as did newspaper accounts. However, parks were not the only sites were conflagrations erupted. One representative headline exclaimed: 'FIRES IN WYOMING. Terrible Timber Fires Raging in the Mountains in all Directions.' In response, men of the Ninth Cavalry from Fort McKinney, Wyoming, 'endeavored to check the fires, but nothing can be done unless it rains' predicted the reporter.[188]

This was only a minor incident to the natural disaster that raged across much of the Northern Great Plains and westward in 1910. During what now sometimes is known as 'The Big Burn' the US Army worked alongside the fledgling US Forest Service.[189] Among those who responded were elements of the Twenty-Fifth US Infantry. A popular national magazine of the era noted: 'Nearly all the regular troops were negroes.' The article continued: 'When negro troops were last in the Coeur d'Alenes' they were cursed, reviled and sneered at … That was the days of the 'bull pen,' the makeshift detention camps guarded years before the fire.

---

186 J. N. Morris, 'Old Nature Trail Is Found Near Wawona,' *Yosemite Nature Notes*, 9 no. 3 (March 1930): 17–18. Additional reference to the Ninth Cavalry's presence in Yosemite National Park include *A&NR*, May 7, 1904, 14; May 7, 1904, 17; Shelton Johnson, *Invisible Men: Buffalo Soldiers of the Sierra Nevada* (nps.gov/parkhistory/hisnps/NPS historians/ invisiblemen2.pdf.) although somewhat disjointed, mentions numerous primary sources worth consulting. Furthermore, the author's arrangement for a contract to copy relevant documents in the National Archives' RG 94.2.2, is a rich resource worth further exploration. See Buffalo Soldier Collection, Collection YOSE 6901/YOSE 120175, Box 1 Rosters and Biographical Files; Box 2 Biographical Files Continued, Yosemite National Park Museum Archives, El Portal, CA. Consolidated information from these files are found at Appendices 18 and 19.
187 Hoverson, 'Buffalo Soldiers at Kīlauea:' 73.
188 *Great Falls Weekly Tribune*, July 28, 1893, Morning.
189 Timothy Egan, *The Big Burn: Theodore Roosevelt and the Fire that Saved America* (New York: Mariner Books, 2009) and Stephen J. Pyne, *Year of the Fires: The Story of the Great Fires of 1910* (New York City: Viking, 2001) are among several narratives of this devastating natural calamity.

Black troops of the 25th Infantry out of Fort Wright in Spokane were detailed to Avery to fight fire and to maintain order through the hectic days of the 1910 fire. As fires raged around the town, the soldiers patrolled to protect the residents and property in Avery. Four of them, posing here with early US Forest Ranger Debitt (on the far left) were thought to have died in the conflagration, but miraculously survived. FI–1-22 (Courtesy Museum of North Idaho)

Now, the situation had changed drastically. During August 1910, Black soldiers 'were hailed as angels of mercy, rather dusky, perspiring angels, but angels at that.' Under dire circumstances, the reporter added: 'Not once, as they worked side by side with the miners they had once herded into bullpens, did race animosity flare up' asserted the reporter. He continued with a tinge of bias: 'The excellent discipline under which the dusky "dough boys" commended itself to all. Although they were sent most dangerous missions, not one lost his life or suffered serious injury.' Four of the infantrymen had been long counted as dead during those desperate days. Soon after arriving to fight the fire, they were detailed on a manhunt after a white marauder, who had shot a victim to death in a local bar. A few hours after 'a seething wall of flame swept across their track. Three days went by – nothing was heard from them.' Company officers began to doubt their safety. Miraculously, on the sixth day, four, 'tattered, scratched, singed' soldiers with belts tightened several notches 'marched up to headquarters with the same cheerful smile with which they had left.'[190]

---

190 *Colliers Magazine*, September 24, 1910, 16.

In Cuba, Black troops not only fought with valor, but also aided the sick and wounded in spite of endangering their own lives. (Courtesy John Langellier)

In certain respects, the Twenty-Fifth's cooperation with the embryonic National Forest Service as firefighters, by assisting in backfiring operations, was crucial in saving the town of Wallace, Idaho. They also took part in evacuating women and children to escape aboard outbound trains; maintained law and order; and in the wake of the fires, undertook the unpleasant retrieval of charred bodies. Consequently, while the Black soldiers' stay in national parks and forests were brief, their performances offered an excellent indicator of professionalism, versatility and reliability achieved during the first half century after the Civil War.[191]

Despite an impressive combat record amassed during the campaigns on the frontier, in Cuba and the Philippines, the American public of the late nineteenth through mid-twentieth centuries remained largely unaware of the valuable service performed by African American soldiers. One scholar went so far as to conclude that they rarely received the recognition due them. Often official reports limited their contributions in campaigns to a terse, 'colored troops … were also engaged.'[192] That pronouncement no longer remains valid. More significantly, the Black soldiers offer considerable prime examples of Michael Tate's 'multipurpose army.'[193]

---

191 fs.usda.gov/detail/r2/home/?cid=fseprd4917690. Also read: *Missoulian*, August 24, 1910; *Alliance Herald* (NE) August 25, 1910; *Courier Democrat* (Langdon, ND) August 25, 1910; *Omaha Daily Bee*, August 25, 1910; *Tacoma Times*, August 25, 1910; *Bottineau Courant* (ND) August 26, 1910; *Free Lance* (Fredricksburg, VA) August 27, 1910; *Bismarck Daily Tribune*, September 21, 1910; *Fargo Forum and Daily Republican*, September 22, 1910; and *Crisis Magazine* 1 (November 1910): 6.
192 Jack D. Foner, *Blacks and the Military in American History: A New Perspective* (New York: Praeger, 1974), 134.
193 Tate, *The Frontier Army in the Settlement of the West*, x.

4

Army Garrisons

Although arduous field service from Mexico to Canada forged many Black regulars into a dependable combat force, both Black and white soldiers spent most of their time in garrison. As was true for all frontier troops, they occupied and maintained outposts that sometimes were isolated and lonely. There, they participated in the whole gamut of commonplace daily duties. The routine seldom broke except during holidays, field service and under certain other circumstances. Towards the late 1800s and into the early 1900s, Black troops enjoyed respites by postings to more populace locales such as Salt Lake City, Utah and the San Francisco Bay Area in the West and to eastern assignments such as Fort Ethan Allen, Vermont, Fort Meyer, Virginia and the United States Military Academy at West Point. By the end of the nineteenth century, Black soldiers also took up stations beyond the Continental United States in Alaska, Hawaii and the Philippines. The same routine tended to prevail at these far off military homes, although the men and their families often found more amenities at these later garrisons.

Far Flung Military Bastions

When first dispatched to the frontier, typically post-Civil War Black and white US Army units replaced Union volunteers at extant outposts. At that time, scores of scattered military reservations dotted the American West.[1] A few of these existed from the antebellum era. Others came

---

1   Numerous publications treat military installations in the West, among them a trio of noteworthy titles remain significant overviews, to wit: Robert W. Frazer, *Forts of the West: Military Forts, Presidios and Posts Commonly Called Forts West of the Mississippi River to 1898* (Norman: University of Oklahoma Press, 1965); Francis Paul Prucha, *A Guide to US Military Posts of the United States, 1789–1895* (Madison: State Historical Society of Wisconsin, 1964); and Willard B. Robinson, *American Forts: Architectural Form and Function* (Urbana: University of Illinois Press, 1977). Several studies specifically address the history of posts garrisoned by Black soldiers, as follows: Eichner, 'Queering Frontier Identities;' Schubert, *Buffalo Soldiers, Braves and the Brass*; Shellum, *Buffalo Soldiers in Alaska*; Michael James Tins Clark, 'A History of the Twenty-fourth United States Infantry Regiment in Utah, 1896–1900,' Ph.D. diss., University of Utah, 1979; Mary Ellen Rowe, 'Fort George Wright, Washington, 1894–1912,' MA thesis, University of Washington, 1980; Steven D. Smith, *The African American Soldier at Fort Huachuca, Arizona, 1892–1946* (Seattle: US Army Corps of Engineer, 2001);

During the 1870s, men from the Ninth Cavalry stand guard at the entrance to Fort Garland, Colorado. (Courtesy Gordon Chappell Historic Trust)

into being during the late war, while a number would be established during the 1860s through 1880s. Regardless of their origins, most of the Trans-Mississippi western sites stood along key routes whether they were overland wagon roads, stagecoach lines, railroad tracks, or other lines of communication, which chiefly meant the telegraph for many decades. As the commanding general of the US Army stated soon after the war ended: 'With a frontier constantly extending and encroaching upon the hunting grounds of the Indian, hostilities, opposition at least, frequently occur. To meet this and to protect the emigrant on his way to the mountain territories, troops have been distributed to give the best protection with the means at hand.' He went to say: 'Few places are occupied by more than two and many by but a single company. These troops are generally badly sheltered and are supplied at great cost.'[2]

    and Laurie A. Wilkie, *Unburied Lives: The Historical Archaeology of Buffalo Soldiers at Fort Davis Texas, 1869–1875* (Albuquerque: University of New Mexico Press, 2021).
2   *ARSW,* 1866, I, 17.

The scattered posts sometimes provided waystations for resupply and other types of support for civilians traversing near a garrison or residing in the vicinity. For the latter group, the post also tended to offer economic benefits to those who provided food, fodder, fuel, labor and more, to sustain the fort's inhabitants.³ Furthermore, the posts represented government power particularly to the Native Americans who lived in the region. Additionally, when required, the military reservations served as bases for preparing and launching campaigns against these earlier inhabitants should they or anyone obstruct the tide of 'Manifest Destiny.'

Even though one monograph correctly concluded that these widely positioned posts were, 'neither monolithic or uniform' the same scholar also relayed that the 'designs of the posts and the buildings that composed them owed much to military tradition.'⁴ As one example of the dichotomy between the appearance of installations, occasionally, yet rarely did the name fort aptly apply in that actual palisades or encircling walls. Defense works of this nature, which provided a semblance of protection from attack, seldom existed in the West.⁵ In fact, only one post manned by Black soldiers could be considered a fortress in the strictest sense – Fort Cummings, New Mexico. Teenaged hospital steward, William Thornton Parker, described the outpost as 'the only walled fort of New Mexico in the sixties.'

Reinforcing his statement, decades after being stationed there, Parker recalled his first military home was: 'A somewhat pretentious front of 'doby' walls with arch entrance and look-out above it and within on either side of the arch were the guard rooms and prison cells with some rooms above it and a tower.' Inside its nearly 12 feet high outer square perimeter stood 'the various buildings occupied by the garrison, i.e., the barracks, the hospital, the officers' quarters, the quarter-master and commissary departments, etc. Opposite the main entrance there was a door going out to the hay stacks in the rear … stored for the use of the cavalry and quarter-master's department.'

He went on to record the bleak living conditions that Black and white frontier troops alike often faced in the years immediately after the Civil War:

> There were no outside windows even in the hospital … The floors were of dirt. In some rooms army blankets were fastened down with wooden pegs for carpets. In one corner of each room was a large open fireplace. The legs of the bedsteads were in good sized tins containing water to prevent red ants form crawling upon the beds. Overhead we nailed up rubber blankets, so that scorpions, centipedes and tarantulas would not slip off on to the floor and be less likely to fall on the sleeper. Rattlesnakes got into our store rooms and into any open boxes, or among blankets and clothing.

Not surprisingly, young Parker summarized: 'The good old fort was a lonely place to live in.'⁶

---

3   Darlis A. Miller, *Soldiers and Settlers: Military Supply in the Southwest, 1861–1885* (Albuquerque: University of New Mexico Press, 1989), remains a key analysis of military posts in terms of economic impact.

4   Alison K. Hoagland, *Army Architecture in the West: Forts Laramie, Bridger, and D.A. Russell, 1849–1912* (Norman: University of Oklahoma Press, 2004), 3 and 5.

5   John S. Billings, *Circular No. 4 Report of Barracks and Hospitals with Descriptions of Military Posts* (Reprint New York: Sol Lewis, 1974), 238.

6   William Thornton Parker, *Annals of Old Fort Cummings New Mexico, 1867–8* (Northampton, MA: WT Park, 1916), 3–5.

More commonly, as one diarist recorded, a frontier post was:

> ... no fort at all; it is simply a collection of houses and buildings set down on the prairie or on the crest of some high bluff, with no bastions, walls, stockade, nor defence of any kind and might better be termed a small settlement than a fort. Select a fairly level piece of ground, say 400 yards square; on two sides build substantial quarters for the officers and on the other two sides rows of barracks for the enlisted men. Erect stables, guard house, post – trader's store, a club - room for officers, another for enlisted men, install hospital for the sick, with capable doctors and attentive nurses, a bakery, reading-room, gymnasium and bathing-rooms and the picture is complete. At regimental quarters a good band was always stationed and, once or twice a week there were hops and dances for both officers and enlisted men. At the post exchange light wines, beer and cider were sold at almost cost prices, but in some cases no whiskey under any pretence was allowed for sale within the limits of a garrison. In the billiard rooms a nominal charge of five cents a game was made, the receipts merely sufficing to pay the attendants and keep the place in repair.[7]

The picture painted in this diary seemed relatively comfortable, but during the 1860s through late 1880s, often that was the exception. US Army inspectors generally noted the substandard conditions that existed at numerous frontier forts whether garrisoned by Blacks, whites, or both groups. One such report found that barracks for the Black troops at Fort Quitman, Texas, were, 'not fit to stable cattle.'[8] Another military facility supposedly amounted to little more than, 'a collection of adobe huts and dugouts' that appeared 'pitiable' and little different from than 'a shabby section of the Bronx in New York' or so recollected Mary Leefe Lawrence, who spent her childhood at such places with her infantry officer father.

Furthermore, she recalled that Fort Dodge, where she first came to live as a toddler in the late 1870s, had many things in common with most Western posts. For instance, it was built in the form of a square. However, many were more rectangular. Regardless of the geometry, regularly officers' and soldiers' quarters faced 'each other across the parade ground.'[9] At the far ends stood support facilities, by and large a headquarters, hospital, warehouses and similar structures. Stables and corrals were situated away from the main complex. Often 'soapsuds row' inhabited by laundresses and the few married enlisted men in the predominantly, bachelor society of the Industrial era US military establishment, stood apart from the main complex.

---

7   Carrie Adell Strahorn, *Fifteen Thousand Miles by Stage; A Woman's Unique Experience During Thirty Years of Path Finding and Pioneering from the Missouri to the Pacific and from Alaska to Mexico* (New York: G. P. Putnam's Sons, 1911), 15.
8   Foner, *Blacks and the Military in American History*, 55.
9   Thomas T, Smith, ed., *Daughter of the Regiment: Memoirs of a Childhood in the Frontier Army, 1878–1898* (Lincoln, NE: Bison Books, 1996), 11. By way of comparison and contrast several official documents describing military installations of the 1870s exists such as *Outline and Descriptions of Posts in the Military Division of the Missouri Commanded by Lieutenant General P.H. Sheridan, Accompanied By Tabular Lists of Indian Superintendencies, Agencies and Reservations, and A Summary of Certain Indian Treaties* (Chicago: Headquarters Military Division of the Missouri, 1876); *Circular No. 4 A Report on Barracks and Hospitals: with Descriptions of Military Posts War Department, Surgeon General's Office, Washington, Dec. 5, 1870*; and Billings, *Circular No. 8 A Report on the Hygiene of the United States Army*.

A soldier at Fort Concho, Texas gazes across the river as a laundress goes about her daily chores. These women often wedded soldiers. Between their earning and their spouse's salary, they were among a small number of military families at a garrison in the West. (Courtesy National Park Service)

Army Families

Typically, the relatively few married enlisted men resided in ramshackle shacks or even tents. As one study concluded, 'enlisted families lived in near squalor … All soldiers' households existed under conditions that severely tested the viability of even the closest families.'[10] Often unsanitary, overcrowded facilities that could be firetraps, proved typical. A tragic example of this last-mentioned factor took place at Fort Robinson, Nebraska at the ramshackle wooden 'Beehive' (the one-time barracks where the ill-fated Cheyenne were held as prisoners of war in 1877) where seven cramped soldiers' families lived side by side. On March 23, 1898, among the residents was Sergeant Harry Wallace from Troop C, Ninth Cavalry, his spouse and their two daughters, Gertrude (four years old) and Mattie (two years old). Mrs. Wallace stepped out momentarily and locked the door to keep the children safe, or so she thought. With both the parents absent, 'a fire broke out' which when men responded 'had gained such headway that it

---

10 Schubert, *Buffalo Soldiers, Braves, and the Brass*, 57.

was impossible to enter that portion of the building. When the word passed that two babies were in the flaming rooms, several soldiers made bold but futile efforts to rescue them. After the fire had burned itself out the two babies were found on a bed, burned to a crisp.'[11]

Substandard or not, the scarcity of suitable housing for rank-and-file families remained a reality well into the twentieth century. In the main, this paucity of quarters stemmed from financial constraints and the long-standing policy to enlist only single men during their first enlistment. Once in uniform, in order to wed, a soldier could do so only with their commanding officer's permission, which was not granted easily. This practice remained in place for many years.[12] As a reflection of military policy, there was little need, or were efforts made, to accommodate enlisted families. Thus, it was not unusual for the ratio of men to women to be off balance at frontier garrisons where bachelors outnumbered husbands, women and children. Given higher reenlistments among the Black regulars, however, there was a tendency for these regiments to have a slightly larger number of married men. As precarious as wedded life could be, a certain level of security existed for families of Black soldiers in terms of pay and food.

Even so, the disproportionate number of men versus women residing at a post continued as the norm. A major contributor to this imbalance was the lack of official status for women, except for laundresses (at least for several years after the Civil War) and hospital matrons. Annie Washington was one of those who served at a medical facility, in her case at Fort Garland, Colorado, when elements of the Ninth Cavalry formed part of the troop complement.[13] Except for these two sanctioned occupations, all other women were classified under the demeaning umbrella of 'Camp Follower.' In this regard, the stanza from Rudyard Kipling's poem, *The Ladies*, was not far off the mark when he rhymed: 'For the Colonel's Lady an' Judy O'Grady Are sisters under their skins!'

By 1878, even the laundresses' standing diminished when General Orders No. 37 disallowed these long-standing fixtures of military posts to relocate at government expense during a unit transfer. Those who had a soldier husband were exempt at least until the expiration of their spouse's enlistment.[14] Although a financial blow, laundresses remained present, but not without competition. Adding steam laundries to a post late in the 1800s, while innovative, deprived the women of revenue. This modernization was looked upon askance by one post newspaper that reported: 'The Chinese laundry is getting too much of the laundrying [sic] that should go to the honest and hard-working women of the garrison.'[15]

---

11 *A&NJ*, April 2, 1898, 590 and Schubert, *Buffalo Soldiers, Braves, and the Brass*, 59. The local *Crawford Tribune*, March 25, 1898, lamented that this was 'one of the 'saddest affairs in this section of the country … for many a long time.'
12 Eichner, 'Queering Frontier Identities,' 49.
13 Gordon Chappell, 'Fort Garland: A United States Army Frontier Garrison in the San Luis Valley of Colorado 1853–1883,' unpublished MS Denver: State Historical Society of Colorado, 2003, end notes 330–332, copy in author's collection.
14 Patricia Y. Stallard, *Glittering Misery: Dependents of the Indian Fighting Army* (Fort Collins: Old Army Press, 1978), 53–73 contains significant details on the subject or launderesses and married men. Jennifer J. Lawrence, *Soap Suds Row: The Bold Lives of Laundresses, 1802–1876* (Glendo, WY: High Plains Press, 2016) adds some additional context. Also consult www.raggedsoldier.com.
15 *Fort Robinson Weekly Bulletin*, February 8, 1893, Vol. 1 no. 3. Collections of the Huntington Library, San Marino, CA.

Whether married or single, as a contemporary newspaper article indicated, many military posts during the 1860s through early 1890s, constituted, 'isolated communities in themselves.'[16] Not only were they physically remote in numerous cases, but in all instances, as indicated, they represented a stratified society. Furthermore, for Black troops, they existed in a racialized landscape.[17]

Common Ties

One commonality at a fort, however, bound the residents together – the parade ground. There, the troops conducted time-honored martial rituals including, as the name implied, parades and guard mounts, as well as raising and lowering of the national colors that floated over the post from a tall flag staff that could be spied from a great distance. Fort Grant, Arizona's parade ground held a unique feature in the form of a small manmade pond dubbed 'Lake Constance' in honor of Constance Mills, the daughter of Tenth Cavalry Major Anson Mills. Replete with a canvas-covered canoe for paddling about this oasis at the extreme south end of the parade ground, added a park-like atmosphere.[18] A tennis court also existed as it did at Fort Bowie and a few other fortunate other posts.[19] The Presidio of San Francisco even boasted a golf course. Such amenities were reserved for 'The Brass' and not the rankers.

As these creature comforts illustrated, some installations could be rated as 'gilt edged assignments,' military slang for select, desirable sites such as Fort Sill, Indian Territory. First occupied and constructed by elements of the Tenth Cavalry, in October of 1873, a correspondent described the place as 'the best arranged and most complete military post I have yet seen. The barracks, officers' quarters and quartermaster's buildings are built of limestone around a square parade-ground of near ten acres area. Hard by are a fine hospital and guard-house. All are kept in fine order by a garrison.'[20]

Elsewhere, one observer pronounced Fort Duchesne guard house ('mill' in soldier parlance) as:

> ... the finest in the land. It is located in the centre of the administration building ... It consists of one large prison room and three prison cells, all ventilated. In the large room the prisoners are provided with mattresses, have benches and a neat dining table. The guard room is large and comfortable. The bunks for the guard are suspended from the wall, which gives them the appearance of folding beds. Each relief sleeps in its separate section and the name of each occupant is placed over his resting place when he is mounted on guard.[21]

16 *St. Paul Daily Globe*, November 7, 1887.
17 Eichner, 'Queering Frontier Identities,' 49, offered a representative picture for the period 1866 and the late 1880s. The entire study is a must read for a better understanding of daily garrison life from the perspective of the soldier, families, and civilians at a post consisting of mixed ethnicities.
18 William T. Corbusier, *Verde to San Carlos: Recollections of a famous Army Surgeon and His Observant family on the Western Frontier 1869–1886* (Tucson: Dale Stuart King, Publisher, 1971), 205, 218–19, 237.
19 Langellier, *Scouting With the Buffalo Soldiers*, 105, 158, 177.
20 *Nation*, October 30, 1873, 286–7.
21 *Salt Lake Herald*, December 7, 1890.

In sharp contrast, an 1871 description by Frances Roe, echoed Mary Leefe Lawrence's memories of Fort Dodge. She declared Camp Supply, Indian Territory was 'quite as dreadful as it has been represented to us.' One positive factor made life a bit more bearable there. Although tinged with racial overtones and smacking of plantation life, Roe recollected: 'There is one advantage of being with colored troops,' she conceded because 'one can always get good servants.' Roe remarked how another officer's spouse had secured, 'an excellent colored soldier cook and her butler was thoroughly trained as such before he enlisted.'[22]

J. Lyman Brown, born on March 9, 1840, apparently plied his culinary skills to the army during his 23 years with the Twenty-Fourth and Twenty-Fifth Infantry that took him to Kansas, Indian Territory and Texas. Allegedly, after his final enlistment, he even cooked for Buffalo Bill and served as the showman's valet.[23]

Daily Routine

Regardless of the amenities or locale, bugle calls punctuated the day at all forts. (See Tables 8 and 9 for examples) Characteristic military routine regularly began at 5:30 a.m. or 5:45 a.m. with a howitzer booming as the Stars and Stripes went aloft to the strain of *To the Colors*. Rising, dressing and eating a boring breakfast, the men preceded to numerous non-military tasks known as fatigues. Duties ran from tending the post garden, picking wild berries as a supplemental food source, cutting ice, securing wood for lumber and fuel, performing construction of post facilities and assignments to the mess hall or company kitchen on what has come to be known by generations of soldiers as 'KP' or 'Kitchen Police.'

Table 8: Bugle Calls Schedule Fort Union, June 1876[24]

Hd. Qtrs., Fort Union, N. M. June 25, 1876 General Orders No. 27	
I. The following list of service calls will take effect on and after the 27th inst. viz:	
Reveille	Sunrise
Stable call	Immediately
Breakfast call	6 A. M.
Sick Call	6:30 A.M.
Fatigue Call	7 A.M.
Guard Mount	8 A.M.
Water Call	8:30 A.M.
Recall from Fatigue	12 M
1st Sergeant's Call	12 M
Dinner	12:15 P.M.
Fatigue call	1 P.M.

22 Roe, *Army Letters from an Officer's Wife*, 54–55.
23 *Winners of the West*, April 1937, 6.
24 RG 93, Fort Union, NM Orders, v. 41, NARA.

Drill Call (Except Saturday and Sunday)	1:30 P.M.
Recall from Drill	3 P.M.
Water and Stable Calls	4 P.M.
Recall from Fatigue	4 P.M.
Drill Call (Except Saturday and Sunday)	6 P.M.
Retreat	Sunset
Tattoo	9 P.M.
Taps	9:15 P.M.
Sunday Morning Inspection	8 A.M.
Target Practice, Friday	9 A.M.
Dress Parade, Sunday	6:30 P.M.
By order of Captain Whittemore	

Table 9: Bugle Calls Fort Union, December 1876[25]

Head Quarters, Ft. Union, NM.	
December 20th, 1876	
General Orders No. 70	
All orders regulating calls at this post heretofore published are hereby revoked. Commencing at Reveille on the 21st inst. the following list of calls will regulate the duties of this garrison.	
1st Call Assembly of Trumpeters	06:25
2d Call Reveille at first note morning gun will be fired	06:35
3d Call Assembly	06:45
4th Stable call immediately after Roll Call	
5th Breakfast Call	07:20
6th Sick Call	07:40
7th Fatigue Call	07:45
8th 1st Call for Guard Mount	08:45
Guard details, Band and field Music will assemble, and be inspected	
9th Adjutant's Call	09:00
10th Water Call	10:00
11th Recall from Fatigue	11:45
12th 1st Sergt. Call	11:50
13th Dinner Call	12:00
14th Fatigue Call	1 P.M.
15th Mounted Drill, Boots and Saddles	01:30
16th Dismounted Drill	01:45
17th Recall from Drill	02:45
18th Water and Stable Call	3
19th Recall from Fatigue	4

[25] RG 93, Fort Union, NM Orders, v. 41, NARA.

20th Dress Parade or Drill every evening except Saturday and Sunday 40 minutes before sunset.	
The companies will be exercised by their respective Company Commanders between the signal for assembly of companies and Adjutant's Call.	
21st Tattoo	8 P.M.
22nd Taps	8:15 P.M.
Sunday morning inspection	9 A. M.
School Call Signal Instructions for Officers, Monday and Thursday	10:00 A.M.
Church call Sunday	10:45
Sabbath School Call	2 P.M.
School Call for Officers recitation in Tactics (Wednesday evenings)	7 P.M.
The prisoners will be worked from sunrise to sunset except one hour for dinner and half an hour for Breakfast. The Prison labor will in no case be regulated by the fatigue calls.	
The Provost Sergt. will be held responsible that the Cavalry prisoners are sent promptly to their respective companies at stable and Water Calls.	
By order of Lt. Col. Dudley	

At times, military prisoners labored at these and other tasks under the watchful eyes of their comrades appointed as guards. Frequently, enlisted men reported for special details or extra duty, requiring soldiers to be absent from their martial schedule much to the chagrin of their commanders. These tasks might necessitate reporting to the quartermaster as teamsters or day laborers, duties in the post library, service as a janitor in the post exchange, carpentry, road construction, maintenance of telegraph lines, cleaning barracks, mucking out stables by cavalrymen and a host of other unpopular chores that started at 7:30 a.m. and continued until approximately 12:15 p.m.[26]

Rank Had Its Privilege

Additionally, some men might secure a position as a 'striker' for an officer. This sinecure permitted earning extra pay. Strikers handled a variety of chores from cleaning boots to household work. Envious soldiers, who failed to secure these limited plums, sometimes called these fortunate few 'dog robbers,' intimating they deprived the family dog of tit-bits from the larder. In fact, strikers not only received supplemental income, but also, might enjoy other benefits. The daughter of a Tenth Cavalry officer expanded on the presence of these manservants, who were ubiquitous, while 'officers' wives employed the wives of the soldiers.' In the Tenth, 'soldiers vied for such jobs' she said, as they had, 'comfortable kitchens to sit in and talk with cooks and

---

26 John P. Langellier, 'Buffalo Soldiers in Big Sky Country, 1888–1898,' *Montana The Magazine of Western History*, 67 no. 3 (Autumn 2017): 46 and 94 n15.

never lacked good things to eat, as they were entitled to their regular meals in the barracks and they were able to devour delicacies prepared for the officer's table.'[27] Also, the memoir revealed that one of her father's soldiers had been assigned to act as a bodyguard for her and 'felt highly honored at the new duty.' Private Michael Finnegan of the Tenth Cavalry would ride twenty feet behind his charge with a full 'cartridge belt about his waist, the pistol and his gun were ready for service' reserving the last round for his captain's daughter rather than allow her to fall into the hands of the Apache.[28]

The young lady and her mother also enjoyed another helpmate. Spending some time at a temporary post named Camp Bonita, Arizona, established during the final stages of the Apache campaigns, the Coopers brought a cook with them. Jenny Miller, the wife of Sergeant Girard Miller, accompanied the family to their dirt-floored, makeshift domicile during their stay in the wilderness.

Fanny Dunbar Corbusier, the spouse of the post surgeon at Fort Grant, also took advantage of 'the crowd of women and children' who accompanied the Tenth Cavalry to that post. Consequently, she 'had no difficulty in procuring servants.' At first, Mrs. Corbusier engaged a woman named Julia as a cook. When beaus arrived to woo her, Julia began to neglect her work. Mrs. Corbusier discharged the woman. A string of enlisted men followed as replacements, trained by the surgeon's spouse until they settled upon Henry Jackson. He endeared himself to Mrs. Corbusier's wild band of five sons. They thought the soldier 'was just about perfection. "It was Jackson this and Jackson that" on just about any subject and soon he was accepted as a very necessary part of our outfit' recalled the youngest lad, Willie. Among Jackson's many accomplishments, he performed as a butler for formal dinners. Incidentally, when not engaged at the doctor's residence, the capable Jackson was one of the post's first members of the newly established, partially integrated hospital corps. He also modeled for some of Frederic Remington's illustrations that accompanied the artist's article 'A Scout With the Buffalo Soldiers.' Fifteen years after they were brought together in Arizona, Jackson enjoyed a brief reunion with Mrs. Corbusier while she visited Washington, DC By then, he was a census taker.[29]

Even if all strikers did not become so closely attached to the household where they worked, they might gain one more advantage. Some of these men could room in the quarters of the officer who employed them rather than live in communal open-bay barracks. Among the drawbacks, privacy was impossible. An historical sketch from the late 1800s, synopsized other disadvantages of these communal living quarters for the enlisted men. 'The appliances for the personal comfort of the soldiers were few,' wrote the observer. This meant soldiers often had, 'to improvise a comfortable resting place out of two blankets.' Moreover, sheets and pillows 'were not dreamed of and bath tubs were unknown, for the water system was limited to a huge tank on wheels, with eight mules and a surly driver.'[30] Even so, for those who had endured the antebellum yoke of enslavement, such conditions were not new, nor necessarily uncomfortable.

27 Steve Wilson, ed., *Child of the Fighting Tenth: On the Frontier with the Buffalo Soldiers Forrestine C. Hooker* (Oxford: Oxford University Press, 2003), 56–57
28 Wilson, *Child of the Fighting Tenth*, 191–2.
29 Corbusier, *Verde to San Carlos*, 216–17.
30 Hutcheson, 'The Ninth Regiment of Cavalry,' 283.

Even on campaign, soldiers experienced idle time. To relieve the tedium of off-duty hours Tenth Cavalry detachments at a camp in Bonita Cañon in present day Chiricahua Monument erected a stone memorial to honor deceased President James Garfield. Later, the building materials were repurposed to build a fireplace for a nearby ranch house. (Courtesy National Park Service)

In 1875, Company I, Tenth Cavalry turned out on the parade ground of Fort Davis in their dress uniforms including a European inspired helmet topped with a yellow horsetail plume – a rather incongruous piece of headgear for the American frontier. (Courtesy National Park Service)

Quality of Life

A few years later, this less than desirable situation remained standard, as exemplified by the lament of a report from the Twenty-Fifth Infantry at Fort Davis, Texas. After a half dozen years, the band and regimental non-commissioned staff roomed in improper shelters. Almost every heavy rain deluged the men for want of an adequate roof. The dirt floor was awash in four inches of deep mud on which the soldiers' feet dangled as they ate their meals, while water drizzled from the leaky ceiling onto their heads and backs.[31]

Over the ensuing decades, the basic layout continued but creature comforts improved. Sometimes this included indoor plumbing, steam heat and other additions from coast to coast, along with facilities in the Hawaiian Islands and Alaska. In the last-mentioned locale, the barracks was unusual in that the Skagway company of the Twenty-Fourth Infantry lived in a two-storey rented facility, purpose-built as a hotel. This meant the soldiers had many amenities that would have been unheard of at a remote frontier post during the 1860s and 1870s.[32] One

---

31 Eichner, 'Queering Frontier Identities' 53–54.
32 David A. Clary, *These Relics of Barbarism: A History of Furniture in Barracks and Guardhouses of the United States Army, 1800–1880* (Harpers Ferry: WV: National Park Service, 1982); Clary, *A Life Which is Gregarious in the Extreme: A History of Furniture in Barracks and Guardhouses of the United States Army, 1880–1945* (Harpers Ferry: WV: National Park Service, 1983); and William L. Brown III, *A Pictorial History of Enlisted Men's Barracks of the US Army, 1861–1895* (Harpers Ferry: WV: National Park Service, 1984), image numbers 12, 22, 31, 35, 36, 39, 60, 61 all add depth details about the evolution of these structures that enlisted men called home. For Alaska review, Bearss, *Proposed Klondike Gold Rush National Historical Park Historic Resource Study*, 173–79 as well as Robert L.S. Spude, *In Skagway, District of Alaska 1884–1912: Building the Gateway to the Klondike*, (Fairbanks:

At their new barracks in Skagway, a corporal in charge of a work party from Company L, Twentieth-fourth Infantry paused before they prepared what would have been an unheard of delicacy at prior assignments in the Continental United States – giant halibut. (William Norton Collection P226_867–1000w. Courtesy Alaska State Archives & Alaska State Library)

general officer of the era would not have been surprised by the accommodations in Alaska. In his report from San Francisco, he expressed the opinion that enlisted quarters were overdesigned and overbuilt with, 'the highest priced plumbing and bath facilities not inferior to those of a first-class hotel.'[33]

Assuredly, as stated, this had not been the situation for a score of years after the mid-1860s. For example, by the early 1880s, Fort Craig, New Mexico exemplified the persistent substandard condition that existed at many posts in the West. The commanding officer deplored the dilapidated disrepair. Roofs and walls were in terrible shape 'and in some cases they had fallen entirely to the ground.'[34] Adding to this view, the commanding general of the Department of Missouri, which included Fort Craig, made it clear that almost all the posts in southern New Mexico were subpar. He lamented:

Anthropology and Historic Preservation, Cooperative Park Studies Unit, University of Alaska, 1983) babel.hathitrust.org/cgi/pt?id= umn.31951 p008901578&view=1up&format =plaint ext &seq =5&skin=2021.
33   *ARSW, 1907*, I, 194.
34   Charles Carroll and Lynne Sebastian, eds., *Fort Craig: The United States Posts on the Camion Real* (Socorro: US Department of Interior Bureau of Land Management, 2000), 31.

> The amounts allowed for building posts on the frontier are so small that … the posts are necessarily of the frailest and least substantial character and require constant repairs, made by the same labor of troops, until within a few years hardly a remnant of the original material remains in the buildings. At the end of that time they are quite as worthless as they were in the beginning.

These make-do structures may have served their purposes in another era and under different circumstances, but with the arrival of the railroad and telegraph lines that 'made communication rapid and transportation of bodies of troops almost equally so all over the Indian frontier' the poor living conditions seemed to the general, that a better solution to repairs could be found if troops could 'be assembled in large garrisons and sheltered decently.'[35]

Taking a page from this proposed remedy, the department commander in New Mexico sought congressional authorisation of over $250,000 for the construction of a major regimental-sized complex at Fort Selden. Once complete, the massive, proposed undertaking was to replace Forts Craig, Cummings, McCrae and Thorn in New Mexico, along with Bowie and Grant in Arizona, most of which had been built prior to 1860. The call for funds prompted a caustic quip from the army's commanding general, William T. Sherman:

> These old posts are a disgrace to civilization and now that the railroads have penetrated that hitherto inaccessible region common decency demands that our officers and men shall have decent and clean habitations. If a citizen of Washington were to stable his horse or cow in an 'adobe' good enough for soldiers in New Mexico [they] would be arrested for cruelty to animals.[36]

In due course, better standards evolved as was true at Fort Robinson, Nebraska. The barracks there had come to represent common, desirable traits for many western posts. After primitive existence in tents and 'all the little adobe and jackal' [*sic*] structures endured in days gone by, improvements materialized, as an 1893 medical report noted.[37] Of eight barracks at Fort Robinson, six of adobe and two of wood, the plan was 'nearly the same for all. In the main building a hall, an orderly room, a 1st Sergeant's room and a store room are at one end and the remainder is a squad room.'[38] Within the basic dormitory-like layout stood approximately 60 'iron cots, with wire springs, cotton mattresses and several blankets.' These metal bunks ran in a neat row on each side of the structure with the bed's head towards the wall and 'at the foot of the cot … a small flat box with a key which serves as the cavalrymen's trunk' in this case for members of the Ninth Cavalry.

---

35 *ARSW, 1881*, I, 123–24. The commander of the Department of Texas voiced similar complaints in one of his reports. *ARSW, 1884*, I, 125. It should be noted that a number of Black regulars served in both of these departments and inhabited several of the forts condemned as woefully inadequate.
36 Ex. Doc. No. 92, 47th Cong. 1st sess. *House Report* (Washington, DC: US Government Publishing Office, 1882), 1.
37 Ex. Doc. No. 92, 47th Cong. 1st sess. *House Report* (Washington, DC: US Government Publishing Office, 1882), 2.
38 As quoted in Gayle F. Carlson, et al, *The Archeology of an 1887 Adobe Barracks (25DW51-B56) At Fort Robinson, Nebraska: Report on the 2000 Investigations* (Lincoln, NE: Nebraska State Historical Society, 2001), 20.

Those items of clothing not stored in footlockers hung at the head of the bunk from pegs. An overhead shelf provided space for the 'fatigue uniform, dress parade, stable clothing and saber,' as well as the various pieces of headgear such as a plumed helmet, forage cap, campaign hat and cork summer helmet, where issued. Furthermore, at the foot of each cot was 'tied a small tin tag in which is inserted a card with the soldier's name and number. Down the center of the barracks are three circular stands holding the carbines and revolvers.'[39] Adding to the comfort: 'A pot-bellied wood stove provided uneven heat' while in daytime, windows plus 'mammoth Rochester burners' fueled with kerosene, lit each squad room.'[40]

Military Fare

Either within these barracks or in an adjacent structure when *Mess Call* rang out, sometime after high noon or whenever set by the commanding officer (who dictated this and every other detail including when to bathe), most of the men marched off from the morning duties for what typically, was a less than memorable meal.[41] The sameness and lack of quality arose as the company cooks tended to be untrained and disinterested in their work. The consequence was as one officer pointed out: 'Nearly as much food is wasted as is issued in the Army from ignorance and experience of company cooks.'[42]

Not until 1896 did the US Army Commissary of Subsistence, charged with providing food, publish the *Manual for Army Cooks*. Two years later, a congressional act assigned one cook to each company. As of March,1899, a second cook would be added to most units. At first, the cooks received the payment and the same allowances as a corporal, which later increased to that of an infantry sergeant. They also gained a new insignia in the form of a brassard bearing a stylized chef's cap in branch colors (white for infantry and yellow for cavalry) sewn to the coat or jacket above the elbow.[43]

Even prior to these changes, the post quartermaster furnished stoves, utensils and rudimentary pots and pans. The first sergeant assigned a waiter to each table and a pair of men to clean up after the meal ended.[44] What they served varied from the locale and the time-period, as well as who commanded. By way of example, in the 1890s and for that matter during much of the

---

39 *Enterprise* (Omaha) January 30, 1897, with supplemental information including the fact that in a connected wing there was a troop library, mess hall, barber shop, china closets, kitchen, tailor shop, and a pair of billiard tables bespeaking of fairly comfortable surroundings. *State Journal* (Lincoln) September 27, 1896.
40 Schubert, *Buffalo Soldiers, Braves and the Brass*, 71.
41 For example, at Fort Huachuca in the early 1890s Companies A, B, C, and H, Twenty-Fourth Infantry were required to bathe twice weekly. Steven D. Smith, *The African American Soldier At Fort Huachuca, 1892–1946* (Seattle: US Army Corps of Engineers, 2001), 17. As with most things facilities for this hygienic practice varied from place and time but by the late 1890s the new brick bath house for enlisted men being built at Fort Douglas was rather typical. *A&NJ*, August 7, 1897, 907.
42 Thomas J. Caperton and LoRheda Fry, *Old Army Cookbook 1865–1900* (Santa Fe: Museum of New Mexico, 1974), 6–7.
43 William K. Emerson, *US Army Soldiers and Their Chevrons: An Illustrated Catalog and History from the Revolutionary War to Present* (San Jose: R. James Bender Publishing, 2013), 143, 157–8.
44 Caperton and Fry, *Old Army Cookbook*, 8.

last part of the nineteenth century, the ration typically consisted of certain quantities of meat, bread, coffee and starches. (See Table 10)

Table 10: US Army Ration[45]

Component. One Article of Each List.
Meat …12 oz.
pork 12 oz.
bacon 22 oz.
salt beef 20 oz.
fresh beef 20 oz.
mutton 14 oz.
dried fish 18 oz.
pickled fish 18 oz.
fresh fish
In 10 days it is usual to give 7 days' of fresh beef, 2 of bacon and 1 of salt pork. The other articles are very seldom issued.
Bread …18 oz. soft bread 10 oz. hard bread 120 oz. corn meal
Soft bread is the invariable issue in garrison.
Dried Vegetables … 2   2–5 oz. beans or peas.
1 3–5 oz. rice or hominy.
Fresh Vegetables … 1lb. potatoes or 9–10 potatoes and
1–10 onions or 8–10 potatoes and 2–10 onions
or 7–10 potatoes and 3–10 canned tomatoes
7–10 potatoes and 3–10 vegetables, such as cabbage, beets, carrots, turnips, squash, etc.
Coffee … 1   3–5 oz. green coffee.
1   7–25 oz. roasted coffee
8–25 oz. tea. Sugar …
2   2–5 oz. sugar.
16–25 gill molasses or syrup.
Condiments and additional articles …
8–25 gill [a gill measure is one fourth of a pint or four ounces.]
vinegar 16–25 oz.
salt 1–25 oz.
pepper 6–25 oz.
candles [In the field] 16–25 oz.
soap, tobacco, lunches, beer, etc., the prices being a slight increase over the cost and the net profits being turned into the company funds – in other words, a cooperative retail store which makes each soldier a silent partner, though not subject to any losses.

Any excess could be sold 'to grocers, settlers, or back to the Commissary Department for non-issue foodstuffs. The money from the sale of this excess was known as the Company Fund.' This practice dated to an 1866 congressional act 'to sell foodstuffs at cost to supplement the monotonous ration. Some of the items sold at these Subsistence Stores included canned vegetables, canned butter, onions, potatoes, oysters, pickles and spices.'[46]

---

45   Charles E. Woodruff, *The U. S. Army Ration and Military Food. Read in the Section of Physiology and Dietetics at the Forty-third Annual Meeting of the American Medical Association, held at Detroit, Mich., June, 1892.* Reprinted from *The Journal of the American Medical Association*, December 3, 1892, 5.
46   Caperton and Fry, *Old Army Cookbook*, 5.

An army surgeon further explained the system. He reported: 'It must not be thought that the soldier is restricted to the actual articles that are mentioned in the table, for by a fairly efficient system, the company commander is permitted to make outside purchases of food.' This was accomplished by selling unused commissary stores, 'technically called the "savings," and with the proceeds buys what he thinks proper.'[47] Having an expendable cash reserve could ease the long-standing, 'crying need' for vegetables, which sometimes might be stored in 'hoards from summer gardens.' Raising fresh food depended on climate and soldiers with experience as farmers, as well as a supportive commanding officer.[48] Failing these agricultural endeavors, the post 'commissary kept only the component parts of the regular ration and the pound of fresh vegetables was not a part of it.'[49] One late twentieth century study, albeit without supporting primary sources, contended: 'What little variety in food the white troops enjoyed – canned tomatoes, dried apples and peaches, molasses, potatoes, onions – was denied the black soldiers.'[50]

Besides a possible lack of certain items critical to a balanced diet, quality also could be wanting. For instance, at Fort Concho, the post surgeon pronounced, 'the bread was sour, the beef of poor quality and the canned peas not fit to eat.'[51] Over time, scrutiny of the prescribed bill of fare and its shortcomings, exposed weaknesses for all troops, regardless of their ethnicity. This led to the realization that the regulation ration did not suit all situations. Local circumstances that varied from halibut in Alaska to fruit in the Pacific Islands, constituted one significant factor to be considered. Cultural proclivities also eventually received consideration.[52] In fact, during the 1880s, the second variable resulted in finding that 'negro companies sold more coffee than the whites and bought more tea.' On the other hand, the whites sold more than twice as much pork or bacon, pepper and rice, more than eight times as much sugar and *mirabile dictu*, more than three times as much soap.[53] In the case of rice, by and large viewed by white Americans at the time as nourishment for the sick, the ingredient was to Black troops raised in the South, especially those on plantations, understood as a food staple.

47 Woodruff, *The U. S. Army Ration*, 5.
48 Vandiver, *Black Jack*, I, 139. As Caperton and Fry, *Old Army Cookbook*, 6 noted: 'The soldiers kept company gardens to provide fresh vegetables' while occasionally 'some companies raised chickens, kept pigs, and occasionally, a milk cow.'
49 Rodenbaugh and Haskin, *The Army of the United States*, 283.
50 Smith and Zeidler, *A Historic Context*, 119.
51 As quoted by Leckie, *Buffalo Soldiers*, 98–99.
52 Shellum, *Buffalo Soldiers in Alaska*, image 20.
53 *A&NJ*, January 15, 1880, 481. *ARSW, 1881*, I, 500–10 divulges extensive data demonstrating the differences as to the rations preferred by Black and white troops. Also see *ARSW 1889*, I, 833–34, which as an interesting aside at Fort Grant, Arizona where elements of the Tenth Cavalry served, Assistant Surgeon William H. Corbusier reported 'the coffee is rarely an infusion, as it should be, but an over-boiled decoction, and sometimes contains considerable charcoal, which, owing to carelessness, is produced during the process of parching the grains. The charcoal robs the beverage of its aroma and strength, leaving it almost odorless and tasteless.' Perhaps this is one reason many Black soldiers preferred tea over coffee.

Education and Training

Whatever the fare, at approximately 1:00 p.m., the troops concluded their midday meal. They returned to their labor details or might attend classes. The latter option was especially evident before 1889 when soldiers lacking an elementary education, were mandated to attend post schools.[54] Almost two decades after the establishment of regiments manned by Black regulars, the need for rudimentary schooling continued. An official report from 1882 indicated that despite post schools receiving much attention and considerable outlay of money, Black enlisted men supposedly manifested limited interest in attendance. Even with low turnout, an unexplained observation by one inspector again illuminated the supposed differences between Blacks and whites. For an unknown reason, 'about one-third more burners [lamps] are required to light a school of colored troops than to light a school of white troops' the inspector related.[55]

Lighting aside, just two years later, military authorities indicated a firm commitment to the school program. Military authorities recommended 'that for posts garrisoned by colored troops teachers be detailed from the white regiments. This chiefly is because the colored soldiers sadly need education, are ambitious to learn and their officers continue to petition that experienced white teachers be sent to them.'[56] That is not to say qualified Black teachers were unavailable, particularly by the next decade.[57] Whomever the mentors were, garrison or regimental chaplains retained their responsibility for oversight of school operations. This practice remained in place through the mid-1890s and even beyond in some instances. Separate facilities and programs for Black and white soldiers tended to be practiced as another example of the US Army's segregation policy of the era.

If not heading off to the schoolroom, men returned to fatigue details or non-academic instruction in signaling with semaphore flags or heliographs that used mirrors to flash messages; hands-on demonstrations of pack train equipment that enabled supplies to keep pace with troops on the move in broken terrain; estimating distances; and a host of other practical exercises offered until 4:45 p.m., when drill commenced.[58]

According to John J. Pershing, who beginning in October 1895, served as an officer with Troop D, Tenth Cavalry at Fort Assiniboine, was pleased with his men's competence. Pershing bragged his horse soldiers drilled to 'perfection.' The lieutenant also contended: 'The troops required little of the officers. The ranks were filled with veterans and the power and prestige of the old top sergeant was sufficient to maintain sufficient discipline and manage the minor details of administration.'[59]

---

54 It seems not only was this requirement ignored but on one occasion, prohibited. *Fort Robinson Weekly Bulletin*, February 1, 1893, Vol. 1 no. 2, which asked why 'eight men of E troop who cannot write their names not allowed to attend school.'
55 *ARSW, 1882*, I, 70 and 192.
56 *ARSW, 1884*, I, 55 and 879.
57 For instance, James W. Abbott of the Twenty-Fourth Infantry and who later would become an ordnance sergeant, had been detailed temporarily from San Carlos, Arizona to Fort Bayard, New Mexico as schoolteacher. Billington, *New Mexico*, 162.
58 Smith, *The African American Soldier At Fort Huachuca*, 13.
59 *Plentywood Herald* (MT) April 17, 1930.

Longtime veteran, Company Quartermaster Sergeant Emmett Hawkins, served with the Twenty-Fourth Infantry when this phograph was taken in 1903. (Library of Congress)

Then, honing combat skills might also entail fording rivers or water obstacles and wielding bayonets by infantrymen and sabers for cavalrymen.[60] Familiarization with new revolvers along with other more advanced firearms that periodically replaced earlier models, or learning about various versions of 'machine guns' and lightweight improved breech-loading howitzers, existed.[61]

Practice marches afoot and on horseback meant leaving the post for maneuvers, which became increasingly significant in the late 1800s.[62] There was skirmish and volley firing, along with practice at the target range particularly after the mid-1870s when emphasis on marksmanship gained momentum.[63] In all cases, duration and frequency varied. For example, in 1893 at Fort Huachuca, Arizona Company C, Twenty-Fourth Infantry averaged three drills a week.[64]

Civilian Interactions

Besides becoming adept with weapons and maintaining their gear, Black troops stood inspection. They did their turn at guard mount and similar military evolutions, plus paraded regularly, on some occasions for high-ranking military and civilian visitors.[65] In the 1890s, one of these notables, Mark Twain, received an invitation from the commanding officer at Fort Missoula, Montana. The famed author accepted, but decided he would rise early to 'walk to the fort slowly; he thought it would do him good.' Unfortunately, he took the wrong route. When the army ambulance with other members of his party appeared, he flagged them down and 'sat quietly inside' until reaching headquarters. As he 'stepped out, a colored sergeant laid hands on him, saying: "Are you 'Mark Twain?" "I am," he replied. "I have orders to arrest and take you to the guardhouse." "All right." And the sergeant walked him across the parade ground to the guardhouse, he [Twain] not uttering a word of protest.'

The post commander then appeared, hurrying 'to relieve the prisoner' after begging his guest's pardon for the practical joke. In response to a proffer for a ride to headquarters, Twain replied: '"Thanks, I prefer freedom, if you don't mind. I'll walk. I see you have thorough discipline here," casting an approving eye toward the sergeant who had him under arrest.'[66]

---

60 Langellier, *Scouting with the Buffalo Soldiers*, 288.
61 Langellier, 'Buffalo Soldiers in Big Sky Country,' 45 and 93 n15.
62 Albert S. Lowe, 'Camp Life of the Tenth US Cavalry,' *Colored American Magazine* 7 (March 1904), 203.
63 For more on the marksmanship program in the last quarter of the nineteenth century consult McChristian, *Regular Army O!*, 75, 200–4, 271, 425, 446 , 539. See also, Langellier, *Scouting with the Buffalo Soldiers*, 147, 168, 183, 231. For examples of notable skill in this area by Black regulars being mentioned in the press and periodicals see *A&NJ*, September 23, 1883, 154; October 20, 1883, 234; November 23, 1883, 355; December 29, 1883, 423; *San Francisco Call* August 21, 1890; August 13, 1903; August 14, 1903; *Evening Star* (Washington, DC) August 16, 1905; August 18, 1905; and *A&NR*, July 9, 1910, 14.
64 Smith, *The African American Soldier At Fort Huachuca*, 13.
65 For example, *A&NJ*, June 22, 1895, 709, reported 'An officer at Fort Robinson, Neb., says: 'We regret exceedingly that you were not with us on Tuesday last, that you might have witnessed a magnificent review and inspection of the 9th Horse before Gen. Schofield and the Department Commander. We are all satisfied with the display made and have reason to believe that the Lieutenant General of the Army and Department Commander were also favorably impressed."
66 J.B. Pond, *Eccentricities of Genius* (New York: G. W. Dillingham Company, 1900), 213–15.

In 1915, Black troops stationed at Fort Apache, Arizona paused for a final rife salute over the grave of one of their officers. (Courtesy Fort Huachuca Museum)

Whether for a special audience or just as a matter of course, a monthly muster would bring out the entire troop complement together 'in full dress and the appearance of the soldiers' often could be 'martial-like and spectacular ... to see the whole command out in all the "pomp and circumstance of war."'[67] At more somber times, the troops formed for memorial ceremonies for the deceased daughter of a comrade where six sergeants acted as pallbearers or performed a similar solemn role for a comrade or superior, such as the one held for the Ninth Cavalry's beloved Colonel Edward Hatch.

At another funeral, this time in Missoula, the Twenty-Fifth Infantry band was among the cortege escorting the remains of Captain C. P. Higgins to his final resting place. There were, 'nearly 150 vehicles with about 600 in attendance' making up the funeral procession.[68] On another sad occasion, men of the Tenth Cavalry's non-commissioned staff and the band assembled at Fort Concho, Texas in 1882.[69] They paid their final respects to Sergeant Major Joseph Parkman, whom they eulogized as 'brilliant' and 'respected by all.' He represented a 'link in its military chain' that cannot 'easily be replaced,' stated the obituary. With his passing, the regiment had, 'lost a kind friend ... one whose soul was centered in its success and whose aim and object was its welfare.' Entering the volunteer service in 1863, his fellow enlisted men supposedly, 'respected him as a man and admired him as a soldier' because of 'his devotion to his profession and his genial manners' he furnished 'an example that should be emulated by all.'[70]

---

67 *Fort Robinson Weekly Bulletin*, April 5, 1893, Vol. 1 no. 11.
68 *Weekly Missoulian*, October 16, 1890, and October 23, 1889.
69 *Salt Lake Herald*, January 16, 1891, noted: 'Miss M. Campbell, daughter of the late Sergeant Campbell, Ninth Cavalry, died at this post on Saturday morning January 3, and was buried January 4, in the post cemetery' carried to her gave by a half dozen of the sergeant's fellow non-commissioned officers. At Fort Robinson, the Ninth Cavalry's senior non-commissioned staff served as Colonel Hatch's pallbearers. Schubert, *Buffalo Soldiers, Braves and the Brass*, 287–89.
70 *A&NJ*, February 11, 1882, 610.

While in many instances barracks remained spartan, until the early 1890s, such as this one at Fort Bayard, New Mexico, military life continued to offer incentives to Black soldiers who joined the army for varied reasons. (Courtesy National Archives and Records Administration)

On a happier note, troops engaged in physical fitness exercises that came into vogue during the late Victorian era. As indicated in the *Annual Report of the Secretary of War* for 1891, military leadership appreciated 'the need for the systematic development of the physique of our troops' which they based in part on 'certain measurements of 161 colored men, 80 of the Tenth Cavalry and 81 of the Twenty-Fourth Infantry, taken by Capt. Edward Everts at Fort Apache.'

Afterwards, 'two months of systematic and well directed exercise' became a regular practice as part of a 'gymnastic course.'[71] Although not a complete success due to what appeared to be a haphazard execution of the trials, the embryonic experiment was only the beginning. By 1904, an impressive new gymnasium at Fort Robinson was under consideration at a staggering cost for the times of $810,000 to provide a facility 'commensurate with its importance as a cavalry post' then garrisoned by the Ninth Cavalry. This substantial sum indicated the extent to which the military embraced physical fitness and offered Black troops facilities comparable to whites.

Whether they worked out to remain in fighting trim, or engaged in other efforts, the men remained active from 4:45 to 5:15 p.m. The daily regimen oft concluded with guard mount at 5:30, then dinner, followed later by *Tattoo* at 9:00 p.m. Finally, came *Taps*, when it was lights' out and time to rest after long hours of toil and activities.

71 *ARSW, 1891*, I, 635.

Pastimes and Recreation

It was not it all work and no play at a fort.[72] For instance, Black soldiers participated in various athletic competitions other than the mandated physical fitness programs. Sometimes it was a bout between two pugilists as demonstrated at Fort Bayard, New Mexico in 1889, where a 'desperate fistic encounter was decided' there between William Wooley of the Twenty-Fourth band and Private John W. Johnson of Company A from the same regiment. The pair donned, 'four ounce gloves for a purse of $40, Richard K. Fox rules to govern.' This was no mean sum, more than equaling three months' pay for a private.

The contenders slugged away for a dozen rounds. 'In the last, Johnson was about done for. Wooley struck at him and he dropped to his knees without being touched. Wooley forced him to his corner and rained neck and face blows,' but Johnson momentarily escaped 'when time was called.' During the final round 'Johnson stepped to the centre of the ring and threw up the sponge.'[73] The referees awarded the decision and purse to Wooley.

While it was one against one in the ring, many more men participated as a team on the diamond. During the half century after the Civil War, baseball grew steadily in popularity, followed to a lesser degree by football. There were also track and field events. Such activities sometimes took place between Black and white troops or white civilian teams from nearby communities.[74] When it came to the gridiron, in early matches, the balls might consist of inflated beef bladders.[75] Over time, some posts such as the Presidio of San Francisco and Fort Huachuca even offered bowling alleys.

The existence of leisure time for these sorts of diversions could be a double-edged sword leading to, 'three related problems of garrison life … boredom, drunkenness and desertion.'[76] Allegedly, boredom's 'chief ally, monotony, sapped spirit and strength.' Included as a culprit was 'the wearied familiarity in food.' Consequently, hunting and fishing supplemented often bland, unvaried rations. Simultaneously these outings provided a break from sameness. Even then, 'long-stocked venison, tasty in moderation, became oddly flavorless with overexposure. Some

---

72 Dale Frederick Giese, 'Soldiers at Play: A History of Social Life at Fort Union, New Mexico, 1851–1891,' Ph.D. diss., University of New Mexico, 1969, should be studied for a contextual overview for several decades in the nineteenth century.
73 *A&NJ*, December 28, 1889, 353.
74 Dobak and Phillips, *Black Regulars*, 148. More information is found in *Arizona Weekly Journal-Miner/Weekly Arizona Miner* (Prescott). December 8, 1886; *Valentine Democrat* (NE) June 17, 1897; *San Francisco Call*, December 3, 1903: December 13, 1903; *Omaha Daily Bee*, February 4, 1904; Thomas J. Clement, 'Athletics in the American Army,' *Colored American Magazine* 8 (January 1905), 21–29; Schubert, *Buffalo Soldiers, Braves and the Brass*, 101–4; Shellum, *Buffalo Soldiers in Alaska*, 2–3, 10, 20; 43, 94–99, 106, 121–22, 133–39, 141, 145, 149, 158, 168, 173, 178–80, 182–85, 188–93, 198, 207, and 209; Robert P. Nash, 'The Buffalo Soldiers Play Ball,' in Angelo J. Louisa, ed., *The African American Baseball Experience in Nebraska: Essays and Memories* (Jefferson, NC: McFarland and Company, Inc. Publishers, 2021), Section I, Chapter 4. Another article indicated that at a major encampment of Black and white troops held at Fort Riley for military maneuvers 'the popular notion of negro inferiority' were supposed at 'the athletic sports' competitions pitting whites against Blacks. The latter athletes put a lie to this notion with Blacks sweeping most of the events. *A&NJ*, November 14, 1903, 280.
75 Eichner, 'Queering Frontier Identities,' 56.
76 Bruno J. Rolak, *History of Fort Huachuca, Arizona* (El Paso, TX: Southwest Antiquarians, 1972), 213.

antelope meat offered variety' but that too could become 'tiresome.' The sutler's store, canteen, or 'post trader's store offered partial relief. Ladies and gentlemen both gathered at this magical place … Here the outer world entered the garrison's closed realm; here gimcracks, liquors, smokes, fashions, cloth and color came to life the drab of isolation.'[77]

At Fort Duchesne, a newspaper report indicated, 'the canteen … is elegantly furnished. Pool and billiard tables of the newest makes are here whilst pictures in profusion ornament the walls. The men could buy beer at 'ten cents a glass and at thirty cents a bottle and must be drank in the canteen building. Billiards or pool ten cents a game or forty cents an hour.' Patrons also could frequent a restaurant where 'anything required to fill up the inner man can be had on short notice and at low figures … the prices charged at the canteen more than bear favorable comparison with western towns located on the line of the railroads.'[78]

While open to all, but with distinctly separate accommodations, this public place was far from a perfect oasis. Yes, there might be rooms for billiards, cards, checkers and chess, but as indicated, alcohol consumption presented a challenge that spawned the exclusion of whiskey sales at army posts as of 1881.[79] Taking more drastic measures, Congress passed legislation that discontinued the post trader's store, replacing it with the more strictly regulated and military governed post exchange. Only beer could be purchased there.

Mixed reactions to this policy arose. Many chaplains favored the more restrictive canteen. Others sought to bar all alcohol purchases.[80] One of these, Reverend Henry Plummer at Fort Robinson, adopted a prohibitionist bent. He decried the 'Curse of the Army' which he singled out as the 'Blighting and demoralizing effects of the system of government liquor selling at Post Exchanges.'[81] Carrying on his condemnation, he disparaged, 'the evil effects of Pay Day' when a nearby local grog shop in town, as well as the 'Trader Store and Post Exchange' not only had remained 'open throughout Saturday, but they were kept open or accessible during the Sabbath day, thus extending an influence which lessens that high regard for the Holy Sabbath that should be inculcated in every young American.' Then, the temperance-minded clergyman ended his sermonizing: 'These Sunday desecrations, if continued and countenanced, will produce a class of men who may so disregard the Christian Sabbath as to wipe out the very name of Christianity.'[82] Plummer condemned his military congregation for spending 'so much money … for bad whisky and beer, instead of real estate.'[83] No doubt, he also wanted them to attend services, which in some ways, was another pastime and break from the daily norm.

---

77 Vandiver, *Black Jack*, I, 139–40. John Thomas Murphy, 'Pistol's Legacy: Sutlers, Post Traders, and the American Army 1820–1895,' Ph.D. diss., University of Illinois at Urbana-Champaign, 1993, furnishes an in-depth narrative on this subject.
78 *Salt Lake Herald*, December 7, 1890, and August 29, 1890.
79 Rickey, *Forty Miles A Day*, 200.
80 Smith, *The African American Soldier At Fort Huachuca*, 20; Eichner, 'Queering Frontier Identities,' 56. *ARSW,* 1887, I, 83–84, 693; *1891*, I, 593; and *1893*, I, 456, also provides comparative statistics for Blacks and white soldiers and incidents of alcoholism.
81 *Fort Robinson Weekly Bulletin*, February 1, 1893, Vol. 1 no. 2.
82 Ibid., March 15, 1893, Vol. 1 no. 8.
83 Ibid., January 25, 1893, Vol. 1 no. 1. Once more Schubert, *Buffalo Soldiers, Braves and the Brass*, 96–100 offers valuable insights into the canteen and exchange system and varying views about these facilities. Likewise examine McChristian, *Regular Army O!*, 392–98.

The Ninth Cavalry's chaplain should not have fretted over this matter if one is to accept an inspection report about the Fort Robinson exchange. This facility could not compare to most others in the military as 'the garrison is composed largely of colored soldiers who do not drink much beer – nor nearly as much as white soldiers – the article on which the greatest profit is derived, that they spend their money for candies and luncheon on which there is little profit.'[84] Although having a sweet tooth may not have been the best for oral hygiene, the results were benign when compared to other more harmful and sometimes fatal practices that arose from overconsumption of liquor. One of these oft dangers existed due to prostitution giving rise to numerous occasions that adversely impacted the army in many ways from health issues to violence and even killings.

That is not to say that socially acceptable pastimes were absent. Decidedly, many wholesome diversions existed. Among these were post libraries funded by the men themselves. They might house an impressive variety of books and periodicals such as *Wilson's Speller and Reader, French's Arithmetic, Harper's Geography, Scott's History of the US and Tactics of the US Infantry* to *Harper's Weekly, The Nation, Army Navy Register, Daily St. Louis, Globe Democrat, Washington Sunday Herald, San Antonio Express, Journal of the Military Service Institution of the United States, Popular Science Monthly, Southern History Papers, Army and Navy Journal, Leslie's Weekly, Sporting Life, Puck, New York Age, World* and *Field and Farm*.[85]

In contrast to his diatribes against the exchange and sutler store, Chaplain Plummer praised the fine library of Troop A, Ninth Cavalry and encouraged them: 'It is a pleasure to see so many young men using the Post Library and filling their minds with useful information. Keep it up, boys, for "reading market a full man." Educate! Educate! Educate!' He followed suit when Troop G was 'getting up a first-class library, which they intend to have well supplied with choice books and the leading magazines and papers. This is a laudable movement and should be done by every Troop in the Regiment,' he applauded. By so doing they emulated, 'the members of Troop A' who had 'long since established a good library for themselves and as a result you will find them bright and well posted on current matters and on the vital issues of the day.'

Correspondingly, the chaplain extolled Troop F for its literary society, which he suggested as a model that should be extended to the entire post in order to 'enlarge its sphere of usefulness.'[86] Reading in a quiet place and away from the buzz of the barracks was a luxury. Those who were literate and who had recipients for their letters, could compose correspondence in the comfort of the library, as well as enjoy hearing from their 'sweetheart, wife or mother' after 'the mail and whether weekly, semi-weekly, or daily' arrived, an event greatly anticipated by 'the entire garrison, from the commanding officer to the latest recruit.'[87]

---

84 RG94, Records of the Adjutant General's Office, Entry 25, Box 480 18833prd 1893, NARA.
85 Eichner, 'Queering Frontier Identities,' 56; Fletcher, *Black Soldier and Officer*, 101.
86 *Fort Robinson Weekly Bulletin*, January 25, 1893, Vol. 1 no. 1; February 15, 1893, Vol. 1 no. 4; March 15, 1893, Vol. 1 no. 8; January 25, 1893, Vol. 1 no. 1; February 22, 1893, Vol. 1 no. 5. For further context regarding schools and libraries consult Schubert, *Buffalo Soldiers, Braves and the Brass*, 115–25.
87 Hutcheson, 'The Ninth Regiment of Cavalry,' 283.

Music and Dance

Other enjoyable occasions involved 'hops' (military slang for dances). As Elijah Cox, an old-timer and fiddle player of the Twenty-Fifth Infantry musician reminisced in a 1924-newspaper interview: 'Folks danced the schottische, the polka, the square dance and the quadrille. We had real music in them days, too. I'll bet I can play 300 waltzes, all of them different without stopping.'[88] The spouse of the post surgeon at Fort Concho, Texas, Mrs. James W. Buell, voiced a different point of view. She recounted: 'We went to a little dance Friday evening at General Grierson's and I nearly killed myself laughing. It was a regular frontier dance with the most absurd old negro to call off the most ridiculous quadrilles and every one danced in true negro style.'[89]

Of a similar mind, Captain George Armes derided his commanding colonel, Benjamin Grierson, as 'a common bone-rattler in a minstrel troupe' referencing his superior officer's former career as a music teacher. Armes accompanied his jibes with a caricature of the colonel seated with a fiddle in the foreground and couples whirling about in an exaggerated manner in the background. The caption below read: 'General Grierson Entertaining His Friends'[90] As might be expected, Alice Grierson offered an opposing perspective. Rather than unsophisticated cavorting, the attendees simply enjoyed themselves at Fort Concho where 'the dancing was lively.'[91]

Be that as it may, finding women as dance partners might present a challenge. When elements of the Ninth Cavalry rode into Fort Wingate, New Mexico, in January 1876, the post surgeon scribbled in this diary, there were 'no Desdemonas with these Othellos.' By August, that situation changed as the same diarist indicated: 'The men of the colored companies have a hop this night ... We have had quite an accession of colored females with the recently arrived cavalry and I hear there will be no lack of partners.'[92] During the immediate post-Civil War years, when insufficient partners were on hand, it also might necessitate enlisted men dancing with each other.[93]

Need for such innovations decreased and eventually disappeared as time passed. At Fort Grant, Arizona, Second Lieutenant Powhatan Clarke divulged that the dances staged by Black soldiers, 'beat them all especially the ladies.'[94] Indeed, these could be occasions to bring out finery as occurred at another Fort Grant gathering. Mrs. Corbusier lent her new blue silk dress trimmed with white lace to the family cook, Julia. As Julia entered, the Black soldier who performed as the usher uttered: 'Ladies and gentlemen let me introduce the "Blue Bird," and soon had a crowd of admirers surrounding her.'[95]

---

88   *San Angelo Standard*, May 3, 1924.
89   Susan Miles, 'Mrs. Buell's Journal,' *Edwards Plateau Historian* 2 (1960): 42.
90   Armes, *Ups and Downs of An Army Officer*, 2.
91   As quoted in Bill Green, *The Dancing Was Lively Fort Concho Texas: A Social History, 1867–1882* (San Angelo: Fort Concho Sketches Publishing Company, 1974), 114.
92   Robert M. Utley, ed., *An Army Doctor on the Western Frontier: Journals and Letters of John Vance Lauderdale, 1864–1890* (Albuquerque: University of New Mexico Press, 2014), 91.
93   Green, *The Dancing Was Lively*, 109.
94   As quoted in Langellier, *Scouting with the Buffalo Soldiers*, 102.
95   As quoted in Corbusier, *Verde to San Carlos*, 216.

After the tragic Wounded Knee debacle, when Ninth Cavalry troops returned from duty at Pine Ridge, they planned 'a fancy dress ball' at Fort Robinson for which 'over 600 invitations were sent out.' To be attired properly, 'several $75 and $100 dresses have been ordered from Chicago and New York by the ladies of the post,' which amounted to an incredible extravagance.[96]

Furthermore, an elaborate masquerade ball in fanciful costumes was staged at Fort Robinson, uncharacteristically 'attended by officers and enlisted men and their wives.'[97] A comparable gathering took place at Fort Bayard, New Mexico. Twenty-Fourth Infantry Sergeant James W. Abbott served as one of three managers of a gathering hosted by his company.[98] Not to be outdone, men of the Ninth Cavalry at Fort Riley, Kansas planned to host a 'masquerade ball' arranged by a senior sergeant'[99] Similarly, Fort Missoula. Montana held 'a domino mask dance until 12 o'clock with supper included at Hotel Florence and "Music by the Fort Missoula string band" all for $5.'[100] Also, a performance by the Black bandsmen from that garrison was termed an 'Old Folks Concert' at which many of Missoula, Montana's, 'best people' attended and the event deemed 'a great success.' The attendees 'were to dress in old fashioned costumes' as part of the theme that included a repertoire of traditional melodies from the past. The proceeds were slated for donation to the Episcopal Church.[101]

These events could take on rather elaborate proportions as evidenced by a holiday celebration held at Fort Supply, Indian Territory. The garrison observed the yuletide with: 'A masquerade and Christmas tree given by the officers of the post' to the children. Then, on Christmas Eve, a full-dress ball was on the tap. For this proposed soiree, members of the garrison bedecked the post library with 'standards, flags and evergreens; over an archway of national flags ran the legend "Merry Christmas, 1884," in gilt, while from numerous tastefully constructed evergreen stars gleamed the naked blades of cavalry sabers; the massive regimental standards, artistically grouped swept the waxed floor with their silken folds.'

Enlisted men from, 'the "Diamond Club," Troop K, 9th Cavalry' matched such labors. This social organization 'came to the front. A grand dress ball was given by them in the Troop quarters Dec. 25. The room was finely decorated with the national colors – a noticeable feature was the American flag grouped with the colors of the republics of Hayti and Liberia. The Troop letter with crossed sabres, wreathed and surmounted by the word "Welcome" in gilt lettering, greeted the eye on entering.'

Elsewhere and at an earlier time, musicians of the Twenty-Fourth Infantry band, 'freely rendered their services until relieved by the Regimental String Band composed of Chief Musician Star and Bandsmen A. Salter, Craycroft and Scott. The utmost decorum prevailed during the entire night. A bountiful repast was served at 11:30 p.m. and at 1 o'clock the last strains of music died away and the guests reluctantly wended their way homeward to dream of "Ye Merrie Christmas."'[102]

---

96 *Appeal: A National Afro-American Newspaper* (Saint Paul, MN) April 25, 1891.
97 *Fort Robinson Weekly Bulletin*, March 1, 1893; Vol. 1 no. 6; March 15, 1893, Vol. 1 no. 8.
98 Schubert, *Voices of the Buffalo Soldiers*, 198.
99 *Omaha Daily Bee*, October 8, 1905.
100 *Weekly Missoulian*, February 6, 1889.
101 *Ibid.*, April 24, 1889.
102 *A&NJ*, January 10, 1885, 471. Several years earlier Fort Sill staged an impressive Christmas as reported in *A&NJ*, January 7, 1882, 495. Likewise, Thanksgiving could be an event of some significance or so an advertisement in the *Tombstone Prospector* for November 16, 1892, indicated

By the early twentieth century, most small one and two company frontier posts had given way to large garrisons such as Fort Lawton, Washington where an infantry battalion and the regimental band provided the garrison. (Courtesy Library of Congress)

Military Bands

Whatever the type of dance there was one commonality – the requirement for music. Bands, which traditionally served at regimental headquarters, would be called upon where available. Other posts might form ad hoc groups such as at Fort Huachuca where individuals from Company B, Twenty-Fourth Infantry developed a string instrument combo to accompany dancers on the 4th of July in 1893.[103] This particular gathering took place under the sponsor-

---

when it promoted a 'Grand Thanksgiving Ball. Skating Rink. Wednesday Eve. November 23,1892. Music Provided by the 24th Infantry Band of Fort Huachuca. Tickets (Ladies Free) $1.50 (Dancing Commences at 9 sharp).' Also see, Schubert, *Buffalo Soldiers, Braves and the Brass*, 108–9 for Fort Robinson references to Thanksgiving and Christmas festivities. Similarly, the December 28, 1890, issue of the *Salt Lake Herald* related that at Fort DuChesne 'sumptuous banquets which every company prepared on the 25th spoke volumes for the chiefs of the culinary departments. All enjoyed their dinner.'
103 *Arizona Citizen/Weekly Citizen* (Tucson) July 15, 1893. The 4th of July regularly capped all celebrations and brought together soldiers and local civilians as reflected by Schubert, *Buffalo Soldiers, Braves and the Brass*, 110–14.

ship of the Army and Navy Union Garrison No. 66, just one of a few different veterans' groups in existence. This also involved examples such as the GAR, as well as widely known fraternal organizations including the Prince Hall Masons, the Grand United Order of Odd Fellows and Knights of Pythias, along with home grown societies, 'organized to meet their social needs.' This included the previously referenced 'Diamond Club' at Fort Robinson and another organization from this garrison, comprised of members of the regimental band, who formed the 'Oak and Ivy' dancing club.[104]

In the case of the 'Oak and Ivy,' the enlisted men established the association. Sometimes officers might take a similar hand. At Fort Duchesne, Utah, during the winter months of 1887 through 1888, officers inaugurated a makeshift orchestra. Captain John F. Stephens, in terms betraying his stereotypical beliefs at that installation stated: 'Naturally the trumpeters were easily taught and several of the colored troops from the Ninth Cavalry had the usual excellent ear for music.'[105] This integrated brass band consisted of Black and white soldiers who played 'grand evenings at parade' under the charge of Lieutenant Charles Young. When the officers of that, 'garrison gave a very pleasant entertainment at post theatre,' other musically inclined enlisted men 'furnished by the string band composed of members of troop B Ninth Cavalry under the leadership of Private Wallace.' Incidentally, this was only one of several stage productions sometimes staged by post personnel and at other times 'by traveling troups' [sic] who performed professionally.[106] In like manner, at Fort Wingate, New Mexico a pair of Ninth Cavalry troopers, one with a banjo, accompanied his bunkie who danced a 'jig,' 'walk around' or 'essence of old virginny.' Incongruous as these antebellum types of performances were, this show was not the only vestige of stereotyping continued from another epoch.

End of the Frontier

Over the 50 years since the end of the Civil War, the military posts, like the men and their missions, had changed. Less than a quarter of a century after the 1866 Army Reorganization Act ushered in the regiments of Black regulars, some 43 frontier forts had closed. Their units transferred to major concentration points where sometimes entire regiments could be billeted.[107] For instance, in places such as Arizona, where dozens of one and two company posts once existed, only Forts Apache, Huachuca and Whipple remained. At these enlarged installations, Troop strength swelled, as did the number and types of improved facilities. The same pattern emerged throughout the former frontier.

104 Schubert, *Buffalo Soldiers, Braves and the Brass*, 93; *Arizona Weekly Journal-Miner/Weekly Arizona Miner* (Prescott) August 7, 1885; *A&NJ*, February 11, 1882, 611. Also consult, Dobak and Phillips, *Black Regulars*, 152, 276–8.
105 Stephen Perry Jocelyn, *Mostly Alkali* (Caldwell, ID: Caxton Printers, Ltd, 1953), 320.
106 *Salt Lake Herald*, December 7, 1890.
107 Discussions in *ARSW, 1881*, I, 123–24; *1884*, I, 84–85; *1885*, I, 167 and *1886*, I, 137 all advocated such actions in keeping with the unpublished proposals by 'the army's leading theorist, the principled, pessimistic Col. Emory Upton' who preached far reaching reforms the gist of which had been 'circulated in unfinished form among interested officers, and Peter Michie's *Life and Letters of Emory Upton* (1885).' Charles Reginald Shrader, gen. ed., *Reference Guide to United States Military History 1865–1919* (New York: Sachem Publishing Associates, Inc., 1993), 39.

This consolidation movement streamlined administration and logistics. Training improved at the battalion, squadron and regimental levels, followed by a combination of two to three companies or troops to form a battalion or squadron with all the companies or squadrons united to form a regiment. This new state of affairs emerged at a time when the military's role as a frontier constabulary drew to a close. A quarter century of facing Native Americans, during more than a thousand engagements of varying magnitude across the West, all but ended.[108]

The focus on pockets of resistance to settler colonial expansion across the Mississippi, morphed into international imperialism. The nation now looked beyond the Continental United States. It gazed ever-more westward towards the Pacific. In the late 1890s, with the emergence of the United States as a world power, the Black regulars no longer lived in arid, sparsely settled pockets of the 'great American Desert' and the bone-chilling blasts of the Great Plains. Instead, they would be scattered from coast to coast, as well as dispersed to Alaska, Hawaii and the Philippines. In part, some of these postings represented a reward for their stalwart performance. Likewise, racial motivations underpinned dispatching Blacks overseas as a means of upholding segregation and isolation from contact with white communities.

The practice of separating the races could not always be maintained. For example, 10 days in advance of the United States' declaration of war against Spain, on April 23, 1898, the Ninth and Tenth Cavalry regiments received orders to entrain for Chickamauga Park, Georgia.[109] Soon thereafter, the Twenty-Fourth and Twenty-Fifth Infantry regiments followed suit. As each of the four regiments arrived, they found themselves in a Jim Crow world, although they generated a good degree of curiosity. Indeed, because the Twenty-Fifth appeared in the vanguard of both Black and white units, locals were drawn to the newly established camp.[110] Many of the curious crowd never had seen a Black soldier. Supposedly, the throngs from the nearby community found the 'behavior of the men was such that not even the most prejudiced could find no fault' [sic].[111]

As other regiments reported, the *New York Tribune* indicated the enthusiasm continued. The paper stated:

> Chattanooga turned out to day and visited the Chickamauga camp grounds. Every vehicle of every description, every bicycle and every horse in the city was called into use and frequent excursion trains ran to the park. Excursions from Cincinnati, Memphis. Knoxville, Huntsville, Ala. and Atlanta and Birmingham were run to Chattanooga, bringing thousands of visitors from out of town to see Uncle Sam's assembling Army.[112]

The crowds personally witnessed the crack troops at drill. This first-time training since the American Civil War, with large scale forces of combined arms, was short-lived. Nevertheless,

---

108 The actual move by the US Army 'to concentrate its forces at the larger and more permanent posts and relinquish numerous smaller installations that had outgrown their usefulness' came to fruition so that 'by 1895 the Army was deployed more or less equally around the country on the basis of regional rather than operational considerations.' Matloff, *American Military History*, 318.
109 *H. Ex. Doc.*, 55:3 *Report of the War Department, Miscellaneous Reports, 1898*, II, 265.
110 *Senate Executive Documents*, 56th Congress, 1st Session, *Report of the Commission Appointed by the President to Investigate the Conduct of the War Department in the War With Spain* (8 vols. 1899–1900), VI, 3005.
111 Quoted in Johnson, *History of the Negro Soldier*, 37.
112 *New York Tribune*, April 25, 1898.

it no doubt impressed some onlookers including a few who might have been skeptical about the capability of Blacks in uniform.[113]

Although living under canvas at Chickamauga, the routine reflected typical garrison duties in a permanent post, along with intensified training. After the Black regulars returned from Cuba and subsequently sailed from the Philippines, they continued this combination of garrison routine and heightened military training. Then, at last Black soldiers rotated for the first time to posts in the East, but often as not, went across the Pacific to the Philippines and even Hawaii. By March 1908, the Twenty-Fourth Infantry sailed back the US shores, boarded a train and during that month, the first and third battalions moved to Madison Barracks, while the second battalion reported to Fort Ontario, both in New York State. They exchanged outpost duty at provincial firebases in the Philippines to intense training in New York that 'consisted of field exercises, annual marksmanship training and the normal garrison duties. They continued to hold their band concerts and parades on holidays, maintaining their reputation as a valued part of the Regular Army.'[114] Even more so than in Salt Lake, they served near a substantial Black civilian population, which proved a good recruiting base.

Similarly, the Tenth Cavalry went to Fort Ethan Allen, Vermont, also known familiarly as '40th and Allen.' After three years in the snowy Vermont countryside, in late 1913, the regiment again received orders returning them to the West. With them was Second Lieutenant John B. Brooks, a recent graduate of the United States Military Academy, who received his first posting, Troop D, Tenth Cavalry. Almost a half century later, Brooks detailed the exchange of stations involving three regiments.[115] During a 1961 interview, he shared: In October when we learned of this movement which was to take place early in December … it was decided to make this switch a three-way affair and the horses, Government mounts, were to remain in place at all three stations involved. The only horses which accompanied us were the private mounts of the officers. The Second Cavalry, then at Fort Bliss, Texas, was designated to relieve us.

On the first portion of the journey to Fort Huachuca, they traveled by squadron via freight trains. On December 8, 1913, the Tenth Cavalry departed Fort Ethan Allen. The regiment proceeded to Weehawkten, New Jersey, thence transferred to the transport *Kilpatrick*. The enlisted men unloaded the freight, boarded the ship and sailed to Galveston, Texas where the men repeated the offloading at the dock to awaiting trains bound for Arizona on the El Paso and Southwestern Railroad. They arrived on December 19 at Fort Huachuca where, 'the whole regiment … except L Troop, which went to Fort Apache' disembarked and took up their new lives along with the horses left behind the Fifth Cavalry.[116] Border duty occupied the regiment in Arizona until being summoned in 1916 to accompany the Punitive Expedition into Mexico.

---

113 Evans, E. Raymond, *Camp Thomas: Chickamauga-Chattanooga National Military Park During The Spanish-American War* (Chattanooga, TN: E. Evans, 2008), combined several sources to produce an overview of the mobilization and camp life at that national military park prior to deployment of US forces to Cuba.
114 Squire Willards, III, 'The 24th Infantry Regiment and the Racial Debate in the US Army,' MA thesis, US Army Command and General Staff College, Fort Leavenworth, KS, 1997, 71–72.
115 *Army and Navy Register*, October 25, 1913, 513, synopsized the three-regiment movement.
116 As reprinted from the 1961 interview in James Finley, *Huachuca Illustrated* I (1993): 14–17.

Garrison Days in Mexico

After facing Villistas in March and April 1916, the Tenth Cavalry went into a permanent camp at Colonia Dublan, Chihuahua, Mexico. Under the circumstances, the troops attempted to make themselves as comfortable as possible. Moreover, after field service took its toll, the cavalrymen refitted with replacement mounts and uniforms, before rotating by troop within their district of responsibility on patrols.[117] Further, at Colonia Dublan, they drilled and performed typical camp functions such as guarding prisoners, kitchen police and a litany of other mundane daily routines.[118]

By early July, the Twenty-Fourth Infantry also consolidated at Colonia Dublan. They made adobe bricks and other mud concoctions for primitive shelter foundations with tent canvas and other makeshift roofing materials to erect a variety of structures. Trenches for defense, which included machine gun positions and even a crude fenced stockade for Mexican prisoners of war, likewise came into being.[119] In due course, many other additions, among which was one amenity which stood out in that Pershing authorised the construction of a theater for nightly motion picture screenings, along with the staging of plays and minstrel shows.

When not engaged in building and housekeeping chores around camp, one company assisted in road building northwards towards the border that opened a logistical lifeline for the Punitive Expedition.[120] Moreover, officers held regular marksmanship training, a three-month machine gun course and daily mock combat, as well as athletic competitions to retain fitness and break monotony. This meant adding a boxing ring plus baseball and football fields. Moreover, sporting events provided both troops and local civilians with diversions. Given that much of the population were members of the nearby Mormon colony, such wholesome pastimes likely were welcomed, as was the prohibition against liquor in camp.

With the ban on alcohol induced nearby entrepreneurs to set up grog shops and small food stalls near camp. Probably, the latter enterprise was viewed more favorably and was indicative of the plentiful supply of fresh produce and other fare.[121] No doubt more destressing to the faithful members of the Church of Latter Day Saints (Mormons) practitioners than the sale of ardent spirts, was Pershing's permission for a 'sanitary village' where prostitutes were available to the

---

117 Rodney, *As A Cavalryman Remembers*, 265.
118 RG393, Returns of the Tenth Regiment of Cavalry, June–December 1916, NARA, delineated of the regiment both on patrol and within the Colonia Dublan basecamp.
119 William G. Müller, *The Twenty Fourth Infantry Past and Present: A Brief History of the Regiment from Official Records Under the Direction of the Regimental Commander* (n.p.: 1923). The publication is unpaginated, but by count, the information about Colonia Dublan appeared on 81.
120 Ernest Graves, 'Road Work on the Punitive Expedition into Mexico,' *Professional Memoirs, Corps of Engineers, United States Army and Engineer Department at Large* 9 no. 48 (November-December 1917:) 662–3, mentioned employment of men from one of the companies from the regiment on the supply road linking the camp to the United States. According to one newspaper report, the route followed one blazed by the Mormons decades earlier. *Cooper Era and Morenci Leader* (Clifton, AZ) July 28, 1916.
121 Perhaps there was too much of a food thing when it came to the quantity of some edibles. Supposedly, a few men from the Tenth Cavalry overindulged in watermelons, and went on sick call. This prompted a temporary embargo fresh fruit consumption. *Weekly Journal-Miner* (Prescott, AZ) August 16, 1916.

soldiers under careful supervision. This practice led to a low venereal disease rate, although some Medical Corps officers protested.[122]

Conversely, evidently the regimental band gained good will amongst all the residents of the area. It contributed to making life somewhat more pleasant. Indeed, music brought civilians and the military together, as had proved a factor for decades at many other posts. As an example, on the 4th of July, one newspaper headline revealed the garrison staged an: 'Old Fashioned Field Day' followed in the evening by a minstrel show to 'Entertain With Songs and Monologues.'[123] To reciprocate, a few weeks later, local civilians produced a pageant that depicted the Mormon's entry into Utah and then Mexico. In the spirit of neighborliness, the Twenty-Fourth Infantry band provided musical accompaniment.[124]

During the next month, some residents must have enjoyed the spectacle of 'Black Jack' Pershing and his staff's inspection of the entire garrison, which culminated in a review of the troops. The Twenty-Fourth Infantry, headed by their band, began the parade past the reviewing party marching, 'with matchless precision.' Then came the Tenth Cavalry with their, 'horses mincing past well fed and glossy.' As the mounted contingent appeared, 'the band's 'brassy blare' was succeeded by the shrill notes of the bugle corps' comprised of trumpeters from the Tenth.[125]

So it was that a garrison, whether long-term or a temporary, not only evolved as its own community, but also often interacted with others in the area. At times, this contact produced accommodation, or occasionally even resulted in mutual respect and friendly relations that broke down barriers and eroded prejudice. In many other instances, familiarity did not eradicate contempt. Regrettably, on numerous occasions, proximity and contact increased racial tensions, which sometimes led to conflict.

---

122 Unless otherwise indicated, the summary of camp details was taken from, Julie Irene Prieto, *The Mexican Expedition 1916–1917* (Washington, DC: Center of Military History United States Army., 2016), 61–62.
123 *Ogden Standard*, July 5, 1916.
124 *El Paso Herald*, July 25, 1916. It should be noted that before departing from Columbus, New Mexico to Colonia Dublan the regimental bands likewise enlivened the Flag Day commemoration in a community where they had been posted prior to marching into Mexico. *Columbus Courier*, June 16, 1916.
125 *Arizona Republican* (Phoenix) August 23, 1916.

5

Segregation, Discrimination and Race Relations

From the mid-1860s to the eve of the nation's entry into the First World War, most of the missions, garrison routine, pay, class divisions between officer and enlisted, postings and supplies from the commissary, ordnance and quartermaster departments, differed little for all soldiers regardless of background or ethnicity. That is not to say that there were not major factors that set Black regulars apart.[1] Significant amongst these was the presence of Black commissioned officers including chaplains. What generally distinguished Blacks in the US Army of the post-Civil War ear, however, was the formidable 'color line.' This ideologically based 'social construct … in which races are created not by nature but human history' separated Blacks within and without of the military, during the half century after the Civil War and beyond.[2]

Segregation

Like their civilian contemporaries, African Americans in the US Army endured Black Laws and Jim Crowism that underpinned thorough and complete racial segregation.[3] Adding to the mix, after Adolph Plessy's challenge to the system when he refused to ride in the 'colored' railway car from New Orleans to Covington, Louisiana, the matter went to the courts. By 1896, *Plessy v. Fergusson* (163 US 537) led to the Supreme Court's majority opinion that equality of accommodation existed, therefore segregation could not of itself, be considered discriminatory. The high court ruled, technically, that violation of the equal rights existed under the provision of the Fourteenth Amendment. For more than half a century, this 'separate but equal' doctrine prevailed in American law. Surely separation existed, but it most certainly was not

---

1 Thompson, 'The Negro Regiments,' 96.
2 Leiker, *Racial Borders*, 7. As this monograph emphasized such 'racialization' was not unique to Blacks. Additionally, he casted the 'border' not as 'a place, but an idea, a separation of groups based on a combination of ethnic and physiological characteristics' that gave rise to especially complex racial relations where whites, Latins, indigenous Native Americans, and Blacks interacted in a variety of ways.
3 Barnard C. Nalty, *Strength for the Fight: A History of Black Americans in the Military* (New York: Free Press, 1986), 2.

The front page of the January 12, 1907 issue of *Harper's Weekly* depicted the sad fate of Mingo Sanders, one of the scores of Twenty-Fifth Infantry soldiers dishonorably discharged as a result of the 'Brownsville Affair.' (Courtesy John Langellier)

equal. Interestingly, a year after the court's opinion in favor of the state of Louisiana, retired Ordnance Sergeant Charles Chinn brought a similar suit against the state of Georgia, but as revealed previously, he did so without success.[4]

As indicated, within the US Army, equality of pay and other material aspects existed, although the extremely limited openings to Blacks as officers constituted a significant example of discrimination. Similarly, from the outset, segregation was the rule as set forth in the legislation of both 1866 and 1869 that gave birth to the Black US Army regiments. A few members of the Black community thought that although not optimal, segregated regiments guaranteed existence of African Americans within the regulars. Some African American leaders even suspected that mixing Blacks and whites in the ranks would eventually end enlistment opportunities for the former group. Trepidation stemmed from concerns that opening assignments to any regiment would prompt recruiters to select only whites to the exclusion of Blacks in order to fulfill their quotas.[5]

A few exceptions to strict segregation emerged. Among these were occasional assignments of Black enlistees in the Signal Corps and hospital corps, which brought about the limited presence of mixed units. Likewise, in a few instances, staff non-commissioned officers including Ordnance Sergeants John Fitzgerald and Jeremiah Jones, reported for duty at posts consisting solely of whites. Furthermore, army shooting competitions, organized to promote military marksmanship, temporarily mixed Blacks and whites. Sometimes athletic competitions did so as well. All these instances greatly differed from integration that followed in the years after the Second World War.[6]

By way of comparison, for considerable time, the United States Army varied to some degree from the United States Navy. The sea service once integrated white seamen with sailors of color until early1890s, when it also adopted strict segregation.[7] In the army, at least in one instance, this staunch commitment to separation adversely impacted a soldier who had been served in a white regiment. After Private Ned C. Harvey of Company G, Twentieth Infantry was classified as 'a colored man,' he could no longer remain with his unit. An exchange of letters ensued including one in which Harvey indicated his desire to remain in the military and another from Captain Charles E. Nordstrom, stating his willingness for the soldier to transfer to his command, which was Troop C, Tenth Cavalry.[8] Indeed, Harvey reported to the Tenth, but not as Nordstrom's subordinate. Instead, he served under another commanding officer in the regiment, Captain John Bigelow. Soon, Bigelow requested the private's dismissal for, 'enlisting under false pretenses.'[9]

---

4   *Morning News* (Savannah, GA) March 31, 1897; *A&NJ*, April 17, 1897, 602.
5   Foner, *Blacks and the Military in American History*, 66.
6   Nalty, *Strength For The Fight*, 255–86, sums up this critical transition phase.
7   Charles Hughes Williams III, "We Have ... Kept the Negroes' Goodwill and Sent Them Away," MA thesis, 2008, Texas A&M University, 4 and 13; and Michael Shawn Davis, "Many of Them are Among My Best Men': The United States Navy Looks at its African American Crewmen,' Ph.D, diss., Kansas State University, 211, 11–58, chart the uneven approach to race and segregation in the US Army through the early twentieth century.
8   May 31, 1893, Vol.,7, Letters Sent, and June 1, 1893, Vol. 18, Letters Received, MC46, Fort Assiniboine, Montana, Montana Historical Society, Helena.
9   John Bigelow, Commanding Officer Troop F, Tenth Cavalry, July 14, 1894, MC46, Fort Assiniboine, Montana, Letters Received, Vol. 19, Montana Historical Society, Helena. Nearly a decade earlier

Army Officers' Divergent Views

During his considerable tenure with Black troops, Bigelow, the son of an early Republican party faithful with direct ties to Abraham Lincoln, held varied, sometimes conflicting views relative to Black soldiers whom he long commanded. Some of these were negative, others positive and a few displayed his acceptance of stereotypes. One of his more damning statements maintained: 'The intelligence of our enlisted men, especially the colored and more especially the colored cavalryman, is not up to the military standards of our age. Work is required of them, both in peace and war, which they must either fail to do or do very imperfectly.'

Bigelow contended that the lack of good non-commissioned officers heightened this challenge. He called for a better class of recruits, as did some others, to fill the ranks in both Black and white units. Bigelow yearned for 'a more honest and generally better class of colored men in the army.' Continuing, the captain expressed his view, 'the cardinal vice of the negro, stealing.' To improve the pool of candidates, Bigelow recommended recruitment be undertaken exclusively by officers from the regiments where Blacks served. He rationalized they were 'better judges of colored people.' Bigelow admitted that to the 'general run of officers,' as was often the case throughout society at large during the era, 'all negroes are alike. Under that condition of mind, an officer recruiting for a colored regiment takes anybody with kinky hair.' Bigelow added more mixed signals when he verbalized, 'a colored soldier will stand more work and hardship without grumbling than a white one,' but countered that a Black would 'exert himself less on his own accord.'

He deduced what might seem strange to later generations aware of Black Olympians and professional sports figures. Bigelow degreed: 'Gymnasiums, foot-balls and bats and such things move him comparatively little.'[10] Elsewhere Bigelow added an offset to his less than glowing reviews: 'These men as soldiers, if properly officered and properly handled, will prove second to none as staunch supporters and defenders of the government.'[11]

Following in Bigelow's rather ambiguous footsteps, John Pershing, although supposedly, 'a man more enlightened regarding minorities than the usual retrograde views held by many white Americans during the era of Jim Crow' also displayed prevailing biases of his times.[12] After Pershing traveled to Fort Assinniboine, Montana, where he had his first taste of command, in particular with Blacks, he discovered men of the Tenth Cavalry were reliable, professional troops.[13] Despite this, Pershing contended: 'Service with colored troops demands greater effort

---

Bigelow called out another private who had reenlisted under false pretenses when he forged his previous 'bobtail discharge, a discharge without character' by producing one that read he had left service with a 'good' character. The same man also had 'sold his carbine to a citizen and pretended to have lost it through no neglect of his.' John Bigelow, Jr., *On the Bloody Trail of Geronimo* (Tucson: Westernlore Press, 1986), 133. This book was a compilation of Bigelow's mid-1880s' serialized articles of his experience in the Southwest for *Outing Magazine*, which one of his brothers edited.

10   Bigelow, *On the Bloody Trail of Geronimo*, 22, 58, 88, 133.
11   John Bigelow, Jr., 'Comments on Leading Colored Troops,' Historical Sketch of the Tenth Cavalry as reprinted in Morris J. MacGregor and Bernard C. Nalty, eds., *Blacks in the United States Armed Forces: Essential Documents* (Wilmington, DE: Scholarly Resources, 1981), 47.
12   Tim McNees, *Time in the Wilderness: The Formative Years of John 'Black Jack' Pershing in the American West* (Lincoln, NE: Potomac Books, 2021), 168.
13   Vandiver, *Black Jack*, 139, and 150.

on the part of officers than that with white troops.' He assumed, 'negro troopers had their limitations and required more supervision and more careful attention to details of instruction.'

As for ever-present military paperwork, such as various reports and troop returns, a much greater responsibility devolved upon the officers, he objected.[14] Even so, Pershing disregarded the complaints voiced by some officers about Blacks being undisciplined and slovenly. With few exceptions, to his surprise and due to tales he had heard from some of those who commanded Blacks during the Civil War, his troops, 'were brave, efficient and cooperative.'[15]

Pershing landed in Cuba with four Black Regular Army regiments. At first, he handled supplies as the regimental quartermaster officer. Eventually, he saw combat, which brought him to the notice of superiors. One of his admirers, Theodore Roosevelt, as commander of the First Volunteer Cavalry ('Rough Riders') was among those who held Pershing in esteem.

To a degree, the future president shared some of Pershing's own thoughts about Blacks, which one biographer indicated, 'were complicated and inconsistent.'[16] Pershing's own words supported this analysis. He candidly remarked: 'My attitude toward the Negroes was that of one brought up among them.' Based on his background as a teacher with Black students in his Missouri public school classroom, Pershing avowed: 'I have always felt kindly and sympathetically toward them and knew that fairness and due consideration if their welfare would make the same appeal to them as to any other body of men.' He ended these remarks by theorizing: 'Most men, of whatever race, creed, or color, want to do the proper thing and they respect the man above them whose motive is the same.'[17]

Yet, arguably the most salient example of Pershing's nuanced perspectives dated from the First World War. In command of the AEF, he issued strict instructions to the French that related to their treatment of American Blacks serving on the Western Front attached to the host nation's forces. The gist of Pershing's directives required maintenance of strict segregation, prohibition of fraternization with French troops and civilians and curtailment of treatment as equals of the Blacks from the AEF. In short, nothing that might undermine racially superior attitudes practiced by many whites in the United States should not be allowed. Later, Pershing also belittled the abilities of the Black soldier.[18]

Long before Pershing wore his four stars, Ulysses S. Grant first sported what was then, a rare insignia. He also displayed mixed attitudes about the Black soldier. At first, after the Battle of Vicksburg (July 24, 1863) Grant concluded: 'The negro troops are easier to preserve discipline

---

14 John J. Pershing, 'Memoirs,' 1, Chap. 6, 9, unpublished draft, Library of Congress, 1937.
15 Vandiver, *Black Jack*, 150.
16 Smyth, *Guerrilla Warrior*, 39.
17 Pershing, 'Memoirs,' 1, Chap. 6, 9.
18 When the first Black regiments reported for duty with the French, Pershing sanctioned secret official circulars to be distributed to commanders of these units. The document outlined American racial preferences and practices as well as warned of 'dangers' inherent in racial mingling. See *The Crisis*, May 1919, 16–18, for the full text of this directive. Further, Pershing later wrote: 'It is well known that the time and attention that must be devoted to training colored troops in order to raise their level of efficiency to the average were considerably greater than the white regiments. More responsibility rested upon officers of colored regiments owning to the lower capacity and lack of education of the personnel ... It would have been much wiser to have followed the long experience of our Regular Army and provided these colored units with selected white officers.' John J. Pershing, *My Experiences in the World War*, vol. 2 (New York Frederick A. Stokes Company, 1931), 228–29.

among than our white troops and I doubt not will prove equally good for garrison duty. All that have been tried have fought bravely.'[19] By late 1865, Grant maintained: 'The presence of black troop, lately slaves, demoralizes labor, both by their advice and by furnishing in their camps a resort for the freedman for long distances around.' Moreover, he thought: 'Colored troops must be kept in bodies sufficient to defend themselves' as some Southerners might take violent action against them. He thought that such a possibility particularly could result as 'the late slave seems to be imbued with the idea that the property of his late master should by right belong to him.' Such a notion, Grant held, could lead to the, 'danger of collisions being brought on by such causes.'[20]

The following year, when United States Senator Henry Wilson introduced a bill to add African Americans to the US Army in peacetime, Grant opposed 'the permanent employment of colored troops.' The general expressed, very possibly based on his belief that Blacks lacked the intellectual capacity to man cannon, that he especially, 'was not in favor of colored artillery regiments.'[21] Incidentally, prohibition of Blacks as artillerymen generally, was the status quo for decades to come.[22]

When Grant became president of the United States, William T. Sherman assumed the mantle of general of the army. His views went beyond the musings of the president. As early as 1863, he confided to his spouse: 'With my opinions of negroes and my experience, yea prejudice, I cannot trust them yet.'[23] In an official communique, he reiterated to the secretary of war: 'I would use negroes as surplus.'[24] Building on this attitude, during the Atlanta campaign of May - September 1864, Sherman opposed Black enlistment. He made no secret of his contempt for Blacks as soldiers. His correspondence bristled with such phrases as 'niggers and vagabonds,' 'niggers and bought recruits,' and 'niggers and the refuse of the South.'[25] Moreover, Sherman officially divulged a strong bias against Blacks as members of the military. Sherman's June 3, 1864, Special Field Order No. 16, offered a prime example. He disallowed the enlistment of Blacks and directed that 'any staff officer having a negro employed in useful labor on account of the Government will refuse to release him from his employment by virtue of a supposed enlistment as a soldier.' Recruiters who violated Sherman's dictate were to be arrested.[26]

---

19 Quoted in Jeremiah Chaplin, ed., *Words of our Hero: Ulysses S. Grant* (Boston: D. Lothrop and Company, 1885?), 13–14. For a brief review of Grant and Black troops during the Civil War see: Robert G. Lambert, Jr. 'Grant and the Black Soldier,' Washington, DC: Army Public Affairs, 1985. files.eric.ed.gov/fulltext/ED269337.pdf.
20 *Dallas Herald*, January 13, 1866, printed the text of Grant's report to President Andrew Johnson, while the former served as commanding general of the US Army.
21 Lt. General Ulysses S. Grant to Senator Henry Wilson, January 12, 1866, in 'The Negro in the Military Service of the United States, 1639–1886,' Microfilm M858, NARA.
22 Morris J. MacGregor and Bernard C. Nalty, eds., *Blacks in the United States Armed Forces: Basic Documents*, vol. 3 (Wilmington, DE: Scholarly Resources, 1977), 207–215; and vol. 4, 374–78.
23 M. A. Dewolf Howe, ed., *Home Letters of General Sherman* (New York: Charles Scribner's Sons, 1909), 252–3.
24 The contents of Sherman's letter to Secretary of War Edwin Stanton appeared in Benjamin P. Thomas and Harold M. Hyman, *Stanton: The Life and Times of Lincoln's Secretary of War* (New York: Alfred A. Knopf, 1961), 343.
25 Clarence Mohr, 'Black Troops in Civil War Georgia,' *New Georgia Encyclopedia*, last modified July 17, 2020, georgiaencyclopedia.org/ articles/history-archaeology/black-troops-in-civil-war-georgia.
26 *The War of the Rebellion: A Compilation of the Official Records of the Union and Confederate Armies* (Washington, DC: Government. Printing Office, 1880–1901) ser. 3, vol. 4, 433–4.

Due to Sherman's blatant stance, one historian charged him with 'the racial views of a Southern slaveholder.'²⁷ Several months later, however, Sherman reversed his ban on recruiting Blacks. In Special Field Order No. 15, January 1865, Headquarters Military Division of the Mississippi he conceded, 'young and able-bodied negroes must be encouraged to enlist as soldiers in the service of the United States, to contribute their share towards maintaining their own freedom and securing their rights as citizens of the United States.'

Nonetheless, after the war, Sherman remained steadfast. He firmly avowed: 'The white man of this country will control it and the negro, in mass, will occupy a subordinate place as a race.'²⁸ Although he allegedly did not oppose Blacks 'as soldiers for I claim for them equality in the ranks,' he declared: 'I honestly think the white race is best' for the duties 'to combat the enemies of civilization.'²⁹ In 1876, during a testimony before a congressional committee, Sherman reiterated his position., He affirmed whites 'were superior to black soldiers in every way.'³⁰

A former Civil War Union general turned US senator, Benjamin Butler, vehemently challenged Sherman. As late as a decade after the establishment of the regiments consisting of Blacks, Sherman remained adamant that they were: 'A quiet, kindly, peaceful race of men.' In this, they were: 'Naturally not addicted to war' but instead 'better suited to the arts of peace.' Sherman indicated the 'experiment of converting them into soldiers' had only 'been partially successful.' The US Army, he said, had made a sincere effort, but it was 'not and should not be considered a charitable institution.' He felt it would be better served if 'the word black be obliterated from the statute Book, that Whites and blacks be enlisted and distributed alike.' Although the general's prescription seemed like an appeal for integration, it represented a coded call for purging the US Army of Blacks.

Senator Butler retorted: 'I utterly dissent from the opinion of the General of the Army as to the employment of blacks as soldiers.' Butler dismissed Sherman as an officer who 'had no experience with them.' Due to the general's lack of personal knowledge, he could not appreciate that the Black soldier was temperate, from a 'rugged race of men' and could 'live on Little,' as well as 'bear privations' longed endured during enslavement.³¹

Sparring over the attributes or shortcomings of Black soldiers remained a leitmotif well into the twentieth century. As demonstrated by Pershing and Bigelow, often officers who served with Black troops exhibited an array of attitudes from negative to paternalistic and in certain cases, even unreservedly positive perspectives. Yet many of those who commanded white troops shared Sherman's disdain. For instance, at Fort Leavenworth, Kansas, Colonel William Hoffman lorded his authority as post commandant over the recently arrived Tenth Cavalry. He demanded the 'nigger troops' maintain their distance.³² Furthermore, he made their stay at his garrison most uncomfortable. This meant he quartered the unit in tents 'on low ground that

---

27 John F. Marszalek, *Sherman: A Soldier's Passion for Order* (Carbondale: Southern Illinois University Press, 2007), 271.
28 Rachel Sherman Thorndike, ed., *The Sherman Letters: Correspondence Between General Sherman and Senator Sherman from 1837 to 1891* (London: Sampson, Low, Marston, and Company, 1894), 263.
29 Endorsement by William T. Sherman to Sec. of War. J.D. Cameron, March 1, 1877, *The Negro In the Military Service of the United States, 1639–1886*, Microfilm M858, NARA.
30 Fowler, *The Black Infantry*, 117.
31 MacGregor and Nalty, *Blacks in the United States Armed Forces* vol. 3 –20.
32 Armes, *Ups and Downs of an Army Officer*, 230.

became a swamp during rainfall' endangering their health. When Benjamin Grierson requested a relocation, as well as wooden sidewalks to improve conditions, Hoffman ignored these pleas.[33]

Ninth Cavalry First Lieutenant Frank B. Taylor, a New Yorker, tended to deal with enlisted men in an imperious manner. Accused of using 'obscene and profane language … toward Trumpeter Benjamin Hockins, Company E. Ninth Cavalry' and abusing of the soldier 'by striking him several blows on the head, face and shoulders with a carbine,' led to an end of Taylor's military career. A courts-martial sentenced him to dismissal from the army. He received a reprieve, however, when the court recommended clemency. Taylor went on half pay for a year, was restricted to post during that time and was suspended from rank until the end of his sentence.[34] At the conclusion of his punishment, Taylor returned to active duty and rose to captain, a grade he held when for a time, he served as Charles Young's commanding officer. Taylor retired in 1891 with the incident of maltreatment towards one of his subordinates having little overall adverse impact on him.[35]

Another example of rank having its privileges, involved a hearing that resulted in two sergeants, three corporals and 27 privates of Company E, Twenty-Fourth Infantry at San Carlos, Arizona being reduced to the grade of private for the non-commissioned officers. They, along with all the privates, likewise received a sentence of forfeiture of pay. These punitive actions emerged from courts-martial proceedings, 'for conspiracy to injure the company commander, Captain A. C. Markley, by making malicious charges against him under the guise of a complaint to the Assistant Adjutant-General of the Department of Arizona.'

Despite confirmation of the multiple sentences:

> The reviewing authority found that the evidence showed that Captain Markley was in the habit of addressing his company while on drill, or other formations, in language that no gentleman and especially an officer of the army, should ever use. It appears also of record that in violation of existing orders he tacitly assented to gambling being carried on daily in the company barracks.

An inspection report further admonished the captain for his failure to comply 'with regulations and orders.' If he had done so 'the unusual spectacle of nearly half a company tried for conspiracy' could have been avoided.[36] In reply, Markley demanded a court of inquiry to challenge the boards' remarks and the damning testimonies of the soldiers.[37]

---

33   Leckie and Leckie, *The Buffalo Soldiers*, 14 and 14 n35. Dobak and Phillips, *Black Regulars*, 303–4 n 46 added, additional evidence about the tyranny of Fort Leavenworth's commander, the Third Infantry's Colonel William Hoffman. This same source presented many examples of race relations and racial confrontations. See pp.1, 20, 21, 24, 41, 84–89, 95, 99, 146–8, 151–2, 189–90, 192–3, 224–7, 235–8, 241–7, 254–8, 260, 263–6, 286–7n 14, 292 n 49, 283 n 7, 309 n 12, 313 n 28, 327–8 n26, 329 n4, 328 nn 31, 33, 331 n 21.
34   General Court-Martial Orders No. 62, Headquarters of the Army, AGO, November 4, 1881.
35   Heitman, *Historical Register*, I, 946.
36   *San Francisco Call*, May 4, 1891.
37   *Ibid.*, June 15, 1891. Also see *Sacramento Daily Record-Union*, April 26, 1891, and May 29, 1891. Edward Valentin, 'Black Enlisted Men in the US-Mexico Border: Race, Citizenship, and Military Occupation 1866–1930,' Ph.D. diss., Rice University, Houston, TX, 2020, 1–62, offers an insightful review of examples of courts-martial proceeding related to Black soldiers.

Such ill treatment of Black soldiers, negative attitudes expressed by certain officers and the refusal of some individuals to serve with the Black regiments, generally reflected personal prejudices. Overall, however, racial motivation supposedly, 'neither shaped nor characterized army policy' or so one source argued.[38]

Clashes Between Black and White Enlisted Men

As an officer, Colonel Hoffman displayed his personal bigotry at Fort Leavenworth whereas at another Kansas garrison, Fort Larned, a series of incidents demonstrated the level of racial tensions that might be extant within the rank and file. There, a mixed garrison of Black and white forces resorted to blows. During late December of 1868, the situation came to a head after some men from Company A, Tenth Cavalry rented a pool table at the post sutler's store. White enlisted men from Company C, Third Infantry, also stationed at the fort, after they entered the facility, made disparaging remarks. Their words provoked a brawl. The post commander unjustly reacted by banishing the Black members of the garrison except for small working parties which he permitted to undertake various labor details at the main post. While the cavalrymen stood guard in the cold at the woodpile a half mile from their warm barracks, in the early morning of January 2, 1869, Company A's stables went up in flames. A review board convened over the matter charged Company A's commander, Captain Nicholas Nolan, over $5,000 for the loss of government property. It took the officer years to overturn the ruling. In the meantime, he and his company removed to Fort Zarah, Kansas, which ended the friction they previously experienced.[39]

In 1888, recruits from both sides of the color line clashed at Jefferson Barracks, Missouri.[40] Two years later, a fierce fight erupted as Black and white enlisted men headed back from town to Fort Leavenworth, Kansas with two of the former group so severely injured that they went to the post hospital.[41] In 1902, Fort Assinniboine, Montana turned into a 'race war' while Black and white soldiers were attending a stag dance. Violence escalated to the level that a Black private and a white private were, 'wounded lying at the point of death' as the 'result of a shooting affray.[42]

---

38 James N. Leiker. *Racial Borders: Black Soldiers Along the Rio Grande* (College Station: Texas A&M University Press, 2002), 49. For further context related Black officers and racism in the US Army from the Civil War to the late twentieth century review, Craig T. Johnson, *Leveling The Competition Not the Playing Field! Perceptions of Racism in the US Army Putting Our National Security at Risk* (Carlisle, PA: US Army War College, 1996). Among other conclusions, thew author asserted: 'Black Americans struggled on four fronts during the late 1890–1930s. They fought to become socially, politically, and psychologically accepted; at the same time, they fought in combat for freedom and democracy against our nation's enemies.' Johnson, *Leveling*, 11.
39 Timothy Ashley Zwink, 'Fort Larned: Garrison on the Central Great Plains,' Ph.D. diss., Oklahoma State University, 1980, 116–18. Also see Geoffrey R. Hunt's 'Race Riot of Fort Larned, Kansas,' unpublished Mss Fort Larned National Historic Site, September 2014, which is a well-documented review largely drawn on NARA Microcopy Number 619, Roll 720 (1869) 434–478M from RG94, Letters Received by the Office of the Adjutant General.
40 *Cheyenne Daily Leader*, January 5, 1888.
41 *Omaha Daily Bee*, January 6, 1890.
42 *Prairie Chronicle* (Cottonwood, ID) August 26, 1902.

Another outbreak similar to the one at Fort Leavenworth, took place in 1903, this time in San Francisco, California. Ninth Cavalry troopers, who recently returned from duty in the national parks, began an altercation with some white soldiers who 'had been drinking and it is claimed that the colored soldiers had been insulted.' When the streetcar on which both groups rode approached Van Ness Avenue, on its way back to the Presidio, the Black troops brought the conveyance 'to a standstill to allow the civilians to reach a place of safety.' A scrap ensued between the Black cavalrymen and the white soldiers whom they claimed had slandered them.[43]

Not too far from the San Francisco Bay Area, in 1904, a drunken brawl in Monterey, California pitted members of the Fifteenth Infantry (white) and the Ninth Cavalry, against each other. The battleground was 'a notorious den in the red light district.' Three Ninth Cavalrymen were believed to have killed an infantry sergeant 'and fatally injured another and then escaped on an early train for San Francisco. A lamp overturned during the fracas set fire to the building, which with the contents and the adjoining building, were totally destroyed.'[44]

On at least one occasion, white soldiers leveled their racial disdain against a Black officer. In the early 1900s, five white soldiers, when they saw African American Captain Charles Young in uniform, walking briskly toward them, 'on account of his color, not wishing to salute him, they turned their backs.' The captain halted and addressed the offenders: 'You refused to salute as the regulations require. Your refusal is an insult to this uniform.' They mumbled, 'but made no move to salute.' Their unresponsiveness prompted Young to remove his coat, hang it on a post and commanded, 'in a tone that enforced compliance, 'Salute that coat and those shoulder straps!' They complied. Young donned his jacket and resumed his walk.[45]

Not only men in ranks refused to accept Young. Although one of his champions optimistically professed:

> It was thought that there would be a severe strain upon discipline when a colored officer rose to the rank of captain and to the command of white officers. But in Captain Young's case his white subordinates seem to have realized that it is the position and rank that they are compelled to salute and obey and not the individual.

Young rarely rated treatment commensurate with his status.[46] As a prime example, after Young became a lieutenant colonel in command of the Tenth Cavalry at Fort Huachuca, Arizona, a subordinate demurred. Southern born First Lieutenant Albert B. Dockery strongly protested. He insisted it was 'not only distasteful but practically impossible to serve under a colored commander.' The matter reached one of Mississippi's US senators. Efforts to transfer Dockery; replace him with a northern born officer; relieve Young due to poor health or transfer the

---

43 *San Francisco Call*, November 24, 1903.
44 *Spokane Press*, October 20, 1904. Also review: *San Francisco Examiner*, October 21, 1904; *San Francisco Call*, October 21, October 22, December 17, 1904; *Tacoma Daily Ledger*, October 22, 1904.
45 *Army and Navy Register*, June 20, 1903, 14. Hereafter referred to as *A&NR*.
46 Villard, 'The Negro in the Regular Army,' 728. While not definitive, Squire Willard III, 'The 24th Infantry Regiment and the Racial Debate in the US Army,' MA thesis, US Army Command and General Staff College, Fort Leavenworth, Kansas, 1997, bears consideration as a point of departure to appreciate the convoluted position of the US Army and Black soldiers prior to the Second World War.

lieutenant colonel to a Black national guard regiment, all received consideration.[47] In the end, Young underwent a medical examination that removed him from active duty. Dockery could remain with his fellow all white officers without fear of service under a Black.[48]

One overview of race and class in the post-Civil War US Army best summarized the situation thusly: 'It might be seen that black soldiers faced unrelenting abuse and scorn.' Nevertheless, the military of the time consisted of a wide 'array of individuals, whose behaviors covered the spectrum. Some were thoroughly racist; others defended the honor of black troops. Some stood up for black soldiers while holding assumptions that were patronizing or condescending; others held black soldiers to be generally ineffective but acknowledged their bravery.'[49] To varying degrees, a similar mixture existed in the civilian populace of the 1860s through well into the twentieth century.

Opposition to Posting of Black Soldiers

Discrimination within the US Army generally reflected the nationwide attitude towards Blacks. As such, an announcement that Black soldiers were on their way to replace white troops could provoke negative reactions. Typically, local newspapers, even prior to Black troops reporting to a nearby post, decried the negative consequences of their replacing whites in a garrison. Predictions that Black prostitutes would be among the negative additions to the community and a rise in violence, even though military records indicated crime rates among white and Black regiments tended to be equal, appeared in print.[50] According to one study, local newspapers tended to be 'more interested in crimes committed by black soldiers than by whites.'[51] Accounts of desertions by white soldiers, if published at all, would be printed on inside pages. Black deserters, particularly if apprehended, made the front page.

As examples, during the mid-1880s, an undeserved reputation preceded the Tenth Cavalry as presented by a few newspapers in southern New Mexico and Arizona. Two contrasting articles illustrated this point. One Arizona editor betrayed his contempt when he stated officers of the Third Cavalry, who exchanged with the Tenth Cavalry, 'predicted Indian outbreaks on account of the colored troops going into Arizona. The Indians call the negroes "buffalo soldiers," and have no fear whatever of them.'[52] Countering this report, another Arizona periodical observed while, 'several of our contemporaries are making great ado because colored troops are to be stationed at several posts in Arizona and before the despised negroes set foot in the territory they were accused of all sorts of immorality.' In contrast, the article reiterated that the Apache did not fear Black troops. Displaying a negative attitude often extant in Texas and along the

---

47 MacGregor and Nalty, *Blacks in the United States Armed Forces*, vol. 3, 106–13.
48 Shellum, *Black Officer in a Buffalo Soldier Regiment*, 252–3. Also review: Louis Sheridan, 'Patriotism Betrayed: How the US Military Segregated From 1913–1939,' *Historical Perspectives: Santa Clara University Undergraduate Journal of History*, Series II 26 (2021): 81–82
49 Kevin Adams, *Class and Race in the Frontier Army: Military Life in the West, 1870–1890* (Norman: University of Oklahoma Press, 2009), 183.
50 Thompson, 'The Negro Soldiers on the Frontier:' 232–23.
51 Frank. N. Schubert, 'Black Soldiers on the White Frontier: Some Factors Influencing Race Relations,' *Phylon* (Winter 1971) 32: 413.
52 *Arizona Weekly Citizen* (Tucson) May 2, 1885.

border in general for the military, the editorial quired, 'but are they [the Apache] any more afraid of white soldiers?' Adding to this this line of reasoning, the writer took an interesting perspective when he concluded: 'The moral tone of the United States army is low, but the negro soldiers are not a whit worse than their white brethren.'[53]

A decade later, in Utah, the *Salt Lake Tribune* of September 20, 1896, carried the headline: 'An Unfortunate Change.' The accompanying editorial protested the proposed posting of 'colored' soldiers to the city that would result in these men riding to town on local streetcars. They would be in the presence of whites, particularly white women. Potential danger lurked. The paper argued a Black enlisted man, when inebriated, 'will be sure to want to assert himself.' This prevalent paranoia about Black men and white women proved unfounded in Salt Lake as it did elsewhere.

When elements of the Twenty-Fifth Infantry reported to Fort Lawton, Washington, Seattle's mayor and some of his constituents fought to have soldiers expelled from the area. President William Howard Taft refused. This rebuff prompted the mayor to order, 'sixty emergency policemen placed in the Fort Lawton district.' Also, the mayor approached the city council 'to authorise the addition of these policemen to the permanent force.' Capping these actions, the mayor 'ordered the closing of negro resorts near the fort where negro soldiers have obtained liquor.' Seattle police simultaneously closed 'the most notorious one of these places whose mistress had been threatened with violence by the whole neighborhood.'

Contrarywise, some citizens of Denver, Colorado indicated that they would be pleased to accept the regiment at nearby Fort Logan. To this end, a circular sent to President Taft asked 'to have the negro troops.' Those favoring the petition asserted that Black troops previously 'had behaved satisfactorily at Fort Logan.'[54]

Taft stood fast in Washington State as had the War Department nearly a quarter of a century earlier in regard to a raid by men of the Twenty-Fifth Infantry from Fort Meade on the town of Sturgis, South Dakota. Locals there protested. The response from military authorities rebutted: 'There is no evidence to show that the peace of Sturgis City, in the future, is threatened.' As the Black 'troops were as well behaved and as amenable to discipline as any white troops' and as they tended to be 'more temperate than our white troops and crime and disorders resulting from intoxication are extremely rare' the clamor to transfer the Twenty-Fifth Infantry from Fort Meade and substitute it with a white garrison received a resounding denial.[55]

In contrast, being sent to Seattle and other urban posts appealed to officers serving with Blacks, who periodically decried remote assignments that they felt had been unfairly assigned to their units. As an example, in 1879, after the Twenty-Fourth Infantry's 'long and arduous service on the Rio Grande frontier' a change of locations seemed appropriate to some advocates. The commanding general of the Department of the South retorted that a transfer to New Orleans or Little Rock would be of no avail. 'However senseless and unreasonable,' the reasons against this relocation might be, the general cautioned, 'the fact that a strong prejudice exists at the South against Colored troops' would mean 'trouble, for these troops' whom he painted as 'easily excited and thoroughly united on any question of insult to their race.' For this and other

---

53   *St. Johns Herald* (AZ) May 28, 1885.
54   *Ogden Standard,* June 9, 1910.
55   MacGregor and Nalty, *Blacks in the United States Armed Forces*, vol. 3, 146–8.

reasons, real or imagined, the departmental commander argued against resettlement in the South.[56]

General Sherman concurred, but not wholeheartedly. His rather convoluted approach was that he understood the political opposition of placing a Black regiment 'in mass in New Orleans, at this time, there are in the welfare of the men themselves very great objections to sending them to Dakota,' which had been a suggested as an alternative. Sherman embraced the stereotype that Blacks 'for half of the year' in that frigid climate would be of little more 'value than an army of dormice or any other hybernating [sic] animals.' Building on his erroneous racial typecasting, the general contended: 'The only non-political reason at this time for keeping up a body of colored troops in the US Army that I know of is their comparative exemption from epidemics and other diseases of the Southern coast,' based on their origins 'from the tropics.' His spurious rationale ended with the remark: 'The Southern climate suits the men.' Likewise, he offered an untenable aside that the officers might be transferred to other regiments and the men left in place. No such option existed in the army of the era, which he well knew.[57]

Returning to Sherman's line of reasoning, Texas may have presented a logical duty station for military authorities, but by the mid-1870s through the 1880s, new orders incrementally dispersed the regiments to a variety of climes. Years afterward, however, the army began to return Black troops to the Lone Star State. That movement once more provoked disapproval. Among those who reacted was powerful Texas Congressman John Nance Garner, a future vice president of the United States. In 1911, President Taft rescinded plans to post Ninth Cavalry detachments along the border. Supposedly, the president reacted because he deplored: 'Violations of Jim Crow Laws' by Black soldiers who increasingly stood up against discrimination after the Spanish American War.[58] Perhaps Taft also bowed to Garner. Regardless, the senator drew praise from citizens in both El Paso and Marfa, who saw him as a staunch supporter of their rights to reject an incursion of Black troops.[59]

Previously, the Ninth Cavalry also 'was not wanted' in Douglas, Arizona as the locals feared the Black troops 'would be a source of trouble.'[60] Douglas' mayor lacked Garner's political clout. The regiment reported as planned. Over time, after the Ninth's arrival was a fait accompli and trepidations decreased considerably.

Prejudice also existed in the heart of former Abolitionist New England. In 1907, former secretary of war from 1889 to 1891, Senator Redfield Proctor previously spoke in a positive light concerning Black soldiers. Now, he led resistance against stationing African Americans at Fort Ethan Allen in his home state of Vermont. He bragged that his efforts to prevent this move represented the 'most arduous struggle of his whole career.'[61] Even in Hawaii, where multiculturalism presumably long existed, influential residents attempted to prohibit the posting of

56 Ibid., 127.
57 Ibid., 131–2.
58 *El Paso Herald*, April 5, 1911.
59 *Waxahachie Daily Light* (TX) April 5, 6, and 8, 1911; *El Paso Herald*, April 7, and 8, 1911, *Bryan Daily Eagle and Pilot*, April 8, 1911. For a summation of the situation read Garna L. Christian, *Black Soldiers in Jim Crow Texas, 1899–1917* (College Station: Texas A&M University Press, 1995), 102–10.
60 *Chicago Defender* July 4, 1914, and September 4, 1915.
61 Stephen Bonsal, 'The Negro Soldier in War and Peace,' *North American Review* 185 no. 616 (June 7, 1907), 322.

Black regulars to Oahu.[62] After the War Department ignored opposition and sent the Twenty-Fifth Infantry to Hawaii, a 'Series of Burglaries, Holdups and Lesser Offenses Committed' by the Black foot soldiers took place. Recruits were blamed. Even so, the provost guard temporarily was increased.[63] With the passage of time, the furor dissipated. Often, civilians and soldiers at a minimum, struck an unwritten truce. Several positive experiences likewise emerged generally at posts near larger cities and especially where a substantial number of Black civilians resided.[64]

Accommodation and Barrier Breaking

As one example of amenable relations, when elements of the Tenth Cavalry reported to Fort Whipple in 1885, outside of Prescott, Arizona, they showed 'no disposition to rival the legendary 'Bloody Fourteenth" Infantry. This was a unit manned by white soldiers previously garrisoned to the post and who periodically ran roughshod over the nearby town. Instead, the Black cavalrymen were 'well behaved and as soldierly looking set of men that have ever been stationed at Whipple.'[65] In contrast, the town's saloonkeepers were not as impressed. The reason for their disappointment arose from a contention that the men of the Tenth spent 'less money on ardent spirits than any other troops stationed at Whipple.' At least merchants purveying male garments benefitted from this sense of style. Instead, 'their special weakness' was 'swell clothing in the ultra dude design.'[66] Years later, when the Tenth Cavalry relocated to Montana, residents of Miles City discovered after the arrival of the paymaster at nearby Fort Keogh that businesses, 'did quite a lively trade from the colored troops.'[67] Furthermore, *The Daily Yellowstone Journal* conceded: 'It was the quietest pay day ever seen in the city, not one arrest had been made.'

These encounters in Arizona and Montana, as well as in other states and territories, were not uncommon. Indeed, as the authors of *The Black Regulars* noted: 'Merchants, saloonkeepers, and owners of gambling halls and brothels usually ignored a soldier's race.' Simply put: 'The color of a man's money was more important than that of his skin.'[68]

More than financial transactions fostered amenable relations between Black soldiers and some of their civilian neighbors. Military bands stood high on the list of forging good relations between Black soldiers and nearby white civilians such as, once again, occurred at Fort Whipple. There the regimental band received praise in the local press for their talent.[69] Prescottonians had the opportunity to judge the quality of these martial musicians from personal experience. Just over a week after the Tenth Cavalry arrived, the band marched in the lead of Decoration

---

62 When it was learned that 'The 25th Infantry ... a colored regiment ... was ordered here nearly a year ago' some of Honolulu's residents protested. The War Department acquiesced, and the regiment went 'to Schofield Barracks and [would] not be camped at Fort Shafter, as was thought by some.' *Honolulu Star-Bulletin*, December 23, 1912, 3:30 Edition.
63 *Ogden Standard*, April 17, 1914, 4 P.M. City Edition.
64 Smith and Zeidler, *A Historic Context*, 120–21.
65 *Prescott Weekly Courier*, May 22, 1885.
66 *Ibid.,* June 5, 1885.
67 *Daily Yellowstone Journal*, May 27, 1892.
68 Dobak and Phillips, *The Black Regulars*, 226.
69 *Prescott Weekly Courier*, May 21, 1885. Schubert, *On The Trail of the Buffalo Soldier*, 232.

On occasion, military bands brought a degree of positive associations between Black troops and civilian communities such as in Douglas, Arizona prior to World War I. (Courtesy John Langellier)

Day observances.[70] On another occasion, one of Prescott's two militia companies secured the band to perform for a benefit they sponsored. In early June, residents were informed that, 'the Promenade Concert given by the 10th Cavalry Band ... at the new City Hall ... Tickets were available for gentlemen and ladies at $2.00.'[71] Such popular recitals prompted a Prescott paper to exhort: 'The excellent band of the Tenth Cavalry would confer a favor on the citizens of Prescott.' They followed the pervious example of the musicians of the Third Cavalry and appeared for a weekly concert at the centrally located Court House Plaza.[72] The considerable attention paid to the band by its long-time champion, Colonel Benjamin Grierson, produced positive results.[73]

Just a few years before the Tenth Cavalry martial musicians gained recognition in Arizona, their counterparts in Minnesota received commendations. During the summer of 1883, the Twenty-Fifth Infantry's band accepted an invitation from Minneapolis' Shattuck Military School to perform. Afterwards, the institution's commandant issued a glowing review. On

70 *Ibid.,* May 30, 1885, and June 5, 1885.
71 *Ibid.,* June 5, 1885.
72 *Ibid.,* July 17, 1885.
73 Grierson, a music teacher before the Civil War, paid considerable attention to the band as indicated in a number of studies such as: John Strauss Buchanan, 'Functions of the Fort Davis Military Band and Musical Proclivities of the Commanding Officer, Benjamin H. Grierson, Late Nineteenth Century,' MA Thesis, Sul Ross College, 1963; and Levern Wagner, ed., *The Benjamin H. Grierson Collection* (Madison, WI: A.E. Editions, Inc., 1998). For background review Anthony Powell, *Keep Step To The Music of The Union, African American Army Musicians 1776–1940* (San Jose, CA: Images in Black, 2020).

September 13, 1883, the Twenty-Fifth Infantry's regimental musicians repeated their success by pleasing crowds at the Minnesota State Fair.[74]

Public performances did not end there; both the Twenty-Fifth's band and two companies were on hand for the completion of the Northern Pacific Railroad where they escorted President Chester A. Arthur, who joined the celebrations. A Minnesota newspaper complemented these troops 'for their proficiency and soldierly bearing.'[75] Such participation by units from the Twenty-Fifth Infantry often brought the men in their military finery into town such as at St. Paul for Decoration (Memorial) Day where their presence in 1883 was a novelty.[76] Even then, not everyone welcomed their participation, as evidenced by a letter to the editor of the *St. Paul Daily Globe*. An outraged white bemoaned the fact that Black bandsmen led the way.[77]

Five years later, the Twenty-Fifth Infantry's band enlivened another Decoration Day parade, but without racist disclaimers. In this instance, they marched through a Montana community where they 'discoursed the sweetest music ever heard in Missoula.' In addition to parades, the band offered regular concerts in town on Thursday evenings. They even headed a funeral procession of a prominent white Missoulian in October of 1889.[78]

In general, the bandsmen in Missoula and their fellow musicians from the Twenty-Fourth Infantry in Salt Lake City, enjoyed popularity with nearby communities consisting mainly of white residents, many of whom belonged to the Church of Latter-Day Saints. At that time, Mormon religious doctrine concerning Blacks tended to be negative, yet this factor proved of little consequence.[79] Actually, relations tended to be unconfrontational in Salt Lake. In fact, during 1898, when the regiment entrained for Chickamauga National Battlefield, the city's population cheered the band and the men as they paraded off to the depot.

So, too, did the Ninth Cavalry, after it disembarked from their train in Ocala, Florida, find their band an asset. There the musicians, the last to dismount the rail cars, rendered tunes including *Dixie* and *Suwanee River*. These sections prompted resounding cheers, 'from the hundreds who had gathered to see the soldiers.'[80] Incidentally, up to that point only a single company of Black troops had served at a post east of the Mississippi River. In this light, as a *New York Times* article noted: 'Very many citizens have never seen a military organization of Negroes since the entire service of those troops has been on the Western frontiers.' With the arrival of the four regiments, on their advance to Cuba, an expanded audience in the United States realized that Blacks served in the US Army.[81]

---

74 Fowler, *The Black Infantry in the West*, 57.
75 *Worthington Advance* (MN) September 13, 1883. Also see *St. Paul Daily Globe*, August 30, 1883, September 2, 1883, September 4, 1883, September 14, 1883.
76 *Worthington Advance* (MN) June 7, 1883.
77 The first letter appeared in the *St. Paul Daily Globe*, May 31, 1883, under the header of 'The Color Line.' The writer who simply signed his name as 'Clay' ranted that the parade was 'a day that should make each and every American heart feel sad while standing over the graves of our fallen heroes ... But what man could stand to-day and see the procession pass without feeling that the white soldiers and white musicians were entirely ignored and placed second in position.' This diatribe drew a thoughtful reply in the same paper on June 5, 1883, titled 'The Color Line from a Colored Soldier's Stand Point.'
78 Langellier, 'Buffalo Soldiers in Big Sky Country:' 53 and 94 nn46–48.
79 Russell W. Stevenson, *For the Cause of Righteousness: A Global History of Blacks and Mormonism. 1830–2013* (Salt Lake City: Greg Kofford Books, 2014) should be consulted for context on this topic.
80 *Ocala Evening Star*, May 16, 1898.
81 Foner, *Blacks and the Military in American History*, 133–4.

Years later, members of the same Ninth Cavalry band gained recognition in southern Arizona. Starting in early 1914 at Douglas, a community that originally sought to bar the regiment, every afternoon the bandsmen helped changed this attitude. The musicians offered 'a short concert when the time comes for changing guard.'[82] During the summer, on many Sundays, the bandsmen appeared at the city park for the pleasure of the local citizenry. The popular players also performed for dances, political rallies and parades on Flag Day in June and for 4th of July.[83]

Other forms of music periodically helped forge a degree of commonality.[84] Of all things, African American soldiers staged incongruous minstrel performances, which had spun off from white troupes in the 1850s. During the post-Civil War, these shows upheld negative stereotypes typically presented by whites in black face. While the traveling groups comprised of civilians were the characteristic, Black military entertainers also assumed minstrel guise. For instance, Silver City residents were treated to a minstrel troupe organized by Black infantrymen at Fort Bayard.[85] Elsewhere in New Mexico, Fort Wingate staged minstrels 'composed of both Black and white soldiers' replete with 'burned cork' makeup for all the members![86] Members of the Tenth Cavalry played the part and 'attracted one of the finest audiences seen in Globe for some time and the entertainment was very fair.'[87] Residents of Tombstone, Arizona enjoyed a similar experience when 'The Great Western Minstrel troupe, composed of colored soldiers from the Tenth Cavalry, stationed at Mescal Springs' appeared in town for a Christmas program.[88]

Other newspaper accounts of such recitals appeared in the 1880s through the early 1900s.[89] Moreover, civilians near a fort might make their way to the neighboring post for more than music. They could observe parades, military drill, maneuvers and inspections. The Third Squadron of the Ninth Cavalry reviewed by their new commanding officer, Major John Bigelow, Jr. represented one such occasion. The exercises took place on a major parade ground in front of the Presidio of San Francisco's general hospital.[90] By the next month, the stage shifted to the expansive Presidio Golf Course where Ninth Cavalrymen quickly established a tent camp then dismantled the canvas city. Their taskings required, 'unpacking, unsaddling, running down picket lines, tying horses, unrolling the packs, buttoning together the shelter halves and pitching the tents.' Troop I, under Captain Charles Young, earned the laurels 'by executing the order, complete in every detail, in thirteen minutes.'[91]

82 *Bisbee Daily Review*, February 7, 1914.
83 *Ibid.*, May 15, 1914; June 10, 1914; June 14, 1914; June 16, 1914; *Phoenix Arizona Republic*, October 25, 1914.
84 Horace D. Nash, 'Community Building on the Border: The Role of the 24th Infantry Band at Columbus, New Mexico, 1916–1922,' *Fort Concho and the South Plains Journal* 2 no. 3 (Summer, 1990): 76–92.
85 *El Paso Daily Herald*, August 14, 1899, Third Edition 4:30 p.m.
86 Utley, *An Army Doctor on the Western Frontier*, 91.
87 *Arizona Silver Belt* (Globe) December 22, 1888. Also see *Daily Tombstone Epitaph*, December 10, Accounts of such performances appeared in the 1880s through the early 1900s. 11, and 22, 1885; *Bisbee Daily Review*, June 8, 1913.
88 *Daily Tombstone Epitaph*, December 22, 1885.
89 *Arizona Citizen/Weekly Citizen* (Tucson) June 13, 1885; *Fort Robinson Weekly Bulletin*, February 22, 1893, 1 no. 5, and March 1, 1893, 1 no. 6; *Anaconda Standard* (MT) November 14, 1896; *A&NR*, December 3, 1905, 27.
90 *San Francisco Call*, January 6, 1904.
91 *Ibid.*, February 27, 1904.

The Golf Course, much to the chagrin of those who took advantage of the links and temporarily lost access to the greens, soon served as a setting for troopers of the Ninth Cavalry. A mock battle plan called for men of the Ninth Cavalry to oppose the landing of a fictional foreign foe. Dividing the units into two teams, 'Troop L, known as the brown troop' played the part of the enemy. The invaders soon faced Uncle Sam's defenders posted at the beach from where they 'dashed up the steep incline and came to a halt under the brow of the bluff, being hidden from view by a clump of dense foliage. From this point scouts were sent out and the enemy located.' Once again Captain Young commanded the heroic defenders. He ordered his men to dismount and lead their horses up the hill from where they commenced firing. This fusillade surprised the enemy whom they routed.[92] Young's troops won the day.

More typically, rather than carry on war games, soldiers paraded with precision in adjacent communities. Their presence marching down the streets of towns large or small, provided another window to observe Black soldiers at their best. During a 1913 appearance in Oneota, New York, a white veteran who served as a lieutenant colonel during the Spanish war congratulated the commander of the Tenth Cavalry for 'the deportment of the colored troops ... I was so favorably impressed ... as to their orderly and courteous behavior. From the excellent discipline shown while here, any competent observer must concede that the colored man makes an excellent soldier and thus have a tendency to change any prejudice now existing against them as soldiers in our regular Army.'[93]

In a similar manner, competitive meets, which allowed military athletes 'to show dexterity in outdoor events' also drew nearby crowds.[94] In addition to tugs of war and track and field events, programs included camp pitching and military related competitions that entertained community spectators. Further, team sports, especially baseball, brought Black soldiers and civilians from diverse ethnic backgrounds together both as participants and onlookers.[95] Indeed, in contrast to first being shunned by some residents of Oahu, Black infantrymen gained acceptance. They competed with other regiments and civilian leagues in track and field events, as well as baseball. In the latter instance, the 'Wreckers' of the Twenty-Fifth Infantry regularly appeared in Honolulu's newspapers as fan favorites.[96] In the far colder climes of Alaska, baseball meant Twenty-Fourth Infantrymen mingled with white civilian teams and onlookers.[97] So also, did Fort Vancouver's 'Hard Hitters' of Company B from the same regiment.[98] Moreover, in Douglas, Arizona, the Ninth Cavalry's nine periodically met civilian opponents.[99]

Remarkably, rivalries on the playing field could induce a certain amount of comradery. A range of responses ran the gamut. More often than not, however, blatant bigotry and the maintenance of distinct, strict ethnic and racial divisions that resembled apartheid, both self-imposed and

92 *Ibid.*, March 9, 1904; March 24, 1904.
93 *A&NR*, July 12, 1913, 54.
94 *San Francisco Call*, December 13, 1903; December 15, 1903; December 16, 1903.
95 As one example of the interest and import of the 'national pastime' Nankivell, *The History of the Twenty-Fifth Infantry*, 163–74, devoted the last chapter to baseball.
96 Hoverson, 'Buffalo Soldiers at Kilauea:' 73–85, treats not only interactivity through sports, but also several other aspects of cross-cultural mingling.
97 Shellum, *Buffalo Soldiers in Alaska*, x-xi, 2–3, 10, 20, 43, 94–99, 106 121–22, 133–139, 141, 149, 158, 160, 173, 178–80, 182–85, 189–93, 198, 207, 209.
98 Shine, 'Buffalo Soldiers at Vancouver Barracks:'196–227.
99 *Bisbee Daily Review*, September 20, 1914; October 2, 1914; October 3, 1914.

Segregation, Discrimination and Race Relations 245

1. BASEBALL TEAM OF 25TH INFANTRY STATIONED AT HONOLULU.
2. "SHAKESPEARE'S DAUGHTERS," DECAGYNIAN CLUB, FISK UNIVERSITY.
3. DEBATING TEAM, VIRGINIA UNION UNIVERSITY.

Sports, especially baseball, meant interactions between civilian and military players along with fans, often improving relations between divergent groups. (Courtesy John Langellier)

Relations between varying groups in the West ranged from romantic liaisons between men and women of different ethnic backgrounds to hostility and violence. The former situation seemed to apply to a soldier stationed in Arizona and an Apache woman possibly from the San Carlos reservation. (Courtesy Arizona Historical Society)

inflicted by outsiders, remained the rule.[100] All too often, where Asians, Blacks, Latinos and whites came into close contact, sporadically many forms of friction emerged. Likewise, this same situation applied to Blacks and Native Americans. Ethnic diversity, rather than being embraced, oft took another form, on more than one occasion encounters ended in bloodshed.

Civilian and Military Clashes

Altercations between citizens and the Black soldiers usually caused the latter group to be blamed. Often the press tried and convicted accused Black soldiers in print. Even when papers reported favorably, minor incidents reversed positive perspectives and brought about undesirable press. More crucially, murderers of Black troops might avoid the consequences and sometimes never faced arrest. On occasion, when indicted, after perpetrators went to trial, juries acquitted them.[101]

An extreme example dating from January 1875 involved the Ninth Cavalry. A detail left Ringgold Barracks on what they believed to be a routine patrol in south Texas. Four privates from Company G under Sergeant Edward Troutman, rode into an ambush staged by local

---

100 Loening Eichner, 'Queering Frontier Identities;' Horne, *Black and Brown*; Christian, *Black Soldiers in Jim Crow Texas*; Dobak and Phillips, *The Black Regulars*; Leiker, *Racial Borders*; Valentin, 'Black Enlisted Men in the US-Mexico Border;' and Wilkie, *Unburied Lives*, are highly recommended for further exploration of this complex, pivotal topic.
101 Smith and Zeidler, *A Historic Context*, 120–21.

ranch hands. Two privates and one of the assailants died in the exchange. The following day, Colonel Hatch, led 60 of his men, along with Starr County's deputy sheriff, to the scene of the clash. There, they located the corpses of the soldiers whose uniforms and equipment inexplicably had been removed and left in an adjacent shed. A grand jury indicted nine Mexicans for the murders, yet only one went to trial. He received an acquittal. The other eight were released.

On the other hand, civilian authorities took the trio of surviving soldiers into custody. They charged them with the murder of one of the attackers. Further, the court indicted Colonel Hatch and another officer for the theft of the uniforms of the two casualties. The defense of the five men from the Ninth Cavalry entailed considerable legal expense, along with a venue change, before they could successfully defend themselves against the preposterous charges! Yet the murderers went free.[102]

Kansas in the 1860s furnished an earlier object lesson of animosity between civilians and the post-Civil War army, this time at Fort Hays. There, elements of the Thirty-Eighth Infantry and Tenth Cavalry clashed on an escalating basis with white civilians. The resulting explosion of 'racial violence … mirrored and even surpassed that in other western communities' at least to that point in time.[103] Senator Willard Saulsbury, Jr., a Democrat from Delaware, might have thought this discord validated his warning that Black troops 'riding up and down the streets … dressed in a little brief authority' would be 'a stench in the nostrils of the people.'[104] Ample military and civilian naysayers agreed with Saulsbury.

Another occurrence took place in New Orleans where a long, complex history existed between various ethnic and national groups. In 1866, four Black soldiers went to jail for a disturbance on a streetcar that ran along St. Charles Street. At a hearing, witnesses testified 'eight or ten colored soldiers, who ran and jumped it while it was in motion. One of them, who was a colored sergeant, gave an order to take possession of the car, although another of the negroes remarked at the time that it was a white car.' Nevertheless, the men complied. Supposedly, one of them remarked 'as he entered that he would kill any man who ordered them out and called them negroes.' After that, the defendants left the car 'but repeated their curses and abuse. They also leaned with their backs against it as if endeavoring to force it off the track.'

The account noted the men received a defense 'or rather were as seen to have a fair trial by the judge advocate of the department, who conceded without argument' that one of the four 'was guilty of violence, but did not think the proof was conclusive against the other.' The alleged ringleader received 'thirty days imprisonment' while two of the privates went to the guard house for ten days and the sergeant received a discharge.'[105] In this instance and a number of others, when the US Army conducted the legal proceedings, soldiers regularly received due process. On the other hand, as one survey remarked, when the offense fell outside the military's jurisdiction: 'In many cases where violence erupted between black soldiers and white citizens, the Army did little to help the soldiers.'[106]

Such a reaction did not always reflect the army's lack of commitment to its men. More than once, the military had little recourse to intervene. This was true when the Tenth Cavalry served

---

102 Leckie, *The Buffalo Soldiers*, 108–109.
103 Leiker, 'Black Soldiers At Fort Hays, Kansas,.' 3–17, explored this cultural collision.
104 As quoted in Macgregor and Nalty, *Blacks in the United States Armed Forces*, vol. 3, 20.
105 *New Orleans Daily Crescent*, October 11, 1866.
106 Smith and Zeidler, *A Historic Context*, 120.

in Arizona. As one of its young officers, Lieutenant Powhatan Clarke related, cowboys from the area, many of whom were Texas transplants, ached for a confrontation. Afterwards, they avoided the consequences of their actions being immune from military sanctions.

As Clarke told the story, one night in Willcox, 'two or three pistol shots' fired by 'drunken cowboys of the Chiricahua Cattle Company' caused concern. The lieutenant 'feared some of our men might get into a scrape.' He later learned racist motives were at play. Even before ascertaining this fact, a cautious Clarke requested permission from his commanding officer to lead a detail of four armed soldiers back to town. He intended to fetch the remaining troopers.

Once back at the saloon with his carbine carrying patrol, Clarke spied a fractious cowpuncher and 'his compadres … taking a drink and as I feared they might bull doze my men I told them to get their pieces ready and if any one hurt one of them I wanted them to fill him full of lead.' Fortunately, none of the civilians made a play. It appeared they did not 'seem inclined to pick a quarrel with carbines.'

The tense situation ended without casualties. This might not have been the case. According to a story C. M. Renaud (a southern Arizona quartermaster agent) if the troopers 'had not a white officer with them they would never have gotten out' alive. Renaud also believed 'there would have some very dead cow boys.' Further, from Renaud, Clarke learned 'that some of the cow boys had been spoiling for a fight saying that they were going to kill a "nigger" that night and at the bar room one of them had jumped up swearing a soldier had hit him,' which the lieutenant dismissed as untrue. The accuser pulled 'his pistol on a soldier trying to shoot him, but the revolver misfired. The soldier instead of running "like a nigger" coolly pulled out his government Colt and opened up on the cow boy who fled.' The lanky lieutenant noted the instigator was a Texan. In a letter Clarke told his father, 'not a civil officer in town even attempted to arrest this man nor any of his friends.' Clarke knew many Arizonans viewed the military with contempt and vice versa.[107] At least, Clarke's detail eluded the fatal exchange of Sergeant Troutman's detachment in Texas, although the instigators in both cases avoided repercussions for their misdeeds.

Lynchings

When a Black soldier stood accused of a crime, he often faced swift punishment, which could take a lethal, unlawful turn. Lynching characterized widespread acceptance of the violence that prevailed as in the South, but likewise existed in the West, as well as regrettably other regions throughout the United States.[108] For instance, during August 1885, mob rule resulted in deaths. The first stage of the convoluted affair began somewhat familiarly with Corporal Ross Hallon (also spelled Hollis and Hallis in various accounts), who served with Company A, Twenty-Fifth Infantry at Fort Meade, South Dakota on the outskirts of Sturgis. Evidently, the corporal beat a Black woman in town and broke three of her ribs. Her injuries required treatment by Dr. H. P.

---

107 The scenario was based on Langellier, *Scouting With the Buffalo Soldiers*,' 196–98.
108 Over 1,697 Blacks were lynched from 1882–97, primarily in the Southern states that formed the old Confederacy. P. Thomas Stanford, *The Tragedy of the Negro in America* (Boston: Boston Press, 1897), 140.

Lynch. After that, one version stated a grand jury called the physician as a witness. When the hearing concluded, supposedly the soldier vowed, 'to kill the doctor.'[109]

One partially contradictory rendering expanded on the soldier's hatred of the doctor. In this version of the tale, following Dr. Lynch's treatment of the battered woman, he:

> ... indignantly denounced Hollis, threatening to file a criminal complaint against him. This warning, coupled with jealousy in the belief that Lynch was too attentive to the injured woman, rankled in the mind of Hollis until Saturday evening, when he deserted the post as guard, exchanged clothing with and borrowed a six shooter of a friend, sneaked into the store, shot his victim and escaped.[110]

According to yet another source, a lengthy newspaper depiction bombastically pronounced that this was the 'darkest and most dastardly deed known to the criminal annals of the [Black] Hills,' Among these statements appeared details of witnesses who heard the gunfire and rushed to the scene. The group included:

> ... a couple of colored women, living in an adjoining building, who stated that they were in bed when the shot alarmed them. Hastily rising and dressing they rushed to the store as the doctor was gasping his last. They heard him calling to Fraser (one of the women) for help, but he was dead before they reached his side. They saw no other person leaving or in the store.

An inquest held the following Monday afternoon concluded the 'deceased came to his death by a pistol shot inflicted with felonious intent by Ross Hallis, corporal Company A, Twenty-Fifth Infantry.' Not waiting for due process, that day, 'the better class of citizens of Sturgis who had determined to unearth the mystery surrounding the death of Dr. Lynch, became satisfied that Hallis was the guilty party and they at once resolved that he should speedily suffer for his great offense.' After satisfying themselves of the corporal's guilt, 'they proceeded with their self-imposed mission.' Then:

> At about 9 o'clock, two score of masked men quietly drew near and in a manner so cautious that not a soul absent from the building was aware of the event ... obtained custody of the prisoner and as silently retired to Fiddler's Tree, rear of the Catholic church, where, with little ceremony and delay the guilty wretch was suspended 'twixt heaven and earth.'

Two hours later, some of the corporal's comrades arrived on the scene under the company commander, 'to protect Hallis from violence.'[111] The rescuers appeared too late.

---

109 *Evening Star* (Washington, DC) August 27, 1885.
110 *Press and Daily Dakotaian* (Yankton) August 29, 1885.
111 *Custer Chronicle* (Black Hills, DT) August 29, 1885. Of note, except for the *Custer Chronicle*, none of the more than half dozen reprints of the murder mentioned that the corporal was Black. For examples see: *Bismarck Weekly Tribune*; *Indianapolis Journal*; *Las Vegas Daily Gazette* (NM); *New York Tribune*; *Portland Daily Press* (ME); *Richmond Dispatch* (VA); *Savannah Morning*; *Wheeling Daily Intelligencer*, all published on August 28, 1885.

At Fort Meade, Black infantrymen headed to town, perhaps to torch buildings there. The post commander responded. He dispatched a 'strong detail' of white Seventh Cavalry troops who met the irate infantrymen. The cavalrymen turned the seething throng back to the fort. Following this, the horse soldiers remained in town to patrol the streets until the following morning, 'as also did many a well-armed citizens' the combination of which, one newspaper contended, averted more violence.[112]

Peace lasted but briefly. By September, the next round resulted in another fatal incident. After being ejected from Sturgis' Abe Hills' saloon for drunkenness, a Black infantryman from the Twenty-Fifth returned to Fort Meade. He rallied 16 soldiers armed with rifles. They marched back to Sturgis, drew up in formation in front of the saloon, whereupon they 'fired a volley into the building killing Richard Bell, a cowboy from Nebraska.' Reportedly, their leader commanded: 'When I say three fire and fire low. One – two – three.' Then, they cut the telephone wires so that news of their conduct did not reach the fort before they made their way back to the barracks. Despite this precaution, town authorities made five arrests. Supposedly, it was said 'the soldiers were prepared and intended to lynch Deputy Sheriff Sauter and a man named Cole who are alleged to have been implicated in the lynching of Corporal Hollis for the murder of Dr. Lynch.'[113]

Three years later, another lynching occurred, this time in Montana. At Sun River, 'jealousy between two soldiers named Matchett [white], of the Third Infantry and Robert Robertson (colored) belonging to the Twenty-Fifth Infantry, over a sporting woman, Quennie Montgomery' exploded into 'a shooting affray ... wherein a man named McGuire ... was instantly killed.' The trouble originated during a ruckus after which Robertson fired at an escaping Matchett. The bullet went wild. It struck McGuire and innocent bystander 'who left a wife and two children.' Military authorities unwittingly turned Robinson over to the sheriff and his deputy. Cooperation with local lawmen ended tragically. On June 10, 1888, 'between 11 and 12 o'clock last night a masked body of men overpowered Deputy Sheriff John Hurley and took the prisoner out in the alley back of the stone store and hung him to a beam,' read the newspaper column about the swift, illegal retribution.[114]

Perhaps learning a lesson from this unfortunate outcome, after a June 1892 clash in Suggs, Wyoming, where a soldier from the Ninth Cavalry, after being insulted, came under fire. He and another trooper returned to camp. Once again, in retaliation, a group of about 20 troopers went back to town where they leveled a barrage into the saloon. Townspeople responded in kind.

They killed Private Willis Johnson. Fearing vigilante action, the commanding officer received permission to provide an escort of sufficient strength for the perpetrators as protection.[115]

Later in the decade, at Cheyenne, Wyoming, 'a certain clique of the soldiers ... threatened to "shoot up" the saloon and gambling house' operated by Harry Hynds. The proprietor boasted that if members of the Twenty-Fourth Infantry stationed at nearby Fort Russell tried to 'carry out their threats, a bloody battle will be the result.'[116] Fortunately, no test of Hynds' bombast occurred.

---

112 *Las Vegas Daily Gazette* (NM) August 29, 1885; and *Memphis Daily Appeal*, August 29, 1885. The latter paper also carried a report of the lynching of a white man who murdered four women and two men near Johnson City, Texas.
113 *Sun* (New York) September 22, 1885; and *Press and Daily Dakotaian.* (Yankton) September 23, 1885.
114 *Missoula Gazette*, June 23, 1888.
115 Schubert, 'The Suggs Affair:' 63–67; and Schubert, *Buffalo Soldiers, Braves, and the Brass*, 33.
116 *Salt Lake Herald*, November 15, 1898.

Far to the north, outbursts flared in Skagway, Alaska where numerous bars and brothels alike made it clear that Black patrons were unwelcome. The one exception related to public places was the YMCA. Even then, a few individuals raised objections to violation of the color line. In this case, protests went unheeded.[117]

Spanish American War Impacts

Given that for more than three decades, the army mainly stationed Black units on the frontier, troops escaped the rabid racism of the South. Some authors maintained that this dispatching Black troops, 'to the most remote regions of the Texas frontier and Indian Territory' represented a major 'example of ... discrimination' by the army. Following this thesis, supposedly white regiments, 'regularly rotated between the frontier and military installations east of the Mississippi River.'[118] In contrast, the War Department avoided sending Black units to posts near predominately white communities, which raised backlashes from citizens and allegedly resulted in heighted violent encounters.[119]

In 1898, that paradigm, regardless of what motivated it, shifted dramatically when the invasion of Cuba escalated. The recognition that these units boasted some of the longest serving veterans in the US Army with many marksmen in the ranks, partially prompted this move. Also, racial stereotypes played out as military authorities continued to embrace William Sherman's attitude of bygone times. One newspaper account reflected a widespread erroneous assumption that Black troops sent were better able to stand the climate of the gulf than the white soldiers.'[120]. This meant the War Department not only called out the regulars, but also raised several regiments of Black volunteer infantry units popularly referred to as the 'Immunes.'[121]

It was the Twenty-Fifth Infantry, however, that first responded to possible shipment to Cuba. One of the officers recalled: 'All along the line of railway from Montana to Chickamauga Park where Headquarters and six companies were finally ordered, the American people gave the regiment an enthusiastic welcome and 'God Speed.'"[122] The regimental sergeant-major's account contrasted somewhat with the lieutenant's portrayal, when he noted: 'All along the route from Missoula, Montana, with the exception of one or two places in Georgia, we had been received most cordially.' Once the Twenty-Fifth detrained and marched into Chickamauga, on April 20, 1898, these previously warm receptions gave way to contempt expressed by some southern whites. An enlisted man's account reported, 'it mattered not if we were soldiers of the United States and going to fight for the honor of our country and the freedom of an oppressed and starving people, we were "niggers."' Rather than laurels, many locals, 'treated us with contempt,'

---

117 Shellum, *Buffalo Soldiers in Alaska*, 72–73, 116, 150, 166–67, 176.
118 Smith and Zeidler, *A Historic Context*, 118. The same source postulated that the closer of the scattered frontier forts and consolidation of larger bodies of troops at the end of the Indian Wars also has an 'effect within the military.' Smith and Zeidler, *A Historic Context*, 120.
119 Foner, *Blacks and the Military in American History*, 56.
120 *Chipley Banner* (FL) April 9, 1898.
121 The four volunteer immune regiments raised consisted of the Seventh, Eighth, Ninth, and Tenth Volunteer Infantry. The Ninth was the only one sent to Cuba. For a brief overview, see Marvin E. Fletcher, 'The Black Volunteers in the Spanish-American War,' *Military Affairs* 38 no. 2 (April 1974): 48–53.
122 Nankivell, *Twenty-Fifth Infantry*, 67.

said the soldier. He wryly ended his observations with: 'That is the kind of "united country" we saw in the South.'¹²³

During the Spanish American War, the return of Black troops to the former Confederacy coincided with a generally heightened, virulent nationwide racism. Legal segregation and disfranchisement of Blacks within the South codified by rulings such as *Plessy v. Ferguson* (1896) and *Williams v. Mississippi* (1898), which sustained poll taxes and voter literacy tests, numbered among the dauting prejudicial barriers that gravely impacted the rights of Black soldiers and civilians alike.¹²⁴

By way of contrast, after decades of relative independence, Black troops resisted the prevalent denigration by whites and others. To a certain degree, they possessed a sense 'their performance as soldiers' in the Spanish American War enabled them 'to be role models in the black community.'¹²⁵ Additionally, as set forth in one late nineteenth century publication about Blacks, many of them, along with several of their civilian contemporaries viewed 'the prospect of war against Spain' as an avenue of 'hope in a time of despair.' Blacks' willingness to sacrifice for their country conceivably could 'lessen white racism as well spell a death knell for disenfranchisement in the South.'¹²⁶ In short, participation in this conflict offered 'a more public arena' for the Black fighting forces 'to regain some of their recently lost rights,' rights they earned through valor in arms during the Civil War. Finally, some saw military service as a means to 'exercise their citizenship and demonstrate their manhood.'¹²⁷ With more than two dozen years of faithful performance of duty, Black soldiers especially, could point to their record and answer in the affirmative, to an age-old question about whether they would and could fight.

To this query, a Florida paper referred to evidence given by the Ninth and Tenth Cavalry officers published in the New York *Sun*. Summarizing the longer article, the column concluded:

> The history of the United States Army gives no account of any body of men in its service who have proved more obedient, tractible [sic], thoroughly disciplined and more efficient in the use of their weapons in battle, than those same black men in the uniform of United States army that fought from the Rio Grande to the British possessions and were bloody participants in every important Indian battle that has been fought and won during the past three decades.¹²⁸

---

123 Quoted in Johnson, *History of the Negro Soldiers*, 37.
124 Richard B. Morris, ed., *Encyclopedia of American History* (New York: Harper & Row, 1965), 494; and Charles H. Wesley, *The Quest for Equality: From Civil War to Civil Rights*. (Cornwells Heights, PA: The Publishers Agency, 1978), 26–27. For added perspective review, Reginald Horsman, *Race and Manifest Destiny: The Origins of American Racial Anglo-Saxonism* (Cambridge, MA: Harvard University Press, 1981).
125 Le 'Trice Danyell Donaldson, 'From Triumph to Tragedy: African American Soldiers Fight For Citizenship and Manhood in the Spanish-American-Cuban-Filipino War,' MA thesis, University of Tennessee, Knoxville, 2006, 32.
126 Michele Mitchell, *Righteous Propagation: African Americans and the Politics of Racial Destiny after Reconstruction* (Chapel Hill: University of North Carolina Press, 2004), 61–63. Also refer to, Piero Gleiieses. 'African Americans and the War Against Spain,' *North Carolina Historical Review* 73 no. 2 (April 1996): 184–214.
127 Donaldson, 'From Triumph to Tragedy,' 21, and 26–27. For more about masculinity, review Darlene Clark Hine and Earnestine Jenkins, 'A Question of Manhood: A Reader' in *US Black Men's History of Masculinity* Vol. 2 (Bloomington: Indiana University Press, 2001).
128 *Ocala Evening Star*, April 14, 1898. Similarly, the *Chipley Banner* (FL) July 23, 1898, repeated a *Boston Herald* piece under the headline 'COLORED SOLDIERS ARE BRAVE,'

Friction on Florida

Despite positive portrayals, the mood in the South tended to be toxic. Clashes in Florida especially marred the vision that Black participation in the Cuban venture would result in an improved racial climate. After an initial incident in May between a white US Marine and a Black civilian, animosity grew.[129] Through the summer of 1898, the arrival of the four Black regiments in Tampa exacerbated local ill-will. Nevertheless, 'the black soldiers displayed restraint against those who insulted them, but it was clear that tensions were rising.'[130] By June, insults by whites, who adopted a superior attitude and the resented Black troops, who had the audaciousness to insist on being treated being as white men, finally provoked a riot. Once the regiments boarded transports for Cuba. the sparring vanished, only to resurface after the Spanish American War on a former familiar racial battleground.[131]

Turbulent Texas

Although duels between locals and Black soldiers emerged in many regions over different time periods, Texas tended to be the most volatile, long-lived arena for conflict. Beginning with Reconstruction, some papers painted the environment there as a: 'Reign of Terror in Texas' singling out 'armed organisations, generally known as Ku Klux Klan.' Klansmen's objectives included disarming, robbing and sometimes murdering Union men, regardless of their color, as well as Black civilians. In the latter instance, both United States officers and soldiers were targets.[132] It seemed anyone wearing the US uniform were resented or even loathed. In this environment, white Prussian-born Captain George Haller was a victim. Tellingly, the officer held a commission in a regiment consisting solely of white enlisted personnel. Supposedly, in 1869, the Klan murdered him near Port Sullivan, Texas, emblematic of the animosity towards any member of Uncle Sam's forces.[133] The withdrawal of numerous federal troops heightened the KKK's activities. Thereafter, Klansmen operated with impunity.

---

129 Representative negative press, which in at least one case was the same periodicals that early on took a more positive stance, included: *Morning Tribune* (Tampa) May 5, 7, 10. 12, 18, 19, 25, June 8, 1898; *Ocala Evening Star*, May 26, 1898, July 29, 1898, August 8, 1898, August 15, 1898; *Daily Kentuckian* (Hopkinsville), June 21, 1898.
130 For a recapitulation of this outburst review, Willard B. Gatewood Jr., 'Negro Troops in Florida, 1898,' *Florida Historical Quarterly* 49 no. 1 (July 1970): 1–15.
131 Elsewhere, however, other battles between whites and Black soldiers including some of the Black volunteers continued as indicated in *Chipley Banner* (FL) December 3, 1898.
132 *Texas Republican* (Marshall, TX) January 8, 1869, and *St. Landry Democrat* (Opelousas, LA) January 8, 1869.
133 *Nebraska Advertiser* (Brownville, NE) October 28, 1869. Months later another release indicated: 'The body of Capt. George Haller, late of the 24th Infantry, United States army, who had been missing for the past six or eight months, was discovered by a citizen, last week, some twelve miles from Cameron, in Milam county, on Elm Creek. His clothes were riddled by balls, but his papers and money were untouched' adding that the documents 'led to the identification of the body.' *Dallas Daily Herald*, March 19, 1870. William L. Richter, *The Army in Texas During Reconstruction 1865–1870* (College Station: Texas A&M University Press, 1987) warrants examination for a better appreciation for this era along the Texas-Mexico border.

Blacks wearing Army Blue especially faced wrath in Texas. Viewed as 'a riotous assemblage of colored soldiers' who brutally sacked communities 'invariably ... when under the influence of liquor' they 'infested (that's the word,)' places like Brownsville. Their 'simple presence' irritated 'the resident population' who daily read 'accounts of the colored soldiers ... robbing market wagons' on the outskirts of town and who supposedly gradually drew closer and finally entering the jacles [sic], on the suburbs; next invading private domiciles, within the corporate limits; and finally, with unparalleled audacity, attempting a burglary within a very short distance of their quarters,' or so one hostile editorial fumed.[134] The diatribe ended with the prediction the, 'citizens of Brownsville are not fearful of the struggle come when it will. Eventually, the boast proved prophetic.

Before then, other confrontations and challenges existed in great part as during the Civil War years, portions of Texas had devolved into chaos and widespread lawlessness. Such conditions persisted after the war. Livestock thieves ran roughshod. Illegal liquor production and sales plus significant smuggling between Mexico and the United States occurred unhindered by the Mexican government, even after April 1878, when the United States officially recognized the strongman regime of President Porfirio Díaz.

Occasionally, the actions of Mexicans in opposition to Díaz spilled over north of the Rio Bravo. Among other accounts, one newspaper mentioned the Ninth Cavalry's 'capture of a gang of horse thieves and murderers near Camp Colorado, Texas, on the 27th of February.'[135] This outlaw band had long terrorized that section or the state. An Arizona editor pretentiously added, 'outrages committed by bandits and Indians from Mexico and the raids have become so frequent [in Texas] that stock raisers, in many instances have been compelled to abandon their ranches and drive their cattle into the interior for safety.'[136]

Besides Klansmen, outlaws and Native Americans, in at least two cases Black soldiers, faced another set of tough Texas characters. A Fort Worth newspaper correspondent mentioned 'a fight between buffalo hunters and colored soldiers stationed at Fort Griffin.'[137] Likewise, during February of 1878, violence with buffalo hunters aided by other whites in the town of San Angela (AKA Angelo), Texas ended in tragedy. After some buffalo hunters and cowboys surrounded a sergeant from Company D, Tenth Cavalry, they cut the chevrons from his sleeves and the stripes from his trousers. After this demotion, they forced him out of a local saloon. In response, First Sergeant George Goldsby unlocked the company's carbine rack. The white bullies did not long savor their bravado. Some of Goldsby's comrades marched to the saloon where this humiliating incident had taken place. With carbines in hand, the revenge-seeking soldiers opened fire, killing one of the whites inside and wounding two more. As the smoke cleared, Private John L. Brown also lay dead. One of his comrades had been wounded. Fearing consequences, Goldsby bolted. He disappeared. His whereabouts remained a mystery for decades.[138]

For nearly three years, a lull ensued. On January 19, 1881, a far more volatile outburst claimed additional lives in San Angelo. A gambler named Pleas Watson shot and killed a white Sixteenth Infantry private, who had attempted to halt the cardplayer from pistol whipping a Black soldier

---

134 *New Orleans Daily Crescent*, October 12, 1866.
135 *National Republican* (Washington, DC) March 23, 1874.
136 *Arizona Weekly Journal-Miner/Weekly Arizona Miner* (Prescott) November 25, 1871.
137 *New Orleans Daily Democrat*, June 9, 1877.
138 Leiker, *Racial Borders*, 90.

in John Nasworthy's Saloon. Watson fled the scene. No one attempted to intercept him. The county sheriff went in pursuit, but to no avail.

A few weeks later, on February 1, local white cowhand Tom McCarthy gunned down Private William Watkins of Company E, Tenth Cavalry. The reason for his actions remained unknown. Regardless, the homicide triggered an unprecedented response from both Black and white members of Fort Concho's garrison. In an uncommon outburst of soldier solidarity, one night, upwards of 130 enlisted men formed an integrated mob. They made their way across the river to the town and demanded the sheriff release McCarthy. The lawman managed to extract his prisoner. Meanwhile, one of the Tenth Cavalry officers discovered the mass movement of soldiers from the post. He rushed with a guard to head them off and escort the men back to their barracks.[139]

When the court released McCarthy on bail, a few of the soldiers, again both Black and white, printed a handbill. The broadside contained a threat on behalf of the soldiers: 'If we do not receive justice and fair play … some one will suffer, if not the guilty, the innocent.' In this lethal atmosphere, on February 4, an infantry officer at Fort Concho claimed he heard 200 shots. In reply, he led a pair of armed Sixteenth Infantry companies to quell what some have styled, a riot or mutiny. After a roll call accounted for most of the men, Colonel Benjamin Grierson ordered the incarceration of five of the ringleaders. He further dispatched a protective detail from the Sixteenth Infantry to town where they remained until morning. A substantial extra guard stood watch for several nights thereafter, at 13 sentry posts that ringed the fort. Calm returned with no further disturbances. In due course, the Tenth Cavalry transferred from Fort Concho, ending all future tensions, as well as this rather atypical banding together of Black and white soldiers.[140]

Unhappily, ill feelings between Texas civilians from many ethnic backgrounds and Black soldiers remained contentious on all sides and for many years.[141] When the US Army dispatched Black regulars to other locales, however, friction temporarily disappeared. That respite came to an end during the late 1890s. After being lauded for their glorious charge at San Juan Hill and overall valor in Cuba, Black veterans returned to the United States. By the following year, freshly won recognition began to fade. Racial bias again overshadowed former patriotic praise. Back on US soil, several outbursts originated in the Old South in such places as Georgia, just as they had during the short-lived billeting in Florida preparatory to sailing to Cuba.[142]

Not surprisingly, against this backdrop, turbulence heightened as Black troops rode the rails westward back to the Lone Star State. The first clash took place in Texarkana where supposedly inebriated Tenth Cavalrymen left their coaches at the depot. An altercation with a policeman escalated. The scuffle eventually provoked more law enforcement and a mob who gathered to hold the troops onboard as hostages. According to a newspaper account, the stand-off continued

---

139 Mutinies were not unknown throughout the first 50 years and beyond of the existence of the Black regulars. Scott F. Thompson, "The Negro had been run over long enough by white men, and it was time they defend themselves': African-American Mutinies and the Long Emancipation, 1861–1974,' Ph.D. diss. West Virginia University, Morgantown, West Virginia, 2021, 163–316 treats this topic in detail.
140 Bruce J. Dinges, 'The San Angelo Riot of 1881: The Army, Race Relations, and Settlement on the Texas Frontier,' *Journal of the West* 41 no. 3 (Summer 2002): 35–45.
141 Christian, *Black Soldiers in Jim Crow Texas*, 29–30, adds a few related details to early adverse actions against Black soldier not long after they reported to Texas in the 1860 and 1870s.
142 *Houston Daily Post*, February 1, 1899, March 19, 1899, for incidences in Georgia.

for 'seven hours and had the soldiers fired a shot the whites would have dynamited the train off the earth.'[143]

At last, the siege broke. The troops steamed on to Fort Bliss. Upon arriving near the El Paso post and without leaving their cars, the soldiers transferred immediately to the White Oaks railway line and went directly to Fort Bliss. At that point, El Paso's daily editorialized: 'Colored soldiers at Fort Bliss will be something of a novelty and it is to be hoped that the members of troops are a quiet and orderly set of men and not imbued with the idea that they own the universe.'[144] A few days later, this wishful postulation vanished.

A headline blazed: 'NEGRO TROOPERS Are Creating Disturbances In This Part of the Country and They Are Banking Too Much On Their Cuban War Record.' The story concerned five soldiers who had been apprehended for firing their revolvers in a residential area on Myrtle Avenue. When Policeman Joe Rogers responded on horseback: 'He rounded up a wagonette containing five negro troopers and brought them back to town.' Two or three others fled 'when the officer approached and made good their escape.' Those he apprehended were unarmed 'but each had a bottle of whiskey concealed under his blouse and all appeared to have been drinking.'[145]

Picking up the thread, Texas papers publicized implicating incidents of Black soldiers in El Paso.[146] A Houston paper reinforced the negativity under such sensational teasers as: 'Men Murdered, Women Violated by Negro Soldiers … wives and children were left to starve and subjected to revolting outrages by the colored soldiers' referring to presence of Black units dispatched to the mine strikes in Idaho.[147]

These skirmishes in print paled by comparison to actual fighting in Laredo, Texas. There, as elsewhere, Black soldiers along the international boundary between the United States and Mexico had been common sight, although far from uniformly embraced. Yet such border duty rarely drew little more than passing mention as in April 1899. Four companies were dispatched from Arizona to locations along the Rio Grande in Texas. Only a fleeting reference to this action appeared regarding the two companies of infantry and two troops of cavalry, who were 'quiet and orderly.' The likelihood that all Black regulars in due course would be 'sent to Cuba and Manila for garrison duty,' further pleased some locals.[148]

---

143 For contemporary newspaper accounts see *Houston Daily Post*, February 1, 1899, and February 3, 1899; *El Paso Daily Herald*. February 4, 1899, Third Edition 4:30 p.m.
144 *El Paso Daily Herald*, February 2, 1899, Third Edition 4:30 p.m.
145 *Ibid.,,* February 6, 1899, Third Edition 4:30 p.m. Elsewhere in this edition appeared a denial by one of the officers of the Tenth United States Cavalry 'that the report from Texarkana that his regiment was drunk and disorderly is absolutely false. He went on to state 'it was unfair to the Tenth Cavalry' of which he argued 'there is no better regiment in the federal service.' Regardless, the paper carried yet another tale about the Black troops passing through Richmond, Texas and claimed 'Their passage through the county was characterized by the most outrageous conduct. Houses all along the line were filled with bullets and several narrow escapes from death are reported[.]' It appears this was not an isolated situation in that barely three years later the *New York Herald*, July 6, 1901, reported 'NEGRO SOLDIERS RAISE A RIOT. Albuquerque. N. M. July 5. Two wounded men. one fatally hurt, and the other shot through the leg, were brought here on one of the soldier trains passing through to the East. Near Holbrook the discharged negro soldiers got to shooting promiscuously through and out of the cars …'
146 *El Paso Daily Herald*, February 8, 1899, February 9, 1899, October 30, 1899, November 6, 1899, and November 7, 1899.
147 *Houston Daily Post*, August 26, 1899.
148 *Ibid.*, April 30, 1899.

Little came of this situation until an outbreak of smallpox in Laredo, the bane of community more than six decades earlier. The epidemic especially ravaged the more impoverished segments of the Latino inhabitants, decidedly the largest portion of the population. In the wake of a health official's dictating a quarantine that required the infected to be transferred 'from their homes to a local pesthouse … an angry mob gathered.' This outburst prompted a call for Texas Rangers to keep order and enforce the required medical measures. Their efforts failed. Government officials resorted to another measure of control. They dispatched Black infantrymen from Fort McIntosh adjacent to Laredo.[149]

A complex mixture simmered to a dangerous level. Perhaps most of the trouble emanated from prevailing perceptions extant among the marginalized Latino community. Often their negative experiences associated soldiers, regardless of skin color, as the force of 'repressive government policies that punished their folk heroes as bandits and revolutionaries.' Enlarging on this theory, ostensibly, 'many of them, through emulation, convenience, or conviction, shared the southern white prejudice against blacks.'[150] Mexican nationalism proved another potent factor, one that remained from the supposed peace between the two neighbor nations codified in the 1848 Treaty of Guadalupe Hidalgo. Adding to the combative mood were the disorderly decades that followed, including the incursion by the Europeans who established Maximilian's puppet empire, through ongoing revolutionary actions tantamount to nascent civil war.

Kinsmen of the Tejanos south of the Rio Bravo, likewise spurned Blacks, if a report of one military commander in Texas could be believed. He called for an increase in his troop strength, 'to continue operations – which are not intended to offend Mexico but are for self-protection with my present force.' To this request, he added the caveat that reinforcements should not include more Black soldiers as their use 'to cross the river [Rio Grande] after raiding Indians is, in my opinion, impolitic, not because they have shown any want of bravery, but because their employment is much more offensive to the Mexican inhabitants than that of white soldiers.'[151]

In turn, Black regulars were supposedly no friend of Latinos in the United States or Mexico. A *New York Times* editorial refuted one commentator 'that the colored man is unworthy to be a soldier in the army and stands ready to abandon his colors and form a conspiracy prejudicial to his country with the Mexican … is altogether the reverse to the real standing.' In fact, no friendship existed, emphasized the reporter 'between the Mexican and the Colored soldier, for the Mexicans do not like a colored man for nothing and show their animosity toward them at all times.'[152]

Proof of a lack of sympatico surfaced as hostility in Laredo. Partially fueled by adverse interplay between local law enforcement, who chiefly consisted of Latinos and Black troops, the stage was set. One of the first accounts appeared not in Texas, but instead far to the north in Minnesota. The brief, graphic piece ran only a few lines that covered a:

RIOT AT LAREDO. Negro Soldiers and Police Collide With Fatal Result … Friction between the Laredo police and the negro soldiers at Fort Mcintosh resulted in a street riot

---

149 Christian, *Black Soldiers in Jim Crow Texas*, 20. This same source offers a succinct narrative of the events which followed on 21–29.
150 *Ibid.*, 19.
151 *ARSW, 1877*, I, 80–81.
152 *New York Herald*, November 8, 1875.

last night, a Mexican, C. Nuncio, receiving a Krag-Jorgenson bullet through the shoulder. Policeman William Stoner was badly beaten with clubbed rifles and at least 100 shots from the army rifles and- pistols were fired by the rioting negroes.'[153]

Texas editors elaborated. Some sensationalized or added highly questionable details. For example, such portrayals as found in the *Brownsville Daily Herald* of Black soldiers going on the 'Warpath ... Armed with Rifles They Made a Raid on the City of Lerado' were not uncommon.[154] The *El Paso Daily Herald* followed with: 'NEGRO OUTRAGES' from Laredo's Fort McIntosh, as well as at another Texas installation, Fort Ringgold, outside Rio Grande City, which reported comparable collisions between Black regulars and townsmen.[155]

In response, the US Army ordered the Black garrison withdrawn from Fort McIntosh. It seemed that military leadership also would do likewise at Fort Ringgold, 'where the negro soldiers bitterly complain of continued insults which they allege they receive at the hands of the white and Mexican population of the town.'[156] Removal of Black soldiers, while welcomed by a considerable element among the citizens, had a downside. The loss of revenue due to the departure of the Blacks from the pair of posts and the possible failure to regarrison them by whites, threatened an economic blow. Despite the initial request of Texas' governor to remove Black troops from the area of Rio Grande City, the War Department refused to transfer the Black cavalrymen at Fort Ringgold.[157]

Thereafter, newspapers continued to fill columns including out-of-state publications.[158] Most reports emanated from Texas. Typically, the stories flatly accused the troops. One such columnist from a Houston paper faulted the soldiers for discharging their weapons 'on themselves to substantiate their claim that they were fired on.'[159] A second comment from El Paso prematurely announced: 'All negro troops will be withdrawn from the frontier posts, including Fort Ringgold and Fort Brown. Continued trouble between negro soldiers and citizens of the border is the cause.'[160]

In contrast, a few reporters acknowledged there were: 'Two Versions of the Difficulty Given, One Placing the Blame On the Negroes and the Other Saying the People of the Town Were the Aggressors.'[161] One writer went so far as to assert the US Army had been the victim not the perpetrator. Another newspaper accused 'several hundred citizens' from Rio Grande City of an 'Outrageous Attack Upon The Ninth Cavalry' with the intent to kill.[162] A version from

---

153 *St. Paul Daily Globe*, October 20, 1899. *Santa Fe Daily New Mexican*, October 24, 1899, carried much the same story.
154 *Brownsville Daily Herald*, October 23, 1899.
155 *El Paso Daily Herald*, October 24, 1899, October 25, 1899, and October 26, 1899. For a recapitulation of events at Fort Ringgold see Christian, *Black Soldiers in Jim Crow Texas*, 29–45.
156 *Houston Daily Post*, November 20, 1899.
157 *Ibid.*, November 22, 1899, and November 23, 1899. That same day the *Alma Record* (MI) November 23, 1899, declared 'QUIET AT FORT RINGGOLD. Because of the Recent Trouble the Post Is to Be Abandoned.'
158 *Santa Fe Daily New Mexican*, November 22, 1899, and November 23, 1899, for instance.
159 *Houston Daily Post*, November 25, 1899, and November 26, 1899.
160 *El Paso Daily Herald*, November 29, 1899, Last Edition 4:30 p.m.
161 *Salt Lake Herald*, November 22, 1899. *Alma Record* (MI) November 22, 1899, correspondingly shared: 'United States Soldiers Declare They Were Attacked, but Are Accused of Bombarding the Town.'
162 *Richmond Planet*, November 25, 1899.

California downplayed the case of Fort Ringgold as, 'Only a Drunken Row.'[163] An Iowa editor dismissed the actions in Rio Grande City as just one more of many examples of,'Southern Outrages' and as 'another time southern people have fired upon the flag of their country.' The author rhetorically asked: 'Just think of it, 3,000 American citizens attack at dusk,' who had to be repulsed after 'white officers ordered the Gatling gun turned on the mob.'[164] In some regards, the 1899 Texas imbroglios not only presaged later Brownsville and Houston upheavals, but also served as portents of the widespread devastation of the 'Red Summer' after the return of Black doughboys from overseas after the First World War.[165]

Relative to Brownsville, James Leiker's thought-proving analysis concluded, 'historical understanding of the Brownsville affair lacks a proper consideration both of its complexity and its many antecedents on the Mexican border.' He challenged: 'Many factors other than racism contributed to the civil-military violence on the Rio Grande.'[166] Stepping back into the late 1800s, he cited the forging of strong nationalism placed Latinos and Black soldiers at odds. The former group, he argued, shifted from a village and province focus to a 'national ethnic identity.' In turn, 'Blacks sought to secure their rights as citizens through national service.'[167]

Loyalty to their military oaths placed Blacks and all soldiers in opposition to Latinos whose perceptions of any US military elements along the border were not unlike negative attitudes of latter generations to the US Border Patrol, whom army personnel predated. This persistent cleft between the military and civilians in Texas shared by varied ethnicities, widened against Blacks for a litany of reasons. As the commander of the Department of Texas wrote in 1900: 'There is unquestionably, a very strong prejudice throughout all the old slave states against colored troops and this is quite a separate feeling from ordinary race prejudice.' Indeed, he added, the 'negro in uniform is frequently subjected to insult, though behaving with perfect propriety, for no other reason than color.'[168]

Yet other motivates compounded the variable equation. Some of the reasons probably stemmed from African American efforts in the late 1800s and beyond, to emerge in 'the position of 'leading minority.'[169] In that regard, Latinos who had constituted 'the vast majority of the counties along the Texas-Chihuahua border' resented incursion of others who might usurp them on the socio-economic ladder. 'Class cleavages and political systems,' further fed the mutual antagonism. The Democrat party machine in such places as Rio Grande City, played into the mix where white politicos gained votes and power 'by casting themselves as the town's protectors against the Army and black soldiers.' Corrupt officials allegedly operated gambling and prostitution establishments, as well as resorted to robbery, extortion and violence against

---

163 *Sacramento Daily Record-Union*, November 23, 1899.
164 *Denison Review* (IA) November 24, 1899.
165 Robert Whitaker, *On the Laps of Gods: The Red Summer of 1919 and the Struggle for Justice That Remade a Nation* (New York: Three Rivers Press, 2009), offers a popular account of this significant episode in US racial history.
166 Leiker, *Racial Borders*, 144. More recently, Edward Valentin Jr, 'Black Enlisted Men in the US-Mexico Borderlands: Race, Citizenship, and Occupation, 1866–1930,' Ph.D. diss., Rice University, 2020, expanded on Leiker's seminal study.
167 Leiker, *Racial Borders*, 96.
168 Lieutenant Colonel Chambers McKibbin to Adjutant General of the Army, March 1, 1900, 'The Brownsville Affray,' Sen. Doc. No. 389, 60th cong., 1st sess., 353–6.
169 Leiker, *Racial Borders*, 117.

Black troops, to appear as supportive of the Latino population, as well as for personal profit and due to their own prejudice.[170]

Analogously, in Loredo, Texas, frequent arrests and fines against Black soldiers resulted in a series of incidences including when a Twenty-Fifth Infantry member experienced an assault and scalp wound then left in a cell untended. Some of his comrades went to town in groups and under arms.[171] Here again, the department commander investigated the matter through an inspector general – Major W. H. H. Crowell. The major underscored the 'feeling of antagonism between the Mexican element of the city of Loredo and the soldiers.' Complicating matters, Crowell lamented the 'youth and inexperience' of the officers and men in the unit stationed in Loredo. His superior, the department commander, concurred. He judged Company D as consisting, 'largely of recruits young in years and, owing to the short period since enlistment, they have not yet acquired the habit of discipline … which would act as a restraint.'[172] In other words, the men would not abide slights and mistreatment, an attitude that grew more prevalent in the wake of earning honors and recognition, which they felt deserving of from their exploits in Cuba.

Chaplain Theophilus G. Steward knew this fact well, as indicated from a passage in his autobiography. He revealed, 'among those who had faced Spanish bullets at El Kaney [sic] a feeling that there were limitations to a soldiers' submission to insults and outrages' remained strong for the sake of the regiment's reputation. This passage seemed to imply that forbearance was not limitless.[173]

As in other aspects, a substantial number of Black males of the era, within and without the military, had adopted the Victorian standards of masculinity, arguably to an even greater degree after having been at length, 'seen as less then human.'[174] When confronted with traditional Latino *machismo*, another possible flashpoint sparked tensions. If yet one more sensational press story about Rio Grande City possessed veracity, a headline from the November 22, 1899, *Galveston Daily News* added a further source of discord. It claimed Black soldiers: 'Smiled on Senoritas [sic] Who Did Not Repel Their Advances and Angered the Mexican Population.' True or not, fraternization occurred between various ethnicities, but was met with mixed responses. Soldiers with a stable life and sound income might have appealed to some Latinas, but simultaneously could have threatened Latinos, who might be abandoned for economic, social and other reasons. Jealousy aside, the late 1890s scuffles served as a prologue to the more well known Brownsville episode that marked yet another stain on peaceful relationships between Texas civilians and Black troops posted to the state.

Brownsville Affair

Following previous patterns, tensions in Texas desisted with the Twenty-Fifth Infantry's redeployed to the Philippines, along with their comrades in the Twenty- Fourth. After their

---

170 *Ibid.*, 124.
171 *Ibid.*, 122–23.
172 RG94, AGO File 292843, Chambers McKibbin, November 13, 1899, NARA.
173 T.G. Steward, *From 1864 to 1914: Fifty Years in the Gospel Ministry* (Philadelphia: A.M.E. Book Concern, 1921), 360.
174 Leiker, *Racial Borders*, 108.

assignments in the Pacific, however, members of both regiments returned stateside. Once more, they found the same racist environment awaiting them that infected much of the nation. After the Twenty-Fifth landed stateside, at first, they enjoyed a relatively quiet respite in Nebraska.[175] Several years later, they drew duty in Texas. Again, a familiar scenario reappeared. On the night of August 13, 1906, a group of a dozen or more men rushed through the border town of Brownsville near the fort where a battalion of the regiment performed garrison duties. The unknown assailants randomly fired into structures for an estimated 10 minutes. Their wild shooting left one dead and several wounded, among these was a policeman.

After the assault, a local ad hoc committee obtained evidence from nearly two dozen witnesses. Eight of them attested, but not under oath, that they witnessed Black soldiers on the rampage. This inquiry ended with the citizens assigning the blame to the soldiers. Five investigations by the army, one by the Texas Rangers, as well as another by a county grand jury, failed to reach a definitive verdict as to the guilty parties. An unsatisfied President Theodore Roosevelt turned to a US Army's inspector to conduct a ninth examination.

This final effort concluded irate Black soldiers violently reacted to a series of slights, harassment and other factors, but once again, despite threats by interrogators of dishonorable discharges, unearthing the actual rioters came to naught. The army took this silence as a conspiracy indicative of guilt. Based on this perspective, the inspector general urged with a few exceptions, a carte blanche dishonorable dismissal of the battalion as an object lesson. Roosevelt concurred. He added the caveat that the dismissal be postponed until after the conclusion of the congressional elections to avoid alienating Black voters.

Ever the savvy politician, Roosevelt's prediction proved correct. After the hiatus called for by the president ended, the military released the verdict and punishment. As expected, adverse reactions rippled through the Black electorate. Black editors castigated Roosevelt for his cavalier treatment of 160 Black soldiers many of whom had served with honor for decades and whose careers ended in ruin. From many pulpits, Black clergyman described T. R.'s actions as 'damnable.'

Efforts to address the wholesale punishment failed, as did a decisive answer as to who participated. Possibly culpability could be found both within the community and in the battalion. Certainly, the outburst harkened to the same convoluted motives and multiethnic milieu present in the late 1890s. Assuredly, Brownville was not a simple white versus Black conflict. Nor was Brownsville the last time there was an outburst involving Black soldiers by the military.[176] Eleven years later, in Houston, a more awesome outbreak brought about the deaths of a pair of Black soldiers and 17 Texas residents. The Houston riot culminated in the mass execution of

---

175 For an interesting contrast as to the relationship of the Twenty-Fourth Infantry to local whites in Nebraska immediately prior to posting to Texas consider: Thomas R. Buecker, 'Prelude to Brownsville: The Twenty-Fifth Infantry at Fort Niobrara, Nebraska, 1902–1906,' *Great Plains Quarterly* 16 no. 2 (Spring 1996): 95–108.
176 Because of extensive literature available on the topics of the 1906 Brownsville affair, where nearly an entire battalion of the Twenty-Fourth Infantry was dishonorably discharged, and the 1917 Houston mutiny leading to the two dozen men being sentenced to execution, 53 life sentences, and 18 more receiving terms from two to 15 years, no further details appear in this narrative. Ann J. Lane, *The Brownsville Affair: National Crisis and Black Reaction* (Port Washington, NY: Kennikat Press, 1971) wrote one of the first succinct references to this event but left certain aspects undeveloped or ignored. Also see John D. Weaver, *The Brownsville Raid* (College Station: Texas A&M, 1992). For context consult: Christian, *Black Soldiers in Jim Crow Texas*, 26–91 and 145–172.

18 members of the Twenty-Fourth Infantry coupled with the sentence of another 54 men to be imprisoned from the regiment for various lengths of time.[177]

One recent appraisal summed up the multi-layered position of Black soldiers on the US-Mexico where 'they assumed hybrid identities; they were border enforcers by day, but often became border people at night. On the one hand, as active agents of the US government, black troops transformed the southwest borderlands by restricting movement of border people and strengthening some of the ethnic and national distinctions based on the boundary between the United States and Mexico.' Conversely, their deployment to 'the US-Mexico borderlands … allowed black men to form relationships with border people that they could use to exploit the porousness and fluidity of the border to improve their material conditions when they were off duty.' Finally, while 'perceptions of racial, ethnic and national difference (and sometimes animosity based on these categories) certainly existed among soldiers and civilians; relationships therefore assumed many forms on a broad spectrum ranging from cooperation to conflict.'[178]

Native Americans

If Texas' troubles could be traced in certain instances to a three-way mix of Blacks, Latinos and whites, there were other groups in the multi-cultural American West. Asians particularly existed on the fringe of this shifting cultural landscape. From the California gold rush onward, the Chinese led the way. They appeared in growing numbers until they, too, fell prey to racism. By the mid-1870s, restrictive legislation arose that discriminated against Asians. By May 6, 1882, the Chinese Exclusion Act brought the force of federal law into play. Any Chinese person found unlawfully within the United States would be deported. Customs agents and other government officials enforced the rules, among them were Black troops in Montana.

However, carrying out legislated policies went far beyond enforcement of the Exclusion Act. For more than nearly three decades, Black soldiers served as one of many government arms of ensuring federal Indian policy. In this, Black soldiers have been cast as one of the agents of settler colonialism.[179] A work focusing on Montana offered but one example of this hypothesis that painted 'Black settler colonialism fundamentally' in terms of a reliance on dispossessing Native Americans from their land. From this point of view, Buffalo Soldiers, 'directly perpetrated or witnessed the violence of the western Indian Wars of the late nineteenth century.' In the process: 'Many Black soldiers became settlers themselves and later served as semi mythical heroes or martyrs for Black settler communities who mobilized the memory of the Buffalo soldiers to legitimize their own continued presence on the land and to bolster emerging ideas of home and belonging in the West.'[180]

---

177 Donaldson, 'From Triumph to Tragedy,' 57. John Minton, *The Houston Riot and Courts-Martial of 1917*. (San Antonio: n.d.); and Robert V. Hayne, *A Night of Violence: The Houston Riot of 1917* (Baton Rouge: Louisiana State University Press, 1976), provide further details.
178 Edward Valentin, Jr., 'Black Enlisted Men in the US-Mexico Borderlands: Race, Citizenship, and Military Occupation, 1866–1930,' Ph.D. diss., Rice University, 2020, 110–11.
179 See Jeffery Ostler, *The Plains Sioux and US Colonialism from Lewis and Clark to Wounded Knee* (New York: Cambridge University Press, 2004), for one representation of this theory.
180 Anthony W. Wood, *Black Montana: Settler Colonialism and Erosion of the Racial Frontier, 1877–1930* (Lincoln University of Nebraska Press, 2021), 9.

During Arizona's Apache campaigns, Tenth Cavalry Second Lieutenant Powhattan Clarke carefully selected troopers from his regiment. He combined them with key Native American scouts to form a mobile strike force. Cooperation between Black soldiers and Native Americans varied from time and place. (Courtesy Hindman Auctions)

Taking a more forceful stand, in *An Indigenous Peoples' History of the United States* Roxanne Dunbar-Ortiz decried, 'the explicit purpose of the buffalo soldiers and the army in the West as a whole' who operated with the primary goal to 'invade Indigenous lands and ethnically cleanse them for Anglo-settlement and commerce.' The author further argued that the Black soldiers were 'a specially organized colonial military unit' comprised 'of oppressed former slaves.' They would be deployed against Native Americans as instruments of 'genocidal warfare' thereby squelching any thoughts of unification between the two groups 'against their common enemy, "the white man."'[181]

Even more damning, Jace Weaver envisioned: 'The Indian Wars' as a deliberate US government policy but 'not fought by the blindingly white American cavalry of John Ford westerns.' Instead, the aggressors were 'African Americans and Irish and German immigrants.'[182] Assuming a more equivocal stance, Stanford L. Davis, who traced part of his ancestry to a Buffalo Soldier, softened the rhetoric with the words quoted by Ortiz: 'Slaves and the black soldiers, who couldn't read

---

181 Roxanne Dunbar-Ortiz, *An Indigenous Peoples' History of the United States* (Boston: Beacon, 2014), 146–8. Following along a similar line of discourse, among other findings, Patrick Wolfe's 'Settler Colonialism and the Elimination of the Native,' *General of Genocide Research* 8 no. 4 (December 2006): 387–409, applied the term 'migratory genocide' in his summary of US Army operations on the frontier.

182 Jace Weaver, 'A Lantern to See By,' *Notes from a Miner's Canary: Essays on the State of Native America* (Albuquerque: University of New Mexico Press, 2010), 315. Likewise review Cynthia H. Enloe, *Ethnic Soldiers: State Security in Divided* (Athens, GA: University of Georgia Press, 1980).

or write, had no idea of the historical deprivations and the frequent genocidal intent of the US government toward Native Americans.' Advancing his explanation further, Davis stated, 'it was business as usual in the name of "Manifest Destiny"' that Blacks along with 'most Americans' accepted along with the dominant belief that Native Americans were 'incorrigible and non-reformable savages.' Given this predisposition, Davis mirrored fellow Buffalo Soldier decedent Anthony Powell, who voiced the opinion, 'many Black men opted for army service for survival reasons, as it gave them food and shelter, pay and a pension and even some glory.'[183]

Further, as one historian mused, there may be justification in questioning 'the morality of driving the Native Americans from their ancient homes, but ethical considerations are rarely the domain of the average soldier.' The Black soldiers who volunteered typically looked upon their role as, 'doing their country's bidding and helping to "win" the West for America.'[184] Veteran Rueben Waller assuredly would have accepted this statement in that he once informed the editor of *Winners of the West* about 'the hardships and experiences that attended my five years of service with the 10th cavalry, which will be the history of the "regular army, making the west safe"'.'[185]

An early overview of the Black soldier added to positive service of the Black soldier, focusing on the Ninth Cavalry who:

> … spent the greater part of their early history on the frontier fighting Indians and paving the way for the American people to establish homes, industries and commerce without fear of the marauding bands of Indians which used to make life of the white man exceedingly dangerous … And to-day the Indian is given more consideration and recognition than the Negro who saved the country from their onslaughts.'[186]

Did this author capture the Black soldiers' perspective relative to Native Americans? Once again, Frank Schubert shed some light on the topic, although his observations fell below a definitive level of proof. He pointed out, among another other things, 'black soldiers writing in pension requests and veterans' newspapers showed no signs of a special regard for the Indians. As evidence, he referred to such dismissive epithets that appeared in prints such as "hostile tribes," "naked savages," and "redskins" – and the same racist caricatures employed by whites.'[187]

---

183 Stanford L. Davis, 'Buffalo Soldiers & Indian Wars,' Buffalosoldier.net.www.buffalosoldier.net/index.htm. David Krueger, 'To Hold What the US Has Taken in Conquest:' The United States Army and Colonial Ethnic Forces, 1866–1914,' Ph.D. diss., Harvard University, Cambridge, MA, 2019, 7, expressed the incentives in another way, writing 'the soldiers in these segregated formations leveraged their service to obtain practical economic and legal opportunities, as well as to support their arguments for more meaningful social and civic participation.' Further, Secretary of War Redfield Procter praised the performance of Black soldiers, noted their low desertion rates, and thought the US Army offered the white man 'often only a refuge' but for Blacks military service was a 'career.' *ARSW, 1889*, I, 5, 8–9.
184 McGlone, 'Monuments and Memorials to Black Military History,' 114.
185 *Winners of the West*, July 1924, 1.
186 Mary Curtis, *The Black Soldier, or The Colored Boys of the United States Army* (Washington, DC: Murray Brothers, 1918), 567–57.
187 Frank N. Schubert, 'Buffalo Soldiers: Myths and Realities,' *Army History: The Professional Bulletin of Army History* 52 (Spring 2001): 13–18 along with 'Buffalo Soldier Contributions: 10th Cavalry Regiment, US Army,' Lecture delivered at The Center for Research on Vermont in Burlington, https://ia601004.us.archive.org/8/items/retncrv 2008franknschubert buffalo soldiers/RETN-CRV–2008-Frank N Schubert_BuffaloSoldiers.ogv are the main sources for most of references to Schubert's debunking many inventions

Additionally, a Ninth Cavalry sergeant was even quoted as calling a Lakota (Sioux) a, 'voodoo nigguh,'[188] Taking another racist page from whites, in 1894 a Black private from Company D, Twenty-Fourth Infantry attended a masquerade ball at Fort Bayard, New Mexico. Akin to donning blackface, a guise that came to be shunned, the soldier appeared as 'an idiotic Indian squaw' much to the admiration of the spectators.[189]

A more concrete incident illuminated that coexistence between Black troops and Native Americans in peacetime could prove as volatile as with other groups. In this example, an 1899 fracas at the San Carlos Reservation resulted in bodily harm. Some members of Company C, Twenty-Fifth Infantry grabbed clubs and assaulted four Apache men 'whom they beat in-sensible.' Evidently, the friction had to do with some soldiers contact with Apache women, 'causing bad blood among the Indians.' In response to the brutality, the Apache vowed vengeance.[190] Fearing unrest, military officials ordered a detachment of the Ninth Cavalry from Fort Thomas to San Carlos. Not long afterwards, it seemed more prudent to assign white troops to the duty at San Carlos and extract the Black garrison. Curiously, during the 1880s and early 1890s, no such clashes had emerged. Further, a deputy marshal arrested a dozen Black infantrymen suspected of the vicious attack. By October 24, the United States commissioner in Globe jailed the perpetrators for later action by the federal grand jury.[191]

Nonetheless, another analyst challenged the view that Black soldiers shared white racist disdain for Native Americans. He proclaimed for the most part, Black soldiers did not embrace the low opinion of Native Americans with their white counterparts.[192] Of note, the author offered little supportive documentation to underpin this thesis. Nonetheless, either viewpoint represented concurrent attitudes that very probably, were present within the ranks. Black soldiers, like any other groups, were not monolithic in this or any other way. Individuals varied as did the cultural environment of their times.

Philippines and Fagen

In contrast to this ambivalence on the frontier, clearly, support for the war in Cuba existed. The Black press, including the publication of Edward Johnson unabashed promotion, *History of the Negro Soldiers in the Spanish-American War*, along with Chaplain Steward, as well as numerous

---

that have been incorporated into Buffalo Soldier canon. As Schubert underscores, these reactions bespeak of 'metaracism' in which differences between races are not primarily biological, but primarily cultural. For more on this phenomenon consult Joel Kovel, *White Racism: A Psychohistory* (London: Free Association Books, 1988), 22–12. Additionally in his Vermont lecture Schubert offered three other quotations from Black frontier veterans implying a certain pride in their achievements asserted that they 'made the West,' by smoothing 'the way for the great West' and helping 'to blaze the right of way for the settlers of the Wild West' all of which at the very least appear to be relevant to the settler colonialism argument.

188 *Richmond Planet*, November 5, 1898.
189 *A&NJ*, February 10, 1894, 407.
190 *El Paso Daily Herald*, October 16, 1899, Third Edition, 4:30 p.m.
191 *Ibid.*, October 18, 1899, Third Edition, 4:30 p.m.; October 24, 1899, Third Edition, 4:30 p.m.; *Dakota Farmers' Leader* (Canton, SD), October 20, 1899.
192 Anthony Powell's statements were taken from August 18, 2020, 'Conflict of Conscience: Buffalo Soldiers,' August 18, 2020, podcast, youtube.com/watch?v=FFHCMjLmK9s.

illustrations reminiscent of lithographs of the Civil War meant to adorn the parlors of homes, all bespoke of a large body within the Black community who viewed the war as positive.[193] This conflict, as one study (referenced earlier) contended, afforded Black soldiers 'more than just citizenship, they fought for their honor, they fought for their pride, they fought because they wanted to be heroes, they fought to be leaders, but most importantly they fought for their manhood.'[194]

This was not always so when it came to the Philippines. Prominent whites among whose ranks numbered Samuel Clemens and notable Blacks, led by such luminaries as Bishop Henry Turner and Booker T. Washington, decried the United States refusal to grant Filipinos their independence after Spain ceded the islands.[195] Even so, backing for the Black soldier remained steadfast.[196] In turn, supposedly: 'The black soldier simply saw the task in the Philippines as a duty that had to be performed, no matter how unjust' although this same thesis added that Black, 'soldiers held a certain level of respect for the Filipinos that was not equally shared by the white soldiers.'[197] As the Twenty-Fourth Infantry's sergeant major, John Galloway, deduced from an interview with a Filipino doctor, 'the colored soldiers do not push them off the streets, spit at them, call them damned "niggers," abuse them in all manner of ways and connect race hatred with duty.'[198]

A humorous but poignant piece in a Texas newspaper, pointed out the dichotomy presented to the Black soldier during their most recent mission. Drawing on Rudyard Kipling, this article indicated:

> The 'white man's burden,' which has been carried by the volunteers and regulars in the Philippine islands for over a year, is now being shared by some of the black boys of the United States. A sergeant in the Twenty-Fourth Infantry said the other day when saluted with the question, 'What are you boy doing here?' The quick reply came: 'Why boss, we'se here to tak up de white man's burden.'[199]

Nonetheless, a goodly number of Black troops looked favorably upon their 'Brown Brothers' to reference another cliché of the era used by whites for Filipinos.[200] Of those, some literally embraced their 'Brown Sisters.' Generally, 'Black soldiers were more welcomed by Filipino women than white soldiers.' Among other factors, romance, economic stability and physical

---

193 J.M. Guthrie, *Campfires of the Afro-American: or The Colored Man as a Patriot*. (Philadelphia: Afro-American Publishing, 1899).
194 Donaldson, 'From Triumph to Tragedy,' 25.
195 *Ibid.*, 46; *Baltimore Ledger*, October 1, 1898.; and Willard B. Gatewood, 'Black Americans and the Quest for Empire 1898–1903,' *Journal of Southern Hist*ory 38 no 4 (November 1972): 65–75.
196 Guthrie, *Campfires of the Afro-American*, 7–10; *Kansas City American Citizen*, July 14, 1899.
197 Donaldson, 'From Triumph to Tragedy,' 47. One example cited by this author was a letter written by M.W. Saddler, a soldier in the Twenty-Fifth Infantry and punished in *Indianapolis Freeman*, November 18, 1899.
198 *Richmond Planet*, December 30, 1899.
199 *Bryan Moring Eagle*, September 17, 1899.
200 Apropos, Leon Wolfe, *Little Brown Brother: How the United States Purchased and Pacified the Philippine Islands at the Century's Turn* (New York: History Book Club, 1960), remains interesting reading.

protection, resulted in marriages and families. Such relationships also led some whites to doubt the loyalty of Black soldiers. The same perspective prompted the revolutionary cause to resort to propaganda bent on enticement of Black troops to come over to the Filipinos.[201] Very few soldiers succumbed to this ploy, but David Fagen, 'along with a few others defected to the enemy.'[202] Other Black soldiers elected to remain peacefully after their term of service expired.

By some estimates, upwards of 1,000 Black soldiers took up life in the Philippines where, in pursuit of opportunities denied them in the United States, they remained. Among these would be veterans who promoted 'the emigration of blacks to the Philippines and even Cuba' in advance of 'the Black Nationalist migration movement' which 'between 1910 and 1920, nearly 500,000 southern blacks moved from the rural South to several major metropolitan cities throughout the north.'[203]

Conclusion

Over the first 50 years of Black regulars' service, a growing self-awareness accompanied, 'unwillingness to accept injustice.' Even as the regiments formed immediately after the Civil War, early opposition to perceived discrimination and slights arose. With heightened racism and prejudice, particularly extent in the civilian sector from the promulgation of Jim Crow laws experienced as the Black soldiers headed via the South to Cuba and subsequent inequalities, these troops endured much. Despite Fagen and a few others in the Philippines, eruptions in Texas after the Spanish American War at such flashpoints as in 1906 Brownsville; 1911 riots in the San Antonio; 1915 protests in Honolulu and the devastating 1917 Houston carnage, the majority of these men honored their oaths to perform faithfully.[204] As Edward Johnson wrote, 'let it be said that the black soldier did his duty under the flag, whether that flag protects him or not.'[205]

201 Donaldson, 'From Triumph to Tragedy,' 50–51.
202 Frank Schubert, 'Seeking David Fagen: The Search for a Black Rebel's Florida Roots,' *Sunland Tribune* 31 Article 5 (2006): 28.
203 Donaldson, 'From Triumph to Tragedy,' 56.
204 Finley, *Huachuca Illustrated* I, 5; and Smith and Zeidler, *A Historic Context*, 120.
205 Johnson, *History of the Negro Soldiers*, 216.

6

Myths, Memorials and Meanings

This maxim: 'The best way to spoil a good story is by sticking to the facts' especially seemed applicable to the Buffalo Soldiers. Beginning with the term itself, for nearly the past century and a half, considerable imagination and manipulation has occurred. Like so much of the narrative surrounding Black regulars, the name itself represents divergent meanings with an uncertain origin. In the process, it has added to the myth rather than shed light on reality.

The Buffalo Soldier Sobriquet

In a well-documented essay, Thomas Phillips plumbed the depths of the sobriquet 'Buffalo Soldier.'[1] He charted what was purported to be the earliest appearances of the term in print from the 1870s onward. Simultaneously, Phillips deconstructed several of the unsubstantiated claims about this malleable appellation. For example, he cited Frances Roe's *Army Letters from an Officer's Wife* as the oft alluded to first usage (1872), followed by several well-reasoned caveats about when the manuscript was produced. Phillips further deliberated whether the source stemmed from her actual correspondence or simply represented a literary device. He then turned to dateable examples from newspapers and periodicals of the 1870s through the early 1890s. While not comprehensive, the selections were extensive.

In his discourse, Phillips singled out the October 30, 1873 issue of the New York *Nation* (reprinted in the *Army and Navy Journal* of November 8, 1873) as the first of a score or so of articles over the last quarter of the nineteenth century to reference 'buffalo soldier.' Sent from Fort Sill, Indian Territory, the unknown 1873 correspondent shared telling observations about the Tenth Cavalry troops stationed there whom he said the Comanches called, '"buffalo soldiers," because, like the buffalo, they are woolly.' This statement matched Frances Roe's narrative. The writer added a further nuance that revealed the: 'Indians at first treated them with utter contempt and when they chanced to kill one would not take his scalp. After a while, when they had had a taste of their fighting qualities, they began to respect them,' demonstrating their

---

1   Tom Phillips, 'Sobriquet: A Chronological Commentary on the Name 'Buffalo Soldier," *Journal of America's Military Past* 35 no. 2 (Spring/Summer 2010): 5–30.

One theory, albeit a questionable one, proposed that the term 'buffalo soldier' arose when Native Americans observed Black soldiers bundled in their heavy winter buffalo hide overcoats. (Courtesy Hindman Auctions)

newfound admiration by taking the scalps of the Black soldiers they killed.[2]

Decades later, in a letter to the editor that appeared in the July 1924 issue of *Winners of the West*, a Black veteran reinforced the 1873 article. Under the headline 'COLORED TROOPERS' HAIR TOO SHORT FOR SCALPING' the story involved an incident of a white scout and five Black horse soldiers setting out from Fort Harker, Kansas to hunt buffalo. After they had made their way 'five miles from camp ... The Indians were surprised and surrounded them and captured the entire party. They scalped the one white scout and burned him alive at the stake, but the five black soldiers were stripped of all the clothing by the Indians and administered an unmerciful beating and admonished to "go home,"' the Indians saying, 'Indians no fight tushi-ti-bi-buthano,' meaning 'black man's scalp no good.' Presumably, their reluctance to treat the Black captives in the same manner as the white adversary did not bespeak of a high regard for the troopers.

---

2 In a letter referenced as dating from June 1872, and written from Camp Supply, Indian Territory, Roe noted: 'The Indians call them 'Buffalo Soldiers' because their woolly heads are so much like the matted cushion that is between the horns of the buffalo.' Roe, *Army Letters from an Officer's Wife*, 1871, 65.

Earlier Roots

While Phillips' sleuthing offered many useful insights, the term 'buffalo soldiers' can be traced earlier than 1873. In fact, according to a lengthy exploration of the expression, it appeared in the 1860s as a 'reproach against' by southerners in reference to follow southern 'men who took up arms against the Confederacy.'[3] These perceived traitors were whites, as were men who became the subject of a derogatory, lengthy private letter from an unidentified US Army officer serving in the Lone Star State, possibly at Fort Richardson. The January 16, 1870 issue of the *New York Dispatch* gave pause to later interpretations of the term's positive meaning. This anonymous army critic expressed poor opinions of the 'little town on the extreme outskirts of civilization,' and generally displayed his low esteem for Texas and its people.

As part of a wordy diatribe, the officer contended that Native Americans shared his contempt. He claimed: 'Indians have, in many instances, had ample opportunity of seeing the unwillingness of the Texans to run much risk in the way of fighting and have, therefore, contracted a most supreme contempt for them, as soldiers or fighters.' They derisively dubbed Texans, '"buffalo soldiers," meaning they are fit to hunt buffalo only and not to take the war path.' Purportedly, one Native American elder went so far as to say: 'Texan, he heap woman; he fight woman.' Whether the informant was speaking the truth, or instead sharing his own bias against Texans, whom he may have viewed as unreconstructed rebels, cannot be substantiated.

What is in a Name?

Although a case exists that 'buffalo soldier' may have a pejorative rather than positive base, at least one late nineteenth century source and several twentieth century writers ignored this possibility without necessarily supplying proof for their interpretation. According to headlines in the November 5, 1898 issue of the *Richmond Planet*: 'BUFFALO TROOPERS. THE NAME BY WHICH NEGRO SOLDIERS ARE KNOWN. Comprise Several of the Crack Regiments of Our Army – The Indians Stand in Abject Terror of Them.' The article that followed drew heavily on the testimony from a white veteran who variously served in both the army and navy and who declared, 'an American Indian has a deadly fear of an American negro. The most utterly reckless, dare-devil savage of the copper hue stands in awe of a negro and the blacker the negro the more the Indian quails.' This piece, which Edward A. Johnson reprinted in toto as part of post-Spanish American War patriotic pamphlet in praise of the Black soldier, was at odds with most previous accounts.[4] It may have been more self-serving than factual.

---

3   Alex Christopher Meekins, 'Unionism and the Arcane Origin of 'Buffalo,' *North Carolina Historical Review* 85 no. 3 (July 2008): 284.
4   Johnson, *History of the Negro Soldier*, 50–55. In another contemporary work extolling the performance of Blacks soldiers during the War with Spain, Miles V. Lynk, *The Black Troopers, Or the Daring Heroism of the Negro Soldiers in the Spanish-American War* (Jackson, TN: M.V. Lynk Publishing House, 1899) 24, the author indicated the Ninth Cavalry was 'popularly known as the 'Black Buffalos" essentially the term Frederic Remington had used nearly a century before in a confidential letter to Lieutenant Powhatan Clarke. Langellier, *Scouting With the Buffalo Soldiers*, 182. Despite this statement, when GO No. 11, February 11, 1911, Headquarters, 10th Cavalry, Fort Ethan Allen, Vermont, RG 391, Miscellaneous Records, 10th Cavalry, National Archives and Records

Decades later, Fairfax Downey, who had been weaned on first-hand tales of the military in the West, added to the growing legend. He reckoned Native Americans prized African American scalps because they came from another fighting man rather than a civilian, in direct contradiction to some sources from veterans.[5] Downey claimed that Native Americans coined the term because of the 'woolly hair and shaggy hide coats' the Tenth Cavalry 'wore on winter campaigns.' If this contention were factual, it would be a case of independent invention from a later era by Native Americans on the northern Great Plains. These overcoats, however, were not issued until 1876, several years after the first mention of the name Buffalo Soldier in print. Moreover, army quartermasters only provided these bulky garments, designed for the harshest winter climates, to infantrymen serving at select posts where the mercury severely plummeted.

The earliest examples went to white troops serving on the Great Plains.[6] The first issue to Black soldiers occurred after 1880, when the Twenty-Fifth Infantry began service in the Dakotas and Minnesota. Moreover, cavalrymen found it nearly impossible to don such a heavy cumbersome garb and still mount their horse. As such, the item primarily was intended for foot soldiers, both Black and white. While possibly Native Americans on these Northern Plains referred to the men arrayed in this item of winter war as 'buffalo soldiers,' the likelihood, 'the nickname for black soldiers was invented at different times and different places by different groups of Native Americans' remains suspect.[7]

Following Downey's lead, William Leckie did more than any latter-day scribe to transform an idea into an icon. In Leckie's original version of *The Buffalo Soldiers: A Narrative of the Negro Cavalry in the West*, he emphasized Black troops 'were dubbed "buffalo soldiers" by their red antagonists. Men of the Tenth and later the Ninth, accepted the title and wore it proudly.' In an accompanying footnote, the author tempered his conclusion. He admitted the term's origin was 'uncertain.' Leckie insisted, however, without providing his sources, that because the 'buffalo was a sacred animal to the Indian … it is unlikely that he would so name an enemy if respect was lacking.' Extrapolating from this assumption, he concluded: 'It is a fair guess that the Negro trooper understood this and thus his willingness to accept the title.'[8]

Administration, was issued, the Tenth Cavalry, and not the Ninth Cavalry, would adopt 'an American bison statant, proper' as its regimental 'blazon' or badge. During the First World War, none other than James Moss, who had headed the bicycle experiment during his stint with the Twenty-Fifth Infantry, and later as a junior officer with the Twenty-Fourth Infantry including duty in Yosemite National Park, would in October of 1918 prepare the design of a black buffalo silhouette on an olive drab circle as the shoulder sleeve insignia to be adopted by the 92nd Infantry Division. Roger D. Cunningham, 'African-American Divisional Shoulder Sleeve Insignia During World War I,' *Miliary Collector & Historian* 56 (Winter 2004): 269–71. It should be noted, that while the unit's rank and file was comprised of Black enlisted men serving in France during the First World War, some of whom had been Black regulars, none of them had input into the selection of this insignia, nor did any enlisted men have a say into the adoption of a buffalo as part of the regimental coat of arms for the Tenth Cavalry.

5   Fairfax Downey, *Indian-Fighting Army* (New York: Charles Scribner's Sons, 1941), 25.
6   For more on this heavy winter wear obtain Jerome A. Greene, 'The US Army Buffalo Overcoat and M1883 Canvas Blanket Lined Overcoat on the Northern Plains,' *Military Collector & Historian* 46 no. 2 (Summer 1992): 73–75, and T.J. Sperry, 'Winter Clothing on the North Plains,' *Military Collector & Historian* 44 no. 44 no. (Fall 1992): 117–19.
7   Phillips, 'Sobriquet:' 12.
8   Leckie, *Buffalo Soldiers*, 25–26.

The operative word in this discourse was 'guess' although on camera for a 1992 A&E Network documentary, Leckie defended his thesis. He shared his recollections of an informal interview conducted during the 1950s, when he asked about the meaning of the name and how it came into existence. The gist of the response received from some Kiowa and Comanche elders at Anadarko, Oklahoma was that their people saw a resemblance of the Black soldiers to the bison. Leckie also asserted that the group confirmed the reference, 'was meant as a compliment.' Said Leckie: 'That Black trooper understood it' as being a form of praise by an enemy. Because of this, Leckie insisted the soldiers themselves, 'not only liked it, they were 'proud of it.'[9] That may be true for later generations of Black soldiers, but no conclusive contemporary evidence has been unearthed that the earlier generations of Black regulars embraced the term during the 1800s.

Despite the author's avowals, in the 2003 revised edition, co-written with Shirley Leckie, the narrative retained Native Americans as the term's origins, but the new interpretation ran: 'The reasons are not entirely known.' Interestingly, no mention appeared referencing the 1950s' interview Leckie cited for television. The altered account likewise included a hope, 'that further research may illuminate this question in the future.'[10]

Leckie was not the only champion of honorific connotations. A National Archives staff member indicated that the correspondence of Colonel Grierson mentioned the term, which had been acquired, 'during the 1871 campaign against the Comanches in the Indian Territory.' Grierson, according to this essay, noted the Comanches respected the Black soldiers for their tenacity and their trailing skills and: 'They had earned the name of the rugged and revered buffalo.'[11] Regrettably, the essayist failed to share a citation for Grierson's alleged statement.

As late as 2016, one long-time student of the subject of Black regulars went so far as to specify that the Cheyenne bestowed the name based on the model of the 'Clan of the Buffalo' that existed among several Native American groups. These societies consisted of the fiercest fighters. Thus, the concept would be transferred to the Black soldiers in recognition of their brave antagonists.[12]

To such assertions Frank Schubert responded: 'There is no contemporaneous evidence that the soldiers themselves actually used or even referred to this title [Buffalo Soldiers].' He determined, 'any claims concerning their views of the usage remained unproved suppositions.'[13] Two other scholars stated, 'to the men … "buffalo" was an insult.' They based their declaration on pair of courts-martial transcripts. The first of these recorded Private Robert Hopkins lashing out against one of his officers who daily drilled the soldiers, 'like black buffalo sons of bitches.'

---

9   *Buffalo Soldiers*, Bill Armstrong Production, 1992. This production may be viewed on YouTube at youtube.com/watch?v=xhX5WNnwwaQ&t=553s.
10 Leckie and Leckie, *Buffalo Soldiers*, 26–27 and 292.
11 Walter Hill, 'Exploring the Life and History of the 'Buffalo Soldiers," *The Record: News from the National Archives and Records Administration* (March 1998): 12–14.
12 Presentation by Anthony Powell, September 29, 2016, Smithsonian Institution's National Postal Museum, youtube.com/watch?v=pBofRUraUMY. In the same program, Powell added several other topics including acknowledging that Black soldiers subjugated the Native Americans and helped place them on reservations, which is a curious in that it raises the issue why would anyone esteem an enemy that wrought this fate on them?
13 Schubert, *Voices of the Buffalo Soldier*, 47 and 261.

Private Peter White mirrored this disparaging usage when he testified that his sergeant was, 'a God damned black, cowardly buffalo son of a bitch.'[14]

That is not to say after the end of the Indian Wars that some veterans viewed the name in a positive light. For instance, Reuben Waller, who enlisted in the Tenth Cavalry on July 16, 1867, described to Roman Nose's siege of Beechers Island. In passing, Waller said the stalemate had been broken by, 'heap too many' (buffalo soldiers).[15] As this account dated from 1929 recollections, it is ambiguous whether the title previously had been accepted by the Black rank and file during the 1800s, or if Waller interjected this statement based on later, growing uses of the term.

Assuredly, during the 1940s, when Vance Marchbank, who had enjoyed a lengthy career as a Black regular, shared his recollections with a positive spin, he referred to the 'famous fighting "Tenth Cavalry" which is also known as the "Buffalo Regiment."'[16] It remains unclear whether his statement emerged from the regimental insignia adopted in 1911, which he well knew, or stemmed from his contact with older Black soldiers earlier in his military life.

Some Native American Views of the Black Soldiers

While much is unknown about the origins of the term and what it meant to the men to whom it referred, at least it is clear that at least a few Native Americans disparaged Black soldiers' warriorlike qualities contrary to Leckie and others. One of those was the powerful Comanche leader Quanah Parker. As a white Texas frontiersman recalled: 'For some reason, I never knew why, the Indians hated the negro soldiers. They called them "Buffalo soldiers." The young Indians took a delight in tantalizing the negroes.' As an example, 'a disturbance between the Indians and the negro soldiers' arose at a military post. In response, through an interpreter, an officer informed: 'Quanah if he did not make the young braves behave themselves that he would take their guns away from them.' Quanah replied in Spanish: 'You can have our guns'; then pointed to some tepee poles and said, 'We will use those on the negroes.' The point was that the Comanche did not need to 'waste any ammunition on these negroes.'[17] If they wanted to kill them, they simply could do so with wooden lodge poles, which meant they did not fear the Blacks, nor particularly respected them.

Referring to the early 1880s, during the Victorio Campaign, purportedly some Mescalero Apache also derided the: '"Buffalo Soldiers," as the Indians call the colored troops' exhibiting an 'intense hatred ... for them.' The correspondent, a US Army officer, further suggested that the antipathy was mutual.[18] Another paper said the Indian agent with the Mescalero Apache warned in order to remove them from their reservation, 'the government had better not send "buffalo soldiers" to make the attempt for the Indians have no fear at all of them.' The agent laughingly added, 'buffalo soldiers' was 'a term of contempt applied by the Indians to our colored

---

14   Dobak and Phillips, *Black Regulars*, xvii and 287n18.
15   Robert Lyman, ed., *The Beecher Island Annual* (Wray, CO: The Beecher Island Memorial Association, 1930), 116.
16   Marchbank, 'Forty Years in the Army,' 79.
17   Harley True Burton, 'History of the JA Ranch,' *Southwestern Historical* Quarterly 31 (October 1927): 107–08.
18   *A&NJ*, April 3, 1880, 704–5.

troops. The Indians have no opinion at all of the bravery of our negro soldiers and always speak of them most contemptuously.'[19]

Similarly, two instances related to the Utes indicated that these people had come to 'despise the negro soldiers.' The first of these was a statement made to a rancher by a member of the tribe that 'One Ute good ten buffaloes (meaning colored soldiers).'[20] A similar account from the era was reported after news of the arrival of Black soldiers among the Uncompahgres (Utes). Negative reactions came from one of their leaders. Sour, an old headman who shouted: 'Buffalo soldiers! Buffalo soldiers! Coming … Don't let them come! We can't stand it! It's bad very bad!' He repeated: 'We cannot stand for them to come on our Reservation. It is too bad!' To make his point, he rubbed the Indian agent's 'black coat sleeve and then over his face and exclaimed with great vehemence in broken English: "All over black! All over black, buffalo soldiers! Injun heap no like him!!"' Gesturing further, he rubbed 'his head all over with a jerk of his hand, he almost screamed: "Woolly head! Woolly head! All same as buffalo! What you call him, black, white man? NIGGER!!! NIGGER!!!"'[21]

Reporter Theodore Davis divulged the application of the same prejudicial epithets from another time and a different Native American people, possible Southern Cheyenne. When a war party 'attacked Wilson Creek Station twice: each time a few colored troops were there,' he reported. A few days later, they launched a third attack against 'a small squad of soldiers, under the command of a colored sergeant, present; but they had nerve and showed it … As soon as the redskins came sufficiently near to be within easy range the black-skins rose and opened a rapid-fire from their breech-loaders. The Indians turned and fled, shouting, "Nigger! nigger! nigger!" and ignominiously abandoned the field.'

What also was interesting, along with Davis' reference to degrading language, he offered a counterpoint to those contemporaries who claimed Native Americans did not fear the Buffalo Soldiers. Davis assured they indeed had 'come to regard a black man with holy horror.'[22]

While periodicals and published accounts provided opposing viewpoints and might display biases one way or the other, sometimes to influence rather than inform their readership, one private piece of correspondence from Benjamin Grierson's niece might be taken as more objective. Helen Davis had married a Tenth Cavalry officer. She was familiar with the regiment. Davis wrote that some Apache had bolted from San Carlos Reservation in Arizona assuming

19　*Daily Bee* (Omaha, NE) September 17, 1885. Like allegations could be found in *Arizona Weekly Journal-Miner/Weekly Arizona Miner* (Prescott), May 8, 1885: 'The Apaches do not fear the colored troops but have a contempt for them. They have received this idea from the New Mexico Indians, who have been in contact with them.' Elsewhere, *Daily Tombstone*, May 8, 1886, chimed in: 'The Apaches from the time negro troops were first sent against them, have called them 'buffalo soldiers' and seem to have the utmost contempt for them.' It should be noted that Arizona's papers often took hostile views towards the military in the territory, and that such reporting may not have been completely accurate, and most unlikely not verified.
20　*Omaha Daily Bee*, August 15, 1887.
21　Eugene R. White, *Service on the Indian Reservations: Being the Experiences of a Special Indian Agent* (Little Rock: Diploma Press, 1893), 147–8. According to one later study, this attitude did not remain indefinitely. See Ronald G. Coleman, 'The Buffalo Soldiers: Guardians of the Uintah Frontier 1886–1901,' *Utah Historical Quarterly* 47 No. 4 (Winter 1979): 427, who concluded the adverse reaction subsided to some degree and 'within several years the initial distrust was diminished.'
22　*Harper's Weekly*, September 7, 1867, 564.

they could do so with impunity, 'because they said, "buffalo soldier no shoot." They do not seem to think very well of the colored soldier's fighting powers.'²³

A parallel commentary from Texan Herman Lehmann, who as a boy was captured by an eastern Apache band and had embraced the ways of his new people, recollected:

> Among the soldiers were some negroes, the first most of the Indians had seen ... We called them 'buffalo soldiers,' because they had curly, kinky hair and heads like bisons. Our arrows would not penetrate their skulls. I remember hearing our chief instruct his warriors one time that in fighting 'buffalo soldiers' never to shoot them in the head, because the skull was too hard..., but to shoot him through the heart and kill him easy.²⁴

Admittedly, these scant examples of the vast cultural gap between Native Americans and Blacks are insufficient to be irrefutable. Moreover, neither the Native Americans nor the Black soldiers, held universal views. For instance, some Native Americans kept slaves. A case in point, the Seminoles enslaved Blacks, yet at the same time, Black freedmen lived among them and fought alongside Native Americans against the US Army.²⁵ How diametrically opposing perspectives existed even within the same , was embodied in a Comanche sub-chief described as 'a Big Negro' who participated in an 1868 raiding party in Texas. Furthermore, Comanche men married Black women and supposedly a Black bugler, who had deserted the army, rode with Quanah.²⁶ Although these negative testimonies contrasted with late twentieth century notions that Native Americans held the Black soldiers in special regard, to date, neither perspective has been proven or disproven regarding this complex, complicated relationship.²⁷

---

23 Helen Davis to Alice Grierson, May 26, 1885, Benjamin H. Grierson Papers, Illinois State Historical Society, Springfield.
24 J. Marvin Hunter, ed., *9 Years Among the Indians 1870–1879 The Story of the Captivity and Life of a Texan Among the Indians Herman Lehmann* (Albuquerque: University of New Mexico Press, 1993), 121. Generally speaking, he maintained that he and his captors 'never feared Uncle Sam's regular soldiers much, for we knew they would take a great deal of time in getting ready to take to the trail.' (115)
25 Kevin Mulroy, *The Seminole Freedmen A History* (Norman: University of Oklahoma Press, 2007), 36, 88, 103, and 192, which also revealed the Cherokee, Chickasaw, Choctaw, and Creek held slaves as well as the Seminoles.
26 Quintard Taylor, 'Shifting Borders of Race and Identity: A Research and Teaching Workshop On the First Nations and African American Experience Intersections between Native American and African American History in the West,' shiftingborders.ku.edu/presentations/taylor.html, which cites these examples taken from Kenneth W. Porter, *The Negro on the American Frontier* (New York: Arno Press and the New York Times, 1971), 414–20. Elsewhere, Professor Taylor offered several generalizations about Native Americans and Blacks including a statement in 1868 from Indian Territory where Chickasaw officials complained about 'former black soldiers' who resided 'illegally in the western section of their nation.' He further pointed out that most African Americans residing in 1870 Indian Territory were formerly enslaved by the various tribes who took an array of approaches to them ranging full participation within the Seminole and Creek nations to having no rights in the Chickashaw and Choctaw nations. Taylor, *In Search of a Racial Frontier*, 117–2. Beyond that, despite a chapter treating buffalo soldiers, this tittle added nothing specific about views held by Native Americans relative to Black regulars, or the corollary of perceptions of the Black soldiers and the Native Americans whom they alternated engaged in battle or conversely helped protect from white settler encroachment.
27 For example, William Loren Katz, *Black Indians: A Hidden Heritage* (New York: Atheneum, 1986), 176, postulated: 'there was something very different between the two dark races [Native Americans

The contention made by some authors that Black regulars received inferior equipment and mounts, had limited basis in fact. For example, as illustrated here, members of Company F, Twenty-Fourth Infantry at Fort Bayard, New Mexico received cutting-edge experimental field equipment designed by First Lieutenant Charles Dodge, Jr. (Courtesy National Archives and Records Administration)

Other Myths or Misconceptions

Besides his take on the term Buffalo Soldiers, Leckie faced other challenges from historians who published after his first book. One of the objections arose to refute the oft-recited statements that Blacks received inferior horses, castoff equipment and the worse postings as compared to white troops. These statements ran contrary to a body of evidence.[28] Further, the charge that

---

and African Americans] than one either of them had with whites.' The author, however, provided scant evidence to support his sweeping statement.

28 Dobak and Phillips, *Black Regulars*, xvi-xvii, and 106–13. Among references that collaborate the authors' repudiations is James S. Hutchins, 'Collectors' Field Book: The Dodge Blanket Roll Support,' *Military Collector & Historian* 20 (Fall 1968): 92–95. *AN&J*, March 14, 1874, 48, and August 8, 1874, 820 as well as the *Dallas Daily Herald*, November 25, 1874, all noted that some Black cavalrymen and even infantrymen received the newly adopted Springfield .45-55 calibre 'trapdoor' carbine in advance of the much vaunted Seventh Cavalry, as well as in some instances received experimental Springfield rifle-carbines as captured by none other than Frederic Remington's work as depicted in Langellier, *Scouting with the Buffalo Soldiers*, 250, and accompanied by a photograph of Troop K. Tenth Cavalry at the Fort Thomas, Arizona target range. They also received the new Colt .45 single-action revolvers prior to or at approximately the same time as white cavalrymen. Finally, posts in Texas including Fort Davis, were be provided with priority with receipt of the new uniform in 1872 as treated in John P. Langellier, *Army Blue: The Uniform of Uncle of Uncle Sam's Regulars, 1848–1873* (Atlglen, PA: Schiffer

Blacks more often served at remote, undesirable duty stations because of race, lacked credibility. In this case, among other things, Department of Missouri commander, Brigadier General John Pope, expressed concern that two regiments, one Black and one white (the Ninth Cavalry and Fifteenth Infantry) had, 'for several years been almost continuously in the field, the greater part of the time in harassing and wearisome pursuit of small bands of Indians who infest the mountains of southern New Mexico and Mexico and are, therefore, much run down in every way. They need rest and recuperation.'[29]

Furthermore, data exists that Blacks and whites both drew less than sterling assignments. Comparisons of regimental rosters regularly indicate Black troops rotating to sites previously garrisoned by white soldiers and vice versa, indicative of little preferential or punitive treatment. Nonetheless, overall, Black troops tended to be shuttled around the frontier as needed at remote places of conflict with at least as much, if not more, regularity than whites during the Indian Wars and were among the first to be deployed to Cuba in 1898.

Even if some early assignments were hardships, the fact that they served in regions of extreme conflict with Native Americans, outlaws and Mexican border disturbances, meant that regardless of ethnicity, in a goodly number of cases, deployments depended on tactical or strategic requirements. Moreover, between the 1890s and into the early twentieth century, Black regulars would be sent to urban sites such as Minneapolis, Salt Lake City and San Francisco, as well as to Hawaii, upstate New York, the Pacific Northwest, Vermont and Virginia, all of which provided more access to the comforts of better facilities and to local communities, but admittedly these posting in the main occurred only after several decades of deployments typically removed from extensive contact with towns dominated by whites.

Also, an erroneous perception that Black soldiers evolved into an elite force and participated in 85 percent or more of every engagement fought by the US Army between the end of the Civil War and 1893, ran contrary to reality.[30] Dobak and Phillips offered strong evidence that demonstrated this contention's flaws.[31] So, too, Schubert's statistics overturned 'the idea that the buffalo-soldier combat record surpassed that of other units.' His careful calculations disclosed Black regulars participated in approximately 13 percent of the engagements fought in the West after the Civil War through the early 1890s, which he pronounced 'just about proportional to their numerical presence in the Army.' Based on this analysis, clearly Black soldiers, while in the field, did not bear more than their share of frontier fighting.[32]

Military Books, 1998), 253 and 274, n232, and *More Army Blue, The Uniform of Uncle of Uncle Sam's Regulars, 1874–1887* (Atlglen, PA: Schiffer Military Books, 2001), 108.

29 *ARSW, 1881*, I, 124–25.
30 Comments from Anthony Powell as set forth in, 'Conflict of Conscience: Buffalo Soldiers,' youtube.com/watch?v=FFHCMjLmK9s&t=15s. He made a similar comment during his September 29, 2016, Smithsonian Institution's National Postal Museum address, youtube.com/watch?v=pBofRUraUMY&list=PLdvULuYSGxbDxaIzwCVBBC8je7Bq6_Z3u.
31 Dobak and Phillips, *Black Regulars*, xvii and 90–105.
32 Selected from Frank N. Schubert, 'The Myth of the Buffalo Soldiers,' *The Black Past*, posted on December 19, 2009, blackpast.org/african-american-history/myth-buffalo-soldiers, an abbreviated version of his article from *Army Historian* and without endnotes.

During the 1880s, Troop K, Tenth Cavalry practiced their marksmanship at Fort Thomas, Arizona's target range. They all fire experimental Springfield .45 calibre rifle-carbines as one more example of Buffalo Soldiers receiving arms and other military issuance on par with white troops. (Courtesy John Langellier)

Faithful Service

In fact, as an early study of the subject found 'with the exception of the desertion and a few other aspects, such as the lack of drunkenness,' the regiments consisting of African American enlisted men 'must be regarded as being more like white units than different from them.'[33] Even so, an argument could be made that while much of the narrative related to Black soldiers paralleled white soldiers, their lot differed in many ways. For instance, in contrast to white troops, Black regulars tended to remain more faithful to their enlistment oaths than whites and for the most part, boasted a worthy record of lower desertions and higher incidences of reenlistment.[34] One author even outlined some of the reasons why such a significant accomplishment existed among the Black regulars.[35] Then, there was the practical side of the matter. In a vast number of

---

33 Thompson, 'The Negro Regiments of the US Army, 1866–1900,' 96. As to the subject of alcoholism among Black troops Miles V. Lynx, *The Black Troopers; or, The Daring Heroism of the Negro Soldiers in the Spanish-American War* (Jackson, TN: M.V. Lynx Publishing House, 1899), 18–19, offers some useful statistics baring out a more positive record during a number of years related to the abuse of liquor and health consequences.
34 Dobak and Phillips, *Black Regulars*, 62–64. The groundbreaking research by Thompson, 'The Negro Regiments,' 9, included the statement: 'an amazingly small percentage of Negro soldiers deserted. Their desertion rate is even more surprising when compared to the amazingly high desertion rate among white troops.' One individual, however, made an antithetical blanket statement without offering accurate figures to substantiate his theory that in the first 20 years or so after the Civil War Blacks 'deserted just as much as whites did. Powell, 'Conflict of Conscience.' Utley, *Frontier Regulars*, 26, underscored the higher reenlistments.
35 McChristian, *Regular Army O!*, 422–24. A contemporary newspaper account provided additional credence observing the Black soldier 'in the regular army sticks to his colors in a way that calls forth the praise of his officers. While 27 per cent of the men of the light [artillery] batteries desert, only 2

Myths, Memorials and Meanings 279

On March 3, 1977, Fort Huachuca's centennial celebrations included the dedication of a heroic-sized bronze Buffalo Soldier statue keynoted by guest speaker Master Sergeant John Campbell, a twenty-seven-year US Army veteran. This was the first monument of many to pay tribute to the African American soldier on the frontier. (Courtesy Fort Huachuca Museum)

postings in the West, Blacks made up only a minute fraction of the population, thereby making it difficult to merge with local civilians and easily hide. Regardless, Black soldiers looked on the military as a profession rather than a mere job of work. Generally, they took pride in service, which much of the Black civilian populace supposedly saw as a well-respected endeavor, in contrast to a general disdain, extent among the white community towards white soldiers.[36]

Monuments and Memorials

Even though these men's records on the frontier may not have been all that extraordinary, and despite some writers who contended the Black soldiers' story had been forgotten, unknown, or unsung, an array of efforts to recognize their history dated back to the late 1800s and continued for decades to come.[37] Frederic Remington's extensive works of art, Buffalo Bill's inclusion of veterans in his Congress of Rough Riders, late 1890s documentary motion picture footage by Thomas Edison, the pre-First World War silent feature *Trooper of Troop K* that portrayed a fictional character gaining manly virtues during the Punitive Expedition and a number of other graphic and written works, often aimed at a Black audience, all existed prior to William Leckie's *Buffalo Soldiers*.[38] With the release of his book, however, scores of other publications followed. Furthermore, larger than life bronzes, such as one of the first to be erected in the 1977 at Fort Huachuca, Arizona, appeared, followed by many other memorials across the nation. Perhaps the most notable of these, unveiled to much fanfare on July 25, 1992, at Fort Leavenworth, would be 'accompanied by a veritable explosion of buffalo soldier commemorations including museum displays, documentaries, newspaper and journal articles and reenactment societies.'[39]

Not everyone embraced the heroic story as the issue of a US postage stamp in 1994, based on the Fort Leavenworth memorial, indicated. One provocative article by Vernon Bellecourt rejected the legend that Black soldiers and Native Americans of old, shared a mutual 'endearment or respect.' Bellencourt's take on the matter was rather than being seen as worthy foes, his ancestors only referred to 'these marauding murderous cavalry units' as buffalo soldiers because of 'their dark skin and texture of their hair.'[40]

---

    per cent of the colored soldiers abandoned their duty. The Twenty-Fourth Infantry, colored, has the champion record of only 1 per cent.' According to one newspaper, 'while on the frontier' they had the reputation of 'being 'tough citizens,' but very hardy soldiers.' *Great Falls Leader*, December 6, 1889.

36 Utley, *Frontier Regulars*, 22.
37 There was a time that this view held weight. It can be argued during the early through mid-twentieth century 'the black soldier's story slipped from the mainstream of American History.' Dobak and Phillips, *Black Regulars*, xviii.
38 Langellier, *Fighting for Uncle Sam*, 192–202, provided a brief overview of Buffalo Soldiers in popular culture.
39 Leiker 'Black Soldiers at Fort Hays:' 3.
40 Vernon Bellecourt, 'The Glorification of Buffalo Soldiers raises racial divisions between blacks, Indians,' *Indian Country Today*, May 4, 1994. For other examples from the period obtain Cornel Pewewardy, 'Buffalo Soldiers Were Federal Hired Guns' *Indian Country Today*, June 23–30, 1997, and for the issue of the stamp by the United States Postal Service see 'US Issues Buffalo Soldiers April 22,' *Stamp Collector*, March 26, 1994. As an aside, the accompanying the US Postal Services' Buffalo Soldier StampFolio 1994 text touted: 'Buffalo Soldiers wore the name with pride and the 10th Cavalry Regiment adopted the buffalo symbol for its regimental crest' much to the later

There are more than two dozen sites that stretch from the Atlantic Seaboard to Hawaii where Buffalo Soldiers once served and now are held in trust by the National Park Service. At the Presidio of San Francisco, California, among the poignant reminders of the presence of Black soldiers, are rows of headstones marking their final resting places. (Courtesy National Park Service)

Conclusions

To condemn or condone the actions of the Black regulars would not only constitute gross presentism but also, ignore the main issue of understanding why these men served a nation that typically failed to treat them with their due. In many ways, the so-called Buffalo Soldiers carried all the anxieties and insecurities of the dominant society that once enslaved them and continued to suppress Black Americans under the yoke of white supremacy, a manifestation of the concept of whiteness once used to justify enslavement.

During westward expansion, adherence to many of the tenants adopted from their former master class meant acceptance of oppressing other people of color. As volunteers in the military, Black regulars obeyed their orders, which at times resulted in the give and take of death against

chagrin of the contract historical consultant, John P. Langellier, who provided the folio's narrative. Finally, another source revealing the complexity of Black soldier versus the Native Americans can be viewed at www.seattletimes.com/life/buffalo-soldiers-played-complicated-and-controversial-role-in-westward-expansion.

Native Americans, while on other occasions they protected the reservations of their sometimes foes, from encroachment by white interlopers. Undeniable instruments of expansion, during the seizure of the Trans-Mississippi West, some Black soldiers of the late 1800s and early 1900s, eventually voiced opposition to US imperial ambitions, but not until much later in their existence when sent to quell unrest in the Philippines. A few echoed the climate of the times, including those who enjoyed higher educational levels than the men who joined the military in the decades immediately after the original cadre of illiterate enslaved recruits. In fact, service in the Philippines revealed the complexity and perhaps the growing awareness of cultural differences and their resultant clashes. By the end of the Victorian era, many Black soldiers served the country, yet among them were those who questioned a conflict that they did not support and that ran contrary to their self-interest, as well as their nation's interests.

Returning to the first generation of Black troops, they often offered prime examples of 'up from slavery' narratives. Many embodied Frederick Douglass's prediction: 'Once let the black man get upon his person the brass letters US, let him get an eagle on his button and a musket on his shoulder and bullets in his pocket and there is no power on earth or under the earth which can deny that he has earned the right of citizenship in the United States.'[41] Likewise, scores of them reflected Douglass's self-realization: 'I was nothing before. I was a man now.' They and those who followed, by their actions persisted in Douglass's demand: 'You're going to look me in the eye and see my humanity.'

Not content to accept slights or subservient treatment, Black soldiers sometimes expressed righteous discontent, occasionally in violent ways. They developed regimental pride or overall pride in military service. Not a few, who believed themselves representative of Black Americans, determined to demonstrate their capabilities to their military superiors and the United States, as a whole whose uniform they wore. At times, when they faced prejudice, solidarity developed, which heightened *esprit de corps* and enhanced morale.

Further, as, Schubert shared, 'the buffalo soldier story' evolved as a blend of 'history with heritage; fact with myth' that gradually 'entered the mainstream with … other iconic western sagas.' By the early twenty-first century, he judged: 'it's now also safe to say, not only is this not just black history, but American history … beyond that we can conclude, it's not just American history, but it's American mythology.'[42] Most significantly, Schubert observed the service record of Blacks in the US Army between 1866 through 1916 represented 'a building block in an ongoing struggle to achieve equality.'[43] Of greatest importance, as General Colin Powell acknowledged at the Fort Leavenworth monument dedication, he and others stood on the shoulders of this vanguard of US Army regulars. For these reasons, their story enriched the national narrative. More remarkably still, the sacrifices of the Buffalo Soldiers, which at times

---

41   Frederick Douglass Speech, 'Should the Negro Enlist in the Union Army?', National Hall, Philadelphia (July 6, 1863); published in *Douglass' Monthly*, August 18, 1863.
42   Schubert, 'Buffalo Soldier Contributions.' Elsewhere, Schubert went beyond dissecting the myths and legends. He pondered why in the absence of data, or even despite the contrary evidence, had the myth taken hold? Further, he asked, 'how much of the myth is a multi-cultural fantasy, an attempt to see the past through a present-day prism? Is it patronizing to give these soldiers more credit than they deserve? Why is a story that has been told repeatedly from multiple perspectives over the last two generations widely labeled 'untold'? The myth raises many questions that still await answers.' Schubert, 'The Myth of the Buffalo Soldiers.'
43   Schubert, 'Remembering the Buffalo Soldiers,' 153.

came at the cost of life to purchase a better future, usually entailed more work than glory as they did their duty for a nation that often scorned them.

Lastly, parallel to their white counterparts, yet differing in many ways, the record of the Black regulars lends credence to Michael Tate's well-crafted thesis of the 'multipurpose army' as set forth in his *The Frontier Army in the Settlement of the West*. Furthermore, studying Black soldiers' experiences after the Civil War to the eve of the First World War, reinforces the specific focus set forth by Garna L. Christian in *Black Soldiers in Jim Crow Texas*, as well as reflects the complex insights found in James Leiker's *Racial Borders*, along with Gerald Horne's broad based contextual views in *Black and Brown*. Conversely, the inclusion of Black regulars as a colonial force as part of a school of thought that adheres to the concept of settler colonialism, is a less supportable contention on several levels. Thus, William Leckie's call for 'further research' that would 'illuminate this question in the future' remains a worthy call to action.[44]

---

44 Leckie and Leckie, *Buffalo Soldiers*, 26–27 and 292.

Bibliography

Institutions and Repositories

Alaska State Library, Juneau, Alaska.
American Heritage Center, University of Wyoming, Laramie, Wyoming.
Arizona Historical Society, Tucson, Arizona.
Cherokee regional Library System, Chickamauga, Georgia
Chickamauga and Chattanooga National Military Park, Georgia and Tennessee
Colorado Mental Health Institute of Pueblo, Colorado.
Denver Public Library, Blair-Caldwell African American Research Library and Western History Collections, Denver, Colorado.
Thomas C. Donnelly Library, Highlands University, Las Vegas, New Mexico.
Fort Bayard Museum
Fort Concho National Historic Landmark, San Angelo, Texas.
Fort Davis National Historic Site, Fort Davis, Texas.
Fort Huachuca Museum, Fort Huachuca, Arizona.
Fort Larned National Historic Site, Larned, Kansas.
Fort Robinson Museum, Crawford, Nebraska.
Fort Sill Museum, Fort Sill, Oklahoma.
Fort Union National Monument, Watrous, New Mexico.
Fort Verde State Historic Park, Camp Verde, Arizona.
Historical Museum at Fort Missoula, Missoula, Montana.
History Nebraska, Lincoln, Nebraska.
Huntington Library, San Marino, California.
Library of Congress, Washington, DC.
McCracken Research Library, Buffalo Bill Center of the West, Cody, Wyoming.
Maureen and Mike Mansfield Library at the University of Montana, Missoula, Montana.
Missouri Historical Society Library & Research Center, St. Louis, Missouri.
Missouri Valley Special Collections Kansas City Public Library, Kansas City, Missouri.
Montana Historical Society, Helena, Montana.
Monterey Public Library California History Room & Archives, Monterey, California
Mountain Empire Historical Society, Campo, California.
Museum of North Idaho, Coeur d'Alene, Idaho
National Archives and Records Administration, Riverside, California and Washington, DC.
New Mexico History Museum, Santa Fe, New Mexico.

Sequoia National Park, Archives and Library, Sequoia, California.
Three Rivers Historical Society, Three Rivers, California.
Tulare County Library, Tulare, California.
United States Army Heritage and Education Center, Carlisle Barracks, Pennsylvania.
United States Army Military Academy Library, West Point, New York.
University of Arizona Library, Special Collections, Tucson, Arizona.
University of Texas Library at El Paso, Texas.
Walton County Historical Society, Monroe, Georgia.
Yosemite National Park, Archies, Yosemite, California.
Charles Young Collection, National Afro-American Museum and Cultural Center, Wilberforce, Ohio.

Archival and Manuscript Materials

Almy, Mary E 'A Fitful Journey.' Transcript 1891 Diary from Fort Washakie, WY to Caspar, WY.' Coll. 3596, American Heritage Center, University of Wyoming, Laramie.
Arizona State Board of Health, Bureau of Vital Statics Original Certificate of Death State Index No. 152.
Buffalo Soldier Collection, Collection YOSE 6901/YOSE 120175, Box 1 Rosters and Biographical Files; Box 2 Biographical Files Continued, Yosemite National Park Museum Archives, El Portal, CA.
Federal Writers' Project: Slave Narrative Project, 16, Texas, Pt. 1.
Grierson, Benjamin H. Papers. Illinois State Historical Society, Springfield.
Harrison, James. Scrapbook and Album. Author's Collection.
Lee, R.V. Official State of Military Service and Death of Louis A. Carter Service Number O 4358, Louis A. Carter File, Fort Huachuca Museum, Arizona.
MC46, Fort Assiniboine Records, Montana Historical Society, Helena.
Neal, William, Collection 1849–1936. MS 579. Arizona Historical Society Library, Tucson.
The Negro In the Military Service of the United States, 1639–1886, Microfilm M858, NARA.
Nicholas, Sergeant W. M. Troop I, Ninth US Cavalry, written in Santa Rosa, California, January 1945, Charles Young Collection, National Afro-American Museum and Cultural Center, Wilberforce, OH.
Papers of the Alexander Family of Helena, AK, HM 28885–28913, Huntington Library, San Marino, CA.
Pershing, John J. 'Memoirs.' unpublished draft, Library of Congress, 1937.
RG 15 Records of the Veterans Administration, pension application file SO 1032593, Cathay Williams. NARA.
RG 21 Records of District Courts of the United States Agency or Division: US Territorial Court for the First Judicial District of Arizona. Series: Criminal Case Files, 1882–1912 Folder Title: C–1114 Philip Lashley Box Number: 70. National Archives at Riverside, CA. NARA.
RG 94 Records of the AGO. NARA.
RG 98, Records of US Army Commands. NARA.
RG 391 Miscellaneous Records, 10th Cavalry, National Archives and Records Administration)

RG 393 Returns From Regular Army Cavalry Regiments, 1833–1916, NARA.
RG 393 Returns From US Military Posts, 1800–1916. NARA.
RG 393 Records of US Army Continental Commands 1821–1920. NARA.
RG 395 Records of US Operations During the Philippine Insurrection 1898–1900. NARA.
Remington, Frederic. 'Journal of a Trip across the Continent Through Arizona and Sonora Old Mexico.' Topeka: Kansas State Historical Society.
'Safe out of Indian Country and very glad of it.' Diary of W.C. Irvine, Carlisle, Cumberland County, Pennsylvania, May 23rd, 1870, Box 3, Folder 1, Coll. 126, John T. Williams Papers, American Heritage Center, University of Wyoming, Laramie.
10th Census 1880 Trinidad, Las Animas County, Colorado. Enumeration District No.66.
12th Census 1900 2nd Precinct, Colorado State Insane Asylum, Pueblo County, Colorado, Enumeration District158, Sheet No. 4.
13th Census 1910 2nd Precinct, Colorado State Insane Asylum, Pueblo County, Colorado, Enumeration District 158, Sheet No. 3b.

Government Documents

Annual Reports of the Department of the Interior, for the Fiscal Year Ended June 30, 1903, 3, pt. 1. Washington, DC: US Government Printing Office, 1903.
*Annual Reports of the Secretary of War, 1866–1906.*Washington, DC: US Government Printing Office, 1866–1906.
Billings, John S. Circular No. 8 *A Report on the Hygiene of the United States Army, with Descriptions of Military Posts*. Washington, DC: US Government Printing Office, 1875.
Cases Argued and Decided in the Supreme Court of the United States, October Terms, 1890, 1891, in 134, 140, 141, 142, US Book 35, Lawyer's Edition. Rochester, NY: The Lawyer's Co-operative Publication Company, 1901.
Circular No. 2, February 11, 1892. Adjutant General's Office, Washington, DC.
Circular No. 4 *A Report on Barracks and Hospitals: with Descriptions of Military Posts War*
Congressional Record. Thirty-Eighth Cong. 1st Sess. Ch. 237. Washington, DC: US Government Publishing Office, 1864.
Department, Surgeon General's Office, Washington, Dec. 5, 1870. Washington, DC: Government Printing Office, 1870.
Ex. Doc. No. 92, 47th Cong. 1st sess. House Report. Washington, DC: US Government Publishing Office, 1882.
General Court Martial Orders, Headquarters of the Army, 1867–1886.
General Orders, AGO, Washington, DC and Courts Martials, 1881–1884.
Holabird, Samuel B. *Some Considerations Respecting Desertion in the Army, Ordnance Notes No. 232*. Washington, DC: US Government Printing Office, 1882.
Report of the Acting Superintendent of the Yosemite National Park to the Secretary of the Interior 1899.
Richardson, William A. Ed. *Supplement to the Revised Statutes of The United States I Second Edition Revised and Continued. 1874–1891*. Washington, DC: US Government Printing Office, 1891.

Senate Executive Documents, 56th Cong., 1st Sess. *Report of the Commission Appointed by the President to Investigate the Conduct of the War Department in the War With Spain*. Washington, DC: US Government Printing Office, 1899. Vol. I.

Senate Executive Documents, 56th Cong., 1st Sess. *Report of the Commission Appointed by the President to Investigate the Conduct of the War Department in the War With Spain* Washington, DC: US Government Printing Office, 1900. Vol. VIII.

Special Orders No. 91, Headquarters of the Army, AGO, April 18, 1892.

Special Orders No. 101, Headquarters of the Army, AGO, April 29, 1892. US Army. *Department of Arizona: Annual Report*, 1886.

The War of the Rebellion: A Compilation of the Official Records of the Union and Confederat Armies. Washington, DC: US Government. Printing Office, 1880–1901) ser. 3, vol. 4.

US Army Register, 1866–1920. Washington, DC: United States Army, 1866–1920.

Published Works

Adams, Kevin. *Class and Race in the Frontier Army Military Life in the West, 1870–1890*. Norman: University of Oklahoma Press, 2009.

Alexander, Charles. *The Battles and Victories of Allen Allensworth*. Boston: Sherman, French, and Co., 1914.

Aleshire, William A. *A Buffalo Soldier's Story: Medal of Honor Recipient Sergeant Thomas Boyne and His Comrades 1864 to 1889*. Westminster, MD: Heritage Books, 2004.

Alshuler, Constance Wynn. *Cavalry Yellow & Infantry Blue: Army Officers in Arizona Between 1851 and 1886*. Tucson: Arizona Historical Society, 1991.

Anderson, Robert B. *From Slavery to Affluence: Memoirs of Robert Anderson, Ex-Slave*. Hemingford, NE: Hemingford Ledger, 1927.

Andrews, George. 'The Twenty-Fifth Regiment of Infantry.' *Journal of the Military Service Institution of the United States* (January 1892): 224–26.

Appiah, Anthony and Henry Louis Gates, Jr. Eds., *Africana: The Encyclopedia of the African and African American Experience* 2d Edition. Oxford: Oxford University Press, 2005.

Arkles, Gabriel. 'No One Is Disposable: Going Beyond the Trans Military Inclusion Debate.' *Seattle Journal for Social Justice* 13 no. 2 (2014): 459–514.

Armes, George. *Ups and Downs of An Army Officer*. Washington, DC: privately printed, 1900.

Baker, Edward L. *Roster Non-Commissioned Officers of the Tenth US Cavalry with Some Regimental Reminiscences, Appendices, Etc., Connected with the Early History of the Regiment*. St. Paul, MN: Kennedy Printing Co.1897.

Ball, Larry D. *Ambush at Bloody Run: The Wham Payroll Robbery of 1889: A Story of Politics, Religion, Race and Banditry in Arizona*. Tucson: Arizona Historical Society, 2000.

Barnett, Louise. *Ungentlemanly Acts: The Army's Notorious Incest Trial*. New York: Hill and Wang, 2000.

Bateman, Cephas C. 'A Group of Army Authors,' *The Californian* 4 (October, 1893): 692–93.

Baumler, Mark F. *The Archeology of Faraway Ranch Arizona: Prehistoric, Historic and 20th Century*. Tucson: Western Archeological and Conservation Center, 1984.

Bearss, Edwin C. *Proposed Klondike Gold Rush National Historical Park Historic Resource Study.* Washington, DC: Office of History and Historical Architecture, Eastern Service Center, National Park Service, 1970.

Beasley, Delilah L. *The Negro Trail Blazers of California: a Compilation of Records From the California Archives In the Bancroft Library At the University of California, In Berkeley, And From the Diaries, Old Papers And Conversations of Old Pioneers In the State of California: It Is a True Record of Facts, As They Pertain to the History of the Pioneer And Present Day Negroes of California.* Los Angeles: Times Mirror Print. and Binding House, 1919.

Berlin, Ira, Joseph P. Reidy and Leslie S. Rowland, Eds. *Freedom: a Documentary History of Emancipation, 1861–1867* Series II *The Black Military Experience.* Cambridge: Cambridge University Press, 1982.

Bierschwale, Margaret. *Fort McKavett, Texas Post of the San Saba.* Salado, TX: Anson Jones Press, 1966.

Bigelow, Donald Nevius. *William Conant Church & The Army and Navy Journal.* New York: Columbia University Press, 1952.

Bigelow, John, Jr., *On the Bloody Trail of Geronimo.* Tucson: Westernlore Press, 1986.

———. *Reminiscence of the Santiago Campaign.* New York and London: Harper & Brothers, 1899.

Billington, Monroe Lee. *New Mexico's Buffalo Soldiers, 1866–1900.* Niwot: University Press of Colorado, 1991.

Bivins, Horace W. 'The Battle of San Juan Hill by a Gunner of the 10th Cavalry.' *Southern Workman* 27 (November 1898), 219–20.

Black, Lowell D and Sara H. Black. *An Officer and A Gentleman: The Military Career of Lieutenant Henry O. Flipper.* Dayton. OH: The Lora Company, Ltd., 1985.

Blanton, DeAnne. 'Cathay Williams: Black Woman Soldier 1866–1868.' *Minerva* 10 nos. 3 (Fall-Winter 1992): 1–12.

Boatner, Mark Mayo III. *The Civil War Dictionary.* New York: David McKay Company, Inc., 1959.

Bogue, Alan G., Ed., *The West of the American People.* Itasca: F.E. Peacock 1970.

Bonsal, Stephen, 'The Negro Soldiers in War and Peace.' *North American Review* 185 (June 7, 1907): 321–27.

Britten, Sophie. *Pioneers in Paradise: A Historical and Biographical Record of Early Days in Three Rivers, California 1850 to 1950s.* Indianapolis: Dear Ear Press, 2013.

Brooks, Charles H. *The Official History and Manual of the Grand United Order of Odd Fellows in America.* Freeport, NY: Books for Libraries Press, 1902.

Brown, Scot. 'White Backlash and the Aftermath of Fagen's Rebellion: The Fates of Three African-American Soldiers in the Philippines, 1901–1902.' *Contributions in Black Studies: A Journal of African and Afro-American Studies* 13 (1995): 165–73.

Barron, R. M. Ed. *Court of Inquiry: Lieutenant Colonel N.A.M. Dudley Fort Stanton, New Mexico May-June-July 1879.* Edina, MN: Beaver's Pond Press, Inc., 2003. 2 vols.

Brown, William L. III. *A Pictorial History of Enlisted Men's Barracks of the US Army, 1861- 1895.* Harpers Ferry: WV: National Park Service, 1984.

Buecker, Thomas R. 'One Soldier's Service: Caleb Benson in the Ninth and Tenth Cavalry, 1875–1908.' *Nebraska History* 74 no. 2 (Summer 1993): 54–62.

Buell, Evangeline Canonizado. *Twenty-five Chickens and a Pig for a Bride: Growing Up in a Filipino Immigrant Family.* San Francisco: T'Boli Publishing and Distributor, 2006.

Burton, Art T. *Black, Red and Deadly: Black and Indian Gunfighters of Indian Territory, 1870-1907.* Austin: Eakin Press, 1991.

Burton, Harley True. 'History of the JA Ranch.' *Southwestern Historical* Quarterly 31 (October 1927): 107–08.

Caperton Thomas J. and LoRheda Fry. *Old Army Cookbook 1865–1900.* Santa Fe: Museum of New Mexico, 1974.

Carlson, Gayle F. Et Al. *The Archeology of an 1887 Adobe Barracks (25DW51-B56) At Fort Robinson, Nebraska: Report on the 2000 Investigations.* Lincoln, NE: Nebraska State Historical Society, 2001.

Carlson, Paul H. *The Buffalo Soldier Tragedy of 1877.* College Station: Texas A&M University Press, 2003.

Carroll, Charles and Lynne Sebastian. Eds. *Fort Craig: The United States Posts on the Camino Real.* Socorro: US Department of Interior Bureau of Land Management, 2000.

Carroll. John M. Comp. *The Black Military Experience in the American West.* New York: Liveright, 1971.

Carsten, James. *Another Custer: Bethel Moore Custer and the Buffalo Soldiers, 1867–1887.* n.p. 2013.

Cashin, Herschel V., Charles Alexander, William T. Anderson, Arthur M. Brown and Horace W. Bivins. *Under Fire with the Tenth US Cavalry: A Brief, Comprehensive Review of the Negro's Participation in the Wars of the United States.* New York and London: F.T. Neely, 1899.

Christian, Garna L. *Black Soldiers in Jim Crow Texas, 1899–1917.* College Station: Texas A&M University Press, 1995.

Clary, David A. *A Life Which is Gregarious in the Extreme: A History of Furniture in Barracks and Guardhouses of the United States Army, 1880–1945.* Harpers Ferry: WV: National Park Service, 1983.

——. *These Relics of Barbarism: A History of Furniture in Barracks and Guardhouses of the United States Army, 1800–1880.* Harpers Ferry: WV: National Park Service, 1982.

Clark, Michael J. *US Army Pioneers; Black Soldiers in Nineteenth-century Utah.* Salt Lake City: Fort Douglas Military Museum, 1988.

Clendenen, Clarence C. *Blood on the Border: The United States Army and the Mexican Irregulars.* New York: The Macmillan Company, 1969.

Coffman, Edward M. *The Old Army: A Portrait of the American Army in Peacetime, 1784–1898.* New York: Oxford University Press, 1986.

Coleman, Ronald G. 'The Buffalo Soldiers: Guardians of the Unitah Frontier 1886–1901.' *Utah Historical Quarterly* 47 no. 4 (Fall 1979): 344–52.

Cool, Paul. *Salt Warriors: Insurgency on the Rio Grande.* College Station: Texas A&M University Press, 2008.

Corbusier, William T. *Verde to San Carlos: Recollections of a famous Army Surgeon and His Observant Family on the Western Frontier 1869–1886.* Tucson: Dale Stuart King, Publisher, 1971.

Cosmas, Graham A. *An Army for Empire: The United States Army in the Spanish-American War.* Columbia: University of Missouri Press, 1971.

Cullum, George W. *Biographical Register of the Officers and Graduates of the US Military Academy at West Point, NY, from its establishment, in 1802, to 1890; with the Early History of the United States Military Academy.* II Boston, Houghton, Mifflin and Company, 1891; III: 1901, IV, 1910, V 1920, VI a, 1920, VI b, 1930.

Culver, Garry Eugene. 'Notes on a Little Known Region in North-Western Montana.' *Transactions of the Wisconsin Academy of Sciences, Arts and Letters* 8 (1892): 187–205.

Cunningham, Roger D. 'African-American Divisional Shoulder Sleeve Insignia During World War I,' *Miliary Collector & Historian* 56 (Winter 2004): 269–71.

———. '"The Loving Touch": Walter H. Loving Five Decades of Military Music.' *Army History: The Professional Bulletin of Army History* 64 (Summer 2007): 4–25.

Cusic, Don. *The Trials of Henry O. Flipper, First Black Graduate of West Point*. Jefferson, NC: McFarland & Co., 2009.

Custer, Elizabeth Bacon. *Tenting on the Plains or General Custer in Kansas and Texas*. New York: Charles L. Webster & Company, 1887.

Dinges, Bruce J. 'The San Angelo Riot of 1881: The Army, Race Relations and Settlement on the Texas Frontier.' *Journal of the West* 41 no. 3 (Summer 2002): 35–45.

Dobak, William A. *Freedom by the Sword: The US Colored Troops, 1862–1867*. Washington, DC: Center of Military History United States Army, 2011.

——— and Thomas D. Phillips, *The Black Regulars, 1866–1898*. Norman: University of Oklahoma Press, 2001.

Dobak, William A. and Thomas D. Phillips. *The Black Regulars, 1866–1898*. Norman: University of Oklahoma Press, 2001.

Dollar, Charles M. 'Putting the Army on Wheels: The Story of the Twenty-Fifth Infantry Bicycle Corps.' *Prologue* 17 no. 1 (Spring 1985): 7–24.

Donaldson, Gary. *The History of African-Americans in the Military, Double V*. Malabar, FL: Krieger Pub. Co., 1991.

Downey, Fairfax. *The Buffalo Soldiers in the Indian Wars*. New York: McGraw-Hill Book Company, 1969.

———. *Indian-Fighting Army*. New York: Charles Scribner's Sons, 1941.

Dunbar-Ortiz, Roxanne. *An Indigenous Peoples' History of the United States*. Boston: Beacon, 2014.

Egan, Timothy. *The Big Burn: Theodore Roosevelt and the Fire that Saved America*. New York: Mariner Books, 2009.

Egerton, Douglas R. *Thunder At The Gates: The Black Civil War Regiments That Redeemed America*. New York: Basic Books, 2016.

Eisenhower, John S.D. *Intervention! The United States and the Mexican Revolution 1913–1917*. New York: W.W. Norton & Company, 1995.

Eldredge, Ward. *In the Summer of 1903: Colonel Charles Young and the Buffalo Soldiers in Sequoia National Park*. Three Rivers, CA: Sequoia Natural History Association, 2003.

Emerson, William K. *Marksmanship in the US Army: A History of Medals, Shooting Programs, and Training*. Norman: University of Oklahoma Press, 2004.

———. *US Army Soldiers and Their Chevrons: An Illustrated Catalog and History from the Revolutionary War to Present*. San Jose: R. James Bender Publishing, 2013.

Enloe, Cynthia H. *Ethnic Soldiers: State Security in Divided*. Athens, GA: University of Georgia Press, 1980.

Eppinga, Jane. *Henry Ossian Flipper: West Points' First Black Graduate*. Fort Worth, TX: Wild Horse Press, 2015.

Evans, E. Raymond. *Camp Thomas: Chickamauga-Chattanooga National Military Park During The Spanish-American War*. Chattanooga, TN: E. Evans, 2008.

Experience of Troop A, 10th Cavalry On the 'STAKED PLAINS', Texas July 1877. Fort Davis, TX: Chas. Krull, Post Printer, 1877.

Finley, James P. 'The Buffalo Soldiers at Fort Huachuca.' *Huachuca Illustrated: A Magazine of the Fort Huachuca Museum* 1 (1993): 42–77; 2 (1996): 1–4, 9–19.

Fitzpatrick, Jim. *The Bicycle In Wartime: An Illustrated History.* Washington, DC: Brassey's Inc., 1998.

Fletcher, Marvin E. *American's First Black General: Benjamin O. Davis, Sr., 1880–1970.* Lawrence: University Press of Kansas, 1989.

——. 'The Black Bicycle Corps.' *Arizona and the West* 16 no. 3 (Autumn 1974): 219–32.

——. *The Black Soldier and Office in the United States Army, 1891–1917.* Columbia: University of Missouri Press, 1974.

Foner, Eric. *Forever Free: The Story of Emancipation and Reconstruction: America's Unfinished Revolution.* New York: Alfred A. Knopf, 2005.

Foner, Jack D. *Blacks and the Military in American History: A New Perspective.* New York: Praeger, 1974.

Foner, Philip S. *Blacks in the American Revolution.* Westport, CT: Greenwood Press, 1975.

Fowler, Arlen L. *The Black Infantry in the American West, 1869–1891.* Westport, CT: Greenwood, 1971.

Franklin, John Hope. *George Washington Williams: A Biography.* Chicago: University of Chicago Press, 1985.

Frazer, Robert W. *Forts of the West: Military Forts, Presidios and Posts Commonly Called Forts West of the Mississippi River to 1898.* Norman: University of Oklahoma Press, 1965.

Gatewood, Willard B. Jr. 'John Hanks Alexander of Arkansas: Second Black Graduate of West Point.' *Arkansas Historical Quarterly* 41 no. 2 (Summer 1982): 103–28.

——. Comp. *'Smoked Yankees' and the Struggle for Empire: Letters from Negro Soldiers, 1898–1902.* Fayetteville: University of Arkansas Press, 1987.

Glasrud, Bruce A. 'Western Black Soldiers Since *The Buffalo Soldiers*: A Review of the Literature.' *Social Science Journal* 36 (1999): 251–70.

Glass, E.L.N. Comp and Ed. *The History of the Tenth Cavalry, 1866–1921.* Fort. Collins, CO: Army Press, 1972.

Gott, Kendall D. *In Search of an Elusive Enemy: The Victorio Campaign, 1879–1880.* Fort Leavenworth: Combat Studies Institute Press, 2004.

Green, Bill. *The Dancing Was Lively Fort Concho Texas: A Social History, 1867–1882.* San Angelo: Fort Concho Sketches Publishing Company, 1974.

Greene, Jerome A. 'The US Army Buffalo Overcoat and M1883 Canvas Blanket Lined Overcoat on the Northern Plains.' *Military Collector & Historian* 46 no. 2 (Summer 1992): 73–75.

Greene, Robert Ewell. *Black Defenders of America 1775–1973 A Pictorial Reference History.* Chicago: Johnson Publishing Company Inc., 1974.

Hampton, H. Duane. *How the US Cavalry Saved Our National Parks.* Bloomington: Indiana University Press, 2017.

Harris, Theodore D. Ed. and Comp. *Henry O. Flipper, Black Frontiersman: The Memoirs of Henry O. Flipper, First Black Graduate of West Point.* Fort Worth: Texas Christian University Press, 1997.

Haymond. John A. *The American Soldier, 1866–1916: The Enlisted Man and the Transformation of the United States Army.* Jefferson, NC: McFarland & Company, Inc., Publishers, 2018.

Heinl, Nancy G. 'Colonel Charles Young Pointman.' *Army* (March 1977), 31.

Heitman, Francis B. *Historical Register and Dictionary of the United States Army* I. Washington, DC: US Government Printing Office, 1903.

Higginson, Thomas Wentworth. *Army Life in a Black Regiment*. Williamstown, MA: Cornerhouse Publishers, 1984.

Hill, Walter. 'Exploring the Life and History of the 'Buffalo Soldiers." *The Record: News from the National Archives and Records Administration* (March 1998): 12–14.

Historical and Pictorial Review Second Cavalry Division, United States Army, Camp Funston – Fort Riley, Kansas, 1941. Baton Rouge: Army and Navy Publishing Company, 1941.

Hoagland, Alison K. *Army Architecture in the West: Forts Laramie, Bridger and D.A. Russell, 1849–1912*. Norman: University of Oklahoma Press, 2004.

Hoffman, Philip W. *David Fagen: Turncoat Hero*. Staunton: American History Press, 2017.

Holterman, Jack. *The Twenty-Fifth Infantry in Glacier National Park Country*. West Glacier, MT: Glacier Natural History Association, 1991.

Holton, Woody. *Black Americans in the Revolutionary Era: A brief History with Documents*. Boston: Bedford/St. Martin, 2009.

Hooker, Forestine C. *When Geronimo Rode*. Garden City, NY: Doubleday, Page & Company, 1924.

Hoverson, Martha. 'Buffalo Soldiers at Kīlauea, 1915–1917.' *Hawaiian Journal of History* 49 (2015): 73–85.

Hughes, Langston. 'Long View Negro: Emancipation, 1865.'

Hutchins, James S. 'Collectors' Field Book: The Dodge Blanket Roll Support.' *Military Collector & Historian* 20 (Fall 1968): 92–95.

Hunter, J. Marvin. Ed. *9 Years Among the Indians 1870–1879 The Story of the Captivity and Life of a Texan Among the Indians Herman Lehmann*. Albuquerque: University of New Mexico Press, 1993.

Internments at Fort Buford 1866 to 1985. Fort Buford, ND: Fort Buford 6th Infantry Regiment Association, 2006.

'John H. Alexander, No. 3205 Class of 1887.' *The Association of Graduates of the United States Military Academy Annual Reunion June 12th 1894*. Saginaw, MI: Seeman & Peters, Inc. Printers, 1894.

Johnson, Barry C. *Flipper's Dismissal: The Ruin of Lt. Henry O. Flipper, U.S.A. First Coloured Cadet of West Point*. London: Privately Printed, c. 1980.

Johnson, Edward A. *History of the Negro Soldier in the Spanish American War*. Cincinnati W.H. Ferguson Company, Publishers, 1899.

Johnson, Jesse J. *A Pictorial History of Black Soldiers (1619–1969) in Peace and War*. Hampton, VA: Hampton Institute, 1969.

Johnson, Nicholas, *Negroes and the Gun: The Black Tradition of Arms*. Amherst, NY: Prometheus Books, 2014.

Jones, Kenneth, Jr. *The Last Black Regulars*. Carlisle Barracks, PA: US Army War College, 2000.

Joslin, Christina. *Fort Bayard: A Post on the Apache Frontier* 3rd ed. n.p: n.p., 2009.

Kenner, Charles L. *Buffalo Soldiers and Officers of the Ninth Cavalry 1867–1898*. Norman: University of Oklahoma Press, 1999.

Kinevan, Marcos. *Frontier Cavalryman: Lieutenant John Bigelow with the Buffalo Soldiers in Texas*. El Paso: Texas Western Press, 1998.

King, James T. *War Eagle: A Life of General Eugene A. Carr*. University of Nebraska Press, 1963.
Koelle, Alexandra V. 'Pedaling on the Periphery: The African American Twenty-Fifth Infantry Bicycle Corps and the Roads of American Expansion.' *Western Historical Quarterly* 41 no. 3 (Autumn 2010): 305–26.
Kovel, Joel. *White Racism: A Psychohistory*. London: Free Association Books, 1988.
Lamm, Alan K. *Five Black Preachers in Army Blue, 1884–1901: The Buffalo Soldier Chaplains*. Lewiston, NY: Mellen Press, 1998.
Lane, Ann J. *The Brownsville Affair: National Crisis and Black Reaction*. Port Washington, NY: Kennikat Press, 1971.
Langellier, John P. *Army Blue: The Uniform of Uncle of Uncle Sam's Regulars, 1848–1873*. Atlglen, PA: Schiffer Military Books, 1998.
———. 'Buffalo Soldiers in Big Sky Country, 1888–1898.' *Montana The Magazine of Western History*, 67 no. 3 (Autumn 2017): 41–56.
———. *More Army Blue, The Uniform of Uncle of Uncle Sam's Regulars, 1874–1887*. Atlglen, PA: Schiffer Military Books, 2001.
———. *Scouting With The Buffalo Soldiers: Lieutenant Powhattan Clarke, Frederic Remington, and the Tenth Cavalry in in the Southwest*. Denton, TX: University of North Texas Press, 2020.
———. 'The Tenth US Cavalry in Prescott, A.T.' *Territorial Times Prescott Arizona Corral of Westerners International* (November 2009) 1: 22–29.
———. and Alan M. Osur, *Chaplain Allen Allensworth and the Twenty-Fourth Infantry 1886-1906*. Tucson: Tucson Corral of the Westerners, 1980.
Laurie, Clayton D and Ronald H. Cole. *The Role of Federal Military Forces in Domestic Disorders 1877–1945*. Washington, DC: Center of Military History US Army, 1997.
Lawrence, Jennifer J. *Soap Suds Row: The Bold Lives of Laundresses, 1802–1876*. Glendo, WY: High Plains Press, 2016.
Leckie, Shirley Anne. Ed., *The Colonel's Lady on the Western Frontier: The Correspondence of Alice Kirk Grierson*. Lincoln: University of Nebraska Press, 1989.
Leckie, William H. and Shirley A. Leckie, *Unlikely Warriors: General Benjamin Grierson an His Family*. Norman: University of Oklahoma Press, 1998.
Leiker, James N. 'Black Soldiers At Fort Hays, Kansas, 1867–1869 A Study In Civilian and Military Violence.' *Great Plains Quarterly* 17 no. 1 (Winter 1997): 3–17.
———. *Racial Borders: Black Soldiers along the Rio Grande* College Station: Texas A&M Press, 2002.
Logan, Rayford. *Betrayal of the Negro, from Rutherford B. Hayes to Woodrow Wilson*. New York, Collier Books, 1965.
Louisa, Angelo J. Ed. *The African American Baseball Experience in Nebraska: Essays and Memories*. Jefferson, NC: McFarland and Company, Inc. Publishers, 2021.
Lowe, Albert S. 'Camp Life of the Tenth US Cavalry.' *Colored American Magazine* 7 March 1904, 203.
Lyman, Robert. *The Beecher Island Annual*. Wray, CO: The Beecher Island Memorial Association, 1930.
Lynch, John Roy. *Reminiscences of an Active Life: The Autobiography of John Roy Lynch*. Chicago: University of Chicago Press, 1970.
Lynk, Miles V. *The Black Troopers. Or the Daring Heroism of the Negro Soldiers in the Spanish-American War*. Jackson, TN: M.V. Lynk Publishing House, 1899.

MacGregor, Morris J., Jr. *Integration of the Armed Forces, 1940–1965*. Washington, DC: United States Army Center of Military History, 2001.

—— and Bernard C. Nalty. Eds. *Blacks in the United States Armed Forces: Basic Documents*, vol. 3. Wilmington, DE: Scholarly Resources, 1977.

McChristian, Douglas C. *Fort Laramie: Military Bastion of the High Plains*. Norman: University of Oklahoma Press, 2009.

——. Ed. *Garrison Tangles in the Friendless Tenth: The Journal of First Lieutenant John Bigelow, Jr. Fort Davis Texas*. Bryan, TX and Mattituck, NJ: J.M. Carroll & Company, 1985.

——. *Regular Army O! Soldiering on the Western Frontier 1865–1891*. Norman: University of Oklahoma Press, 2017.

McKay, D. B. *Pioneer Florida*. Tampa: Southern Publishing, 1959.

McNees, Tim. *Time in the Wilderness: The Formative Years of John 'Black Jack' Pershing in the American West*. Lincoln, NE: Potomac Books, 2021.

McWhorter, John. *Woke Racism: How a New Religion Has Betrayed Black America*. New York Portfolio/Penguin, 2021.

Marriott, Barbara. *Annie's Guests: Tales From a Frontier Hotel*. Tucson: Catymatt Productions, 2000.

Marszalek, John F. *Court Martial: A Black Man in America*. New York: Charles Scribner's Sons, 1972.

——. *Sherman: A Soldier's Passion for Order*. Carbondale: Southern Illinois University Press, 2007.

Mason, Kathy S. 'Buffalo Soldiers as Guardians of the Parks: African-American Troops in the California National Parks in the Early Twentieth Century.' *The Historian* (Spring 2019) 81 no 1: 84–98.

Mattes, Merrill J. *Fort Laramie Park History, 1834–197*. Denver, CO: Rocky Mountain Regional Office National Park Service, 1980.

Matthews, Matt. *The US Army on the Mexican Border: A Historical Perspective*. Fort Leavenworth, KS: Combat Studies Institute Press, 2007.

Matson, Simon E. Ed. *The Beecher Island Annual: Ninety-third Anniversary of the Battle of Beecher Island, September 17, 18, 1868*. Wray, CO: Beecher Island Battle Memorial Association, 1960.

May, Robert E. 'Invisible Men: Blacks and the US Army in the Mexican War.' *The Historian* 49 no. 4 (August 1987): 463–77.

Meekins, Alex Christopher 'Unionism and the Arcane Origin of 'Buffalo.' *North Carolina Historical Review* 85 no. 3 (July 2008): 282–316.

Merriam, H.G. Ed. *Montana Adventure: The Recollections of Frank B. Linderman*. Lincoln: University of Nebraska Press, 1968.

Meyerson, Harvey. *Nature's Army: When Soldiers Fought for Yosemite*. Lawrence: University Press of Kansas, 2001.

Miller, Albert G. *Elevating the Race: Theophilus G. Steward, Black Theology and the Making of an African American Civil Society, 1865–1924*. Knoxville: The University of Tennessee Press, 2003.

Miller, Darlis A. *Soldiers and Settlers: Military Supply in the Southwest, 1861–1885*. Albuquerque: University of New Mexico Press, 1989.

Morey, Michael. *Fagen: An African American Renegade in the Philippine-American War.* Madison: University of Wisconsin Press, 2019.

Morris, J.N. 'Old Nature Trail Is Found Near Wawona.' *Yosemite Nature Notes*, 9 no. 3 (March 1930): 17–18.

Moss, James A. *Military Cycling in the Rocky Mountains.* New York American Sports Pub. Co., 1897.

Müller, William G. *Twenty-Fourth Infantry Past and Present a Brief History of the Regiment Compiled from Official Records, Under the Direction of the Regimental Commander.* n.p.: n.p., 1923.

Mulroy, Kevin. *The Seminole Freedman: A History.* Norman: University of Oklahoma Press, 2007.

Nalty, Bernard C. *Strength for the Fight: A History of Black Americans in the Military.* New York: Free Press, 1986.

—— and Morris J. MacGregor. Comps. and Eds. *Blacks in the Military: Essential Documents* Wilmington, DE: Scholarly Resources, 1981.

Nankivell, John Henry. *History of the Twenty-Fifth Regiment, United States Infantry, 1866–1926.* Denver: Smith-Brooks Printing, 1926.

Nash, Horace D. 'Community Building on the Border: The Role of the 24th Infantry Band at Columbus, New Mexico, 1916–1922.' *Fort Concho and the South Plains Journal* 2 no. 3 (Summer, 1990): 76–92.

Parker, James. *The Old Army: Memories, 1872–1918.* Philadelphia: Dorrance and Company 1929.

Paul, Eli. Ed. *The Frontier Army.* Pierre: South Dakota Historical Society Press, 2019.

Perry, Alexander W. 'The Ninth United States Cavalry in the Sioux Campaign of 1890.' *Journal of the United States Cavalry Association* 4 no. 12 (March 1891):37–40.

Phillips, Tom. 'Sobriquet: A Chronological Commentary on the Name 'Buffalo Soldier." *Journal of America's Military Past* 35 no. 2 (Spring/Summer 2010): 5–30.

Powell, Anthony. *For the Love of Liberty: The African American Soldier in the Post Civil War Army, 1866–1897.* San Jose, CA: Portraits in Black, 2020.

——. *Keep Step to the Music of the Union the African American Soldier Musician 1776–1945.* San Jose: Portraits in Black, 2020.

Powell, William H. *List of Officers of the Army of the United States from 1779 to 1900 Embracing a Register of All Appointments by the President of the United States in the Volunteer Service During the Civil War and of Volunteer Officers in the Service of the United States June 1, 1900.* New York: L R. Hamersly & CO., 1900.

——. *Powell's Records of Living Officers of the United States Army.* Philadelphia, L.R. Hamersly, 1890.

Price, George. *Across the Continent with the Fifth Cavalry.* New York, D. Van Nostrand, 1883.

Programme Farewell Service and Exercise for Louis Augustus Carter Colonel, Chaplain Corps, U.S.A. Fort Huachuca, Arizona October 29–30, 1939.

Prucha, Francis Paul. *A Guide to US Military Posts of the United States, 1789–1895.* Madison: State Historical Society of Wisconsin, 1964.

Pyne, Stephen J. *Year of the Fires: The Story of the Great Fires of 1910.* New York City: Viking, 2001.'None Beautiful.' *Fort Concho Report* (Winter 1964–85): 35–36;

Radbourne, Allan. *Corporal Edward Scott, Frontier Cavalryman.* London: English Westerners' Society, 2014.

Railsback, Thomas C. and John P. Langellier. *The Drums Would Roll: A Pictorial History of US Army Bands on the American Frontier 1866–1900*. London: Arms and Armour Press, 1987.

Rawick, George P. Ed., *The American Slave: A Composite Autobiography*. Westport, CT: Greenwood, 1972. pt. 1.

Reddick, L.D. 'The Negro Policy of the United States Army, 1775–1945.' *Journal of Negro History* 34 no. 1: 9–29.

Remington, Frederic. 'A Scout with the Buffalo Soldiers.' *Century* 37 (April 1889), 899–912.

———. 'Vagabonding with the Tenth Horse.' *Cosmopolitan* (February 1897). 347–54.

Rhodes, [Charles D.] 'Charles Young No. 3330 Class of 1888.' *Annual Report of the Association of the Graduates United States Military Academy June 12, 1922*. Saginaw: Association of the Graduates United States Military Academy, 1922.

Richter, William L. *The Army in Texas During Reconstruction 1865–1870*. College Station: Texas A&M, 1987.

Robbins, James S. *Last in Their Class: Custer, Pickett and the Goats of West Point*. New York: Encounter Books, 2006.

Robinson, Charles M. III. *The Court Martial of Lieutenant Henry Flipper*. El Paso: University of Texas at El Paso, 1994.

Robinson, Michael C. and Frank N. Schubert. 'David Fagen: An Afro-American Rebel in the Philippines, 1899–1901.' *Pacific Historical Review* 44 no. 1 (February, 1975): 68–83.

Robinson, Willard B. *American Forts: Architectural Form and Function*. Urbana: University of Illinois Press, 1977.

Rodenbough Theo. F. and William L. Haskin. Eds. *The Army of the United States: Historical Sketches of Staff and Line with Portraits of Generals-in-Chief*. New York, Maynard, Merrill, & Co., 1896.

Rodney, George Brydges. *As a Cavalryman Remembers*. Caldwell, ID: Caxton Printers, Ltd., 1944.

Roe, Frances *Army Letters from an Officer's Wife, 1871–1888*. New York, D. Appleton, 1909.

Rolak, Bruno J. *History of Fort Huachuca, Arizona*. El Paso, TX: Southwest Antiquarians, 1972.

Romeyn, Charles A. 'The First Sergeant.' *Cavalry Journal* No. 140 (July 1925): 296–98.

Roth, Russell. *Muddy Glory: America's 'Indian Wars' in the Philippine, 1899–1935*. West Hanover, MA: Christopher Publishing House, 1981.

Royal, Alice C. *Allensworth The Freedom Colony*. Berkely: Heyday, 2008.

Rutledge, Lee. 'The Buffalo Soldiers: Unsung Guardians of the Frontier.' *Guns and Ammo* (1986) 30 no. 1, 56–57, 69–70.

San Juan, E., Jr. 'An African American Soldier in the Philippine Revolution: An Homage to David Fagen.' academia.edu/242727/A_.HOMAGE_TO_DAVID_ FAGEN AFRICAN_AMERICAN_ SOLDIER_IN_THE_PHILIPPINE_REVOLUTION

Santala, Russel D. *The Ute Campaign of 1879: A Study in the Use of the Military Instrument*. Fort Leavenworth: US Army Command and General Staff College, 1994.

Santoro, Gene. *Myself When I am Real: The Life and Music of Charles Mingus*. Oxford University Press, 1994.

Savage, W. Sherman. *Blacks in the West*. Westport, CT: Greenwood Press, 1976.

Sayre, Harold Ray. *Warriors of Color*. Fort Davis, TX: published by the author, 1995.

Schubert, Frank N. *Black Valor: Buffalo Soldiers and the Medal of Honor, 1870–1898*. Wilmington, DE: Scholarly Resources, 1998.

———. *Buffalo Soldiers, Braves and the Brass: The Story of Fort Robinson, Nebraska.* Shippensburg, PA: White Mane Publishing Company Inc., 1993.

———. 'Buffalo Soldiers: Myths and Realities.' *Army History: The Professional Bulletin of Army History* 52 (Spring 2001): 13–18

———. *On the Trail of the Buffalo Soldier: Biographies of African Americans in the US Army 1866–1917.* Wilmington, DE: Scholarly Resources, 1995.

———. 'Seeking David Fagen: The Search for a Black Rebel's Florida Roots.' *Tampa Bay History* 22 no. 1 (2008): 1–17.

———. 'The Suggs Affray: The Black Cavalrymen in the Johnson County War.' *Western Historical Quarterly* 4 no. 1 (January 1973): 57–68.

———. 'Seeking David Fagen: The Search for a Black Rebel's Florida Roots.' *Sunland Tribune* 31 Article 5 (2006): 29–40.

———. Ed. and Comp. *Voices of the Buffalo Soldiers: Record, Reports and Recollections of Military Life and Service in the West.* Albuquerque: University of New Mexico Press, 2003.

———. 'The Violent World of Emanuel Stance, Fort Robinson, 1887.' *Nebraska History* 55 (Summer 1974): 203–19.

Schubert, Irene and Frank N. Schubert, *On the Trail of the Buffalo Soldiers: New and Revised Biographies of African-Americans in the US Army, 1866–1917.* Lanham, MD: The Scarecrow Press, 2004.

Scipio, Albert II. *Last Black Regulars: A History of the 24th Infantry Regiment, 1869–1951.* Silver Spring, MD: Roman Publications, 1983.

Seraile, William. *Voice of Dissent: Theophilus Gould Steward (1843–1924) and Black America.* Brooklyn, NY: Carlson Publishing, Inc., 1991.

Shellum, Brian. *Black Officer in a Buffalo Soldier Regiment: The Military Career of Charles Young.* Lincoln: University of Nebraska Press, 2010.

———. *Black Cadet in a White Bastion: Charles Young at West Point.* Lincoln: University of Nebraska Press, 2006.

———. *Buffalo Soldiers in Alaska: Company L, Twenty-Fourth Infantry in Skagway, 1899–1902.* Lincoln: University of Nebraska Press, 2021.

Sheridan, Louis. 'Patriotism Betrayed: How the US Military Resegregated From 1913–1939.' *Historical Perspectives: Santa Clara University Undergraduate Journal of History.* Series II 26 (2021): 78–92.

Shine, Gregory Paynter. 'Respite from War: Buffalo Soldiers at Vancouver Barracks, 1899–1900.' *Oregon Historical Quarterly* (Summer 2006) 107 no. 2: 196–227.

Shrader, Charles Reginald. Gen. Ed. *Reference Guide to United States Military History 1865-1919.* New York: Sachem Publishing Associates, Inc., 1993.

Sinclair, Donna L. *Part II, The Waking of a Military Town: Vancouver, Washington and the Vancouver National Historic Reserve, 1898–1920, with Suggestions for Further Research* Vancouver, WA: Fort Vancouver National Historic Site, 2005.

Smith, Mrs. George W. in Association of Survivors, Regular Brigade, Fourteenth Corps, *Army of the Cumberland Proceedings of reunions held at Pittsburgh, Pa., Sept. 11–12, 1894, Crawfish Springs, Ga., Sept. 18–19, 1895, St. Paul, Minn., Sept. 1–2, 1896, Columbus, Ohio, Sept. 22–23, 1897/Association of Survivors, Regular Brigade, Fourteenth Corps, Army of the Cumberland. Historical sketch/by Frederick Phisterer. Roster of membership and death roll of the brigade during the war. Official reports of the Battle of Stone River, Tenn.* n.p.: n.p., 1898.

Smith, Steven D. *The African American Soldier At Fort Huachuca, Arizona, 1892–1946.* Seattle: US Army Corps of Engineer, 2001.

—— and James A. Zeidler. Eds. *A Historic Context for the African American Military Experience.* Champaign, IL: US Army Construction Engineering Research Laboratories, 1998.

Smith, Thomas T. Ed. *Daughter of the Regiment: Memoirs of a Childhood in the Frontier Army, 1878–1898.* Lincoln, NE: Bison Books, 1996.

Smyth, Donald. *Guerrilla Warrior: The Early Life of John J. Pershing.* New York: Scribner, 1973.

Sperry, T.J. 'Winter Clothing on the North Plains.' *Military Collector & Historian* 44 no. 3 (Fall 1992): 117–19.

Spude, Robert L.S. *In Skagway, District of Alaska 1884–1912: Building the Gateway to the Klondike.* Fairbanks: Anthropology and Historic Preservation, Cooperative Park Studies Unit, University of Alaska, 1983.

Stallard, Patricia Y. *Glittering Misery: Dependents of the Indian Fighting Army.* Fort Collins: Old Army Press, 1978.

Stevenson, Russell W. *For the Cause of Righteousness: A Global History of Blacks and Mormonism. 1830–2013.* Salt Lake City: Greg Kofford Books, 2014.

Steward, T.G. Ed. *Active Service, or, Religious Work Among US Soldiers. A Series of Papers by Our Post and Regimental Chaplains.* New York: US Army Aid Association, 1897.

——. *The Colored Regulars in the United States Army.* Philadelphia: A.M.E Book Concern, 1904.

——. 'Starving Laborers and the 'Hired Soldier.' *The United Service Journal* (October 1895), 363–6.

Stiles, T.J. 'Buffalo Soldiers.' *Smithsonian Magazine* (December 1998), 84–85.

——. *Custer's Trials: A Life on the Frontier of a New America.* New York: Alfred A. Knopf, 2015.

Stover, Earl F. *Chaplain Henry V. Plummer, His Ministry and His Court Martial.* Lincoln, NE: Nebraska Historical Society, 1975.

——. *Up from Handymen: The United States Army Chaplaincy, 1865–1920.* Washington, DC: The Office of Chief of Chaplains, 1977.

Strahorn, Carrie Adell. Fifteen *Thousand Miles by Stage; A Woman's Unique Experience During Thirty Years of Path Finding and Pioneering from the Missouri to the Pacific and from Alaska to Mexico.* New York: G. P. Putnam's Sons, 1911.

Stubbs, Mary Lee and Stanley Russell Connor. *Armor-Cavalry Part I: Regular Army and Army Reserve.* Washington, DC: Office of the Chief of Military History United States Army, 1969. *Monument Arizona.* Tucson: Western Archeological and Conservation Center, 1987

Tate, Michael L. *The Frontier Army in the Settlement of the West.* Norman: University of Oklahoma Press, 1999.

Taylor, Alfred O., Jr. *Following the Trail of Trooper Alfred Pride Buffalo Soldier (1865–1893): A Patriot and A Pawn.* n.p.: Alfred O. Taylor, 2022.

Taylor, Quintard. *In Search of the Racial Frontier African Americans in the American West, 1528–1990.* New York: W.W. Norton & Company, 1998.

Terrell, Mary Church. 'A Sketch of Mingo Saunders Late First Sergeant Company B, Twenty-Fifth Infantry, United States Army Dismissed Without Honor After Serving Twenty-Six Years.' *The Voice of the Negro* 4 no. 7 (March 1907): 128–31.

Torrans, Thomas. *Forging the Tortilla Curtain: Cultural Drift and Change Along the United States-Mexico Border from the Spanish Era To the Present.* Fort Worth: TCU Press, 2000.

Thompson, Erwin N. *Defender of the Gate: The Presidio of San Francisco A History of 1846 1995*, II. San Francisco: Golden Gate National Area National Park Service, 1997.

———. 'The Negro Soldiers on the Frontier: A Fort Davis Case Study.' *Journal of the West* 7 no. 2 (April 1968): 217–35.

——— and Sally B. Woodbridge. *Special History Study Presidio of San Francisco An Outline of Its Evolution as a US Army Post, 1847–1990*. Denver: Denver Service Center National Park Service, 1992.

Tucker, Philip Thomas. *America's Female Buffalo Soldier: A New Look at the Life of Cathy Williams in History and Memory*. n.p.: n.p., 2017.

———. *Cathy Williams: From Slave to Female Buffalo Soldier*. Mechanicsburg, PA: Stackpole Books, 2002.

Tye, Larry. *Rising from the Rails: Pullman Porters and the Making of the Black Middle Class*. New York: Henry Holt and Company, 2004.

Utley, Robert M. Ed. *An Army Doctor on the Western Frontier: Journals and Letters of John Vance Lauderdale, 1864–1890*. Albuquerque: University of New Mexico Press, 2014.

———. *Frontier Regulars: The United States Army and the Indian, 1866–1891*. New York: Macmillan, 1973.

———. *Frontiersmen in Blue: The United States Army and the Indian, 1848–1866*. New York: Macmillan, Co., 1967.

———. *The Last Sovereigns: Sitting Bull and the Resistance of the Free Lakotas*. Lincoln, NE: Bison Books, 2020.

Vandiver, Frank E. *Jack: The Life and Times of John J. Pershing* I. College Station: Texas A&M Press, 1977.

Villard, Oswald G. 'The Negro in the Regular Army.' *Atlantic Monthly* 91 (June 1903), 721–29.

Voelz, Peter M. *Slave and Soldier: The Military Impact of Blacks in the Colonial Americas*. New York: Garland, 1993.

Wagner, Levern, Ed. *The Benjamin H. Grierson Collection*. Madison, WI: A.E. Editions, Inc., 1998.

Washington, Booker T., et al. *The Negro Problem: A Series of Articles by Representative American Negroes of Today*. New York: J. Pott & Company, 1903.

Watt, Robert N. *'Horses Worn to Mere Shadows': The Victorio Campaign 1880*. Warwick, England: Helion & Company Limited, 2017.

———. *'I will Not surrender the Hair of a Horse's Tail': The Victorio Campaign 1879*. Solihull, West Midlands, England: Helion & Company Limited, 2017.

———. *With My Face to My Bitter Foes': Nana's War 1880–1881*. Warwick, England: Helion & Company Limited, 2019.

Weaver, Jace. *Notes from a Miner's Canary: Essays on the State of Native America*. Albuquerque: University of New Mexico Press, 2010.

Weaver, John D. *The Brownsville's Raid*. College Station: Texas A&M, 1992.

———. *The Senator and the Sharecropper's Son: Exoneration of the Brownsville Soldiers*. College Station: Texas A&M University Press, 1997.

Welch, Richard E., Jr. 'American Atrocities in the Philippines: The Indictment and the Response.' *Pacific Historical Review* 43 no. 2 (May, 1974): 233–53.

Whitbeck, Donald Richard. *A Man Named Moses: The Military Life of a Heroic Buffalo Soldier*. Los Angeles: WT Records and Publishing, 1996.

White, Eugene R. *Service on the Indian Reservations: Being the Experiences of a Special Indian Agent*. Little Rock: Diploma Press, 1893.

White, Virgil D. *Index to Pension Applications for Indian War Service between 1817 and 1898*. Waynesboro, TN: The National Historical Publishing Company, 1997.

Whitaker, Robert. *On the Laps of Gods: The Red Summer of 1919 and the Struggle for Justice That Remade a Nation*. New York: Three Rivers Press, 2009.

Wilkes, Laura E. *Missing Pages in American History, Revealing the Services of Negroes in the Early Wars of the United States of America, 1641–1815*. Washington, DC: Press of R.L. Pendleton, c. 1919.

Wilkie, Laurie A. *Unburied Lives: The Historical Archaeology of Buffalo Soldiers at Fort Davis Texas, 1869–1875*. Albuquerque: University of New Mexico Press, 2021.

Williams, George Washington. *A History of the Negro Troops in the War of the Rebellion, 1861-1865*. New York: Harper & Brothers, 1888.

Williams, Vernon L. *Lieutenant Patton: George S Patton, Jr. and the American Army in the Mexican Punitive Expedition, 1915–1916*. Abilene: TX: Old Segundo Companion Book, 2003.

Wilson, Joseph T. *The Black Phalanx: A History of the Negro Soldiers of the United States in the Wars of 1775–1812, 1861–1865*. Boston: Robert F. Walcutt, 1865.

Wilson, Steve. Ed. *Child of the Fighting Tenth: On the Frontier with the Buffalo Soldiers Forrestine C. Hooker*. Oxford: Oxford University Press, 2003.

Wister, Owen. 'Specimen Jones.' *Harper's New Monthly* 80 no. 530 (July 1894).

Wolfe, Patrick. 'Settler Colonialism and the Elimination of the Native.' *General of Genocide Research* 8 no. 4 (December 2006): 387–409.

Wood, Anthony W. *Black Montana: Settler Colonialism and Erosion of the Racial Frontier, 1877–1930*. Lincoln University of Nebraska Press, 2021.

Woodruff, Charles E. *The U. S. Army Ration and Military Food. Read in the Section of Physiology and Dietetics at the Forty-third Annual Meeting of the American Medical Association, held at Detroit, Mich., June, 1892*. Reprinted from *The Journal of the American Medical Association*, December 3,1892.

Work, David K. 'The Buffalo Soldiers in Vermont, 1909–1913.' *Vermont History* 73 (Winter/Spring 2005): 63–75.

Work, Monroe N. Ed. *Negro Year Book: An Encyclopedia of the Negro 1921–1922*. Tuskegee: The Negro Year Book Publishing Company, 1922.

Wynn, Bill. 'Old Cox.' *Junior Historian* 6 no. 5 (May 1946): 1–4.

Unpublished Sources

Buchanan, John Strauss. 'Functions of the Fort Davis Military Band and Musical Proclivities of the Commanding Officer, Benjamin H. Grierson, Late Nineteenth Century.' MA Thesis, Sul Ross College, 1963.

Baumler, Mark F. and Richard V.H Ahlstrom. 'The Garfield Monument: An 1886 Memorial to the Buffalo Soldiers in Arizona,' MS. Western Archeological and Conservation Center, NPS, Tucson, AZ, 1986.

Bowmaster, Patrick A 'Occupation 'Soldier' – The Life of 1st Sergeant Emanuel Stance of the Ninth US Cavalry 'Buffalo Soldiers,' The First African-American to win the Medal of

Honor for Action in the post-Civil War Period.' unpublished MS. Special Collections Department, Newman Library, Virginia Polytechnic Institute and State University, Blacksburg, VA, 1995. .

Braddock, Thomas. Biographical File, Fort Verde State Park, Camp Verde, Arizona.

Chappell, Gordon. 'Fort Garland: A United States Army Frontier Garrison in the San Luis Valley of Colorado 1853–1883.' Denver: State Historical Society of Colorado, 2003.

Cheatham, Alexander 'Sandy.' Biographical File, Fort Verde State Park, Camp Verde, Arizona.

Clark, Michael James Tins. 'A History of the Twenty-fourth United States Infantry Regiment in Utah, 1896–1900.' Ph.D. diss., University of Utah, 1979.

Conrad, George, Jr. Federal Writers' Project Collection. Ex-Slave Narratives. 1935–1942. B Box 25, Folder 7, M1981.105 location 0924.03. Oklahoma Historical Society,

Cox, Elijah. Biographical File, Fort Concho National Landmark and Museum Library. San Angelo, TX.

Davis, Michael Shawn. "Many of Them are Among My Best Men': The United States Navy Looks at its African American Crewmen.' Ph.D, diss., Kansas State University, 2011.

Fletcher, Marvin E. 'Negro Soldier and the United States Army 1891–1917.' Ph.D. diss., University of Wisconsin, 1968.

Forstchen, William Robert. 'The Twenty-Eighth United States Colored Troops: Indiana's African Americans Go to War, 1863–1865.' Ph.D. diss., Purdue University, 1994.

Giese, Dale Frederick. 'Soldiers at Play: A History of Social Life at Fort Union, New Mexico, 1851–1891.' Ph.D. diss., University of New Mexico, 1969. n.d.

Gomez, Philip. 'The Mystery of the President Garfield and Lieutenant Henry O. Flipper in the Water Hole Campaign.' MS. Chiricahua National Monument Accession No. 134, n.d.

Hamilton, George F. 'History of the Ninth Regiment US Cavalry.' MS. US Army Heritage and Education Center, Carlisle Barracks, PA. n.d.

Harris, Theodore Delano. 'Henry Ossian Flipper: The First Black Graduate of West Point.' Ph.D. diss., University of Minnesota, 1971.

Harris, Thomas H. H. 'The Life and Times of a Buffalo Soldier, Sergeant Thomas Shaw, Ninth United States Cavalry: Medal of Honor Recipient.' Unpublished MS. 1999, MS–20 Series 2, Box 6, File 17, Northern Kentucky University.

Hunt, Geoffrey R. 'Race Riot of Fort Larned, Kansas.' unpublished MS. Fort Larned National Historic Site, September, 2014.

James, Jeremy Wayne. 'Alone in the Profession of Arms: America's First Three African American West Point Graduates.' MA thesis, Texas A&M University, 2007.

Krueger, David. 'To Hold What the US Has Taken in Conquest:' The United States Army and Colonial Ethnic Forces, 1866–1914.' Ph.D. diss., Harvard University, Cambridge, MA, 2019.

Langellier, John P. 'Bastion By the Bay: A History of the Presidio of San Francisco, 1776–1906.' Ph.d diss., Kansas State University, Manhattan, KS, 1982.

Leiker, James N. 'The Buffalo Soldiers at Fort Hays.' MA thesis, Fort Hays State University, 1992.

Loening Eichner, Katrina Christiana. 'Queering Frontier Identities: Archaeological Investigations at a Nineteenth-Century US Army Laundresses' Quarters in Fort Davis.' Ph.D. diss., University of California, Berkeley, 2017.

Lynx, Miles V. *The Black Troopers: Or, the Daring Heroism of the Negro Soldiers in the Spanish-American War*. Jackson, TN: The M.V. Lynk Publishing House, 1899.

Marchbank, Vance Hunter, Sr. 'Forty Years in the Army.' unpublished MS c. 1940, Transcription. Fort Huachuca Museum, 2006.

Mazique, Sancho. Biographical File, Fort Concho Library, San Angelo, Texas with a portion of a typescript dated November 1879 from Alice Grierson.

McClung, Donald B. 'Henry O. Flipper: First Negro Officer in the United States Army.' MA thesis, East Texas State University, 1970.

Murphy, John Thomas. 'Pistol's Legacy: Sutlers, Post Traders and the American Army 1820 1895.' Ph.D. diss., University of Illinois at Urbana-Champaign, 1993.

Potts, Benjamin Franklin. Biographical File, Fort Verde State Park, Camp Verde, Arizona.

Rickey, Don, Jr. 'Interview with Sampson Mann, February, 1965, Wadsworth VA Hospital, Leavenworth, KS.' Photocopy of Notes, Buffalo Soldiers File AA5. Fort Union National Monument, New Mexico.

———. 'Negro Regulars in the American Army: An Indian Wars Combat Record.' Photocopied typescript, Falls Church, VA, May 1965, Fort Union National Monument, New Mexico.

Riggs, Lilian Erickson. Letter to National Park Service Volunteer-in-Parks Richard Murray, February 1966. Western Archeological and Conservation Center, NPS, Tucson, AZ.

Simpson, Robert Steven, 'The Regular Soldier in the Campaign for Santiago de Cuba, 1898.' MA thesis, University of Colorado, 1949.

Thompson, Scott F. "'The Negro had been run over long enough by white men and it was time they defend themselves': African-American Mutinies and the Long Emancipation, 1861-1974.' Ph.D. diss., West Virginia University, Morgantown, West Virginia, 2021.

Torres, Louis and Mark Baumler. 'A History of the Buildings and Structures of the Faraway Ranch, Historic Structures Report, Historical and Archaeological Data Section.' MS, Western Archeological and Conservation Center, Tucson, AZ, 1984.

Valentin, Edward. 'Black Enlisted Men in the US-Mexico Border: Race, Citizenship and Military Occupation 1866–1930.' Ph.D. diss., Rice University, Houston, TX, 2020.

Walker, James. Biographical File, Fort Concho National Landmark and Museum Library, San Angelo, TX.

Wheeler, Clara C. Taped Interview, 1970, Chiricahua National Monument, AZ.

Wilkes, Jacob. Biographical File, Fort Concho National Landmark and Museum Library, San Angelo, TX.

Willard, Squire III. 'The 24th Infantry Regiment and the Racial Debate in the US Army.' MA thesis, US Army Command and General Staff College, Fort Leavenworth, Kansas, 1997.

Williams, Charles Hughes III. "We Have…Kept the Negroes' Goodwill and Sent Them Away." MA thesis, August 2008, Texas A&M University.

Work, David K 'The Fighting Tenth Cavalry: Black Soldiers in the United States Army 1892-1918.' MA thesis, Oklahoma State University, 1998. Yancy, James Walter. 'The Negro of Tucson, Past and Present.' MA thesis, University of Arizona, 1933.

Zwink, Timothy Ashley. 'Fort Larned: Garrison on the Central Great Plains.' Ph.D. diss., Oklahoma State University, 1980.

Newspapers and Periodicals

Age-Herald (Birmingham, AL)
Alliance Herald (Alliance, NE)
Alta Advocate (Dinuba, CA)
Anaconda Standard (Anaconda, MT)
Appeal: A National Afro-American Newspaper (Saint Paul, MN)
Arizona Silver Belt (Globe, AZ)
Arizona Weekly Citizen (Tucson, AZ)
Arizona Weekly Journal-Miner/Weekly Arizona Miner (Prescott)
Arkansas Mansion (Little Rock, AK)
Army and Navy Journal
Army and Navy Register
Atlanta Constitution
Baltimore Evening Sun
Barton County Democrat (Great Bend, KS)
Bee (Washington DC)
Belmont Chronicle (St. Clairsville, OH)
Billings Gazette
Bisbee Daily Review
Bismarck Daily Tribune
Border Vidette (Nogales, AZ)
Bottineau Courant (Bottineau, ND)
Broad Ax (Salt Lake, UT)
Brownsville Daily Herald
Bryan Moring Eagle/Bryan Daily Eagle and Pilot
Burlington Weekly Free Press
Butler Weekly Times (Butler, MO)
Butte Inter Mountain
Butte Miner
Camden Chronicle (Camden, TN)
Chariton Courier (Keytesville, MO)
Choteau Acantha (Choteau, MT)
Cheyenne Daily Leader
Cheyenne State Leader
Chicago Defender
Chicago Tribune
Cincinnati Commercial
Circle Banner (Circle, MT)
Cleveland Gazette
Clifton Clarion (Clifton, AZ)
Coeur d'Alene Press
Colliers Magazine
Colored American (Washington, DC)
Colored American Magazine

Colorado Statesman (Denver)
Columbus Journal (Columbus, NE)
Commercial (Union City, TN)
Cook County Herald (Grand Marais, MN)
Courier Democrat (Langdon, ND)
Crawford Tribune
Crisis Magazine
Daily Bee (Omaha, NE)
Daily Evening Bulletin (Maysville, KY)
Daily Dispatch (Richmond, VA)
Daily Kennebec Journal (Augusta, ME)
Daily Morning Oasis (Nogales, AZ)
Daily Tombstone
Daily Visalia Delta
Dakota Farmers' Leader (Canton, SD)
Dallas Daily Herald
Dallas Weekly Herald
Delaware Gazette and State Journal (Wilmington, DE)
Democratic Northwest and Henry County News (Napoleon, OH)
Denison Review (Denison, IA)
Denver Star
Deseret Evening News (Salt Lake, UT)
Dodge City Times
East Oregonian (Pendleton, OR)
El Paso Daily Herald
Emporia Weekly News
Enterprise (Omaha, NE)
Evening Star (Washington, DC)
Evening Times-Republican (Marshalltown, IA)
Fisherman & Farmer (Edenton, NC)
Fort Robinson Weekly Bulletin
Fort Worth Daily Gazette
Elk Mountain Pilot (Irwin, CO)
Fargo Forum and Daily Republican
Flagstaff Sun-Democrat
Free Lance (Fredericksburg, VA)
Freeland Tribune (Freeland, PA)
Fergus County Argus (Lewiston, MT)
Globe-Republican (Dodge City, KS)
Graham Guardian (Safford, AZ)
Great Falls Tribune
Great Falls Weekly Tribune
Hartford Herald (Hartford, KY)
Harper's Weekly
Harrisburg Telegraph

Havre Herald
Hartford Herald (Hartford, KY)
Helena Independent/Helena Independent Record
Honolulu Star-Bulletin
Hopkinsville Kentuckian
Hot Springs Sentinel
Houston Daily Post
Huntsville Gazette
Indianapolis Journal
Interior Journal (Stanford, KY)
International Review
Iowa State Bystander (Des Moines, IA)
Jersey City News
Juniata Sentinel and Republican (Mifflintown, PA)
Kootenai Herald (Kootenai, ID)
Lafayette Advertiser (Lafayette, LA)
Las Vegas Daily Optic (Las Vegas, NM)
Leavenworth Echo (Leavenworth, WA)
Leslie's Illustrated
Lincoln County Leader (Toledo, OR)
Lindsay Gazette (Lindsay, CA)
Los Angeles Herald
McCook Tribune (McCook, NE)
Memphis Daily Appeal
Mesilla Valley Independent
Midland Journal (Rising Sun, MD)
Mineral Point Tribune (Mineral Point, WI
Missoulian
Mitchell Capital (Mitchell, SD)
Mohave County Miner (Mineral Park, AZ)
Montana Oil and Mining Journal (Great Falls, MT)
Montana Plaindealer (Helena, MT)
Montanian and Chronicle (Choteau, MT)
Morning News (Savannah, GA)
Mount Whitney Club Journal
National Republican (Washington, DC)
Nebraska Advertiser (Brownville, NE)
New Bloomfield, Pa. Times
New Era (Monterey, CA)
Newport Miner (Newport, WA)
New North-west (Deer Lodge, MT)
New Orleans Daily Democrat
New York Age
New York Daily Tribune
New York Globe

New York Freeman
New York Sun
New York Times
Nogales International
North American Review
North Platte Tribune (North Platte, NE)
Oasis (Nogales, AZ)
Ogden Standard
Omaha Guide
Omaha Daily Bee
Pierre Weekly Free Press
Philipsburg Mail (Philipsburg, MT)
Phoenix Arizona Republic
Phoenix Index
Phoenix Tribune
Phoenix Weekly Herald
Plentywood Herald (Plentywood, MT)
Prairie Chronicle (Cottonwood, ID)
Prescott Weekly Courier
Pullman Herald (Pullman, WA)
Public Ledger (Maysville, KY)
Ravalli Republican (Stevensville, MT)
Rawlins Republican
Red Cloud Chief (Red Cloud, NE)
Red Lodge Picket (Red Lodge, MT)
Richmond Planet
River Press (Fort Benton, MT)
Roanoke Times Review (Kevin, MT)
Rock Island Daily Argus
Rocky Mountain News (Denver, CO)
Rosebud County News (Forsyth, MT)
Russellville Democrat (Russellville, AR)
St. Johns Herald (St. John, AZ)
St. Landry Democrat (Opelousas, LA)
St. Louis Daily Times
St. Paul Appeal
St. Paul Globe
Sacramento Daily Record–Union
Salt Lake Herald
Salt Lake Tribune
San Angelo Evening Standard
San Angelo Standard Times
San Francisco Call
San Francisco Chronicle
San Francisco Examiner

Santa Fe Daily New Mexican
Seattle Northwest Enterprise
Seattle Post-Intelligencer
Semi-weekly South Kentuckian (Hopkinsville, KY)
Shoshone Journal
Silver Blade (Rathdrum, ID)
Southern Workman
Spokane Press
Springfield Daily Republic (Springfield, IL)
State Journal (Lincoln, NE)
Sully County Watchman (Clifton, SD)
Tacoma Times
Tacoma Daily Ledger
Taney County Republican (Forsyth, MO)
Times (New Bloomfield, PA)
Tonopah Daily Bonanza
Tulare Times (Visalia, CA)
True Northerner (Paw Paw, MI)
Washington Bee (Washington, DC)
Washington Times (Washington, DC)
Waterbury Evening Democrat
Weekly Democratic Statesman (Austin, TX)
Weekly Herald (Cleveland, TN)
Weekly Louisiana Journal
Western Kansas World (WaKeeney, KS)
Western News (Stevensville, MT)
West Tennessee Star (Bolivar, TN)
Wilson Times (Wilson, NC)
Winners of the West
Wolf Point Herald
Wood County Reporter (Grand Rapids, WI)
Worthington Advance (Worthington, MN)
Yellowstone Journal (Miles City, MT)
Yorkville Enquirer (Yorkville, SC)

Electronic Sources

archives.nypl.org/scm/20643#access_use.
armyhistory.org/the-black-immune-regiments-in-the-spanish-american-war.
azcentral.com/story/news/local/inspire/2015/05/24/buffalo-soldiers-long-journey-peace/27876453.
blackoncampus.com/2008/09/09/the-troubling-case-of-william-hallett-greene.
blackpast.org/african-american-history.
buffalosoldier.net.

cem.va.gov/cems/nchp/ftlogan.asp#np.
enotes.com/homework-help/what-religion-for-colonel-charles-young–69855.
fs.usda.gov/detail/r2/home/?cid=fseprd4917690.
georgiaencyclopedia.org/ articles/history-archaeology/black-troops-in-civil-war-georgia.
history.house.gov/People/Detail/17259.
houstonchronicle.com/texas-sports-nation/college/article/Texas-A-M-s-first-black-football-starter-favors–15345087.php.
loc.gov/item/00694419.
loc.gov/item/mm78031989.
military.com/history/cathay-williams-was- armys-only-female-buffalo-soldier-and-first-black-female-enlistee.html.
nkaa.uky.edu/nkaa/items/show/884.
nps.gov/chir/learn/historyculture/garfield-monument.htm.
nps.gov/chir/learn/historyculture/soldier-roster.htm.
nps.gov/civilwar/search-soldiers-detail.htm.
nps.gov/civilwar/search-battle-units-detail.htm.
nps.gov/parkhistory/hisnps/NPS.historians/invisiblemen2.pdf.
nps.gov/yose/learn/historyculture/buffalo-soldiers.htm.
oregonencyclopedia.org/articles/buffalo_soldiers_at_vancouver_barracks/#.Wm3 r5OplE5.
oxfordaasc.com/browse;jsessionid=03D16ECC20DCDD6D34368467D5212E0D?   isQuick Search=true&pageSize=20&sort=titlesort&t=AASC_Occupations%3A349&t_1=AASC_Occupations%3A659.
poddtoppen.se/podcast/1375326879/jack-dappa-blues-podcast/the-african-american-folklorist-ep–2-elijah-cox.phmc.state.pa.us/bah/dam/rg/di/r19–65RegisterPaVolunteers/r19–65 Regt182/r19–65Regt182%20pg%20100.pdf.
rediscovering-black-history.blogs.archives.gov/2022/02/07/iron-riders–25th-infantry-regiment-part-i.
senate.gov/senators/FeaturedBios/Featured_Bio_Sumner.htm.
si.edu/object/ytpBofRUraUMY.
spanamwar.com/Tenth cav.htm.
spanamwar.com/24thinf.htm.
spotsylvania.va.us/783/23rd-US-Colored-Troops.
starexponent.com/news/local/freedom-foundation-plans-to-spruce-up-historic-shiloh-church-cemetery/article_0e936026-b618–53bb–93ee–8d2a66526139.html.
wikitree.com/wiki/Frierson–425.
yellowstone.org/safeguarding-yellowstone-the-us-army–1886–1918.
youtube.com/watch?v=FFHCMjLmK9s&t=15s
youtube.com/watch?v=NQhk4b8DbgA.
youtube.com/watch?v=pBofRUraUMY&list=PLdvULuYSGxbDxaIzwCVBBC8je7Bq6_Z3u.
youtube.com/watch?v=xhX5WNnwwaQ&t=553s.

Index

Accomack County, VA 42
Accoutrements 24, 100, 177.
Adam, Klide 78
Adams, John 121
Adair, Hank 161
African Methodist Episcopal Church 119, 129, 120 n148, 220
Agua Caliente, Mexico 108
Aguinaldo, Emilio 160
Ahern, George P. 182-3
Ahumada, Chihuahua, Mexico 161
Alabama Agricultural and Mechanical College 55
Alcatraz, California 151, 168
Alcohol- Liquor 28, 64, 64 n215, 72-3 n261, 79, 114-15, 167, 217-18, 225. 238, 254, 278 n33
Almy, Mary Elizabeth Allen Richards 171-2
Alexander,
    Frances "Fannie" 99-100
    James 98-99
    John Hanks 98-104
Alexandria, VA 20
Allen Chapel 129
Allensworth, Allen 52. 110, 115-22, 124
    Josephine 53
Allensworth, California 52-4
Allison, Clay 184
American Legion 127
Anadarko, OK 272
Anderson, John R. 56
Anderson, Marian 82, 135
Anderson, Richard 26-8
Anderson, Robert 26
Anderson, William T. 126-7
Andrews, George L. 74, 85 n6, 95
Angel Island, CA 119, 168 n117
Annin, W.E. 103

Anthony, Hugh 77
Apache (*Inde*) 27, 70, 78, 87 n12, 96, 138-44, 148. 150-2, 159, 203, 237-8, 246, 263, 265, 273-5
    Chiricahua 150
    Lipan 139, 148
    Mescalero 138-41, 143, 149, 162, 164, 273
    White Mountain 151
"Apache Kid" (*Haskay-bay-nay-ntayl*) 150-1
Apadaca, José 71
"Are You Coming Home Tonight" 44
Arizona Territorial Legislature 69
Arlington National Cemetery 56, 132
Armament - Carbine - Firearms - Pistol - Revolver 24, 35, 47, 53, 66, 68, 72-4, 145, 148, 151, 182, 203, 213, 230 n9, 234, 248-9, 254, 276
Armes, George 134, 146, 219
Army Chaplain's School 133
Army of Northern Virginia 22
Army Reorganization Act of 1866 xi, 84, 222
Army Reorganization Act of 1869 xi, 26, 84
Army War College 56
Arthur, Chester A. 242
Artillery 15, 56, 87, 156, 158, 168 n117, 171, 185 n174, 232, 278 n35
Assault 64, 74-5, 157, 176, 260-1
Athletics-Sports 134, 216, 216 n74, 225, 229-30, 244-5
Atlanta, GA 223, 232
Auburn, AL 132
Augur, Christopher C. 97
Axtell, Samuel 164

Bachelor, Joseph B. 160, 177
Badie, David 91
Bakery 112, 114-15, 196
Baltimore, MD 18, 20, 28, 44

309

Baltimore National Cemetery 44
Band-Music 41, 47, 55, 61, 91, 97 n47, 108,
    118-19, 130-31, 196, 201, 205, 214, 216,
    219-22, 226, 241-3
Banks, Frank 54
Baptist 25, 34, 114, 120-21, 128-29, 132
Barnes, William 93
Barr, D. Eglinton 113
Barry, A. 71
Baseball 89, 174, 176, 216, 225, 244-5
Baton Rouge, LA 19, 26-27, 89
Barber 16, 48, 69, 208 n39
Barber, John R. 107
Barber, Merritt 97
Beall, F.M.M. 39-40
Bear Valley, AZ 161
Beaver Creek, KS 147
Bedford Springs, PA 34
Beecher's Island, CO 147
Bell, Richard 250
Bellecourt, Vernon 280
Benjamin, Robert 33 n73, 115
Benteen, Frederick W. 92
Bentley, George 35, 48
Bellingham, WA 22
Bi-the-ja-be-tish-to-ce 151
Bicycle iii, 179 n159, 181-2, 223, 271
Bigelow, John 21, 77, 150 n43, 185 n172, 189,
    229-31, 233, 243
Big Foot 145
Billiards 217
Billings, MT 43-44, 175-6
Birmingham, AL 223
Birth of A Nation 130
Bivens, Claudia 43
    Horrace 42-44
Black, Soloman "Black Sol" 49
Blackfeet Agency, MT 154
Blakely, Belle 73
Bledser, Nathaniel 75
Blunt, James G. x
'Boomers' - Oklahoma Movement 163
Bonita Canyon - Camp Bonita, Arizona 48, 70
    n244, 203-4
Bonnie, William 'Billy the Kid' 165
Border xii, 13, 21, 111, 125, 139, 143-4, 147,
    149, 156, 165-7, 224, 227 n2, 238-9, 256,
    258-9, 261-2, 277
Border Patrol, US xii, 166, 259

Bordinghammer, Edward 61
Bowling Alley 216
Boxing 225
Boyd, Charles T. 161
Boyer, Eli 139
Boyne, Thomas 141
Braddock, Thomas 28
Bradford, Harrison 77
Brady, William 164
Brandy Station, VA 25
Brazos River, TX 155
Brest, France 56
Bronx, NY 196
Brooks, John B. 224
Brooks, Preston 23, 128 n182
Brown, Benjamin 141
Brown, Catherine (nee Johnson) 28
Brown, John L. 254
Brown, J. Lyman 200
Brown, Sally 68
Browne, George 65
Brownsville, TX 138-9, 254
Brownsville Affair 122, 228, 259-61, 267
Bruin, Madison 35
Bryant, Samuel 62
Buckner, Benjamin 64
Buckner, Rosa E. 56
Buell, Mrs. James W. 219
Buffalo Soldier 237, 262-4, 268-82
Buford,
    Eliza 50
    James 50
    Parker 50
Bugle Calls 200-1
Bullis, John 35, 155
Bunche, Ralph 82
Burglary- Robbery - Theft 64, 71, 78-79, 240,
    247, 254, 259
Burley, Robert 91
Burt, Andrew S. 80, 83
Butler 16, 200, 203
Butler, Benjamin 233

California Colony and Home-Promotion
    Association 52
Camp
    Bettens, WY 165
    Bonita, AZ 48, 203
    Colorado, TX 254

Nelson, KY 28, 49
Stephen D. Little, AZ 133
Supply, OK 147, 171, 200
A.E. Wood (Camp Hoyle), CA 190
'Camp Follower' 198
Carriso Mountains, TX 148
Carbondale, IL 60-61
Cardoza Military Academy 124
Cards 217
Carlisle Barracks, PA 34
Carpenter 16, 45, 47, 56, 62
Carpenter, Louis H. 87 n12, 147
Carr, Eugene Asa 92, 147
Carranza, Venustiano 160-1
Carrizal, Mexico 143, 161-2
Carter, Louis Augustua 132-4
Carver, George 53
Carver, George Washington 135
Cathay, William AKA Cathey, Cather, Cathy Williams 28-33
Castillo, Maximo 167
Casualties 34, 96, 139, 145, 151, 158, 160, 162, 171, 247-8
Cavalry Regiments
   First Colorado 85
   First, Volunteer 'Rough Riders' 55 n181, 157, 231
   Second, US 224
   Second, US Colored 86
   Third, US 142, 237, 241
   Fourth, US 89, 140
   Fifth, US 89, 92, 142-3. 147, 224
   Sixth, US 88, 143
   Seventh, US 85, 92, 145, 161, 250, 276 n28
   Ninth, US xi, 18-19, 21-3, 25, 27-8, 36, 38 n98, 46, 48, 51, 55,-7, 59-60, 64-6, 71, 74, 76-7, 79, 81 n299, 82, 83 n1, 84-5, 87, 89-90, 92, 92 n27, 98, 100-4, 106-7, 109, 110 n108, 112. 114, 124-5, 133, 135, 138-40, 142-6, 148, 157, 162, 162 n92, 163-7, 169-72, 178, 185-90, 194, 197-8, 214-15, 218-20, 222, 234, 236, 239, 242-4, 246-7, 250, 252, 254, 258, 264-5, 270-2
   Tenth, US vi, ix, xi, 17, 19-22, 26-28, 33-34, 38, 42, 46-50 52-3, 55 n181, 56, 58, 64, 66, 69, 72-3, 76-9, 82-3, 87 n12, 88, 90-4, 96-7, 107-8, 110 n108, 113, 124, 126-7, 131, 133-5, 138, 143, 146-51, 153, 155, 157, 160-2, 167, 170-2, 175-6, 182-3, 199, 202-5, 210-11, 214-15, 223-6, 229-30, 233, 235, 237, 240-1, 243-4, 247, 251-2, 254-6, 263, 268, 271, 273-4, 276 n28, 278
   Tenth US Colored 17 n12
Cayagan River-Valley, PI 160
Certificate of Merit 21-22, 51-52
Chaplain 42, 52, 54, 80, 82, 110, 112-35
Chattanooga, TN 59, 223
Cheatham,
   Alexander 20
   Annie 20
Checkers 217
Cherry Creek, AZ 152
Chess 217
Cheyenne 146-7, 154, 197, 272. 274
Cheyenne Agency 147
Cheyenne, WY 55, 250
Chicago, IL 48, 53, 75, 112, 117, 120-1, 174, 179, 220
Chickamauga, GA 72, 126, 223-4, 242, 251
Chinese -Chinese Exclusion Act 198, 262
Chinn, Charles 22-25, 229
Chiricahua see Apache
Chiricahua Cattle Company 248
Chiricahua National Monument 204
Chiricahua Mountains, AZ 48
Christian, Garna L.283
Christmas 103, 130, 220-1, 243
Church of Latter-Day Saints/Mormons 49, 225, 242
Cincinnati, OH 25, 223
City College of New York 38
City of Para 139
Civil Rights xi, 23, 55 n182, 82, 135
Civil War xi, 9, 16, 25-26, 33-6, 38, 45, 47, 49, 72, 76-7, 83, 85-7, 89, 92, 112, 114-15, 120-22, 125, 136 n2, 139, 168, 193. 195. 198, 202, 216, 219, 222-3, 227, 231-3, 237, 252, 254, 266, 277
Clafin University 124
Clay, John 70
Clark, William 135
Clarke, Powhatan 149, 152-3, 172, 219, 248, 263
Clemens, Samuel AKA Mark Twain 266
Cleveland, OH 124, 126-7
Cleveland Homeopathic Medical Clinic 126

Cleveland, Grover 104, 116
Clous, John W. 97
Cody, William 'Buffalo Bill' vii, 42, 48 n142
Coeur d'Alene Reservation, WA 163, 173-4, 190
Colchester (now Winooski), VT 52
Cole, Pollard 50
Colladay, Samuel 148
Collins, Tom 66
Colonia Dublan, Chihuahua, Mexico 132, 225-6
Columbia, SC 47
Columbia, TN 60
Columbus, NM 108, 226 n124, 243 n84
Columbus, OH 129
Columbus, OH 61
Columbus Business College 129
Comanche 138, 141, 147, 149, 155, 159, 272-3, 275
Comancheros 139
Commissary - Commissary Department - Commissary Sergeant 25, 27, 38, 41, 85, 89, 97, 102, 127, 195, 195, 208-10, 227
Conner, Charles 167
Cook 16, 29, 45, 111, 162 n94, 200, 203, 208, 219
Corbusier, Fanny 203, 219
  William 210 n53, 219
Corps of Discovery 136
Couch, William 163
Court-Martial 25, 63-4
Covington, LA 227
Cox, Elijah 45, 47
Coxey, Jacob 174
Crawford, NE 72, 115, 170
Crowell, W.H.H. 260
Creek, Charles 20-21
Christy, W. 146
Cuba 21-22, 43, 52-6, 59-60, 72, 81 n299, 88-9, 112, 124, 126-7, 141, 154, 156, 158-9, 162, 167, 182, 192, 224, 231, 242, 251, 253, 255-6, 260, 265, 267, 277
Culpeper County, VA 25
Culver, G.E. 183
Cumbre Tunnel, Chihuahua, Mexico 167
Cusack, Patrick 139
Custer, Bethel Moore 85
Custer, Elizabeth Bacon 80
  George Armstrong 92, 179
Cynthiana, KY 21

Dances – 'Hops' 94, 131, 145, 196, 219-21
Daniels, James T. 152
Danilson, William 83
Davis, Benjamin F. 34 n73
Davis, Benjamin O., Sr. 41, 109-10
Davis, Helen 274
Davis, Martin 149
Davis, Stanford L. 263-4
Davis, Theodore 274
Deadwood, SD 43
Decoration (Memorial) Day 240-2
Defiance Normal College 129
Democrat- Democratic Party 111, 116, 247, 259
Denny, John 102, 141
Department of
  Arizona 149, 153, 254
  Dakotas 142, 183
  the Gulf 89, 154
  Interior 187
  Mananillo, Cuba 127
  Missouri 207, 277
  South 93, 238
  Texas 259
Desertion 15, 60, 63-5, 76-9, 216, 265, 278
Detroit, MI 46, 66
Diamond Club 220, 222
Díaz, Porfirio 141, 156, 254
Dickerson, Richard 76
Discrimination-Prejudice 39, 52, 59, 82, 92-3, 98, 115, 131, 135, 140, 176, 226, 232, 237-9, 244, 251, 257, 259-60, 262, 267, 277, 282
Disease-Illness 32, 43, 49, 56 n185, 64 n215, 127, 144, 153, 159 212, 226
Dixie 242
Dobak, William 90, 277
Dockery, Albert B. 236-7
Dodge, Charles 68, 276
Dodge, Francis 86-7, 142
Douglas, AZ 239, 24, 243-4
Douglass, Frederick 118
Douglass, Primas 69
Downey, Fairfax 271
Drew Theological Seminary 129
Drexel Mission, SD 145
Dubois, W.E.B.108, 135
Dubose, Edward A.65
Dudley, N.A.M. 97 165, 202
Dunbar-Ortiz, Roxanne 263

Eagle Springs, TX 96, 148
East St. Louis, IL 126
East Tennessee Banker's Association 132
Edison, Thomas 280
Education-Schools 19, 36, 80, 56, 106, 112, 127-8, 202, 211, 231 n18
Edwards, David 69
El Caney, Cuba 72, 158
Ellis, Ben 165
Ellis, William 'Dead' 44-6
El Paso, TX 50, 138-9 161, 224, 239, 256, 258
El Paso County, TX 166
El Paso and Southwestern Railroad 224
El Pozo Hills, Cuba 157-8
Embezzlement 25 n47, 97
Enlist - Enlistment 19, 27, 20 n62, 33-5, 46-7, 60, 62, 198, 229, 232-3, 260, 278
Episcopal 97, 220
Escort Duties 104, 138, 145, 147, 170-1, 183, 250
Everts, Edward 215
Extortion 259

Factor, Pompey 141
Fagen, David 62-3, 265, 267
Fairmount Cemetery, San Angelo, TX 46-7
Farrier 16, 52, 64
Faulkner, Charles 50
Finley, Leighton 96, 148
Finnegan, Michael 203
Fitzgerald, John 24 n42, 229
Fires 22 n31, 51 n157, 122, 190-1, 197-8
First Sergeant 21, 23, 26-7, 38, 53, 76, 91, 93, 141, 208, 254
Fleming, William 69-70, 72
Fletcher, Nathan 92
Flipper, Henry O. 41, 95-8, 115, 134-5, 167
Florence, AZ 70
Food-Rations 33, 195, 198, 200, 208, 209-10, 216, 225, 264
Football 216, 225
Ford, J.E.121
Forest Service, United States 190, 192
Forgery 79
Forsyth, George A. 147
Fort
　Ethan Allen, VT 127, 133, 170, 193, 224, 239
　Apache, AZ 27, 38, 42, 54, 57, 149, 214-15, 222, 224

Arbuckle, OK 34
Assiniboine, MT 58, 74, 123, 126-7, 154, 183, 211
Bayard, NM 14, 27, 29, 41, 53-4, 88, 117, 142, 144, 149, 21 n57, 215-16, 243, 265, 276
Benning, GA 133
Bliss, TX 224, 256
Bowie, AZ 25 n42, 88, 199, 207
Brown, TX 258
Bufford, ND 175
Clark, TX 39, 72, 74. 89
Concho, TX 44, 74, 89, 147-8, 155, 162, 197, 210, 214. 219, 255
Craig, NM 206
Cummings, NM 29, 195
Custer, MT 25, 69 n233, 175, 177 n143, 178
Davis, TX 28, 44-5, 48, 63, 74, 89, 95-7, 138-40, 205
Dodge, KS 147, 171, 196, 200
Douglas, UT 41, 51-3, 56 n185, 117-8
Duncan, TX 39, 74, 155
Duchesne, UT 51, 66, 100-2, 106, 109, 145, 199, 217, 221-2
Elliott, TX 167-8
Ethan Allen, VT 127, 133, 170, 193, 224, 239
Garland, CO 142, 194, 198
Gibson, OK 147
Griffin, TX 147-8, 254
Grant, AZ 38, 42, 48, 73, 78, 172, 149, 199, 203, 207
Harker, KS 269
Harrison, MT 121, 181
Harrison, VA 34
Hays, KS 27, 74. 146, 247
Sam Houston, TX 72
Huachuca, AZ 49, 53-4, 56, 68, 93 127, 131, 133-4, 174 n132, 209 n41, 213, 216, 221-2, 224, 236, 280
Lancaster, TX 139
Laramie, WY 178
Larned, KS vi, 235
Lawton, WA 61, 75, 221, 238
Leavenworth, KS 17, 93-4, 102, 133, 146, 233, 235-6 280, 282
Logan 238
McDowell, CA 56, 119
McKavett, TX 28, 36, 46, 74
William McKinley, PI 127

McKinney, WY 66, 116, 145, 190
McPherson, GA 25, 167
McRae, NM 142
Marcy, NM 27
Massachusetts, MS 77
Meade, SD 218, 238, 249-50
Missoula, MT iv, 43, 76, 78. 137, 173-4, 176, 180-2, 213, 220
Myer, VA 39
Omaha, NE 102, 114
Ontario, NY 43 n118, 224
Niobrara, NE 53, 100, 145
Pulaski, GA 24
Quitman, TX 45, 96, 139, 148, 196
Reno, OK 14, 61, 67
Richardson, TX 147, 270
Riley, KS 27, 29,107, 114, 216 n74, 220
Ringgold, TX 258-9
Robinson, NE 217-18, 220, 222
D.A. Russell, WY 143, 250
Selden, NM 27, 46, 142, 207
Shaw, MT 66, 182-3
Sheridan, IL 42
Sherman, ID 173
Sidney, NE 101
Sill, OK 73, 147, 199, 220 n102
Sisseton, SD 66
Stanton, NM 142, 164-5
Stockton, TX 74, 89, 138
Stotsenberg, PI 59
Thomas, AZ 73, 149, 153, 172, 220, 265, 276 n28
Union, NM 17 n12, 29, 142, 164 200-1
Verde, AZ 149
Wallace, KS 147
Washakie, WY 100, 172
Whipple, AZ (Whipple Barracks) 222
Wingate, NM 142, 219, 222, 243
George Wright, WA 75, 129 n185
Fort Robinson Punch 114
4th of July 119, 173, 221, 226, 243
Fox, Richard K. Boxing Rules 216
Fox, William 53
Franklin, Henrietta 49
  Selim 49
Freedman's Bureau 116, 139-40
Fresh Fork, TX 155
Frierson, E.P. 52
Fulton, Davis 88

Gadsden Purchase 166
Gallipolis, OH 128
Galloway, John 266
Garner, John Nance 239
Gatling Gun 164, 259
Gavilan Canyon, NM 27
Gem Mine, ID 174
Gender 29 n62, 33 n67
General Grant National Park 183, 185, 187
Geneva Convention 127
Georgetown, KY 48
Germantown, KY 49
Geronimo 48, 149-50
Gettysburg, PA 39
Ghost Dance 136 n2, 145-6
Givens, William 20-22
Glacier National Park 181, 183
Gladden, Elizabth 124
Gladden, Washington 120 n148, 128-32
Glasrud, Bruce viii
Glendive, MT 175
Globe, AZ 151-2, 243, 265
Goldsby, George 255
Goodloe, Thomas 54
Graham, George W. 147
Graham County, AZ 152
Graine, John H. 60
Grand Army of the Republic 120, 187
Grant, Ulysess S. 231-2
Great Migration 36, 62
Greaves, Clinton 141
Green, Henry 71
Green, John Ernest 110
Greene, William 38-41, 103, 116
Greenleaf, Charles 139
Greenville, LA 19
Grierson,
  Alice 219
  Benjamin 47, 90-1, 96, 146, 148, 153, 156, 219, 234, 241, 255, 272
  Charles 78
  Edith 47
Grimes, James 'Bunky' 54
Grimes, Washington M.113
Guadalupe College, TX 132
Guadalupe Hidalgo, Treaty of 166, 257
Guadalupe Mountains, TX 149
Guion, Elijah 113

Haiti-Hayti 108, 120, 122
Hale (Miguel) 151
Hall, One 66
Haller, George 253
Hallon, Ross (AKA Hollis and Hallis) 248
Hamlin, Thomas 53
Hammond, Wade H. 55
Hanging 69, 73
Harrison, Benjamin 68, 173
Harrison, James 60-1
Harvey, Ned C. 229
Hatch, Edward 84, 90, 138-43, 163-5, 214, 247
Hatcher, Willis 52
Hawaii Volcanoes 183
Hawkins, Emmett 212
Hays City, KS 66
Hazen, William 39
Health 15 n7, 19 n22, 32, 43-4, 119, 121, 131, 218, 234, 236, 257, 278
Helena, MT 175, 181
Helena High School, AR 99, 104
Heliographs 211
Henson, John 72
Herbert, George 152
Herkness, Bernard 77
Heyl, Edward 77
Hicks, G.W. 54
Hicks, WIliam 62
Higgins, C.P 214.
Hills, Abe 250
Hindsman, Sarah 53
Hixon, George 53
Hoffman, William 233-5
'Hog Ranch' 73
Holabird, Samuel 35
Holmes, W.A. 'Hunkydory'151
Homicide-Murder 54, 65-6, 68-74, 151, 164, 247, 249 n111, 251, 255
Homosexuality 76
Honey Spring AR, Battle of xi
Honolulu, HI 61, 78, 130, 267
Horses 23, 26, 35, 49, 138-9, 143-8, 151, 153, 155, 161, 164-5, 170-1, 185, 187, 223-4, 226, 243-4, 271 276
Hospital Corps 41, 57, 203, 229
Houston, TX 72, 76, 257-9, 261, 267
Howard, Michael 94
Howard, Robert 53

Howard County, MD 28
Howard University 82, 126
Howitzer 165, 200
Huff, Albert 65
Huntsville, AL 223
Hurley, John 66, 250
Hynds, Harry 250

Iba, Zimbales, PI 160
Illiteracy-Literacy 19, 24, 36, 38, 56, 62, 112. 119, 252, 282
Indian Bureau, United States 141
Indianapolis, IN 38
Infantry Regiments
    African American Charlotte Light (Raleigh, NC) 102
    First South Carolina 82, 112
    First, USCT 26, 84
    Second Regiment of Missouri Colored 26
    Second, US 145
    Third, US 235, 250
    Fourth, US 5, 142, 173
    Eighth, US 145
    Eight, US Volunteer 252 n121
    Ninth Battalion, Ohio National Guard 104
    Ninth, U.S. Volunteer 26, 252 n121
    Tenth, U.S. Volunteer 252 n121
    Eleventh, USCT 85
    Fourteenth, US 240
    Fifteenth, US 164, 236, 277
    Fifteenth, USCT 94
    Sixteenth, US 97, 254-6
    Eighteenth, Kansas Volunteers 146
    Twenty-Fourth, US xi, 14, 23, 26, 35-6, 41, 49-50, 52-6, 59-60, 62, 67-8, 72-3, 78-9, 82, 84, 87-9, 97, 108, 110, 113, 115-21, 128, 155, 157-60, 163, 167-8, 172, 174, 177-8, 180, 184-5, 200, 205, 212-13, 215-16, 220-1, 223-6, 234, 239, 242, 244 250, 260, 262, 265, 276
    Twenty-Third, USCT 22
    Twenty-Fifth, US vii, xi, 36, 44, 46, 54, 61, 65-6, 73-5, 78, 80, 82, 89, 93, 110, 113, 121-3, 125, 129, 131, 134, 137, 155-8, 160, 167, 173-8, 180-5, 190, 200, 205, 214, 219, 223, 228-9, 238. 240-2, 244, 248-51, 260-1, 265, 271
    Twenty-Eighth, USCT 20, 22
    Thirty-Second, USCT 25, 85

Thirty-Eighth, US x-xi, 17, 29, 66, 74, 77, 83-5, 154-5, 247
Thirty-Ninth, US x-xi, 19
Fortieth, US x-xi. 18, 83, 19
Forty-First, US x-xi., 19, 26, 84, 89, 140
Forty-First, USCT 34
Forty-Fourth USCT 49
Forty-Eighth, US Volunteer 25, 38, 159, 252 n121
Forty-Ninth Illinois Volunteers 111
Forty-Ninth, US Volunteer 159, 252 n121
Fifty-Seventh, USCT 17
Sixty-Fifth, USCT 26, 85
Eighty-First, USCT 84
116th, USCT 28, 46
Israel Methodist Church 20
Insurrectos 159

Jackson, Thornton 51
  Viola 51
Jacobi, John C. 113
Jeffers, David 25-6
Jefferson, William 69
Jefferson Barracks, MO 17, 2942, 47, 65, 77, 235
Jefferson City, MO 31
Jennings, Maggie 68
Jenkins, Jerry 35
Jenkins, William 53
Jim Crow Laws 25, 223, 230, 239, 267
Johnson, Henry 141, 143
Johnson, John W. 216
Johnson, Joshua 33
Johnson, Nathan 139
Johnson, Silas 52
Johnson, Willis 250
Johnson County War 165, 175
Jones, E.T. 138
Jones, Jeremiah 115, 229
Jordan, George 141
Juarez, Benito 13, 141
Judge Advocate General Department 89, 97, 102, 247

Kanto, Japan 90
Kean, Jefferson 178
Kelvin Grade, AZ 151
Kendell, Fred 74
Kent, Jacob F. 157

Kickapoo 138, 141, 148, 155
Kickpoo Springs, TX 44
Kilpatrick 224
King, Leslie 130
Kiowa 138, 141, 147, 149, 272
Kipling, Rudyard 266
'Kitchen Police' (KP) 200
Knights of Pythias 222
Knights Templar 103
Knoxville, KY 132, 223
Kornegay, James 14
Kosterlitzky, Emilio 151
Krag-Jorgenson 258
Ku Klux Klan 69. 253

Labor Disputes 173-8
Laborer 16, 28, 32 n70, 4853, 62, 103
The Ladies 198
Lake Constance, AZ 199
Lansing Penitentiary, KS 79
Larceny 77
Las Guasimas, Cuba 157
Lashley, Phillip 68-9
Latina-Latino 166, 257, 260
Laundry-Laundress 29, 32, 197
Lawrence, Mary Leefe 196
Lawton, Henry W. 157-8
Lebo, Thomas 148-9
Leckie, William H. 271-3, 276
Lee, Joseph 53, 65
Lehmann, Herman 275
Leiker, James N. vi
Lemmons, David 67-8
Lewis, George 78-9
Lewis, Meriwether 136
Lincoln County War 164-5
Lincoln, Abraham 122, 129, 230
  Robert 39
Lipan 138-9, 141, 148, 155, 138-9, 140 n15, 141, 148
Little Bighorn, MT 92, 178, 182
Little Rock, AK 31, 238
Livingston, MT 175-6
Llano Estacado (Staked Plains) 148, 162
Lockwood, Benjamin 175
Logan, Rayford 82
Loredo, TX 260
Los Angeles, CA 59, 121, 126, 128
Louis, Joe 82, 135

Louisville, KY 19, 38
Loving, Walter 41
Ludlow, William 182
Lunenburg County, VA 54
Luzon, PI 160
Lynch,
    John Roy 111-12
    Patrick 111
Lynching 248-50
Lyons, John 52

Mackenzie, Ranald 89, 140, 156, 167
McBryar, William 141, 152-3
McCabe, William 44
McCarthy, Tom 255
McCaw, Melvin 60
McClelland, Kate 73
McCoy, Charles 65
McCoy, Frank 90
McDonald Lake, MT 181
McElroy, George 75-6
McGhee, Elizabeth 52-3
McGuire, Charles 66
McIntyre, Henry 112
McKinney, Susan 124
McKinzie, Edmund 91
McSween, Alexander 164-5
Machine Gun 108, 157, 213, 225
Madison Barracks, NY 55, 128, 133, 224
USS *Maine* 156
Mallets Bay, VT 52
Mangus 150
Mangus Coloradas 150
Manifest Destiny 195, 264
Manila, PI 41, 61, 118, 127-8, 256
Mann, Sampson 35
Mann, E.C. 70
Manslaughter 66
Marchbank, Vance H., Sr. 58, 273
Maricopa County Jail, AZ 70
Marine Corps, US 55, 253
Markley, A.C. 234
Marksman-Sharpshooter 47, 60
Marriage 28, 43-4, 52, 124
Marshall, George C. 90
Martial Law 174
Martin, John 49
Masons (Prince Hall) 38, 222
Mauna Loa Trail 183

Maury County, TN 54
May's Lick, KY 105
Mays, Isaiah 141
Mazique, Edward ('Sancho' also spelled
    Maziche and Mozique) 45-7
Medal of Honor xii, , 22, 39, 51, 71, 87, 91,
    102, 141, 143-4, 146, 149 152, 153 n55
Meeker, Nathan 142
Memorials 279-80
Memphis, TN 19, 56, 65, 224
Merced River, CA 189
Merritt, Wesley 89, 139, 177, 183
Mescal Springs, AZ 243
Metropolitan Church, Washington, DC 129
Mexican Border Service Medal 133
Michie, Peter S. 95
Middleton, Eugene 151
Miles, Nelson A. 150, 179, 182
Milk River, CO 142-3
Miller, Charles 65
Miller,
    Girard 203
    Jenny 203
Mills,
    Anson 199
    Constance 199
Mineral Point, WI 38
Mingus, Charles, Jr. 58-9
    Charles, Sr. 58-9
    Harriet 59
    Jacob 58
    Sarah 58
    Vivian 58
Minneapolis, MN 182, 241, 277
Minstrels 219, 225-6, 243
Mississippi River xii, 136, 242, 251
Missoula, MT 176, 214, 220, 251
Mogollon Mountains, AZ 142-3, 149
Mollie Maguires 69
Monrovia, CA 122
Monterey, CA 189, 236
Moore, Francis 164
Montgomery, Quennie 66, 250
Monihan, James 28
Morey, Lewis 161
Moros 129
Morrow, Albert 151
Moscow, Russia
Moss, James 168, 179-82, 185

Mt. Whitney, CA 188
Muir, John 183
Mulatto 68
Mullins, G.G. 80
Murphy, William 177
Music 41, 55, 109, 118, 130-1, 219-220
Mutiny 76-7, 138, 255

Nagasaki, Japan 61
Namiquipa District, Mexico 161
Nana 27, 144, 149
Nasworthy's Saloon 255
National African American Press Association
National Archives and Record Administration 118
National Association for the Advancement of Colored People (NAACP) 15
National Educational Association (NEA) 117
National Park Service, US vi, 178, 281
National Regular Army and Navy Union 38, 222
National Soldiers Home 28
Native American 154, 162, 263, 270, 272-4
Nave, Orville 114
Navy, US ix, xi, 55, 114-16, 120, 158, 229, 270
Nelson, Frank 72-3
Neuman, Maria 42
Neutrality Laws 166
New Orleans, LA ix, 89, 138, 226, 238-9, 247
New York, NY 118, 196, 220
Nicholas, W.M. 186-7
Nolan, Nicolas 162, 167, 235
Nordstrom, Charles 229
Northern Pacific Railroad 175, 242

Oahu, HI 240, 244
Oak and Ivy Club 222
Oakley, Annie 162
Oberlin College 99-100
Ocala, FL 242
Oconaluftee Valley, NC 58
Ohio Wesleyan University 129
Ojo Caliente, NM 142
Old Mount Zion Church, Knoxville, KY 132
Oliver, Fannie 73
O'Neil, Joseph 176
'Outlook for the Race' 118
Overr, Cora 53

Paiute 144
Panic of 1893 174
Parang, PI 61
Parker, Joseph 26
Parker, Montgomery 171
Parker, Quanah 273
Parker, William 195
Parkman, Joseph 214
Parmer, Amos 66
Parmly Billings Memorial Library, MT 43
Paseños 166
Pash-ten-tah (Bach-e-on-al) 151
Patton, George S., Jr. 90
Pay 22 n31, 24, 28, 40, 43, 47-8, 51, 79, 84, 97, 131 198, 202, 216-17, 227, 229, 240, 264
Paymaster Department 79, 87, 111-12, 172, 240
Payne Theological Seminary, OH 124
Payne, Adam (AKA Paine) 141
Payne, David 162-3
Payne, Isaac 141
Payne, William 52
Pecos River, TX 38, 155
Pedee, Martin 74
Pensacola, FL 39
Pension 48-49, 51, 53, 59, 100 n64, 264
Pepper, George 113
Pershing, John ("Black Jack") 88-90, 108, 161, 211, 225, 230-1, 233
Peterson, P.J. 74
Philadelphia, PA 19, 118
Philippines 88, 110, 112 118-19, 124, 127, 129, 133, 159-60, 183, 192-3, 224, 260, 265-7, 282
Phillips County. 99
Phillips, Birdie 53
Phillips, James 53
Phillips, Thomas 90, 268, 270, 277
Phoenix, AZ 29, 49, 70-1
Plessy, Adolph 227
Plessy v. Fergusson 227, 252
Pierce, Charles 114
Pine Camp, NY 133
Pineto Mountains, Mexico 149
Pinkerton detectives 177
Pipes, Henry 189
Platte River, NE 172
Plummer, Henry 41, 112, 114-15, 125, 134-5, 217-18
Poindexter, Max 131

Pope, John 80, 277
Porter, Sarah 53
Porters 17, 48
Port Said 58
Post Sullivan, TX 253
Posse Comitatus Act 174
Post Exchange/Sutler 102, 127, 196, 202, 217-18
Post Library 127, 134, 202, 218, 220
Powell, Anthony 264
Powell, Colin 282
Prescott, AZ 28, 149, 240-1
Presidio of San Francisco, CA v, 56, 59, 118-19, 128, 169, 185, 199, 216, 236, 243, 281
Price, UT 101
Pride, Alfred 64
Prioleau, Ethel 131
Prioleau, George 124-6
Proctor, Redfield 33, 239
Prostitution 67, 73, 218, 259
Pulaski, TN 50
Pullman Car Company 174
Pungoteague, VA 42
Punitive Expedition 107-8, 111, 130, 161, 224-5, 280

Race 25, 33, 63, 80-82, 104, 107, 110., 116-19, 126, 128, 130, 135. 190, 227-35
Railroads vii, 25, 48, 83, 101, 156, 170, 174-7, 195, 207, 224, 242
Rattlesnake Springs, TX 156
Reade, Robert 176
Reconstruction xi, 13, 96, 111, 168, 253
Recruiting xii n10, 17 n12, 18 n14, 19, 35, 38, 61-2, 117, 124, 127, 132, 224, 230, 233
Red River War 148
'Red Summer' 259
Reenlistment 21, 27, 33, 48, 53, 56, 58-9, 230 n9, 278
Reeves, Jesse 77
Remington, Frederic vii, viii, 94, 153
Renaud, C.M. 248
Republican Party 85, 94, 99, 111-13, 120, 126, 147, 230
Revolutionary War ix, 5 122
Rhodes, Charles Dudley 105
Richmond, VA 48, 58
Rio Bravo-Rio Grande 139-41, 148-9, 154, 155-6, 238, 252, 254, 256-7

Rio Grande City, TX 258-60
Rip 150
Ripley, OH 105
Road building 101, 184, 187-8, 190, 202
Robertson, Robert 66, 250
Robinson, Jackie 82, 135
Robinson, Mansfield 35
Rochester, NY 39, 208
Rodney, George 93, 166
Roe, Frances 200, 268-9
Roggenstrohs's Ranch, AZ 152
Roman, Nose 147, 273
Rome, GA 49
Romeyn, Charles 93
Roosevelt, Theodore 90, 120-1, 129, 146, 169-70. 231, 261
Rosebud Reservation, SD 145
Rouse, O.T. 69
Rowdy 152
Royal Military School of Music, London 55
Royer, D.F. 145
Rucker, Alfred 51
Russell, Lewis 65
Russum, Louis 78

Saber 49, 77, 170, 208, 213, 220
Saddler 23, 26, 115
St. John's Church 126
St. Louis, MO iv, 137, 181-2
St. Paul, MN 242
San Angelo, TX 28, 44-7, 254
San Antonio TX 89, 138, 267
San Carlos Reservation, AZ 42, 50, 69, 71, 78, 142-3, 150-1, 153, 254, 246, 265, 274
San Elizario, TX 166
San Francisco, CA 53, 56, 59, 61, 89, 119, 121, 128, 169-70, 182, 185, 187, 193, 199, 207, 236, 243, 277, 281
San Felipe, TX 156
San Joaquin Valley, CA 121
San Juan Hill 26, 43. 60, 118, 157-8, 255
San Mateo, PI 159
Santa Fe, NM 27, 142-3, 150, 166
Santa Fe Ring 164
Sanders, John 68
Sanders, Mingo 81, 228
Santiago, Cuba 21, 52, 60, 157-8, 170
Santo Domingo 18
Santo Domingo Ranch, Mexico 161

Saragossa, Mexico 155
Saulsbury, Willard, Jr. 247
Savage, W. Sherman 63, 80
Savannah, GA 24
Say-es 151
Schofield Barracks, HI 126, 129-30, 190
Schubert, Frank 264, 272
Schuller, Charles 65
Schultz, John N. 133
Scott, Edward 149
Scott, E.J. 41
Scott, John. 66
Scott, O.J.W. 128-32
Seattle, WA 61, 75, 238
Segregation 227-9
Seguin, TX 126
Seminole 140-1, 155
Sequoia National Park, CA v, 107, 183-8, 190
Settler Colonialism viii, 262, 283
Sewall, Alexander 55
Shafter, William 'Pecos Bill' 89, 97, 155, 158
Sharpe, William 139
Shaw, Thomas 91, 141
Sheridan 61
Sheridan, Philip 100
Sherman, William 32, 207, 232-33, 239
Shiloh Baptist Church 25
Ship Island, MS 77, 168
Shipman, Lee 49-50
Shorter Chapel, Denver, CO 129
Shropshire, Shelvin 72, 94
Sierra Diabola, TX 148
Signal Corps 39-41, 229
Sioux /Lakota 144, 265
Sitting Bull 145
Skagway, AK 2056, 251
Smith, James Webster 24
Smith, John 78
Smith, Laura 53
Smith, George Washington 143
Snoten, Augustus 61
'Solid South' 111
Sour 278
Spalding Company 182
Spanish American War 117, 128, 142, 156-9, 167, 180, 239, 244, 251-3, 260, 267
Spaatz, Carl 91 n21
Spartanburg, SC 47
Spencer, Jeremiah 65

Spokane, WA 75, 191
Springfield, OH 103
Springfield Carbine-Rifle 67, 77, 276 n28, 278
Stagecoach 139, 172, 195
Stance, Emanuel 71-2, 140-1
Starbird, A.V. 117
Starr County, NM 247
Starr, Stephen 26
Steward, Theophilus G. 82, 122-4, 175
Stokes,
   Ernest 59-60
   Roberta 59
'Striker' AKA 'Dog Robber' 172, 175-6, 202-3
Sturgis, SD 238, 248-50
Suwanee River, 242
Suggs, WY 250, 165
Sullivant, James 25
Sumner, Charles 23
Sun River, MT 66, 250
Supreme Court, US 70, 227
Sutler's Store (See Post Exchange)
Swain, Sampa 75
Swain County, NC 58
Sweet, Owen 178-9
Sykes, Zekiel 91

Tacony Plantation, LA 111
Taft, William Howard 132, 238-9
'Talented Tenth' 41, 135
Talliaferro, Daniel 74
Tampa, FL 62, 157, 253
Tate, Michael viii, 192
Taylor, Charles 178
Taylor, Frank 106, 234
Taylor, John 53
Taylor, Stephen 91
Telegraph 40, 101, 171, 194. 202, 207
Tennis 199
Texarkana, TX 255
Texas Rangers 166, 257, 261
Thompson, Allen 76
Thompson, John 83
Thompson, J. Milton 174
Thompson, Samuel 65
Thornton, Beverly 52
Tirona, Daniel 160
Tinaja de las Palmas, TX 96
Tockes, William 148
Tombstone, Arizona 243

Tongue River Agency, MT 154
Topeka, KS 104
Trent, Louis 66
Trimble, Andrew 139
Trinidad, CO 29, 32
Trooper of Troop K 280
Troutman, Edward 246
Tucson, AZ 48-9, 52, 70, 134, 152
Tugeraroa, Cayagan, PI 160
Tulare County, CA 52, 187
Tunstall, John 164
Turner, Charles 38
Turner, David 154
Turner, Frederick Jackson 54
Turner, Henry 266
Tuskegee Institute-University 129, 132

Uniforms 35-6, 100, 208, 236, 253, 276 n28
United Order of Odd Fellows 38, 187, 222
United States Colored Troops (USCT) See Cavalry Regiments and Infantry Regiments
US Military Academy West Point, NY 100 xii, 60, 85, 87-9, 93-6, 98-100, 105-6, 179-80, 193
University of Denver 129
Upper Gila River 142
Ute (Uncompahgre) 142, 274

Valentine, NE 74
Vancouver Barracks, WA 79
Van Vliet, Fredrick 149
Varnon, William (AKA Varnum and Henry Varnom) 48-9
Vega, Cruz 164
Victorio 21, 27, 96, 142-4, 148, 156, 273
Villa, Francisco 'Pancho' vii, 108, 160-1
Villistas 108, 161
Villard, Oswald 15
Vidalia, LA 111

Waiter 17, 208
Waites, William 99
Walker, Adelaide 128
Walker, James 48
Wall, Archy 54
Walla Walla Penitentiary, WA 76
Wallace, ID 173-4, 177, 192
Wallace, Lew 165
  Harry 197, 222

Gertrude 197
Mattie 197
Waller, Rueben 264, 273
Waller, Samuel 56
Walley, Augustus 141
Walter Reed Hospital 43
War Department 78-7, 103-4, 120, 122, 131, 159, 161, 187 238, 240, 251, 258
War of 1812 ix, 136
Ward, John 141
Wardner, ID 173-4, 177
Washington, Andrew 65
Washington, Annie 198
Washington, Booker T. 41, 96, 117, 126, 129-30, 187, 266
Washington, DC 18, 20, 37, 43, 56, 58, 78, 109, 114, 126, 129, 203
Washington High School Cadet Corps 41, 58, 109
Watkins, William 255
Watson, James 152-3
Watson, Pleas 254-5
Weaver, Asa 148
Weaver, Jace 263
Webb, Alexander 39
Webster, Peter 67-8
West, Julia 43
Western University 55
Wham, Joseph 51, 172
Wheeler, Joseph 157
'White Man's Burden' 266
White Rose Society 118
Wilberforce University/ Wilberforce, OH 98, 102-4,107, 110, 122, 124, 126-7
Wilks, Jacob (AKA Wilkes) 46-7
Williams v. Mississippi 252
Williams, Annie 74
Williams, Cathy see William Cathay/Cather
Williams, George W. 34
Williams, James 77
Williams, Moses 24 n43, 141
Williams, Squire 51
Wilson, George 91
Wilson, Henry 65
Wilson, Jefferson 69-71
Wilson, William O.141, 146
Wilson, Woodrow 160
Wilson Creek Station, KS 274
Winooski United Methodist Church

Wister, Owen 142
Wokcoff, Green E.N. 75
Woods, Brent 51, 141, 144
Wooley, William 216
World War I 241
World War I Victory Medal 133
World War II 57
Wounded Knee 145, 154, 220
Wright, Emanuel 138
Wright, William vi

Yaqui 162
Yavapai 151
Yellowstone National Park iii, 181-3, 185
Yosemite National Park, CA v, 183-6, 190
Yukon Territory 167
Young, Charles 170, 186-8, 222, 234, 236-7, 243-4, 104-9, 127, 132, 135, 161, 170, 186-8, 222, 234, 236-7, 243-4

Zamboanga, Mindanao, PI 61
Zion Baptist Church 121

The period 1815-1914 is sometimes called the long century of peace. It was in reality very far from that. It was a century of civil wars, popular uprisings, and struggles for Independence. An era of colonial expansion, wars of Empire, and colonial campaigning, much of which was unconventional in nature. It was also an age of major conventional wars, in Europe that would see the Crimea campaign and the wars of German unification. Such conflicts, along with the American Civil War, foreshadowed the total war of the 20th century.

It was also a period of great technological advancement, which in time impacted the military and warfare in general. Steam power, electricity, the telegraph, the radio, the railway, all became tools of war. The century was one of dramatic change. Tactics altered, sometimes slowly, to meet the challenges of the new technology. The dramatic change in the technology of war in this period is reflected in the new title of this series: From Musket to Maxim.

The new title better reflects the fact that the series covers all nations and all conflict of the period between 1815-1914. Already the series has commissioned books that deal with matters outside the British experience. This is something that the series will endeavour to do more of in the future. At the same time there still remains an important place for the study of the British military during this period. It is one of fascination, with campaigns that capture the imagination, in which Britain although the world's predominant power, continues to field a relatively small army.

The aim of the series is to throw the spotlight on the conflicts of that century, which can often get overlooked, sandwiched as they are between two major conflicts, the French/Revolutionary/Napoleonic Wars and the First World War. The series will produced a variety of books and styles. Some will look simply at campaigns or battles. Others will concentrate on particular aspects of a war or campaign. There will also be books that look at wider concepts of warfare during this era. It is the intention that this series will present a platform for historians to present their work on an important but often overlooked century of warfare.

Submissions

The publishers would be pleased to receive submissions for this series. Please contact series editor Dr Christopher Brice via email (christopherbrice@helion.co.uk), or in writing to Helion & Company Limited, Unit 8, Amherst Business Centre, Budbrooke Road, Warwick, Warwickshire, CV34 5WE.

Books in this series:
1. *The Battle of Majuba Hill: The Transvaal Campaign 1880–1881* John Laband (ISBN 978-1-911512-38-7)
2. *For Queen and Company: Vignettes of the Irish Soldier in the Indian Mutiny* David Truesdale (ISBN 978-1-911512-79-0)
3. *The Furthest Garrison: Imperial Regiments in New Zealand 1840–1870* Adam Davis (ISBN 978-1-911628-29-3)
4. *Victory Over Disease: Resolving the Medical Crisis in the Crimean War, 1854–1856* Michael Hinton (ISBN 978-1-911628-31-6)
5. *Journey Through the Wilderness: Garnet Wolseley's Canadian Red River Expedition of 1870* Paul McNicholls (ISBN 978-1-911628-30-9)
6. *Kitchener: The Man Not The Myth* Anne Samson (ISBN 978-1-912866-45-8)
7. *The British and the Sikhs: Discovery, Warfare and Friendship c1700–1900* Gurinder Singh Mann (ISBN 978-1-911628-24-8)
8. *Bazaine 1870: Scapegoat for a Nation* Quintin Barry (ISBN 978-1-913336-08-0)
9. *Redcoats in the Classroom: The British Army's Schools For Soldiers and Their Children During the 19th Century* Howard R. Clarke (ISBN 978-1-912866-47-2)
10. *The Rescue They Called a Raid: The Jameson Raid 1895–96* David Snape (ISBN 978-1-913118-77-8)
11. *Hungary 1848: The Winter Campaign* Christopher Pringle (ISBN 978-1-913118-78-5)

12. *The War of the Two Brothers: The Portuguese Civil War 1828-1834* Sérgio Veludo Coelho (ISBN 978-1-914059-26-1)
14. *Forgotten Victorian Generals: Studies in the Exercise of Command and Control in the British Army 1837–1901* Christopher Brice (editor) (ISBN 978-1-910777-20-6)
15. *The German War of 1866: The Bohemian and Moravian Campaign* Theodore Fontane (ISBN 978-1-914059-29-2)
16. *Dust of Glory: The First Anglo-Afghan War 1839–1842, its Causes and Course* Bill Whitburn (ISBN 978-1-914059-33-9)
17. *Saarbruck to Sedan: The Franco-German War 1870–1871 Volume 1* Ralph Weaver (ISBN 978-1-914059-88-9)
18. *The Battle of Lissa 1866: How the Industrial Revolution Changed the Face of Naval Warfare* Quintin Barry (ISBN 978-1-914059-92-6)
19. *The Zulu Kingdom and the Boer Invasion of 1837–1840* John Laband (ISBN 978-1-914059-89-6)
20. *The Fire of Venture Was in His Veins: Major Allan Wilson and the Shangani Patrol 1893* David Snape (ISBN 978-1-914059-90-2)
21. *From the Atacama to the Andes: Battles of the War of the Pacific 1879–1883* Alan Curtis (ISBN 978-1-914059-90-2)
22. *The Rise of the Sikh Soldier: The Sikh Warrior Through the Ages, c1700–1900* Gurinder Singh Mann (ISBN 978-1-915070-52-4)
23. *Victorian Crusaders: British and Irish Volunteers in the Papal Army 1860–70* Nicholas Schofield (ISBN 978-1-915070-53-1)
24. *The Battle for the Swiepwald: Austria's Fatal Blunder at Königgrätz, the climactic battle of the Austro-Prussian War, 3 July 1866* Ernst Heidrich (ISBN 978-1-915070-49-4)
25. *British Military Panoramas: Battle in The Round, 1800–1914* Ian F.W. Beckett (ISBN 978-1-915113-84-9)
26. *Onwards to Omdurman: The Anglo-Egyptian Campaign to Reconquer the Sudan, 1896–1898* Keith Surridge (ISBN 978-1-915070-51-7)
27. *Hungary 1849: The Summer Campaign* Christopher Pringle (ISBN 978-1-915113-80-1)
28. *Line in the Sand: French Foreign Legion Forts and Fortifications in Morocco 1900-1926* Richard Jeynes (ISBN 978-1-915113-83-2)
29. *The Republic Fights Back The Franco-German War 1870-1871 Volume 2* Ralph Weaver (ISBN 9781915070500)
30. *Controlling the Frontier Southern Africa 1806–1828, The Cape Frontier Wars and The Fetcani Alarm* Hugh Drive (ISBN 978-1-915113-78-8)
31. *The Battle of Magersfontein Victory and Defeat on the South African Veld, 10–12 December 1899* Garth Benneyworth (ISBN 978-1-915113-79-5)
32. *Too Little Too Late The Campaign in West and South Germany June-July 1866* Michael Embree (ISBN 978-1-804513-77-4)
33. *The Destruction of the Imperial Army Volume 1: The Opening Engagements of the Franco-German War 1870-71* Grenville Bird (ISBN 978-1-915113-81-8)
34. *Kitchener: The Man not the Myth* (paperback) Anne Samson (ISBN 978-1-804513-84-2)
35. *From Ironclads to Dreadnoughts: The Development of the German Battleship, 1864-1918* Dirk Nottelmann and David M. Sullivan (ISBN 978-1-804511-84-8)
36. *The Destruction of the Imperial Army Volume 2: The Battles around Metz* Grenville Bird (ISBN 978-1-804511-85-5)
37. *More Work Than Glory: Buffalo Soldiers in the United States Army, 1866–1916* John P. Langellier (ISBN 978-1-804513-34-7)